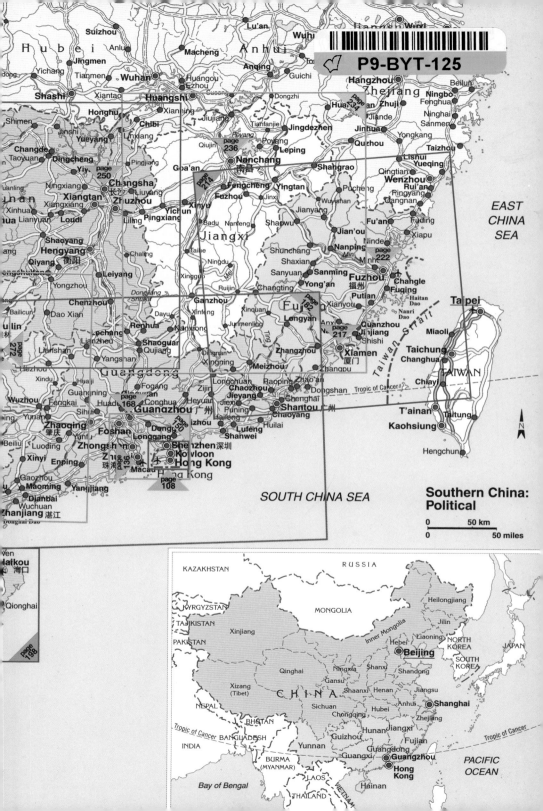

# INSIGHT GUIDES

# SOUTHERN
# CHINA
# & HONG KONG

# Discovery
## CHANNEL

# APA PUBLICATIONS L

Part of the Langenscheidt Publishing Group

**✵ INSIGHT GUIDE**

# SOUTHERN
# CHINA

*Editorial*
**Managing Editor**
**Tom Le Bas**
*Project Editor*
**Ruth Williams**
*Editorial Director*
**Brian Bell**
*Photographic Director*
**Hilary Genin**

## Distribution

*UK & Ireland*
**GeoCenter International Ltd**
Meridian House, Churchill Way West
Basingstoke, Hampshire RG21 6YR
Fax: (44) 1256 817988

*United States*
**Langenscheidt Publishers, Inc.**
36–36 33rd Street 4th Floor
Long Island City, NY 11106
Fax: 1 (718) 784 0640

*Australia*
**Universal Publishers**
1 Waterloo Road
Macquarie Park, NSW 2113
Fax: (61) 2 9888 9074

*New Zealand*
**Hema Maps New Zealand Ltd (HNZ)**
Unit D, 24 Ra ORA Drive
East Tamaki, Auckland
Fax: (64) 9 273 6479

*Worldwide*
**Apa Publications GmbH & Co.
Verlag KG (Singapore branch)**
38 Joo Koon Road, Singapore 628990
Tel: (65) 6865 1600. Fax: (65) 6861 6438

## Printing

**Insight Print Services (Pte) Ltd**
38 Joo Koon Road, Singapore 628990
Tel: (65) 6865 1600. Fax: (65) 6861 6438

©2007 Apa Publications GmbH & Co.
Verlag KG (Singapore branch)
*All Rights Reserved*

*First Edition 2007*

**CONTACTING THE EDITORS**
We would appreciate it if readers
would alert us to errors or out-
dated information by writing to:
**Insight Guides, P.O. Box 7910,
London SE1 1WE, England.
Fax: (44) 20 7403 0290.**
**insight@apaguide.co.uk**

**www.insightguides.com**
*In North America:*
**www.insighttravelguides.com**

# ABOUT THIS BOOK

The first Insight Guide pioneered the use of creative full-colour photography in travel guides in 1970. Since then, we have expanded our range to cater for our readers' need not only for reliable information about their chosen des-tination but also for a real under-standing of the culture and workings of that destination. Now, when the internet can supply inexhaustible (but not always reliable) facts, our books marry text and pictures to provide those much more elusive qualities: knowledge and discern-ment. To achieve this, they rely heavily on the authority of locally based writers and photographers.

*Insight Guide: Southern China* is structured to convey an under-standing of the region and its people as well as to guide readers through its attractions:

◆ The **Features** section, indicated by a orange bar at the top of each page, covers the natural and cultural history of the region as well as illu-minating essays on the southern Chinese economy, daily life, archi-tecture and the arts.
◆ The main **Places** section, indi-cated by a blue bar, is a complete guide to all the sights and areas worth visiting. Places of special interest are coordinated by number with the maps.
◆ The **Travel Tips** listings section, with a yellow bar, provides full infor-mation on transport, hotels, activi-ties from culture to shopping to sports, an A–Z section of essential practical information, and a handy phrasebook with Mandarin and Can-tonese words and expressions. An easy-to-find contents list for Travel Tips is printed on the back flap, which also serves as a bookmark.

China-based writer who has written or collaborated on some 30 travel guides to China and the region, and contributed articles to the *Asian Wall Street Journal* and *South China Morning Post*, among other publications.

**Pete Spurrier**, a writer and publisher who has lived in Asia since 1993, described northern, eastern and western Guangdong, and the southern parts of Guangxi. The Hainan chapter was written by features and travel journalist **Andrew Dembina**, whose work has appeared in several international publications since 1988. Hong Kong-based writer **Jane Ram**, who has been travelling all over China since the 1970s, contributed the Fujian chapter. Writer, photographer and adventurer **Brice Minnigh** described Jiangxi province, while the Hunan chapter was written by **Sam Chambers**, former East Asia Editor for Lloyd's List. The Guizhou chapter was covered by another Hong Kong-based writer and photographer, **David Wilkinson**, who has been documenting the minority peoples of southwest China and their festivals for over a decade. **Peter Holmshaw**, who provided the Lijiang and Northwest Yunnan text, has travelled extensively throughout the country.

Insight regular **Andrew Forbes** wrote the introduction and the history chapters, while the Chinese diaspora was described by **Meiling Voon**. Journalist and Shanghai resident **Brent Hannon** wrote the Life in Modern China chapter and adapted the text for the Food, Arts and Architecture sections. The principal photographer was **David Henley**. The book was proofread by **Neil Titman** and indexed by **Helen Peters**.

### The contributors

This book was commissioned and edited by ex-Hong Kong resident **Tom Le Bas** at Insight Guides' London office. To oversee the work in China and Hong Kong, he enlisted the help of **Ruth Williams**, a freelance writer, editor and regular contributor to Insight Guides and Asian travel trade magazines, who first visited China in 1992 and now calls Hong Kong home. In addition to her project managing role, she also wrote the sections on Guilin and Yangshuo.

The Hong Kong, Macau, Shenzhen, Pearl River Delta and Guangzhou text was the work of **Ed Peters**, a long-standing Insight regular and resident of Hong Kong's New Territories for two decades. **Chris Taylor**, who wrote the chapters on Kunming and southeastern Yunnan, Xishuangbanna, Dali / Burma Road, and the Chinese economy, is a

**Map Legend**

| | |
|---|---|
| —··— | International Boundary |
| —––– | Province Boundary |
| —·•·— | National Park/Reserve |
| ———— | Ferry Route |
| ✈✈ | Airport |
| ✝✝ | Church (ruins) |
| ✝ | Monastery |
| ∴ | Archaeological Site |
| ∩ | Cave |
| ★ | Place of Interest |
| ↰ | Beach |
| ❄ | Viewpoint |
| Ⓜ | Metro |
| ❶ | Tourist Information |
| ☾ | Mosque |
| ⚊ | Statue/Monument |

The main places of interest in the Places section are coordinated by number with a full-colour map (e.g. ❶), and a symbol at the top of every right-hand page tells you where to find the map.

**LEFT:** letting off steam on a tea plantation, Fujian. **BELOW:** temple statue at Humen, Guangdong.

# Contents

**ABOVE:** a wine vessel from
the Shang Dynasty.

**LEFT:** a stall selling well-wishing ribbons.
**RIGHT:** traditional Chinese symbol for good fortune and longevity.

## Maps

A political map of southern China is on the front inside cover; a physical map of southern China is on the back inside cover.

## Travel Tips

**LEFT:** Dai minority children in Xishuangbanna, southern Yunnan.

# THE BEST OF SOUTHERN CHINA: TOP TEN SIGHTS

From the crowded streets of Hong Kong to the remote villages of Guizhou, the tropical beaches of Hainan to Yunnan's Jade Dragon Snow Mountains, a rundown of the best of southern China

△ **Lijiang** is a beautiful old Chinese town set against a backdrop of awesome mountain scenery in the northwest of Yunnan province. Visit in winter for the best views. *See page 337.*

▽ The amazing landscapes along the **Li River** south of the city of Guilin have inspired countless poets through the ages. In the heart of the region, the town of Yangshuo is one of the most relaxed and most attractive places in all of China. *See page 271.*

▷ The numerous **festivals of Guizhou** province's various ethnic minorities are a fascinating spectacle, a riot of colourful costumes, music and dancing. *See pages 292 and 295.*

△ The **Xishuangbanna** region of southern Yunnan borders Laos and Burma, a land of Buddhist temples, jungles and a laid-back ambience that feels like tropical southeast Asia. *See page 313.*

△ The sandy southern shores of **Hainan Island** offer clear waters, year-round warmth and a growing number of international-standard resorts. *See page 197.*

◁ In the northwestern corner of Hunan province, the dramatic landscapes of **Wulingyuan Scenic Reserve** make for some fantastic hiking. *See page 254.*

▷ The ancient town of **Dali**, set picturesquely beneath the towering Cangshan Mountains and Er Hai Lake in western Yunnan, makes a peaceful retreat. *See page 323.*

△ **Macau** has a split personality all of its own: on the one hand is the Portuguese colonial architecture and haphazard charm of the old city; on the other, a massively expanding Las Vegas-style casino industry. *See page 135.*

▽ The city of **Xiamen** in Fujian province is one of the most attractive in China, particularly the car-free island of Gulangyu with its old mansions and meandering pathways. *See page 215.*

△ No visit to China would be complete without taking in the sights and sounds of **Hong Kong**. A trip on the venerable Star Ferry makes a perfect introduction to this amazing city. *See page 111.*

# THE BEST OF SOUTHERN CHINA: EDITOR'S CHOICE

Unique attractions, festivals, urban highlights, fabulous landscapes, dim sum and dragon boats, theme parks and trekking in the wilds ... here are our recommendations, plus some essential tips for travellers

## URBAN HIGHLIGHTS

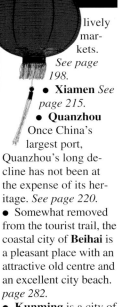

- **Central District, Hong Kong** Vibrant streets with countless shopping and entertainment options, amazing vistas and contrasts – all packed into a narrow strip of land on Hong Kong Island's north shore. *See page 111.*
- **Guangzhou** is a great place to feel the pulse of modern China, with top-notch nightlife and shopping. *See page 167.*
- **Chaozhou** in eastern Guangdong has largely escaped redevelopment and retains an unusually large number of attractive old buildings. *See page 190.*
- With its palm-lined streets, **Haikou** is a laid-back kind of place with a pleasantly preserved old centre and lively markets. *See page 198.*
- **Xiamen** *See page 215.*
- **Quanzhou** Once China's largest port, Quanzhou's long decline has not been at the expense of its heritage. *See page 220.*
- Somewhat removed from the tourist trail, the coastal city of **Beihai** is a pleasant place with an attractive old centre and an excellent city beach. *page 282.*
- **Kunming** is a city of pleasant parks and a relaxed feel, partly due to its wonderful climate. The surrounding hills are great for walking. *See page 302.*

## TOWNS AND VILLAGES

- **Fenghuang, Hunan** Get a glimpse of old China at this gorgeous river town. *See page 256.*
- **Yangshuo, Guangxi** It's hard to think of a more picturesque setting than that provided by the limestone pinnacles around Yangshuo. The town itself is full of cosy bars, restaurants and guesthouses. Simply one of the nicest places in China. *See page 272.*
- **Dong villages, Guizhou** These villages of the Dong minority have barely changed in centuries. Wooden buildings cluster around fabulously ornate "drum" towers and unique covered bridges. *See page 290.*
- **Ruili, Yunnan** Its location on the Burmese border makes Ruili an enjoyably edgy kind of place, and there is a fantastic night market. *See page 334.*
- **Dali and Lijiang, Yunnan** *(see pages 323 and 337).*

**Top:** the view from the Peak, Hong Kong.
**Above:** traditional New Year lantern.

## SPECTACULAR LANDSCAPES

● **Danxia Shan, Guangdong** A scenic forested area in the north of Guangdong province. *See page 186.*
● **Wuyi Shan, Fujian** These eastern backwoods are home to an impressive array of flora and fauna. *See page 224.*
● **Lushan, Jiangxi** Beautiful mountain area rising abruptly from the Yangzi plains. *See page 238.*
● **Heng Shan, Hunan** One of China's sacred Daoist mountains, with a network of hiking paths. *See page 252.*
● **Wulingyuan, Hunan** This UNESCO World Heritage Site protects some of the most stunning scenery in all of China. *See page 254.*
● **Guilin area, Guangxi** The famous karst landscape of the Guilin area is one of the iconic sights of China. Take a river cruise along the Li River to fully appreciate the beauty of the scenery. *See page 263.*
● **Longsheng Terraces, Guangxi** These dramatic rice terraces in northern Guangxi rise 800 metres (2,620 ft) from the valley floor. Best seen in spring when the water within the fields reflects the light in ever-changing ways. *See page 277.*
● **Huangguosho Waterfall, Guizhou** Like a smaller version of Niagara Falls transported to the misty highlands of Guizhou, Huangguosho is a breathtaking sight – especially after heavy rain (common in this part of China). *See page 297.*
● **Stone Forest, Yunnan** This weird "forest" of eroded limestone rocks is best seen early or late in the day to avoid the tour groups. *See page 308.*
● **Tiger Leaping Gorge, Yunnan** The turbulent waters of the Jinsha Jiang (which downstream becomes the Yangzi) have cut a 4,000-metre (13,200-ft) chasm through the highlands west of Lijiang. This is one of China's finest treks. *See page 343.*

## TEMPLES, PAGODAS AND MUSEUMS

● **Wong Tai Sin Temple, Hong Kong** Lively temple dedicated to the Daoist god of good fortune. *See page 125.*
● **Hong Kong Heritage Museum** Visit for an excellent and thorough introduction to Hong Kong and the region. *See page 126.*
● **Guangzhou Museum of Art** One of China's leading art museums. *See page 174.*
● **Sun Yatsen Residence Memorial Museum** In the village of Cuiheng in the southern Pearl River Delta, this is a reconstruction of the great man's childhood home. *See page 163.*

● **Kaiyuan Temple, Quanzhou** Fine carvings are a feature of this magnificent 7th-century temple. *See page 221*
● **Kunming temples** The hills west of Kunming have a rich variety of temples in superb natural settings. *See page 302.*
● **Bamboo Shoot Pagoda, Damenglong** Deep in tropical Xishuangbanna, this exotic nine-spired pagoda was founded in 1204. *See page 321.*
● **Three Pagodas, Dali** Ancient tiered pagodas. *See page 325.*

**LEFT:** a Miao village in Guizhou province.
**RIGHT:** The Sun Yatsen Mausoleum, Guangzhou.

## BEST FESTIVALS

● **Mid-autumn Festival, Hong Kong** At its best in Causeway Bay's Victoria Park, when the park is illuminated by lanterns. *See page 118.*

● **Dragon Boat Festival, Dongting Hu, Hunan** The internationally-popular sport of dragon boat racing originated here, and its annual festival (5th day of 5th lunar month) around the town of Yueyang is a great spectacle. The festival is observed all over southern China – Hong Kong and Xiamen are also good places to see it too. *See page 248.*

● **Tin Hau/Mazu festivals** The birthday of the Goddess of the Sea (Tin Hau to the Cantonese, Mazu to the Fujianese) is marked with lively festivities in coastal communities. *See page 79.*

● **Lusheng festivals, Guizhou** These colourful gatherings of Miao and other minority groups feature spectacular costumes, music and dancing. Almost every village in the Miao areas has its own festival at different times through the October–April period, so there's a good chance of catching one. *See page 295.*

● **Water-splashing in Xishuangbanna** Celebrated in mid-April, this riotous festival involves drenching passers-by with buckets of water. Leave your camera at the hotel. *See page 313.*

## LEISURE PURSUITS

● **Disneyland, Hong Kong** Asia's first such theme park has been packing in the crowds since opening in 2005. *See page 130.*

● **Macau's casinos** The ex-Portuguese enclave has long been known for its gambling, but the advent of new, gargantuan mega-casinos marks its intention to become Asia's leisure capital. *See page 135.*

● **Shenzhen theme parks** Visit the Eiffel Tower, explore the Great Wall or witness life in a tribal village in this triumvirate of parks. *See page 154.*

● **Hainan Island beaches** White sands, warm water, quality accommodation and facilities: southern Hainan is now established as a viable alternative to the resorts of southeast Asia. *See page 197.*

● **White-water rafting in Wuyi Shan** The green hills of northern Fujian form the backdrop to one of China's best rafting rivers. *See page 225.*

● **Trekking in northern Yunnan** Near-endless possibilities, from Tiger Leaping Gorge to Lugu Lake and the Himalayan areas of the far north. *See page 343.*

**TOP LEFT:** Yao minority woman.
**ABOVE:** seaside pursuits at Yalong Bay, Hainan.
**ABOVE RIGHT:** jade for sale.
**BELOW LEFT:** dragon boat racing at Yueyang.
**BELOW:** ersatz sights at Window of the World, Shenzhen.

## SHOPPING

● **Hong Kong** One of the world's great shopping destinations. Clothing, Chinese arts and crafts and antiques can all be good buys. *See page 111.*
● **Shenzhen** A favourite with bargain-hunting Hong Kongers, particularly good for designer clothing and Chinese-made electronics. *See page 154.*
● **Guangzhou** Plenty of choice in southern China's largest metropolis, from shiny new malls to raucous street markets. *See page 167.*
● **Jingdezhen** China's porcelain capital. *See page 241.*

## HISTORIC SIGHTS

● **Monte Fort, Macau** This 17th-century fort looms large over old Macau, with views across the city and a fine museum. *See page 138.*
● **Opium pits, Guangdong** This was where the Chinese publically disposed of a consignment of "foreign mud", sparking the First Opium War. *See page 160.*
● **Hakka round-houses, Fujian** These circular, fortified clan dwellings make a dramatic sight. *See page 214.*
● **Jiangxi and the Long March** Jiangxi province played a pivotal role in the early years of the Chinese Communists. The area around Jingganshan is full of memorials and museums. *See page 240.*
● **Shaoshan** Visit Mao's home town to witness the veneration the Great Helmsman still attracts from the faithful. *See page 252.*

## CUISINES OF SOUTHERN CHINA

● **Cantonese** Fresh ingredients and subtle flavours which have been exported around the world. **Chaozhou** (Chiu Chow) cuisine is similar but with a stronger emphasis on seafood. *See pages 73–4.*
● **Hakka** Traditional peasant cuisine, with plenty of meat and liberal use of ginger. *See page 74.*
● **Hunanese** Spicy food similar to the more famous Sichuanese, with lots of chilli. *See page 75.*
● **Hainan** Plenty of seafood, chicken and mild flavours including coconut. *See page 75.*
● **Yunnan** An often-delicious fusion with a wide range of influences from around the region. *See page 75.*

**ABOVE:** Hakka roundhouse.
**BELOW:** delectable Cantonese dim sum.

## TRAVELLERS' TIPS

● **Tourist Information** Most CTS (China Travel Service) and CITS (China International Travel Service) offices exist to sell tours – rather than to impart free information to tourists. There are, however, exceptions – for instance the CITS in Kaili, Guizhou, is usually very helpful. All CTS/CITS offices should be able to assist with tickets for air and rail travel.
● **Buying rail tickets** For overnight journeys, you should purchase your tickets (hard or soft sleeper) 2–5 days in advance (5 days is usually the maximum), as they often sell out – more of a problem if you are joining the train a long way into its journey. If you are told there are none left, it may still be possible to buy from a travel agent such as CTS. Railway stations in large cities will usually have a dedicated ticket window for foreigners. *See pages 351–2.*

● **Buses** Some long-distance buses (mostly those between smaller cities) will only set off once every last inch of space is occupied. Tickets are usually easy to buy at bus stations on the day of travel. Note that most cities have several bus stations, often miles apart.

# CHINA'S DEEP SOUTH

Spanning eight provinces and two Special Administrative Regions, southern China is culturally diverse, colourful, confident and increasingly prosperous. There has never been a better time to visit

C hina is many things, most of them involving superlatives. It's the oldest continuous single civilisation in the world, dating back some five thousand years. It's the most populous country in the world, dominated by the ethnic Chinese Han who constitute around 92 percent of the population, and also home to a further 55 recognised ethnic minorities, most of whom live in the south and west of the country.

The traditional Chinese heartland is the valley of the Huang He (Yellow River), where more than four millennia ago the ancestors of today's Han Chinese first developed intensive agriculture and established city-states. During this legendary period the foundations of modern China were first laid, and as the city-states unified and prospered, they expanded south and west to colonise new areas. This inexorable expansion into the warm and exotic south – perceived as a rich but potentially dangerous land (yet not as dangerous as the territories to the north and west) – has been a consistent theme in the long history of the Chinese people.

As a result of this expansion, much of the region covered in this book has been part of the Chinese world for around two millennia, and fully assimilated into the empire since the time of the Tang Dynasty (618–907) or earlier. The exceptions are the southwestern areas (Guizhou and Yunnan), where large swathes of territory remained effectively independent of the Chinese empire until the 14th century – later in some areas – and where sizeable ethnic minority populations remain to this day.

Yet despite the apparent uniformity – demographic, cultural and political – with central and northern China, southern China's separate identity is clearly visible. Environmentally, there are obvious differences: the subtropical climate brings a longer growing season; the well-watered landscape is a vivid green for much of the year, the soil a rich red. And even though all are ethnically Han Chinese, the Cantonese and Fujianese are smaller and

**PRECEDING PAGES:** terraced rice fields in southeastern Yunnan; Miao festival parade, Guizhou. **LEFT:** Chinese New Year at a Guangzhou flower market. **ABOVE LEFT:** the Dali pagodas. **ABOVE RIGHT:** the view from Moon Hill, Yangshuo.

darker than their northern counterparts. Rightly or wrongly, northerners also have a reputation for being more stolid and more serious than the southerners, who are in turn viewed by their northern counterparts as shrewd, sharp, noisy and a trifle untrustworthy. The multiplicity of widely differing dialects – Cantonese and Mandarin share the written form but pronunciation and vocabulary are very different between the two – greatly enhances the division.

Compared with the more culturally homogenous north, southern China is a diverse ethnic, linguistic and cultural tableau. By virtue of their proximity to the sea and longer exposure to the West, great port cities like Guangzhou and, of course, Hong Kong are more cosmopolitan than northern cities such

as Beijing and Tianjin. Southerners have long had a tradition (and disposition) that encouraged trade and even migration overseas. Most "Overseas Chinese" in Southeast Asia, as well as in such far-flung centres of Han settlement as San Francisco, London, Amsterdam and Sydney, hail originally from the south, and especially from Guangdong province. The southerners have stronger links with other countries and a more accommodating – perhaps more open-minded – attitude than is sometimes apparent with the more conservative northerners.

Much of the southern region is benefitting hugely from China's new-found prosperity, particularly in the vibrant and increasingly wealthy cities of the coast, although large parts of the hinterland remain relatively poor and the growing economic divide is problematic.

For the tourist, there has never been a better time to visit. Access becomes ever more comfortable and straightforward, with new, state-of-the-art airports opening seemingly every year, excellent provincial highways, and improving trains and buses. Politically, too, the situation has never been more free, and virtually everywhere, from the beaches of Hainan Island to the wild Tibetan borderlands of western Yunnan, is opening up to tourism.

## Dividing lines

China is traditionally split into North and South by the mighty Yangzi River, but for the purposes of this book we have only described provinces in their

entirety, so those small sections of Sichuan (and its eastern offshoot, Chongqing Shi), Hubei and Anhui lying to the south of the Yangzi are not included. Shanghai, southern Jiangsu and the province of Zhejiang were considered to be outside the true southern area. Instead we have focused on those provinces along the South China Sea – Fujian, Guangdong, Hong Kong and Macau, Hainan Island and Guangxi – and their neighbours to the north – Jiangxi, Hunan and Guizhou. We have also included Yunnan, tucked away in the far southwest and in some respects closer to both Southeast Asia and Tibet than to the rest of southern China. ❑

---

**TOP:** Quanzhou's Guan Di Temple. **ABOVE:** Xiamen is one of the region's wealthiest cities. **RIGHT:** much of rural Guizhou remains poor.

# THE SOUTH AND THE CHINESE EMPIRE

**The long history of southern China is marked by the slow expansion of the Han Chinese into the area from their northern homeland.**

It is clearly impossible to write a history of southern China without looking briefly at the history of China as a whole. It should be possible, though, to examine the special role played by the south in Chinese history, and to look in greater detail than usual at the divergent histories of southern regions as diverse as Yunnan and Guangdong, Fujian and Hainan. Properly speaking, Taiwan should also feature in any historical survey of the south, even though the breakaway island currently maintains its independence as the Republic of China and as such does not form part of this book. Until at least 1949, Taiwan's historical links with the southern mainland have been strong, especially with neighbouring Fujian Province.

## IN THE BEGINNING

Histories of China generally begin with the Shang Dynasty (16th–11th centuries BC), when Han Chinese civilisation was centred on the Huang He (Yellow River) and when the Yangzi River, which runs through the centre of China, represented the nation's southern frontier – where it remained through the later Zhou Dynasty (11th century–256 BC). It was not until the Qin Dynasty (221–206 BC) that Han power extended in any meaningful way far south of the Yangzi – in 211 BC Qin Shi Huangdi (r. 221–210), the first emperor of a unified China, conquered the area around Guangzhou for China for the first time – though not yet Fujian or even Jiangxi further to the north, which were bypassed.

One constant factor in Chinese history – at least until the coming of Western colonialism in the 19th century – has been the southern expansion of the Han Chinese people. Historically, China has been driven by a southward territorial imperative that would eventually see all the territories between the Yangzi and the current frontiers with mainland Southeast Asia and India gradually conquered and settled by Han Chinese, the indigenous peoples either being absorbed, surrounded and marginalised, forced into infertile highland areas, or migrating south ahead of the Chinese to avoid subjugation. In this way Chinese control was extended over Fujian, Jiangxi, Hunan, Guangxi and Hainan Island for the first time under the Three Kingdoms (AD 220–265), while Yunnan was not properly absorbed until the Yuan Dynasty (1279–1368), and Taiwan as recently as 1683.

**LEFT:** the Qin Emperor, Qin Shi Huangdi, persecuted Confucian scholars. **RIGHT:** Wei-dynasty tomb guardian.

Southern China as a fully integrated part of the Han Chinese homeland, then, did not come fully into existence until about seven centuries ago – almost three millennia after Chinese civilisation first emerged in the valley of the Yellow River.

## EARLY CHINESE PERCEPTIONS OF THE SOUTH

For Han Chinese right up to Tang Dynasty times (618–907) and even beyond, the far south – as it then was – remained a little-known land of dangers and temptations, a place of exile where, nevertheless, it was always summer. A place to dream about, but not necessarily to visit, home to

The American sinologist Edward Schafer believed that "respectable Chinese opinion" saw something unnatural in the prevalence of the female spirit in the south, citing the 1st-century *Han Shu:* "The land of Viet abounds in women. Male and female share the same river. The wanton female is dominant." A legend popular in China for many centuries tells how the King of Viet educated a beautiful country girl, Xi Shi, in the "feminine arts", then sent her north to corrupt his rival, the Han Chinese King of Wu. The 8th-century poet Li Po celebrates her as: "Xi Shi, a woman of the streams of Viet, luminous, ravishing, a light on the sea of clouds". Given such precedents and

strange but delicious fruits, exotic but dangerous animals, and tempting but wanton women. The culture of the Chinese heartland around the Yellow River was strongly patriarchal, but further south women wielded more influence and authority – a phenomenon both appealing and worrying to the men of Han, who desired yet felt threatened by such confident and assertive females.

> *"The Southern Country has neither frost nor snow. Year in, year out you see the flourishing of nature."*
>
> *Sung Chih-wen (c.650–712), on visiting Wuzhou (Guangxi) in the early Tang period.*

viewed from the perspective of Chinese men of the time, southern women seemed dangerous and wanton creatures indeed.

And yet this very lustfulness clearly exercised a strong appeal. By Tang times Chinese control had been asserted over the entire coast as far south as Tonkin (modern north Vietnam), but not over the interior. Chinese men who had visited or lived in this land of plenty waxed lyrical about the beauty of the women. One Tang poet, Wang Changling, links the "enchantress of Viet" with "a playful tussle in the lotus boat, water dampening her dress". Just as evocative is his near-contemporary Han Yu: "a Viet woman's single laugh – a three year stay."

The Chinese were also distinctly superior in their attitude towards the "southern barbarians" they were slowly conquering and attempting to absorb. Just like the French in the 19th century, they saw themselves with a "civilising mission" that was reflected in their march to the tropics. In 939 the Vietnamese drove the occupying Han forces out of Tonkin, prompting the furious Song Emperor Taizong to demand of the "ingrate Viets":

*You fly and leap like savages, we have horse-drawn carriages. You drink through your noses, we have rice and wine. Let us change your customs. You cut your hair, we wear hats; when you talk, you sound like birds. We have examinations and books. Let us teach you the knowledge of the*

## THE SOUTHERN EXPANSION OF THE HAN CHINESE

Han Chinese troops had been active on and off along the coastal strip around Guangzhou since Qin Shi Huangdi's conquest of the area in 211 BC. Three years later, Chinese troops conquered Tonkin and began their long, 1,000-year occupation of An Nam, the "pacified south". As we have seen, Vietnam would eventually break away from Chinese tutelage, but not before becoming so thoroughly sinicised as to become a satellite of the Chinese cultural constellation.

Meanwhile, Guangdong was emerging as the main centre of Chinese power in the south. When

*proper laws... Do you not want to escape from the savagery of the outer islands and gaze upon the house of civilisation? Do you not want to discard your garments of leaves and grass and wear flowered robes embroidered with mountains and dragons?*

In fact, it was only Vietnam that would manage to throw off the Chinese yoke, with the rest of the south gradually succumbing to Chinese rule and subsequently Chinese customs over a long period of many centuries.

---

**LEFT:** *The Journey of Emperor Ming Huang to Shu –* traditional landscape painting.

**ABOVE:** a bronze wine vessel from the earliest years of Chinese civilisation (Shang Dynasty).

Qin Shi Huangdi's troops first arrived in the region, it was populated by Yue people thought to have been related to the Zhuang of modern Guangxi. The Chinese, however, set up their military headquarters – the Nanhai, or "South Seas" Commandery – at Panyu near present-day Guangzhou. The Han Dynasty (206 BC–AD 220) then administered the three provinces of Guangdong, Guangxi and Tonkin as the Province of Jiao.

In AD 226 **Guangdong** was made into a separate province called Guang, or "broad". Meanwhile, the ethnic balance shifted slowly but inexorably in favour of the Han Chinese invaders as more and more settlers moved south into warmer and more fertile climes, often escaping political troubles further to the north. For example, dynastic records suggest that, as a result of the political turmoil caused by the rebellion of An Lushan (755–63), the Han population of Guangzhou Prefecture increased by about 75 percent. Inevitably, as more migrants moved in, the indigenous Yue population either assimilated through marriage or moved away further south and inland to the hill country.

Nearby **Hainan Island**, known as Qiongzhou or "Agate Region", perhaps because of its green forests and azure waters, was first settled by a Chinese garrison in 110 BC, but in the circumstances at the time was considered a "bridge too far" for ordinary Han settlement and became

Minyue capital, Fuzhou, to surrender. From this time a process of sinicisation began in the area, though it is noteworthy that the people of northern Fujian still honour their early Minyue monarchs in their temples today.

At the time of the Three Kingdoms Period, the entire southern coastal region, including Fujian, Guangdong, Hainan Island and Tonkin, passed under the control of the Kingdom of Wu. Far to the north, meanwhile, the original Han Chinese heartland around the Yellow River came under the rule of the rival Kingdom of Wei. Finally the inland Kingdom of Shu emerged, extending Han Chinese control and influence westwards, for the

instead a place for exiles. During the Three Kingdoms Period (AD 220–265), Hainan was home to the Zhuya Commandery, but it wasn't until the Song Dynasty (960–1279) that the remote tropical island would come fully under Chinese control and Han Chinese emigration would begin to assimilate or displace the local Li people.

Further to the north, Chinese troops had bypassed the difficult terrain of present-day **Jiangxi**, **Fujian** and southern Zhejiang, large parts of which were inhabited by indigenous Austronesian peoples known to the Han Chinese as Min or Minyue. Minyue remained a de facto independent state until Han Dynasty times. In 111 BC the Han Emperor Wudi (r. 141–87 BC) invaded simultaneously with land and sea forces, obliging the

first time, through **Guizhou** and Sichuan into eastern **Yunnan**.

For all this expansion, Han Chinese control over the south and, in particular, the southwest, remained relatively tenuous under the Sui and Tang Dynasties (581–907) and under the Song (960–1279). During this long period internal conflicts and foreign invasions from Central Asia and Manchuria continued to destabilise the north on a regular basis, causing increased migration to the south. By the time of the Southern Song (1127–1279) the southeastern frontier had, to a large extent, solidified along ethnic lines that more or less match today's borders. **Fujian, Guangdong, Jiangxi, Hunan** and **Guangxi** were all increasingly assimilated and part of "China

Proper", while Han settlement proceeded apace in northern Hainan Island, causing the indigenous Li people to withdraw into the southern highlands where some of their descendants continue to live today. To the south, Vietnam had broken away decisively from the Chinese Empire, and to the west, in Guizhou and Yunnan, Chinese influence and control remained limited.

## MONGOL CONQUESTS IN THE SOUTHWEST

China came much closer to attaining its current territorial limits under the Mongol or Yuan Dynasty (1279–1368). During the declining years of the Song, China was increasingly harrassed by the powerful Mongol tribes to the northwest. In 1223 Genghis Khan seized control of all Chinese territory north of the Huang He, and although the great Mongol warrior died in 1227 before he could further extend his Chinese conquests, his grandson, Kublai Khan (r. 1271–94), completed the conquest of China and established the writ of the Yuan Dynasty as far west as Yunnan, Burma and Tibet.

In 1253, when his elder brother Mongke was Khan (1251–59), Kublai Khan was ordered to invade Yunnan. He did so, successfully capturing the ancient walled city of Dali. In 1258 Kublai was once again active on the Yunnan and Sichuan fronts, this time as Commander of the Army of the East. One year later, in 1259, Mongke was dead and Kublai claimed the throne. In 1271 Kublai Khan officially proclaimed the establishment of the Yuan Dynasty with its capital at Dadu (Beijing), finally destroying the last of the Southern Song Dynasty in 1279 and unifying China, from Manchuria and Mongolia in the north to Hainan Island in the south. Kublai would attempt to extend China's frontiers to the east and south, attacking Japan by sea in 1274 and again in 1281, but without success. He was similarly unsuccessful in Vietnam, which he attacked in 1257, 1284 and 1287, taking and sacking Hanoi, but being ignominiously defeated and driven out by the great Vietnamese general Tran Hung Dao (1228–1300).

### The Turkic legacy

But in the west Kublai Khan was more successful. In the time-honoured tradition of any major

---

**LEFT:** a Dutch engraving dating from 1665 showing Chinese peasants at work in the fields.
**RIGHT:** Genghis Khan.

empire, the Mongols used mercenary and conscript troops. In remote frontier areas – such as southern Yunnan – they also borrowed from Chinese tradition, "using barbarians to control barbarians". To suppress the remnants of the Southern Song and to reinforce and extend their control over Yunnan, they employed professional Uzbek fighters from the Khanate of Bukhara in Central Asia.

By the late 13th century Yunnan had been successfully incorporated into the Mongol realm, and Kublai Khan turned his attention further afield. Some of his Turkic mercenaries were sent to attack Burma – the likenesses of two are still

recorded in frescoes at Pagan, one officer supporting a fierce hunting falcon on his wrist. Others were ordered to settle in newly conquered Yunnan to ensure the continued pacification of the province. They were given Chinese wives, and one – Sayyid Ajall Shams al-Din al-Bukhari – was made governor. As a further reward, the faithful Muslims were given control over roads and communications. From that time, their grip on the trade of Yunnan has rarely slackened. Even today most out-of-the-way hostelries are Muslim-run, and truck drivers, as much as muleteers, are likely to be followers of the Prophet Mohammed.

During the centuries following their settlement in Yunnan, the Uzbek followers of Shams al-Din gradually became assimilated into the local population through intermarriage – a process which continues today. They became increasingly Chinese in appearance (though some are still noticeably more hirsute, with longer noses than their Han neighbours), and adopted Chinese as their language, retaining Arabic only for religious instruction, and forgetting Turkish completely. To their Han neighbours they became a part of the minority group known as Hui, or Chinese-speaking Muslims *(see panels on page 81 and 308)*. Relations weren't always good, but they got along fairly well until the mid-19th century, when oppression by the Qing authorities would spark a major Muslim rebellion.

## SOUTH CHINA UNDER THE MING DYNASTY

After Kublai Khan's death, Yuan power rapidly disintegrated and the Mongols were replaced, in 1368, by the Han Chinese Ming Dynasty. The Ming consolidated China's hold over Yunnan and Sichuan provinces, also making an attempt in 1407 to reconquer Vietnam – though ultimately they failed, and were driven out in 1428. The Ming also secured China's control over Guizhou, making it a Chinese province for the first time and encouraging Han Chinese emigration into the area from Sichuan and Hunan to the north and east. The pressure of migration and increasing Han

### CHINESE INVENTIONS

The ancient Chinese were world leaders in technology: monumental inventions such as paper and printing, magnetic compasses, gunpowder and irrigation were familiar to them hundreds of years before they were developed in Europe.

The Chinese first made paper around 200 AD, while printing evolved around eight centuries later – albeit with carved stamps rather than moveable type. Imperial geographers were busy with the deviation of magnetic north from true north before Europeans were even aware that the earth had a magnetic field. Around 1,100 iron foundries in China were already producing quantities of iron and steel unmatched in Europe until the 18th century. Technology to pump water for irrigation was in use by

the 1st century AD, and the water wheel 400 years later, again well in advance of Europe. In the 9th century, Daoist monks, searching for the elixir of eternal life, mixed charcoal, saltpeter and sulphur to accidentally make gunpowder. The mixture was later used for fireworks, and by imperial troops in bombs and grenades. And by the 13th century, using precision instruments, the astronomical observatory in Beijing had calculated the length of one year to an astonishing degree of accuracy.

Yet the Chinese never developed their precocious technology – and it was to cost them dear: by the late Middle Ages they were falling rapidly behind the Europeans, with costly implications *(see page 190)*.

control over the region prompted numerous revolts by the indigenous Miao people, some of whom were captured and sent to Hainan Island to compete with the indigenous Li for control over the central hills in another case of the Chinese "using barbarians to control barbarians". Nevertheless, the Miao long remained restive, rebelling against Han control from time to time until the late Qing period *(see page 32)*. Under the Ming, Guangdong, too, was given its current provincial name, "broad east", to distinguish it from Guangxi or "broad west".

## Yongle and maritime expansion

The third Ming Emperor Yongle (r. 1402–1424) was both ambitious and far-sighted. In 1403 he transferred the imperial capital from Nanjing back to Beijing, ordering the construction of the Forbidden City (1406–20) and the Temple of Heaven (1420). But Yongle wasn't only interested in promoting Beijing and the north. He consolidated China's hold across the south, from Guangdong to Yunnan, setting up military bases at Tengchong and Yongchang (Baoshan), close to the Burmese frontier in the far southwest in 1403. He also developed the city of Quanzhou in Fujian as a major port. Yongle was unique in the annals of Imperial China in that he pursued an active maritime policy – a thing previously unheard of in this very continental, land-based empire – sending his favourite admiral, the Yunnanese Muslim eunuch Zheng He (1371–1433), to explore Southeast Asia and the Indian Ocean as far as the Red Sea and the coast of East Africa.

Starting in 1405, Emperor Yongle dispatched Zheng He on six major naval expeditions at the head of a fleet of hundreds of "treasure ships". Yongle's purpose was to extend Chinese control over Nan Yang, the "southern seas", by imposing imperial control over trade and forcing the peoples of the littoral into paying tribute to the Ming throne in Beijing. Zheng He developed Quanzhou into the main base for his "treasure fleets", bringing wealth and development to the Fujian coast. Significantly, he also visited Taiwan on at least one occasion, signalling developing Chinese interest in that island– although it wasn't until 1683 that this final piece of territory was absorbed into China by the Qing Dynasty.

---

**FAR LEFT:** a Mongol battleship. **LEFT:** a giraffe presented to Ming Emperor Yongle. **RIGHT:** early English impressions of Chinese aristocrats.

## Foreign threats

Yongle died in 1424 and was succeeded by his son, Hongxi (r. 1424–25) who was both more traditional and more inward-looking. Hongxi halted Zheng He's great maritime expeditions, and also stopped sending missions to Yunnan and Vietnam in search of pearls and gold. He was succeeded by Xuande (r. 1425–35), who allowed Zheng He to make one more overseas voyage, though the era of Ming maritime explorations ended definitively in 1434, when Xuande ordered the navy disbanded and the dynasty turned decisively in on itself, outlawing overseas voyages *(see panel, page 190)*.

It was unfortunate timing. Even though the Ming had decided to turn China's back on the outside world, there was little Beijing could do to prevent the outside world beating a path to China's door. To begin with, this threat was regional, in the form of raids carried out by Japanese pirates known as *wako* (*woukou* in Chinese) who had been raiding the coast of Korea and China as far south as Hainan from the 13th century, and whose activities grew bolder and more destructive in the 15th and 16th centuries.

Nor was it any longer just a regional threat. The first Portuguese ships, under Fernão Peres de Andrade, anchored off Guangzhou in 1514, signalling the arrival for the first time of European ships in Chinese waters. In 1535, Portugal obtained the right to anchor shipping in **Macau** harbour and to trade there, making Macau another enclave in the string of forts and harbours established to gain control of the trade of the Indies. By 1557 the Portuguese were permitted to start a settlement in recognition of their services in fighting *wako* pirates – the first and by far the earliest of numerous European settlements to be established in China. At this early stage, Portuguese administration was limited to the Macau peninsula, with neighbouring Taipa and Coloane islands remaining under Chinese administration.

In 1544 Portuguese mariners also sighted the island of **Taiwan**, which they named Ilha Formosa

or "Beautiful Island", although they made no attempt to settle. Chinese control of the island was still 150 years in the future, and at the time it was only visited occasionally by Chinese and Japanese adventurers and fishermen. In 1624, however, the Dutch East India Company, operating from its headquarters at Batavia in Java, set up an administration at Tainan in the south of the island. Three years later their Spanish rivals set up a fort at Keelung in the northeast, where they remained until they were driven out by the Dutch in 1642. During this period, and with Dutch encouragement, Han Chinese from the mainland began to settle on the island in serious numbers for the first time. It is interesting that an island so close to the Chinese mainland – and today so vigorously claimed by

Beijing as an integral part of the Chinese motherland – should have been settled by the Dutch and Spanish before any Chinese administration was set up. Certainly the Straits of Taiwan are both wider and more difficult to navigate than the narrow Qiongzhou Straits separating Hainan from the Guangdong coast, and it seems that Taiwan had an evil reputation with Chinese traders and sailors, who sometimes referred to the island as the "Gate of Hell". Even so, with the fall of the Ming Dynasty in 1644, all this was about to change.

## 1644–1800: THE EARLY QING DYNASTY

In 1644 the Manchus sacked the Ming capital at Beijing, and shortly thereafter the Ming General Wu Sangui (1612–78), who commanded 100,000 troops at the strategic garrison of Shanhaiguan on the Great Wall, threw in his lot with the invading Manchus and opened the gates to their forces. The Mandate of Heaven had passed from the Ming, and in 1644 the Shunzhi Emperor (r. 1644–61) proclaimed the Qing Dynasty, becoming the first Manchu emperor to rule over China.

The last Ming pretender, Prince Gui (1623–62), fled south to Guangzhou where he was crowned king in 1646, but he was closely pursued by Qing troops and soon fled west, crossing to seek sanctuary at Sagaing in Burma. Under Qing pressure, the Burmese handed Prince Gui over to that implacable enemy of the Ming, General Wu Sangui, who executed him personally in Yunnan by strangling him with a bowstring in April 1662.

Under the Qing, the Chinese Empire would reach its greatest extent, controlling not just the whole of southern China (initially with the important exception of Taiwan), but also Tibet, Xinjiang, all of Mongolia and a large slice of Kazakhstan and Kyrgyzstan. In the mould of its Han Chinese and Mongol predecessors, however, it would develop as and remain very much a continental, land-based power, exercising little influence at sea.

### Koxinga and Taiwan

By the time of the first great Qing Emperor, Kangxi (r. 1661–1722) the Qing Empire had been fully consolidated across the south, and all southern provinces, from Yunnan to Fujian, were firmly under Qing administration. One exception was Taiwan, which remained under Dutch control in the north and west of the island, while the aboriginal tribes of the mountainous interior and remote east coast remained independent. Strangely, it was the defeat of the Ming – who had ignored Taiwan during their 276 years in power – that would at last bring Taiwan into the Chinese fold.

In 1624, at Nagasaki, Japan, a male child was born to a Chinese merchant and pirate called Zheng Zhilong, and his Japanese wife, Tagawa Matsu. He was given the Japanese name Tei Seiko and the Chinese name Zheng Chenggong, though he is better known to history by the name Koxinga – apparently an unlikely Portuguese Romanisation of the Taiwanese pronunciation of his Chinese name. The young Koxinga moved to Quanzhou in Fujian at the age of seven, before going on to study at Nanjing Imperial University and becoming a Ming official. Following the collapse of the Ming Dynasty in 1644, Koxinga's father, Zheng Zhilong, surrendered to the invading Qing. Soon after, Qing armies seized Quanzhou as part of their conquest of southern China, and Koxinga's mother either committed suicide or was raped and killed by the Manchu troops.

Koxinga's response was to swear continuing fealty to the Ming. He raised new forces and fought against the Qing for a number of years, on one occasion reaching Nanjing – but his resources were no match for those of the imperial army, and in 1661 he led a fleet of warships to invade Taiwan and drive out the Dutch. Koxinga was successful in this, capturing the Dutch fort of Zeelandia in Tainan after a nine-month siege on 1 February 1662. The Ming loyalist went on to establish his Kingdom of Tungning (1662–83) on the island, with its capital at Tainan.

Koxinga then devoted himself to making Taiwan into an effective base for anti-Qing sympathisers who wanted to restore the Ming Dynasty to power, but he died unexpectedly of malaria in 1662 at the age of 38. He was succeeded by his son, Zheng Jing (r. 1662–81) and then by his grandson, Zheng Keshuang (r. 1681–83), both of whom continued to launch maritime raids against the Qing Empire in a futile attempt to retake the mainland for the Ming. In 1683 the Qing admiral Shi Lang responded by invading Taiwan and deposing Zheng Keshuang, making Taiwan – for the first time in history – a

**LEFT:** Koxinga (Zheng Chenggong) brought Taiwan under Chinese control after expelling the Dutch in 1662. **RIGHT:** Emperor Qianlong meets a foreign delegation.

part of China, and more specifically part of Fujian province. The island would eventually become a province of China in its own right in 1887. Koxinga remains honoured as a Chinese patriot today, both in Taiwan and on the mainland, but his greatest achievement was not his unsuccessful struggle to "overthrow the Qing, restore the Ming", but rather to unify Taiwan with the mainland and complete the socio-political map of southern China more or less as it is today.

## Qianlong and the British

After Qing Emperor Kangxi died in 1722, he was succeeded by his son, Emperor Yongzhen

(r.1722–35), and he in turn by his son, Emperor Qianlong (r. 1735–96). Both were strong-willed, hard-working rulers, and during their reigns – especially that of Qianlong – the Qing Empire was at its peak, ruling virtually unchallenged over an area in excess of 13 million sq. km (5 million sq. miles), an area almost 40 percent larger than that currently ruled by the People's Republic. The south was, by and large, peaceful, and both Yongzhen and Qianlong relied on trusted Han Chinese soldiers and administrators to govern the area. And yet the writing was on the wall. When Qianlong came to the throne in 1735, he inherited a treasury with 30 million taels from his father, Yongzhen. At the peak of his prosperity, Qianlong's treasury held around 74 million taels. And yet, at the end of his reign in 1796, the imperial treasury was virtually bankrupt as a result of military campaigns, palace-building, and the growing problem of paying for imported opium with silver specie, which was impoverishing China at about the same rate as it enriched British East India Company coffers in India.

In 1760 Qianlong, disturbed by the rising tide of opium arriving on Western shipping and the corresponding depletion of the national treasury, especially in silver coinage, had attempted to limit further overseas commerce by issuing an edict restricting all foreign trade to Canton (Guangzhou). In fact it proved all but impossible to

Emperor concluded: "Do not say that you were not warned in due time! Tremblingly obey and show no negligence!"

This was a magnificently haughty imperial response, no doubt. But it was also quite unrealistic, and showed that the Qing Dynasty, having largely barred its gates to the outside world, was rapidly losing touch with reality. And in the 19th century, that reality would be one of internal rebellion and external invasion, growing opium addiction and colonial interference. With the death of Qianlong in 1799 (three years after he abdicated in favour of his son, Emperor Jiaqing, r. 1796–1820), the empire had already started on a

restrict the trading activities of either his own subjects or the foreign merchants. Meanwhile, Qianlong came under increasing pressure from the British to rescind this legislation and open China fully to overseas trade. He famously resisted, refusing the requests of the Macartney Embassy in 1793, while informing King George III by imperial decree that: "As your ambassador can see for himself, we possess all things. I set no value on objects strange or ingenious, and have no use for your country's manufactures." Qianlong made it quite clear that he regarded the Macartney Embassy as a tributary mission, and sent a message to King George III warning that British vessels putting ashore at any point other than Guangzhou would be immediately expelled. The

long, steady decline that would lead, eventually, to the establishment of the Chinese Republic in 1912.

## 1800–1911: DECLINE AND FALL OF THE QING

The traffic in opium, meanwhile, continued to expand, mostly shipped by the British from their colonies in Bengal. By the end of Qianlong's reign, imports had reached around 1,000 chests annually. By the time Emperor Daoguang ascended the imperial throne in 1820, this figure had grown to 30,000 chests annually. Each chest held 140 pounds (64 kg) of opium, making a total of almost 2,000 tons. By the beginning of the 19th century there were already millions of addicts in China, and the country was paying for its spiralling drug habit with silver specie, disastrously depleting the national treasury. Clearly, from a Qing perspective, something had to be done.

In 1799 Emperor Jiaqing reaffirmed the ban on opium promulgated by his father, but without noticeable effect. In 1810 he went further, announcing that: "Opium is a poison, undermining our good customs and morality. Its use is prohibited by law." His son, Daoguang, continued to issue edicts after he came to the dragon throne in 1820, but to no avail – the British weren't listening, and nor, apparently, were the opium addicts. Accordingly, in 1838 Daoguang sent Lin Zexu, the formidable Governor-General of Henan and Hubei, as his commissioner to impose Qing anti-opium legislation on the unruly foreign traders in Guangzhou. To the fury of the Westerners – at whose head stood the British – Lin confiscated and destroyed more than 20,000 chests of opium and blockaded the port to foreign shipping. Lin also wrote to Queen Victoria, asking why the British prohibited opium imports into their own country, but forced it on China. "Was this a morally correct position?", the commissioner asked rhetorically.

Lin's letter was never delivered to the queen, although it was published in *The Times*. And while it may have given liberal anti-opium campaigners in Great Britain pause for thought, it raised no sympathy at all with the opium merchants of India and Canton, who loudly demanded compensation for their lost opium, and pressed for military retaliation. This came in 1840, with the arrival of warships and soldiers from India. European military superiority ensured the First Opium War (1840–42) was short, sharp and one-sided. The British seized control of Guangzhou and sailed up the Yangzi to interdict tax barges carrying grain to the Imperial Court at Beijing. In June 1842, they also sailed up the Huangpu, storming and capturing the walled city of Shanghai in a single night.

Shortly after the fall of Shanghai, the Qing authorities sued for peace, and the Treaty of Nanking was signed in August, transferring Hong Kong Island to the British "in perpetuity", awarding Britain 21 million ounces of silver in compensation for the seized opium, and opening five "Treaty Ports" to foreign shipping and residence including Guangzhou, Xiamen and Fuzhou in the south, as well as Ningbo and Shanghai.

**LEFT:** an opium den in the late 19th century.
**RIGHT:** French troops in combat against Taiping rebels, 1862.

Suddenly southern China was exposed to a new and troublesome "enemy at the gate", and the Portuguese settlement at Macau was joined by a British colony at Hong Kong.

## The Taiping Rebellion

This decline in Qing fortunes led to an increase in nostalgic and patriotic memories of earlier times, sparking a series of increasingly violent uprisings across China, and especially in the south. In 1851 a rising broke out at Jintian (today's Guiping) in Guangxi, when a 10,000-strong rebel force led by Hong Xiuquan defeated the Qing garrison forces. This was the beginning of the great Taiping Rebel-

lion (1851–64), an uprising that would strafe southern and central China, causing at least 20 million deaths, and up to 50 million according to some estimates – the bloodiest conflict in the history of the world up to this time, and since superseded only by World War II. The supreme leader and Heavenly King of the Taipings was Hong Xiuquan (1814–64), who received revelations causing him to believe he was the younger brother of Jesus Christ. In 1851 Hong set out to overthrow the despised Qing, who as Manchus were still considered foreign invaders, and replace their dynasty with the Han Chinese *Taiping Tianguo* or "Heavenly Kingdom of Great Peace".

The rising had begun in Guangxi in January 1851, but rapidly spread northwards. In March

1853, a force of more than half a million Taiping soldiers captured Nanjing, killing an estimated 30,000 Qing defenders and making the city the rebel capital, in earnest of which it was renamed Tianjing or "Heavenly Capital". At its height, the Taiping controlled much of China's territory south of the Yangzi River. Attempts to extend Taiping control north of the Yangzi were less successful, with a rebel thrust against the Qing capital, Beijing, being repelled.

From 1853, Hong Xiuquan became increasingly introverted, devoting more time to sensual pursuits, including his harem and delegating power to various subsidiary kings and princes. An

attack against Shanghai in August 1860, brought disaster upon the Taiping forces in the form of the "Ever Victorious Army" fighting for the Qing but led by General Charles "Chinese" Gordon, who would be killed at Khartoum in 1885. Gordon's army was later reorganised under two Qing officers of military genius, Zeng Guofan (1811–72) and Li Hongzhang (1823–1901). Hong Xiuquan declared that he would defend Tianjing (Nanjing), but died – possibly from taking poison, possibly from food-poisoning – in 1864. By this time the Qing reconquest was assured, and the once mighty Taiping forces were rapidly rolled up by the imperial armies. Hong's body was cremated at the former Ming Imperial Palace in Nanjing; the ashes were subsequently fired from a cannon by the victorious Qing so that the spirit of the deceased would find no resting place, but wander as a "restless ghost" in an eternal punishment for leading the rising.

## Further unrest and division

The Qing may have defeated the Taipings, but it was at a terrible cost in human life, as well as silver specie, and increasing Western involvement in Chinese affairs. Up to 1842, only Portuguese Macau and the Qing port of Guangzhou (Canton) had been open to foreigners, but after the First Opium War and the cession of Hong Kong Island to the British, a rash of so-called "treaty ports" opened along the southern coast. In addition to Guangzhou, Xiamen and Fuzhou (1842), these included Swatow (Shantou, Guangdong, 1860), Qiongzhou (Hainan, 1876), Beihai (Guangdong, 1876), Sanshui (Guangdong, 1897), Wuzhou (Guangxi, 1897), Santuo (Fujian, 1898), and Jiangmen (Guangdong, 1904). In addition, the Portuguese took advantage of Qing weakness to occupy Macau's offshore islands Taipa (1851) and Coloane (1864), as well as signing the Beijing Treaty with the Qing in 1887 by which China ceded to Portugal "the right to perpetual occupation and government of Macau".

As if this were not enough, the Qing faced a series of continuing rebellions elsewhere across the empire. These included a series of Hui Muslim uprisings across the northwest (1862–73), and the Xinjiang Muslim Rebellion of Yaqub Beg (1867–78). Nor was the south immune: between 1855 and 1873 a large part of western Yunnan broke away from the Qing Empire as local Hui Muslims set up their own state, Ping Nan Guo, or "Kingdom of the Peaceful South". Their leader,

### THE MIAO REBELLION

At about the same time as the Taiping Rebellion, the Miao minority in much of Guizhou and parts of Yunnan rose up against Qing oppression, discrimination and Han migratory pressures in the Miao Rebellion (1854–73). Sometimes joining with the Taiping, and with Hui Muslim insurgents further west, the rebels engendered a response of extreme brutality from the imperial authorities. Policies of ethnic cleansing known literally as "washing" were used, with entire towns effectively depopulated; in 1863 Guiyang was "washed", with mass deportations and executions. Time, technology and sheer force of numbers was on the side of the authorities, and the last resistance was mopped up in 1873. .

Du Wenxiu, also styled himself Sultan Sulayman and – tellingly – donned Ming Dynasty costume, indicating loyalty to the Qing's predecessors rather than to some distant Middle Eastern potentate. In the end the relatively powerful Qing armies triumphed, massacring innocent Hui, as well as rebels, as they advanced.

## Foreign power and the Boxers

By 1887, France had established itself as China's new southern neighbour along the Vietnamese and Lao borders, while to the west the British were similarly established in Burma. Both France and Britain used their influence to open "frontier

(1894–95) was fought mainly for control over Korea and ended in victory for Japan at the Treaty of Shimonoseki (17 April 1895), by which Japan not only gained primacy in Korea, but were also awarded part of the Liaodung Peninsula, and considerable war reparations from China. In southern China, the Japanese fleet also seized control of the Penghu Islands in the Straits of Formosa, as well as Taiwan itself, making both into Japanese colonies.

In 1899 the stuttering Qing Dynasty, now ruled by Empress Dowager Cixi (who exercised effective control over the empire from 1861 to her death in 1908), suffered another near-fatal blow

ports" – the inland equivalent of maritime "treaty ports" – in Yunnan and Guangxi, and in 1898 the French forced China to lease them the port of Zhanjiang on Guangdong's Leizhou Peninsula for a (theoretical) period of 99 years. As "Fort Bayard" this port would be administered by the French as part of their Indochinese Empire until it was formally returned to China by President Charles de Gaulle in 1946.

Meanwhile, further to the east, Imperial Japan was also flexing its muscles and detaching bits of Qing territory. The First Sino-Japanese War

**LEFT:** Boxers engage in battle with German troops during the Boxer Rebellion. **ABOVE:** a Chinese painting depicts foreign troops carrying their national flags.

when the "Boxers" – Yihetuan Qiyi or "Harmony of Righteous Fists Society" – started a rising against foreign influences in China. In 1900 the Boxers seized Beijing, killing some 230 foreigners and thousands of Chinese Christians. The remainder of the foreigners, together with many Chinese Christians, withdrew to the Foreign Legations where they held out for 55 days until a multinational coalition of some 20,000 troops could be sent to the rescue, eventually crushing the rising by 7 September 1901. Once again, China was forced to pay a huge indemnity, while Empress Dowager Cixi was outmanoeuvred and humiliated. She died in 1908, leaving the two-year-old heir, Puyi, to become the last Qing Emperor (1908–12). ❏

# POST-IMPERIAL HISTORY

China's turbulent 20th century saw the collapse of the ancient imperial system, a series of bloody civil wars, a brutal foreign invasion, and three decades of hardline communist misrule. Yet pragmatism has comprehensively replaced ideology to spur a remarkable recovery: China is now poised to become the world's leading economy

At the beginning of the 20th century, most Chinese felt that Qing imperial rule had lost any legitimacy. Secret societies like the Xingzhonghui or "Revive China Society" and the Tongmenghui or "United Allegiance Society" were dedicated to its overthrow and the establishment of Han Chinese government. These movements spread across the country, but were especially active in treaty ports where they could operate beyond the reach of the Qing authorities. Southern China had by this time become very much a part of the Chinese body politic, tending towards the rebellious and becoming a focus for nationalist sympathies.

## Sun Yatsen and the Republic

A key figure in the anti-Qing revolutionary movement was Sun Yatsen (1866–1925), now popularly known as the "Father of Modern China" both on the mainland and in Taiwan. Sun – whose name is pronounced Sun Zhonghsan in Mandarin – was born in Guangdong but studied in Hawaii, where he acquired good English. He returned to China and studied medicine, graduating as a doctor from the Hong Kong College of medicine for Chinese (later the University of Hong Kong). But Sun was dismayed at the conservatism of the Qing government and concerned that China was being left behind, not just by the nations of the West, but by Japan as well. In 1894 he founded the Xingzhonghui *(see above)* at Honolulu in Hawaii, using the slogan "Expel the foreigners, revive China, and establish a unified government". In 1905, under his direction, the Xingzhonghui merged with several other revolutionary groups to form the Tongmenghui. Later, in 1912, the latter would form the nucleus for Sun's Nationalist Party or Guomindang (often written KMT, derived from the old Wade-Giles transliteration "Kuomintang"),

which still survives on Taiwan today.

On 10 October 1911, the first shots of the Xinhai Revolution that would replace the Qing Dynasty with a Chinese Republic broke out at Wuchang on the Yangzi. Rebellion quickly spread throughout the southern provinces, resulting in the abdication of Puyi, the last Qing Emperor, on 12 February 1912. The revolution replaced China's three-millennia-old monarchy with a republic notionally wedded to democratic ideas and principles. A group of revolutionaries in Nanjing elected Sun Yatsen provisional President of the Republic of China, but further north in Beijing Sun had a rival for power in the person of Yuan Shikai (1859–1916), commander of the powerful Beiyang Army, and a man who aspired to become a new emperor. The revolutionaries were as yet in no position to fight the Beiyang Army, so it was agreed that Sun should step down and Yuan become President of the Republic of China. A new period of warlord government was beginning.

In December 1915, the ambitious old-school warlord Yuan Shikai proclaimed himself the new Emperor of China, taking the reign name Hongxian – but times had changed, and ordinary Chinese were clamouring for accountability and democracy, not for a new autocracy. The strongest opposition to Yuan's government was in the south, and not just in traditionally rebellious Guangdong. The Military Commander of Yunnan Province, Cai

the north, the warlord Duan Qirui (1864–1936) took over command of the Beiyang Army and dominated Beijing. In the south, Sun Yatsen established a rival revolutionary government in Guangzhou, with the backing of six separate southern provincial cliques, as well as – an increasingly important factor – Overseas Chinese communities in Southeast Asia, America and Australia. Sun's regional allies included the **Yunnan Clique** of Tang Jiyao (1883–1927), the **Old Guangxi Clique** of Lu Rongting (1856–1927), the **New Guangxi Clique** of Li Zongren (1890-1969), the local **Guangdong Clique** of warlords and, of course, the Guomindang Party (KMT).

E (1882–1916) was a follower of Sun Yatsen and a member of the Tongmenghui. When Yuan Shikai proclaimed himself Emperor in 1915, Cai and his military allies confronted him, defeating his 80,000-man army in Sichuan with just 20,000 Yunnanese troops. Yuan was forced to abandon his imperial dreams. The old warlord died a few months later, from kidney failure and damaged pride.

Unfortunately, Yuan Shikai's death did not lead to a unified Chinese Republic – except, perhaps, in theory. In reality China was divided along regional lines, with powerful warlords seizing control of private fiefdoms, sometimes of immense size. In

In 1920, Sun Yatsen and the KMT set up a new administration in Guangzhou, but were denied recognition by the Western powers, who perceived them as dangerously leftist. The newly established Soviet Union had no such compunctions, and saw in the Chinese nationalist movement a potential ally. By 1923 Sun Yatsen and his government were receiving aid and advice from the Soviets, and Mikhail Borodin, a senior Comintern agent, had arrived in south China to advise on the restructuring of the KMT along Leninist lines. The Comintern also instructed the Chinese Communist Party (CCP), which had been founded in Shanghai in 1921, to cooperate with the KMT, leading to the establishment of the First KMT-CCP United Front in 1924.

**LEFT:** Sun Yatsen, still revered as the father of modern China. **ABOVE:** pedlar, 1898. **RIGHT:** "Big Ears Du".

Meanwhile, Sun had been planning to mount a "Northern Expedition" to overthrow the northern warlord cliques and reunify China under KMT rule. But by 1924 he was terminally ill with cancer – and died in Beijing the following year, aged 58, mourned by patriotic Chinese everywhere. Under these circumstances, the task of leading the Northern Expedition fell to Chiang Kaishek (1887–1975), a Zhejiang native who had studied at Baoding Military Academy and later in Japan, rising rapidly through the ranks to become Sun Yatsen's senior military commander in charge of the Whampoa Military Academy at Guangzhou. Chiang was also closely associated with the powerful Shanghai

During the "White Terror" thousands of communists and left-wing sympathisers were rounded up and killed. Chiang went on to establish the new KMT capital at Nanjing, moving the political centre of gravity back to the centre and north, away from Guangdong and the south.

## Civil War and World War (1927–49)

The CCP, although badly mauled in Shanghai, still had a number of revolutionary rural areas in the south to fall back on, most significantly the self-styled "Chinese Soviet Republic" centred on Ruijin in Jiangxi province. Chiang, obsessed with

"Green Gang" and its notorious hoodlum leader "Big Ears Du" (Du Yuesheng, 1887–1951). He was also passionately anti-communist and distrustful of the KMT-CCP United Front.

The long-planned Northern Expedition set out from the KMT powerbase of Guangzhou on 9 July 1926. Chiang Kaishek had 100,000 soldiers of the National Revolutionary Army (NRA) at his disposal, though this would increase to more than 250,000 as he advanced north towards his main targets, the northern warlords. By 1927 Chiang's NRA had entered Shanghai and Nanjing, and won control of half of China. But at this stage the revolutionary forces split, with Chiang Kaishek turning on his erstwhile communist allies in Shanghai with the help of "Big Ears Du" and his hoodlums.

removing the communists from the scene, adopted a disastrous policy of ignoring Imperial Japanese provocations (the occupation of Manchuria and the unprovoked attack on Shanghai in 1932) until he could root out and destroy the CCP. During this period Chiang famously defined the Japanese as "a disease of the skin" and the communists as "a disease of the heart".

From 1931 to 1935 KMT troops systematically surrounded and attempted to eliminate the various communist base areas across southern China, but ultimately to no avail. The Red Army was forced to make a series of strategic withdrawals, but eventually escaped west on the Long March (1934–36) across the southern Chinese provinces of Guangdong, Guangxi, Guizhou, Hunan and Yunnan, before turning north across eastern Tibet, Sichuan and Gansu before re-establishing itself in a new and safer base area at Yan'an in Shanxi Province. This would remain the communist capital until 1948.

Japan, meanwhile, was on the move, largely unchallenged by Chiang Kaishek who was too busy prosecuting the Civil War to oppose foreign invasion. In 1931 the Japanese used a staged incident of "sabotage" on the Mukden Railway to justify invading and occupying China's vast Dongbei (Northeast) region, which they renamed "Manchukuo" or "Country of the Manchus" and administered through the puppet Emperor Puyi. By 1936, with the Red Army safely relocated to Yan'an

Throughout the war, the Japanese attempted to extend the areas under their control across the whole of China's vast land mass – but the distances were too great and the resistance too determined, while Japan was increasingly distracted by the inexorable advance of the US military machine across the Pacific towards their own home islands. In south China things were bad, but not as desperate as further to the north, around Nanjing and Shanghai, or in Manchuria. Taiwan had been occupied by Japan since 1895, but apart from the coastal areas around Fuzhou and Xiamen, Fujian and Jiangxi Provinces remained, by and large, unoccupied. Guangdong, Guangxi and

and Mao Zedong securely in power as the chief military tactician and head of the CCP, Japan had already helped itself to further territories across north China, as well as bombing and invading Shanghai. In 1937, the "Marco Polo Bridge Incident" outside Beijing led to the outbreak of full hostilities between China and Japan. From 1937 to 1941, China fought alone – but following Japan's unprovoked attack on Pearl Harbor on 7 December 1941, the Sino-Japanese War became part of the much larger World War II, and China gained important allies in the USA and the British Empire.

**LEFT:** Mao and Zhang Guotao at the 1935 reunification of the communist armies on the Long March.
**ABOVE:** Guomindang troops on the Burma Road, 1945.

large parts of Hunan and Guizhou fell to the invader, however, and Hong Kong was seized from the British by Japan just one day after the attack on Pearl Harbor.

Elsewhere in southern China, power remained in the hands of local warlords and military men owing allegiance, more or less, to the KMT. In Yunnan, the American Volunteer Group or AVG, better known as Claire Chennault's "Flying Tigers", were busy battling the Japanese on behalf of the KMT government, while other allied airmen flew "the Hump" from India, across Japanese-occupied Burma, to southwest China. Yunnan and Sichuan were also supplied overland by the Burma and Ledo Roads across northern Burma, but with the dropping of atomic weapons on Hiroshima and

Nagasaki in August 1945, followed by Japan's pre-cipitate surrender, the importance of the south-western front vanished almost overnight.

With Japan defeated, full-scale civil war between Chiang Kaishek's KMT and Mao Zedong's CCP was not long in coming. But this time the scales had turned. The CCP had a new and immensely powerful ally in the north. On 8 August 1945, less than a week before Japan's sur-render, the Soviet Union entered the Pacific War, seizing Manchuria, as well as northern Korea and a small part of the Japanese home territory. Between 1945 and 1949 the area of CCP control continued to expand, while that of the KMT

shrank commensurately. In January, 1949, Beijing fell to the communists, followed by Nanjing in April. Mao proclaimed the establishment of the People's Republic of China at Beijing's Tianan-men Square on 1 October, and in December the defeated KMT government fled to the island of Taiwan, where Chiang Kaishek resumed his posi-tion as President of a much-reduced Republic of China on 1 March 1950.

## The Mao years

The CCP's reunification of China (less Taiwan) in 1949 left the country as unified as it had ever been in its long history. The south was set to suf-fer the same vicissitudes and privations as the rest of the nation as Mao Zedong spent the next 27

years pursuing a series of ruthless and sometimes bizarre revolutionary policies designed, primarily, to keep his position as supreme ruler unchallenged. Between 1958 and 1961, in the disastrous Great Leap Forward, as many as 30 million people died in famine across China, including the south. Similarly the Great Proletarian Cultural Revolu-tion, which began in 1966 and dragged on, in places, until after Mao's death a decade later, affected hundreds of thousands of people across China, with the bodies of feuding Red Guards and their opponents being washed down the Zhu Juang (Pearl River) that drains south China, and out to the South China Sea past Macau. In December 1966 Macau itself was shaken by pro-Red Guard riots, and a few months later, in May 1967, Hong Kong, too, was affected.

While minorities such as the Zhuang in Guangxi enjoyed nominal autonomy during this period, all minority groups suffered ethnic and cultural per-secution at the hands of the Red Guards, and it was not until the Deng Xiaoping era that a more mean-ingful autonomy began to be established in the hills of Yunnan and Guizhou. Today the minori-ties, while still experiencing strict political con-trol, enjoy more religious, linguistic and cultural freedom than at any time in their long history of association with the Han.

From the late 1950s to mid-1970s, Guangdong, Guangxi and Yunnan all found themselves on the frontline of the Second Indochina War (1954–75). China supported communist North Vietnam in its bid to take over South Vietnam which, in turn, was backed by the USA. Interestingly, despite the volume of matériel and other supplies entering North Vietnam from southern China, the USA prohibited bombing in any of the North Viet-namese provinces contiguous with China, and no bombs fell on China itself.

On 30 April 1975, Saigon fell to the North Viet-namese Army and the Second Indochina War came to an end. On 9 September 1976, Mao Zedong died, and with him the last vestiges of the Cultural Revolution.

## Deng Xiaoping and the recovery

In 1978 the tough-minded reformist Deng Xiao-ping became paramount leader, setting the nation on a new economic course that would transform China and bring prosperity to many, especially in the southern coastal provinces. But Deng was vigorously opposed to what he per-ceived as Vietnamese hegemonism in Southeast

Asia, and when Hanoi overthrew Beijing's Cambodian Khmer Rouge allies in 1979, Deng ordered PLA units stationed in southern China to invade Vietnam's northern provinces in retaliation. Chinese units advanced into Vietnam from Guangzhou and Yunnan, occupying and subsequently bombarding five Vietnamese provincial capitals. Road and rail links were cut, and normal diplomatic relations between China and Vietnam were not restored until 1989.

Deng was keen to settle the outstanding colonial issues surrounding Hong Kong and Macau as swiftly and amicably as possible. In 1984 the United Kingdom and China signed the Sino-

Deng Xiaoping died in February 1997, just four months before the return of Hong Kong to the Chinese motherland. Since his death, China has continued to follow the free-market economic policies he introduced, enjoying spectacular rates of growth and levels of prosperity quite unforeseen just two decades ago. South China is now more prosperous and peaceful than it has been at any time in its history. Relations between China and Vietnam, though still suspicious, continue to improve, and trade between the two old rivals – prosperity always being the key to stability – is booming.

Perhaps the biggest problem facing the region, as indeed China as a whole, is the increasing

British Joint Declaration agreeing to transfer sovereignty over Hong Kong to the People's Republic of China in 1997, conditional on Hong Kong being governed as a Special Administrative Region (SAR) retaining a high degree of autonomy and its own legal system for at least 50 years. The transfer went ahead smoothly on July 1, 1997, leaving Macau, the first European colony in China, as the last – though not for long. In December 1999, under a similar Sino-Portuguese Joint Declaration, Macau became a Special Administrative Region, ending more than three centuries of Portuguese rule.

**LEFT:** remembering the Long March. **ABOVE:** Shenzhen was China's first Special Economic Zone.

disparity in income between rich and poor. The southern coastal provinces are among the richest in China, and Hainan today is becoming China's tropical Riviera. Yunnan, too, is increasingly prosperous, having emerged as an important destination for domestic, as well as international tourism. Hong Kong and Macau are rich and increasingly free Special Administrative Regions, apparently thriving under China's "two systems" government. Meanwhile, despite the continuing political dispute over Taiwan's status, cross-straits trade between Taiwan and the mainland – especially Fujian province – is huge and growing exponentially. This should help guarantee regional stability if carefully managed. *For more on the Taiwan situation, see pages 228–9.* ❑

# DECISIVE DATES

## The Early Empires

**c. 16th–11th century BC**
Shang Dynasty established in
north China (above, writing on
tortoise-shell oracle from era).

**c. 11th century–256 BC**
Zhou Dynasty. Capital established at Chang'an (Xi'an).

## Han Dynasty (206BC–AD220)

**206 BC**
Han capital at Chang'an (Xi'an).

**111 BC**
Minyue Kingdom under
Chinese control.

## Three Kingdoms Period (220–265)

**220**
Zhuya Commandery set up on
Hainan Island; Nanhai Commandery near Guangzhou.

**c. 220–260**
Chinese control consolidated
over Fujian, Jiangxi, Hainan and
Guangxi, bringing most of
southern China under Han rule.

## Sui Dynasty (581–618)

**581**
Sui Dynasty reunifies China.

**589–610**
Construction of a system of
canals linking northern and
southern China.

## Tang Dynasty (618–907)

**618**
A new and powerful dynasty
develops around Chang'an
(Xi'an). Buddhism and Confucian
bureaucracy flourish. The Silk
Road promotes deeper contacts
with Central Asia and the West.

**907**
Five Dynasties and Ten
Kingdoms rule divided China.

## Song Dynasty (960–1279)

**960**
Northern Song reunites China,
capital established at Kaifeng.
Hainan Island finally brought
under full Chinese control.

**1127**
Southern Song Dynasty establishes capital at Hangzhou.

**1223**
Mongol leader Genghis Khan
seizes control of territory north
of the Huang He (Yellow River).

**1253**
Mongols invade Yunnan.

## Yuan Dynasty (1279–1368)

**1279**
Mongols owing allegiance to
Kublai Khan defeat the Southern
Song. Beijing is made capital.
Tibet and Yunnan added to the
Empire. Silk Road flourishes.

## Ming Dynasty (1368–1644)

Ethnically Chinese Ming
Dynasty replaces Mongol Yuan
and consolidates control over
Yunnan and Sichuan provinces.

**1403**
Beijing re-established as Ming
capital.

**1405–24**
Maritime expeditions to Southeast Asia; Quanzhou in Fujian
becomes a major port.

**1553**
Macau becomes a Portuguese
trading port and the first European settlement in China.

**1624**
Dutch establish settlement on
Taiwan and encourage Han Chinese migration to the island.

**1627**
Spanish establish fort at
Keelung on Taiwan.

## Qing Dynasty (1644–1911)

**1644**
The Manchus seize Beijing,
beginning the Qing Dynasty.

**1661–2**
Ming loyalist Zheng Chenggong
seizes control of Taiwan.

**1661–1722**
Qing dominion over all of southern China except Taiwan.
Kangxi (pictured below) is ruler.

**1683**
Qing admiral Shi Lang invades
Taiwan. Taiwan becomes part
of China for the first time.

**1736–96**
Qing Empire reaches its zenith.

**1839–42**
First Opium War. British force China to open up to Western shipping. Hong Kong Island is transferred to Britain.

**1851–64**
Taiping Rebellion.

**1854–73**
Miao and Muslim rebellions in the southwestern provinces.

**1860**
Kowloon Peninsula ceded to Britain.

**1895**
Japan defeats China in Sino-Japanese War; acquires Taiwan.

**1899–1901**
Boxer Rebellion against foreign influences in China.

**1911**
Republican Revolution: provisional republican government established in Nanjing. Sun Yatsen is named president, but soon steps down.

**1912**
Abdication of the last emperor, Puyi *(above)*.

## Post-Imperial China (1912–1949)

**1916–27**
Civil war in Chinese Republic.

**1919**
May 4th Movement in Beijing demands Chinese unity and independence.

**1921**
Chinese Communist Party founded.

**1926**
Chiang Kaishek leads Northern Expedition from Guangzhou in a bid to unify China.

**1927**
Nationalists split with the communists; civil war across southern and central China.

**1931–41**
Second Sino-Japanese War. Japan conquers the greater part of southern China. Yunnan, Guizhou and parts of Fujian and Jiangxi resist successfully .

**1934–36**
Chinese communists withdraw from southern China to Yan'an in the Long March.

**1946–9**
Civil War results in Nationalist defeat and Chiang Kaishek's withdrawal to Taiwan.

## People's Republic of China

**1949**
Mao Zedong declares People's Republic in Beijing on 1 October.

**1950–53**
China joins Korean War in support of the communist north, supplies arms and equipment to the Viet Minh in the First Indochina War against France.

**1958–61**
Great Leap Forward results in a mass famine that kills upwards of 30 million Chinese.

**1966–76**
Cultural Revolution *(below, a march during that era)*.

**1976**
Mao Zedong dies.

**1978**
Deng Xiaoping institutes a policy of economic reform and opening to the West.

**1979–80**
China invades North Vietnam.

**1980–88**
Special Economic Zones (SEZs), most notably at Shenzhen, kick-start the remarkable growth of the southern economy.

**1988**
Hainan Island, formerly part of Guangdong, becomes a province and an SEZ.

**1989**
Tiananmen Square demonstrations.

**1997**
Deng Xiaoping dies in February; Hong Kong reverts to China.

**1999**
Macau reverts to Chinese sovereignty.

**2000–2007**
Rapidly expanding economy, led by the south, becomes the world's second strongest.

# GEOGRAPHY AND WILDLIFE

The southern Chinese provinces encompass a range of
habitats from tropical lowlands to high mountains, and are
home to a rich array of plant and animal life

China's southern provinces straddle both the temperate and tropical biological zones and, containing elements of both, can be considered some of the richest wildlife and plant-life habitats anywhere on Earth. The region encompasses the tropical regions of Hainan Island and Xishuangbanna in the deep south of Yunnan, the alpine zones of the sub-Himalaya, a large swathe of subtropical hill-forest country, and a long subtropical coastline. It all adds up to a tapestry of varied topography, offering habitats for a vast array of wild animals and plants.

Yet the region is not especially well known as a naturalist's paradise. This is partly due to the fact that its rich heritage has been substantially degraded by the pressures of a large population, a situation that has been exacerbated by a lack of environmental awareness. Nonetheless, if you know where to look, there is still much to see, and more and more locations are becoming accessible to birdwatchers and other ecotourists.

Some highlights are the lush forests of Xishuangbanna, where elephants still lurk in a few sites, the tropical island of Hainan, with its endemic birds and the rare Eld's deer, and the spectacular limestone landscapes of northwestern Hunan, home to clouded leopards and giant salamanders. The Mai Po Marshes in Hong Kong are the finest tidal reserve in southeast China, attracting huge numbers of waders and wildfowl, and breeding colonies of green turtles can be seen at the Huidonggang reserve further east on the Guangdong coast. Less well known, except amongst keen birders, is Chebaling Nature

Reserve, also in Guangdong which has some of the best lowland forest in the region. The vanishingly rare South China tiger may still roam here, along with clouded leopards, and there are special birds too, such as white-eared night herons, Blyth's and crested kingfishers, and silver pheasants.

## Overview

The whole of southern China covered in this book, from Yunnan in the west across to the eastern coastal province of Fujian, experiences an essentially subtropical or tropical monsoon climate, though considerably influenced locally by montane climates on the hills and mountains.

Southern China has some of the richest subtropical forests in the whole of Asia, partly

**PRECEDING PAGES:** young girls at a Miao festival in Guizhou. **LEFT:** red pandas live at moderate elevations in the mountains of Yunnan. **RIGHT:** a blood pheasant.

because this region has had a fairly stable climate for a very long time. Another reason is that temperate, subtropical and tropical habitats exist here often in close proximity, aided by the many variations in altitude. The southern Chinese climate also plays a part: winters in much of the region (Hainan and Xishuangbanna are exceptions) are considerably colder than other areas of similar latitude – for instance, the coastal city of Fuzhou lies at the same latitude as Miami, but has an average January temperature of just 13°C (55°F) compared with 20°C (68°F). This allows temperate species to thrive, but the cool temperatures are sufficiently short-lived and sufficiently mild to ensure tropical species can also survive.

The subtropical evergreen forests of the southeast mainland and the monsoon rainforests of Hainan Island include a remarkable 1,700 families of higher plants, including many endemic species, amongst them well-known rarities such as dawn redwood and ginkgo. The latter is often seen at temples where it is widely planted, but is rare in a truly wild state, persisting in just a handful of sites, such as in the hills of the lower Yangzi and in Guizhou.

From the viewpoint of natural habitats, the following **major regions** can be recognised, although these do merge together to some extent. It is no surprise that most of the areas of high biodiversity

## ENVIRONMENTAL DEGRADATION

China's huge population and high demands for energy, coupled with the recent headlong rush towards the perceived rewards of modern life, have taken their toll of the natural world. To make matters worse, the widespread use of wild animals and plants for food and in traditional Chinese medicine continues to impact on the natural populations of many species. Although there are encouraging signs that high-technology solutions and cleaner, greener industrial development is beginning to appear (Beijing announced encouraging moves in this direction at the G8 summit in 2007), China still has thousands of antiquated, highly polluting industrial plants, such as chemical factories, old-fashioned coal mines, coal-burning power stations, and cement works.

China's rivers are also being used increasingly for hydro-electric power generation – most famously the Three Gorges Dam on the Yangzi. The Mekong (Lancang Jiang) has also recently been dammed in southern Yunnan, and this is already having negative environmental consequences as it affects the natural flow and levels of this mighty river (not just in China, but also downstream in neighbouring Laos and Vietnam). One-third of China suffers from severe acid rain, more than 300 million people have no access to clean water, and half of the country's waterways are badly polluted. Habitat loss for wildlife is a long-running problem. Deforestation has been rampant in the past, and is still a problem in many areas, outside of designated reserves.

are associated with upland or mountain ranges, since so much of the low-lying land has long been intensively cultivated.

## Low mountain ranges behind the coastal plain

A large part of the lands of southern China described in this book, from Fujian and Jiangxi in the east across to Hunan, Guangdong and Guangxi in the west, comprises the hills and low mountain ranges that form a near-continuous swathe of land between the southern coastal plains and the basin of the lower reaches of the Yangzi River.

The natural vegetation of this area consists of composition varies with altitude, aspect and geology, and is richly varied, with evergreen broadleaved and coniferous communities as well as deciduous woodland. Groves of bamboo also dominate in patches, and at high levels there are cloud-forests of pine, birch and cypress. Rare birds include David's parrotbill and Elliot's pheasant.

Wedged between Fujian to the east and Hunan to the west, **Jiangxi Province** abuts the southern bank of the mighty Yangzi. The climate here is subtropical, and in the mountainous areas the rainfall is high – up to 2,000 mm (almost 80 inches) a year. While mountains dominate in the

rich subtropical forests, grading into the broader subtropical plains in the south. **Fujian Province**, on the southeast coast, has a narrow but extremely convoluted coastal fringe extending only a few miles inland, but some 3,300 km (2,050 miles) in length. While the coastal strip is highly developed and populated, the interior of Fujian is rather mountainous and relatively sparsely inhabited.

**Wuyi Shan Nature Reserve**, in the north of the province, protects one of the largest tracts of humid subtropical forest in the world. It has high biodiversity and several threatened species. Forest

southern third, to the north the hills gradually give way to lowland and a flat plain around the vast lake of **Poyang Hu**. Poyang Hu expands in wet summers to become China's largest lake at 5,500 sq. km (2,100 sq. miles). This is an important habitat for wetland birds and migratory species: around 4,000 Siberian cranes (95 percent of the world population) winter here, as do white-naped and hooded cranes.

The area's rich mineral deposits have resulted in many mines and substantial environmental degradation. Yet despite the industry and agriculture, the mountain regions have some beautiful scenic spots with fascinating wildlife. The holy mountain of **Lushan** is a beautiful World Heritage Cultural Site, and other important

---

**FAR LEFT:** northwestern Yunnan contains several impressive snow peaks. **LEFT:** a François langur. **RIGHT:** the landscape near Kaili, eastern Guizhou.

natural sites include Jinggangshan, Longhushan and Sanqingshan.

The southern and eastern mountains of **Hunan Province** also fall within this region, although those of western Hunan form part of the Guizhou plateau *(see below)*. **Nanling** is an important range in the south of the province, while the **Mufu** and **Luoxiao** mountains are in the east. The forests here are dominated by oaks, chestnuts and laurels, with cinnamon, elm and many shrubs on the lower slopes. Protected plants here include *Liriodendron chinense*, the tree fern *Cyathea spinulosa* and *Camellia chrysantha*.

In the northeast of Hunan, the land is rather flat

Marine turtles breed on some of the sandy beaches, and the rare Chinese dolphin still survives in the murky waters of the Pearl River estuary. This is a form of the Indo-Pacific hump-backed dolphin, which is a striking pinkish colour when adult.

Tucked between Guangdong and Yunnan, **Guangxi Province** has a rather short coastline. The land is highest in the northwest and lowest in the south and east. Guilin is the most famous tourist site on the Li River, with its incredible karst landscapes. In southwest Guangxi, close to the Vietnam border, the hillside forests take on a more tropical character with trees including members

with wetlands and rivers draining north to the Yangzi. The largest lake, **Dongting Hu**, is an important refuge for wildlife, especially in winter.

**Guangdong Province** occupies the south-centre, its coast washed by the South China Sea. Biologically, the territories of Macau and Hong Kong are part of this region, lying on either side of the huge estuary of the Pearl River. The low-lying land near the coast is heavily populated and also cultivated with rice, and a wide range of fruits. Away from the Pearl River Delta, most of the province is covered with irregular ranges of low hills.

There are important nature reserves in **Hong Kong**, such as **Hoi Ha Wan**, a marine reserve with coral reefs, the mangrove-rich marshes of **Mai Po**, and the islands of **Lamma** and **Lantau**.

of the dipterocarp family, such as the endemic *Parashorea chinensis*. Many fascinating animals live in this region. Notable mammals are white-headed and Francois' leaf monkeys, pangolin and serow, while the birds include black stork, Cabot's tragopan and silver oriole. Some of the streams are still home to the bizarre giant salsamander.

## The Guizhou plateau

This region of higher ground at 1,000–1,400 metres (3,280–4,600 ft) covers most of the province of **Guizhou**, overlapping into the western parts of **Hunan**. This is an important region for wildlife. Lying south of the Yangzi River, it covers some 269,500 sq. km (104,000 sq. miles). This is one of the wettest areas in China, and the principal vegetation is that of subtropical moist broadleaf forests. The landscape is dominated by limestone peaks and rivers, and while the original forests have been largely destroyed, there are several protected remnants.

The World Heritage Site of **Wulingyuan** in northwest Hunan is a fine assemblage of quartzite sandstone peaks, with extensive forests, rich in rare animals and plants. The **Wuling** and **Xuefeng** ranges, again in western Hunan, are also considered part of the Guizhou plateau. Across the provincial border in northeastern Guizhou is the mountainous **Fanjing Shan** area, with a forest reserve and sacred Buddhist site famous for its

75 metres (250 ft) in the far southeast to 4,060 metres (13,320 ft) near the border with Tibet in the northwest. Much of the province is comprised of a huge upland plateau, connecting to the Tibetan foothills via the Hengduan Mountains in the north. The altitude falls gradually towards the south, the habitats becoming increasingly tropical. The plateau itself has a mild climate (and removed from the often grey, chilly weather so typical of much of the rest of southern China between January and March), the subtropical latitude being ameliorated by the altitude, which varies between about 1,700 and 2,300 metres (5,570 and 7,550 ft). The natural vegetation is mainly evergreen broadleaved forest,

population of rare Guizhou snub-nosed monkeys, numbering just a few hundred. It is also home to macaques and clouded leopards.

To the west of Guizhou province the landscape becomes gradually more and more mountainous, rising towards the border with Yunnan.

## The Yunnan plateau

Yunnan is the largest of southern China's provinces. Bordered in the southwest by Myanmar, to the northwest by Tibet and to the south by Laos and Vietnam, it has a large range in altitude, from about

---

**LEFT:** pangolins are hard to spot, but are still relatively common in forested areas. **ABOVE:** the Chinese giant salamander can reach a length of 1.8 metres (6 ft).

but most has been removed or replaced with forestry. Some of the higher ridges support fern- and moss-rich cloud forest with bamboo.

Located within the southeasternmost strand of the Himalayan chain, the **Ailao Shan Nature Reserve** has a population of black gibbon, a severely threatened species, as well as Asiatic black bears. Today, Yunnan pine covers many of the slopes – often planted, but possibly native in some sites. Many local birds inhabit this region, notably Yunnan nuthatch, white-speckled laughing thrush, white eared pheasant, brown-winged parrotbill and peacocks.

**The Three Parallel Rivers Protected Area** in the far west of Yunnan is probably the most important wildlife refuge in the province. Three major rivers run close together and almost parallel here, in a fabulously remote mountain landscape with habitats ranging from alpine to subtropical, before parting company to drain in very different directions. These are (from west to east) the Salween (Nujiang), Mekong (Lancangjiang) and Yangzi (Changjiang). The Salween continues straight south through Myanmar to reach the Andaman Sea; the Mekong veers southeast to Laos, Cambodia and Vietnam; and the Yangzi makes a number of sharp turns before flowing east right across the heart of China to emerge near Shanghai, and forms the traditional border between northern and southern China.

Here are some of southern China's finest and richest forests. This is also the place of origin of many familiar garden flowers: there are over 300 species of rhododendron and dozens of gentians, lilies and orchids. Rare mammals include the Tibetan water-shrew, the endemic Yunnan snub-nosed monkey, the capped leaf monkey, wild dog, red panda, Asian black bear, smooth-throated otter, leopard, clouded leopard and even the elusive snow leopard on the high slopes. Other notable mammals include musk deer, takin, and red and long-tailed gorals.

The birds are equally fascinating, with Lady Amherst's pheasant, white-eared pheasant, blood

## SAVING CHINA'S DRAGON

The Chinese alligator has played a major role in the folklore and culture of China – not least because it almost certainly gave rise to the myth of the dragon – a fierce-looking, mysterious predator capable of moving rapidly from land to water and associated with wetlands and hence with rainstorms.

Yet persecution and habitat destruction have combined to bring this charismatic reptile to the very brink of extinction. Its loss would be not only an international scandal, it would also be a blow to the Chinese character – China without a real dragon is unthinkable.

The total wild population of the world's most endangered crocodilian is now reckoned at fewer than 150 individuals, although there are now more than 10,000 animals in two main breeding centres.

The good news is that, unlike some species, the alligator needs a relatively small area habitat within which to thrive, and reintroduction from captive animals is certainly feasible – as shown by trials in Anhui province. Plans are now underway to release 1,000 alligators into existing suitable areas over the next 10 years. If successful, this would be a major conservation success story for China. Efforts are centred on the National Chinese Alligator Reserve in Anhui, and there are plans to involve nearby wetlands such as **Xiazhu Hu** and **Xixi Wetlands Park** in Zhejiang and Hunan provinces.

pheasant, Sclater's monal, Blyth's tragopan, black-necked crane, Ward's trogon, Giant and Yunnan nuthatches, white-speckled laughing thrush and brown-winged parrotbill.

## The tropical south and Hainan

In southern Yunnan the landscape becomes gradually greener and lower, the hills clad with forest, or given over to plantations of rubber, tea and tropical fruits, while in the valleys and basins rice paddies shimmer in the sunshine. The Xishuangbanna region lies sandwiched between Myanmar and Laos, well to the south of the Tropic of Cancer. It is a fertile landscape, dominated by tropical

or significantly altered from its original state, often replaced by bamboo, rubber plantation or grassland. The rivers here are fast-flowing, and frequently an opaque red-brown colour due to the effects of soil erosion. The latter has become worse with the replacement of much forest and removal of the natural ground cover. In areas up to about 800 metres (2,600 ft), the natural vegetation is tropical evergreen forest, and in mature stands the largest trees, such as the dipterocarp *Parashorea chinensis*, may reach 50 metres (160 ft) or more. These forests abound with epiphytes, including many ferns and orchids. Palms such as *Calamus* and *Caryota* are also locally abundant.

forests, and drained by the mighty Lancang (upper Mekong) River and its tributaries. The altitude ranges from 420 to 2,400 metres (1,370 and 7,870 ft), and the rainfall is generally high, between 1,200 and 1,700 mm (47 and 67 inches) per year, falling mainly from May to October. Xishuangbanna is the only area in China with a large amount of relatively undisturbed tropical forest, and consequently it has a high biodiversity. Forests are important to the local people, and over 65 percent of the land is still covered by forest or scrub of one sort or another. Most of this is either secondary

**LEFT:** China's dragon, the indigenous alligator.
**ABOVE:** the clouded leopard is one of the few remaining big cats in China.

At somewhat higher altitudes, between about 800 metres and 1,000 metres (2,600 and 3,300 ft), the natural cover is a monsoon semi-evergreen forest. Here the emergent trees shed their leaves in the dry season, but the lower layers are mainly evergreen.

Although large tracts of tropical forest do remain, many of the hills are covered with rubber plantations. Fortunately, the Chinese government now supports the traditional lifestyles of the Dai people, very much to the benefit of conservation, and earlier efforts to extend the rubber plantations at the expense of the natural or managed forests have been largely abandoned. That said, China's huge and expanding car industry has led to an increased demand for rubber in recent years. Rubber is still a major crop, and there are also plantations of pineapple and lychee. The rubber trees are also used as firewood, as are *Cassia siamea* trees, which are planted by the villagers in special fuelwood groves and coppiced regularly for a supply of logs and poles. The *Cassia* trees quickly produce fresh growth from the stumps.

The local philosophy reveres nature, certain areas being designated as sacred, and these are traditionally conserved. In some Dai communities individual trees, usually sacred fig and lofty fig, are revered. Almost every village in Xishuangbanna has sacred trees, which are the location for performance of rituals and traditional ceremonies.

gibbons, peacocks, leopards, lorises and tree shrews. Interesting birds to be seen in the area include the Asian palm swift, Himalayan swiftlet (whose nests are still eaten as bird's-nest soup in some areas), red-whiskered bulbul, speckled piculet, bronzed drongo, sunbirds, bush robins, and hornbills. Conservation is becoming more of a priority nowadays, not least to meet the lucrative eco-tourist trade, and over a quarter of a million hectares of forest is now designated as reserve.

The island province of **Hainan** is the second largest of China's coastal islands, after Taiwan. Its climate is tropical, with a moist, monsoonal summer and a cooler, drier winter. Over its

A distinction can be made between sacred trees dating back to pre-Buddhist, animistic beliefs, and those attributable to Buddhism. The former grow wild, and are worshipped through collective rituals, whereas the latter are planted, and are often worshipped in individual acts. Sacred fig is usually planted as a sacred tree for family cult activities, and can often be found near a village.

Tropical and subtropical crops grow well in the fertile soil, farmers enjoying two or three harvests a year. Home to the famous Pu'er tea, the region also produces quinine, rubber, camphor, coffee, cocoa, and a wide range of fruits.

Its warm, humid forests and nature reserves are home to gaur (a large wild cattle-relative) and even the occasional elephant. There are also

million-year history many endemic species have evolved here. In all there are 4,200 plant species, about 100 mammals and 300 species of bird. Endemic species include the Hainan gibbon, Hainan flying squirrel, Hainan moonrat, Hainan leaf warbler and Hainan partridge. Other notable birds are pale-capped pigeon and ratchet-tailed treepie. Although plantations of rubber, eucalyptus, coffee and oil-palm have replaced the natural vegetation in most of Hainan's lowlands, and deforestation affects many of the mountain slopes, there are important remnants of the original forests on some of the mountains, such as **Bawangling** which still supports Hainan gibbons and Hainan partridge. **Datian** reserve has a population of the rare Eld's deer. ❏

# Too Late?

The story of the **South China tiger** is not a happy one. Once found across a wide belt of central and eastern China, this is the smallest and rarest of the subspecies of tiger found across Asia. It is also thought to be closest to the ancestor of all the existing tiger subspecies. The

historical range included the coastal areas (the last tiger was shot in Hong Kong as recently as 1942), but habitat destruction has meant it has been driven out of the lowlands into the forests and scrub of the hills and mountains.

Only 40 years ago there were thought to be at least 4,000 individuals, but in recent decades these have been hunted almost to extinction, partly for their pelts, and partly for their body parts which, regrettably, are used in traditional Chinese medicine. In 1993 China banned domestic trade in all tigers and derived body parts, but poaching is still a problem, as is the illegal importing of tiger parts from India. Organs, teeth, bones and penises continue to fetch high prices on the black market, and are used to treat many ailments and are also said to act as an aphrodisiac.

In 1995 the Chinese Ministry of Forestry indicated a wild population of fewer than 20, and no wild tigers have been seen by officials in more than 20 years. It is thus quite probable that this wonderful animal is already extinct in the wild. Detailed field surveys were undertaken in 2001 and 2002 in eight reserves across five provinces, but sadly found no trace of the tiger. Interviews with locals came to the same conclusion. It is just possible that a few remain in the wild, but extinction has

**LEFT:** ladyslipper orchids, Yunnan. **ABOVE:** tigers at Xiongsen breeding centre. **RIGHT:** A Yangzi porpoise.

either already occurred, or is imminent. Reintroduction from captive-bred stock may now be the only hope. A small population of about 70 are held in zoos in China, but since these are all descended from six wild tigers the future prospects look rather bleak. Further attempts at captive breeding are being made in South Africa. However, reintroduction cannot really be expected to succeed unless the dreadful trade in body parts can be stamped out (see page 271 ).

The **Yangzi River dolphin** (Baiji) is a remarkable freshwater mammal once common in the waters of the Yangzi and other Chinese rivers. In the 1950s this shy creature was still quite widespread, but it is

now virtually, if not completely, extinct. The Yangzi also hosts the world's only freshwater porpoise, the **Yangzi finless porpoise**. Although it has full legal protection, it is now critically endangered and may well follow the baiji into extinction. Fishing, increased river traffic and pollution have combined to reduce numbers from nearly 3,000 in the late 1980s to well below 2,000, and it is declining at an estimated 7 percent a year. The good news is that the finless porpoise is being bred successfully in protected semi-natural reserves, and reintroductions into the wild may well be possible. On the other hand, pollution in the Yangzi continues to worsen, and unless this can be reversed – and encounters with fishing gear and boat traffic reduced – then even reintroduction may be ultimately unsuccessful. ❑

# LIFE IN MODERN CHINA

China's headlong rush into the 21st century is bringing enormous changes to people's lives right across the region, as the state welfare system begins to fall apart

The people of modern China enjoy a higher standard of living than any of their predecessors have experienced in the country's entire 3,400-year history. They have more opportunity than Chinese people have ever had: more freedom to move around and travel overseas, more opportunity to seek better jobs and better education, and more chance to work and save money and prepare for a better future. The outlook has never been so good for so many people, and the southern regions of the country have fared best of all.

But at the same time, inevitably, huge problems exist. A wide gap separates rich from poor, and the gap is growing, as many of China's poor struggle just to survive. Farmers suffer from inflation and low prices for their crops, and some have been pushed off their land by developers. In the cities, many people make relatively good money, but free access to schools, hospitals and housing, as well as other services which were taken for granted a generation ago, are increasingly threatened by privatisation, as China's brave new world of market economics sweeps away the socialist past.

## Migrant workers

Contemporary southern China is the scene of a huge population movement, as tens of millions of migrant workers, lured by the sudden spectre of wealth, have abandoned the still-poor villages and towns of their home provinces – Guizhou, Jiangxi, Yunnan and Hunan, inland areas of Guangxi and Fujian – and headed for the coastal cities in search of opportunity.

And what have they found? Better lives, mostly. Many are content living in dorms, working long hours, saving money. Most of the successful

migrant workers are young, and often single. When conditions are favourable – reasonable hours, comfortable dorm rooms, decent working conditions and prompt payment of wages – this can be a good life. And the money they send home does a great deal to support the rural countryside, especially in the poorest provinces.

But the less fortunate migrants have found only struggle and hardship. The Chinese have a phrase, *chi ku*, to eat bitterness, that describes the lives of these unlucky ones. Many of them are older men, often with families far away, who work in dangerous, dirty factory jobs, or on dangerous, dirty construction sites. They are everywhere in southern China, in the railway stations, on the streets, in the factories and on the building sites, always

**LEFT:** posing for a photo call at a Sanya beauty pageant. **RIGHT:** loading waste for recycling, Guiyang.

without helmets or safety goggles. With their dirty clothes, unkempt hair and ceaseless energy, they are easy to spot.

Like itinerant workers everywhere, the migrants of southern China face discrimination. With their provincial dialects – many don't speak Putonghua (Mandarin), the national language – and grinding poverty, they make easy targets. Some of the native residents of the south have lost their jobs in struggling state-run factories, and blame the migrants for taking their jobs at lower wages. The migrants also get blamed for crime, and, indeed, they are guilty of many muggings, purse snatchings, and pick-pocketings (bigger crimes, such as

And profit margins for the factory owners and construction companies employing migrant workers are often paper-thin, as huge retail chains like Wal-Mart and Target, with their massive economies of scale, beat down prices to the last fraction of a penny. As wages rise throughout China – a trend that began in 2004 and has been accelerating ever since – margins are further squeezed. Local Triads (mafia) routinely harrass factory owners in the coastal provinces, demanding protection money or goods. In one recent case, a producer of high-end golf clubs in Guangdong was told to deliver 100 sets of brand-new clubs to a local Triad gang, or face the consequences.

extortion, kidnapping and drug smuggling, are usually the work of resident local gangs).

Perhaps the most serious problem for the migrant workers is non-payment of wages. Some factory owners pay wages only once a year, at Chinese New Year. But on pay day, many a migrant has discovered that his or her pay packet is far short of the promised amount, and in some cases, they are not paid at all. But what recourse do they have? Local officials are often in the pockets of the factory owners, and while the central government is concerned about their plight, resolving such issues can take months or years, and pursuing a case requires time and money. Lacking the means, most workers have little choice but to accept whatever deal their employers offer.

The owner flew to Beijing to appeal his case, which helped temporarily. But he also set up a second factory in Vietnam, and if the extortion continues, he says, he will move out of Guangdong altogether.

## The breakdown of the old system

In the old days, before market reforms and the lure of wealth changed everything, China was a place where lifetime employment was largely guaranteed, and people tended to remain in the same town or village for life. This stability was underpinned by the *hukou* system, whereby everyone in the country was registered at a particular address and which subsequently restricted movement as this required permission from the *danwei* (work unit).

This has been breaking down since the 1990s, a process which has made it far easier for people to move around the country seeking work. (With more and more Chinese employed by private – or foreign – companies, the concept of the *danwei* has also broken down.)

Accompanying this freedom of movement is a growing lack of security. Migrant workers are not often eligible for national health insurance, cannot afford private insurance, and their employers seldom provide it. Hospitals routinely turn away those who can't afford treatment, so an injury can mean the end of employment, or the end of a life. And then there is the lack of access to medical care and schooling.

It is important to stress, however, that it is not just the migrant workers who have suffered from the collapse of the state welfare system in matters of health, education and housing. If you are a Party worker and employed by the state, then you will benefit from free healthcare and schooling, but this is not the case for much of China these days. For most, free housing is no longer provided, and for good medical treatment or schooling, payment is essential. These services are increasingly privatised, a process at the heart of a profound transition as China switches from a centrally controlled socialist system to a market economy.

## The urban-rural divide

Farmers, who live far from media centres and big-city spotlights, are southern China's forgotten demographic. The migration from countryside to city is the largest movement in human history – so far, some 115 million people have relocated – and it is hollowing out the rural heartland. Many rural dwellers are lonely: ageing parents with sons and daughters working far away, families with absentee fathers, wives living without husbands. Even in the richer areas of Guangdong, Fujian and Hainan, the farmers have their problems. As farmland gives way to industry and urban sprawl, they are often removed from their land. Compensation is supposed to be mandatory, but the amounts can vary according to the whims of local officials.

Farmers, poor rural residents and other have-nots, most of them in the countryside, have been fighting back, often by gathering in huge, hard-to-ignore protests. Sometimes the protests get violent, and sometimes, too, they get the attention of

the rulers in Beijing, who generally side with the peasants. But the central government has limited power in the rural areas of southern China. Given the fact that farmers officially lease their land from the government *(see also page 68)*, this is a major political issue. Provincial, city and local officials all have much to gain by luring big-money projects to their districts, often in defiance of directives from Beijing. Local officials will usually green-light any project that delivers the cash, while the central government wants cleaner factories that produce higher-value goods. The tug of war between low-level officials and the central government has become one of China's defining

issues, with those in the middle – the rural poor – awaiting the outcome.

## The urban middle class

In southern China, the middle class is clearly on the rise, growing in both numbers and general prosperity. These are the men and women who commute to work in the cities, the secretaries and salespeople and accountants and other service sector workers. They tend to be educated, computer literate and sometimes English-speaking. They have disposable income and leisure time, they watch movies and go to restaurants, buy purses and tailored suits and cellphones and cars and watches. They travel, too, at first to domestic hot spots like Hainan Island and Guilin, and then

**LEFT:** hard-seat class on one of the older trains.
**RIGHT:** roller-coaster ride at a Shenzhen theme park.

overseas. Some are now seasoned travellers, and have visited cities in Europe and the US. On the negative side, the collapse of the state welfare system is a burden for many, and the rich southern cities in which they live are starting to experience many of the problems familiar to so many in the West: high property prices, crowded commutes and rising crime.

## The changing world of the family

The people of southern China fully reflect their Han Chinese heritage: they are generally hard-working and thrifty, they value education and tradition, they cherish family ties and are suspi-

college degree, proficiency in English, and, more than anything else, youth. The kids, drawn by the bright lights of the coastal cities, don't wish to work on farms. They feel they have nothing to learn from their parents, and their parents sometimes feel they have nothing to teach. The communist dogma that provided direction to their parents is gone, and nothing has replaced it except a love of money.

The traditional rural lifestyle, in which extended families worked the land together, is under pressure from another angle: the one-child policy, which was implemented in 1978. Although it is starting to loosen, and was never evenly enforced, the one-child policy has been effective: by some estimates,

cious of strangers. These Confucian values are still alive, but with the rapid changes that are sweeping through the country, the time-honoured bonds are beginning to erode.

For one thing, the generations are fractured as never before. Young people can usually speak the national language, Putonghua (Mandarin), and sometimes even English, while their parents often speak only a local dialect. The older generation knows nothing of the obsessions of youth: cell-phones, video games, designer clothes, comic books and foreign fashions. Thirty or forty years ago, a city dweller's ticket to security was a good job in the Communist Party. On the farm, it was even simpler: plant the crops, work the fields and hope for the best. But the new ticket to wealth is a

it has prevented 300 million births. Labour-dependent rural China is missing a lot of farmhands.

In the cities, the one-child policy has given birth to a generation of kids who are catered to by doting parents. These are the *xiao huangdi*, or little emperors, the children of one-child families. And upon these emperors, the parents heap all of their hopes and dreams and money. Nothing is too much for little Wing-Fat: golf and piano lessons, etiquette courses, language instruction, special get-ahead tutoring programmes. The one-child parents are determined to give that single child every possible chance to succeed in the new China.

**ABOVE:** sharp-suited urbanites. **RIGHT:** a TV audience at the vastly popular *Supergirl* show.

## Minority groups

Southern China is crowded with a plethora of dialects and ethnic (ie non-Han) tribes, especially in Yunnan, Guangxi and Guizhou provinces. The largest single minority are the Zhuang, with 16 million people centered mostly in Guangxi. The Miao are probably the best-known group, with some 8 million scattered across Guizhou, Yunnan, Guangxi, Hunan and Hainan Island. There are many more ethnic groups in Xishuangbanna, while travellers in northwestern Yunnan are likely to come across the Naxi and the Bai.

In many cases, the poor rural minority tribes reflect the broader changes that are affecting China. Some groups, especially the Zhuang, have left the countrysides for city jobs, where they face the same challenges as other rural migrants. Other groups have proven more resistant to integration, particularly in out-of-the-way areas such as Guizhou, where the high mountains and poor roads help insulate them from outside influences. There, they grow traditional crops, weave embroidery, and live their lives much as they have in the past.

China's constitution guarantees minorities certain rights and privileges, including the right to use their own language. But in practice, even in the most isolated parts of Guizhou and Yunnan, fluency in Mandarin tends to be the best way to get ahead. ❑

## MEDIA AND POPULAR CULTURE IN TODAY'S CHINA

In their leisure time, the Chinese middle classes do what their counterparts do the world over: they watch TV. As Hong Kong industrialist Gordon Wu famously pronounced in the early 1990s: the people of southern China don't care about politics, what they want is to watch television in air-conditioned comfort. On one channel is Yao Ming playing basketball for the Houston Rockets, or coverage of a football match from England. On another channel is one of the ever-popular historical costume dramas. On still another is a news programme, a bit stiff and "correct", or a foreign movie or TV show from Japan, Korea or the US. But by far the most popular programmes are the "American Idol" clones, such as the wildly successful "Supergirl" contests.

The Internet is also immensely popular. Chat rooms and websites hum with discourse, as millions of people weigh in the price of houses, the availability of jobs and the best schools, along with shopping, cellphones and television shows. Internet usage in China jumped 30 percent in 2006, as 132 million people logged on. Naturally, the government is aware of this trend, and has erected the "great firewall of China" to monitor sensitive topics such as Tibet, Taiwan, and democracy. Nonetheless, southern China is increasingly wired, and the technology has trickled down to some migrant workers and farmers, in the form of cellphones. If a nearby factory raises its wages, for example, thousands of workers will instantly get the news via text message.

# The Overseas Chinese

China has a long history of emigration that has spawned Chinese communities in virtually every country in the world. As far-flung as Fiji, Peru, Italy and Mauritius, Chinese people can be found living in their adopted countries, some first-, second-, third-, and even fourth- or fifth-generation. They represent one of the great success stories of international migration.

There are about 34 million people of Chinese descent living in more than 130 countries outside China, Taiwan and Hong Kong. Yet the vast major-

ity of this number originated from the two southern coastal provinces of Guangdong and Fujian, and even within those provinces, from a limited number of districts and villages.

The Chinese populations have adapted well to the local cultures in their host countries and achieved a good degree of economic success. And despite years of living in these different lands, there is an underlying "Chineseness" that resonates throughout the diasporic community and maintains its affinity to China, which sees many returning as tourists or as investors.

## The early migrants

China's history of emigration has been characterised by three significant waves marked by economic and political change. The first phase came during the Ming Dynasty between 1405 and 1433, when the intrepid navigator and admiral, Zheng He, set sail with a huge fleet of 300 ships and 28,000 men bound for Southeast Asia and the Indian Ocean in search of trading opportunities and to flaunt the superiority of Chinese power.

Following in the wake of these pioneering voyages a fairly modest number of peasants and villagers looking to escape the hardship and poverty of life in rural China (they were mainly from the poorest districts of Guangdong and Fujian) began to emigrate overseas with the ultimate intention of returning home with their new-found wealth. They become some of the first Chinese settlers in Thailand, Malaysia, the Philippines and Indonesia. Migration took place despite imperial edicts forbidding foreign travel, laws established by Ming emperors who feared those disaffected by Chinese rule would be pushed outside China's borders, thus laying the empire open to invasion from rebel armies. So entrenched was the paranoia that the edicts continued in place right through to the 19th century.

## The second wave

A new, and far more significant, surge of migration from China took place in the 19th century during the European colonial period, when millions of Chinese were transported across the globe on European ships. They can be considered economic migrants, fleeing poverty and famine in China. The Qing rulers were now compelled to permit emigration by the European powers, hungry for a cheap and plentiful labour supply for the colonies. As "coolie" labour, the Chinese were put to work in mines, plantations and railroads across the globe. Records show that between 1848 and 1888, more than 2 million people departed, and like their forefathers, many originated from the provinces of Guangdong and Fujian.

Those that survived the perilous journeys and working conditions settled, usually unable to afford the fare back to China. Once free from the shackles of their exploitative employers, and unable to return their homeland, the Chinese – wherever they found themselves – adapted well to what was available to them. Despite some discrimination, overall they prospered through hard work and a flair for business, and became respected members of the wider community. In Southeast Asia, many of the big tycoons and political figures of the last century have come from humble Chinese beginnings and built up their wealth and reputations.

It is not surprising that today Southeast Asia has the largest population of people of Chinese origin. Estimates place more than 23 million ethnic Chinese in the region, which adds up to fully 80 percent of the world's Overseas Chinese. Although – with the exception of Singapore – they are minorities in their adopted countries, they are a universally significant group in terms of their economic contribution.

### Recent emigration

The most recent wave of migration has followed the series of political upheavals in the 20th century. With the opening up of the economy in the 1980s and a newly open attitude towards the outside world, China's citizens were able to take advantage of greater mobility, and increasing numbers moved abroad. In 1989, the situation was brought to a head with the Chinese government crackdown in Tiananmen Square. The international outrage at the strong-armed tactics used by the government opened the doors of many Western nations to Chinese students, with the United States taking on the largest portion, granting 80,000 green cards to students already on US territory under the Chinese Student Protection Act. There followed a steady outflow of migrants, some fleeing the political situation, but the majority taking advantage of the economic and professional opportunities of living in the West.

This episode of Chinese migration continues today, with the preferred destinations being North America, Europe and Australasia. The Chinese communities in certain North American and European cities in fact date back to the second wave of migration – well known examples being San Francisco and New York in the United States, Vancouver and Toronto in Canada, and Liverpool and London in the United Kingdom. Therefore, these Chinese communities tend to be comprised of a mix of earlier Cantonese- and Hokkien-speaking immigrants

with those fresh out of China who speak the official language, Mandarin, and who are just as likely to come from the north of the country, and who are usually highly educated and highly skilled.

### Links with the motherland

The spread of Chinese people across the globe have done little to diminish their ties with their ancestral homeland. In fact, with the many families and relatives left behind in their villages, the Overseas Chinese *(Huaqiao)* have been assiduous in giving back to the places from whence they came. Donations are collected and given on an informal basis through family connections, temple networks

or community organisations, which then go on to contribute towards the development of the area. So prolific is this practice that some counties in Guangdong and Fujian (known as the *Quaoxiang* – Overseas Chinese counties) have been transformed. Through the donations, hospitals, schools, ancestral halls, bridges and roads have been built to better the home villages, and the family clans (denoted by the surname) are noted on tablets or by the naming of the place.

This allegiance to China has also drawn many to return to explore their cultural and family roots, an extension of the Confucian practice of filial piety. Migrants return to pay homage to their ancestors and to validate their identities and histories as part of the fabric of China's long history. ❑

---

**LEFT:** Chinatown in Vancouver. **ABOVE LEFT:** indentured Chinese labourers arrive in 19th-century Singapore. **RIGHT:** a typical new building in coastal Guangdong, funded by Overseas Chinese money.

# THE NEW CHINESE ECONOMY

China's extraordinary economic progress has brought
unprecedented prosperity to millions in the southern
provinces, but there is a growing inequality between the
rich cities and poor rural areas

In 1992, Deng Xiaoping, who had gradually emerged as de facto leader of China after the death of Mao Zedong in 1976, embarked on a tour of southern China, visiting Guangzhou and the two special economic zones (SEZs) of Shenzhen and Zhuhai. In the aftermath of the Tiananmen protests of mid-1989 – the heady student protests for liberalisation and vaguely democratic principles that were brutally put down on 4 June – leftist forces had been pressing to rein in the limited reforms of the 1980s and put China back on a more solidly centralised track. Deng's tour was, then, a deliberate intervention, and he took the tour as an opportunity to repeat the phrase with which he had jump-started rural reforms in 1982, "To get rich is glorious." Chinese needed to go into business "even more boldly" and "more quickly" to create a socialist market economy with Chinese characteristics, said Deng.

Deng's power had been greatly diminished since the Tiananmen protests, and his tour had little initial impact. Nevertheless, a series of articles he published (under a pseudonym) in Shanghai's *Liberation Daily* won over local elites, and before long the calls for economic liberalisation began to become orthodoxy nationwide. The result has been an explosion of economic growth probably unparalleled in human history, and in the early stages – and even to a significant extent today – it has been largely led by southern China.

China's GDP growth has averaged more than 9 percent for the past two decades since Deng's tour, and it is now reckoned to be the world's fourth-largest economy. In 1985, foreign direct investment (FDI) inflows amounted to around

US$2 billion, but by 2006 had exploded to around US$63 billion. Meanwhile, China's share of world exports was around 7 percent in 2007, according to the World Bank, and that percentage is doubling every three years. In the same period, China's economy has gone from being exclusively state-owned, to one in which the private sector now accounts for 70 percent of tax receipts.

Whether such heady growth can be sustained is uncertain, however, and observers tend to be divided over whether China is set for global economic domination or global economic destabilisation, when the mother of all bubbles finally bursts. All the same, whatever the future holds, in the short space of some 20 years, China has flung

**LEFT:** shoppers on Dongmen Lu in Shenzhen.
**RIGHT:** an educational initiation ceremony.

open its doors to the global economy and emerged as a major economic power.

## Reform beginnings and the southern connection

China first began to turn its back on the collectivised economy it had practised since the communist revolution of 1949 when it started to dismantle the agricultural commune system in the 1970s, allowing "village enterprises" to be established. In the early 1980s, it became possible for individuals to set up one-person enterprises *(getihu)*, while by the mid-1980s families were permitted to establish businesses with up to seven

textiles industry, and later branching out into electronics. Deng's "open-door policy", however, was to mark the beginning of a new era for Hong Kong, making it the trading gateway to the world's most populous nation.

## The rise of the Pearl River Delta

Between 1978 and 1997, when Hong Kong returned to Chinese rule as a Special Autonomous Region (SAR), its reported trade with China grew at a spectacular average of 28 per cent per year. The period saw Hong Kong manufacturing relocate into the so-called Pearl River Delta (PRD) region – a broad triangle of eight Guangdong provincial pre-

employees. At the same time the government began to allow foreign investment, in the form of joint ventures, with the opening of 14 coastal cities to outsiders. This was boosted by the establishment between 1980 and 1988 of Special Economic Zones (SEZs) in Shenzhen, Zhuhai, Shantou and Xiamen, as well on Hainan Island.

The SEZs were all essentially harbour interfaces with the outside world, which had been long been kept at bay by the political Great Wall of the Mao era. Shenzhen was to become the most successful of this privileged elite due to its proximity to that bastion of free trade, Hong Kong. In the 1950s and 1960s, the economy of the British colony had centred on manufacturing, with small family-run businesses largely specialising in the

fectures, with the capital Guangzhou at its western head, and Hong Kong and Macau on either side of the mouth of the Pearl River. For Hong Kong, this resulted in remarkable growth in the service sector, and for the PRD, an average annual GDP growth rate of some 16 percent, far exceeding the annual Chinese average of 10 percent.

Hong Kong's investment in the PRD (and later Taiwan) has been such that it has become common to call the region "the world's workshop", though in recent years Shanghai and the Yangzi River Delta (YRD) have been catching up. In 1981, Hong Kong employed just under 900,000 manufacturing workers on its territory. By 2002 that figure had dropped to around 200,000, but had grown in the PRD to between 10 and 11 million, with Hong Kong providing some two-thirds of foreign direct investment inflows to the region.

Since the 1997 handover, this relationship has increasingly become a two-way street. The Closer Economic Partnership Relationship (CEPR), established in 2004, has facilitated cross-border economic exchanges between mainland China and Hong Kong. In 2005, Chinese investment in Hong Kong reached US$1.3 billion, or around 42 percent of all Chinese direct investment abroad. Meanwhile, Shenzhen – little more than a fishing village when it was appointed an SEZ – has grown into a Chinese immigrant city of anywhere between 9 and 17 million people, depending on

in Shenzhen, Dongguan and Guangzhou, and is today a leading global source for electronics, electrical and electronic components, textiles and garments, shoes, toys, watches and clocks, and everything from clothes hangers to cocktail mixers. Accounting for just 0.4 percent of China's total land area, the PRD is responsible for a whopping 29 percent of the nation's total trade (imports and exports).

## West and south of the river

Macau, which reverted to Chinese rule in 1999, and the prefectures to the south and west of the Pearl River – Zhuhai, Zhongshan, Jiangmen,

who is doing the counting. It is thought to have the highest per capita GDP in all of China.

The rest of the delta region has also prospered from its proximity to Hong Kong, identified for 16 consecutive years as the world's freest economy by the World Bank. In 1980 the region's GDP was estimated at around US$8 billion, but by 2005 it had grown to more than US$221 billion, making it the fastest-growing region in the world's fastest-growing economy. Indeed, for the first 10 years of China's reforms, the PRD led China into the global economic order via foreign-invested firms

Foshan and Zhaoqing – have been lesser beneficiaries of the PRD success story. One of the main reasons for this is a patchy transportation infrastructure that provides limited access to the booming Hong Kong-side PRD cities. Since the boom in border traffic got under way in the early 1980s, Hong Kong and Shenzhen have continued to upgrade border crossings (there are currently four, along with an extensive ferry network). However, connections between the PRD east and the PRD west remain weak. Efforts to alleviate this have been underway since Beijing authorised the Hong Kong, Macau and Zhuhai governments to cooperate on assessing the feasibility of a 29-km (18-mile) bridge linking the three cities. The bridge may cost as much as US$4 billion.

**FAR LEFT:** a toy factory in the Pearl River Delta.
**LEFT:** migrant workers looking for work, Guangdong.
**ABOVE:** cellphone-toting policemen.

In the meantime, the western PRD has also focused, to some extent, on tourism – which in the industrialised eastern region is almost non-existent outside the profusion of high-end golf courses catering largely to factory owners and investors, and theme parks aimed at package tourists en route to shopping tours of Hong Kong. Macau is leading the way, by transforming itself into a major gaming centre. Rule changes after the 1999 handover resulted in tycoon Stanley Ho losing a monopoly on gambling in Macau, and players from Las Vegas have poured in, investing around US$25 billion into the former Portuguese colony. Sceptics were silenced in early 2007,

1990s, as its freewheeling economy attracted investors from all over China. By 1993, the central government had intervened to rein in rampant corruption, prostitution and other "evils", and the boom came to an end. Today, Hainan is a far cry from its SEZ rivals, a recovering economy that is marketing itself as the "Hawaii of the East", admittedly to good effect, attracting more than 10 million (overwhelmingly domestic) tourist arrivals a year. It may not be quite Phuket or Bali or indeed Waikiki, but the beaches of Sanya are overlooked by outposts of international five-star hotel chains, while Bo'ao, to the north, is transforming itself into the Davos (the Swiss

when it was revealed that Macau had officially outstripped Las Vegas as world's biggest-earning casino centre, raking in US$6.95 billion in 2006, compared to US$6.69 billion in Vegas.

Like Macau, Hainan Island, China's southernmost province, is staking its future mostly on tourism. Of all the SEZs, Hainan was the least successful. In fact, many Chinese economists simply refer to it as a "failure". In the mid-1980s, central government funds earmarked for infrastructure development on the island were instead funnelled into the re-shipment to the mainland – at huge profits – of Japanese cars and electronics goods purchased in Hong Kong. After recovering from this scandal, the island entered a speculative boom – mostly in real estate – in the early

home of the World Economic Forum) of the East, regularly hosting the Bo'ao Forum for Asia, an initiative aimed at improving the regional exchange of information.

## Competition and response

If there is unevenness in the southern Chinese economic powerhouse, in recent years the PRD has found itself increasingly challenged by competition from Shanghai and its Yangzi River Delta (YRD) hinterland, as well as the so-called Bohai Sea Economic Zone, which includes the municipalities of Beijing and Tianjin, and the city of Qingdao in Shandong province. With annual GDP growth of some 11 percent, it is calculated that Shanghai will overtake Hong Kong in less than

10 years. This is perhaps a projection that overlooks Hong Kong's enormously efficient service sector, legal framework and economic transparency, but it has also prompted calls in the PRD to begin working to stay on top. Meanwhile, the rise of the YRD and other regional economies is placing a strain on the availability of the migrant workers who have formed the low-cost labour pool that has powered the PRD's rise. Despite the fact that anywhere from 150 to 200 million migrant workers have left their fields in the countryside to work in China's factories, in the past few years there have been consistent reports of labour shortages in the PRD.

The Pan-PRD accounts for approximately a third of China's GDP, and with a population of some 450 million around 35 percent of the country's population. However, the push for closer economic integration in the region also underscores the fact that a legacy of the SEZ model of economic development is the serious inequality of prosperity in the southern Chinese hinterland, and throughout China as a whole. In southern China, for example, 2005 per capita GDP in Shenzhen was thought to be more than US$12,000, on a par with Russia, while in the southwestern province of Guizhou per capita GDP is a little over US$600 a year, which compares with the some of the

In the eyes of the rest of southern China, another problem is that the PRD encompasses such a tiny area, and small population – 45.5 million according to a 2005 census – while the YRD includes a much larger area with a population of some 200 million. Small surprise, then, that there has been talk of creating a so-called "Pan-PRD" economic region: in 2003, officials from the nine provinces of Guangdong, Fujian, Jiangxi, Hunan, Guangxi, Guizhou, Sichuan, Yunnan and Hainan met in Guangzhou to discuss ways of strengthening economic cooperation within this zone.

**LEFT:** St Peter's Square, Window of the World theme park, Shenzhen. **ABOVE:** the arrival of supermarkets is a sign of the times in China.

world's poorest nations, such as Somalia and Malawi.

At the time of writing, there was agreement that transport infrastructure was key to expanding the PRD hinterland, and a Unified Road Transport Agreement was signed. The agreement envisions Guangzhou as the heart of a sprawling roll-out of highways that would facilitate the transportation of goods, while the second phase of development at Guangzhou's state-of-the-art Baiyun International Airport, due for completion in 2010, will turn it into a major international air hub.

This urgency to achieve greater integration can be applied to China as a whole. At present, the nine coastal provinces are the recipients of more than 80 percent of all of China's inward foreign direct investment, with the remaining 20 provinces receiving just 12 percent. This has led to tensions that often bubble over into social unrest, a problem that the central government is seriously concerned about, and which has led to a nationwide campaign for "social harmony."

## Social unrest

In 2005, Beijing estimated there were some 85,000 uprisings nationwide, a 6 percent increase on the previous year, and approximately four times more than a decade earlier. By and large, such uprisings are troubling not the relatively affluent areas that the majority of foreign tourists

developments, hotels, factories, and in some cases infrastructure build-outs. The response to this in Beijing – apart from the issuing of edicts banning the practice, and the arrest or dismissal of officials who are involved – has been a 14-years-in-the-making property law, which was finally passed in early 2007, and effective from October of the same year. The central clause of the law states: "the property of the state, the collective, the individual and other obligees is protected by law, and no units or individuals may infringe upon it." However, critics of the law say that until there is a meaningfully independent judiciary, or land passes officially into private ownership, the cor-

travel through, but the huge swathes of rural China where as many as 80 percent of the population live in poverty and look on as a small minority profit from China's juggernaut acceleration towards economic superpower status. Triggering these protests are a host of factors, but chief among them are land and environmental issues.

Land is a particularly contentious issue in modern China because it is still state-owned, and in the countryside farmers have leases of between 30 and 70 years. With real-estate speculation rife throughout the nation, this provides ample opportunity for corrupt officials to cooperate with developers, evicting rural dwellers from their properties with minimal compensation and allowing business to make handsome profits from housing

ruption of local officials seeking easy money will inevitably remain.

## Environmental problems

The environment is another source of conflict, as China's race to the future has largely been run at the expense of massive environmental degradation. China is something of an environmental pariah, its status as the world's largest polluter confirmed in 2007. The explosion of manufacturing in the PRD has led to a situation where, on a bad day, visibility can be so poor it is barely possible to see across Hong Kong's (shrinking) harbour.

Hong Kong bemoans its environmental woes, but the situation in the Chinese hinterland is positively calamitous. According to the World Bank,

China is home to 16 of the world's 20 most polluted cities, and more than 400,000 premature deaths occur annually due to air pollution. In a rare admission in 2007, China's Environment Minister told the press that environmental issues were behind more than 50,000 protests and riots across the country in the previous year. Generally, very few of these are reported in the press, but a case in Zhejiang province in that year involving thousands of villagers fighting for the closure of polluting chemical factories made headlines, and the villagers eventually succeeded in shutting them down.

The reality is that, for all the talk of the coming China century, the rise of the world's most populous nation is a far more complex phenomenon than many commentators give credit to. A visitor who touches down in cosmopolitan, spectacularly affluent Hong Kong, and travels on to one of the new five-star hotels soon to open in Guangzhou, could be forgiven for thinking China has arrived. But, lurking in the wings of China's success story are a host of problems that mostly impact on those who have not prospered from the past two decades of meteoric growth. After all, despite all the hype, the World Bank estimates that China's per capita GDP, in terms of purchasing power parity, is only equal to that of Japan in 1950, when it was still a ravaged economy, struggling to recover from the catastrophic results of its WWII defeat.

Land and environmental issues usually top the lists of China's woes, but access to water, and failing health and educational systems also deserve a mention. It is thought that some 300 million Chinese have no access to clean drinking water. In a country that has more than 200 cities with populations greater than 1 million (and an increasing number with populations over 10 million), urban development at a rate unprecedented in history is siphoning water away from rural hinterlands. Meanwhile, privatisation and reforms means that the state no longer provides guaranteed free healthcare, and reportedly as many as 700 million people now lack access to even basic healthcare. These same reforms have also resulted in a largely pay-as-you-go education system that puts an enormous strain on the poor who make up the majority of China's population.

How successful China will be in resolving these issues remains to be seen, but there is no doubt that people in high places are aware of the urgency of implementing initiatives such as the Pan-PRD economic region. The failure to do so will be the emergence of an "economic giant" that lives up its name only in isolated, mostly coastal, urban pockets, while the remainder of the country simmers in discontent. ❑

**LEFT:** a power station in the Guizhou countryside; China is gradually waking up to its environmental problems. **ABOVE:** Guangzhou's Olympic Stadium.

# SOUTHERN CHINESE FOOD

Cantonese cuisine, exported by generations of émigres, is familiar around the world. Other regional cuisines are less well known, but every bit as good – fiery dishes from Hunan, simple Hakka fare and the highly varied flavours of Yunnan

The basic pleasure of eating in China lies in the good food. For freshness, variety, flavour and sheer adventure, few cuisines can match Chinese. Compared with a typical experience in the West, in China the dishes arrive in glorious abundance, a parade of fresh crunchy vegetables, succulent fried meats and steamed fish, fragrant with the exotic flavours and spices of the Middle Kingdom, from ginger and sesame oil to black bean sauce and Shaoxing wine.

The atmosphere is also different. Chinese diners cherish a lively, boisterous environment, filled with toasts and jokes and conversation. This is called *re nao* – hot and noisy – and it is the hallmark of a good meal. And what's true of China generally is doubly true of southern China. Few dining experiences are more *re nao* than a Hong Kong dim sum restaurant, or a Yunnanese café, or a busy night market in Fujian province.

One variety of southern Chinese cuisine – Cantonese – is disproportionately familiar around the world; in fact for many people in the USA or Europe, Cantonese food (often in modified form) *is* Chinese food *(see page 73)*.

## Southern characteristics

The approach to food is similar to that in the rest of the country, and some of the ingredients and preparations are similar, too – but they are not identical. Seafood features heavily along the southern coasts, as do fresh green vegetables. Rice is ubiquitous, and appears on the table as simple steamed rice *(bak fan* in Cantonese, *mee fan* in Mandarin), or as rice flour, which finds its way into wonton wrappers, noodles, desserts, and other dishes.

**LEFT:** Cantonese dim sum.
**RIGHT:** a simple meal.

In the far south, wheat dishes are almost absent from the menu. Pork and chicken rule the meaty end of the spectrum, especially in *jia chang* (home-style) cooking. Vegetables are key, including southern Chinese classics such as *bak choi* and *choi sum* (varieties of Chinese cabbage), *dou miao* (snow pea shoots) and others. Tofu, a versatile dish made from pressed bean curd, is popular in this land of historical food shortages, and egg dishes are numerous, particularly in home-style restaurants.

The preparations are also subtly different to those elsewhere in the country. Along the southern coast, most ingredients are steamed, stir-fried or flash-fried in oil, and ginger, garlic, spring onion, sesame and soy are the essential flavours. Southern China features fewer of the stewed and braised dishes, usually pork, that are so common further north.

Related to this is the overwhelming popularity of the wok and the cleaver: historical shortages of fuel, always a problem in this populous region, made quick cooking a necessity. Peer into any southern kitchen, and you will see one or more blast-furnace-fired woks – great spouts of high-pressure flame sear the bottom of the wok, and the sizzle and crackle of ingredients are the essential sounds of southern cookery. Standing over the blazing wok, normally, is a very busy and very hot cook. Ingredients cooked this way are crisp, fresh and tasty; they retain much of their original

Eddie Liu, who works at a five-star hotel in Taipei. "We don't use many different materials because they won't all be fresh, so we have many kinds of cooking. There is one kind of fish, but 10 kinds of cooking. You can steam, deep-fry, cook with garlic sauce, or cook with ginger, orange peel, black bean. There are many things you can mix together, but it is still the same fish."

## AROUND THE REGION

In southern China, as elsewhere in the country, unique local crops and cooking styles combine to generate disinctive regional cuisines. Few regions in the world boast as large a spectrum of flavours.

flavour, and they arrive at the table piping hot.

To keep cooking times to a minimum, most food is cut into small, cookable pieces in the kitchen. There are few items in southern China that can't be hacked to pieces with a cleaver. Chickens, ducks, ribs and vegetables all get the chop-chop in the kitchen, and arrive at the table in chopstick-friendly chunks. One exception is fresh fish, which is commonly served whole, along with crabs, lobsters, shrimp and other seafood.

As elsewhere in China, these few key ingredients and techniques undergo the endless permutations that lend such variety to Chinese dining. "A menu can have hundreds of items, but the material is all the same: beef, pork, chicken, fish, vegetable, tofu, shellfish," says Cantonese chef

In **Yunnan** province, the abundance of certain crops such as crunchy mushrooms, along with subtle influences from Burma and Thailand, have created a cuisine that is beginning to appear in upscale restaurants around the country. In tropical **Hainan**, coconut and pineapple flavour many of the dishes, while in **Macau**, Portuguese, Indian and African spices have seeped into the cuisine, imported from the former Portuguese empire.

**Hunanese** cuisine is considered the "hottest" of all Chinese foods, even spicier than its famously fiery cousin, Sichuanese. **Guangxi**, **Jiangxi** and **Guizhou**, those in-between provinces, share some of the features of their neighbours, including liberal use of chilli peppers and other spices.

In general, the farther south one goes, the less spice is used, until in **Guangdong**, especially for those accustomed to the fiery cuisines of Hunan or Sichuan, or the sweet and salty richness of Shanghai, the lack of oil, pepper, chilli and other spices can take some getting used to. Watch a Cantonese diner – a drop of soy sauce is enough to flavour a bowlful of food, while the mustard and chilli, often served as condiments, are routinely ignored. This is true of the Cantonese cuisine of **Hong Kong** and **Guangzhou**, the Chiu Chow dishes of eastern Guangdong, that of **Hainan Island** and, to a lesser extent, **Fujianese** cuisine. That said, most menus, even in Cantonese restau-

The classic Cantonese dish is steamed fish, which is dipped alive from a tank, and shown to the dinners, still flapping – freshness is paramount in this subtle cuisine. The fish is lightly steamed, then doused in smoking hot oil and topped with a mild sauce of coriander, ginger, pepper, sesame and soy. Other famous Cantonese dishes are too numerous to list fully – they include beef and broccoli with oyster sauce, diced chicken with cashew nuts, barbecue pork and steamed lobster. The Cantonese repertoire also includes the priciest of Chinese foods, including shark-fin soup, bird's-nest soup, abalone and sea slug, as well as dim sum, those tasty wrapped

rants, feature at least one dish that makes use of chilli peppers.

## Cantonese

Of all the cuisines of China, **Cantonese** is the most famous. Few cuisines have so thoroughly swept the world, in part because so many of the people of Guangdong province moved overseas. Food-wise, the Cantonese were far ahead of their time. In the past couple of decades, the world has discovered the virtues of fresh, simple ingredients, quickly cooked and lightly seasoned. The Cantonese have been doing this for centuries.

snacks that form the southern China version of Sunday brunch.

Cantonese chefs like to mix fruit with meat or poultry, and lemon-roasted chicken and duck with pineapple are both typical (and excellent). This balances the flavours, and also looks good. For all Chinese chefs, north and south, colour is important. They pride themselves on creating pleasing colour combinations, and diners like to see an eye-catching array of dishes. That's why sweet and sour pork is a perennial Cantonese favourite – the green pepper, yellow pineapple, brown pork and red tomato create a rainbow of attractive hues. There is a Chinese phrase that describes the perfect dish: *si xiang wei ju quan*, or colour, fragrance and taste in complete harmony.

**LEFT:** Hainan chicken rice is one of the region's best known dishes. **ABOVE:** communal dining.

## Macanese

Among all the foods of southern China, the real oddball is Macanese, a full-flavoured combination of spices and techniques that is found nowhere else in the world. It is a melting-pot blend of African, Portuguese, Indian and southern Chinese influences, along with a hint of Southeast Asia. And the flavours of the former Portuguese empire are here, too, including turmeric, tamarind, coconut milk, cinnamon, cloves, coriander and chilli peppers (which later found their way to Hunan and Sichuan provinces). Baking and roasting are common in Macau, unlike anywhere else in southern China.

The most famous Macanese dishes are chilli shrimp, African chicken and curried crab. Depending on the recipe, African chicken is dusted in garlic, chilli pepper and turmeric, roasted, and served with a rich peanut sauce. Macanese egg tarts, another curiosity, are a variation on the egg tarts that are ubiquitous throughout south China. But in the early 1990s, an enterprising Macau chef caramelised the tops of the tarts, and a famous new dessert was born.

## Hakka

A less well-known cuisine is that of the Hakka people. The Hakka, or *ke jia ren* (literally, guest people), are the wandering tribe of China. Originally from the central plains of north China, they settled throughout the south, usually in less fertile areas. Traditionally poor and often transient, the Hakka's food features preserved meats and vegetables, sun-dried sausages and liver, fermented bean curd, and plenty of cabbage and pork. The signature flavours are vinegar, sliced ginger, and pickled, fermented vegetables, especially mustard greens. Clay pots filled with pungent pickled vegetables, some up to 40 years old, are a hallmark of Hakka villages.

Hakka food has enjoyed a recent revival in China, as diners rediscover the virtues of simple peasant cooking. Pork features heavily in many Hakka dishes. *Di bang* is a thick leg of stewed pork, covered with tangy pickled vegetable and rich, sweet sauce. The defining Hakka dish, shredded beef and ginger, is superb, and the thinly sliced ginger has a remarkable mildness. Nobody knows how they achieve this flavour – it is a Hakka secret.

## Chaozhou

Chaozhou (formerly Chiuchow) food is a close cousin to Cantonese, although you wouldn't know it if you asked anyone in either Hong Kong or Shantou, where the battle lines are drawn and arguments are fierce. But like Cantonese, it is mild and relies heavily on seafood and fresh vegetables, although it has some unique dishes. One of these is cold crab, which is steamed, then chilled and served with ginger and vinegar. Shrimp balls, steamed dumplings with dried radish, peanuts and pork, and steamed pork are famous, and, in common with the rest of Guangdong province, the people of Chaozhou often eat snake, dog, monkey, pangolin, civet cat and other animals from the distant ends of the food chain. Chaozhou meals often finish with a very strong tea called *kung fu cha*. This is the espresso of teas, a strong, bitter brew served in the tiny, delicate, eggshell-thin teacups that are made in the famous ceramic kilns of eastern Guangdong.

## Fujianese

Further up the coast in Fujian province, the food shares much in common with Taiwan, which makes sense, since most Taiwanese trace their ancestry to Fujian. This cuisine is characterised by soups and seafood, and it features strong salty flavours and heavy use of organ meats. One dish stands out as unique to Fujian province (and Taiwan): oyster omelette. A half-dozen oysters are placed on a very hot grill, followed by rice batter, then an egg. This is flipped over and smothered in green vegetables, then turned again and cooked, then served with a spicy, sweet sauce. In some restaurants, the oyster omelettes are served sandwich-style in toasted sesame buns.

Perhaps the most famous Fujian dish is Buddha Jumps the Wall, a delicious salty stew cooked in a clay pot. The broth is pork-based and flavoured with pepper, rice wine and black vinegar, and the ingredients vary, but often include bacon, pork rib, taro root, black mushroom, bamboo, chestnut and sometimes expensive items like abalone and sea cucumber. As the story goes, a Buddhist monk smelt the dish and jumped over a wall to try some.

## Hainan Island

Hainan Island is the most tropical province in China, and the seafood-rich cuisine reflects this warm, wet location. Coconut features heavily, especially in dishes containing crab, mutton, duck and chicken, and unlike in other coastal provinces, goat and mutton are popular in Hainan. The food here is not generally spicy; it is instead light and tasty, with an emphasis on fresh, lightly cooked flavours. The local Hele crab finds its way onto many menus, where it is fried or steamed, and often mixed with fresh local mushrooms.

The most famous Hainan dish is Wenchang chicken, which is known throughout Southeast Asia as Hainan chicken rice. Wenchang chickens are famous for their sweet flavour, and they are "crystal cooked", that is, lightly boiled, to preserve this taste. The cooked chicken is then chopped and served with a delicious dip made from oil, ginger, salt and scallions. Hainan chicken rice is identical, but it uses ordinary chickens.

## Hunanese

If the mild, fresh flavours of coastal China begin to seem a bit punchless, travellers can always visit the "spice belt" of interior China, a region that includes Hunan, Jiangxi, Guizhou, Yunnan and Sichuan provinces. Here, the hot climate, mountainous terrain and lack of fresh seafood and vegetables has promoted cuisines that are spicy, peppery and pungent.

Hunanese cuisine, in common with its close relative Sichuanese, has proven popular throughout China, and has migrated to big cities like Shanghai, Hong Kong and Beijing. Besides its liberal use of chilli, black pepper, Sichuan pepper and other spices, Hunanese also features stewed, braised and smoked dishes, in contrast to the mostly stir-fried coastal cuisines. Hunan ham is rightly famous, and finds its way into hundreds of dishes, including the ever-present Hunan ham stir-fried with green vegetables. The ham is rich and sweet and smoky, and the scallions and chili are pungent and spicy, a perfect combination. Stewed tofu and hot-and-sweet braised chicken are also perennial favourites.

## Yunnanese

Another cuisine that has started to migrate from interior southern China to the capital cities is Yunnanese, a mixture of Dai and Miao tribal flavours, unusual local ingredients, Chinese cooking techniques, Sichuanese spices and Southeast Asian influences. The key combination is sour and spicy, and the food is highlighted by tropical flavours such as coconut milk, pineapple and lemon grass, and features items like mountain vegetables and crunchy local mushrooms. Dairy products are popular here, unlike in the rest of China, and goat's cheese and delicate custards are used. The most famous dish is "crossing the bridge noodles", a hot noodle soup that features many of the province's signature flavours. ❑

**LEFT:** a food-processing factory. **RIGHT:** chillis add heat to the cuisine of Hunan and Jiangxi.

# BELIEFS AND RELIGION

**Religious faith in southern China is an amalgam of formal religions and philosophies. These are interwoven with a plethora of folk superstitions and beliefs, and the worship of a colourful array of deities**

Chinese religion is often described as a synthesis of the "three teachings" of Confucianism, Daoism (Taoism) and Buddhism: Confucianism teaches ethical and pragmatic standards of behaviour, while Daoism has a religious and also a philosophical dimension. Buddhism, imported from India in the 1st century AD, has since evolved into a uniquely Chinese form that is influenced by Confucianism and Daoism.

Yet these mainstays are only part of the picture. Most day-to-day religious practices adhere to a form of "folk" or "popular" tradition that has its roots in the three religions, but also includes a broad mixture of other beliefs, including feng shui and ancestor worship. Indeed, the religions practised in southern China are, for the most part, fusions of different beliefs. The people of the region welcome different deities and influences into their belief systems. And in particular it is Daoism, especially influential in the south, that embraces multiple gods.

## Home worship

Many Chinese, even those who don't profess a religious belief or routinely worship at a church or temple, nonetheless engage in religious activity. It is common in southern China, especially in Hong Kong and Macau, to see homes and shops decorated with an illuminated shrine, or people burning incense to honour a deity, hero or ancestor. Many families perform ancestor worship, and at important times, for example when a son or daughter takes a university entrance exam, parents will visit a temple to burn incense, light candles and solicit divine help. Some drivers decorate their cars with

charms, statuettes and religious slogans for protection against accidents, and many shopkeepers place a "wealth-beckoning" cat next to their cash registers. These small golden figurines perpetually wave one paw back and forth, to welcome the arrival of wealth.

A family altar sits in the main room of many homes in southern China, again more often in Hong Kong and Macau, where traditions were not disrupted by the Cultural Revolution. On this altar, household gods and ancestors are venerated in an ancient tradition that has changed little over the centuries. The altar contains small statues of the household god, while to the left are ancestral tablets that contain family records, including the names of ancestors dating back many generations.

**LEFT:** Tin Hau statue, Repulse Bay, Hong Kong.
**RIGHT:** "wealth-beckoning" cats.

On special days, offerings of food are placed on the family altar. The altars take many forms: in some homes a simple shelf hangs on the wall, while others boast large, intricately carved shrines that take up a great deal of space.

The approach to prayer is essentially pragmatic: what has this god done for me lately? If a god fails to deliver the goods, usually money, marriage, a child or a promotion, he can be replaced by another deity. But it works both ways: worshippers can ask gods for better health or more money, but they must give something in return, by burning paper "spirit" money, lighting incense and candles, or offering fruit or drinks or

food. If a petitioner fails to return a favour, bad fortune may follow.

Religious customs, icons and beliefs once permeated all levels of society in China, but after the founding of the People's Republic in 1949, religion was deemed "counter-revolutionary", with repression culminating in the widespread destruction of temples, mosques and churches during the Cultural Revolution. Following Mao's death conditions became less hostile and in 1982, freedom of religious belief was guaranteed by law.

## Fortune-telling, lucky numbers and feng shui

In China, the idea of fate began in feudal Chinese society, when it was believed that "the god" – ie the Emperor – decided one's destiny. With the Tang (618–907) and Song (960–1279) dynasties, people became more concerned with fate, and fortune-telling grew popular.

Fortune-tellers make predictions by reading faces and palms, or performing complicated calculations based on a person's name and the time and date of birth. This takes reference from the system of the 12 animal signs of the Chinese zodiac – rat, bull, tiger, rabbit, dragon, snake, horse, goat, monkey, chicken, dog and pig – dividing people into the 12 categories according to the year they were born. Fortune-tellers also predict the future with the Chinese tradition of lucky, and unlucky, numbers. The number two stands for easy, three for living or giving birth, four for death, six for longevity, eight for prosperity and nine for eternity. Combinations of numbers can also make a difference. For example, 163 means "live for ever" or "give birth non-stop." The number 8222 assures that attaining prosperity is easy.

Such emphasis on numerology brings its own oddities: vehicle licence plates containing auspicious numbers can change hands for astronomical prices. Some Hong Kong tower blocks avoid having a 14th floor (going straight from the 13th to the 15th). Even mobile phone numbers come in a wide range of prices: those containing the number eight are more expensive, and those with the number four are cheaper.

*Feng shui* (wind and water), or geomancy, is a set of spatial guidelines that are used to attract good luck and prevent bad fortune. The theory is largely based on the principle of *qi* – life spirit or breath – divided into *yin* and *yang*, the female-passive and male-active elements of life. Feng shui is taken very seriously in south China, especially by the Cantonese, and virtually every office and every building in Hong Kong and Macau has had a feng shui "consultancy". The feng shui master's prescriptions can range from a wholesale remodel to a few simple correctives like hanging a gourd or a mirror to deflect bad energy, or placing a fish tank to limit the outflow of wealth.

The concept of *wuxing* also has a prominent standing in Chinese medicine, astrology and superstition. The term translates as "five elements", in which five types of energy dominate the universe at different times. Water dominates in winter, wood in spring, fire in summer, and metal in the autumn, while earth is a transitional period between seasons.

## Tin Hau and other folk deities

Tin Hau (Tian Hou in Mandarin; Mazu in Fujianese), the patron saint of seafarers, is by far most popular folk deity in coastal southern China, where many of the people are fishermen or sea traders. According to legend, Tin Hau was born Lin Mo, the daughter of a fisherman, on an island near Fujian. Using mystical powers in her dreams, the young Lin Mo tried to save her father and brothers after a typhoon sank their ship. After waking, she learnt that her brothers had been saved. She died at 28, but continued to save other seafarers, and became affectionately known as Mazu, or maternal ancestor. Her spirit is believed to appear

Gods of Wealth, divided into civil and martial camps, are also common. The martial god of wealth is often represented by Guan Yu, recognisable by his bright red face, while the most popular civil icon of prosperity is the God of Increasing Wealth, who is depicted as an elegant scholar with a long beard. Besides these, there is a very long list of additional folk deities who remain very popular.

## Daoism (Taoism)

A central concept of Daoism is the *dao*, which means the way or the path, but it also has a secondary meaning of method or principle by which the universe operates. Another important premise

on the sea, and many rescued sailors have reported seeing a red fire, called the Fire of Mazu, upon the surface of the sea.

Dozens of other folk gods are also popular in southern China. Immortality is a major theme, and these icons include the Eight Immortals, which are Daoist deities who died and were reborn into new bodies. Some gods are "appropriated" from Buddhism, the most prominent example being Guanyin (the Buddhist bodhisattva Avalokitesvara); Guanyin is generally interpreted as the Goddess of Mercy, protector of the sick, poor or generally unfortunate; to others she is the Goddess of Good Fortune.

**LEFT:** Daoist statue at Qingyuan Shan near Quanzhou, Fujian. **ABOVE:** incense at Yuantong Temple, Kunming.

of Daoism is *wu wei*, which is sometimes defined as passivity, or "swimming with the stream". The Chinese martial art of *tai ji* (t'ai chi) is inspired by this concept. The notion of *de* (virtue) is also central; it is a virtue that manifests itself in daily life when *dao* is put into practice.

Daoism perceives the course of worldly events to be determined by the forces of *yin* and *yang*. The yang forces are masculine, bright, active and heavenly, while the yin forces are feminine, weak, dark and passive. Daoism is especially vibrant in southern China, where, in its many folk forms and permutations, it is by far the leading religion.

Laozi was the founder of Daoism, and he lived at a time of crises and upheavals. It is said he was born in a village in the province of Henan in 604

BC, into a distinguished family. He was a contemporary of Confucius, and ancient chronicles record that the two met.

Religious Daoism developed in various directions from Laozi's teachings. The ascetics retreated to the mountains and devoted all their time to meditation, or else lived together in monasteries. Priests had important functions as medicine men and interpreters of oracles. They carried out exorcisms and funeral rites, and read special services for the dead or for sacrificial offerings. The classic work of Daoism is the *Dao De Jing* (or *Tao Te Ching)*, "the Way of Power." Attributed to Laozi, it now seems likely it was written by more than one author.

## Confucianism

While Laozi was active in the south of China, Kong Fuzi, or Confucius, lived in the north. For Confucius, too, *dao* and *de* were central concepts. For more than 2,000 years, the ideas of Confucius (551–479 BC) have profoundly influenced Chinese culture, which in turn coloured the worldviews of neighbouring lands such as Korea and Japan. Confucianism is not a religious philosophy in the strictest sense, rather it is a moral code for society. But Confucius is sometimes worshipped as a deity, and was officially made equal to the heavenly god by an imperial edict in 1906. In south China, people visit Confucius temples during exam times, to ask this patron saint of scholars for divine intervention.

Confucius came from an impoverished noble family that lived in the state of Lu (in the west of Shandong province). For years, he tried to gain office with one of the many feudal lords, but was repeatedly dismissed. So he travelled with his disciples and instructed them in his ideas. All in all, Confucius is said to have had 3,000 disciples, 72 of whom are still worshipped today.

Confucianism is largely a creed of law and order. Just as the universe is dictated by order, and the sun, moon and stars move according to the laws of nature, so a person, too, should live within a framework of order. This idea, in turn, is based upon the assumption that people can be educated.

Confucius was a conservative reformer, yet he changed the idea of the *junzi*, a nobleman, into that of a noble man, whose life is morally sound and who is therefore legitimately entitled to reign. Confucius believed that he could create an ideal social order if he reinstated the culture and rites of an earlier time. Humanity *(ren)* was a central concept, its basis being the love of children and brotherly love, and rulers would meet success if they governed society according to these principles. The Chinese word *ru*, which is usually translated as "Confucian", actually means "someone of a gentle nature" – a trait that was attributed to a cultured person.

Confucius defined social positions and hierarchies very precisely. Only if every member of society took full responsibility for his or her position would society function smoothly. Family and social ties were considered to be of fundamental importance: between father and son (son must obey father without reservations); man and woman; older brother and younger brother; and ruler and subject. As it evolved, Confucianism reached canonical status in Imperial China; it formed the basis of all civil service examinations, a determining factor for Chinese officialdom until the 20th century.

## Buddhism

The Chinese initially encountered Buddhism at the beginning of the 1st century, when merchants and monks came to China on the Silk Road. The prevalent type of Buddhism in China today is the Mahayana, which as opposed to the Theravada form (practised in southern Yunnan), promises all creatures redemption through the bodhisattva, or redemption deities. Today, there are Buddhists among the Han Chinese, Mongols, Tibetans, Manchus, Tu, Qiang and Dai peoples.

Two aspects of Buddhism particularly appealed to the Chinese: the teachings of karma provided an explanation for individual misfortune, and there was a hopeful promise of existence after death. Nevertheless, there was considerable opposition to Buddhism, which contrasted sharply with Confucian ethics and ancestor worship.

Modern China has three schools: Chan, or Zen Buddhism; Amitabha, or Pure Land Buddhism; and Tantric Buddhism. The most influential is the Zen school, developed during the Tang Dynasty, which preaches redemption through enlightenment, which anyone can attain. It denounces knowledge gained from books or dogmas; the masters of Zen consider meditation to be the only path to knowledge.

In the 7th century AD, another type of Buddhism, called Tantric Buddhism or Lamaism, was introduced into Tibet from India. Eventually, it replaced the indigenous Shamen Bön religion, while absorbing some of its elements. Combining these teachings, Tibetan monasteries later developed into centres of intellectual and worldly power.

The most popular form of Buddhism in the deep south of Yunnan is Theravada, the oldest surviving school of Buddhism. This sect is popular in Southeast Asia, and it flowed across the southern borders into Yunnan province. Further north, Theravada fades away, and the Mahayana Buddhism typical of most of China, Japan and Korea predominates. Generally, Theravada Buddhism teaches that insight must come from experience and advice, not blind faith; the goal is freedom from suffering, and practitioners believe that enlightenment is achievable in a single lifetime. Pagodas are central to the religious life of Theravada believers, and many of China's most dramatic pagodas are in Yunnan.

## Christianity

Christianity was first brought to China by the Nestorians, in 635. For a period, in spite of persecution, the religion spread to all the regions of the empire, and survived in some parts of the country until the end of the Yuan Dynasty.

Later, contacts were made between China and the Roman Catholic Church. The first Catholic church in China was probably built by a Franciscan monk from Italy, who arrived in Beijing in 1295. During the Ming period, Catholic missionaries were active in China. A leading figure among the Jesuit missionaries who played an important

role was an Italian, Matteo Ricci. When he died, there were 3,000 Christians in China.

The Jesuits used their knowledge of Western sciences to forge links with Chinese scholars, but other Catholic orders were more dogmatic and caused tension. The Chinese emperors, fed up with the squabbling, persecuted them all. The Vatican took a strong anti-communist stance after World War II, and the Chinese ordered that Catholics in China could no longer be accountable to the Vatican. Protestant Christianity in modern southern China is tolerated, although not exactly encouraged. Despite this, the number of people practising the religion appears to be growing. ❏

### CHINA'S MUSLIMS

Ten of the 56 recognised nationalities in China define themselves as Muslim: Hui, Uzbek, Uighur, Kyrgyz, Kazakh, Tatar, Tajik, Dongxiang, Salar and Bao'an – a total of 20 million people. Of these groups, the Hui (among whose number are the descendants of the 13th-century Uzbek mercenaries in Yunnan, *see page 26)* are unique in being Chinese-speaking and living in every province across the country. The Hui are more integrated into mainstream Chinese life than the other groups, and it is possible to argue that most Hui are really Han converts to Islam, and therefore not an ethnic minority at all, but a religious minority. However, neither the Han, nor the Hui themselves, readily accept this.

**LEFT:** small household shrines are a feature of southern China. **RIGHT:** Yunnanese Muslims.

# CHINESE MEDICINE

Traditional Chinese methods of treating illness and pain – herbal medicine, acupuncture and remedial massage – are increasingly popular in the West

The mention of traditional Chinese medicine often conjures up images of magical needles, aromatic herbs and strange animal parts. Yet, despite its exotic stereotype, traditional Chinese medicine is increasingly gaining respect from both scientists and the general public in Europe and the US, particularly with regard to the alleviation of pain. In China, scepticism and debate arose as to the value of traditional medicine in the first half of the 20th century. Intellectual and political groups, such as the Nationalists and Marxists, were particularly disapproving, and the medical establishment suffered greatly at their hands. After the founding of the People's Republic of China, competition between Western and Chinese medicine was eradicated for practical as well as ideological reasons, with an attempt to integrate the two systems.

This approach has persisted, and today, medical care in China often consists of a mixture of both Western and traditional Chinese medicine, although Western-style medicine, or *xiyi*, tends to be dominant. Large public hospitals *(renmin yiyuan)* in cities across the country offer both traditional Chinese and Western approaches to medical treatment. Hospitals dealing exclusively with traditional Chinese medicine, or *zhongyi*, tend to be smaller, less well equipped and harder to find.

The Chinese will usually visit a doctor trained in Western medicine if they feel that they are seriously ill and need to be treated quickly. If the problem is not too serious or urgent, the patient will most likely seek out a traditional doctor, who is thought to be better able to restore harmony to the body.

**BELOW:** *A Village Doctor Using Acupuncture*, print from the Song Dynasty (960–1279).

## The pharmacy

A traditional Chinese apothecary has a unique smell made up of thousands of scents emanating from jars and cabinets stocked full of dried plants, seeds, animal parts and minerals. Among them are the well-known ginseng roots, dried or immersed in alcohol and often looking much like a human figure. In fact, the Chinese word for ginseng contains the character ren, which means person. You will also recognise the acupuncture needles and the cupping glasses made of glass or bamboo. And then there are the myriad kinds of dried herbs, blossoms, roots, berries, mushrooms and fruits.

**LEFT:** The Chinese herbal tradition is said to date back 5,000 years to the time of Shennong, a farmer who tasted thousands of different varieties of herb. These were later described in the *Shennong Bencaojing*, the earliest complete Chinese pharmacopoeia, which lists 365 medicines.

**ABOVE:** a traditional Chinese apothecary is full of dried seeds, herbs and plants, not to mention parts of unfortunate animals – sometimes endangered species which have been illegally killed.

**BELOW:** the Chinese medical treatment of cupping, a method of applying acupressure by creating a vacuum next to the patient's skin. The vacuum is made by heating the air in the cup.

## THE ORIGINS AND UNDERSTANDING OF CHINESE MEDICINE

Traditional Chinese medicine is based on an array of theories and practices from both foreign and native sources. It was during the Zhou period (11th century–221 BC) that many of these theories first emerged. This stage of Chinese history, marked by fighting and misery, lasted several centuries. Considering the turmoil of the period, it is hardly surprising that people began to search for a solution to the endless strife. Innumerable thinkers, philosophers and social reformers with as many diverse ideas emerged, forming a collection of thought often referred to as the "hundred schools". Many ideas took root that were to influence all aspects of life in China for the next 2,000 years – including medicine. Medicine itself was influenced by the teachings of Confucianism and Daoism.

Holism, or the idea that parts of a human body form an integral, connected and inseparable whole, is one of the main distinguishing features of traditional Chinese medicine. Whereas Western medicine tends to treat symptoms in a direct fashion, Chinese medicine examines illnesses in the context of the whole person.

Yin-yang philosophy and the theory of five elements form a system of categories that explain the complex relationships between parts of the body and the environment. Yin and yang represent two opposite sides in nature such as hot and cold, light and dark. Each of the different organs is said to have yin or yang characteristics, and balance between the two is vital for maintaining health. Likewise, each organ is linked directly to a particular element: fire for the heart, earth for the spleen, water for the kidneys, metal for the lungs and wood for the liver. The way in which they interact affects a person's health, so, for example, the kidneys (water) nourish the liver (wood).

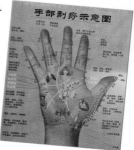

**TOP:** acupuncture is based on the theory that currents of energy *(qi)* flow through channels, or meridians, in the body.
**RIGHT:** diagram of pressure points.

# ARTS AND CRAFTS

With its long history and inward-looking tradition,
China has developed and refined a resplendent catalogue
of fine arts and exquisite crafts

The world of Chinese art is an intoxicating one. First, there is the superb detail found in the intricate ink lines of the paintings, the cleverness of the carvings, the historical precision of the bronzes, and the ceramics' explosive, vibrant colours. Then there is the near-perfection of the individual pieces, with some objects as close to perfect as it is humanly possible to get. And there is the sheer variety of mediums, from bronze to jade to ceramic to silk to stone to paper, and that doesn't even include folk arts such as paper cutting, lacquerware and woodcarving.

Chinese art begins with the jade disks and oracle shells of the Yellow River era, at the dawn of Chinese civilisation, then proceeds forward in time through the rustic simplicity of the Han bronzes, the graceful statues of the Tang, and the rich paintings of the classical Song, one of the high points of Chinese culture. Next come the beautiful soft jades and fine calligraphy and scrolls of the Ming, then the vibrantly colourful ceramics of the Qing, followed at last by the East-meets-West oil paintings that are currently in vogue in modern China.

## Painting and calligraphy

There has always been a close connection between Chinese painting and calligraphy. Ancient Chinese written words started as pictures (pictograms), and while each has developed in a separate direction, there has nonetheless remained inextricable ties between the two. Classical Chinese painters usually have extensive training in calligraphy, while calligraphers have experience in painting. Both forms are created with the same brushes and are often present together in one piece of work.

**LEFT:** a hanging scroll painting of the southern Chinese landscape style. **RIGHT:** calligrapher at work.

What elevated the status of painting from other crafts was its similarity to calligraphy. Both calligraphy and painting are considered scholarly pursuits with esteemed traditions, but calligraphy was once held in higher regard. Literati painters, for example, judged works by their combinations of painting, poetry and calligraphy. Success in all three areas deemed paintings to be art. According to such standards, paintings that lacked calligraphy were merely crafts, regardless of their level of technical brilliance.

Writing and painting utensils are referred to in China as the Four Treasures of the Study. They consist of the brush, ink, rubbing stone and paper – tools held in high regard by poets, scholars and painters. Brushes are made from bamboo and various kinds of animal hair, such as rabbit's fur, horsehair and even mouse whiskers, and come in a wide variety of sizes.

Ink was widely used in China during the Han period. It was made from the soot of coniferous resin with the addition of glue. Ink of good quality has perfume added – musk in the former days, but cloves are now commonly used. The substance is pressed into the shape of slabs, bars or prisms. Ink in solid form is used for writing and painting, although liquid ink is now available. But using liquid ink removes one of the more contemplative and ritualistic aspects of traditional Chinese painting: making the ink, in which one

ings" in Chinese, this style features mountains and water accented with clouds, mist and trees. By contrast, human figures are small specks in the landscape and lack the detail lavished on the vegetation, water and mountain. These proportions reflect Chinese philosophies on the relationship between individuals and the outside world; Chinese paintings often show people as a small part of their surroundings.

Chinese painting reached its peak during the Song Dynasty. This period was typified by a love of art and widespread collecting, particularly by the ruling class, and especially the Emperor. The paintings are typified by what critics call a

first drips water onto a rubbing stone, then rubs the ink stick on it. The resulting ink is an intense black, but can be diluted to the lightest of greys as necessary.

Paper is the usual medium on which to paint. Itself a Chinese invention, developed by Cai Lun and used from the 2nd century AD onwards – it is now produced in different qualities, each offering the painter new possibilities depending upon absorption and texture. Silk was once the standard of professional painters, as it gave better control over graded ink and colour washes, but scholar-painters preferred paper for its immediate response to the brush.

One of classical China's favourite forms was landscape painting. Called "mountain water paint-

"blanketing simplicity," with spare, clean lines, large open spaces, exquisitely rendered details and simple, often natural, themes. They were once much brighter, but the reds and yellows and oranges have faded with time, and some of the original vibrancy has been lost. Classical Song paintings have mountains at the centre, and common themes are village life, water, hills, skies and animals.

Animals were of particular interest to the Song-era painters. For example, in the 11th-century painting *Magpies and Hare*, by Ts'ui Po, a curious rabbit looks over his shoulder at two magpies that are scolding him. The magpies are at the top right of the painting, and the rabbit is in the lower left. Between them, as is typical of Song paintings, is a large open space. The open space is key: it exactly balances the frame, and the eye is drawn to the emptiness, and from there to the interaction between the three animals. The artist sees the essence of the animals and captures it perfectly, another feature of Song paintings. The masterpiece is rendered on a human scale, and is more immediately accessible than the dramatic, sweeping Song landscapes.

Of special note is the scroll, a form of painting unique to China. After being painted on silk or paper, the painting is backed with stronger paper and mounted on a long roll of silk or brocade. Then a wooden stick is attached at the lower end (or left end, if the scroll is to be displayed horizontally). Typically, the picture was stored away rolled up and brought out only on special occasions, to be unfurled slowly, revealing only parts of a scene that were pieced together in the mind of the observer, subtly drawing him into the picture. Like an early cinema reel, the pictures were rarely displayed for long.

In modern China, painting as an art form – and as a business – has grown rapidly in popularity. Two broad forms have emerged: one is traditional, and has attracted a Chinese audience, and the other is pop-oriented, and has attracted an overseas following. In general, the "modern traditional" form focuses on technique and uses familiar themes, like landscapes and village scenes, or city life, or a girl with a birdcage, often with a hint of the erotic. The "overseas" form is a sort of political pop art, featuring icons and imagery from communist China, but using modern materials and an Andy Warhol-type approach.

## Silk

Calligraphy, painting, poetry and music were historically regarded in China as noble arts, and every scholar was required to know them. By contrast, applied arts such as silk and carving were considered merely honourable crafts, performed by craftsmen and ladies of leisure. All the same, these skilled crafts have always held a special fascination.

The cultivation of the silkworm is said to go back to the 3rd century BC. The planting of mulberry trees and raising of silkworms is credited to Fuzi, a legendary figure of prehistoric China. For centuries, silk held the place of currency: civil servants and officers as well as foreign envoys were frequently presented with bales of silk. The precious material was transported to the Middle East and the Roman Empire, mostly via the Silk Road.

The Chinese maintained a monopoly on silk until about 200 BC, when the secret of its manufacture became known in Korea and Japan. In the West – in this case the Byzantine Empire – such knowledge was acquired in the 6th century AD. The Chinese had long prohibited the export of silkworm eggs and the dissemination of knowledge of their cultivation, but a monk is said to have succeeded in smuggling – an offence punishable by death – some silkworm eggs to the West.

The centres of silk production are traditionally concentrated in central-eastern China – mainly Zhejiang and Jiangsu provinces. Southern China has featured more in silk embroidery, with Hunan and Guangdong two important and ancient centres for this art.

## Porcelain

The Chinese invented porcelain sometime in the 7th century, although the history of Chinese pottery goes back to the Stone Age. Along the Huang He (Yellow River) and Chang Jiang (Yangzi), 7,000 year-old pottery vessels – red and black clay with comb and rope patterns – have been found. The Yangshao and Longshan cultures of the 5th to 2nd millennium BC developed new types of vessels in a diversity of pat-

**LEFT:** an array of calligraphers' tools.
**RIGHT:** *Quails Among the Chrysanthemums*, from the Song Dynasty (1131).

terns in red, black and brown. Later, light-grey stoneware with green glazes, known as yue ware – named after the kilns of the town of Yuezhou – were designs of the Han period (206 BC–AD 220). By the time of the Tang Dynasty, Chinese porcelain was famous in the Middle East and Europe, where it became known as "China". Jingdezhen *(see page 241)* in Jiangxi province became China's porcelain capital from around the 13th century, a status it retains today.

The most widespread form of ancient Chinese porcelain was celadon, produced by blending iron oxide with a special glaze that resulted, during firing, in a green tone. Sancai (three-colour) ceram-

ics from the Tang Dynasty also became world-famous. The colours were mostly green, yellow and brown. Sancai ceramics were also found among the tomb figurines of the Tang period in the shape of horses, camels, guardians in animal or human form, ladies of the court and officials.

The Song period celadons – ranging from pale or moss green, pale blue or pale grey to brown – were also technically excellent. In the Yuan period, the first "underglaze blue" ceramics appeared, a technique that would reach its zenith with the celebrated ceramics of the Ming period. Some common themes seen throughout the Ming period were figures, landscapes and theatrical scenes. By the beginning of the Qing Dynasty, blue-and-white porcelain attained its highest level of quality.

But it was the during the Qing Dynasty that ceramics reached a whole new level, with the bright, vibrant colours called polychrome enamels. The plates and bowls and vases of this period, aside from their exquisite shapes and forms, feature a remarkable combination of vivid colours and evocative designs, such as maroon dragons, aqua-blue clouds, lime-green swirls, and backgrounds of rich mustard yellow. Many of the pieces are elegant yet playful, and in their exquisite perfection, though they are from the last of the dynasties, they carry echoes of the magnificence of 25 centuries of Chinese classical art.

## Jade

Jade is China's most precious stone, and it was one of the earliest art forms to reach a superior level of achievement. According to a Chinese creation myth, when the god Pan Gu died, his breath became the wind and clouds, his muscles became soil, and the marrow of his bones jade and pearls. Chinese valued the stone for its beauty and for its attributed magical powers. In early times, jade was used for ritual and religious purposes, but it later came to be used for ornamentation and jewellery.

The oldest jades so far discovered come from the neolithic Hemadu culture of about 7,000 years ago. The finds are presumed to be ritual objects. Many small circular discs with holes in the centre, called *pi* discs, given to the dead to take with them, have been found. These round discs represent the harmony between heaven and earth. Even today, many Chinese wear *pi* discs.

Jade was believed to have preserving powers, and burial suits were made with the precious stone. The Han Dynasty saw an early peak in the jade carving. During this time, the corpses of high-ranking officials were clothed in suits made of more than 1,000 thin slivers of jade sewn together with gold wire. The Hebei Provincial Museum in Shijiazhuang displays the jade suits of Prince Liu Sheng and his wife. It is said that jade glows with the vitality of the owner. If the owner became ill, for example, the jade would tarnish. Jade ornaments were believed to impart good health, luck and offer protection.

Jade is not a precise mineralogical entity, but rather comprises two minerals, jadeite and nephrite. The former is more valuable because of its translucence and hardness, as well as its rarity. Nephrite is similar to jadeite, but not quite as hard. Colours vary from white to green, but also black, brown and red. The Chinese most value a clear, emerald-green stone. Jade is an especially difficult material to shape due to its hardness.

In the jade-carving workshops of present-day China, there are thought to be as many as 30 kinds of jade. Famous among the jade workshops are those in Hetian (also called Khotan; Xinjiang), Shoushan (Fujian) and Luoyang (Hunan).

In government shops, jade can be trusted to be genuine. On the open market and in private shops, however, caution is advised. Genuine jade feels cool and cannot be scratched with a knife. Quality depends on the feel of the stone, its colour, transparency, pattern and other factors. If in doubt, a reputable expert should be consulted.

astonishingly intricate. Traditional paper cuts are black or red, but recently, more modern-looking rainbow-coloured works have become popular.

Lacquerware is another time-honoured folk art: lacquered objects date back to the Warring States period (403–221 BC). At that time, lacquerware was already an everyday material: bowls, tins, boxes, vases and furniture made of various materials (wood, bamboo, wicker, leather, metal, clay, textiles, paper) were often coated with lacquer. Emperor Qianlong (r. 1735–1796) had a special liking for carved lacquerware; he was buried in a coffin carved and preserved using this technique.

## Folk arts

Aside from the classical "high" arts, China features a number of folk arts, including woodcarving, paper cuts, embroidery, and lacquerware. Woodcarving has a long history; many of the carvings are richly detailed, and some are unbelievably precise. Common subjects include gods, literary figures, and mythical animals like dragons and phoenixes. Paper cutting is another ancient art that is still widely practised; sheets of paper are folded and carved with scalpels, rendering mirror images that are

The glossy sheen of lacquerware is not only attractive but also strong and lightweight. The bark of the lacquer tree, which grows in central and southern China, exudes a milky sap when cut, which solidifies in moist air, then dries and turns brown. This dry layer of lacquer is impervious to moisture, acid and scratches, and is therefore ideal protection for materials such as wood or bamboo.

To make lacquerware, a base coat is applied to a core material, followed by thin layers of fine lacquer that, after drying in moist, dust-free air, are smoothed and polished. If soot or vinegar-soaked iron filings are added to the lacquer, it will dry into a black colour, while cinnabar turns it red. ❑

**LEFT:** porcelain at a market in Jingdezhen, Jiangxi.
**ABOVE:** jade, formerly the preserve of China's elite, is extremely popular throughout the country.

# CHINESE OPERA

The emphasis in Chinese opera is on Confucian ethics and morality. Stories invariably have endings in which goodness is upheld and evil is punished

Although Chinese theatre in the form of skits, vaudeville, puppet shows and shadow plays has existed since the Tang Dynasty, formal music-drama had its origins in the Yuan era (1279–1368). Today there are more than 300 different styles of Chinese opera. By far the most popular is the highly stylised *jingxi* (Beijing or Peking opera) form, which dates from the 1800s and is prevalent across the country. The major southern regional form is Cantonese opera; apart from being performed in the Cantonese dialect, it has only subtle differences from Beijing opera, the most noticeable being that Western musical instruments such as saxophones are sometimes used. Fujian province specialises in puppet operas, whilst Chaozhou in eastern Guangdong has its own opera of the same name (and also known as Teochew opera). Yue (Shaoxing) opera is another southern form.

While there are endless variations among the different opera styles, all of them share some general characteristics. Almost all operas are based on popular legends, folk or fairy tales with which audiences are already familiar, and almost all forms are a composite of dialogue, song, dance, mime and martial arts. Time is marked with the aid of a redwood clapper that produces a high-pitched clicking sound when struck. The accompanying musical instrument in Beijing opera is usually the *huqin*, a Chinese fiddle, although cymbals are sometimes, if not usually, employed in action scenes.

Mastery of singing is essential, while clowns are required to demonstrate acrobatic prowess. All actors must hone the fine body movements that are the opera's style. An actor's training includes applying the elaborate make-up that identifies the character. Actors often undergo seven years of training as children.

**ABOVE:** the words used in any performance are colloquial – opera was meant to be watched by the common people.

**ABOVE:** changes in time and place are evoked through speech, action and the ritualised use of props. Walking in a circle is symbolic of a journey, while circling the stage with a whip indicates riding a horse.

Red make-up on a male character indicates bravery and loyalty, while white denotes a powerful villain. Clowns have their own special make-up, often with a white patch on the tip of the nose to indicate wit or playfulness.

## VISITING THE OPERA

A visit to the Chinese opera is a relaxed though occasionally quite noisy experience; formal dress is not the norm. Be warned, however, that this exotic art form doesn't appeal to everyone: once you've got over the visual spectacle of the elaborate costumes and startling make-up, you might find the strangled singing style, the atonal music and the plot too much to take for a whole performance – and performances can be long. Of course, it helps if you have a good grasp of the language (although some theatres will have subtitles in English). If you are in Yangshuo, you can catch a performance of Zhang Yimou's spectacular "concept opera" *Impressions of Liu Sanjie* (pictured above; details on page 275). See *Travel Tips, page 368,* for a list of venues in major cities.

**ABOVE:** the long flowing sleeves in certain costumes can be manipulated in more than 100 movements. Costumes are based on those of the court of the Han, Tang, Song and Ming dynasties, although they are symbolic rather than realistic.

**LEFT:** the female role *(dan)* is often the most important part, and usually played by men. The *dan* usually has a white make-up base with various shades of carmine.

# ARCHITECTURE

In Imperial China, architectural principles were dictated by the cosmology defining heaven and earth, and there are plenty of examples of this in the south. Some extraordinary minority architecture, a scattering of colonial relics and gleaming modern skyscrapers are also characteristic of the region

Southern China lacks the spectacular architectural highlights found in the north of the country, but there is, nonetheless, plenty of interest – from the hi-tech skyscrapers of Hong Kong to the covered wooden bridges of Guizhou, the Buddhist pagodas of Xishuangbanna, and the circular Hakka roundhouses of Fujian and Guangdong provinces. As elsewhere in China, much was lost during the vandalism of the Cultural Revolution. Most of what has survived – the old clan houses, ancient pagodas, traditional temples and quiet gardens – is classical Chinese, reflecting the twin philosophies of order and authority.

## Classical architecture

Feng shui ("wind and water"), the Chinese practice of placement to achieve harmony with the environment, has been a significant factor in the construction of buildings, and indeed whole cities, since records began. A sheltered position, facing the water and away from a hillside, is considered auspicious.

Chinese households were centered around courtyards; the higher the rank, the greater the number of courtyards. The home of the head family is situated in the north of the compound, and faces south. The side buildings facing the central courtyard might belong to sisters and brothers, while more distant relatives might live around courtyards further south. In more modest homes, a similar layout prevails, with parents living in the main northern quarters facing south and children occupying the side quarters facing the courtyard. Surrounding and enclosing every classical Chinese residence is a wall, which normally forms part of the courtyard. Walls are very important to the Chinese; not only do they provide protection and privacy, but they symbolise the containment and group mentality that are such

important aspects of Chinese society. The longest wall of all, the Great Wall, reflects this concept.

A so-called spirit wall was usually put up behind the entrance of apartments and palaces to bar the entry of evil spirits, believed to be able to move in a straight path only and not around corners. In large palaces, the splendid Nine Dragon Walls, fulfilled this function, while many pagodas, teahouses and other structures are approached by nine-cornered bridges.

## Pagodas and temples

Majestic and ornate, pagodas are an integral part of any romantic image of the Far East, and yet they are not indigenous to China. They originated in India, where they were made of brick and used to enshrine sacred objects. During the first centuries AD, Buddhist missionaries spread the teachings of Buddha to China. Many Chinese monks later travelled the same route back to India and in this way, reports of burial rites, religious art and impressive monastic and temple architecture filtered into China. Through the centuries, Chinese pagodas lost their religious associations and incorporated traditional Chinese architectural styles.

One of the earliest surviving – and tallest – pagodas in China is the Ornamental Pagoda at Temple of the Six Banyan Trees, in Guangzhou *(see page 172)*. This octagonal tower first appeared in 537 and was rebuilt in 1097; much of

with their own building traditions. Examples of Daoist, Buddhist and Confucian temples include the Kaiyuan Temple at Quanzhou in Fujian province, the Confucius Temple at Wenchang on Hainan Island, and the Nanyue Temple in Hunan.

## Chinese construction

From the earliest days, wood was favoured as a building material as it was easily transported and practical. Residences were designed to be rebuilt, not to be permanent monuments. Brick and stone were used, however, for the construction of important buildings intended to withstand the elements for a prolonged period, such as imperial tombs

the present pagoda dates from the second rebuild. The classical pagodas of Guangdong and Fujian provinces, many of them rebuilt over the years using original materials, are among the top architectural highlights of southern China.

The secularism of Chinese society (and architecture) is also reflected in the temple design of various religious sects. Buddhist temples, for example, have the same general design as Daoist and Confucian temples. They are built and designed by the same craftsmen as those who build homes and palaces, just as they adapted Buddhism by mixing the original style of the Buddhist pagoda

**LEFT:** pagoda at Kaiyuan Temple, Quanzhou, Fujian.
**ABOVE:** Tianxin tower, Changsha, Hunan.

and ceremonial structures, and, occasionally, bridges. As a result of the widespread use of wood, few of the original ancient remnants remain.

Chinese craftsmen developed timber-frame construction into its ultimate form. Traditional Chinese buildings rest on a floor made of beaten earth, brick or stone; heavy columns set in stone bases carried the roof and could also be carved for decoration and embellishment. Partitioning the interiors were walls made of light materials that could easily be built up or removed. In summer, the panels between the load-bearing columns of simple houses could be easily removed.

Colour and construction material varied according to the significance of the building and social status of the owner. Yellow tiles, for example, were used for imperial buildings. In addition, different roof shapes were used to denote the importance of a building. The most important buildings had hipped roofs, while unimportant ones had simple gabled roofs. The overhanging eaves, which give the structure an air of weightlessness, are not just pleasing to look at; they also keep out rain and control the amount of light entering the building, keeping out the sun in summer and allowing it in during winter.

## Minority architecture

One of south China's signature architectural features, the circular Hakka roundhouses, are found are covered – and the Drum towers in Guizhou province, Buddhist pagodas in Xishuangbanna and Tibetan hillside architecture in the rugged northwest corner of Yunnan province. The bridges are lovingly decorated by master Dong carpenters and are built of mortise and tenon joinery, without nails. The Chengyang Wind-and-Rain Bridge in Sanjiang county is one of the best examples. The drum towers – seven, nine, or 11 storeys tall – are the dominant structures in Dong villages, and like the bridges, they display the building skills of these remarkable craftsmen.

Xishuangbanna, with its Buddhist tradition, offers another architectural treat: traditional pago-

in western Fujian and eastern Guangdong provinces. The four-storey structures – there are square ones, too – are made of clay, sand, lime, sticky rice and sugar, reinforced with wood or bamboo. These roundhouses are not museums: Hakka people still live in them, and often, tourists will be invited inside for tea.

In typical roundhouses, the kitchens, dining areas and common spaces are on the ground floor. Old folks live on the second floor – fewer stairs – while younger Hakkas live on the top two floors. In the courtyards are the wells, grain mills, ancestral halls and other features of daily life.

In the minority areas further west are many structures reflecting local building styles, including the wind-and-rain bridges – so called because they

das. Each pagoda is built in a different style, and all are unique, but the most famous is the Bamboo Shoot Pagoda at Damenglong (see page 321): Made from brick and clay, it is over 800 years old and features a tall central tower and several satellite pagodas, typical of the regional style.

## Colonial relics

Casino-dominated Macau also has its modern architectural extravagances, including Las Vegas-style attractions like spouting volcanoes and replicas of the Potala Palace and the Colosseum. But, unlike Hong Kong, Macau has managed to preserve many of its colonial-era charms; it recently earned a World Heritage listing from UNESCO for 29 key historical sites. These include the Sam

Kai Vui Kun and A-Ma temples, Guia Fortress, and the dramatic facade of São Paulo church. Many of these Portuguese structures were the first of their kind on Chinese soil. There are only a handful of comparable buildings in Hong Kong, including Flagstaff House in Hong Kong Park, the nearby St John's Cathedral. A slightly more recent gem is the Old Bank of China Building in Central district, a 17-storey Art Deco classic that opened in 1937. It was designed by Palmer and Turner, a firm that became famous for designing many structures on Shanghai's Bund, including the Peace Hotel.

Another area of traditional Western architecture is Gulangyu Island, a five-minute ferry ride from the city of Xiamen in Fujian province. Xiamen, a former English treaty port, was one of the busiest colonial enclaves in China in the late 1800s and early 1900s, and Gulangyu is home to dozens of examples of the large, graceful colonial-era structures that once served as consulates, residences and offices. Among and between the colonial buildings are some equally well-preserved Chinese courtyard mansions.

Fifteen Western-style buildings in Beihai, on the coast of Guangxi, were recently included on a list for top state protection, including the sites of the British, German and French consulates, a nunnery, a Catholic church, a hospital, a school for girls and a Customs building; most were built between 1870 and 1902. Beihai used to be one of the starting ports on the sea for China's "maritime silk road". After the Opium War, it was turned into a port for free trade.

## Modern architecture

No cityscape on earth can rival the sight of Hong Kong Island from the southern tip of Kowloon peninsula. There, tucked between the mountains and the harbour, is a dramatic skyline – rambling, chaotic and unplanned, but nonetheless very impressive. Buildings are shooting up at a breakneck pace in Shenzhen, Guangzhou, Fuzhou, Xiamen, Changsha, Kunming and elsewhere, but those cities lack the remarkable density, and therefore the drama, of Hong Kong. Guangdong province has two of the world's tallest skyscrapers: the CITIC Plaza in Guangzhou and the Shun Hing Square in Shenzhen.

China is paying a very high price for economic expansion, as old buildings are making way for residential towers, office blocks and motorways. From Lhasa to Beijing, historic structures are rapidly disappearing. Even many so-called "heritage" schemes have a dubious value. The popular Xintiandi area of Shanghai was flattened and rebuilt in an "old style" – which included a Starbucks, several bars and boutiques, and many other municipalities consider it a model for "cultural renovation". Tong Mingkang, deputy director of cultural heritage, said this faking of history made the country poorer. "It is like tearing up an invaluable painting and replacing it with a cheap print." ❑

**LEFT:** the spectacular Zhencheng Lou, a Hakka roundhouse near Yongding, Fujian.
**RIGHT:** colonial remnant, Beihai, Guangxi.

### IDENTICAL CITIES

The speed of China's modernisation is having a devastating effect on its cultural heritage. Some have compared the damage to that wrought by the Red Guards during the Cultural Revolution of 1966–76, when temples were ransacked in the name of revolutionary politics. Today the damage is being done by urban developers in the name of economic progress. Even the vice-president for construction, Qiu Baoxing, has criticised the destruction of historical sites and cultural relics. Developers have torn down tens of thousands of traditional homes and countless colonial-era neighbourhoods across southern China. In their place are identikit tower blocks flanking identikit wide boulevards.

# PLACES

A detailed guide to the region, with the
principal sites clearly cross-referenced by
number to the accompanying maps

Isolated, aloof, for much of its history known only to the outside world through rumour spread along the threads of the Silk Road, the ancient land of Cathay still retains an enigmatic hold on the traveller's imagination. And its southern regions are among the most enigmatic of all: behind the long, convoluted coastline of the South China Sea lies a broad subtropical hinterland of endless green hills and narrow valleys, where emerald rice fields occupy every available inch of flat land; further west, as the terrain rises towards the Himalayas, the picture becomes ever more alluring, a landscape of misty heights and remote villages home to exotically-clad minority peoples.

Of course, this romantic view isn't the whole story. As elsewhere in China, the south has its share of bland, grey, concrete cities, Dickensian coal mines and other industrial monstrosities, some world-class environmental problems and all the other ills that afflict a fast-developing economy. Indeed, the southern coastal provinces are riding the wave of economic advance as much as, if not more than, anywhere else in China – most obviously in the Pearl River Delta, where an area half the size of Belgium produces a large proportion of the world's clothing, shoes and toys, is criss-crossed by modern

highways and peppered with teeming cities. This is about as far from mysterious Cathay as it is possible to get.

Much of the interest in travelling through 21st-century China, though, is to experience these contrasts – an experience likely to be enormously enhanced given that most people begin their journey in glittering Hong Kong. A possible itinerary would be to take a train from there up to Shenzhen or Guangzhou in the delta, and spend a couple of

days acclimatising before heading east to the absorbing cities of Chaozhou, Xiamen and Quanzhou, and then north to Jiangxi and Hunan. Or go west, to the unforgettable landscapes of Guilin, remote, fascinating Guizhou, and then on to explore the wonderful riches of Yunnan. ❑

**PRECEDING PAGES:** the ethereal beauty of the Li River near Yangshuo, Guangxi; the new China, Guangzhou; mountain scenery at Lu Shan, Jiangxi.
**LEFT:** trekker at Tiger Leaping Gorge, Yunnan. **TOP:** Man Mo Temple, Hong Kong.
**ABOVE LEFT:** tropical beach, southern Hainan. **ABOVE RIGHT:** Chaozhou, Guangdong.

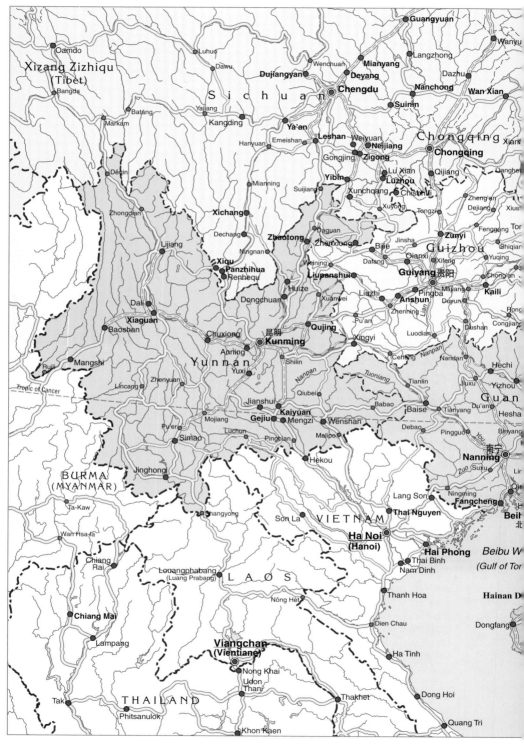

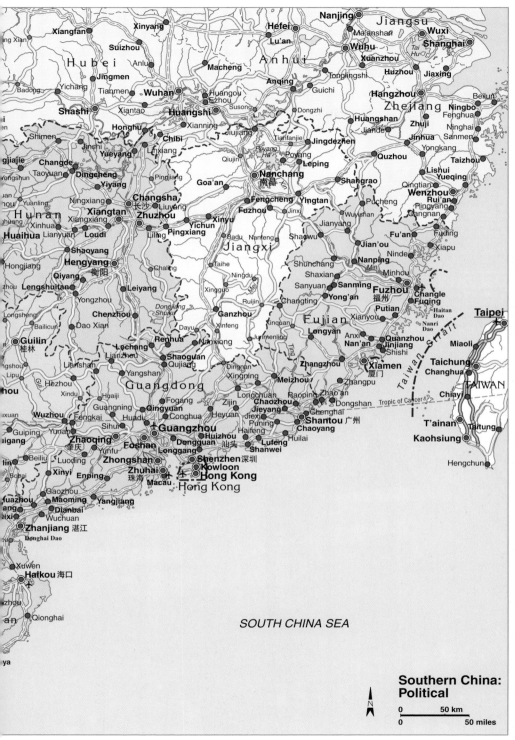

**Southern China:
Political**

0       50 km

0       50 miles

SOUTH CHINA SEA

# HONG KONG AND MACAU

### Colourful, vibrant, exciting Hong Kong makes a perfect introduction to China, while nearby Macau is an intoxicating blend of old Europe and new Asia

Gateway to southern China, yet in some ways a million miles away from it, Hong Kong makes a spectacular start- or end-point to a Chinese odyssey. This crowded, noisy, energising place is utterly unique in its juxtaposition of East and West, its role in recent Chinese history and even its topography.

A Special Administrative Region (SAR) of China since the British packed their bags in 1997, Hong Kong can be divided into four parts: Hong Kong Island, Kowloon, the New Territories and the numerous outlying islands. Hong Kong Island is a bizarre mix of steep forested mountains and dense urban jungle dominated by grand financial institutions, futuristic skyscrapers, opulent hotels and shopping malls, splendid residences and – contrastingly – some of Hong Kong's oldest Chinese communities. Beyond, the southern side of the island is completely different to the north, with a scattering of beach resorts and wealthy residential communities.

Across the harbour at the southern tip of the Kowloon peninsula is the neon-lit Tsim Sha Tsui district with its many hotels, bars and shopping centres, and views of Hong Kong Island. To the north, past grittier Yau Ma Tei and Mong Kok, Boundary Street marks the demarcation line between the old British colony and the New Territories, which were leased in 1898 for a 99-year period. The British also leased 233 outlying islands, only four of which are inhabited by sizeable communities. Contrary to most people's image of Hong Kong, large areas of the New Territories, and many of the islands, are uninhabited, their empty grassy hills popular with hikers.

Across the mouth of the Pearl River, the former Portuguese enclave of Macau makes a wonderful day-trip. It's a heady mix of southern Europe, the Orient and Las Vegas: a sizeable Portuguese community remains, with their restaurants and cafés; the colonial architecture is well-preserved, yet the city is still unmistakeably Chinese; and gigantic Nevada-style casinos are springing up as Macau strives to cash in on the economic boom to become Asia's leisure capital. ❏

---

**LEFT:** the view across Chater Garden and Statue Square and the bright lights of Hong Kong Island's Central District. **TOP:** fishmonger in Western District. **ABOVE LEFT:** a Hong Kong tram. **ABOVE RIGHT:** the facade of São Paulo, Macau.

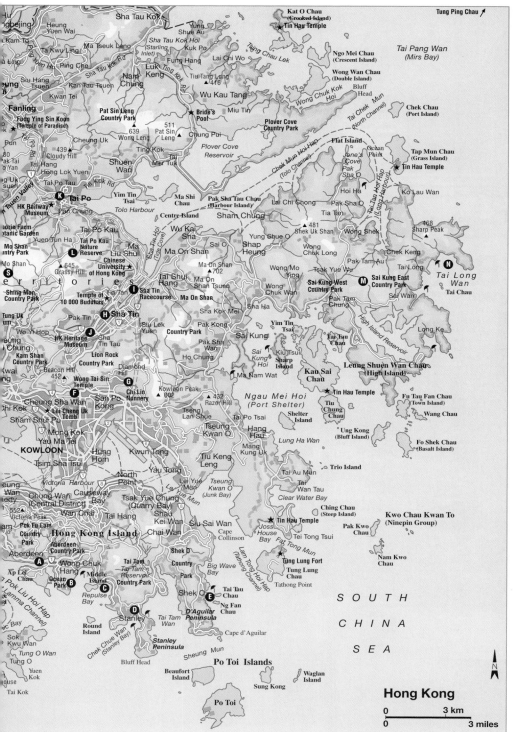

Hong Kong

*Recommended Restaurants & Bars on pages 132–3*

# HONG KONG

Taken from China during the Qing Dynasty, Hong Kong – having returned to Chinese sovereignty – is as colourful, vibrant, chaotic and appealing as ever

The entry point into southern China for most tourists, Hong Kong makes a memorable introduction to the Chinese world. Glamorous, hectic, exciting and spectacular, with fabulous food, nightlife and shopping, this is a place like no other.

## HONG KONG ISLAND

Central – still occasionally marked on maps as "Victoria", and Chung Wan in Cantonese – is Hong Kong's business and financial hub, at the heart of the incredible cliff face of high-rise buildings that extends along the north shore of Hong Kong Island. Squeezed between the harbour and the precipitous slopes of Victoria Peak, this is where the money is, the financial powerhouses, the glamorous high-end shopping malls, overlooked by the multi-millionaires' mansions on the Peak. And in the midst of all the glitz, there are still strong elements of former days, with wayside hawkers dangling novelties and knock-offs, incense sticks smouldering by tiny shrines, and delivery boys pedalling serenely through red lights with a cargo of fresh meat balanced in their bike's cast-iron basket. It all adds up to one of the most fascinating areas of modern Hong Kong.

### The financial centre

The **Central Ferry Pier** ❶, the new terminal for the Star Ferry on Hong Kong Island, is as good a place as any to begin exploring Central. With reclamation continually narrowing the harbour, the pier was forced to relocate in 2006. Now situated next door to the Outlying Island Ferry Piers, it features Edwardian-style embellishments and is more user-friendly than its predecessor. The iconic green-and-white ferries, however, remain unchanged: old-fashioned, functional and reliable. A trip across the harbour to Kowloon is essential for any visitor, with wonderful views of the famous skyline. Fares are extremely low – splash out an extra 50 cents to travel on the "deluxe" upper deck. The crossing takes 7 or 8 minutes (6.30am–11.30pm).

**LEFT:** a typical Hong Kong street.
**BELOW:** tai chi by the harbour.

*IFC2 is the world's sixth-tallest building, and dominates the Hong Kong skyline.*

**BELOW:** rush hour on Des Voeux Road Central.

The prosaically named **International Finance Centre (IFC)** , a combination of smart shopping mall and offices, sits atop the Airport Express Central terminal. Just to the north in front of the ferry piers, and part of the same complex, is the tallest of Hong Kong's 7,500-odd high-rise buildings, the **International Finance Centre Two (IFC2)**, finished in 2003. It stands at a staggering 420 metres (1,378 ft), which makes it currently the sixth-tallest building in the world (fully 39 metres/128 ft higher than the Empire State Building). Unfortunately people are not normally allowed up to the 88th floor to admire the views.

Walkways connect the IFC to the rest of Central via **Exchange Square** ❸, home of the Hong Kong Stock Exchange and featuring a collection of sculptures by Henry Moore and Ju Ming in the adjacent plaza. Head east along the walkway to **Jardine House** ❹, whose distinctive 1,700-plus round windows have inspired the nickname "House of a Thousand Orifices". Opened in 1973, it was for many years the tallest building in Hong Kong. Just behind is the **General Post Office** (GPO).

Back on street level and inland from the GPO, an underpass will take you to **Statue Square** ❺, on either side of Chater Road. On Sundays, throngs of Filipina maids gather here on their day off in a festive, chaotic outdoor party. The 143,000 Philippine nationals, most of whom work here as maids, now form by far the single largest foreign community living in Hong Kong.

Chinese and expatriate victims of World Wars I and II are commemorated at the **Cenotaph**, and Hong Kong's war veterans gather here on Remembrance Day every November. Nearby, the **Mandarin Oriental Hotel** ❻ is one of the oldest and grandest hotels in Hong Kong, and a favourite meeting place for the captains of industry.

This part of Central District is the financial hub of Hong Kong, home to the headquarters of several major banks. Facing Statue Square is Norman Foster's US$1 billion **Hongkong & Shanghai Bank Building (HSBC Building)** ❼, the most expensive building in the world when it was completed in 1985. A short distance along Des Voeux Road is the dramatic 368-metre (1,209-ft) **Bank of**

**China Tower ❽**, designed by the American-Chinese architect I. M. Pei, and one of Hong Kong's most famous buildings. Opened in 1990, it is surmounted by two antennae resembling a pair of chopsticks. The 43rd-floor observation area is open to the public (Mon–Fri 9am–6pm, Sat 9am–1pm; free).

East of Statue Square is the colonial-style former Supreme Court Building, which is now the **Legislative Council (Legco) Building** *(see margin)*. Across Jackson Road, **Chater Garden** is a rare (but not especially pleasant) open space that may host demonstrators, off-duty Filipina maids or munching office workers on their lunch break. Until the 1970s, the site was occupied by the Hong Kong Cricket Club. When the 1967 pro-communist riots shook Hong Kong, a photographer captured the ultimate clash of cultures – English colonels playing cricket against a backdrop of Mao posters draped all over the old Bank of China Building.

## Des Voeux and Queens roads

Much of Central District is easily navigated via the elevated **walkways** which run from the GPO (first floor) past Exchange Square to the Macau Ferry Terminal, and via Chater House and adjacent buildings as far as the bottom of Lan Kwai Fong. Heading inland from the GPO on these pedestrian thoroughfares takes you over Connaught Road Central to **Des Voeux Road**, named after Sir George William Des Voeux, governor from 1887 to 1891. The tram stop here, at the junction with Pedder Street, is one of Central's most photographed spots, a blur of traffic and people.

Across the street, **The Landmark ❾** is a prestigious shopping mall with enormous stand-alone stores dedicated to luxury brands. Five floors surround a vast atrium, around which walkways connect with neighbouring buildings such as **Chater House** and **Prince's Building**, flaunting a further abundance of marble and relentlessly upmarket shops.

The next east–west road away from the harbour, **Queen's Road Central** marked the waterfront before land reclamation began in the 1850s. Running between its shops and emporia and those of Des Voeux Road are two narrow alleyways, **Li Yuen Street East** and **Li Yuen Street West ❿** – also known as **The Lanes**,

*Built in 1912, the Legislative Council Building was used as a torture chamber by Japanese police during World War II, and wartime shrapnel damage can still be seen on the eastern wall. It is not open to the general public.*

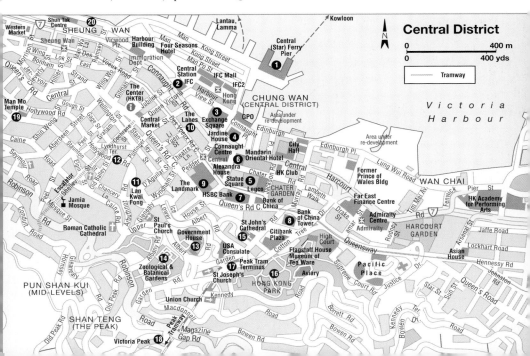

*The steps up Pottinger Street from Queen's Road Central mark the start of the steep ascent from the harbour. Queen's Road was once on the waterfront.*

**BELOW:** Lan Kwai Fong nightlife.

lined with stalls and outlets selling clothing, fabrics and counterfeit designer fashion accessories. The atmosphere is a complete contrast to the glamorous highrises on the larger avenues nearby, and bargaining is still expected.

### Lan Kwai Fong and beyond

Behind Queen's Road Central the terrain rises steeply. D'Aguilar Street leads up to **Lan Kwai Fong ⓫**, which together with neighbouring SoHo is a prime nightlife area. Modern cuisine, modish bars, clubs, English pubs and tiny snack shops generate dollars and testosterone in equal measure, and late-night revellers can get everything from pizza to sushi in the wee hours. At weekends many bars stay open until 5am or later.

At the top of Lan Kwai Fong, winding Wyndham Street is lined with small antique and crafts shops, and leads on to **Hollywood Road ⓬**, packed with shops selling top-dollar antiques, furniture, rattan and second-hand books, and the nightlife area of **SoHo** (SOuth of HOllywood), accessed via the useful Central-Mid-levels Escalator, which starts by Central Market.

### Colonial relics

The higher up one gets on the Island, the more desirable the property and the higher the rents – a pattern established in the early colonial years, when the upper slopes were considered less prone to malarial mosquitoes.

Just above Lan Kwai Fong on Upper Albert Road, the rarefied air is immediately apparent at **Government House ⓭**, grand home of the former colonial leaders of Hong Kong and now the official residence of the Chief Executive. The mansion dates from the 1850s but was remodelled by the Japanese during World War II, who added a tower with a vague Shinto look. There is a clear view of the building through the wrought-iron gates, which are opened to the public only a couple of times a year, usually in spring and autumn (no set dates).

Opposite Government House are the **Zoological and Botanical Gardens ⓮** (open daily 6am–7pm; free), a lush tropical area housing a small assortment of wildlife. It opened in 1864 and still retains elements of its original Victorian gentility, with the added Eastern spirituality of elderly Chinese performing their

t'ai chi exercises each morning. From here it is just a short stroll to the Victorian Gothic **St John's Cathedral ⓯**, consecrated in 1849 and the city's oldest Anglican church. In nearby **Hong Kong Park ⓰**, **Flagstaff House** is another example of bespoke architecture. It is home to the **Museum of Tea Ware** (open Wed–Mon 10am–5pm; tel: 2869 0690; free) and completed in 1846. The building – of more interest than the museum – is reputedly Hong Kong's oldest surviving colonial structure.

## The Peak

Make your way along to the **Peak Tram terminus ⓱** on Garden Road to ascend Hong Kong's most notable natural landmark, properly though rarely called **Victoria Peak ⓲** (Shan Teng in Cantonese). "The Peak" is the residential aspiration of most of the population, not to mention the goal of more than 3 million visitors a year. The vertiginous tram, which runs from 7am to midnight, ascends to 396 metres (1,299 ft) above sea level in just seven minutes.

The upper terminus at the **Peak Tower** is shaped like a wok, and is for many people one of the ugliest buildings in Hong Kong. Of course, the main reason for coming up here is to marvel at some of the world's finest vistas. Many find the nighttime views even more incredible, a vast glittering swathe of electric light, most spectacular immediately below in Central and Wan Chai as the buildings attempt to outdo each other in their eye-catching displays. The **viewing platform** has been raised 30 metres (100 ft) to the top of the "wok" for a 360-degree panorama. Attractions inside the tower include Hong Kong's own **Madame Tussaud's** waxworks (open daily 10am–10pm; entrance fee). The area around the Peak Tower is in fact Victoria Gap, whereas the summit of Victoria Peak itself (552 metres/ 1,811 ft) lies to the west.

## Western District

Just to the west of Central, this area offers a glimpse of a more traditionally Chinese Hong Kong, complete with mah-jong-makers, herbalists and craftsmen. But don't expect a sanitised, tourist-orientated experience: it's all quite gritty and dirty.

Begin a tour of Western with a ride on the **Central-Mid-Levels Escalator** from

**TIP**

There are a variety of superb walks from the Peak Tower. The Peak Circle Walk is a gentle 3-km (2-mile) stroll, well signposted and shaded from the sun; allow about 45 minutes for a round trip from the Peak Tower. Alternatively, turn off onto Governor's Walk, which winds up to the attractive Victoria Peak Garden. The summit itself is out of bounds. For the more ambitious, the Hong Kong Trail heads east along the spine of Hong Kong Island for some 50 kms (30 miles), all the way to Tai Tam and on to Shek-O.

**BELOW:** Peak view.

*The Central-Mid-Levels Escalator, opened in 1992, has transformed the neighbourhood of steep streets on the western edge of Central. Once rather run-down and seldom visited by outsiders, there is now an abundance of restaurants, cafés and bars here.*

**BELOW:** inside Man Mo Temple.

Queen's Road/Central Market. This lowest section passes bustling, noisy Chinese markets on small, steep thoroughfares such as **Peel, Gage** and **Graham streets**. Get off at **Hollywood Road** and follow it west to the corner of Ladder Street and the wonderfully dark and atmospheric **Man Mo Temple** ⓲ (open daily 9am–6pm; free), built around 1842. Tourists regularly throng through Man Mo, but this doesn't inhibit the temple's regular worshippers from visiting to fill the space with thick clouds of smoke from their joss sticks. The immense incense spirals hanging from the ceiling can burn for weeks.

Just past the temple is **Ladder Street**, zigzagging down steep inclines from Caine Road to Hollywood Road and down again to Queen's Road Central. The broad stone steps were built so that sedan-chair bearers could more easily carry their human cargo from Hollywood Road to residential Caine Road. Ladder Street contains some of Hong Kong's oldest houses, including shuttered buildings with wooden balconies and elaborate carvings.

Where Ladder Street meets Hollywood Road is the street officially called Upper Lascar Row but much more commonly known as **Cat Street**, because the odds and ends you can buy here are known in popular Chinese as "mouse goods", and those who trade in them are known as "cats". The lanes are filled with bric-a-brac, real and fake antiques, set out on myriad stalls.

Continue west to **Possession Street**, so called because it was here that Captain Sir Edward Belcher landed in January 1841 to plant the Union Jack and take possession of Hong Kong for Britain. No monument marks the exact spot where the British flag was planted. The only memento to the HMS *Sulphur*, whose crew was the first to step ashore, is Belcher Street, west of Possession Street.

Head back towards Central through the **Sheung Wan** area ⓴, along either Queen's Road West or Des Voeux Road; both are lined with aromatic Chinese pharmacies, traditional wedding-dress stores, and merchants selling paper lanterns and incense. Take a look at the fascinating range of dried seafoods, including abalone, sea cucumber and shark's fin, which can sell for up to several thousand dollars a kilo. Between Bonham Strand and Des Voeux

Road is colourful **Wing Lok Street**, with shops selling herbs, ancient medicines, preserved seafood and tea.

**Man Wa Lane** is lined with chop-makers, who carve elaborate name stamps from blocks of stone *(see margin note)*.

On Morrison Street, close to the harbour, stands a red-brick Edwardian-style building called **Western Market**, opened in 1906 and a food market until the 1980s. Recognised as a historical landmark, its elegant architectural features were preserved and restored, and in 1991 it was converted into a shopping complex. It offers a diversity of handicrafts, fabric and souvenir stalls.

## Wan Chai and Causeway Bay

To the east of Central lie two vibrant districts which embrace the hedonistic Hong Kong pleasures of eating, drinking and, of course, shopping. Wan Chai and Causeway Bay are, in general, architecturally undistinguished, but they are among the territory's most crowded and active areas, revealing the authentic flavour of modern Hong Kong. The tram line (which was on the waterfront when it was built at the beginning of the 20th century) runs right the way through these districts, and provides cheap and convenient transportation.

**Admiralty**, between Central and Wan Chai, is an agglomeration of gleaming office towers and shopping malls. Its epicentre is **Pacific Place** ㉑, one of Hong Kong's ritziest shopping malls. From Admiralty, it is a few minutes' walk to Wan Chai itself, originally a red-light district, though in the past decade or so girlie bars have been eclipsed by trendy bars.

Close to the waterfront (north of multilane Gloucester Road) are the **Academy for Performing Arts** ㉒ and the **Hong Kong Arts Centre** ㉓, two of the most popular venues for theatrical and cultural performances, while right on the harbour is the futuristic **Hong Kong Convention and Exhibition Centre** ㉔, which underwent a HK$4.8 billion extension in order to serve as the venue for the formal handover ceremony in 1997 – the building work was completed days (some say

hours) before the ceremony. The complex is fringed on the harbourside by a waterfront **promenade**, and at its northernmost point are two rather odd-looking statues. The tall black obelisk is the **Reunification Monument**, erected to commemorate the handover, and the gaudy, golden statue is the **Forever Blooming Bauhinia Sculpture**, the bauhinia flower being the territory's emblem since 1997 (its five petals are printed on the Hong Kong flag). Further on, past the tourist cruise operators, is Wan Chai's own Star Ferry Pier, with ferries to Tsim Sha Tsui.

Elevated walkways lead south from the Convention Centre to the 78-storey **Central Plaza** ㉕ office tower, currently Hong Kong's second-highest building at 374 metres (1,227 ft), and on into the heart of Wan Chai around the MTR station and **Lockhart Road** ㉖. From here westwards is a lively neighbourhood with numerous bars and restaurants.

Three blocks to the south of Lockhart Road, **Queen's Road East** ㉗ is notable for its rattan and rosewood furniture shops. This area also has two traditional Chinese temples that provide a glimpse of the old way of life in stark contrast to

*Chops are not only practical instruments (formal documents in Hong Kong still require a "chop", used as a signature), but works of ancient Chinese craftsmanship. Your name can be carved out of stone, ivory, jade or wood; when background material is carved out, the chop is male; when the characters are carved out, it's female.*

**BELOW:** the mall at Pacific Place.

*The Noon-Day Gun is fired daily from the Causeway Bay waterfront. The salute dates back to the 1860s when the governor was miffed that a mere trader received a 21-gun salute, and gave the order that it should be fired in perpetuity at noon every day.*

their modern surroundings. On Queen's Road East next to a narrow lane of steps leading up towards the Mid-Levels is the tiny, dark **Hung Shing Temple**. Much more impressive, however, is the **Pak Tai Temple** ❷❽ at the top of Stone Nullah Lane, a triple-halled temple noted for its 400-year-old, 3-metre (10-ft) statue of the deity Pak Tai, who assures harmony on earth. There are usually old men and women pottering around in the dark recesses, lighting incense sticks or laying out offerings.

Just before Stone Nullah Lane, along Queen's Road East, is the circular, 66-storey **Hopewell Centre** ❷❾. A rooftop restaurant offers an inspiring view of the city below but serves food that is far from inspirational.

At the eastern end of Queen's Road East is one of the oldest settlements on Hong Kong Island, developed after the early colonial settlers abandoned Western District because of malaria. This second settlement was named **Happy Valley**, reportedly because a cartographer's girlfriend accepted his proposal of marriage there. Residents created the greensward and edifice that has made the

area world-famous amongst horse-racing fans: the Hong Kong Jockey Club's **Happy Valley Racecourse** ❸⓪. If you can't make it to the actual races, visit the **Hong Kong Racing Museum** (open Tues–Sun 10am–5pm; free) inside the racecourse.

East of Wan Chai, **Causeway Bay** (Tung Lo Wan) is one of Hong Kong's top shopping areas, with large department stores – many of them Japanese. The streets are often crowded to the point of being uncomfortable, even by Hong Kong standards, and pollution levels are notoriously bad. **Times Square** ❸❶, a few blocks south of the main crossroads of Causeway Bay, is a large modern mall with restaurants, shops and a cinema.

Two blocks east is **Victoria Park** ❸❷, named after Queen Victoria, whose statue can be seen surveying the activities of her former subjects. Tens of thousands of people gather here during the Mid-Autumn Festival, when the park is illuminated with lanterns – a beautiful sight.

Travelling by MTR (or tram) to the east leads past the old Shanghainese residential neighbourhood of **North Point** to the bars and restaurants of Quarry Bay,

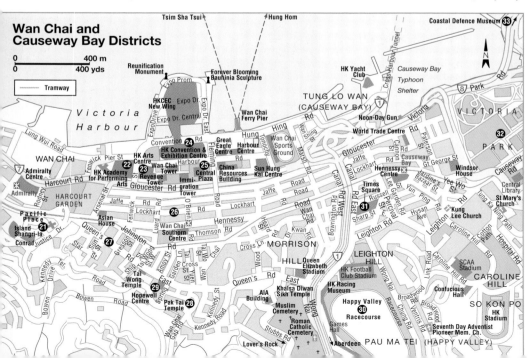

**Wan Chai and Causeway Bay Districts**

the large shopping centre of Tai Koo Shing, and the well-interpreted **Coastal Defence Museum** ㉝ (open Fri–Wed 10am–5pm; entrance fee) near Shau Kei Wan, which details the maritime military history of Hong Kong.

## The south side

In comparison with the densely urban strip along the northern coast of Hong Kong Island, the rocky southern shore remains more or less as nature intended.

The harbour town of **Aberdeen** Ⓐ is notable for the huge numbers of floating vessels bobbing in the water along its shoreline. This natural typhoon shelter is home to what remains of Hong Kong's "boat people" and their raggle-taggle collection of junks and sampans. Tourists are usually impressed by the colourful 30-minute ride through the harbour to the flamboyant Jumbo floating restaurant – one of the world's largest, with seats for over 4,000.

From Aberdeen, head east to one of Hong Kong's biggest home-grown attractions, even if it has been usurped by the shiny new Disneyland on Lantau *(see page 130)*. Opened in 1977 at a cost of HK$150 million, **Ocean Park** Ⓑ (open daily 10am–6pm; tel: 2552 0291; entrance fee) is a combination of theme park and oceanarium. The complex is divided into two sections, a lowland site and a headland site, linked by a 1.4-km (1-mile) cable-car. Ocean Park has responded to the Disney challenge by opening more attractions, and now has two extra pandas to pull in the crowds.

Beyond to the east is a region of rocky coasts and smooth, white sands – home to 14 of Hong Kong's 36 designated beaches. On summer weekends it can seem as if most of the population of Hong Kong has made its way here.

**Repulse Bay** (Cheen Soy Wan) Ⓒ was named after the battleship HMS *Repulse*, which took an active part in thwarting pirates who plundered here in the mid-19th century. Now widened to several times its original size and developed into a playground for tourists as well as urban Hong Kongers, Repulse

Bay Beach has everything except peace and quiet.

The resort is well known for a large blue apartment building with a big square hole in the middle. Some say the hole is a passageway for the heavenly dragon to come down from the mountains; others say it was put there to generate good feng shui; still others say it was just the architect's attempt at being funky.

Fifteen minutes' drive further southwest is the popular tourist magnet of **Stanley** (Chek Chu) Ⓓ. Named after Lord Stanley, a 19th-century Secretary of State for the Colonies, Stanley was the largest indigenous settlement in Hong Kong when the British first set foot here in 1841. **Stanley Market** draws thousands of visitors at weekends – locals in search of a bargain as well as tourists looking for souvenirs to take home.

Hong Kong residents come to Stanley for its restaurants and seaside feel. A modern shopping mall occupies a site at the end of Main Street, directly opposite one of the SAR's most amazing modern architectural projects. **Murray House**, a former British Army barracks built around 1848, was moved stone by stone from

*During the September–June racing season, the Hong Kong Jockey Club attracts up to 75,000 punters a race. The atmosphere is frenetic and makes for an enjoyable night out, with the entrance fee still only HK$10. Most of the profits are donated to charity.*

**BELOW:** on board a Hong Kong tram.

*The early British settlers regarded a posting to Stanley as highly dangerous. Only a dirt track connected the town to the city of Victoria (now Central), and pirates frequently attacked and robbed the garrison. Stanley was all but abandoned in the 1850s, until the original police station was replaced by the building which stands today. The station is also thought to have been the last point of resistance to the advancing Japanese forces in World War II.*

**BELOW:** Repulse Bay beach.

Central and rebuilt on the waterfront. The ground floor is home to the **Hong Kong Maritime Museum** (open Tues–Fri 10am–6pm, Sat 10am–7pm; entrance fee), which traces Hong Kong's long connection with the sea and trade with China. Upstairs there is a choice of airy restaurants.

East of the bus station is the **Old Stanley Police Station**, built in 1859 and one of only 30 protected historic buildings in Hong Kong – even if it is now being used as a grocery store. Down the road is **Stanley Prison**, which is still in use, while the two-storey building topped with a mock guard tower next to its parade ground houses the quirky **Correctional Services Museum** (open Tues–Sun 10am–5pm; free). Its nine galleries chart the history of Hong Kong's penal system. To the right of the prison is **Stanley Military Cemetery**, whose tombstones date back to early colonial times. It was also in Stanley – at both the prison and at nearby St Stephen's College – that the Japanese interned British prisoners of war. Near the cemetery is **St Stephen's Beach**, cleaner and more pleasant than Stanley's main beach. The last tiger ever shot in

Hong Kong (in 1942) was killed in the hills above Stanley, and its pelt can be seen at the Tin Hau Temple in the village.

The beaches east of Stanley are a little less accessible and therefore less crowded. A little way inland, **Tai Tam Country Park** is a popular picnic and hiking spot. At the far end of the island **Shek O Village ⓔ** is a pleasant place with a modest collection of shops selling beach paraphernalia. There are also a few restaurants and bike-rental shops. As the name suggests, nearby **Big Wave Bay** has Hong Kong's best surf.

## KOWLOON

The Kowloon Peninsula is in many ways very different from the glittering island across the harbour, more down to earth and more Chinese. Yet, somewhat paradoxically, Tsim Sha Tsui – its southern tip – is the location of the majority of Hong Kong's tourist hotels. Nathan Road is host to the quintessential Hong Kong image of gaudy neon signs and hundreds of small electronics shops. Save for the waterfront views, it is not an especially attractive place. But few can deny the electricity that charges life here, especially at night.

*Recommended Restaurants & Bars on pages 132–3*

Lacking the steep mountainsides that hem in the north shore of Hong Kong Island, Kowloon sprawls. Until Kai Tak Airport closed in the late 1990s, regulations restricted its buildings to a modest height. Now, they shoot skywards as never before, a process most obvious above Kowloon Station on the West Kowloon Reclamation, where the Union Square development is to include a 484-metre (1,588-ft) skyscraper. This sister building to the IFC tower across the harbour will usurp its sibling as the city's tallest when completed in late 2007. The reclaimed area itself is set to become the "West Kowloon Cultural District", with hi-tech arts and cultural venues in place by 2011.

## Around the waterfront

The obvious place to start in Tsim Sha Tsui is the **Star Ferry Pier** ㉞, where the ferries land from Central and Wan Chai. The adjacent **Railway Clock Tower** *(see margin)* dates from 1921. Immediately behind is the unmistakable **Hong Kong Cultural Centre** ㉟, a minimalist structure with a sweeping concave roof covered in ugly pink tiles. Its construction caused a great deal of controversy in 1984, as it was designed without windows – thereby inexplicably turning its back on one of the world's most dramatic views. Nonetheless, it is there to stay and to be used. During the Hong Kong Arts Festival in January and February, the centre stages local and international opera, classical music, theatre and dance.

This complex abuts the igloo-like **Hong Kong Space Museum** ㊱ (open Mon, Wed–Fri 1–9pm, Sat–Sun 10am–9pm; tel: 2721 0226; entrance fee, but free on Wed), with IMAX movies on space travel and exhibitions of Chinese astronomical inventions. The **Hong Kong Museum of Art** ㊲ (open Fri–Wed 10am–6pm, closed Thur; tel: 2721 0116; entrance fee, but free on Wed) displays traditional and contemporary calligraphy and painting, along with historic photographs, prints and artefacts of Hong Kong, Macau and Guangzhou. Other galleries exhibit Chinese antiquities and travelling exhibitions of fine art.

One of the unfortunate losers to suffer from the construction of the Cultural Centre was the venerable **Peninsula Hotel** ㊳, directly across Salisbury Road. Its exquisite rooms lost their classic harbour views but regained them with the addition of a tower grafted onto the original 1928 building. The Pen's sumptuous gilt-corniced lobby is accented by a string quartet on the balcony, and from rooftop helipad via swish restaurants, pool, spa and bars, this remains the acme of Hong Kong's accommodation, however hard the new kids on the block may try to emulate it.

Situated immediately north of the Star Ferry Pier is **Star House**, where *cheongsams*, porcelain, and what appears to be almost every conceivable kind of Chinese handicraft available, are on sale at the huge Chinese Arts and Crafts Store. Adjoining Star House on Canton Road is the mammoth **Harbour City** ㊴ complex, encompassing **Ocean Terminal** and **Ocean Centre** and filled with hotels, antique stores and designer boutiques. The deep-water mooring means that cruise ships regularly tie up here, disgorging their passengers directly into

*The clock tower next to Kowloon's Star Ferry Pier is the final vestige of the original Kowloon-Canton Railway (KCR). Kowloon station stood here until it was replaced by a new station to the east at Hung Hom.*

**BELOW:** Tsim Sha Tsui is full of electronics shops.

*The gaudy, neon-lit strip along Nathan Road and neighbouring streets in Tsim Sha Tsui is an iconic image of Hong Kong.*

the malls and other entertainments of downtown Tsim Sha Tsui.

From the Star Ferry Pier eastward along the harbour, a **waterfront promenade** extends past the Cultural Centre and Inter-Continental Hotel towards **Tsim Sha Tsui East** and **Hung Hom Bay**, a stretch of reclaimed land packed with hotels, offices and shops. This provides a great vantage point for viewing the north shore of Hong Kong Island, one of the most spectacular cityscapes in the world. At 8pm each night the promenade is the place to be for watching the Symphony of Lights, the world's largest sound and light show, which lights up the glittering skyline more than ever. The promenade itself – dubbed the **Avenue of Stars** ⓸ – is decorated with tributes to the famous and less so of Hong Kong and Chinese cinema, with Hollywood-style stars set in the pavement.

In Hung Hom, the **KCR Station** ⓹, built in 1975, was the terminus for trains to the New Territories until the new extension to Tsim Sha Tsui East opened in 2005. However, this is still the place where through trains to China begin their journeys – every two or three days to Beijing and Shanghai, much more frequently

to Guangzhou – and the forecourt feels more like mainland China than Hong Kong. The **Cross-Harbour Tunnel** between Hong Kong Island and Kowloon emerges immediately west of Hung Hom Station. The tunnel took three years to construct, and by the time it opened in 1972 it had cost a total of US$427 million. Of the harbour's three tunnels, it remains the busiest, with more than 150,000 vehicles passing through it every day. Ten minutes' walk away is **Hung Hom Ferry Pier**, with services to Central, Wan Chai and North Point.

On the other side of the harbour-tunnel approach road, in **Tsim Sha Tsui East**, are two of the best museums in Hong Kong. The **Hong Kong Science Museum** ⓸ (open Mon–Wed, Fri 1–9pm, Sat–Sun 10am–9pm; tel: 2732 3232; entrance fee, but free on Wed) displays more than 500 scientific and technological interactive exhibits, including robotics, computers, phones, a miniature submarine and a DC-3 aeroplane.

Just opposite is the **Hong Kong Museum of History** ⓸ (open Mon, Wed–Sat 10am–6pm, Sun and public holidays 10am–7pm; tel: 2724 9042;

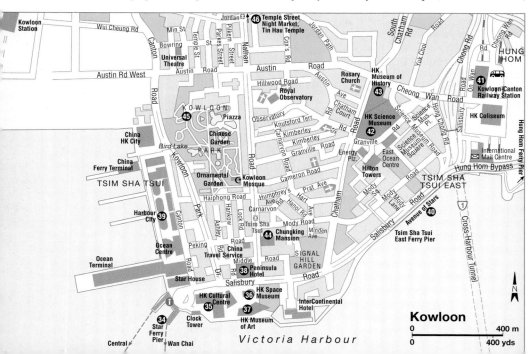

entrance fee, but free on Wed), charting the 6,000-year story of Hong Kong from neolithic times right up to the handover.

## The heart of Tsim Sha Tsui

Introductions to Tsim Sha Tsui always used to churn out the phrase "Golden Mile", the nickname for **Nathan Road**, its central axis. The main shopping and entertainment area extends from here along Peking, Hankow and Haiphong roads, as well as to Carnarvon and Kimberley roads on the eastern side. But things are changing, as an enormous construction project is sidelining Nathan's slightly outré strip of shops and their touts. The area around Mody Road, which links Nathan and Chatham roads, is being turned into a large shopping mall, and bars and restaurants are springing up nearby.

Tsim Sha Tsui is also home to a series of run-down mansion blocks, oddly wedged in amongst the shops and luxurious hotels, the most infamous being **Chungking Mansion** ㊹, a teeming labyrinth of cheap guest houses (there are few alternatives in budget accommodation in Hong Kong), curry restaurants, sweat-shops and sari stores right in the middle of the most commercial stretch of Nathan Road.

A few minutes further north along Nathan Road is the pleasant expanse of **Kowloon Park** ㊺ with its aviary (open daily 6.30am–8pm) housing a colourful collection of rare birds. The Sculpture Walk displays work by local artists, while at the northern end of the park past the flamingos' pond a bridge leads over Kowloon Park Drive to the lurid gold **China HK City Building**, departure point for ferries to various Chinese cities.

The southeastern corner of the park is marked by **Kowloon Mosque**, with its four minarets and large, white-marble dome standing out from the clutter of shops and restaurants opposite. Built in 1984, it serves the territory's 50,000 Muslims, of whom about half are Chinese. On the other side of Nathan Road, **Carnarvon** and **Kimberley** roads are both stuffed with clothing and electronics shops, while nearby **Knutsford Terrace** hosts a couple of dozen bars and restaurants.

## Yau Ma Tei

From Tsim Sha Tsui, Nathan Road slips into Yau Ma Tei, a more traditional area

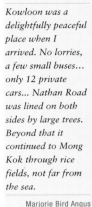

*Kowloon was a delightfully peaceful place when I arrived. No lorries, a few small buses... only 12 private cars... Nathan Road was lined on both sides by large trees. Beyond that it continued to Mong Kok through rice fields, not far from the sea.*

Marjorie Bird Angus

**BELOW:** the sumptuous lobby of the Peninsula Hotel.

*Around 80 per cent of Hong Kong's smog is thought to originate over the border, and the number of smoggy days had risen from one in 10 in 2002 to one in five in 2007. Investment bank Merrill Lynch even recommended investors sell shares in Hong Kong property in late 2006 due to pollution concerns.*

of old Chinese shops and trades but expanding inexorably westwards with the West Kowloon reclamation project.

At the junction of Jordan and Canton roads there are several jade and ivory shops selling mah-jong sets. At the junction of Kansu and Battery streets the **jade market** (open daily 9am–6pm) is packed with stalls. Unless you are an expert, take along a Hong Kong Tourist Board (HKTB) information leaflet on jade, and spend wisely, as not all the artefacts on offer are genuine.

Shanghai Street continues north into an area once famous for its temples, now renowned for the **Temple Street night market ㊻** that lights up after dusk. Palmists, physiognomists, and a fortune-teller whose trained bird selects slips of paper to predict the future, vie to reveal your destiny. This area has numerous open-air restaurants, where oysters, prawns, clams, lobsters and fish are laid out on beds of ice to tempt diners.

Dating back over a century, the **Tin Hau Temple** complex (open daily 7am–5.30pm) is in Public Square Street. This is Hong Kong's principal Tin Hau temple (there are scores throughout the territory,

Tin Hau being the protector of fishermen, *see page 79*), originally built closer to the harbour. Land reclamation forced it to move inland.

## Mong Kok

Mong Kok (properly Wong Kok in Cantonese: a long-dead sign writer got his letters mixed up) is famous for having the world's most densely crowded population. For many years this gritty neighbourhood was associated with sleaze, but things are changing, and there are distinct signs of gentrification.

On the east side of Nathan Road, on Tung Choi Street, the so-called **ladies' market** (open daily noon–10.30pm) sells everything from fake designer accessories and clothing to cheap cosmetics and toys. Hundreds of colourful song-birds in beautifully crafted cages can be seen at the well-known **bird market** (open daily 10am–6pm), on the other side of Nathan Road on Yuen Po Street.

Kowloon comes to an end at Boundary Street, which originally defined the frontier between Hong Kong and China. Although officially part of the New Territories, the districts immediately north

**BELOW:** Hong Kong Science Museum.

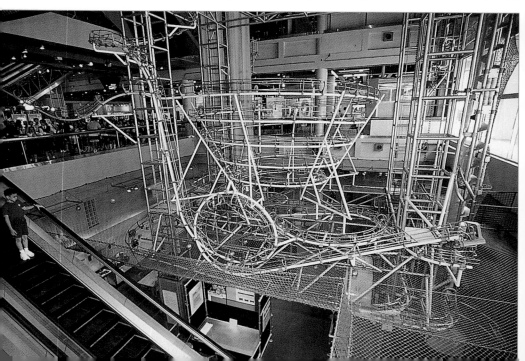

*Recommended Restaurants & Bars on pages 132–3*

of this street are more commonly known as New Kowloon. Most of the area is crammed with densely populated housing estates and shopping malls, juxtaposed with historic architecture, temples and archaeological ruins.

Stuck on the harbour at the eastern edge of this crowded part of the city is the forlorn site of **Kai Tak**, Hong Kong's former international airport. The airport site is set for redevelopment, which is likely to include a cruise terminal, park and multi-purpose stadium.

### A lucky temple

Probably the liveliest and most colourful place of worship in Hong Kong, and the most rewarding for outsiders to visit, is **Wong Tai Sin Temple ⑦** (open daily 7am–6pm; free), which sits opposite the eponymous MTR station. Wong Tai Sin is the Daoist god of healing and of good fortune. The Chinese, who are too cautious to rely solely on luck, flock to the temple to ask him for advice on all matters, including horse-racing and stockmarket tips. One stop to the east on the MTR, the **Chi Lin Nunnery ⑥** (open Thur–Tues 9am–4pm; garden open

7am–7pm; free) is the largest Buddhist nunnery in Southeast Asia.

Close to Cheung Sha Wan MTR station is the **Lei Cheng Uk Tomb** (museum open Fri–Wed 10am–1pm and 2–6pm, Sun 1–6pm; free), a Han Dynasty burial vault dating back to between AD 100 and 200, when the area was under the administrative control of the Wu Empire.

## THE NEW TERRITORIES

The buffer between the urban area of Kowloon and the boundary with Shenzhen and Guangdong province, the New Territories are an odd mixture. Nobody is ploughing with water buffalo any longer, but there are corners where time seems to have not so much stood still as gone into reverse. Conversely, other areas are as modern as anywhere else in the SAR, notably the New Towns such as Sha Tin and Yuen Long. There is scenic beauty aplenty, with calm beaches to seek out and lofty mountains to hike.

### Sha Tin and surroundings

**Sha Tin ⑭** is one of Hong Kong's largest New Towns, with gargantuan housing projects occupying what were once lush rice

*The sound of rattling chim – a container holding dozens of bamboo fortune sticks – resounds all day long at Wong Tai Sin, as people shake them until a single stick falls out. Each has a number that is later interpreted, for a fee, by an on-site fortune-teller.*

**BELOW LEFT:** Temple Street night market.
**BELOW:** Mong Kok's bird market.

*The main altar room at the Temple of 10,000 Buddhas actually has a total of 12,800 Buddha statues lining its walls.*

**BELOW RIGHT:** the Walled City, shortly before demolition in 1992.

paddies whose produce was reserved for the Emperor.

One of the foremost attractions is the **Temple of 10,000 Buddhas** (open 9am–5pm daily; free), reached by climbing 431 steps flanked by gold-painted effigies of enlightened beings up the hillside above Sha Tin Station. The temple is guarded by huge, fierce-looking statues of various gods, and by similarly ferocious watchdogs that are chained up in the daytime. The complex also contains an impressive nine-storey pagoda of Indian architectural design.

A major destination in the valley is the **Sha Tin Racecourse** ❶, which has its own station. Up to 75,000 punters flock here at the weekend on race days.

Just south of Sha Tin, the KCR forks, with a new line branching east to Ma On Shan and providing a possible alternative route round to the district of Sai Kung *(see page 127)*. A five-minute walk from the first station, Che Kung Temple, is the highly praised **Hong Kong Heritage Museum** ❶ (open Mon, Wed–Sat 10am–6pm, Sun 10am–7pm; tel: 2180 8188; entrance fee, but free on Wed), which opened in 2000. This is

Hong Kong's largest museum, with 12 exhibition halls including a gallery of Chinese art, an exhibition entirely devoted to the development of the New Territories, one on the history of Cantonese opera and another detailing the evolution of local toys.

Further north (back on the main KCR East Rail line) past the **Chinese University of Hong Kong**, with its highly respected **art museum** (open Mon–Sat 10am–5pm, Sun 12.30–5.30pm; free), lies the market town of **Tai Po** ❶, which means "buying place". The old town is at the northeastern end of Tolo Harbour. The **Hong Kong Railway Museum** (open Wed–Mon 9am–5pm; tel: 2653 3455; free), complete with vintage train carriages, is housed in the former station.

### The call of the wild

One of the best places to escape from urban Hong Kong is the **Tai Po Kau Nature Reserve** ❶, a short taxi ride from Tai Po Market KCR station. The oldest of Hong Kong's reserves and spread over 460 hectares (1,136 acres), planting began here in 1926 as part of the government's attempt to reforest the

## The Walled City

In the east of Kowloon City is Kowloon City Walled Park, built on the site of the infamous Walled City. This peculiar anomaly persisted for several generations, a little piece of mainland China right in the heart of Hong Kong. Before the British arrived, the neigbourhood was governed by a Manchu magistrate, and through a legal loophole it was excluded from the treaty that granted Britain the New Territories on a 99-year lease in 1898. As a result, British law was never fully implemented within the claustrophobic confines of the City, and the area deteriorated into a semi-lawless enclave which was left to its own devices. After World War II, illegal low-rise blocks sprang up on the site, resulting in a multi-storey squatter area with unauthorised electricity and water supplies. By the 1950s, the dank alleyways of the city had become a notorious haven for drug addicts, Triad gangs, illegal immigrants – and unlicensed doctors and dentists. The Walled City remained a thorn in the side of the authorities. Beijing (and Taiwan) vehemently opposed plans for its demolition during the 1980s, regarding it as Chinese territory. Eventually, 35,000 residents were resettled in housing estates, with several tenants forcibly removed by the police, and the entire block was bulldozed to the ground in 1992. A few remnants have been preserved in the Walled Park, which opened in 1996.

*Recommended Restaurants, Cafes & Bars on pages 132–3*

New Territories (much of the original forest cover had long since disappeared, and what was left was destroyed during the Japanese occupation). Today, the forest shelters a good proportion of Hong Kong's flora and fauna.

To the northeast, the coast around **Tolo Harbour** has become more built up in recent years, but once past Shuen Wan, Ting Kok Road must rank among the most picturesque routes in Hong Kong, leading round to the Plover Cove Reservoir, Bride's Pool and Starling Inlet. At weekends and on public holidays, the roadside barbecue areas teem with noisy groups, but even then, a five-minute walk into the hills brings peace and solitude.

Out in the waters of Mirs Bay (Tai Pang Wan) in the far northeast of the SAR, is **Tung Ping Chau**. City people like to come to the island to have picnics and enjoy the silence surrounded by long white beaches of smooth sand scattered with seashells, starfish and spiked sea urchins. **Tap Mun Chau** (also called Grass Island) is another remote and atmospheric island, with a famous Tin Hau Temple.

## Sai Kung

In the eastern part of the New Territories is the scenic area centered on **Sai Kung**. The eponymous town and neighbouring villages retain a strong seaside flavour and have some good restaurants, but the real attraction here is to head off into the hills – where some of the SAR's best hiking is on offer, as well as the sumptuous white-sand beach at Tai Long Wan.

The road from town runs out to **Sai Kung Country Park Ⓜ**, the starting point of the **MacLehose Trail**. The well-marked trail stretches for 100 km (60 miles) through mostly open country, from one side of the New Territories to the other.

The jewel in Sai Kung's crown is **Tai Long Wan** beach **Ⓝ**. Getting there involves an hour's trek, either around the High Island Reservoir or by cutting across the hills along the MacLehose Trail from the road at Pak Tam Au. Either way, it's more than worth it. There are two long swathes of very pale and powdery sand, and enough surf to make it

worth lugging a surfboard over the hill. There is also a café selling cold beer and hot noodles.

## The west

Heading west from Kowloon, the **Tsing Ma Bridge Ⓞ**, sometimes referred to as Hong Kong's "Golden Gate", links Kowloon with Lantau and the airport (there are actually two bridges, the longer one from Tsing Yi Island to Lantau, a shorter bridge from Tsing Yi to the Kowloon mainland). Tsing Ma's 200-metre (650-ft) high twin towers are visible along much of the highway that leads to Kwai Chung, an extensive complex of container terminals, and the industrial community of **Tsuen Wan Ⓟ**. The main attraction here is the **Sam Tung Uk Museum** (open Wed–Mon 9am–5pm; free), a beautifully restored Hakka walled village. The narrow alleyways trace a path past a central ancestral hall, an exhibition room and rows of tiny cubicles stocked with period furniture and farming tools.

Beyond Tsuen Wan, the Tuen Mun Highway passes another very impressive airport-related bridge – **Tsing Long** – before reaching the sprawling New Town

*The forest reserve at Tai Po Kau protects the greatest concentration of wildlife in Hong Kong. Mammals are well represented, although mostly difficult to observe – the exception being the rhesus macaque monkeys, which can be quite aggressive (avoid feeding them). Numerous exotic bird species breed here too, as does the extremely rare Romer's tree frog (pictured).*

**BELOW:** Plover Cove Country Park.

*Water transport the traditional way. It is possible to charter small boats to access the numerous small islands scattered off the coast of the New Territories.*

**BELOW:** junks at Tai Long Wan, Sai Kung.

of **Tuen Mun**. North of **Yuen Long**, another redevelopment project, lies the **Mai Po Marshes ⓠ** (open Mon–Fri 9am–5pm, Sat–Sun 9am–6pm; entrance fee; permits must be booked in advance, tel: 2526 4473), an expanse of mangroves and mudflats which are a stopping point on the migratory routes of more than 400 species of birds. To the south, the 61-hectare (150-acre) **Hong Kong Wetland Park** (open Wed–Mon 10am–5pm; entrance fee) is a more accessible place to experience Hong Kong's bird life. Easily reached by the Light Rail network close to Tin Shui Wah New Town, the park has well-planned wooden walkways and an impressive visitor centre.

Another quick trip from Yuen Long is the walled villages of **Kam Tin ⓡ**. The most popular for visitors is the Kat Hing Wai village, which stands rather incongruously across the road from a supermarket. Some 400 people live there, all with the same surname, Tang. Built in the 1600s, it is a fortified village with walls 6 metres (20 ft) thick, guardhouses on its four corners, arrow slits for fighting off attackers, and a moat. Visitors can enter for a nominal admission fee.

From **Shek Kong** a scenic road, the **Route Twisk**, ascends quickly to the high mountains, seemingly far from all human habitation. From the top, close to Hong Kong's highest peak, **Tai Mo Shan ⓢ** (957 metres/3,140 ft), one can look over to China and down to Hong Kong Island. This is the only part of Hong Kong ever to have experienced frost.

Alternatively, continue on Lam Kam Road to Pak Ngau Shek in the Lam Tsuen Valley, and the **Kadoorie Farm and Botanic Garden** (open daily 9.30am–5pm; free), a conservation centre sheltering a wide range of local wildlife.

## THE OUTLYING ISLANDS

A substantial majority of Hong Kong's visitors arrive at the state-of-the-art international airport on what used to be an "outlying island", but one which is now joined by road-and-rail suspension bridge to Kowloon. Within a short space of time they are being whisked into the city aboard the smooth Airport Express train, passing Lantau's lofty mountains. Neighbouring Cheung Chau is a unique island, heavily urbanised but sporting some pleasant beaches and a village atmos-

phere, while the other major outlying island, Lamma, is far less developed. The remainder of the islands – more than 230 of them – are either uninhabited or support small rural communities.

## Lantau

**Lantau** ("broken head" in Cantonese) is by far the largest of Hong Kong's islands. Its north and east are dominated by the new airport, a four-lane highway, and double railway lines which thunder along the shore to the apartment blocks of Tung Chung, Tsing Ma Bridge and the new Disneyland theme park. The rest of the island largely rural. In the south are long beaches and small townships such as Silvermine Bay (Mui Wo), linked by ferries with the city's Central District. In the west, Tai O and Fan Lau are favourite destinations for day-trippers, and there are good coastal and hill walks.

Up on Lantau's mountainous spine is one of Hong Kong's best-known attractions, **Po Lin Monastery** ❶ (Precious Lotus Monastery; open daily 10am–6pm; free). The large complex, which dates back to the 1920s, is busier and noisier than the average Buddhist retreat. Its

canteen serves good vegetarian meals 11.30am–4.30pm. The real crowd-puller, however, is the **Big Buddha**, at 24 metres (79 ft) the world's largest outdoor bronze statue of a seated Buddha, completed here in 1990. A long flight of steps leads up to the statue, with fantastic views from the top, while an exhibition in the base of the statue explains how it was built. Po Lin can be reached by No. 2 bus from Mui Wo, bus nos. 11 or 23 from Tung Chung, or by taxi).

West of Po Lin, in the direction of Tai O on Lantau's northern coast, is an excellent walking path that traverses mountain ridges, canyons and streams en route to Lantau's **Yin Hing Monastery** ❶, a haven rich with traditional Buddhist paintings and statues.

One of Lantau's older communities, **Tai O** ❶ is located on the northwest coast. Here, the island's Tanka "boat people", have converted some of their larger junks into three-storey permanent living structures. Further up at Tai O Creek, they have also built homes on stilts where the water rises during tide changes.

Lantau is famed for the long, smooth and often empty **beaches** that line much

*One of Hong Kong's newest attractions, the Ngong Ping 360 Skyrail cable-car offers a spectacular route between Tung Chung (close to the airport) and the Big Buddha at Po Lin. However at the time of going to press, the cable-car has been temporarily closed following technical problems in June 2007.*

**BELOW:** the Big Buddha at Po Lin.

**TIP**

Ferries run from the Outlying Districts ferry piers in Central to Silvermine Bay (Mui Wo) on Lantau approximately every 30–50 minutes throughout the day. Ferries from Central to Cheung Chau run every 30 minutes daily. Lamma ferries are run by Hong Kong and Kowloon Ferry Ltd (HKKF) – services run at 20–60 minute intervals to Yung Shue Wan, less often to Sok Kwu Wan. For information contact:

**First Ferry**, tel: 2131 8181, www.nwff.com.hk;

**HKKF**, tel: 2815 6063, www.hkkf.com.hk/en/

**BELOW:** Buddhist monk, Lantau.

of its southern coastline. The most popular and crowded beach (probably because it is the easiest to reach) is at **Silvermine Bay (Mui Wo)** . A clutch of bars and restaurants has opened in the village, roistering affairs that become extremely busy at weekends. There are also numerous Chinese restaurants.

## Hong Kong Disneyland

Hong Kong **Disneyland** (open Mon–Fri 10am– 7pm, Sat–Sun 10am– 9pm; tel: 1 830 830; entrance fee, *see margin page 131*) opened its doors to the public in 2005, complete with its own link to the MTR, two hotels, shops, restaurants and the sort of amusements that thrill at more-or-less similar venues in Paris, Tokyo and the US. Learning from past mistakes, efforts have been made to reflect the local culture – feng shui experts were consulted on the layout of the 126-hectare (310-acre) site, while Chinese numerology was also taken into account: on-site hotels avoid the number four when numbering their floors because it's considered bad luck to the Chinese, and one of the main ballrooms covers an area of 888 square metres,

reflecting the perceived good fortune of the number eight.

Disneyland is divided into themed areas. The nostalgic **Main Street USA** evokes a typical small town in the American Midwest from the early 1900s, with marching bands, rides on old-time buses and other contraptions, plus the largest concentration of shops and restaurants on site. **Fantasyland** is set around a fairytale castle where stories and characters such as Winnie the Pooh, Dumbo and Snow White are brought vividly to life, much to the delight of small children. **Adventureland** includes a Jungle River Cruise and Tarzan's Treehouse, while **Tomorrowland** focuses on space exploration. Highlights for Disney fans include an all-singing all-dancing parade of characters every afternoon, and the nightly fireworks display.

## Cheung Chau

**Cheung Chau** ("long island" in Cantonese) is the most densely populated of the outlying islands. The curving waterfront promenade, the *praya,* is one of the most pleasant places in Hong Kong, especially after sunset, when its alfresco restaurants burst into life only yards from the fishing vessels bobbing at anchor. Home to Hong Kong's first and so far only Olympic gold medallist (from Atlanta 1996), Lee Lai-shan, Cheung Chau has a strong windsurfing tradition, centered on Afternoon Beach (Kwun Yan Wan).

The village of **Cheung Chau** , near the ferry dock, is a tangle of alleyways. There are no vehicles on the island apart from small motorised carts and an amusing bonsai-sized police car, fire engine and ambulance. Head off in any direction from the ferry terminal and you will pass both modern and traditional shops and restaurants.

A short distance to the left of the ferry dock, up the main road, is **Pak Tai Temple**, dedicated to the protector of fishermen and the island's saviour from plague during the late 1700s. Cheung Chau was once the haunt of pirates, including the notorious Cheung Po Tsai. As on the other outlying islands, "Family Trail" walks are clear and well marked, and lead to **Cheung Po Tsai Cave** as well as other scenic spots.

Each year the island hosts the colourful **Bun Festival**, usually in May. Giant bamboo towers covered with edible buns are erected in the courtyard of Pak Tai Temple. In the past, the local men would climb up the towers to pluck their lucky buns – the higher the bun was, the more luck it would bring. After one of the towers collapsed in 1978, bringing broken bones and bruises rather than luck, the free-for-all was stopped. The ritual was revived in 2005 – now trained athletes risk their necks.

There are some good beaches on Cheung Chau. The main strand is **Tung Wan** on the eastern, side of the narrow isthmus from the harbour.

## Lamma

The second-largest of the outlying islands is **Lamma ❷**. Rich in grassy hills and picturesque bays, the island has a population of around 8,000, mostly concentrated in and around the village of Yung Shue Wan. Among them are a sizeable number of expatriates, who value the peace and quiet: despite a frequent ferry service to Central, this roadless island remains slow-paced, although it can get crowded with day-trippers at weekends.

**Yung Shue Wan** (Banyan Bay), at the northern end of Lamma, is one of two ferry gateways to the island. The village has a good supply of restaurants serving Japanese, Thai, Mediterranean and Indian cuisine, as well as several Chinese seafood establishments on the waterfront.

It is only a short stroll out into the countryside. The most popular walk runs much of the length of the island, to the village of Sok Kwu Wan. The well-marked concrete path passes neat vegetable plots and three-storey buildings (nothing higher is permitted, with the exception of the power-station chimneys that loom behind the hill to the right of the path), then goes along **Hung Shing Ye Beach**, a pleasantly clean stretch of sand.

**Sok Kwu Wan** is famous for its seafood restaurants, lined up one after the other along the waterfront. Most walkers reward their efforts with a slap-up meal here before taking the ferry (from Sok Kwu Wan) back to Central. ❑

*A Disneyland ticket gives a full day in all four themed parks. Adults: HK$295 (peak days HK$350); children (3–11 years): HK$210 (HK$250); over-65s: HK$170 (HK$200). Buy online or collect from Disneyland Ticket Express at the Hong Kong MTR.*

**BELOW:** welcome to Disneyland.

# RESTAURANTS & BARS

## Restaurants

Prices for a three-course
dinner per person with
one beer or glass of
house wine:
$ = under HK$150
$$ = HK$150–300
$$$ = HK$300–500
$$$$ = over HK$500

Hong Kong Island's
main eating-out and
nightlife areas are
around Lan Kwai Fong
and SoHo in Central,
around Lockhart Road in
Wan Chai, and also – in
less concentrated form
– in Causeway Bay. Over
in Tsim Sha Tsui
(Kowloon), most of the
action is focused on the
cluster of streets south
of Kowloon Park, and
also around Mody Road
a little further east.
There is a strip of bars
and restaurants on
Knutsford Terrace.
Some of the best
restaurants are in the
large five-star hotels.

### Hong Kong Island
**Cantonese**
#### Dynasty
3/F Renaissance Harbour
View Hotel, 1 Harbour Rd,
Wan Chai. Tel: 2802 8888.
Open: L & D daily. $$$
Dynasty's palatial dining
hall, with its tasteful
décor and selected
antiques, is the setting
for a truly exceptional
dining experience. The
kitchen excels in all
areas. Look for sea-
sonal delicacies like
snake soup.

#### Luk Yu Teahouse
24–26 Stanley St. Tel: 2523
1970. Open: L & D daily. $$
This traditional Can-
tonese teahouse in the
heart of Central is
legendary for its bad-
mannered manage-
ment. Despite that,
chauffeurs tend the
lined-up Mercs outside
while tycoons and crim-
inal kingpins in dark
glasses take their yum
cha. Tourists take sec-
ond place, but the food
can be excellent.

#### Victoria City
2/F Sun Hung Kai Centre, 30
Harbour Rd, Wan Chai. Tel:
2827 9938. Open: D daily. $$
Seafood heaven for local
Cantonese. One of the
best for daily dim sum.

#### Yung Kee
32–40 Wellington St.
Tel: 2522 1624.
Open: L & D daily. $$
A true Hong Kong institu-
tion, with a rags-to-riches
history spanning almost
70 years. Justly famous
for its roast goose and
the obligatory 1,000-
year-old eggs. Also great
for dim sum.

**Other Chinese**
#### Chuen Cheung Kui
108–120 Percival St, Causeway Bay. Tel: 2577 3833.
Open: L & D daily. $$
Long-standing Hakka
cuisine specialists
famous for chicken
cooked in salt and
served with a pungent

garlic and scallion
sauce. The main event
is up the stairs on the
first floor.

#### Red Pepper
G/F 7 Lan Fong Rd, Cause-
way Bay. Tel: 2577 3811.
Open: L & D daily. $$$
Long-established
Sichuanese restaurant
serving up authentically
fiery dishes.

#### Yellow Door
6/F, 37 Cochrane St.
Tel: 2858 6555. Open: L & D
Mon–Fri, D only Sat. $$
Owned by one of Hong
Kong's best-known
artists – obvious from
the simple but inventive
interior. High-quality
Sichuanese and Shang-
hainese menus are
served at lunch and din-
ner respectively.

**International**
#### Harlan's
Shop 2075 IFC 2. Tel: 2805
0566. Open: L & D daily.
$$$$
Brash and moneyed,
Harlan's aims to attract
Hong Kong's hoi polloi
and succeeds. High-
class "modern West-
ern" cooking featuring
fine ingredients pre-
pared with panache.

#### M at the Fringe
1/F, 2 Lower Albert Rd. Tel:
2877 4000. Open: L & D
Mon–Fri, D only Sat–Sun. $$$
A perennial favourite
with a unique ambience
and a dedicated clien-

tele. The satisfying mod-
ern Oz menu overflows
with French and Middle
Eastern influences. The
rooftop bar above is a
great place for a drink.

#### Peak Lookout
121 Peak Rd. Tel: 2849 1000.
Open: L & D daily. $$
This historic building on
Victoria Peak is like an
Alpine hunting lodge
transported to the trop-
ics. Vivid, lively and
colourful, with great
views.

**French**
#### Le Tire-Bouchon
45a Graham St. Tel: 2526
5965. Open: L & D Mon–Sat.
$$$
This long-standing
French restaurant has
the feel of a subter-
ranean wine cellar. A
traditional menu offers
rich, tasty and satisfying
food and vintages from
a comprehensive cellar.

**Italian**
#### Toscana
1/F Ritz-Carlton Hotel,
3 Connaught Rd. Tel: 2877
6666. Open: L & D Mon–Sat,
D only Sun. $$$$
Sublime Italian dining in
one of the most elegant
hotel restaurants in
town.

**Indian**
#### Tandoor
1/F Lyndhurst Tower, 1
Lyndhurst Terr. Tel: 2845
2262. Open: L & D daily. $$
Classy Indian restaur-

ant featuring a top-notch lunchtime buffet.

## Indonesian
### Indonesia 1968
G/F 28 Leighton Rd, Causeway Bay. Tel: 2577 9981. Open: L & D daily. $
Serving up favourites like *gado gado*, *sambal rending* and *nasi goreng* since 1968, this Indonesian restaurant has smartened up its décor to meet the high quality of its food – but remains good value.

## Kowloon
### Cantonese
### Hoi King Heen
B2, Grand Stanford Inter-Continental Hotel, 70 Mody Rd, Tsim Sha Tsui East. Tel: 2731 2883. Open: L Mon–Sat, D daily. $$$
Endlessly creative Cantonese fine dining, adapting novel ingredients into classic Cantonese cooking. A quality operation.

### T'ang Court
1/F, Langham Hotel, 8 Peking Rd, Tsim Sha Tsui. Tel: 2375 1333. Open: L & D daily. $$$
Among the most stylish Cantonese restaurants in town. The lush interior brims with sumptuous opulence, but don't let that distract you from a menu that dotes on shark's fin, bird's nest and abalone.

### Other Chinese
### City Chiu Chow
East Ocean Centre, 98 Granville Rd, Tsim Sha Tsui East. Tel: 2723 6226. Open: L & D daily. $$

A great place to sample Chiu Chow specialities like cold crab, *e-fu* noodles or chicken in *chin jiu* sauce.

### Hutong
28/F, 1 Peking Rd, Tsim Sha Tsui. Tel: 3428 8342. Open: L & D daily. $$$
Serious Sino-chic featuring an intoxicating mix of the antique and up to date. The menu offers classic northern Chinese cuisine with a contemporary twist.

### Peking Restaurant
1/F, 227 Nathan Rd, Jordan. Tel: 2730 1315. Open: L & D daily. $
The Peking restaurant is a nostalgic blast from the past, manned by white-gloved geriatrics with limited attention spans. The Peking menu features good-quality roast duck and traditional accompaniments.

### Japanese
### Aqua
29/F, 1 Peking Rd, Tsim Sha Tsui. Tel: 3427 2288. Open: L & D daily. $$$
Panoramic vistas and a glamorous interior design, with high-quality Japanese (Aqua Tokyo) and Italian (Aqua Roma) cuisine.

### Hibiki
15 Knutsford Terrace, Tsim Sha Tsui. Tel: 2316 2884. Open: L & D daily. $$
Neo-Japanese temple to tempura, sushi, sashimi and Kobe beef. Dark wooden textures and subdued

lighting promote a cozy atmosphere.

## French
### Gaddi's
The Peninsula, Salisbury Rd, Tsim Sha Tsui. Tel: 2315 3171. Open: L & D daily. $$$$
The historic Peninsula Hotel's French haute cuisine legend is a high-society magnet, serving flawless food in splendid surroundings. Jacket and tie required. The chandeliered dining room exudes opulence.

## Bars

### Hong Kong Island
### Carnegie's
53–55 Lockhart Rd, Wan Chai. Tel: 2866 6289.
A rowdy bar that is packed and boisterous at weekends and fun most nights. Hosts live music events.

### Club 97
Lan Kwai Fong, Central. Tel: 2810 9333.
One of the longest-running but still one of the hippest clubs in town.

### Club Feather Boa
38 Staunton St, Central. Tel: 2857 7156.
Like a regency drawing room; amazing, eclectic and very SoHo.

### Dublin Jack
1/F, 40 D'Aguilar St, Central. Tel: 2543 0081.
Lively Irish bar in Lan Kwai Fong. Plenty of Irish-style comfort food, Guinness and screens for sports.

### Fringe Club
2 Lower Albert Rd, Central. Tel: 2521 7485.
Live bands downstairs, or a relaxing beer garden on the roof. Along with reasonable drinks prices, this place is a rare gem.

### Mes Amis
83 Lockhart Rd, Wan Chai. Tel: 2527 6680.
Open-fronted bar on the corner of Luard and Lockhart roads for both relaxed early-evening people-watching and late-night dancing.

### Staunton's
10 Staunton St, Central. Tel: 2973 6611.
Long-running bar next to the Mid-Levels escalator.

### Vodka Bar
13 Old Bailey St, Central. Tel: 2525 1513.
Hip bar and gallery on the fringe of SoHo.

### Kowloon (Tsim Sha Tsui)
### Aqua Spirit
1 Peking Rd. Tel: 3427 2288.
Amazing views of the skyline in this trendy, expensive bar.

### Chillax Bar & Club
G/F, The Pinnacle, 8 Minden Ave. Tel: 2722 4338.
One of the livelier of several bars and clubs sprouting up on Minden Avenue.

### Rick's Café
53–59 Kimberley Rd. Tel: 2311 2255.
Loud basement bar/club, usually packed.

# MACAU

**Following in the steps of Hong Kong, Macau has become a Special Administrative Region of China, but its Portuguese colonial ambience and numerous casinos continue to offer a very different experience to that found elsewhere in the region**

I n 1557 the Portuguese established the first European colony on Chinese soil in Macau, almost 300 years before the British claimed Hong Kong. For much of recent history it was a sleepy outpost, playing second fiddle to its high-profile neighbour on the opposite shore of the Pearl River. Things have changed quickly since Lisbon returned the enclave to China in December 1999 and Macau became a Special Administrative Region like Hong Kong. While the population of Macau remains fairly constant around half a million people, by 2006 annual visitor arrivals had risen from 9 million in 1999 to just under 22 million. These figures reflect the change that has swept in with new casinos opened since the government ended Macau tycoon Stanley Ho's four-decade monopoly of the gaming industry.

Macau's premier entertainment rumbles to the rattle of the roulette ball with the speed of a croupier shuffling a deck of cards. Gambling – or gaming as the industry would have it – is Macau's principal revenue-earner, fleecing the pockets of millions of Chinese and other nationalities every year, but equally sending a few on their way with riches beyond the dreams of avarice. With 26 casinos open and plenty more on the way, "Asia's Las Vegas" has overtaken the original in terms of gaming revenue – Macau made US$6.95 billion in 2006 while Las Vegas made US$6.69 billion. Among the six new companies with gaming licences in Macau are some of the biggest players

in the US: Wynn Resorts, MGM Mirage and Las Vegas Sands Corp.

Yet away from all the glitz, glamour and mega developments the old Macau survives – graceful old buildings redolent of southern Europe, overlooking cobbled streets shaded by ancient banyan trees. The historic centre of Macau was added to UNESCO's World Heritage list in 2005, acknowledging its importance as the first example of European architecture on Chinese soil and one of the first places where Eastern and Western cultures met.

**Main attractions**
SÃO PAULO FACADE
FORTALEZA DO MONTE
WALKING TOUR OF THE
    SOUTHERN PENINSULA (LEAL
    SENADO TO BARRA FORT)
COLINA DA GUIA / LIGHTHOUSE
CASINOS

**LEFT:** Largo do Senado Square, the hub of old Macau.
**BELOW:** the casino industry is going from strength to strength.

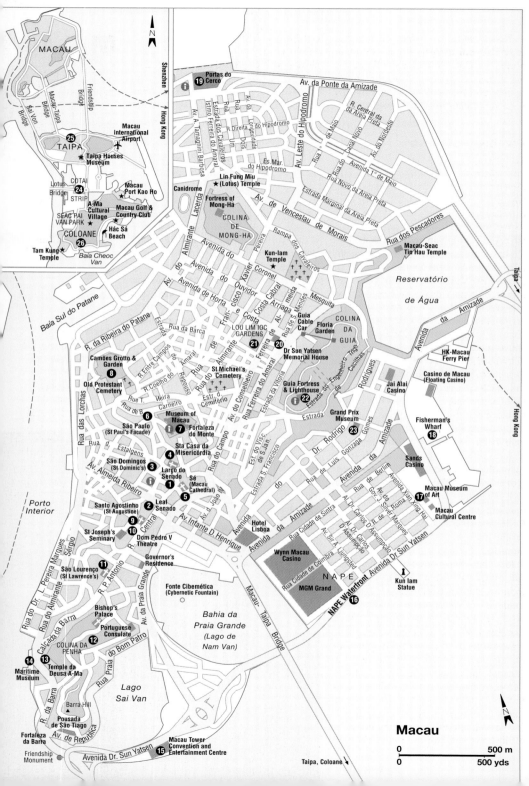

N

MACAU

Shenzhen →

← Hong Kong

Friendship Bridge

Sai Van Bridge

Macau-Taipa Bridge

**TAIPA**

Macau International Airport

COTAI ★ Taipa Houses Museum

Lotus Bridge

**②④** STRIP

Macau Port Kao Ho

**②⑤**

SEAC PAI VAN PARK

A-Ma Cultural Village ★

Macau Golf & Country Club

**COLOANE**

Hác Sá Beach ★

**②⑥**

Tam Kung Temple ★

Baía Cheoc Van

---

**⑲** Portas do Cerco

Av. da Ponte da Amizade

R. Central da da Areia Preta

Av. A. Tamagnini Barbosa

Estrada dos Cavaleiros

Ístmo Ferreira do Amaral

R. da Lavandeira

Av. do Conde de S. Januário

Rua do Hipódromo

R. Direita

R. da Madre de Deus

Rua 1 de Maio

R. do Canal Novo

Av. do Nordeste

Av. do Hipódromo

Es. Mar. do Hipódromo

Avenida 1° de Maio

Rua Nova da Areia Preta

Canidrome

Lin Fung Miu ★ (Lotus) Temple

Estrada Marginal da Areia Preta

Fortress of Mong-Ha

COLINA DE MONG-HA

Av. de Venceslau de Morais

Rua dos Pescadores

Macau-Seac Tin Hau Temple

Kun-lam Temple

Rampa dos Cavaleiros

Avenida do Almirante Lacerda

Xavier Coronel

Avenida do Ouvidor

Francisco Xavier Pereira

Avenida de Horta e Costa

Rua da Barca

Costa Cabral

Al. de Mendes

Mesquita

**Reservatório de Água**

COLINA DA GUIA

Guia Cable Car

Floria Garden

Dr Sun Yatsen Memorial House

Av. Sidónio Pais

Avenida da Amizade

HK-Macau Ferry Pier

R. da Ribeira do Patane

Camões Grotto & Garden **⑧**

R. Entre Campos

R. do Almirante Costa Cabral

Ferreira do Amaral

LOU LIM IOC GARDENS **②①**

**②⓪**

Casino de Macau (Floating Casino)

**Baía Sul do Patane**

Old Protestant Cemetery

R. Coelho do Amaral

St Michael's Cemetery

Estr. do Cemitério

Rua Ferreira da Vinha

Guia Fortress & Lighthouse **②②**

Estrada do Engenheiro Trigo

Rua do Cuartel

Jai Alai Casino

Rua das Lorchas

São Paulo (St Paul's Façade) **⑥**

Museum of Macau **⑦**

Fortaleza do Monte

Estr. do Repouso

Grand Prix Museum **②③**

Fisherman's Wharf **⑱**

Sta Casa da Misericórdia **④**

Av. do Conselheiro Ferreira de Almeida

Estr. de S. Francisco

Dr. Rodrigo

Dr. de Luis Gonzaga Gomes

Sands Casino

São Domingos (St Dominic's) **③**

Largo do Senado **①**

Sé (Macau Cathedral) **⑤**

Estrada S. Francisco

Rua de Berlim

Porto Interior

Av. Almeida Ribeiro

Santo Agostinho (St Augustine) **②**

Leal Senado

Av. Infante D. Henrique

Avenida do Dr. Mario Soares

Hotel Lisboa

Macau Museum of Art **⑰**

Macau Cultural Centre

St Joseph's Seminary **⑨ ⑩**

Dom Pedro V Theatre

Governor's Residence

Rua Cidade de Sintra

Al. Dr. Carlos d'Assumpção

Gov. J. Silva Marques

São Lourenço (St Lawrence's) **⑪**

R. P. Antonio

Fonte Cibernética (Cybernetic Fountain)

Avenida Dr. Sun Yatsen

NAPE Waterfront

Kun lam Statue

Calçada da Barra

Bishop's Palace

Portuguese Consulate **⑫**

COLINA DA PENHA

**Bahia da Praia Grande (Lago de Nam Van)**

Rua Cidade de Coimbra

Wynn Macau Casino

**N A P E**

MGM Grand **⑯**

Maritime Museum **⑭ ⑬**

Temple da Deusa A-Ma

Pousada de São Tiago

Barra Hill

**Lago Sai Van**

Fortaleza da Barra

Av. da República

Friendship Monument

Avenida Dr. Sun Yatsen

Macau Tower Convention and Entertainment Centre **⑮**

Taipa, Coloane ↘

N

**Macau**

| 0 | | 500 m |
|---|---|---|
| 0 | | 500 yds |

Taipa

→ Hong Kong

Amizade

Walk from Largo do Senado to Barra, or drive from the gargantuan Venetian Macau on Cotai to Coloane village for lunch in one of the restaurants on the square, and you could be on the Iberian Peninsula rather than in the heart of the Orient.

## The historic centre

The obvious place to start any foray into this old city is the **Largo do Senado** ❶ (Senate Square), Macau's largest piazza, which has been paved with a bold Portuguese wave-pattern mosaic. A handy tourist information centre is situated on the square (open 9am–6pm daily).

Across the main road (Almeida Ribeiro) is the **Leal Senado** ❷ (Loyal Senate; open daily 9am–9pm) building, regarded by most as the best example of Portuguese architecture in Macau. It now houses the Institute of Civil and Municipal Affairs. The Leal Senado was dedicated in 1784 and its facade completed in 1876. It was restored in 1939, with further internal restoration completed in the late 20th century. An inscribed tablet here, dating from 1654, declares: "City of the Name of God, Macau, There is None More Loyal." Head up the staircase to the fine wrought-iron doors and beyond to a small courtyard with traditional blue and white *azulejos* tiles. Up more stairs, the library (open Mon–Fri 1–7pm) and council chamber show fine examples of Old World woodwork. Half the offices on the ground floor have been converted into a gallery (open Tues–Sun 9am–9pm).

It is easy to spend hours exploring the side-street shops, markets, cafés and historic buildings on and around Largo do Senado. Facing the Leal Senado, at the northern end of the square is **São Domingos** ❸ (St Dominic's). A chapel was established here in 1597 by Spanish Dominicans who came to Macau from Acapulco in Mexico. The current yellow-walled church dates from the 17th century. At the back is the **Museum of Sacred Art** (open daily 10am–6pm).

The white building on the eastern side of the square is **Santa Casa da Miser-**icórdia ❹ (Holy House of Mercy), which was established as a charitable mission in 1569. Wake a short walk up a *travessa* (side street) to the **Sé** ❺ (Macau Cathedral). In 1850 it was declared the mother church of the Macau diocese, which then included all of China, Japan and Korea.

From São Domingos follow the pavement north along one of Macau's main shopping streets before turning uphill to the ruins of **São Paulo** ❻ (St Paul's; open access). Its towering facade and impressive grand staircase are the most striking of all Macau's churches. Unfortunately, the site must have bad feng shui. The first church on the site was destroyed by fire in 1601, and construction of a new one began the following year. Japanese Christians who had fled persecution in Nagasaki crafted the present classical facade between 1620 and 1627. In 1835 another fire destroyed São Paulo, the adjacent college and a library. In 1904, efforts were made to rebuild the church, but little progress was achieved. Still, today the grand facade of São Paulo remains as Macau's most enduring icon.

Overlooking the facade of São Paulo

*Authentic 17th-century cannons overlook the city of Macau from the battlements of Fortaleza do Monte.*

**BELOW:** a typical pastel-hued Portuguese church.

*The Macau Grand Prix takes place on the third weekend of November, with the 6-km (4-mile) circuit using the city streets. There are 3 events: the main Formula 3 race, the Guia touring car race, and the motorcycle grand prix.*

**BELOW:** Macau's casinos are a mainstay of the local economy.

are the massive stone walls of the **For-taleza do Monte 7** (open Tues–Sun 7am–7pm; free), often simply called Monte Fort, built in the early 1600s. When Dutch ships attacked and invaded Macau in 1622, the half-completed fortress was defended by 150 clerics and African slaves. A lucky cannon shot by an Italian Jesuit, Geronimo Rhu, hit the powder magazine of the Dutch fleet's flagship and saved the city. The **Museum of Macau** (open Tues–Sun 10am–6pm; entrance fee) on the site of the fortress has well-captioned exhibits that chart the history of the enclave and its citizens, from its first settlement through to the handover to the Chinese.

A short stroll to the west will take you to picturesque **Camões Grotto 8**, where Luís de Camões, the celebrated Portuguese soldier-poet, is said to have composed part of the national epic, *Os Lusíadas* (The Lusiads). A bronze bust of Camões rests in the garden's grotto. Nearby are the Casa Garden built in 1770 and the **Old Protestant Cemetery** (open daily 9am–5.30pm) that was the final resting place of many an East India Company official.

## South to Barra

More of the UNESCO historical sites lie along an easy-to-follow route from Largo do Senado to the southern tip of the peninsula. From Leal Senado, follow the bottle-green signposts up Rua Dr Soares and Calcada Tronco Velho to Largho de Santo Agostinho (St Augustine's Square), which is surrounded by four noteworthy buildings. The Baroque-style **Santo Agostinho 9** (St Augustine's) organises Macau's Easter procession every year. Spanish Augustinians founded a church here in 1586, but the present structure dates from 1814, and its ornate facade from 1875. Across the square and on the UNESCO list is the **Sir Robert Hotung Library** (open Mon–Sat 1pm–7pm). Originally built in 1894, it was later bought by Hong Kong businessman Sir Robert Hotung, who bequeathed the building to the Macau government as a library.

The beautifully restored **Dom Pedro V Theatre 10** was built in the 18th century. It has 350 seats and is closed during the day, but often opens for concerts and performances during Macau's many arts festivals. Also on the square, though

accessed from Rua do Seminario around the corner, is **St Joseph's Seminary** (church open 10am–5pm). Dedicated in 1728, its sole purpose was to establish Jesuit missions in China, a task it performed with gusto. Today its vast halls, classrooms and living quarters have mostly disappeared, but its architecture and sculptures are worth viewing, and its beautiful chapel is open to the public (daily 10am–5pm). The statues in the chapel were salvaged from the fire at São Paulo in 1835.

Further south on Rua de São Lourenço the church of **São Lourenço ⑪** (St Lawrence's) is raised up above street level and surrounded by a small garden. The church was originally built in the 1560s, and most families of Portuguese sailors used to gather on the front steps of the church to pray and wait for their return, so it was known in Cantonese as Feng Shun Tang (Hall of the Soothing Winds). The elegant church was most recently rebuilt in 1846.

Take a detour up **Colina da Penha ⑫** (Penha Hill) for sweeping views and to visit the Chapel of Our Lady of Penha, which was first built in 1622 and last rebuilt in 1837. While not listed as a UNESCO site, the chapel and Bishop's Palace next door were important centres of Roman Catholic missionary work. The marble statue of the Virgin Mary on the exterior wall facing China symbolises this mission.

Continuing on the UNESCO World Heritage route, there are more examples of different cultures' architectural styles. The peaceful piazza of **Largo do Lilau** marks one of the first areas of Portuguese residential areas. Nearby, the **Casa da Mandarin** (Mandarin's House) on Antonio da Silva Lane is a traditional Chinese courtyard-style residence, dating back to 1881. Further south, the **Moorish Barracks** (open daily 9am–6pm) were built in 1874 to house policemen recruited from another Portuguese enclave, Goa.

Heading down to the foot of Barra Hill to Largo do Barra is **Temple da A-Ma ⑬** (open daily 7am–6pm). This temple at the entrance to Macau's Porto Interior (Inner Harbour) is the oldest temple in the territory, said to date back 600 years to the Ming Dynasty. It was certainly there in 1557, when Macau was ceded to Portugal. The original temple was built

*Macau is the only place in China where casinos are legal. Chinese people love to bet and are travelling in ever increasing numbers, and it is this winning combination that makes the global gaming industry so interested in Macau. Ambitious reclamation has created plenty of land on which to build new casinos – most dramatically on the Cotai strip, home to a rapidly developing series of gambling "resorts".*

**BELOW:** New Year dragon dance on the steps in front of São Paulo.

**TIP**

Take a high-speed elevator to the top of the Macau Tower for panoramic views across the city and islands. This is the best way to appreciate the scale of Macau's massive programme of reclamation and construction as it strives to tap into the new Chinese wealth and establish itself as the leisure capital of Asia.

**BELOW:** the historic library at the Leal Senado.

by fishermen from southeast China and dedicated to Tin Hau, the patron goddess of fishermen and called A-Ma in Macau. It was then called Ma Kok Miu (Ma Point Temple). The Chinese named the area A Ma-Gao, or the Bay of A-Ma. The oldest surviving part of this temple is a lower pavilion to the right of its entrance. There is a coloured, bas-relief stone carving here, said to be a rendering of a Chinese junk that carried the goddess A-Ma from Fujian province through typhoon-ravaged seas to Macau, where she walked to the top of Barra Hill and ascended to heaven. Near the temple is the **Maritime Museum** ⑭ (open Wed–Mon 10am–5.30pm; entrance fee, but free on Sun), with various displays tracing the history of shipping in the South China Sea.

## New Macau

Macau's most prominent new tourist attraction is the 338-metre (1,110-ft) **Macau Tower** ⑮, a concrete totem on the tip of the Sai Van and Nam Van artificial lakes. Take the lift to the observation deck (open daily 10am–9pm; entrance fee) for 360-degree views of Macau, and look through its glass floors (not recommended for vertigo sufferers). Thrill-seekers can "skywalk" around the edge of the clear handrail-free platform, climb all the way to the top of the mast or leap off in a controlled bungee jump.

From the tower it's easy to see Macau's changing shape and other new landmarks. The orange-and-white Hotel Lisboa that was once the main landmark now looks quaintly retro and is dwarfed by new developments, including owner Stanley Ho's monstrous 44-storey Grand Lisboa Hotel and Casino, modelled on a lotus root but resembling a giant mirror-covered turnip.

Across Nam Van Lake (also called the Baia da Praia Grande), a series of brash new casinos are the glistening landmarks of Macau's burgeoning skyline. The copper-coloured **Wynn Macau**, the gold-and-silver **MGM Grand**, the 34-storey **StarWorld Casino** and the golden **Sands Macau** symbolise the new breed of Vegas-style gambling palaces for which Macau is becoming famous. Bounded on the north by the Avenida da Amizade, the rectangle of reclaimed land on which they sit is known as the **NAPE** (Porto Exterior Outer Harbour, or Novos Aterros do Porto Exterior in Portuguese).

In addition to the casinos, the area is also home to a growing number of small restaurants, cafés and bars. The **NAPE waterfront** ⑯ faces Taipa and is marked by the beautiful bronze statue of Kun Iam, designed and crafted by Portuguese artist Christina Reiria. The **Macau Cultural Centre** is located at the far end of the NAPE and has two auditoria that host a regular programme of performances. It is also home to trendy lounge bar Bex. Next door, the **Macau Museum of Art** ⑰ has spacious art galleries over five floors (open Tues–Sun 10am-5pm; entrance fee), which houses a permanent collection of over 3,000 works of Shiwan ceramics, calligraphy and art from Macau and China.

Further east towards the ferry terminal, an artificial volcano marks the entrance of the **Fisherman's Wharf** ⑱ entertainment area, which is open 24 ours a day. Admission to the 93,000-sq. metre (111,000 sq. yds) complex is free, but there are charges for the rides. Inside the volcano there's a roller coaster and a water-ride, and for younger visitors the Children's Fort has a bunch of Aladdin-themed rides and amusements. The mixed bag of architectural styles in three themed sections – Dynasty Wharf, East Meets West, and Legend Wharf – range from old Cape Town and Miami to the Tang Dynasty and have shops, a bou-ique hotel and dozens of restaurants, including Japanese, American and African cuisines.

## South from the border

At the northern end of Macau is the mod-ern border gate between the Special Administrative Region and the city of Zhuhai in mainland China. A park has been created around the former gateway, **Portas do Cerco 19**, which was built in 1870 and is inscribed with a quote from Portuguese poet Camões: "Honour your country for your country is watching you." The crossing is open from 7am to midnight, and the casino shuttle buses line up to meet the many punters arriving from Zhuhai and elsewhere in China.

Protecting the other approach to the city was the **Fortress of Mong-Ha**, on Colina de Mong-Ha, constructed to pro-vide a defensive vantage point to guard the Portas do Cerco. Built in 1849, the fort's barracks now hold the 24-room Pousada da Mong-Ha and Macau's Insti-tute of Tourism Studies, whose students now staff the small hotel and restaurant.

Most organised tours make a quick visit to the **Dr Sun Yatsen Memorial House 20** (open Wed–Mon 10am–5pm; free). The memorial is near the Kiang Vu Hospital, where Sun practised medicine as one of the first Western-trained Chi-nese doctors in this area before he became known as the father of modern China. Nearby is the Suzhou-style **Lou Lim Ioc 21** (open daily 6am–9pm) with lotus ponds, bridges and ornamental mountains, resembling a classical land-scape painting.

The hill of **Colina da Guia**, the high-est point in Macau, rises east of the Sun Yatsen memorial and Lou Lim Ioc, and is home to the **Guia Fortress and Light-house 22** (open daily 9am–5pm; free), which is one of Macau's landmarks. This

*The Kun Iam statue on the NAPE waterfront. Kun Iam is the Macanese name for Tin Hau, the patron saint of seafarers.*

**BELOW:** the new Macau–Taipa bridge, with the Macau Tower in the background.

**BELOW:** old-fashioned barber shop.

17th-century Western-style lighthouse – the oldest on the Chinese coast – stands atop Colina da Guia and used to guard coastal approaches. Besides the views, there is a small art gallery. A cable-car links the hilltop with a small park and aviary at **Flora Garden** below (open 7am–6pm).

Every year, in the last weekend of November the streets of Macau are taken over by the Macau Formula 3 Grand Prix and the Macau Motorcycle Grand Prix. Learn more about the "Guia Race" history of these exciting road races at the **Grand Prix Museum ㉓** (open 10am–5pm, closed Tues) at 431 Rua Luis Gongazaga Gomes in the basement of the Tourism Activities Centre. Next door, the **Wine Museum** (open 10am–5pm, closed Tues) tells the story of Portuguese wines.

## Taipa and Coloane

The "other" Macau is not on the peninsula that is generally regarded as Macau, but consists of what were until recently the two outlying islands of Taipa and Coloane – now melded together by the **Cotai strip ㉔**, 620 hectares (1,550 acres) of reclaimed land either side of the 1.3-km (¾-mile) road that used to link the two (and connected to Macau proper by a series of bridges and causeways). Cotai is the focus for Macau's drive to become Asia's leisure capital, a vast playground of casinos, hotels and entertainment centres; some casinos have already opened, including the gigantic **Venetian** *(see margin)*. The Venetian will be joined by at least 12 more hotels and casinos before 2010, including Australian James Packer's Publishing and Broadcasting US$1.5 billion joint venture, the underwater, Atlantis-themed City of Dreams casino, with Hyatt, Hard Rock and Crown hotels on site.

**Taipa ㉕** was once the centre for junk building and firecracker manufacture and in the early 1700s became the busy centre for Western trade with China when an imperial edict banned English and French ships from Guangzhou insisting they moor at Taipa instead. Today, it is home to Macau's International Airport and has its share of new casinos, including the amusing Greek Mythology Casino, complete with Roman centurions, and the more sophisticated Crown Macau. Bets can be placed on horses at the Macau Jockey Club Racecourse, which has racing on Friday nights and Saturday afternoons apart from in August and September.

A few bits and pieces of old Macau survive. In **Taipa Village** local history and developments are explained in the three-storey mint-green **Museum of Taipa and Coloane History** (open 10am–6pm, closed Mondays; entrance fee). Head east along Rua Correia da Silva to Largo to explore the narrow streets around the village square and Our Lady of Carmel, a neoclassical church built in 1885. It is close to one of Taipa's greatest treasures, the **Taipa Houses Museum** (open Tues–Sun 9.30am–5pm; entrance fee), also painted mint-green.

On the Avenida da Praia, five beautifully restored houses are now home to the Macanese House, House of the Islands, House of the Portugal Regions, Exhibition Gallery and House for Reception. Pause

between the different exhibitions at the Taipa Houses Museum, and glance across the water to the 32 storeys of The Venetian Macao Resort-Hotel and its 3,000 rooms, casinos, shops, canals and gondolas; nowhere is the contrast between new and old Macau more striking.

A short drive across the Cotai strip takes you to the still relatively quiet island of **Coloane** ㉖, almost twice as big as Taipa. What was once the last hiding place for pirates is now a green retreat from the SAR's bustle, casinos and construction with beaches, country parks and a moderately picturesque village to explore. On the southern side of the island at the pretty bay at **Cheoc Van** there's an open-air pool next to the white sandy beach. The Pousada da Coloane overlooks the bay, and from this pleasant family-run hotel and restaurant you can follow a well-signposted trail for 45 minutes up to the island's peak and the **A-Ma Cultural Village** (open daily 8am–6pm). When you are close to the village you will hear piped music coming from speakers hidden in the bushes before being rewarded by the sight of a vast, newly built Qing Dynasty-style complex with temples, bell tower, drum tower, Tian Hou Palace and museum. The 170-metre (560-ft) peak is marked by an impressive 20-metre (65-ft) statue of the goddess A-Ma, which can be seen from the sea. Nearby, there's a recreational fishing area, picnic tables and an Arboretum with more than 100 species of trees. Shuttle buses run between the complex and the Façade at Estrada de Seac Pai Van every 30 minutes.

Coloane's other hotel is the grander Westin Resort Macau. The Westin is built into the hillside overlooking Hac Sa (Black Sands) beach, and **Macau Golf and Country Club**'s 18-holes begin on the hotel's "roof". Close to the black sand beach (Hac Sa) is the ever-popular Fernando's restaurant, where lunches rarely finish before dusk.

Peaceful **Coloane Village** lies in the southwest of the island. **The Chapel of St Francis Xavier**, built in 1928, commemorates the successful recapture of a group of children kidnapped by pirates in 1910. The chapel looks onto Coloane's tiny Portuguese-style village square, which comes alive with restaurant tables and festivities at weekends and holidays. From the square you can explore the lanes and backstreets which have a few furniture shops and cafés, or walk down the recently restored waterfront along Avenida da Republica to the Kun Lam Temple, which was built in 1677 and is dedicated to the gods and goddesses of heaven, war, wealth, medicine and carpenters.

A short walk away along Loc Ium Lou is the **Tam Kung Temple** (1862), where there is a dragon boat carved from a whalebone by the local fishermen as a gift for Tam Kung. Head back to the village, and among the narrow lanes of Coloane the maze of houses and few small furniture shops and cafés to discover which makes this an easy place to spend half a day exploring. And an even easier place to sit with some Portuguese wine and Macanese food and watch the world go by while others lose and win fortunes at the gaming tables a few miles away.                    ❏

*Speedy jetfoils and catamarans travel the 70-km (45-mile) Hong Kong–Macau route in under one hour. There is also a helicopter service (16 minutes).*

**BELOW:** Coloane village.

# RESTAURANTS & BARS

## Restaurants

Prices for a three-course dinner per person with one beer or glass of wine: (MOP$ = patacas)
$ = under MOP$150
$$ = MOP$150–300
$$$ = MOP$300–500
$$$$ = over MOP$500

Macau is a great place for eating out. It's cheap, and the local cuisine features elements from the far-flung Portuguese colonies of old, with African, Brazilian, Goan and Chinese influences combining with those from the European homeland.

### Portuguese/Macanese

#### A Lorcha
289 Rua Almirante Sérgio. Tel: 2831 3193. Open: L & D Wed–Mon. $$
One of the best of Macau's Portuguese restaurants, serving pork with clams, *feijoda* (pork-and-bean stew) and seafood rice.

#### A Petisqueira
15A & B Rua São João, Taipa. Tel: 2882 5354. Open: L & D Tues–Sun. $$
Fish and seafood are a must here: prawns, seafood salads, sea bass and Portuguese-style cod dishes.

#### Clube Militar de Macau
975 Avenida de Praia Grande. Tel: 2871 4009 Open: L & D daily. $$$
Former officers' mess

dating from 1870, Clube Militar still attracts the cream of the city's Portuguese and Macanese society. Truly Portuguese cuisine and an excellent wine list.

#### Estalagem
Estrada Gov. Albana de Oliveria, 410 Edificio Nam San, Bloco 1, Taipa. Tel: 2882 1041. Open: L & D daily. $$$
Located near the racecourse on Taipa, Estalagem is known for its remarkable veal medallions with bacon. Traditional Portuguese fare includes *bacalhau* – Portuguese-style cod.

#### Fernando's
9 Praia Hac Sa, Coloane. Tel: 2888 2531. Open: L & D daily. $$
At weekends, and on many weekdays, scores of diners queue for tables at this beachfront institution on Coloane Island. Crispy African chicken, prawns in clam sauce and casseroled crab are all excellent, and even the salad is exceptional.

#### IFT-Educational Restaurant
Colina da Mong-Ha. Tel: 2856 1252. Open: L & D Mon–Fri only. $$
Exploring the north of Macau is a good excuse to visit this old fort where culinary and hospitality students at Macau's Institute for

Tourism Studies prepare international and Macanese favourites.

#### Lord Stow's Bakery
Rua da Tassara, 1 Coloane Square, Coloane. Tel: 2888 2534. Open: B, L & D daily, Wed B & L only. $
Well known locally for its take on Macau's traditional *pastel de nata* (Portuguese egg tart), Lord Stow's is also good for fresh bread, snacks and coffee.

#### Nga Tim Café
8 Rua Caetano, Coloane Village, Coloane. Tel: 2888 2086. Open: L & D daily. $$
Eat alfresco on Coloane village square at Nga Tim. It satisfies its many regular customers with a straightforward menu of Portuguese and Macanese classics, like African chicken and garlic prawns.

#### O Manuel
90 Rua Fernão Mendes Pinto, Taipa. Tel: 2882 7571. Open: L & D daily. $$$
This unassuming but popular restaurant highly deserves its following. Portuguese treats include cod fish cakes, grilled sardines and *calde verde* (Portuguese vegetable soup).

#### O Porto Interior
259 Rua Almirante Sérgio. Tel: 2896 7770. Open: L & D daily. $$–$$$
Enjoy fine Macanese

classics in an attractive restaurant decorated with interesting prints and artefacts.

#### O Santos
20 Rua da Cunha, Taipa. Tel: 2882 5594. Open: L & D Wed–Mon. $$–$$$
Tuck into filling fare such as stuffed pork loin and curried crab, surrounded by football memorabilia.

### French

#### La Bonne Heure
12A & B Travessa de São Domingos. Tel: 2833 1209. Open L & D Thur–Tues. $$
French cuisine prepared by chef who trained under Robuchon. Cosy bistro has art exhibitions and stays open for postdinner drinks and music until 1am Friday nights.

#### La Comédie Chez Vous
Avenida Xian Xing Hai, Edificio Zhu Kuan (opp. Cultural Centre). Tel: 2875 2021. Open: B, L & D daily. $–$$
The ground-floor café, serving memorable crêpes, is popular for breakfast (8am–noon). Lunch or dine in the upstairs restaurant.

#### Robuchon A Galera
3/F Hotel Lisboa, 2 Avenida de Lisboa. Tel: 2857 7666. Open: L & D daily. $$$$
Joel Robuchon, lauded by the Parisian media as "chef of the century", chose the Lisboa Hotel as the location for his first establishment out-

side France, now regarded as one of the best restaurants in Asia. Fiendishly expensive for dinner; good value for lunch.

### Italian

#### Antica Trattoria

40–42 & 46 Avenida Sir Anders Ljuungstedt, NAPE. Tel: 2875 5103. Open: L & D daily, closed 2nd Tues each month. **$$**
One of three restaurants run by different members of the same Italian family, Antica Trattoria serves up great pasta, pizza and Italian snacks.

#### Bistro Italiano

66C Rua de Pequim. Tel: 2878 9701. Open: L & D noon–1am. **$$**
Bistro Italiano is a pleasant contrast to its slightly seedy back-street location behind the Diamond Casino and has good-value traditional Italian dishes.

#### Caffé Toscana

11 Travessa de São Domingos. Tel: 2837 0354. Open: L & D daily. **$–$$**
Small Italian café with a mezzanine dining area. Stop off for antipasti, pizza or fresh focaccia while exploring the Largo do Senado area.

#### Il Teatro

Wynn Macau, Rua Cidade de Sintra. Tel: 2888 9966. Open: D only. **$$$$**
Classy southern Italian restaurant overlooking the lake where the

choreographed fountains perform nightly.

#### Pizzeria Toscana

Calcada da Barra, 2A Edificio Cheong Seng. Tel: 2872 6637. Open L & D daily. **$$**
A Macau institution, now located in the Barra area near the Moorish barracks. Always excellent value and good for a romantic dinner or group lunch. Clam linguine and the giant profiteroles are recommended.

### Asian

#### Star Hub Café

3 Rua Francisco H. Fernandes, NAPE. Tel: 2875 7733. Open: L & D daily. **$–$$**
This colourful no-frills café delivers its promise of a "uniquely Singapore and Vietnam dining experience", with tasty and inexpensive dishes such as *laksa*, *pho bo* and Southeast Asian curries.

#### Tung Yee Heen

1/F Mandarin Oriental Macau, Avenida da Amizade. Tel: 2879 3821. Open: B, L & D daily. **$$–$$$**
Classic Cantonese fare with dim sum available all day. Well worth trying are deep-fried prawns with garlic chilli sauce.

#### Wong Chi Kei Congee & Noodle

17 Largo do Senado. Tel: 2833 1313. Open: L & D. **$**
Step off the main square to grab a bowl of wonton noodles and a seat in this traditional-style restaurant.

## Bars

#### Al's Diner,

Block 1, New Orleans, Fisherman's Wharf. Tel: 297 2818.
Well-known, lively Hong Kong bar brings American beer, burgers and music across the delta.

#### Bex

Macau Cultural Centre, Avenida Xian Xing Hai, NAPE. Tel: 797 7755.
Trendy lounge bar in unlikely location has raised the cool factor of Macau's nightlife.

#### Casablanca

1369–73 Avenida Dr Sun Yatsen, NAPE. Tel: 2875 1281.
One of the many open-fronted bars in NAPE, a good place to bar-hop.

#### MP3

1333 Avenida Dr Sun Yatsen, NAPE. Tel: 2875 1306.

With dancing girls, DJs and an all-you-can-drink happy hour (6–9pm), MP3 is one of the loudest bars in NAPE.

#### Old Taipa Tavern

21 Rua dos Negociantes, Taipa Village. Tel: 2882 5221.
Pleasant pub in Portuguese-style building. Live music and sports screens.

#### Oparium

1399 Avenida Dr Sun Yatsen, NAPE. Tel: 2872 7222.
Good range of beers and extensive wine list, plus outdoor seating.

#### Vasco

1/F Mandarin Oriental Macau. Tel: 793 3831.
Sip away on a themed cocktail in cool and sophisticated hotel lounge bar. Piano music in evening.

**RIGHT:** Fernando's in full swing.

# THE COASTAL SOUTH

The provinces of Guangdong, Hainan Island and
Fujian are home to some of China's wealthiest cities,
beach resorts and a less-developed hinterland

The coastal provinces of southern China are among the wealthiest in the country, and several centuries of contact and exchange with the outside world has made their cities relatively cosmopolitan. This coast, most notably along the stretch from eastern Guangdong through to Fujian, is traditionally the exit point for generations of émigres who set sail to establish Chinese communities across Southeast Asia and beyond. Today, there is more of an influx than an outflow, as thousands upon thousands of migrants from the poorer interior move southwards to seek employment in the increasingly prosperous southern cities.

Guangdong province, to which Hong Kong and Macau are joined, occupies the central part of the coast. Right on the Hong Kong border is Shenzhen, an economic success story which showed the rest of China the way ahead after it became the pioneering Special Economic Zone (SEZ) in the 1980s. At the other end of the Pearl River Delta is the vibrant city of Guangzhou, formerly known in the West as Canton, with a long tradition of trading and entrepre-

neurial zeal. Highlights elswhere in Guangdong are the old city of Chaozhou, the landscapes of Zhaoqing ("little Guilin") and the gone-to-seed charm of Kaiping in the west.

Part of Guangdong until it became a province in its own right in 1988, Hainan Island is marketed as China's tropical paradise, and the beach resorts at the southern end of the island do indeed have palm-fringed white sands and warm clear waters – this is just about the only place in China to remain warm throughout the year. Haikou, the capital, is a pleasant city and the interior highlands have much to offer.

To the east of Guangdong is Fujian province, which has several highlights. Xiamen is an attractive city, with a real gem in its offshore island of Gulangyu. Just along the coast, Quanzhou was once China's leading port and has a wealth of history to explore. Inland are the astonishing Hakka roundhouses and the Wuyi Shan mountains. ❑

**PRECEDING PAGES:** the island of Gulangyu, Xiamen, Fujian. **LEFT:** the beach at Xiaomeisha, east of Shenzhen. **TOP:** Hakka roundhouse near Yongding, Fujian. **ABOVE LEFT:** banyan tree and a quiet path. **ABOVE RIGHT:** the Tianhe shopping mall in eastern Guangzhou.

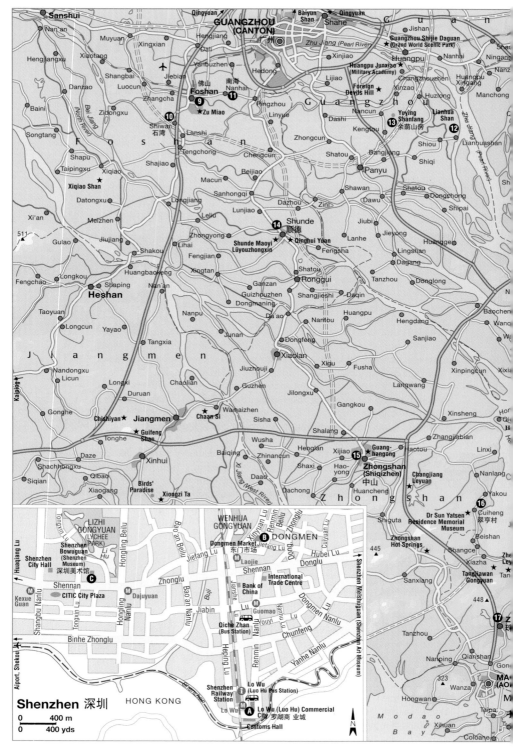

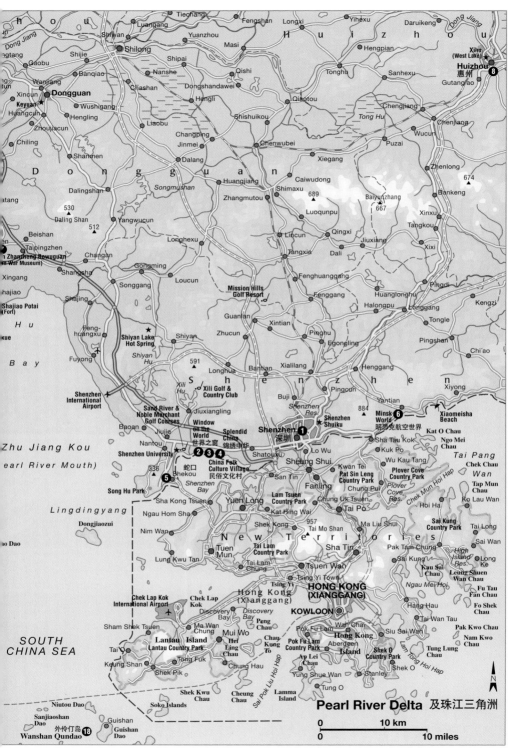

**Pearl River Delta** 及珠江三角洲

# SHENZHEN AND THE PEARL RIVER DELTA

**One of the fastest-growing cities in the world, Shenzhen is a symbol of the new China, its population spilling over into the surrounding cities of the Pearl River Delta**

Ever since the groundbreaking utterance "to get rich is glorious" was ascribed to Deng Xiaoping on his grand tour of southern China in 1992, the Pearl River Delta (PRD) has revelled in its economic success. Within one generation a land of farmers and fishermen eking a living from paddy fields, fish farms and duck ponds has been taken over by urban sprawl and factories that generate a GDP of US$113 billion and rising – an average increase of 11 percent per year over that time.

The superlatives are arresting: the PRD is home to two of the three most prosperous cities in all of China, Shenzhen and Dongguan; as a country on its own, it would be the world's 11th-largest trading economy; it has the world's busiest border crossing; it attracts almost half of the total foreign investment in China. It is the world leader in light manufacturing – churning out vast quantities of everything from hi-tech electronics to garments, footwear and toys.

The development has been as spectacular as it has largely due to the proximity of Hong Kong, whose legions of entrepreneurs, many of whom had long family associations with the region, quickly spotted a good opportunity and cheap labour on their doorstep and swiftly switched much of their production to the PRD in the 1980s and 1990s. Millions of dollars has been enthusiastically invested in the rising businesses of the PRD from the former British colony and Hong Kong's financial and man-

agerial expertise, legal system and efficient port that has played a key role in the economic success story.

For the typical overseas tourist venturing into mainland China for a day or two from Hong Kong, the PRD provides a decidedly unrepresentative, but fascinating, glimpse of "the other side". Conventional tourist sights – some venerable temples, attractive gardens and assorted historical sights – are well scattered, although the excellent roads and a good network of bus, rail and ferry routes make getting around straightforward. And

**Main attractions**
SHENZHEN SHOPPING
SHENZHEN THEME PARKS
OPIUM WAR MUSEUM
HUIZHOU
FOSHAN
ZHONGSHAN

**LEFT:** the urban sprawl of Shenzhen.
**BELOW:** Lo Wu Commercial City.

**BELOW RIGHT:** the Shenzhen Development Centre building.

sightseeing isn't really the point anyway: the main purpose of a visit is to witness at first hand this remarkable distillation of modern China – and, of course, to go shopping.

## SHENZHEN

If the Pearl River Delta is the economic engine of the new China, then **Shenzhen** ❶ (深圳) is, without doubt, its starter motor, an economic success story almost without equal in the modern world. But while a new city centre and seat of government has been raised in Futian, adding a little order to the maelstrom, Shenzhen is less than postcard-perfect. It may contain the eighth-tallest building in the world, the 384-metre (1,260-ft) Shun Hing Square, but much of the urban area is unprepossessing to look at, with construction work a constant eyesore.

On the plus side for the visitor, there's a cornucopia of shops, some very good and reasonably priced food, a cluster of kitsch theme parks and the world's biggest golf course. Hong Kongers make regular trips across the border here, in search of shopping bargains and high jinks at low prices.

Shenzhen is a very large and sprawling city. Bounded by its eponymous river to the south (marking the border with Hong Kong), it is laid out on a grid system, so orientation is quite simple.

### Luo Hu (Lo Wu)

If you are coming up from Hong Kong on the train, you will arrive at **Luo Hu** (Lo Wu when transliterated from the Cantonese; 罗湖). After disembarking at Lo Wu station in Hong Kong, it's simply a case of walking across the border (indoors) to emerge into a large open area on the Chinese side. The gargantuan **Lo Wu Commercial City** ❹ (罗湖商业城; Luohu shang yecheng) is a little way ahead on the right. This is one of Shenzhen's largest retail centres, selling a vast array of electronics, leather goods, jewellery and a medley of other merchandise that is packed layer upon layer. Shops selling the same sort of items tend to cluster together, and tailors can be found on the upper levels. *For more on shopping in Shenzhen, see page 374.*

Opposite is Shenzhen's railway station, with frequent trains to Guangzhou and various PRD destinations (see panel,

## The Rise and Rise of Shenzhen

The creation of Special Economic Zones (SEZs) during the 1980s, with their modern and relaxed business and tax regulations, kickstarted the transformation of the Pearl River Delta, and nowhere was this more pronounced than in Shenzhen. Pell-mell, the factories and skyscrapers grew almost overnight, immigrants from all over China poured into the burgeoning city to make their fortunes, highways were rolled out, airports and railways constructed, and arable land smothered in concrete. The few hundred peasants who once eked out a living here dispersed in a phenomenon that was to become a byword for fast living, cheap shopping and a no-holds-barred race to the future.

Two decades later and Shenzhen is the second-richest city in China. Per capita income is around eight times the national average, and the population has risen from 700,000 to 11 million in 25 years. Between 1992 and 2004, the city's GDP increased ten-fold, from Rmb 32 billion to 342 billion – so rapidly in fact, that reining in the economy (thus making it more efficient by preventing "over-heating") has become government policy. Of course, the relentless growth has its downside. As inequality rises, so does crime: you are around nine times as likely to be mugged in Shenzhen as in Shanghai, and the pollution is notorious – on average, the air is classed as hazardous 130 days of the year.

## TRANSPORT TO/FROM SHENZHEN

**Flights**: Most large Chinese cities have flights to Shenzhen. For a list of international destinations connected with Shenzhen, *see page 351*.

### Hong Kong–Shenzhen

**Trains**: 3 per hour (5.30am–10.20pm) from Kowloon to the border terminus of Lo Wu (40 mins). Shenzhen station is just over the border.

**Ferries**: 20+ daily between Hong Kong/Kowloon and Shekou port (50 mins); 11–13 daily between Hong Kong Airport and Shekou (30 mins); 5–8 daily between Hong Kong Airport and the Fuyong Ferry Terminal (Shenzhen Airport; 45 mins).

**Buses**: Frequent shuttle buses (typically every 30 mins) run from several locations in Hong Kong, including the airport, to downtown Shenzhen, Shekou and Shenzhen Airport.

### Shenzhen–Macau

**Ferries**: 3 daily to/from Shekou port (80 mins). Also hourly Shekou–Zhuhai (1 hr).

### Shenzhen–Guangzhou

**Trains**: 3–5 express per hour (55–70 mins), plus slower trains (1½–2 hrs).

**Buses**: frequent departures (1½ –2 hrs).

### Shenzhen–elsewhere in the region

There are good **train** and **bus** links with cities across Guangdong and beyond *(see page 185)*, plus **ferries** from Shekou to ports across the delta, and to Haikou (daily, 18 hrs).

*Fast turbo-jet vessels link Shenzhen's port (Shekou) with several other delta towns. There are also frequent services to Hong Kong.*

*above*), and the new Metro, which can whisk you north to the downtown area and on to Futian District and the theme parks west of town.

## Jianshe Lu and Downtown

The major thoroughfare of Jianshe Lu arrows north from Luo Hu, with large department stores and hotels on either side. Binhe Lu strikes off to the west, past the municipal area of Futian to the theme parks, Shekou and the airport (40 km/25 miles west of town).

Continue north along Jianshe Lu and after 2 km (1¼ miles) you'll reach the intersection with Shennan Lu, central Shenzhen's main east–west drag. This crossroads can be thought of as the

**BELOW:** busy Downtown intersection in Shenzhen.

**BELOW:**
contemporary art exhibition at the Shenzhen Art Museum.

centre of Downtown, lying at the heart of the remnants of the original town of **Baoan**. It is perhaps fitting that this area, now known as the Dongmen District, is the site of China's first McDonald's (on Qingyuan Lu): Baoan was renamed Shenzhen in anticipation of the city becoming China's first Special Economic Zone (SEZ) in 1980.

Some of the best tailors in Shenzhen cluster together in the streets around **Dongmen Market** (东门市场; Dongmen Shichang) on Hu Beilu. Customers are welcome to choose their fabrics in one shop and then get them made up by the tailor of their choice. A pair of trousers, for example, can be made in a couple of hours and should cost less than Rmb 100.

Despite appearances, Shenzhen is not entirely devoted to relentless consumerism. To the northeast of Dongmen, at 32 Donghu Lu, the **Shenzhen Art Museum** (深圳美术馆; Shenzhen Meishuguan; open Tues–Sun 9am–5pm; entrance fee but free on Fridays; www.szam.org) hosts an ever-changing programme of exhibitions – mainly consisting of contemporary art.

## Futian District

The Shennan Lu drag stretches west from Dongmen towards **Futian District** (福田区), Shenzhen's financial hub. Along the way, at No. 1008, is the **Shenzhen Museum** (深圳博物馆; Shenzhen Bowuguan; open Tues–Sun, 9am–5pm; entrance fee), which borders Lizhi Park on Tongxin Lu. By any standard the museum is comprehensive, well interpreted and thoughtfully laid out, with exhibits devoted to history, art, culture and nature, with more than 20,000 relics, including bronze, china, jade, calligraphy and paintings.

The main shopping area in Futian is **Huaqiang Beilu**, running north from the Huaqiang Lu metro station and around 3 km (2 miles) west of the downtown Jianshe Lu / Shennan Lu intersection. The prominent Sundan Department Store makes a good reference point, with the Sege computer market standing more or less opposite, and a watch and clock mart is a short walk away on Zhenxing Lu. International chains have not been slow to realise Shenzhen's potential, and there are cavernous offerings from both Britain and America in the shape of Wal-Mart,

*Recommended Restaurants & Bars on pages 164–5*

**THE SHENZHEN METRO**

Shenzhen's metro system opened in 2004. There are currently two lines: line 1 runs from the border crossing at Luohu to the central Dongmen area and then through Futian District all the way out to the Window of the World theme park; line 4 is shorter and runs north–south. Fares are cheap and trains run every 6–8 minutes 6.30am–11pm. Shekou and the airport will be linked to the network by 2010.

on Hongu Lu, and the B&Q store on Baon'an Jie, both with familiar logos but with products aimed squarely at the burgeoning Chinese middle class.

After dark, the Futian area reverberates with cheap, raw fun. As is the case across Shenzhen, the scene has developed rapidly, vaulting from bars with a keg of beer and a suspect stereo into themed entertainment venues. Note that this is not a place for women to party alone. *For more details, see Travel Tips, page 371, and for bar listings see page 165.*

## The Theme Parks

In Nanshan District, some 14 km (9 miles) west of downtown Shenzhen and about halfway between the city and Shekou, is a cluster of theme parks based around replicas of tourist attractions across the world and around China.

**Window of the World ❷** (世界之窗; Shijie Zhichuang; open daily 9am–10pm; entrance fee), a sort of global Lilliput, showcases scaled-down facsimiles of everything from Thai palaces to Japanese teahouses – to say nothing of the Eiffel Tower, one of the area's most prominent landmarks. Legend has it that the project architect's budget stretched no further than one overseas trip, hence this 108-metre (354-ft) souvenir from the City of Light which is visible across the border from Hong Kong. Besides generating income from admission fees, the rationale behind Window of the World was to encourage Chinese to travel overseas: you've seen the copy, now how about the real thing? The park is certainly deluged with tour groups from all over China, and foreign visitors may find themselves the focus of some curiosity, or even the vague supposition

*Window of the World brings Europe to China. Some sights are smaller than others... the 108-metre (354-ft) Eiffel Tower being the largest.*

**BELOW:** re-enactments of historical events are part of the Spendid China experience.

# The Golf Scene

In the space of two decades, China has gone from a nation of card-carrying communists to scorecard-carrying faddists. Golf is the new opiate of the masses, a social accolade, an entrée to the higher realms of business, played by everyone who can afford it and aspired to by those who cannot. It's said that nowadays you talk business on the course and golf in the office and, naturally, the Chinese love to gamble, too, so you might find US$10,000 riding on a single hole.

Crème de la crème of Shenzhen's scores of golf clubs is the 12-course, 72-par, 216-hole **Mission Hills** (观澜湖; Guan Lan Hu), conceived and built with a fair measure of élan by cardboard-packaging tycoon David Chu and ranked by Guinness World Records as the largest on the planet. A shuttle-bus service plies the 20-minute drive from the border with Hong Kong to Mission Hills (which is en route to Dongguan). Mission Hills' 7,500 members (each of whom pays up to US$102,600 to join) and its 2,400 caddies (all emphatically female, some of whom can talk golf in English, Cantonese, Putonghua and Japanese) all share a passion for what G. K. Chesterton called "an expensive way of playing marbles".

For anyone who witnessed Shenzhen in the late 1970s when it was a rural backwater, Mission Hills

is little short of miraculous. But Mission Hills should not be seen solely as an agglomeration of golfing, but rather as symptomatic of the new China and its burgeoning band of plutocrats, to say nothing of the increasingly prosperous middle classes.

The courses are surrounded by vaguely surreal spas and dozens of shopping outlets that are emphatically designer-label, for the amusement of golf widows and widowers as well as the players themselves. And overlooking the greens stand a couple of hundred mansions, each with palatial interiors and grounds (think *Dallas* or *Dynasty* with oriental characteristics), not so much somewhere to raise a family as a place to dazzle business associates in the wine-flown minutes before they ink the big deal.

Perhaps the most beautiful club in Shenzhen belongs to the Kuok family dynasty, who originally hail from Malaysia. **Xili** (西丽) is not normally open to non-members, however guests of the Shangri-La hotels in Hong Kong and Shenzhen may play its four Nelson, Wright, Haworth-designed, nine-hole courses and retire to its villa-like clubhouse which stands beneath an imposing tree-clad granite monolith.

Closer to Hong Kong, and within easy reach of Macau and Shenzhen International Airport, two clubs lie more or less side by side. **Sand River** (沙河; Sha He) and **Noble Merchant** (名商; Ming Shang) are more modest than Xili and Mission Hills, yet still imaginatively designed and backed up with a full range of facilities. Each features two nine-hole courses, though Sand River is developing a third.

Most Shenzhen courses are relatively empty on weekdays, but getting a tee-time at weekends and holidays is by no means easy. Mao Zedong may have declared "The East is Red" but nowadays China's more concerned with its greens. *For more details on the golf courses, see page 376.*

**ABOVE:** the entrance to the Conghua White Swan golf course. **LEFT:** the 15th hole at Mission Hills.

that they have been shipped in to add some authenticity to the exhibits. It is easy to draw comparisons between this temple of artifice and the nearby plethora of copy goods in the city's marts, not to mention the nation's new-found fascination with kitsch. Suffice to say, this is a fun day out, if only to observe other visitors.

The nearby **China Folk Culture Village** ❸ (民俗文化村; Minsu Wenhuacun; open daily 9am–9.30pm; entrance fee) recreates the homes and lifestyles of the country's ethnic minorities, with Buyi stone villages, Dai bamboo huts and Mongolian yurts. Torch-lit parades, dragon-boat races and water-splashing festivals are also staged according to the time of year. Rather more authentic than Window of the World, the China Folk villagers are genuine tribespeople and, language permitting, are friendly and informative about their traditions.

**Splendid China** ❹ (锦绣中华; Jinxiu Zhonghua; open daily 9am–6pm; entrance fee) is the third member of this triumvirate, and a good option for anyone without the time to travel the entire country. For here are the Terracotta Warriors, the Great Wall, the Old Summer Palace, the Forbidden City and much more besides, all replicated in miniature, spread over 30 hectares (75 acres) and doable in a couple of hours.

A short distance east of Splendid China in the Overseas Chinese Town (OCT; Huaqiao Cheng; metro Qiaochengdong) is the **He Xiang Ning Art Museum** (何香凝 美术馆; Xiang Ning Meishuguan; open daily 10am–6pm; entrance fee) , a showpiece for the paintings and calligraphy of the museum's namesake.

Beyond the western theme parks is the town of **Shekou** ❺ (蛇口), well endowed with expat-oriented restaurants and bars catering to Westerners who work in the district's oil industry. It's a place to dine and drink away from the more frenetic atmosphere of downtown Shenzhen. Shekou is well connected; there are frequent ferries to Macau, Hong Kong and Zhuhai, and its hilly peninsula has been linked to Hong Kong's northwest New Territories since 1 July 2007 by a 5-km

(3-mile) bridge across Deep Bay. A further 15 km (9 miles) north is Shenzhen International Airport, also connected to Hong Kong by direct ferry.

On the other (east) side of Shenzhen an alternative theme park experience awaits the curious. **Minsk World** ❻ (明思克航空世界; Mingsike Hangkong Shijie; open daily 9am–7.30pm; entrance fee), situated in the docks on Dapeng Bay, has a 40,000-tonne former Soviet aircraft carrier as its centrepiece, with MiG aircraft, a Soyuz space capsule and other assorted Soviet paraphernalia also on show. Despite the owners' (unsuccessful) attempts to auction off their assets following bankruptcy in 2006, the theme park was still in operation at the time of writing. Beyond to the east are some reasonable beaches centered on the resort of **Xiaomeisha**.

## AROUND THE PEARL RIVER DELTA

Much of the Pearl River Delta is accessible in a two- or three-day tour from Hong Kong, Guangzhou or Macau, but at times the pollution belched out by the "Workshop of the World" can make a trip

*The Beijing Quadrangle at Splendid China.*

**BELOW:** deck action at Minsk World.

*Sizhou Pagoda towers above the shores of West Lake, Huizhou.*

**BELOW:** the entrance to the Opium War Museum at Humen.

unpleasant. The PRD is made up of vast sprawling urban and industrial areas. The eastern side of the delta was developed first and has the greatest concentration of industry; some areas have metamorphosed into a netherworld of endless factories and migrant-worker dormitory blocks. Still, the landscape is occasionally broken up with relics from another time: scenic gardens, monuments, historic treasures offering occasional glimpses of the old way of life.

## Humen to Dongguan

While international trade is now all the rage in the delta, early attempts by western traders to introduce opium to China in the 19th century met with stiff official resistance, commemorated at both a park and a museum in the town of **Humen** ❼ (虎门), south of the booming city of Dongguan. It was at Humen that Commissioner Lin Zexu contaminated several thousand chests of opium with quicklime in 1839, then deposited the haul in the so-called opium pits on the shore to the south of town. The British retaliated, sparking the First Opium War, and Lin was exiled. Much is made (and rightly so)

of the perfidiousness of foreign merchants in the **Opium War Museum** (鸦片战争博物馆; Yapan Zhanzheng Bowuguan; open daily 8am–5.30pm; entrance fee) in Zhixin Park, who subsequently started the conflict that ended with the Chinese forces vanquished and the ceding of Hong Kong in 1841. On the coast 5 km (3 miles) south of Humen town, the original **opium pits** and the **fortress of Shajio** (沙角炮台; Shajiao Potai) are worth a visit (open 8am–5pm; entrance fee).

**Dongguan** (东莞) itself is not on the tourist trail. It is home to one of the world's largest shoe factories and is a major centre for car manufacturing.

## Huizhou

Easily reached from either Guangzhou or Shenzhen, **Huizhou** ❽ (惠州; Wai Chau in Cantonese) sits in the northeastern corner of the delta region on the Dong River. Compared to more polluted PRD cities it seems sparklingly modern, its evening lights reflected to enchanting effect in the still waters of **West Lake** (西湖; Xihu), but it has a long history dating back to Song times. The flagstone causeway across the lake was laid in 1096 with the sponsorship of Su Dongpo, a Song-dynasty poet who spent three years in exile governing Huizhou, and who is remembered in many spots around town.

West Lake is in fact five lakes connected by bridges and dotted with islands and pavilions. The main entrance lies across the road from the Xihu Hotel on Huancheng Xilu, and leads directly onto the famous causeway. On the far side stands the octagonal **Sizhou Pagoda**, built in 1618 to replace a Tang-dynasty tower – an elegant outline both night and day. On the same hill is a small museum of items associated with Su Dongpo, and close by lies the tomb of Wang Zhaoyun, the only one of Su's concubines loyal enough to follow him to Huizhou.

At the foot of the hill, the Underground City is a subterranean maze of creepily lit chambers holding animated tableaux of Chinese legends, bound to terrify children.

Opposite, a zigzag bridge stretches across the lake to islets in the middle and then to an old nunnery on the north side. Bearing right here, you can follow the shore back to the Xihu Hotel, passing the pedestrianised Zhongshan Xilu on the way.

North of the bus station on Eling Beilu, **Fei'e Park** occupies a hill which functioned as a defensive position for Huizhou's now-vanished old town. An artillery emplacement was constructed during the Eastern Expedition of 1925, the remains of which can be found on the brow of the hill, and an old People's Liberation Army fighter plane continues the military theme.

## Foshan and Nanhai

**Foshan** ❾ （佛山）, a dusty centre of ceramic production around 20 km (12 miles) southwest of Guangzhou, draws its main spiritual guidance from the 1,000-year-old **Zu Miao temple complex** (祖庙; 21 Zumiao Lu; open daily 8.30am–7.30pm; entrance fee), which centres around a 15th-century bronze statue of Beidi, the Daoist god of water. This well-preserved temple, surrounded by an elevated garden, dates back to the Song Dynasty and is packed with finely carved friezes depicting the key fables of Foshan's history. The temple has long served as a protection against the flooding of the Zhu Jiang (Pearl River): look out for carvings of turtles and snakes, thought to ward off the floodwaters. The magnificent glazed roof tiles were a 19th-century addition. The surrounding courtyards and halls display antique weapons, iron bells, porcelain figures and a series of stone-carved street markers from the Qing Dynasty.

Kung Fu fans will be aware that grand master Huang Fei-Hong was born in Foshan, but souvenir-seekers will probably head for the **Shiwan** ❿ （石湾） area, where the **Nanfeng Ancient Kiln** （南风古灶; Nanfeng Guzao; 6 Gaomiao Lu; open daily 8am–6pm; entrance fee) turns humble clay into some very attractive pottery. Dating from the Ming era, the kilns have reportedly never gone out, and the four-day firing process is explained by way of a series of English signs.

The city of **Nanhai** ⓫ （南海） lies within Foshan's orbit, though the inhabitants like to brag about the settlement's past as a pioneering centre of Chinese maritime trade. Excavations have revealed that merchants of the Qin and Han dynasties used the area as a launching point for seaborne traffic, which eventually replaced the Silk Route in importance. The city is also home to the ancient Nanhai Temple, built 1,400 years ago.

Nanhai lies within a less densely industrialised area and an interesting backdrop to its mix of factories and fields is the wooded slopes of **Lianhua Shan** ⓬. The cable-car is open intermittently, but you can walk to the top of the hill in half an hour or so to view the contradictions of the landscape and visit a 17th-century pagoda and a bronze statue of Guanyin, the goddess of mercy; at 41 metres (135 ft) tall the largest such statue in the world. The mountain was quarried 2,000 years ago, though the stone edges have now eroded and regained a natural appearance.

To the west is the town of Nancun with the gardens of **Yuying Shanfang** ⓭ （余荫山房; open daily 8am–5.30pm; entrance fee). Created by a wealthy Qing-

*Ceremony at the well preserved Zu Miao ancestral temple in Foshan.*

**BELOW:** Huizhou's West Lake.

dynasty scholar, they remain an attractive and peaceful spot.

## South to Zhuhai

Leaving gritty air behind as you travel south through more rural countryside towards Zhuhai and Macau, **Shunde**  (顺德) is home to the renowned **Qinghui Garden** (清晖园; Qinghui Yuan; open daily 8am–5.30pm; entrance fee). The gardens display all the features of a classical Chinese courtyard garden, with a series of fish ponds, kiosks, bamboo groves and fanciful engravings. As famous as the gardens themselves is the Qinghui Yuan restaurant, situated within the gardens and serving classical Cantonese cuisine.

Shunde is cashing in on its tentative associations with Bruce Lee: construction has begun on an extravagant theme park in honour of the martial arts legend. Lee's grandfather emigrated from Shunde in the late 19th century, and Bruce Lee himself spent a day or two here at the age of five – excuse enough for a dedicated theme park. Shunde is also the ancestral home of Stanley Ho, the Macau casino kingpin who made bil-

*Classical Chinese gateway at the Zu Miao temple, Foshan.*

**BELOW:** ceramics for sale at Shiwan.

lions from a decades-long monopoly of the enclave's gambling trade, just a few miles down the river.

**Zhongshan** ⑮ (中山) is one of the more attractive cities in the region, largely thanks to its central pedestrianised shopping street, Sunwen Xilu, whose construction was funded by wealthy emigrants in the early 20th century. At No. 152, the **Commercial Culture Museum** (商业文化博物馆; Shangye Wenhua Bowuguan; open daily 9am–5pm; entrance fee), housed in an elegant three-storey building that was once the chamber of commerce, is well interpreted and relates the stories of more than a few local lads who made good. A stroll along Sunwen is one of the most enjoyable pastimes in Zhongshan, a city favoured by Hong Kongers as a weekend retreat. The street is lined with twin colonnades, painted in a variety of pastels and housing various shops and boutiques staffed by lively youngsters whose enthusiasm is infectious – although they are mainly selling cheap fashion items and kitschy souvenirs. The street is backed by Zhongshan Park, which is topped by the 400-year-old Fufeng Cultural Pagoda.

The village of **Cuiheng** ⓰ (翠亨村), where Sun Yatsen was born in 1866, lies to the southeast of Zhongshan. The man most frequently described as the Father of Modern China spent only part of his childhood here, and the original house was demolished in 1913. However, it has since been reconstructed and turned into the **Dr Sun Yatsen Residence Memorial Museum** (孙中山故居; Sun Zhongshan Guju; Cuiheng Dadao; open daily, 9am–5pm; entrance fee), standing as a suitable testament to his life as well as an illuminating illustration of rural existence in pre-revolutionary days.

Continue southwards to reach **Zhuhai** ⓱ (珠海) on the border with Macau, a Special Economic Zone in its own right – albeit one which has not progressed quite as fast as Shenzhen. It's chiefly noticeable for its parks; Haibin is set by the waterfront, while Jingshan includes the boulder-dotted Paradise Hill, best scaled via cable-car. If the weather's dodgy, you can always pop into the **Zhuhai City Museum** (珠海市博物馆; Zhuhaishi Bowuguan; 191 Jingshan Lu; open daily 9am–5pm; entrance fee), some of whose exhibits date back 5,000 years.

Zhuhai is popular with Hongkongers for its hot spring resorts – these lie west of the city, and weekend breaks can be booked directly with Hong Kong travel agents.

## Wanshan Archipelago

The **Wanshan Islands** ⓲ (万山群岛; Wanshan Qundao) extend from the mouth of the Pearl River estuary far to the south of Hong Kong, giving Zhuhai, from where they are accessed, reasonable cause to call itself "the city of islands". There are more than 130 isles in all, but only five are easily reached by ferry. Departure point is the Xiangzhou (Heung Chau) pier at the northern tip of Zhuhai.

**Dongao Island** (东澳岛) is the pick of the bunch, with decent beaches, offshore coral and villa accommodation. The ferry from Zhuhai (departs 9.45am) calls in on its way to **Wanshan Town** (万山镇), the main hub of the archipelago. Beyond somewhat desolate **Guishan Island** (桂山岛) (ferry departs 8.40am) the ferry proceeds to rocky **Wailingding Island** (外伶仃岛), a locally popular resort from which the southern shores of Hong Kong are visible. ❏

*Guishan Island in the Wanshan archipelago is a major port for Chinese shipping.*

**BELOW:** Zhuhai's Lianhua Lu pedestrian street at Chinese New Year.

# RESTAURANTS & BARS IN SHENZHEN

## Restaurants

Average price for a meal for one, with one drink:

**$** under US$12 (under Rmb 100)
**$$** US$12–20 (Rmb 100–160)
**$$$** over US$20 (over Rmb 160)

Shenzhen has a wide range of restaurants, a result of its status as an international businesss centre. Regional Chinese cuisines are especially well represented here. There are numerous options in all price ranges, from extremely cheap canteens and street food to upmarket (but still affordable) hotel restaurants. The Downtown area around Jianshe/Shennan Lu and Heping Lu is well supplied, as is Luohu. Futian District's shopping area further west has plenty more and also numerous bars (try International Bar Street). Luohu and Shekou are the other main nightlife areas.

### Cantonese
#### Phoenix House
2/F The Pavilion Hotel, 4002 Huaqiang Donglu, Futian. Tel: 0755 8207 8888. **$$$**
Hankering for dim sum? This is the place, very Hong Kong and with a very good ambience. Book one of the 30 VIP rooms for a (relatively) quiet meal.

### Beijing
#### Gou Bu Li
Lo Wu Building, Jianshe Lu, Lo Wu. Tel: 0755 8223 9325. **$$$**
Beijing duck is the obvious choice, but other northern fare – in particular the dumplings – are equally good.

### Hakka
#### Hakka King
14 Zhenhua Lu. Tel: 0775 8336 0892. **$$**
Freshly-made tofu and sausages top the varied menu at this very traditional and amenable Hakka eatery.

### Seafood (Chinese)
#### Fenghuang Zhanjiang Fishing Village Wineshop
Xiyuan Hotel, Dongmen Nanlu. Tel: 0755 8217 7328. **$$$**
Daily fresh and very extensive selection of crab, lobster and just about every other sort of seafood.

### Sichuanese
#### Lao Yuan
2/F Qiche Building, intersection of Zhenhua and Yan'an rds. Tel: 0755 8332 8400. **$$**
Super-spicy, and a touch of theatre, too, as the trad-garbed waiters wield long-necked teapots. A must for fans of chilli.

### Yunnanese
#### Yunnan Guoqiao Rice Noodle
F/1 Xianggui Building, Xiangxi Lu. Tel: 0755 8239 6175. **$**

Oodles of noodles and other Yunnanese favourites are dished up in a regionally traditional wooden house. Often filled with migrant workers homesick for home cooking.

### French
#### The Paris Restaurant
57–58 Sea World Shekou, Nanshan. Tel: 0755 2683 9629. **$$$**
Kitchen, cellar and ambience may not quite add up to the City of Light, but it's pretty close; great for a date or celebration.

### Indian
#### Spice Circle
Tianjun Mansion, Dongmen Nanlu. Tel: 0755 8220 2129. **$$$**
Having imported chefs from India, Spice Circle provides not only excellent fare but an imaginative drinks list, too.

#### Taj Indian Restaurant
G/F Lianhua Building, Renmin Nanlu. Tel: 0755 8236 2782. **$$**
A praiseworthy selection of dishes spicy and less so from across the Sub-continent, tastily served with style.

### International
#### 360 at the Shangri-La
Shangri-La Hotel, Jianshe Lu, Luohu. Tel: 0755 8396 1380. **$$$**
The views are top-notch, ditto for the

cuisine, to say nothing of the wine list and décor at this world-class fine-dining venue.

### Italian
#### Polo
5F MOI World Finance Center, Shennan Donglu. Tel: 0755 2598 0981. **$$$**
While essentially Italian (pizza, pasta, etc), Polo also does some good burgers and ribs. Free Internet access too.

#### Prego Italian Restaurant
2/F 3018 Nanhu Lu, Landmark Hotel, Luohu. Tel: 0755 8217 2288. **$$$**
The catering at Shenzhen's hotels is usually pretty up to par, and nowhere more so than in this relaxing and fulfilling Italian joint.

### Japanese
#### Kada
2/F The Pavilion Hotel, 4002 Huaqiang Beilu, Futian. Tel: 0755 8207 8888. **$$$**
The seafood is jet-fresh, and so is the ambience at this calming and traditional corner of Japanese cuisine.

#### Tairyo Teppanyaki Restaurant
2/F Fumin Jiayuan, Fumin Lu, Futian. Tel: 0755 8830 7658. **$$**
Delicious (the steaks in particular), and deliciously inexpensive. Fast catching on as a hip place to dine.

### Korean
#### Sorabol
4/F Citic City Plaza, 1093
Shennan Zhonglu, Futian.
Tel: 0755 2598 8822. **$$**
Kimchi doesn't come
spicier, nor *bulgogi*
tastier, than in this
tribute to the cuisine
of the Land of the
Morning Calm.

### Mexican
#### Amigos
G/F E06, Carriana Friendship
Center, Renmin Nanlu, Luohu.
Tel: 0755 8422 0052. **$$**
Following the success
of its Shekou outlet,
Amigos is now open in
Lo Wu: an accomplished
(if Chinese) take on
Mexican cuisine.

### Vegetarian
#### Dengpin
3/F Jun Ting Ming Yuan,
Bao'an Nanlu, Luohu.
Tel: 0755 2590 8588. **$**
Something of a rarity in
carnivorous Shenzhen:
excellent range of vege-
tarian dishes, and
extremely well priced.

### Turkish
#### Mr Kebab
Building 14, 105 Jinghua-
dayuan, Huafa Beilu, Futian.
Tel: 0755 8320 6465. **$$**
Kebabs, kebabs and
more kebabs, well priced
and done to a turn.

## Bars

#### Bear Paradise
07–08 Central Square, Sea
World, Shekou. Tel: 01324
291 2500 (mobile phone).
A very creditable

attempt to ensure that
nobody should want for
good ales from around
the world. Matey staff
round things off.

#### Capital Bar
G33B Boulevard East Pacific
Garden, Agricultural &
Science Park, Futian.
Tel: 0755 8313 6861.
Very hip, and very
much the place to get
in as far as Shenzhen
cognoscenti are con-
cerned.

#### Captain's Club Wine and Cigar Bar
Minghua Boat, Sea World
Square, Taizi Lu, Shekou.
Shenzen's new-found
love affair with grape
and leaf meets its full
measure here, amid a
slightly irrational naut-
ical theme. Plenty of
whiskies, too.

#### Class Club
5th Floor Century Plaza
Hotel, 1 Chun Feng Lu,
Luohu. Tel: 0755 8236 3999.
www.classclubsz.com
It's certainly classy for
Shenzhen, with state-
of-the-art hi-tech stuff
and well-known inter-
national DJs spinning
all hours of the night.

#### Coko Club
Shenzhen International Bar
Street, Zhongxin Citic Plaza,
Shennan Zhonglu, Futian.
Tel: 0755 2598 9998.
The largest of the estab-
lishments on Bar Street,
which benefits from a
lively office crowd who
call in on the way home.

#### Demon
Block C, Citic Plaza, Futian.
Tel: 0755 2598 9118.
One of two bars of the
same name (the other
is in the COCO Park
Shopping Mall),
Demon's outside seat-
ing makes it a popular
choice when good
weather puts in an
appearance.

#### Eye's
Ying Chun Lu, Luohu.
Tel: 0755 8236 8398.
The Eye's have it. Great
for a quiet drink with
a bunch of friends:
excellent cocktails and
friendly service.

#### The French Kiss Club
57–58 Sea World, Shekou.
Tel: 0755 2683 9629.
One of the area's better
nightclubs, popular with
the trendy set, which
lives up to its name
most evenings.

#### Ibiza
1024 Huafu Lu. Tel: 0755
8326 6996.
If it's not quite as wild
as its island namesake,
it's still loads of fun.

#### In Club
King Glory Plaza, Renmin
Nanlu, Luohu. Tel: 0755
8261 1111.
Having taken on a new
lease of life with a
change of manage-

ment, the In – famous
for its drinks specials –
is very much on the
party people's circuit.

#### Lace Club
G/F 114 Citic City Plaza.
Tel: 0755 8212 0022.
Innovative design,
rather than just another
copy-cat Shenzhen
watering hole. Bag a
VIP booth if you want
some privacy.

#### Soho
Bitao Club, Taizi Lu, Shekou.
Tel: 0755 2669 0148.
An outdoor garden pro-
vides a measure of
relief from the top vol-
umes within, but there's
no doubting that this is
one of the best places
to kick up your heels.

#### Sugar
Fuhua 3 Lu, Coco Park L3,
Luohu. Tel: 0755 8290 3234.
As sweet as might be
imagined. Handy
location and top spins
from a very cool DJ.

#### V Bar
Crowne Plaza Shenzhen,
9026 Shennan Dadao,
Overseas Chinese Town.
Tel: 86 755 2693 6888.
A crescent-shaped
stage draws everyone
into the action, at this
pricey yet smart joint
that's a cut above the
rest of Shenzhen.

**RIGHT:** Shenzhen has a lively nightlife scene.

# GUANGZHOU

Echoes of old Canton can still be traced in Guangzhou, a city with an independent streak and a long history of economic development

**B**uy it. Sell it. Trade it. Lend it. For centuries **Guangzhou ❶** (广州), formerly known to Westerners as Canton, has been synonymous with commerce, and for many years it was – by imperial decree – the country's only international port. While the city has since been overtaken, first by Hong Kong, more recently by Shanghai, it retains a strong presence on the global stage, not least because of its best-known export, the cuisine universally dubbed Cantonese. Guangzhou's character is markedly independent, and its plain-speaking citizens make no bones about their hometown pride and the machinations of big government further to the north.

## The historical background

Guangzhou was most likely founded in 214 BC as an encampment by the armies of the Qin Emperor, Qin Shi Huangdi (r. 221–210 BC). At first the town was called Panyu; the name Guangzhou first appeared during the period of the Three Kingdoms (AD 220–265). During the Tang Dynasty (618–906), the city was already an international port, but ranked behind Quanzhou to the east. After the overthrow of the Ming Dynasty by the Manchu (Qing) in 1644, nationalist ideas survived longer here than in other parts of China, although at the same time, close contact with Overseas Chinese *(Huaqiao)* ensured the continuation of an openness to the world and a desire for reform in the city.

From 1757 until1842, Guangzhou held a trade monopoly in China, as it was the only Chinese port open to foreigners (the Portuguese had been a presence in the area since the 16th century, and had been followed by the Dutch and British). Traders – many of whom dealt in opium – were obliged to cooperate contractually with Chinese merchant guilds, an arrangement that eventually planted the seeds for the subsequent *comprador* bourgeoisie. Later, matters came to a head in the 19th-century furore with the British over the opium trade, which resulted in the First

**Main attractions**
SHAMIAN ISLAND
PEARL RIVER CRUISE
TEMPLE OF THE SIX
   BANYAN TREES
CHEN FAMILY TEMPLE
SUN YATSEN MEMORIAL HALL
YUEXIU PARK
GUANGZHOU MUSEUM OF ART
WHITE CLOUD HILLS

**LEFT:** view from the Temple of the Six Banyan Trees.
**BELOW:** the butterfly dance greets visitors.

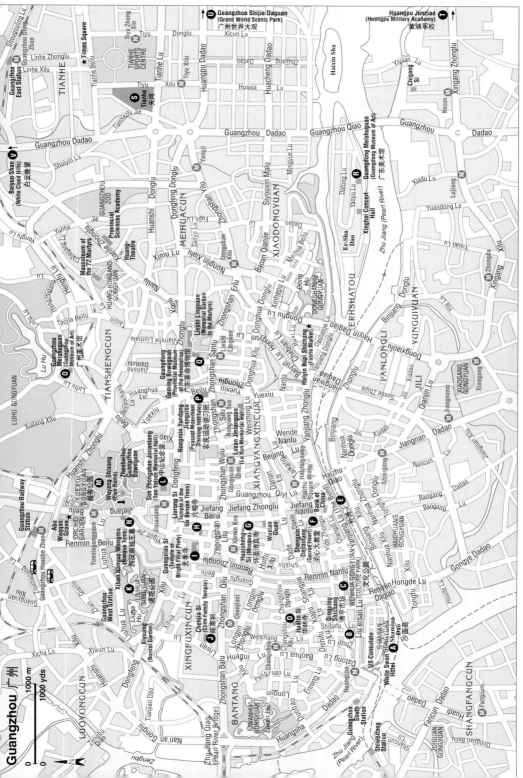

Guangzhou / 广州

Opium War (1840–42). This resulted in the city – together with Xiamen and Fuzhou in Fujian, and Ningbo and Shanghai further north – being formally opened to foreign trade.

Following the overthrow of the Qing in 1912, Guangzhou became the centre of a movement led by Sun Yatsen and the headquarters of the Guomintang, or Nationalist Party, the first modern political party in China. During a rather brief period of cooperation between the Guomintang and the communists, Mao Zedong worked and taught at Guangzhou's Institute of Peasant Movements, and Zhou Enlai and Lin Biao at the Military Academy.

The city was occupied by the Japanese during World War II, followed by the Guomintang for a few brief years before the PLA arrived in 1949. Mao then earmarked Guangzhou as China's principal industrial centre and international port. While the rest of China was isolated from the world, Guangzhou did business with the West at the biennial Canton Fair, which runs to this day. In the post-Mao era, the city has remained a centre for business and trade: it is still one of the richest cities in China and continues to expand – if not at the same frenetic pace as some of its neighbouring cities.

Around 6 million people live in the main urban area, with a total of over 12 million in the sprawling conurbation as a whole. The population has swelled rapidly in the past two decades with the large numbers of migrants who come to the city in search of work.

## Old Guangzhou

**Shamian Island Ⓐ** (沙面岛; Shamian Dao) is without any doubt the city's most picturesque area. It is connected to the rest of Guangzhou by several bridges, and its avenues, colonial buildings and open spaces exude an air of brisk gentility.

Rather than feeling like an artificial enclave for tourists, Shamian is a thriving community, with century-old mansions forming an attractive backdrop, and antique cannons pointing out over the river as a reminder of more turbulent

times. The more significant buildings sport plaques outlining their antecedents, while statues are dotted about depicting rickshaw pullers, tradesmen and – rather daringly – a trio of women from down the ages, the most recent of whom wears tight shorts and gabbles on her mobile phone.

Originally a sandbar, Shamian was reclaimed from the river in 1842 and subsequently expanded and divided in 1859 into several foreign concessions, primarily French and British. (The previous year, the Chinese had limited foreign traders' base of operations in the city to Shamian – although this was a short-term arrangement: after the Second Opium War (1856–60), foreigners settled in other parts of the city and continued trading.) A canal was built, and two iron gates and narrow bridges served to keep the Chinese off the island after ten o'clock every evening.

The most significant change to the island in recent years was the construction of the multi-storey White Swan Hotel in 1983. However, despite its architecture being sharply at odds with its surroundings, its presence scarcely affects Shamian's true character. **Shamian Park**

*A Pearl River cruise is a pleasant way to see the city, particularly at night.*

**BELOW:** colonial architecture on Shamian Island.

*Scorpion kebabs at a street stall. Guangzhou is as good a place as anywhere to sample some of China's more outlandish delicacies.*

**BELOW RIGHT:**
Guangzhou's riverside buildings are imaginatively illuminated at night.

(沙面公园; Shamian Gongyuan), a few steps from the White Swan, is chock-a-block with people most hours of the day, performing t'ai chi, ballroom dancing, kicking feathered quoits back and forth, playing mah-jong, breast-feeding babies and generally revelling in their own mini-island resort. Schoolchildren pour forth at break time to disport themselves in Friendship Square, more or less in the centre of the island, and the tennis club next to the park resounds to the gentle ricochet of well-served balls.

Hardly a shopping Mecca, Shamian's retail options include a few oddities like a tyre warehouse, some wedding boutiques and a clutch of souvenir shops nearby the White Swan. Most of these include baby clothes and pushchairs among their stock, marketed at the many Americans who come here to adopt, basing themselves near the US Consulate at the western end of the island, and providing an unintentionally ironic endnote to foreign occupation of Shamian.

### Qingping to Haizhu Bridge

On the mainland immediately to the north of Shamian Island is **Qingping Market** **Ⓑ** (清平市场; Qingping Shichang; open daily 8am–6pm), a large, noisy enterprise that has spilled into the side streets around Renmin Nanlu and Nuren Jie. This is one of the first parts of the city to develop under China's gradual adoption of market economics, and, as such, it was for a long time something of a rarity in China, with its carnival-like atmosphere and crowds of shoppers. Ironically, the market's name translates as "peaceful". Nowadays, Qingping is best-known for the wide range of meats on its market stalls, from dogs and cats, to owls and insects – although the authorities intervene from time to time to protect endangered species. For jade, jewellery, old timepieces, Mao paraphernalia and reproductions of antique porcelain, head for the stalls lining Dishipu Lu and Daihe Lu.

East of the market, at the end of Liu'ersan Lu, is **Culture Park** **Ⓒ** (文化公园; Wenhua Gongyuan), where an open-air theatre and separate theatre halls host performances by the School of Acrobats. There are regular art exhibitions here, too, as well as roller-skating rinks. Nearby, on the corner of Renmin Nan Lu, is the state-run Department

## Cruising the Pearl River

Like many Chinese cities, Guangzhou is pervasively grey and drab. The fact is, it looks better by night: after dusk the construction crews go home, the neon comes out to play, and the roar of the city traffic subsides somewhat. The best way to appreciate all this is aboard one of the gentle river cruises, which depart from the Tianzi Pier on the north bank, between Haizhu and Jiangwan bridges. Cruises generally last 90 minutes, with the option of dining aboard, though the buffet fare is hardly gourmet, and you should aim for the front of the surging queue.

The usual route is to sail as far as the Liede Bridge, past the Guangdong Museum of Art and Concert Hall, and then to double back to where the Pearl River divides at Shamian before returning to the starting point. All the bridges along the way, and many of the skyscrapers on either bank, are imaginatively festooned with lighting displays, and the prolix-taped commentary will be happily unintelligible to non-Putonghua speakers. Chinese travellers equipped with the latest in digital-camera technology usually outnumber foreign visitors, and the former's patent enthusiasm for all they behold is half the fun of the trip. Miss out on this and you neglect one of the best aspects of Guangzhou. The Guangzhou Passenger Ship Company (tel: 020 8333 0397) operates several cruises each evening; buy tickets at Tianzi Pier.

## CITY TRANSPORT

Getting about the city is easier than it used to be. The **metro system** (www.gzmtr.com/en/) is extensive, with four lines and more under construction (one of which will extend south to Foshan), and the network connects most of Guangzhou's sites of interest. Trains are spotlessly clean and run every few minutes from 6am to midnight. Tickets (actually a disc which is inserted in the turnstile) cost from Rmb 2, and stored-value cards are an option. Stations are marked by red signs with a split Y symbol, and signage and ticket machines are bilingual – which is more than can be said for the city's cab drivers. That said, **taxis** do fill in the gaps that the metro has yet to reach; ask your concierge to write your destination in Chinese. All cabs have meters. The **bus** network is comprehensive, but slow and crowded. There are fewer **bicycles** these days, but this can still be a good way of getting about – bike hire is available at a few places on Shamian Island.

Store of the South (sometimes called Nanfang Department Store), which still lags behind the city's newer malls, despite making a determined effort to bridge the gap.

Around 1 km (⅔ mile) north of the Culture Park run the parallel streets of Xiajiu Lu and Changshou Lu, which together form the centre of a lively shopping and dining area. If you head down Shangxia Jie, a narrow side alley behind the Guangdong Restaurant, you'll come across **Hualin Temple ⓓ** (华林寺). Although the existing buildings date from the Qing Dynasty, the temple is said to have been founded by an Indian monk in 526. In the main hall, 500 statues of *luohan* – pupils of the Buddha – are the object of veneration for many residents.

East of Shamian, **The Bund ⓔ** (外滩; Yanjiang Lu) runs alongside the Pearl River (Zhu Jiang) as far as **Haizhu Bridge** (海珠桥; Haizhu Qiao), built in 1933. The Bund might not be quite as attractive as its more famous namesake in Shanghai, but it is a good place to take the pulse of the city. All day long it is populated by tourists from out of town, families taking the air, itinerant peddlers and mendicants, as well as office workers

*The forecourt of Guangzhou's Central Railway Station is a ceaseless maelstrom of human activity.*

**BELOW:** the Pearl River runs through the heart of the city.

**BELOW:** looking down on the Temple of the Six Banyan Trees from the Flower Pagoda.

taking a break from their drab routine. By night it assumes a more alluring character, when the main skyscrapers are floodlit, the traffic on the river takes on a vaguely ghostly air, and there are fewer pedestrians about to impede your progress.

Face northwest on Haizhu Bridge and you'll spot the **Sacred Heart Cathedral** **F** (圣心大教堂; Shengxin Dajiaotang), its double 50-metre (160-ft) towers plainly visible beyond Haizhu Square. Built from granite in neo-Gothic style, the cathedral was completed in 1888, but left to decay before being neatly restored in the 1980s. It now holds services under the auspices of the Patriotic Catholic Church, which the government has prohibited from contacting the Vatican.

## Temples near Zhongshan Lu

There are a cluster of historic buildings around **Zhongshan Lu**, the main east-west thoroughfare in central Guangzhou. Directly north of the Sacred Heart Cathedral is an older place of worship, **Huaisheng Mosque** **G** (怀圣清真寺), dating back to AD 627 and founded by a trader who was reputed to be an uncle of the Prophet Mohammed. Arab traders

were frequent visitors to China at the time, so the legend may well have some truth to this. The 25-metre (82-ft) minaret which towers above the mosque's onion-shaped dome is called the **Naked Pagoda** (Guang Ta) and dominates the area, although ever-increasing numbers of high-rises are competing to capture the skyline. Huaisheng Si is a cultural centre for Guangzhou's substantial Muslim community.

A narrow street north of Zhongshan Lu leads to the **Temple of the Six Banyan Trees** **H** (六榕寺; Liurong Si; open daily 8.30am–5pm; entrance fee), with its **Flower Pagoda** (Hua Ta), built in 1097. From the outside, the pagoda appears to have nine storeys, each with doorways and encircling balcony, but there are actually 17 levels. Visitors can climb to the top for a bird's-eye view of Guangzhou's sprawling streets. The main hall contains three brass statues of the Buddha, eight *luohan* figures, statues of the god of medicine, and an image cast in 1663 of the goddess of mercy, Guanyin. Today, the temple is the local headquarters of the Chinese Buddhist Association. The trees which gave the

emple its name are, needless to say, no onger in evidence.

A short distance to the west lies the **Temple of Bright Filial Piety** ❶ (光孝寺; Guangxiao Si; open daily 8.30am–5pm; entrance fee), preserved during the Cultural Revolution on orders from Premier Zhou Enlai. In all probability, the temple is older than the city itself, dating back to around AD 400. Parts of the complex were rebuilt after a fire in 1629, and then further expanded in the 19th century. The entrance is marked by a brightly painted laughing Buddha, and in the main courtyard a huge bronze incense burner fills the air with smoke. The ceiling in the main hall is distinctive for its red-lacquered timber, while the **Western and Eastern Iron Pagodas** (Dongtie Ta and Xitie Ta) in the rear courtyard are two of the oldest iron pagodas in China. Behind the main hall stands a 7-metre (23-ft) stone pagoda with sculptures of the Buddha placed in eight niches. It is thought to have been built in 967, and was moved to its present location at the beginning of Mongolian rule in the Yuan dynasty.

Further west, off Zhongshan Lu, and close to the subway station of the same name, is the **Chen Family Temple** ❿ (陈家祠; Chenjia Si; open daily 8.30am–5.30pm; entrance fee), one of China's more whimsical temples, built in 1894 and restored after the Cultural Revolution. The temple has six courtyards and a classical Chinese layout, and is decorated with friezes crafted in Shiwan, near Foshan *(see page 161)*. The largest frieze depicts scenes from the epic Romance of Three Kingdoms, with thousands of intricate figures against a backdrop of ornate houses, grandiose gates and pagodas. There is a giant altar of gold-leaf plating and additional wood, brick and stone friezes along the rooftops. The temple was named after descendants of the Chen clan, who funded its construction. Chen is one of the commonest clan names in Guangdong province.

A few hundred metres north on Liuhua Lu is green **Liuhua Park** ❿ (流花公园;

Liuhua Gongyuan), featuring a series of expansive artificial lakes built as part of the government's Great Leap Forward Campaign in 1958. Rowing boats can be hired.

## Remembering Sun Yatsen

Although economics rather than politics hold sway nowadays, Guangzhou was a hotbed of Chinese nationalism during the early 20th century, in part due to its exposure to the outside world. Dr Sun Yatsen, considered the founding father of contemporary China, was born nearby *(see page 34)*. The **Sun Yatsen Memorial Hall** ❿ (中山纪念堂; Sun Zhongshan Jiniantang; open daily 8am–6pm; entrance fee) is easy to spot with its eye-catching blue roof tiles. Work began shortly after Sun's untimely death in 1925 and was completed in 1931. The hall sits in a lush 6-hectare (15-acre) park and houses a large theatre and lecture hall with seating for 5,000 people.

On a hill above the Memorial Hall, within Yuexiu Park *(see following page)*, is the marble-and-granite **Sun Yatsen Monument**. Visitors can climb to the top for a great view of the city.

*Fierce-looking temple guardian at the Temple of Bright Filial Piety.*

**BELOW:** calligraphy on an incense burner.

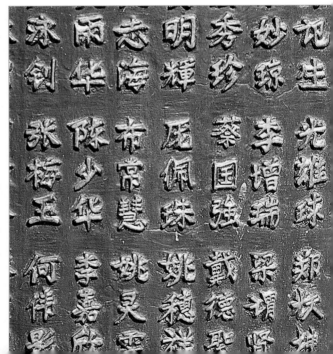

*The impressive Tower Overlooking the Sea is the centrepiece of pleasant Yuexiu Park.*

**BELOW:** fishmonger at Qingping Market.

## Around Yuexiu Park

**Yuexiu Park** (越秀公园; Yuexiu Gongyuan) is Guangzhou's largest and most attractive open space, skilfully landscaped with three artificial lakes, rolling hills, rock sculptures and lush greenery. Its centrepiece is the **Tower Overlooking the Sea** (镇海楼; Zhenhailou), built in 1380 as a watchtower and forming part of the long-disappeared city walls. Today it houses a **municipal museum** (open Tues–Sun 9am–4pm; entrance fee), which displays an assortment of archaeological finds and documents showcasing the history of the city. The park also contains a golf driving range, bowling alley and swimming pool. Look out, too, for the **Sculpture of Five Rams**, the symbol of Guangzhou (the five heavenly creatures are said to have flown over the city and relieved the people of famine).

Just west of the Sculpture of Five Rams, across the road from the park on Jiefang Beilu, is the fascinating **Nanyue Tomb** (西汉南越王墓; Xihan Nanyue Wangmu; open daily 9.30am–5pm; entrance fee), the resting place of the Emperor Wen Di, who ruled southern China from 137 to 122 BC. The tomb was discovered in 1983 when bulldozers were clearing the site for construction of a hotel. The site is now a **museum** housing the treasures found in the tomb, along with the remains of the emperor himself and 15 of his courtiers – including concubines, guards, cooks and a musician – all of whom were buried alive with the emperor. The museum recreates the original setting of the tomb, and visitors can walk down into the chambers. Thousands of funerary objects, from jade armour to bronze music chimes, are displayed in adjoining rooms. The museum also features a rare collection of porcelain from Tang and Yuan times.

East of Yuexiu Park, on the edge of Luhu Park, is the **Guangzhou Museum of Art** (广州美术馆; Guangzhou Meishuguan; 13 Luhu Lu; open Tues–Fri 9am–5pm, Sat & Sun 9.30am–4.30pm; entrance fee), not to be confused with the Guangdong Museum of Art (*see page 176*). It houses an impressive collection of ancient and contemporary art and sculpture (including genuine terracotta warriors from Xi'an). There is a special section devoted to a body of work by the political cartoonist Liao Bing Xiong, who

was sent into exile in 1958. A frank admission of some of the upheavals that characterised China in the 20th century is very much a departure from the norm, at least as far as officialdom is concerned. Nearby Luhu Lake, lined with cooling trees, is a nice place for a stroll.

To the north, there's a chance to take in the new face of Guangzhou. Construction being the city's leitmotif, new buildings and glittering malls are springing up everywhere. The **GITIC Plaza Arcade** on Huanshi Dong Lu (not to be confused with the 80-storey CITIC Building in Tianhe district) is typical of the breed that are rising above the city streets, with smart boutiques, sparkling window displays, self-important security guards, packs of teenagers and plenty of others flexing their gold credit cards.

## Revolutionary reminders

Yuexiu Lu, the busy S-shaped street which runs from Yuexiu Park down towards the river, forms the approximate eastern boundary of the older part of the city. Halfway along is the former Kongzi Miao, or Confucius Temple, which lost its religious function during the "bour-

geois revolution" in 1912. Twelve years later the **Peasant Movement Training Institute P** (农民运动讲习所; Nongmin Yundong Jiangxisuo; open daily 8.30–11.30am, 2–5pm; entrance fee) was opened here as the first school of the Chinese Communist Party. The elite of the Communist Party taught here: Mao Zedong (his work and bedroom are on show), Zhou Enlai, Qu Qiubai, Deng Zhong, Guo Moruo and several others. It was here that Mao developed his original theory of peasant revolution.

In 1927 a workers' uprising in Guangzhou was stamped out by Nationalist forces, who slaughtered all those involved. A park and memorial, the **Memorial Garden to the Martyrs** (烈士陵园; Lieshi Lingyuan) was created in 1957 in memory of the uprising and its nearly 6,000 victims. Nearby is the **Provincial Museum of the Revolution Q** (广东革命博物馆; Guangdong Geming Bowuguan; open daily 9am–5pm), a reminder of the role of the Guomintang (Nationalist Party) and its predecessors since the First Opium War.

Lu Xun, considered China's first modern author, is remembered at the **Lu Xun**

*Guangzhou has a subtropical climate. The Tropic of Cancer runs just to the north of the city, and for a few days in June and July, the sun lies directly overhead. During the hot summer months, daily afternoon showers are typical. Winters are mild but often grey.*

**BELOW:** a shady path at Yuexiu Park.

*The outdoor sculpture garden at the Guangdong Museum of Art.*

**BELOW:** one of the city's large nightclubs.

Memorial Hall (鲁迅纪念馆; Luxun Jinianguan; open daily 9am–5pm; entrance fee), set in the old buildings of Guangdong University, south of Zhongshan San Lu, where he lectured in 1927.

## The eastern waterfront

Northwest of the Hai Yin bridge is the **Hai Yin Fabric Market** (海印布匹市场; Haiyin Bupi Shichang) on Donghu Lu, where more than a thousand stalls in hundreds of rows sell wool, fine silk and locally made textiles at bargain prices. It's one of the largest fabric markets in China.

East of the bridge on Er-sha Island is the **Guangdong Museum of Art** **R** (广东美术馆; Guangdong Meishuguan; 38 Yanyu Road; open Tues–Sun, 9am–5pm; entrance fee). Its dozen exhibition halls display some of the more avant garde examples of Chinese art, with frequent exhibitions of work by local students as well as special events celebrating artists from overseas. There is also an outdoor sculpture area.

## Eastern suburbs

Northeast of central Guangzhou, near the zoo on Xianlie Lu, is the **Huang Huagang**

**Memorial Park** (黄花岗公园; Huang Huagang Gongyuan), built in 1918 in memory of the 72 victims of an uprising in 1911. The large park features monuments symbolising democracy and peace.

Further east lies Guangzhou's most prominent financial and shopping centre, **Tianhe** **S** (天河). The giant sports centre here takes up several city blocks with basketball courts, Olympic-size swimming pools, running tracks and football pitches. Across the street is Team Plaza, a six-storey shopping mall with a Japanese department store on the bottom level and expensive shops spiralling upward. Just north of the stadium is Times Square; it doesn't really compare to its namesake in New York or even Hong Kong, but there are some good restaurants inside.

Deep in the eastern suburbs, **Huangpu Military Academy** **T** (黄埔军校; Huangpu Junxiao; open Tues–Sun 9am–5pm; entrance fee) was established by Sun Yatsen. Zhou Enlai and other prominent communist officials were educated here. The remaining buildings now serve as a museum detailing the history of the Communist Party, though little of the history is displayed into English.

*Recommended Restaurants & Bars on pages 178–9*

## TRANSPORT TO/FROM GUANGZHOU

**Flights**: For a list of international destinations connected with Guangzhou, *see page 351*. Almost every sizeable Chinese city has flights to and from Guangzhou.

**Trains** arrive either at the Central station (Guangzhou Huochezhan) or at Guangzhou East railway station (Guangzhou Dong) in Tianhe. Both are linked to the metro system. There are several long-distance **bus stations**, many clustered near the Central rail station.

### Guangzhou–Hong Kong

**Trains**: 7 daily direct between Guangzhou East and Kowloon's Hung Hom station (1¾ hrs).
**Buses**: frequent (2½ hrs).**Ferries** no longer run Guangzhou–Hong Kong.

### Guangzhou–elsewhere in the region

*for Guangzhou–Shenzhen, see page 155.*
**Trains**: Shaoguan (frequent, 2½ hrs); Meizhou (3 daily, 6 hours); Chaozhou/Shantou (2 daily, 6½/7 hours); Zhaoqing (10 daily, 2 hours); Haikou/Sanya (3 daily, 11/15 hrs); Xiamen (2 daily, 14 hrs); Nanchang (7 daily, 10½–16 hrs); Changsha (frequent, 7¼–9 hrs); Guilin (2 daily; 11 hrs); Nanning (3 daily, 11–12 hrs); Guiyang (7 daily, 21–25 hrs; Kunming (2 daily, 25 hrs).
**Buses**: Frequent departures to Zhuhai/Macau (2–2½ hrs), Qingyuan (1½ hrs), Kaiping (2 hrs) and Zhaoqing (1½ hrs), also Meizhou (8 hrs) and Chaozhou/Shantou (5–6 hrs). Overnight sleeper buses run to Haikou, Xiamen, Fuzhou, Guilin, Nanning and other regional centres.
**Hydrofoils** operate from nearby delta ports (Nanhai, Huangpu) to Hong Kong and Haikou.

*The name "Canton" derives from the Portuguese attempt at pronouncing the province's name – Guangdong – from which the Portuguese somehow derived the name of Cantào. From Cantào came Canton.*

Similar to Shenzhen's Window on the World theme park, the large **Grand World Scenic Park** ⓤ (广州世界大观; Guangzhou Shijie Daguan; open daily 9.30am–8.30pm; entrance fee), across the river from Huangpu Miltary Academy, is aimed squarely at the local market and showcases the sights and sounds of some of the more significant parts of the planet.

## Baiyun Shan

For some much-needed fresh air, peace and quiet, make the easy half-day trip north of the city to the **White Cloud Hills** ⓥ (白云山; Baiyun Shan), a series of hills overlooking Guangzhou's urban sprawl whose highest point reaches almost 400 metres (1,300 ft). The area is only around 8 km (5 miles) from the city centre, and you can get there either by taxi or on bus No. 24 from the south side of Renmin Park by Gongyuan Qian metro station – journey time around 30 minutes.

A paved road and stone footpaths make it possible to walk into the hills, although most people take the cable-car which ascends to one of the peaks from the southern side. Souvenir stands and tea-houses at various viewpoints in the area are ideal places to sit back and take in the scenery. As you would expect, it all gets very crowded at weekends and holidays.

Nengren, an active Buddhist temple, is situated halfway up the peak of **White Cloud Evening View** (白云晚望; Baiyun Wanwang). There is also an old swimming pool nestled among the trees used by locals in summer, while at the base of Baiyun Shan is the well-manicured garden of Yun Tai.   ❑

**BELOW:** Tianhe Plaza, one of the main shopping malls in Guangzhou.

# RESTAURANTS & BARS

## Restaurants

Average price for a meal for one, with one drink:
**$** under US$12
(under Rmb 100)
**$$** US$12–20
(Rmb 100–160)
**$$$** over US$20
(over Rmb 160)

Guangzhou is a great place for eating out. The city is the home of Cantonese cuisine, and there are hundreds of good restaurants in which to sample it. There is also a good supply of dining options from elsewhere in China and, reflecting Guangzhou's cosmopolitan nature, from around the world.

There are numerous restaurants on Shamian Island and in the nearby streets north of Qingping Market, but overall they are spread quite evenly around the city.

### Cantonese and other southern Chinese

**Bei Yuan Jiujia**
202 Xiao Beilu.
Tel: 020 8356 3365. **$$**
While the dim sum here is served all day, it's at its best first thing in the morning. There are plenty of other classic Chinese dishes, too.

**Chiu Chou City**
Landmark Canton Hotel, 8 Qiao Guang Lu.
Tel: 020 8335 5988. **$$$**
Shantou-style goose is very popular here, as

indeed is the whole restaurant, whose private rooms and tables are invariably packed.

**Guangzhou Restaurant**
2 Wenchang Nanlu, Shangxiajiu Lu. Tel: 020 8138 0388. **$$**
Ranged over several floors, signature dishes include Wenchang chicken and double-boiled shark's fin soup with black chicken. Very popular with local residents for dim sum.

**Tao Tao Ju**
20 Dishipu Lu, Liwan District.
Tel: 020 8139 6111. **$$$**
Historic place that makes the most of its location and reputation. The dim sum menu runs to 200 items.

### Seafood (Chinese)

**Dong Jiang Haixian Da Jiulou**
2 Yanjiang Lu.
Tel: 020 8318 4901. **$$**
"Noisy but tasty" best sums up this monster seafood eatery. Stick to steamed crab and prawns if water beetles (a delicacy) lack appeal.

**Dongjiang Seafood Restaurant**
276 Huanshi Zhonglu, Tinahe District.
Tel: 020 8322 9188. **$$**
Downtown and downright excellent. There are non-seafood choices, but regulars sing the praises of the stuffed giant crabs.

### Northern Chinese

**Dong Bei Ren**
36 Tianhe Nanerlu.
Tel: 020 8750 1711. **$$**
Dong Bei Ren is renowned for its myriad Manchurian *jiaozi*, or mini dumplings, and its sweet red wine.

### Indian

**Haveli**
2 Aiguo Lu. Tel: 020 8359 4533. **$**
Haveli's fulsome Indian fare tastes even better beneath the trees of its picturesque garden. Very well priced.

### Japanese

**Japan Fusion**
2/F Metro Plaza, 358–378 Tianhe Beilu. Tel: 020 8388 5109. **$$$**
Gigantic restaurant, gigantic menu; come here with an appetite to match.

### Korean

**Qing Wa Ju**
117-14 Shuiyin Lu.
Tel: 020 8725 1929. **$$**
The many expatriate Koreans who have come over to do business in Guangzhou flock here for a taste of home: there's no higher recommendation.

### Muslim

**Nur Bostan**
43 Guangta Lu.
Tel: 020 8187 4919. **$**
Uighur-style halal food – with lamb predominating – at this inexpen-

sive reminder of the city's sizeable Islamic population.

### Nepali

**Nepal Royal Cuisine**
21 Lianxin Lu.
Tel: 020 8338 3409. **$$**
Something of a surprise for Guangzhou. Palace recipes include Himalayan rabbit and curried lamb chops. Fun and friendly.

### Thai & Vietnamese

**Cow and Bridge**
2/F Xianglong Huayuan, 175–181 Tianhe Beilu.
Tel: 020 8525 0821. **$$**
Great name, great atmosphere, and the Cow is into its second decade of serving top Thai dishes to very satisfied customers.

**Vietnamese**
**Lemon House**
Ground Floor, 11 Jianshe Liu, Ma Lu/507 Huifu Donglu.
Tel: 020 8375 3600. **$$**
There are some Thai dishes on the menu, but concentrate on the Vietnamese, especially the range of *pho*.

### Continental

**Silk Road Grill Room**
White Swan hotel, Yi Shamian Lu, Shamian Island. Tel: 020 8188 6968 ext. 18. **$$$**
A very sophisticated establishment with a price tag to match, and service that would not be out of place in a capital city.

## International

### 1920

183 Yanjiang Zhonglu.
Tel: 020 8333 6156.
www.1920cn.com **$$**
A charming riverside café
that's just the place for
lunch, Sunday brunch, or
somewhere to kick back
and listen to live jazz of
an evening.

### Backstreet Restaurant

Guangdong Museum of Arts,
38 Yanyu Lu, Ersha Island.
Tel: 020 8735 396. **$$$**
Arty ambience, as
might be expected, and
plenty of platters from
around the planet
dished up in chic
surroundings.

### Lucy's

3 Shamian Nanjie,
Shamian Island.
Tel: 020 8121 5106. **$$**
A menu that embraces
the world, and smiles
that embrace all diners,
pretty much sums up
this Shamian stunner.

## Italian

### Di Mateo

1/F, Westside, 175–181
Tianhe Beilu. Tel: 020 8525
1300. **$$**
Flashy Italian job,
where the manage-
ment has ambitions to
introduce real Euro-
pean cuisine to the
city. The menu fea-
tures Italian restaurant
staples like carpaccio,
frittata and a range of
well-prepared pasta.
The desserts and the
espresso are authentic
and high-quality.

## Bars

### Baby Face

83 Changti Lu.
Tel: 020 8335 5771.
A high-decibel club that
really gets going as the
night wears on. Can be
very busy – getting
served at the bar can
take a while.

### Café Elles

2/F Huaxin Dasha, 2 Shuiyin
Lu. Tel: 020 8761 2939.
No prizes for guessing
that this very Gallic
hang-out is a popular
rendezvous for the
French and Franco-
phones in the area.

### China Box Bar

3 Heping Lu, Overseas
Chinese Village. Tel: 020
8359 6868.
One of several bars at
the Overseas Chinese
Village, the Box attracts
mainly young profes-
sional types.

### Elephant & Castle Bar

363 Huanshi Donglu.
Tel: 020 8359 3309.
The Elly's two bars and
pool table blend sports
and socialising nicely,
pulling in the after-work
crowd on a nightly basis.

### F4

1/F TP Plaza, 109 Linhua Lu.
Tel: 020 8666 8070.
"Build up the prices
and they will come" is a
business motto which
seems to have proved
true for this club. Much
favoured by the city's
smart set.

### Hare & Moon

White Swan Hotel, Yi Shamian
Lu, Shamian Island.
Tel: 020 8188 6968.
A very relaxing bar, not
least for the riverine
panoramas beyond the
picture windows.

### Hill Bar

367 Huanshi Donglu.
Tel: 020 8359 0206.
An old favourite, and
deservedly so. There's
usually something going
on in this straightforward
drinking den every night
of the week.

### Kathleen's

60 Taojin Lu.
Tel: 020 8359 8045.
Going stronger than
ever, these days
Kathleen's is as
popular with locals
as with the expats
who were the original
target clientele.

### L'Africain

2/F Zi Dong Hua Building,
707 Dongfeng Zhonglu.
Tel: 020 8762 3336.
Beats from around the
world and not just the
African continent keep
L'Africain throbbing till
the small hours.

### The Paddy Field
### Irish Pub

Central Plaza Grd Floor, 38
Huale Lu. Tel: 020 8360 1248.
Excellent craic guaran-
teed in this first outpost
of Erin in Guangzhou.
Plus, of course, Guin-
ness and Jameson's.

### Tang Club

1 Jianshe Liu Malu.
Tel: 020 8384 1638.
This place is fun – not
least for its maze of
floors and lounges. At
weekends, elbow room
only at the bar and
adjacent dance floor.

**RIGHT:** a typically gaudy restaurant entrance.

*Recommended Restaurants on page 195*

# ELSEWHERE IN GUANGDONG

**Beyond Guangdong's Special Economic Zones lie a surprising variety of sights, from Stone Age relics and striking limestone karst formations to Ming architecture in ancient Chaozhou**

A way from the teeming Pearl River Delta, with its booming megacities and pervasive industrial smog, Guangdong province quickly assumes a more traditional Chinese flavour. As its name implies, Guangdong ("broad east") is a large province, encompassing much of the southern Chinese coast – all the way from the Gulf of Tonkin in the west to the borders of Fujian in the east – and such a sizeable area guarantees geographic diversity: the hilly north is less intensively populated than the lower-lying east, which has a cluster of major cities around Chaozhou, while the south-west is characterised by karst formations and a more tropical climate. The long, indented shoreline is fringed by hundreds of islands, including tropical Hainan – which only became a separate province in 1988.

## NORTHERN GUANGDONG

Northern Guangdong forms part of a near continuous line of hills that stretch right across southern China. Relatively unknown to tourists, the area is fairly attractive and a world away from the booming cities further south in the province. The main sights are strung out along the hilly corridor linking Guangzhou to Hunan and the centre of China.

## Qingyuan

**Qingyuan ❷** (清远), 75 km (47 miles) northwest of Guangzhou and around an hour by bus, promotes itself as Guangzhou's back garden – or '"rear garden" on the road signs – but it's the riverine attractions upstream that visitors come for. The town itself has a striking setting on the Beijiang (North River), but is modern and provides few reasons to linger. Buses to the surrounding sights leave from two different bus stations, old and new, on the northern and southern sides of town respectively. The No. 6 bus runs between the two.

Running southwards from the old bus station, **Beimen Jie** is a buzzing semi-pedestrianised street of shops and food

**LEFT:** Hakka women.
**BELOW:** the rice harvest at Kaiping against a backdrop of *diaolou* watchtowers.

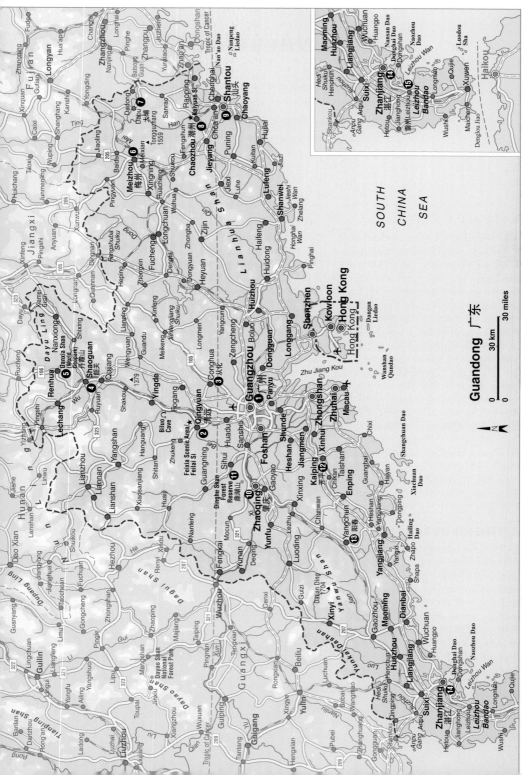

talls with specialist bazaars branching off in different directions. It continues across Xianfeng Zhonglu to the river banks, where there are cafés and bars with outdoor seating. If you're killing time at the new bus station, it's a 10-minute walk to **Jiangbin Park**, a landscaped section of waterfront with a 180-degree view of the wide, sandy river, the other half of town and the ring of hills around it. Locals swim out to the sand flats, though it's not entirely safe to do so.

## Feixia and Feilai Si

The **Feixia Scenic Area** (飞霞风景区; entrance fee), an attractive riverside site of hills and temples upstream from Qingyuan, is an hour away by bus from Qingyuan's old bus station. There's only one useful departure from Qingyuan, at 8.45am; the bus departs Feixia at 4pm for the return journey.

Upon arrival, walk down to the river from the ticket office to where a waiting barge will take you over to the north shore of the Beijiang. The shallow river is exceptionally wide for one so far from the sea. A track runs above the river bank past a ceremonial gateway to a bus rank, from where a minibus will take you on a switchback journey to a point high in the hidden valley behind.

Walking ahead from this stop will take you to a picturesque series of temples and terraced halls rising up a hillside, all interconnected by winding paths, stairways and verandas, and collectively known as **Feixia Gusi** (飞霞古寺). One hall is devoted to the three religions – Buddhism, Daoism and Confucianism; another houses a statue of the Monkey King. The temple keepers are friendly and welcoming, and the complex enjoys an air of antiquity and a remote forested location which has evidently protected it since its establishment in the Qing dynasty. Behind it, steep woodland paths lead up to the **Endless Sky Pagoda**, the highest point of the area.

To return to the river, you can wait for the bus or simply follow the old temple trail downhill – a natural stone path

descending through a damp valley which, in season, is a riot of butterflies, dragonflies and small lizards. The path passes the beautifully sited **Jinxia Si**, surrounded by peach trees on the banks of a stream, and gaps in the forest allow views of the brown river far below. The descent takes an hour at sightseeing pace.

**Feilai Si** (飞来寺), a smaller collection of temple buildings on the riverfront further downstream, is older than Feixia. To reach it, you'll need to negotiate a price with the boatmen at the Feixia wharf: reckon on Rmb 100 for the hour-long round trip. You can also take a hired speedboat in the other direction to the Feilaixia Great Dam, which blocks and calms what was previously a turbulent stretch, but it's further away than Feilai Si and boatmen will quote prices of Rmb 250 and up. In both cases, take care not to miss the return bus to Qingyuan.

## Conghua

Two to three hours northeast of Guangzhou by long-distance bus is the town of **Conghua** ❸ (从化), home to **Conghua Hot Springs** (从化温泉; Conghua Wenguan), a well-known des-

*Doorway at the Kaiyuan Temple in Chaozhou. The symbol confers good fortune and longevity.*

**BELOW:** eggplants, chillis and peppers at a Qingyuan market.

*The hills surrounding Conghua are known for the production of lychees and tea. Tour groups visit during summer and autumn, when lychees are in season. It is also possible to visit the Conghua Tea Farm, which organises tours from Guangzhou.*

**BELOW:** traditional Chinese playing cards.

tination for local and overseas Chinese. Known for its clean air and serene setting, many long-term expats have cottoned on to a good thing and use Conghua as a city escape. Unfortunately, expensive hotels have effectively annexed the area around the hot springs north of the town itself, so it is difficult for the traveller to negotiate the aqua-green hot springs.

## Shaoguan

**Shaoguan ❹** (韶关; Siu Gwan in Cantonese) occupies a strategic position on the old route north to Hunan province, downstream on the Bei River from Meiguan, the main pass north out of Guangdong. Situated on a spit at the confluence of two rivers, the city has waterfront promenades on all sides. It's one of the cleanest cities in Guangdong, and its compact size keeps it walkable.

The Ming Dynasty **Fengcai Tower** (风采楼; Fengcai Lou) was built in the same era as Beijing's imperial palace, and matches its style of upturned eaves – although the current building is a reconstruction. The friendly gents drinking tea in the room at the top will turn on the lights for you to view a small photo exhibition, and once you leave, will go back to sitting in the dark.

Walking away from the river, you can take the second left turn after the Fengcai Tower onto **Fuxing Road**, a traffic free stretch of shops and food stalls. Several first-floor restaurants and bars overlook the street scene. Running parallel with and to the east of Fuxing Road a series of narrow lanes and alleys is a great mishmash of old and new houses, shops with bags of spices and chillies, vegetable hawkers and a streetside fish market. At the southern end you'll find the compound of **Dajian Monastery** (大鉴禅寺; Dajian Chansi). Founded in 660 during the Tang Dynasty, the monastery was used as workers' housing during the early communist period but was restored to the monks in 1985.

**Zhongshan Park**, like thousands of others across China, is named after Sun Yatsen. The great man passed through Shaoguan on his anti-warlord Northern Expeditions in 1922 and 1924, but had to turn back both times due to rebellions in Guangzhou. South of the park, a promenade overlooks the spot where the

## GETTING AROUND GUANGDONG

**Chaozhou and Shantou**: Trains between Shantou, Chaozhou and Guangzhou (2 daily) take 6½ to 7 hours (add 30 minutes for Shantou) and stop at Longchuan and Huizhou. There are also trains to Meizhou (2 daily, 2½ hrs), Nanchang (2 daily, 14 hrs) and an overnight train to Shenzhen (10 hrs). There are several buses daily from both cities to Meizhou (3–3½ hrs), Guangzhou (5½ hrs), Shenzhen (4 hrs) and Xiamen (3½–4 hrs), and from Shantou to Fuzhou (7 hrs).

**Kaiping**: Buses to Guangzhou (2 hrs) run every 20 minutes or so. There are also buses to Shenzhen, Zhuhai and Zhaoqing.

**Meizhou**: Two daily trains, and several buses, run from Meizhou to Chaozhou and on to Shantou (2½–3 hrs). Meizhou is on a slow rail line, and the 3 daily Guangzhou trains take at least 6 hours. Buses take 8 hours to Guangzhou.

**Qingyuan**: Buses to Guangzhou (1½ hrs) are frequent throughout the day.

**Shaoguan**: The city lies on a major north–south rail route and there are numerous trains to/from Guangzhou (1½ hrs) and Changsha (6–8 hrs). Guangzhou buses take around 4 hours.

**Zhanjiang**: There are 4 daily trains to/from Guangzhou (6½–8 hrs; 3 of them originate from/continue to Hainan Island via a ferry). There are also 3 daily trains to Nanning (6 hrs) and Guilin (8½ hrs) and an overnight train to Kunming (21 hrs). Buses to Guangzhou (several daily) take around 5 hours.

**Zhaoqing**: Ferries run direct from Hong Kong daily (4 hrs). Frequent trains and buses to Guangzhou take 1½–2 hours. Zhaoqing is also linked by train, bus and ferry to Shenzhen, and is on the main Guangzhou–Haikou rail line.

**TIP**

There is a tourist office directly in front of Shaoguan's railway station, and the staff there are, atypically, willing to share their knowledge of the local sights and bus routes. Buses for Maba and Nanhua Si leave from a spot on the edge of the railway station forecourt, close to the river; those for Danxia Shan depart from a different bus station directly south of the train station.

---

Wujiang and Zhenjiang rivers become the Beijiang. Here, as is the case on other parts of the waterfront, you can watch the locals practising their ballroom dancing.

## Trips from Shaoguan

**Shizi Yan** (狮子岩; Lion Crag) is a pair of limestone outcrops near the outlying town of Maba (also known as Qujiang), 16 km (10 miles) south of Shaoguan. In the 1950s, archaeologists discovered the remains of "Maba Man" – an early version of homo sapiens thought to have lived 130,000 years ago – in a cave system inside the peaks. The surrounding area is now contained inside the **Maba Man Historical Relics Park** (马坝人历史遗产公园; Mabaren Lishi Yichan Gongyuan; open daily 9am–4pm; entrance fee), reached by bus from Shaoguan to Maba and then a five-minute taxi ride. After passing the sculpture of noble-looking Maba Men (and Maba Women), head first for the pleasing little **museum**. Its dioramas and relics are sparsely labelled, but little is needed. Cross a lily-filled moat to reach the nearest limestone peak, inside which

you can explore the dark, slippery cave system that the Maba Men inhabited. The fields around the crags have also yielded archaeological evidence of more

**BELOW:** prehistoric insights at Maba Man Historical Relics Park.

*To the east of Shaoguan, **Chebaling Nature Reserve** has some of the best forest in the region. It's an important sanctuary for birdlife, while mammals include civet cats, pangolins and porcupines, a few clouded leopards and – possibly – some of the last surviving South China tigers.*

**BELOW:** the China Sex Museum.

recent neolithic settlement; the path which circles the first peak is an easy 15-minute amble which gives you an idea of the surrounding terrain.

Not far from Maba, **Nanhua Si** (南华寺; entrance fee) is a temple of great significance for Chinese Buddhists. Founded in AD 502 during the time of the Northern and Southern dynasties, after a travelling Indian monk had recommended the site for its natural beauty, it became the residence of Huineng, the Sixth Patriarch of Chan (or Zen) Buddhism. Huineng taught here for 37 years, training 43 disciples who spread Chan Buddhism far and wide. Today, the temple is regarded as a spiritual home of the Chan school.

The large complex is laid out along a symmetrical axis, central halls one behind the other. The highest hall contains a figure of Huineng said to have been made from a cast of his corpse, and behind the hall you can walk among ancient yew trees to the spring where he washed his robe. Nanhua Si is still a working monastery, and you may come across large groups of monks and nuns chanting verses; photography is discouraged.

## North of Shaoguan

Around 50 km (30 miles) northeast of Shaoguan, **Danxia Shan** ❺ (丹霞山; Danxia Shan World Geopark open 6.30am–7pm; entrance fee) is an area of high eroded peaks of red sandstone, sculpted by time and water into shapes resembling elephants, tortoises, candles, giant teapots and various genitalia. The entry fee is as steep as the rock formations, but the price does include transport around the large park area on a fleet of buggies. The Yangyuan Mountain area is closest to the entrance. Its most famous rock formation is Yangyuan Stone, poetically described on a guide map as a "peak of eternal masculinity". The local tourism bureau puts it more directly: "It looks from a distance very much like a male genital." The Yinyuan Stone elsewhere represents the female counterpart.

A cable-car will take you up to the top of Danxia Shan itself, one of the larger ridges. From here, you can survey many of the park's major geological features during a two-hour walk via viewing stations to the **Biechuan Monastery**, a temple which seems almost Tibetan in its cliffside setting. Along the way you pass

the Dragon King Spring and several caves used as shrines or once inhabited by monks. Red stone steps lead down the cliff face to the monastery – an attractive set of buildings around a flagstoned courtyard – and then down further, beside sets of rock engravings, to a line of shops by the road where you can catch another buggy.

Most locals, as well as the monks, walk up rather than take the cable-car; there is a group of sedan-chair bearers waiting to carry those less sure of their fitness. The park itself extends far to the south, encompassing further mountains, lakes and villages, and one could easily spend a full day touring around.

Doubtlessly inspired by the Yangyuan and Yinyuan Stones, the **China Sex Museum** (中国性爱博物馆; Zhongguo Xingai Bowuguan; open daily 9am–midday, 1–6pm, until 7pm Fri and Sat; entrance fee) has opened its doors beside the roundabout at the entrance to Danxia Shan. It's easy to find: you can't miss the large phallic sculpture outside. The three-room museum has collections of coinage used in ancient brothels, erotic paintings on porcelain plates, Kama Sutra-like ivory

carvings and displays with names like "Popularity of Dildo in Ancient China". It covers the period from 500 BC to the present with surprising openness.

An hour's scenic railway journey to the northwest of Shaoguan leads to **Pingshi** (坪石), a hilly market town surrounded by red Danxia-style peaks. This is the departure point for an exhilarating rafting trip down the **Wujiang River** (武江) – a stretch of white water known as the **Nine Torrents and Eighteen Shoals**. Turn left upon exiting the railway station to find the building marked "Ticket Office for Floating". The staff will provide you with watertight bags for your belongings and will then transport you to the wharf, where you mount an inflatable raft with outboard engine which carries eight people.

The Wujiang follows a broad route through a steep gorge, but its initially gentle demeanour masks its capabilities in times of flood. High on the left bank, the remains of a railway line jut at crazy angles over the water – sagging iron tracks hanging across ravines without the bridges which once supported them, like a Salvador Dalí impression of a hillside

*White-water rafting on the Wujiang River north of Shaoguan.*

**BELOW LEFT:** the red sandstone hills of Danxia Shan.
**BELOW:** mushrooms from the Danxia Shan forests.

*Abandoned Hakka house at Meizhou.*

**BELOW:** Meizhou is one of the sleepier towns in Guangdong.

railway. A line of rusting carriages sit where they were trapped between landslides. On the right bank, bridge pillars and the foundations of waterworks buildings litter the shore. The tops of old trees are wrapped tightly with broken stands of bamboo, marking the high-water limit of the last flash flood.

The torrents and shoals are spread apart, with long stretches of calm water between, but some of them are rough: you will need to hold on tight. The three-hour trip ends at **Lechang**（乐昌）, a small town itself recovering from disastrous flooding in 2006. From here you can connect with a train back to Shaoguan.

## EASTERN GUANGDONG

Moving to the eastern edge of Guangdong, three of the province's best-known cities – Meizhou, Chaozhou and Shantou – are found close to the Fujian border. Meizhou and Chaozhou are historically distinct from the rest of the province, both traditional homelands to their respective ethnic groups – the Hakkas and the Chiu Chow (commonly known overseas as Teochew). This corner of

Guangdong is historically one of the main centres of emigration from China, with many Hakka and Chiu Chow people forced overseas during the 19th century, thanks to the Opium Wars and famine. Many successful Overseas Chinese have since fed money back into the region, keen to preserve the traditions of their ancestral homeland *(see page 61)*.

## Meizhou

**Meizhou ❻**（梅州）and the adjoining town of **Meixian**（梅县）are considered the home of the Hakka people, migratory members of which are spread all over China and in Overseas Chinese communities worldwide. Arriving in southern China later than other Chinese groups (having originated in the central Yangzi region), the Hakka found the best arable land already taken and often had to make do with less productive hill country. The resulting lack of agricultural employment led many Hakka men to pursue alternative careers in academia or the military, and this strategy paid handsome dividends: Hakkas who have risen to become heads of state include Deng Xiaoping, Lee Teng-hui, Lee Kuan Yew (Singapore)

and Thaksin Shinawatra (Thailand).

Bisected by a loop of the Meijiang (Plum River), Meizhou is a small city, but that doesn't mean taxi drivers are any more likely to know their way around it. Thankfully, minibuses run around town on set routes: No. 6 runs between the coach station and the railway station, passing the Jiangnan bus station on the way. There's a section of old town between the coach station and the north bank of the river which has plenty of traditional shophouses, food stalls and animated street life.

For a fine example of late Qing Dynasty architecture, visit **Renjinglu** (人境庐), to the north of Dongshan Bridge. The former home of Meizhou intellectual Huang Zunxian, it's a house of impressive size and artistry. Another building over a moat houses thousands of books from Huang's library. At the time of writing, both were being intensively restored and landscaped. The neighbourhood around Renjinglu is made up of dozens of traditional walled compounds with ornate gates and courtyard fish ponds. Within walking distance east of here, the Buddhist **Qianfo Pagoda** (千佛寺; Qianfo Si; entrance fee) features intricate stone carvings, although it is completely new, having been rebuilt with Overseas Chinese investment. It's well known for its vegetarian restaurant (*see page 195*).

The far side of the lake in Jianying Park is where you'll find the modest **Historical Museum**. No opening hours are posted, and the museum closes for a long lunch break.

## Hakka villages

The valleys between Meizhou and **Dabu** ❼ (大埔), 100 km (62 miles) to the east near the border with Fujian, are filled with countless traditional Hakka villages, square, symmetrical and well kept, and set in pleasant scenery. Dabu itself is a small but rapidly-expanding town with little to see in its centre, but on its outskirts, **Fangshilou** (泰安楼; entrance fee) is well worth a visit. Also known as Taianlou, it's a three-storey square house built in 1764 to accommodate a single clan. The outer walls are made of stone, except the third storey, which is brick; inside, the pillars and floors are wooden. The 200 rooms look out upon a cobbled

*The **Huidonggang Nature Reserve** on the Guangdong coast around 100 km (60 miles) east of Shenzhen protects colonies of green turtles which come ashore to lay their eggs between June and September.*

**BELOW:** communal Hakka housing in eastern Guangdong.

**BELOW RIGHT:**
paper was invented in China around 200 AD – centuries before it was used in Europe.

central courtyard, in which chickens and ducks congregate around an ancestral hall. Members of the clan will let you wander freely around the upper storeys, from where you can view the attractive tiled roofs and hanging lanterns; many units are empty in preparation for the building's transformation into a museum. Next door to Fangshilou, the newly laid **Xihu Park** is set to include an exhibition of Hakka culture when it is completed.

The most spectacular Hakka round-houses are concentrated in Fujian province's Yongding county (*see page 218*), but an hour east of Dabu, on the provincial border, **Hua'e Lou** (花萼楼) is one of Guangdong's examples of the style. Like Fangshilou, it is built around a cobbled courtyard, although round in shape, with the eaved roofs of two terraces overlooking it. Hua'e Lou is close to Dadong; it's best to charter a taxi to take you there from opposite Dabu's bus station.

## Chaozhou

**Chaozhou** ❽ (潮州) is a city of great antiquity with its own very distinct language and culture. Like the Hakka, many

Chaozhou people emigrated overseas during periods of poverty and made their fortunes in places like Malaysia, Thailand and Singapore. Overshadowed since the late 19th century by Shantou, a newer settlement downriver, it has escaped redevelopment (for now) and retains the architecture and atmosphere of an ancient city.

The Tang Dynasty **Kaiyuan Temple** (开元寺; Kaiyuan Si; open 8am–6pm; entrance fee) should be your first stop. Built in 738 on a grand scale and inevitably reconstructed many times since, it features many examples of ancient-looking stonework and several great old trees. A pair of stone pillars in the courtyard date back to Tang times. The main hall features three Buddhas, while another hall is dedicated to Guanyin.

Directly east from the square in front of the temple you'll find a long section of the **Old City Wall**, the largest remaining in Guangdong. The nearest opening is **Guangji Gate** (广济门; Guangji Men); you can climb steps here to reach a three-storey watchtower on top of the wall. Opposite, the **Guangji Bridge**, a

## The Decline of Chinese Technology

As described on page 26, Chinese technology was generally well in advance of the rest of the world until around 1300 AD. Thereafter, the rapid advances made by European civilisations, coupled with certain characteristics of Chinese society, soon put China at a disadvantage.

For all their precocious ingenuity, the Chinese inventions were the exclusive preserve of the uppermost echelons of society and of scarce benefit to commoners. This had the effect of restricting the further development of existing technologies, in sharp contrast with what was happening in Europe in the later Middle Ages.

The Chinese world was, above all, an insular one. Just when the rich and powerful Ming dynasty was poised to reach outwards and develop trade with Southeast Asia and beyond (*see page 27*), an imperial edict – essentially the result of nothing more than a court argument – banned foreign voyages by the Ming fleet, and at a stroke comprehensively changed the course of Chinese history. Within 100 years, the first European adventurers were guiding their ships, equipped with guns developed from Chinese gunpowder technology, into the region, eventually to devastating effect. Before long, China was being subjugated and humiliated by the European colonial powers.

medieval trading link between Guangdong and Fujian, stretches across the wide Hanjiang River. Originally a pontoon bridge made up of over 80 boats, stone and brick piers were gradually extended from each bank to lay a proper bridge across. Shops were built on it to cater to river as well as caravan trade. One can imagine what a sight the walled city of Chaozhou would have made for travellers approaching the long bridge from the far shore.

The river is named after Han Yu, a Tang official who promoted Confucianism in the face of Daoism and Buddhism, which were increasing in popularity at the time. For this act of dissent he was banished to Chaozhou for eight months. He made a great impact on the local people, promoting education and clearing the river of crocodiles. Han is also commemorated at the **Hanwengong Memorial Temple** (韩文公寺; Hanwengong Si; open 8am–5.30pm; entrance fee) just northeast of Guangji Bridge. The temple was established in 999, a century after Han Yu lived in Chaozhou, and was moved to the present site, where Han had planted an oak tree, in 1189.

The area between the hefty city wall and Huancheng Xilu is a dense warren of courtyard homes, shrines, market streets and alleyways, some of them partly covered. On Changli Lu, a narrow street south of Zhongshan Lu, the former Haiyang Confucian Academy is now operated as a **city museum**.

## Shantou

An almost continuous strip of development links Chaozhou with its sister city of **Shantou** ❾ (汕头), an hour south by bus. Better known in the 19th century as Swatow, it was opened to foreign trade in 1858 as part of the settlement of the Second Opium War, and by the 1930s had grown into China's third-largest trading port. In the 1980s it was designated as one of the first Special Economic Zones, but although industry is very much in evidence, the city lacks the modernity and prosperity of Shenzhen or Zhuhai. Again, the Chaozhou language is spoken here; the shared culture of the two cities is known as Chaoshan.

If you're not visiting on business, the southwest section of town, poking out into the harbour, contains almost all

*Hakka food is a feature of the eastern parts of Guangdong; it is straightforward and simple, with an emphasis on pork and other meat, combined with preserved vegetables.*

**BELOW:** Guangji Gate, Chaozhou.

Shantou's Stone Fort Park is a reminder of the city's role as a foreign Treaty Port in the latter part of the 19th century.

**BELOW:** Xinghu Lake, Zhaoqing.

points of interest. Radiating from the crimson pavilion on Shengping Lu, all streets are lined with beautiful but decaying examples of **colonial-era mansions** and public buildings, remnants of Shantou's time as an international treaty port. Many are in shocking disrepair, and the crumbling plastered facades are generally ignored by the people at street level; see them now, as some blocks are being demolished and the rest may not exist for much longer. There is a small but lavishly decorated **Tianhou temple** at the junction of Shengping Lu and Waima Lu, and another group of halls around the corner to its right with painted doors, potted plants and an attractive flagstone courtyard.

South of here, boats depart from the Xidi and Guangchang piers to make the quick crossing to the **Queshi Scenic Resort**, a hillside area of pavilions, grottoes and gardens. From the piers, you can also join daytime or evening boat tours, which take around 90 minutes to take in the harbour's attractions. From the Guangchang Pier, a well-used **promenade** runs east along the waterfront. Shantou people come out in force here,

practising t'ai chi or simply brewing and drinking *gongfu* tea, a regional pastime.

The promenade comes to an end opposite the **Stone Fort Park** (石炮台: Shipaotai; open daily 7.30am–6pm; entrance fee), a moated fortification built in 1879 for coastal defence. The fort is low but solidly built: the 5-metre (16-ft) thick outer wall is made of granite, glutinous rice, brown sugar and crushed seashells. Atmospheric arched tunnels run around its base, with chambers on either side. Enter the circular central courtyard to see the wavelike steps which allowed cannons to be rolled up to the battlements. A total of 18 cannons face the harbour.

## WESTERN GUANGDONG

The lands to the west and southwest of the Pearl River Delta are less industrialised than those to the east. This may change as cross-delta transport links improve, but for now, agriculture still holds sway in these parts of the province. If you're heading from Hong Kong to Vietnam, the overland route through Guangdong and Guangxi is easy to follow. Trains and express buses run between Guangzhou

and Nanning, and then to Pingxiang on the Vietnamese border.

## Zhaoqing

**Zhaoqing ⑩** (肇庆) is located around 110 km (70 miles) west of Guangzhou and is known as "Little Guilin", thanks to the surrounding limestone karst formations – though these are on a much smaller scale than their more famous counterparts.

Overlooking the river at the eastern end of Jiangbin Lu stands **Chongxi Pagoda** (崇禧塔; Chongxi Ta), a Ming Dynasty pagoda (open daily 8.30am–5pm; entrance fee). The main attraction in Zhaoqing, however, is **Seven Stars Crag** (七星岩; Qixing Yan): according to legend, the crags are stars that fell from the heavens. The surrounding area to the north of the city has been made into a large **park** (open daily 8am–5.30pm; entrance fee). Stone paths lead through the gentle limestone hills, which are surrounded by artificial lakes and modern pagodas that float over the water. Each of the crags is named after what its shape symbolises – a toad, a stone house, a jade curtain. There are plenty of sou-

venir and refreshment stands scattered throughout the park.

**Dinghu Shan ⑪** (鼎湖山), a forest reserve 20 km (12 miles) east of Zhaoqing, is famous for a Ming-era Buddhist temple as well as many villages scattered over the mountain. Less touristy than its neighbour, Dinghu Shan offers scenic walks through lush subtropical forests, complete with babbling streams and waterfalls. To get there, take a taxi or bus No. 21 from Zhaoqing.

## Kaiping and surroundings

South from Zhaoqing, **Kaiping ⑫** (开平) has historically been a centre of emigration from China. It is famous for its hundreds of ornate *diaolou* watchtowers, which were built from the early 17th century to the 1930s. The remaining *diaolou* – more than 1,800 in all – are scattered over a wide area, some hidden beside duck ponds in the backstreets of Kaiping, but most in the villages around the city.

A wonderfully cohesive example of early 20th-century architecture can be found at **Chikan** (赤坎), a river town 20 minutes west of Kaiping by taxi or bus.

*Originally intended as fortifications for villages, Kaiping's* diaolou *watchtowers evolved into showpieces of wealth and style, as locals who had made their fortunes overseas returned home. Many display Western European, Greek and even Arabic influences in their architectural details.*

**BELOW:** opening an athletics event.

*Boat dwellers, as here at Leizhou, are a feature of the southern Chinese coast.*

**BELOW:** palm-lined promenade at Zhanjiang.

Its varied and graceful colonnaded buildings are dilapidated but still very much in use, making it somewhat reminiscent of Georgetown in Penang, Malaysia. One section near the river has been restored and appropriated for use by film studios for shooting costume dramas. It also houses an exhibition covering the emigration of Kaiping people to North America and other places overseas.

At the same distance west of Kaiping lies **Li Yuan** (立园; entrance fee), a collection of villas, *diaolou* and pavilions in attractive garden surroundings. It was originally built as the home of Xie Weili, an Overseas Chinese who returned from America in 1926. The Xie family fled in advance of the Japanese occupation in the late 1930s and never returned. The main houses contain period furniture and fittings, all is shaded by trees, and the canal running through the compound is full of coloured carp. It's authentic and relaxing enough to merit an hour or two looking around.

Kaiping city is intersected by a maze of rivers and channels, with waterfront promenades along many stretches. As an amalgamation of three port towns, it is rather spread out; you'll need to take buses or one of the ubiquitous motorbike taxis to get around. For shopping, head to Jiachong Xilu – which is one long pedestrian street crammed with clothes and food stalls – or to the busy Musha Lu and Xijiao Lu.

## Southwest to Yangchun

Limestone formations rise from the flat paddies like giant canines and molars as you approach **Yangchun** ⓮ (阳春), an unsophisticated country town which fancies itself as a Guilin-in-waiting. Yangchun has the hotels and facilities, while most of the natural karst attractions are clustered around the smaller town of **Chunwan**, 40 minutes to the north. Buses run frequently between the two towns. En route you get a view of **Fish King Rock** – the top-heavy riverside crag used as the area's emblem. Chunwan may be the scrappiest town in the whole of Guangdong, and there's no need to hang around: buses, taxis and motorbikes all depart from the dusty crossroads which serves as the town centre.

For large-scale karst scenery both above and below ground, visit **Lingxiao Cave** (凌霄洞; entrance fee), an hour's drive north of Chunwan through attractive scenery of villages and mountains. A shingly river runs out of the mouth of the cave, which rises to a height of 180 metres (590 ft). Stalactites and stalagmites meet and merge to give the impression of giant cathedral columns holding up the remote ceiling. A bridge beside a small temple gives access to a sandy bank inside the cave, where you can enjoy tofu dessert while waiting for a group to gather. Local students will then lead you on a guided tour of the cavern's upper levels, lit at intervals by gaudy fairy lights. You'll get a demonstration of the Chinese predilection for assigning characteristics to nature: this stalactite looks like a little goose; this one looks like a monk laughing; this one is a dragon's spine, and so on. Finally you have the chance to take a short boat trip along the inky subterranean river. Further up the road from Chunwan, there is

another group of similar karst caves at **Yuxi Sandong**.

## The far southwest

Under the name of Kwangchowan, **Zhanjiang** ⑭ (湛江) was a French colony from 1898 until World War II, but absolutely nothing has survived from that period – there is a Catholic church on Yan'an Lu, but it is a modern pastiche with coloured cement in place of stained-glass windows. Since the 1950s, the city has been developed into a major shipping port, and is usually visited only in transit to the city of Beihai or Hainan Island.

The main bus station is inconveniently remote from the city centre at Haitian, a 10-minute taxi ride from the Xiashan area where hotels and street life are located. The long waterfront promenade runs from Haibin Park up to **Sea City**, a passenger ship permanently docked and used as a seafood restaurant. If you want to meet English-speaking locals, the town's "English corner" regulars meet in Renmin Square on Friday evenings.

You can use Zhanjiang as a base for day trips to the beach resorts on Donghai and Nansandao islands, or more prof-itably to the ancient town of **Leizhou** ⑮ (雷州), 90 minutes further down the peninsula. Strangely, the people of Leizhou speak a version of Minnan (Fujianese) rather than Cantonese; the town is also notable for the large numbers of unexplained dog figurines which have been unearthed in several locations around the area.

Leizhou is much smaller and older than Zhanjiang, and though lacking in major sights, the narrow streets south and east of the bus station hold a wealth of Qing Dynasty houses, temples and wells. The **Fubo Temple** (伏波寺; Fubo Si) on Leizhou Dadao is finely decorated with gilded carvings, old stone inscrip-tions and beautifully painted panels below its eaves. Be sure to find the graceful **Sanyuan Pagoda** (三元塔; Sanyuan Ta; entrance fee), overlooking thatched village houses on the eastern edge of town. Set in gardens which include a gate tower, a small museum and a collection of the city's stone dogs, it's a peaceful and beautiful place, far removed from the chaotic overdevelop-ment which characterises much of southern China. ❏

*A modern version of Leizhou's unexplained dog statues.*

## RESTAURANTS

**Regional cuisine**

Chaozhou (Chiu Chow) restaurants are found in Chinatowns the world over, with cuisine primarily based on seafood – but also featuring vegetarian dishes made from pump-kin and taro. A meal starts with cold starters such as spiced goose or boiled crab, served with sweet dipping sauces. Main dishes may include bird's-nest soup, steamed fish and shrimp balls.

Hakka cuisine features dried and preserved ingredients, such as fermented tofu, fried pork, preserved vegeta-bles, leaves and fungus – seafood is not a major feature. Dishes include salt-baked chicken; beef ball and lettuce soup; and tofu stuffed with pork and herbs.

**Chaozhou**

**Kaiyuan Vegetarian Shop**
16–17 Kaiyuan Lu, Chaozhou
Tel: 0768 225 2665. **$**
A good place to see Chiu Chow-style vegetable carving, where delicate figures of flowers, birds and dragons are used as garnishes. Situated next to the Kaiyuan Temple.

**Meizhou**
Browse local restaurants and food stalls in Meizhou's old district around Zhongyuan Lu.

**Qianfo Pagoda Canteen**
Qianfo Pagoda (east of town). **$**
The canteen at this temple complex serves authentic Buddhist vegetarian dishes.

**Shantou**

**Chaozhou Restaurant**
2 Changping Lu
Tel: 0754 854 6498. **$**
One of the best places for Chiu Chow specialilties.

**Shaoguan**
A number of first-floor restaurants and cafés on pedestrianised Fengdu Lu allow you to eat while watching the shoppers and street life below.

**Kaiping**
Stroll along Jiachong Xilu or Xijiao Lu to graze from streetside food stalls. Pavement restau-rants are found all over the busy central area.

• • • • • • • • • • • • • • •
*Average price for a meal for one, with one drink:*
**$** = under US$12 (Rmb 100),
**$$** = over US$12 (over Rmb 100).

*Recommended Restaurants on page 211*

# HAINAN ISLAND

**The transformation of China's tropical southern island into a hassle-free tourist destination over the past few years is astonishing. The palm-fringed beaches are more accessible than ever, while swish hotels offer a new level of comfort**

Hainan Island, also known in Chinese as Qiong'ai, covering approximately 34,000 sq km (13,000 sq miles), is situated just 30 km (20 miles) off the coast of Guangdong province at the southernmost tip of China. Lying on the same latitude as Hawaii, leading to a long-tired "Hawaii of China" tag, it is a tropical isle with Chinese characteristics: alongside extinct volcanoes, palm trees and white-sand beaches sit Buddhist and Daoist temples, busy markets and a few lingering Soviet-style state buildings. Together with southern parts of Yunnan, it is the only place in China to bask in reliably warm weather year-round, particularly along its southern coast. Sunshine and 25°C in January and February, combined with comfortable water temperatures for swimming, guarantee its popularity as a winter escape from the chillier mainland.

During the Ming and Qing dynasties Hainan was an island exile for statesmen and popular poets who spoke out against China's imperial rulers. Tombs and monuments for some of the better-known imperial critics exist in the provincial capital, Haikou, on the island's northeast coast. Meanwhile, Sanya, on the southern tip, has been home to fishing communities for centuries, and on some of the town's nearby beaches exiles, in their isolation, inscribed rocks with phrases such as "The End of the Sky and the Corner of the Sea". Today, the mood is infinitely more upbeat. Around Sanya luxury global hotel brands have suddenly

arrived, fronting some of the best of the powdery sand.

The year-round warmth, white sands and clean water has attracted a slow trickle of Western holidaymakers that is expected to grow – the island is being aggressively marketed in Europe and America – alongside increasing numbers of affluent mainland Chinese. Tropical beauty and an improving infrastructure, coupled with an increase in the use of English and an undeniable novelty appeal will, no doubt, lure a few tourists away from Southeast Asian holiday spots.

**Main attractions**
HAIKOU OLD CITY
WENCHANG
XINGLONG TROPICAL
  BOTANICAL GARDEN
DADONGHAI BEACH
YALONG BAY BEACH
NANSHAN BUDDHIST
  CULTURE PARK
JIANGFENG PRIMEVAL
  FOREST RESERVE
WUZHISHAN AREA

**LEFT:** the beach at Tianya Hajiao.
**BELOW:** actor Jackie Chan at a Miss World event, Sanya.

Most visitors will only see the east coast as they travel along the fast-moving Haikou–Sanya highway, a strip which is dotted with fishing and pearl-cultivating communities. The west of the island has always been sparsely settled and remains relatively undeveloped, and was off-limits for years due to sensitivity about PLA military bases located on this strategic southernmost island. Today there are no restricted areas.

Hainan has been a province since 1988 (previously it had formed part of Guangdong), and was awarded Special Economic Zone (SEZ) status at the same time, a fact which has contributed a great deal to its prosperity.

*Dragon fruit and other tropical produce at a Haikou market.*

## HAIKOU

About as laid-back as Chinese cities get, **Haikou** ❶ (海口) is well endowed with a pleasant tropical ambience – roads are planted with shady banyan trees and palms, exotic fruits overflow from street stalls, people are friendly, and a pervasive sleepiness is in evidence. The cycle lanes, once busy with the country's previously favoured form of two-wheeled transport, still remain, but with less traffic, as the increasingly affluent population of some 650,000 upgrade to motor-scooters. This is a prosperous place, although its role as the gateway to China's tropical paradise has diminished as Sanya's airport becomes ever more established.

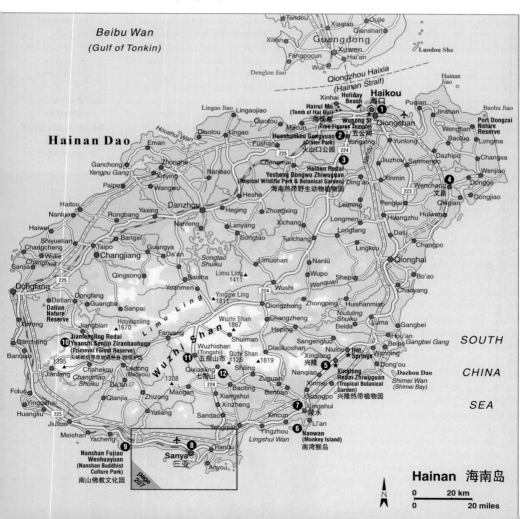

## The old centre

The most attractive part of Haikou is the old quarter in the north of the city centre, where a promenade beside Changdi Lu (also known locally as Haikou Zhonglu, meaning "Central Street") stretches past clipped lawns along the banks of **Haidian River**. Along the way is a replica of a 1940s clock tower, built to replace the dilapidated tower dating from the Japanese occupation.

Nearby, arcaded Bo'ai Lu and Zhongshan Lu contain a mellow small-scale **wholesale and retail market** within European colonial-style buildings, many of which were restored in the 1990s. A large proportion of the old quarter's buildings were designed by early 20th-century French colonial architects by order of warlord Deng Benyin. Xinhua Lu runs south from the river through the heart of the district to **Haikou Park**, a pleasant open space almost always busy with a peculiarly Chinese assortment of keep-fit enthusiasts, ballroom dancers, musicians and chess players.

Alfresco hot-pot restaurants and other street food appear in this part of town at dusk, offering mostly seafood – the main cluster is around Jiefang Lu and Xinhua Lu. On Renmin Dadao on the far (northern) side of the river is a night market selling clothing and household products.

## Further out

In the west of the city, around 4 km (2½ miles) from the old centre, lies the **Tomb of Hai Rui** (海瑞墓; Hairui Mu; open daily 8.30am–5pm; entrance fee). Hai Rui was an upright 16th-century statesman and outspoken critic of imperial excesses and corruption of his day. As a county magistrate in Zhejiang province (situated on the east coast south of Shanghai), he dared to speak out against Ming Emperor Jia Jing, resulting in his exile to Hainan, from where he returned home and resumed his post following the Emperor's death.

Fond of his time in the deep south, it was Hai Rui's wish to be buried in Hainan, and his tomb was built here in 1589. Remnants of the original structure remain, along with weathered stone sculptures of animals; landscaped grounds with colourfully painted memorial pavilions around a rock pool were added in the 1990s.

*Most of Hainan's residents speak a Hainanese dialect as their first language. The dialects change every 50 km (30 miles) or so, with a total of around 15 on the island. Mandarin is taught in schools, but is not always widely understood in rural areas. Despite Hainan's administrative links to Guangdong and the popularity of Hong Kong television, Cantonese is rarely spoken outside the cities.*

**BELOW LEFT:** the clock tower in Haikou's old quarter.
**BELOW:** typical old Haikou street.

**TIP**

Other than the pleasant central Haikou Park (see page 199), Haikou has plenty of green spaces, including Wanly Park with its lakes and a decent restaurant. Jinniuling Park (Haixiu Road; open daily 8.30am–5.50pm; entrance fee) contains well-kept botanical gardens – and a zoo that is best avoided.

**TRANSPORT TO/FROM HAINAN**

There are numerous **flights** to Haikou and Sanya from all major Chinese cities. There are also a few international flights to both airports – for details see page 351.

The new **railway line** between Sanya and Haikou via Dongfang on the east coast (3 hrs), and an improved rail link (including a ferry – which the train itself actually boards) between Haikou and Guangzhou (3 daily, 11 hrs), make rail an alternative to planes or ferries.

Long-distance **sleeper buses** run between Haikou and Guangzhou (daily, 12 hrs).

Several **ferries** ply the straits between the Leizhou Peninsula (Hai'an) and Haikou every 1½ hours, journey time 1½ hours. There are also overnight boats to Beihai. Longer-distance ferries operate Shekou (Shenzhen)–Haikou (daily except Sat, 18 hrs).

**GETTING AROUND HAINAN**

**Haikou:** Trains to Sanya via Dongfang take just under 3 hours, and currently there are 6 services per day. Buses to Sanya take 3 hours.

**Sanya:** Trains and buses (far more frequent) to Haikou take approximately 3 hours. Wenchang is 3½ hours away. Minibuses ply the routes between the south coast resorts.

**Tongzhi:** There are plenty of buses to Haikou (3 hrs) and Sanya (1½–2 hrs).

**Wenchang:** Buses to Haikou take 1½ hours hours, while Sanya is 3½–4 hours away.

Around 3 km (2 miles) southeast of the city centre, **Five Figures Temple** (五公祠; Wugong Si; open daily 8.30am–5pm; entrance fee) is a pleasant Qing Dynasty complex, dotted with fragrant frangipani trees, again built in honour of exiled Tang and Song Dynasty imperial critics. Noth-ing remains of the original Ming Dynasty compound. The five in question, Li Deyu, Li Gang, Li Guang, Hu Quan and Zhao Ding, were all state officials. The high-ceilinged, two-storey Watching Crop Hall carries stone carvings of each, with bio-graphical inscriptions carved in Chinese characters.

Adjacent **Xuepu Hall** (学甫大厅; Xuepu Dating), displays local relics that include a Han Dynasty ceremonial drum, a large Ming Dynasty iron bell and Qing Dynasty cannons. There is also a com-memorative temple to the poet Su Dongpo, one of the island's most famous exiles, and poetic inscriptions on a stone tablet by Huizong Zhao Ji, who called himself the father of Daoism in the Song Dynasty.

## Day trips from Haikou

A little under 10 km (6 miles) northwest of the city centre lie low rolling sand dunes that most people would assume are natural, if not told otherwise. A natural sandy stretch was enhanced some 20 years ago, to stretch around 5 km (3 miles) of dunes, shaded lawns and cycling tracks – well used by picnickers, joggers and t'ai chi practitioners. **Holiday Beach** (假日海滩; Jiari Haitan) lies at

**BELOW:** the Five Figures Temple.

the hub of this city seaside escape, with its slew of aquatic and sand-bound beach buggies for hire. Normally it is laid-back on weekdays and buzzing at weekends, when it is fun for people-watching. Holiday Beach also has an outdoor swimming pool (open daily from sunrise until sunset; entrance fees), with kids' area and water slide. To get here from the city centre you can take bus No. 40 from the south side of Haikou Park.

Some 15 km (9 miles) south of the city lies **Horse Saddle Mountain** (马鞍山; Maan Shan), which is riddled with 72 extinct volcanic craters, caves and tubes. On its slopes, **Crater Park ❷** (火山口公园; Huoshankou Gongyuan; open daily; entrance fee) is a landscaped area of lava rock-slab paths and stairways that ascend a 222-metre (728-ft) peak for good views of three other overgrown craters and surrounding rural villages, before descending into the small crater core. Nearby, and accessible by hired vehicle, is the **Cave of Heavenly Spirits**, a 2-km (1¼-mile) lava tube that ends in a tall-ceilinged wide chamber. There is no need for tickets here, but local old men provide flare-light illumination and act

as informal guides for those keen to explore. These senior entrepreneurs will charge anything up to Rmb 30 to assist small groups for half an hour or so.

With a collection of around 4,000 birds and animals, which reside in relative space and comfort, the **Hainan Tropical Wildlife Park and Botanical Garden ❸** (海南热带野生动物植物园; Hainan Redai Yesheng Dongwu Zhiwuguan; www.hntwzoo.com; open daily 8am–6pm; entrance fee), 12 km (7 miles) southeast of Haikou, is an illuminating experience. Indigenous inhabitants include white buffalo, black mountain goat, Hainan peacock pheasant, Eld's deer and a rare subspecies of the rhesus macaque.

The sprawling park is really designed for the drive-through visitor, with dirt roads wending their way through mature rainforest. Big cat enclosures are reached via electronically activated double gates (which can take a while to open). Less threatening animals, such as Asian elephants, Bactrian camel, Sika deer and Eld's deer can be observed from outside a visitor's vehicle on the other side of moats or low wooden fencing. As if by

*Commemorating the Song-dynasty poet Su Dongpo at Haikou's Five Figures Temple.*

**BELOW:** Hainan Tropical Wildlife Park is one of China's best zoos, not least in terms of its animal welfare.

*The Bayi Stone Flower Cave (open daily 8.30am–5.30pm; entrance fee), 180 km (112 miles) southwest of Haikou, makes a worthwhile day trip. A small punt takes visitors on to the small "stone forest sanctuary", a clump of weathered vertical rocks.*

**BELOW:** taking it easy on holiday.
**RIGHT:** tropical flora.

magic, park attendants appear at these points, offering fruit and veg that visitors can feed to the animals for a small fee.

## ALONG THE EAST COAST

A town commonly overlooked by tourists, **Wenchang ❹** (文昌) – 70 km (44 miles) southeast of Haikou and set back from the coast to the west of the Sanya highway – has distinct charm and is worth an overnight stay. Its once-ramshackle centre, through which a small canal runs, was built up as a commercial centre last century by the French, and is now undergoing gradual modernisation.

The **Confucius Temple** (孔庙; Kong Miao; open daily 8am–6pm; entrance fee) is today one of the best-preserved examples of ancient architecture on the island. Dating all the way back to the 11th century, repeated renovation and expansion since the Ming Dynasty has continued to the present day, with a major spruce-up in September 2006. The entrance moon gate leads past a small landscaped terrace, a life-sized statue of Confucius, and on to wooden halls, where the calligraphy and ink paintings

illustrate some of the philosopher's maxims. Carved stone memorial tablets dedicated to Confucius and 12 of his disciples are also displayed. In the temple, altars are dedicated to the virtual Chinese saint.

Throughout China, Wenchang is well known for two other associations: first, as the birthplace of the famous Chinese dish "Hainan chicken rice" (boiled chicken with a ginger and garlic dip and an optional serving of seasoned rice cooked in chicken stock); and second, as the birthplace of the Song sisters.

Political and social heroines, Song Qingling and Song Meiling were the respective wives of legendary political figures Sun Yatsen and Chiang Kaishek. **Song Qingling's former residence** (宋庆龄故居; Song Qingling Guju; near Changsa village, and signposted in Chinese only from the town; open daily 8.30am–5pm; entrance fee) is a well-kept example of a late Qing Dynasty family courtyard home, built by her father Song Yaoru. A permanent exhibition of photographs and artefacts depict the life of a moneyed Chinese family with Communist Party ties, whose life flitted between

the PRC and the USA, rubbing shoulders with international politicians. Unfortunately, almost all explanations appear without English translation.

Wenchang's spreading suburbs spill out towards the nearby coastal village of **Qinglan** (清澜). A natural beach close to a tiny harbour is being developed as Qinglan Port Scenic Area, with tasteful resorts under construction.

From Qinglan, vehicle ferries hop across a small inlet to **Dongjiao Yelin** promontory, usually known simply as Dongjiao, which was home to Hainan's first coconut plantation and now has several, set back from a fine stretch of sandy coastline. Small resorts and family hotels are mushrooming here.

## Xinglong and Shimei Bay

Around 100 km (62 miles) south of Wenchang, **Xinglong** ❺ (兴隆) is another Hainanese town that is famous for two things: natural spring water and coffee. Both are found some distance from the dusty dirt-road village itself. Some visitors stay around the spring area, which has spawned a collection of hotels that all claim to offer both outdoor hot and cold spring-water pools and spring water piped into guest bathrooms. With the large volume of rooms available, it would seem unlikely that they all tap into the actual mineral source.

This is a fertile agricultural area. In the 1950s, Chinese émigrés from Indonesia, Thailand and Vietnam first planted coffee and peppercorn in the vicinity, and later began making a variety of coconut sweets. Nearby is the superb **Xinglong Tropical Botanical Garden** (兴隆热带植物园; Xinglong Redai Zhiwuguan; open daily 8.30am–5.30pm; entrance fee). Founded in 1957 for government-funded botanical research, laboratory buildings remain and are off-limits. At the well-landscaped gardens, knowledgeable guides expound on the grounds' lush contents. Of all the introduced produce grown here, gargantuan vanilla pods from South America are the most prized, although they are not considered viable for commercial farming on the island. The gift shop here sells some of the best-quality produce available in Hainan – including an unusual variety of green tea flavoured with vanilla. Close to the botanical gardens is **Xinglong Indonesian and**

*Look at a Chinese map of China and you will see the border extending far to the south to encompass a cluster of tropical reefs and atolls, some 1,000 km (600 miles) beyond Hainan. These are the Paracel and Spratly Islands (Zhongsha and Nansha Qundao), also claimed by Vietnam, the Philippines – and Taiwan, whose army occupies the largest island. Various skirmishes have resulted, most seriously in 1988, when China sank two Vietnamese patrol boats. There are thought to be oilfields in the area.*

**BELOW:** Hainan chicken rice.

**TIP**

A cautionary word: monkeys on Nanwan Island have been known to jump on visitors and are regularly chased off by park staff; they have only been known to bite when a visitor panics to throw them off.

**BELOW:** resort life at Yalong Bay.

**Thai Village**, where dance performances take place daily; it's a shoddy theme park, best avoided.

On the other side of the expressway from Xinglong is Hainan's surfing centre, **Shimei Bay**, which seems set to develop a significant tourism industry. For now, the palm-fringed beaches are idyllic and relatively unspoilt, and there is little of the hubbub of the southern resorts. As well as surfing, there are diving trips and excursions to nearby Jiajing Island.

## Nanwan Island and Xincun

Otherwise known as **Monkey Island** ❻, Nanwan (南湾猴岛) is actually a 10-sq km (4-sq mile) peninsula that is only accessible by boat or cable-car from the tiny port of **Xincun** (新村) – a ramshackle village with a couple of shops selling locally made pearl jewellery.

In such isolation and with government protection, a colony of around 1,500 macaque monkeys have thrived for decades. Though still benefiting from official state care, the grey primates and their environs have been turned into the stars of an overly commercial park. It makes for an unusual and family-friendly

excursion, but the recent addition of outdoor performance stages seems less than ideal for those concerned with animal welfare. On the plus side, the peanut and sweet-potato vendors that used to supply snacks for visitors to feed the monkeys have now been removed.

A high admission charge has been introduced; while this includes the return cable-car ticket, local fishermen still offer a boat ride over, which passes the cluster of floating fish farms off Xincun. Should you negotiate a private charter a ticket is still required (purchased from the cable-car office), and there is no reduction in its cost.

## Lingshui Village

Ten kilometres (6 miles) north of Xincun is **Lingshui** ❼ (陵水), an appealing little village and one of the oldest settlements on the island. Once past some dull residential blocks near the highway, narrow arcaded streets and alleys comprise low-rise buildings full of character – several of them around a century old.

The **Lingshui History Museum** (陵水历史博物馆; Lingshui Lishi Bowuguan; open daily 8.30am–5pm;

ntrance fee) is worth a visit; much of Hainan's archaeological finds from the Stone Age hail from this area. The ornate building was built as a wealthy businessmen's club in 1921, becoming a communist club in 1927. Exhibits document modern eras including the Japanese occupation.

A small Qing Dynasty monastery nearby with upturned eaves, tall ceilings and a courtyard operates as something of a community centre, with pool tables, a teahouse and VCDs shown on a large-screen television.

## SANYA AND THE SOUTH

Hainan's tourist boom has focused on this beautiful beach-fringed area on the southern tip of the island. Although Sanya Airport has whisked in visitors from the mainland and a handful of Asian cities since it opened in 1994, it's only since 2003 that airport traffic has significantly increased, with long-haul visitors a relatively new phenomenon – most staying in the out-of-town resorts of Dadonghai and Yalong Bay (see below).

## Sanya

Sanya ❽ (三亚) was originally one of several fishing villages on the southern tip of Hainan, and fishing docks still occupy a focal point at the town's hub. Large trawlers are on the move both day and night, despite recent government restrictions as a result of the waters being overfished. The trawlers' wharf was pedestrianised in mid-2006, and makes for a pleasant stroll.

The Sanya River divides the town from north to south, with the original settlement lying to the west. New hotels have sprung up on both sides of the river, and are more reasonably priced than those on nearby beaches. The town is pleasantly relaxed; shabbiness now rubs shoulders with a form of gentrification – witness the recent opening of several good restaurants and a trend for upmarket teahouses.

The main market on and around Xinian Lu witnesses possibly Sanya's only bustle, as traders and locals haggle over tropical fruit, live and dried seafood, clothing and much more. Hainan's best mangoes and pink-fleshed guavas are found here. Headscarf-wearing Hui (Chinese Muslim) women are evident in town, and 3 km (2 miles) west of Sanya lies the predominantly Hui Yanglang village with its large mosque.

### Luhuitou Hill

Luhuitou ❹ (鹿回头) means "Deer Looking Back" and denotes a legend, which appears as a giant sculpture that tops this rocky peninsula within view of downtown Sanya. The story relates how a hunter had a deer in the sights of his drawn bowstring on the hill. The deer turned towards the hunter and transformed into a beautiful maiden. As you would expect, the hunter dropped his bow and the two fell in love.

The statue is at the centre of a landscaped **park** (open daily 8.30am–6.30pm; entrance fee) that is also home to a few tacky amusements and vendors hiring out costumes and props to those wishing to take outlandish photographic keepsakes. From the summit there are superb views of Sanya City, Dadonghai Bay and other nearby beaches.

*Sanya has made considerable efforts to raise its international profile. Three successive Miss World competitions were held here from 2003, and April 2007 saw the launch of the annual Beach Jazz Festival.*

**BELOW:** beach volleyball at Dadonghai.

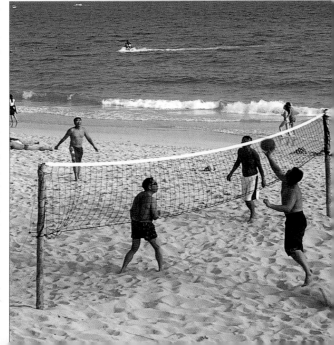

## Dadonghai

Five minutes south of Sanya by road, or a 45-minute walk, lies the long fine-sand bay of **Dadonghai ⑬** (大东海). The whole of its beachfront has been developed, with mostly high-end hotels and villa resorts. Off the main drag, side streets are wall-to-wall with seafood restaurants and beachwear and souvenir knick-knack shops; it's all fairly relaxed, with little hard sales pressure.

Palm-tree shade is a little scarce, although it's possible to rent chairs and tables under parasols. The water is clean, but deceptive currents mean that it's not suitable for children or weaker swimmers.

Another fine stretch of sand, this time just north of Sanya city, **Sanya Bay** is home to both reasonably priced and mid-priced hotels; it's also one of the best spots to rent a holiday apartment, with plenty of shops and a good choice of local restaurants in the neighbourhood.

## Yalong Bay

Around 20 km (12 miles) to the east of Sanya lies **Yalong Bay ⓒ** (亚龙湾; Yalong Wan), a stunningly beautiful 8-km (5-mile) bay that has everything you would expect of a tropical beach: palm trees, warm, clear water, and endless fine white sand. Despite being listed a protected marine park, development has been allowed to go ahead, and a number of resorts have been built along the fringes of the beach. Fortunately, most of the design and landscaping has been reasonably well integrated with the natural beauty of the bay.

Relaxing in the sun and swimming are the order of the day here. Watersports on offer include diving, paragliding and jet skiing; the quality of equipment is variable. For now, those staying here are captive to five-star resort prices come mealtime, but a new dining and retail area called Lakeside Commercial Street is set to offer a somewhat cheaper alternative.

In the vicinity is the **Yalong Bay Seashell Museum** (亚龙湾海洋贝壳馆; Yalong Wan Haiyang Beike Guan; open daily 8.30am–6.30pm; entrance fee), and the beautifully landscaped **Yalong Bay Butterfly Park** (same hours; entrance fee), which houses a butterfly museum that holds a comprehensive selection of species from across the world. The highlight, though, is a net-enclosed landscaped

**BELOW:** Dadonghai beach.

garden. Avoid the middle of the day, when the heat renders the insects inactive.

**Yalong Bay Underwater World** (亚龙湾海底世界; Yalong Wan Haidi Shijie; open daily; various activity fees) offers glass-bottom boat tours, snorkelling, scuba diving, deep-sea fishing trips and more from its pier at the bay's eastern end.

## Tianya Hajiao

Not to be confused with a standard sun-worshipping and swimming beach, **Tianya Hajiao** ① (天涯海角; open daily 7.30am–7pm; entrance fee) literally translates as "The End of the Sky and the Corner of the Sea" or is sometimes more simply referred to as "The End of the Earth" in English. This stretch of coastline, 25 km (15 miles) due west from Sanya, was so named by exiles from the mainland from dynasties past, who, in their desperate isolation carved this and other poignant observations, such as "The Pillar of the Southern Sky" into large rocks that mark the end of a long sandy stretch.

The ever-expanding area around the beach includes landscaped gardens (with some adventurous dragon-shaped topiary), sculptures of historical Chinese figures, souvenir stalls, and somewhat over-persistent "pearl" vendors and photo opportunists.

## Nanshan

Further west again, some 50 km (32 miles) from Sanya, **Nanshan Buddhist Culture Park** ⑨ (南山佛教文化园; Nanshan Fujiao Wenhuayuan; open 8.30am–6.30pm; entrance fee) was developed as a major tourist attraction in the mid-1990s. As a break from beach life, it's easy to spend half a day or so exploring the 40 hectares (5,000 acres) of landscaped Chinese, Japanese and European gardens dedicated to Buddhism. While enlightenment is made easier if you can read Chinese, the park has some of the island's most interesting Buddhist temples, and the rolling landscape enjoys ocean views. The park's lawns are the backdrop for impromptu Li- and Miao-inspired music and dance performances.

The centrepiece of the park is the huge multi-tiered and fabulously restored **Nanshan Temple and Monastery complex** (南山寺; Nanshan Shi), which was originally built in the 1950s. Near the

*Dragon topiary at Tianya Hajiao's landscaped gardens, a popular photo-spot for tourists.*

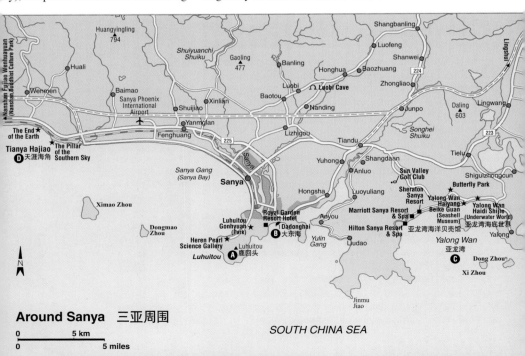

**Around Sanya** 三亚周围

| 0 | 5 km |
| 0 | 5 miles |

*SOUTH CHINA SEA*

*Nanshan Buddhist Culture Park is not just for tourists.*

entrance, the **Guanshi Yin** (Goddess of Mercy) Temple charges a separate admission fee on account of its 4-metre (13-ft) Tibetan eight-armed altarpiece being made of solid gold and jade. That's not to mention 120 carats of diamonds, pearl, red coral and turquoise.

Take the time to cross the causeway from the park's beachfront to visit the small man-made island, which is dominated by a giant statue of Guanyin. At 108 metres (354 ft) in height, this is the world's largest standing statue of the Buddhist goddess of mercy and infinite compassion. One hundred and eight monks attended the statue's enshrinement in 2005, and it was said that the statue's three faces were looking at the Chinese mainland, Taiwan and the rest of the world respectively – which suggested that the goddess would bestow her blessings and protection not only on China but on the rest of the world, too.

The park as a whole is enormous, so make sure you purchase a hop-on-and-off buggy pass. If you're really taken with the place, you can stay on-site in a hotel, or at the more unusual Nanshan Treehouse accommodation *(see page 360)*.

## Jiangfeng Primeval Forest Reserve

The sprawling 9,700-hectare (24,000 acre) **Jianfengling Primeval Forest Reserve** ❿（尖峰岭热带原始森林自然保护区; Jiangfengling Redai Yuanshi Senlin Ziranbaohuqu) was set up by the local government in 1976, after large areas of forest had been felled to make way for rubber plantations. Located in Ledong County in the southwest of the island, a trip to the reserve is best done as an overnighter from Sanya with a car and driver. Tour agents in Sanya will arrange the required admission pass and a guide; if visiting with a driver, passes are available at the park entrance lodge. Guest houses and a few eateries in Jiangfeng Village stoke up visitors before entering the reserve.

From the village, the reserve drop-off point is a further 45 bone-rattling minutes away, where there is also modest hotel accommodation and a restaurant. From here, marked trails wind through the mature forest, home to some 2,000 species of plant life, 1,000 types of insect and 148 varieties of bird and beast. These include Eld's deer, black-headed gibbon

## Tourism in Hainan

A decade ago Hainan Island was little-known outside of mainland China as a destination. Even then, with a poorly developed tourism infrastructure, it was mostly favoured by well-heeled Chinese from the north of the country, who would descend here to escape their bitter winters; a significant amount of government officials made up their number.

Fast-forward to 2007, and a transformation of the tourist infrastructure, coupled with some aggressive marketing, has brought a huge boost to visitor numbers. Of these, more than 90 percent are Chinese nationals, with a large portion travelling from southern China. Of some 600,000 international visitors annually, approximately 200,000 are from Hong Kong and Macau. The most prevalent foreign tourist by far has been from Russia, since direct charter flights were launched from Moscow in 2005; the impact has been so strong that the Dadonghai area has Chinese and Russian signs and menus, with English thrown in as an afterthought. This may change, though, as May 2007 marked the beginning of UK charter flights. Korean visitors – who have reciprocal relaxed entry into China – are also much in evidence. Meanwhile, clean beaches, golf courses and a very relaxed vibe have visitor figures on a continuing upward curve.

nd Hainan partridge. As in most places f natural beauty in China, physical features are romantically named after what hey subtly resemble: Buddha Hill and Moonlit Pond are such examples. Visors to the reserve will also see some of he lesser-visited western side of Hainan, where villages reflect a more modest evel of economic growth compared with hose to the east of the island.

## THE CENTRAL HIGHLANDS

Hainan's hilly centre, always something f a backwater to say the least, has ecome even sleepier since the mid-990s when the completion of the eastrn Haikou–Sanya highway diverted most traffic from the old central route cross the island. Highland towns are nore than a bit shabby around the edges, ut very relaxed, and the ever-changing mountain vistas are easy on the eye. iuided walks can be arranged through nost of the hotels in the region.

The Li and Miao minorities are rarely een elsewhere on the island, but are still n evidence in these parts, having been isplaced into the more marginal highnds by the arrival of the Han Chinese –

a relatively recent process on Hainan. Although victim of relentless logging, this area is still home to some indigenous forest, particularly around Wuzhi Shan and Qizhi Shan mountains, in the heart of the Li autonomous counties.

## Wuzhishan (Tongshi)

At the centre of the Hainan's Li Autonomous Region, the quiet town of **Wuzhishan** ⓫ (五指山市), known as Tongshi until it was recently renamed after the nearby mountain (30 km/20 miles northeast), has a laid-back feel. Thankfully, a tacky Li and Miao "cultural experience" has relocated to Sanya, but the real thing can still be witnessed in villages all around Wuzhishan's periphery, albeit without the song, dance and colourful costume. The truth is that these ethnic minority villages have almost all upgraded from thatched mudand-straw hut dwellings to tiled concrete with satellite TV dishes.

Named best museum in China in 1995 by Beijing's minister for South China, Li Peng, the **Museum of Nationalities** (民族博物馆; Minzu Bowuguan; open daily 8.30am–5.30pm; entrance fee) has

**TIP**

The rock calligraphy of the undesirables banished to southern Hainan is one of the main sights at Tianya Hajiao. On a blazing hot day, pay for the privilege of a passenger buggy ride to and from the path to the rocks, which is otherwise a 20- to 30-minute walk.

**BELOW:** the gigantic Guanyin statue off the coast at Nanshan.

*Li minority textiles on display at the Nationalities Museum, Wuzhishan.*

**BELOW:** central Highlands resort at Qixianling.

since slipped into disrepair. There are still several interesting exhibits, though, some with explanations in English. Hainan's history is tracked from the Stone Age to 1990s sporting trophies. Notable inclusions are Li and Miao hunting and trapping implements and beautifully woven textiles, and nationalist, communist and Japanese weapons and uniforms from China's turbulent 1930s and 1940s.

The southern bank of the river that bisects Wuzhishan buzzes with outdoor restaurants and tea and coffee houses. The market is another source of colour, and the occasional woman in Li or Miao headgear may be glimpsed.

**Wuzhishan** (Five Finger Mountain) was named after its subtle structural similarities to a hand, and is shrouded in folklore. The 1,867-metre (6,125-ft) peak is the highest on the island, and can be explored via a series of marked trails that pass through some beautiful protected mature forest. The most popular circuit takes four to five hours, taking in pine-fragrant vistas of local ranges and valleys. Guides and tents can be hired at hotels in the vicinity.

## Elsewhere in the highlands

Some 35 km (22 miles) due south o Wuzhishan, the highland village o **Qixianling** ⑫ (七仙岭) shelters unde the seven jagged peaks of Qizhisha (Seven Finger Mountain), close to th village of **Baoting**. Qixianling is idea for some serious down time. The villag itself – "Seven Fairy Maidens Spa" i English – where mythological woodlan nymphs are said to have bathed in the ho springs, is very laid-back, and there ar hikes up into the surrounding mountai slopes, lush and often mist-shrouded Hotels and resorts, ranging from th modest to the thatched Bali-inspired typ complete with piped-in hot spring wate and massage menus, make a pit-stop her appealing.

Accessible from Ba Cun, a short rid from Baoting, **Qizhishan** (七指山） sacred to the Li people, is less often vis ited than Wuzhishan, and the climb i shorter but steeper – this is a fairl demanding hike and requires decen footwear. To the north of Wuzhishan o the main road to Haikou, **Qiongzhong** i a pleasant hill town surrounded by attrac tive countryside.

# RESTAURANTS

## Restaurants

Average price for a meal for one, with one drink:
**$** under US$12 (under Rmb 100)
**$$** US$12–20 (Rmb 100–60)
**$$$** over US$20 (over Rmb 160)

## Haikou

Reasonably priced noodle and congee restaurants abound. Jinlong Road has become known as "Food Street", popular with well-heeled locals and tourists, and features Japanese, Korean and regional Chinese fare – but, surprisingly, no Hainanese menus.

### Fusion Restaurant

Sheraton Haikou Resort, 199 Bin Hai Lu. Tel: 0898 6870 8888.
www.sheraton.com/haikou **$$$**
Western fine dining, with a European Continental bent and wine to match, is served in the city's most elegant restaurant.

### Lu Zhi Hai Xien Mai Tze Chen

38 Hai Shu Donglu. Tel: 0898 6672 3925. **$–$$**
Bang in the centre of the city, what used to be a street vendor became so popular that the local government granted a two-storey expansion. Its open ground floor displays locally caught seafood

and "wild" vegetables.

### Pu Qian Hai Xian Han Niu Ji Fandian

13 Long Hwa Lu. **$**
You will find no better Hainan chicken rice than at this downtown specialist restaurant. Hotel staff will point you in the right direction. Other signatures include rice noodles and wild veggies.

### Sheng Long Jiu Jia

Lao Cheng Zhen, Cheng Mai Xian. Tel: 0898 6748 8235. **$**
On a no-nonsense suburban strip with no numbers on its four large restaurants, this is a local favourite for fair-priced seafood that you select yourself in the kitchen.

## Sanya Area

Sanya Market area is dotted with small restaurants where fresh seafood costs significantly less than in the beach resorts. The numerous live-aquarium eateries of Dadonghai are a step up in the comfort and selection stakes. Yalong Bay's restaurants are only in the resorts.

### Asia Café

Eadry Resort, Yuya Lu. Tel: 0898 8860 9999.
www.eadryresort.com **$$**
Open-sided restaurant with a can't-go-wrong

menu spanning Asia and the West – despite its name. Its Saturday night barbecue buffet comes highly recommended.

### Bai Yun

1st Floor, Sheraton Sanya Resort, Yalong Bay. Tel: 0898 8855 8855.
www.sheraton.com/sanya **$$$**
Classy regional Chinese renditions. Local specialities include octopus, dim sum-style dumplings, coconut rice and chilled steamed duck with vinegar dip.

### Indochine

Ground Floor, Sanya Marriott Resort & Spa, Yalong Bay. Tel: 0898 8856 8888.
marriott.com/SYXMC **$$$**
From a cool steel open kitchen come surprisingly traditional Vietnamese recipes – albeit with modern touches.

### IZE

Ground Floor, Hilton Sanya Spa & Resort, Yalong Bay. Tel: 0898 8858 8588.
www.sanya.hilton.com **$$$**

Western-style fine dining uses local ingredients where possible – the spiny lobster main is served with oxtail ragout and sweet pea sauce, vegetable foam and oyster mushroom.

### Sanya Hai Yun Hai Shan Da Pai Dong

Shengli Lu, corner of Xinjian Lu. Tel: 0898 8826 2145.
www.haiyunhx.com **$–$$**
This clean and cheerful seafood restaurant also operates as a casual noodle shop. It has no street number but is a couple of doors away from the Bank of China.

### Spice Garden

2nd Floor, Sheraton Sanya Resort, Yalong Bay. Tel: 0898 8855 8855.
www.sheraton.com/sanya **$$$**
Casual indoor and outdoor restaurant serving quality Southeast Asian and Japanese cuisine, with seating also set at sushi and tepanyaki grill counters.

**RIGHT:** typical Hainan cuisine.

*Recommended Restaurants & Cafés on page 227*

# FUJIAN

Fujian province is split down the middle, with steep mountains to the north and subtropical valleys to the south. Firmly off the beaten track, this is nevertheless one of China's most varied and interesting destinations

Fujian is seldom visited by foreign tourists, but within its 121,700 sq km (47,000 sq miles) it offers enough history, spectacular scenery, folk traditions, fine food and other attractions to rank alongside some of China's more lauded destinations.

For military reasons, much of the province was closed for 30 years, and access from the coast to the interior was deliberately restricted to resist what was thought to be an imminent invasion from Taiwan. Times have changed, however, and these days domestic tourism is well established, although international tourism has barely begun.

This part of China was part of the Minyue Kingdom for aeons, not fully integrated into the Chinese Empire until the Tang Dynasty (618–906). To this day most Fujianese people refer to themselves as Minnan, after the Min River that flows from Wuyishan to Fuzhou.

International traders are familiar with Fujian as the source of most of the world's footwear, and it is a global manufacturing base for companies like Honda, Yamaha, Daimler Chrysler, Dell and Kodak. But international trade is nothing new here. Several hundred years ago, Fujian's subtropical coastline was the starting point for some of the great seafaring expeditions of all time. Coastal cities were the transshipment ports for exports of fine silks, porcelain and the teas that flourish on the wet mountain slopes of the interior. Inbound cargoes included spices and, in later centuries, opium.

A thousand years ago Quanzhou was arguably the world's most important port, and all of Fujian's coastal cities have more than their share of historic attractions. Down through the centuries the rugged coastline, mountain ranges and generally sparse soil have discouraged all but the most intrepid spirits from inland exploration. Fujian has more dialects than any other Chinese province, and neighbouring coastal villages often lack a common spoken language, let alone a land link. Instead of exploring opportunities near home, it was traditionally

**Main attractions**
GULANGYU ISLAND, XIAMEN
ZHENCHENG LOU (HAKKA HOUSE)
MARITIME MUSEUM, QUANZHOU
KAIYUAN TEMPLE, QUANZHOU
WUYISHAN SCENIC DISTRICT
NINE BEND STREAM RAFTING
MINYUE KINGDOM MUSEUM

**LEFT:** Zhencheng Lou Hakka roundhouse.
**BELOW:** child at Wuyi Square, Fuzhou.

*Typically grand colonial architecture on the peaceful island of Gulangyu, Xiamen.*

easier to set sail for foreign lands in search of fame and fortune, or even a spouse. This explains why most of the Overseas Chinese of Singapore, Malaysia and the Philippines trace their ancestral roots to this corner of China. Some left as indentured labourers, but Fujian has long been notorious as the starting point for illegal emigration, by young men desperate to escape at any price the grinding poverty of much of the interior.

Only a short distance from Fujian's cities you enter a time warp where accommodation is basic, roads are rough and English is rarely spoken. Inland are sights that rival the wonders of the world; head for the mist-laden northernmost moun-

tains of the province to explore deep river gorges and one of the largest and most sophisticated capitals of 2,000 years ago, or track down the *tulou*, fortified Hakka roundhouses around Yongding, built on a scale that boggles the mind. Across the province you'll find delicious local food and a warm and old-fashioned sense of hospitality, all washed down by the fragrant Oolong tea that is Fujian's lifeblood, flowing almost non-stop into thimble-sized cups 24 hours a day.

## Orientation

Despite the opening of new airports and grandiose plans for rail expansion, much of the province remains isolated. Still

Fujian 福建

ʷujian is the midpoint between Shanghai ɑnd Hong Kong, and, more importantly, ɪt is the stepping stone between Taiwan ɑnd China. As scheduled cross-Strait ʰlights become a reality, and passenger ʲerries follow the freighters that already ɔly the Formosa Strait separating Taiwan ɑnd Fujian, this part of China can be ᵉxpected to do well.

Even with the promised new transport ɪinks, it would take years to explore ᵉverything that this fascinating province ʰas to offer. Concentrate on one area or ɔick a few highlights. Fuzhou and Xiaᴍen are major gateways thanks to their ɪnternational airports, and they form natᵘral starting or finishing points for ᵉxploration off the beaten track.

## XIAMEN

Once better-known by its Fujian name of Amoy, **Xiamen** ❶ （厦门）remains one ɔf China's most appealing cities, full of ʷell-maintained streets lined with 19thᶜentury shophouses. However, the main ɑttraction is, without doubt, the enchantɪng island of Gulangyu, with its quiet ᵊtreets and colonial mansions, just a few ᴍinutes away by ferry.

Xiamen itself is an island, linked to mainland Fujian via a 5-km (3-mile) causeway. The **old town** ❹, full of character and charm, is focused around the lower (western) end of Zhongshan Lu, and is a pleasant place to wander around, although lacking in any notable sights. At the harbourside here, ferries cross the narrow channel to Gulangyu every 10–15 minutes from 5.30am until 9pm, and then every 20–30 minutes until 12.20am. The journey time is 5–7 minutes.

### Gulangyu Island

Following the First Opium War, Xiamen was declared an international settlement, and the tiny island of **Gulangyu** ❸ （鼓浪屿）became the preferred environment for foreigners and residents who had made good overseas. It has been preserved largely intact, a living museum of refined late 19th- and early 20th-century buildings. Mellow granite, brick and plaster, weathered terracotta roof tiles and fanciful towers and turrets adorn churches, consulates and clubs, private residences, hospitals, convalescent homes, law courts and schools from another era to create a

*Door panel gracing an old Chinese house in central Xiamen.*

**BELOW:** the view across Xiamen harbour to Gulangyu.

*The lack of vehicles makes Gulangyu one of the most relaxing places in China.*

**BELOW:** looking across Gulangyu to the modern city of Xiamen.

harmonious ensemble. Peace and quiet is a big part of the experience – there are no cars, motorbikes or even bicycles allowed on the island, although electric trains now trundle along the pleasant leafy lanes. Anachronistic they may be, but these space-age vehicles certainly make thorough exploration more manageable in Xiamen's long, hot and humid summers.

But Gulangyu offers more: beaches, an Undersea World theme park, with no lack of teahouses and excellent seafood restaurants for refreshment along the way. Domestic tour groups tend to be less interested in the buildings than in the many curiously shaped rocks and other natural formations scattered around the place, where they pose for their friends to snap souvenir shots.

The most enjoyable way to explore is simply to stroll (and get lost) wherever your inclinations lead you through the winding, tree-shaded lanes. Even if you try to follow the souvenir map (best bought in the city as supply on the island is unreliable), the turns and curves threaten to defeat even the most expert map readers. The reward for an unstructured approach to sightseeing will be many a crumbling treasure – elaborate wrought-iron railings, lovingly moulded stucco, and a thousand fascinating details awaiting discovery, like Sleeping Beauty's castle, almost hidden under layers of green.

## Gulangyu's sights

The ferry from the city brings you to the main Gulangyu Pier, inland from which is the main commerical centre with shops and restaurants aplenty. Only a few metres from the ferry pier is the **Xiamen Undersea World C** (海底世界; Haidi Shijie; open 9.30am–4.30pm; entrance fee), which boasts a variety of attractions including a walk-through aquarium. To get here, turn right past the bank – the entrance ahead of you is clearly marked by a large octopus.

Heading in the other direction from the ferry pier will bring you to **Haoyue Gardens** and the **Koxinga statue** (郑成功铜像; *see margin on opposite page*) at the easternmost point of the island. Continue along the coast to reach one of the most picturesque places on Gulangyu, the **Shuzhuang Garden D** (菽庄花园; Shuzhuang Huayuan; open daily 6.30am–8pm; entrance fee) in the

*Recommended Restaurants & Cafés on page 227*

southeast, with its zigzag bridge that enables you to believe that you "walk on water" at high tide. Beyond the garden, the pleasant sandy beach extends along much of the island's southern coast.

The leafy sanctuary at Shuzhuang was the pet project of Mr Lin Er Jia, who is believed to have brought the first piano to Gulangyu, starting a musical tradition that continues to this day. The island is said to have some 1,800 pianos, which earns Gulangyu the common nickname "Piano Island". Many of China's leading classical musicians were born on Gulangyu, or have their roots here. Some say that the many subtle microtones in the local dialect account for the survival of strong musical genes over the centuries. Be that as it may, you can't miss the point that music plays a major role in life on the island once you spot the pier – shaped like a grand piano – looming towards you as your ferry approaches the island. Gulangyu has its own concert hall where the Xiamen Philharmonic Orchestra gives regular concerts. With the absence of any vehicles it is still possible to hear the tinkling scales and trills that still cascade out of many an open window around the island.

Appropriately enough, Shuzhuang Garden houses the **Piano Museum** (鼓浪屿钢琴博物馆; Gangqin Bowuguan; open daily 8.15am–5.15pm; entrance fee), established by an Australian-Chinese musician who felt that this was the ideal resting place for the collection of a lifetime.

**Sunlight Rock** Ⓔ (日光岩; Riguang Yan; open daily 6.30am–8pm; entrance fee), a favourite photo opportunity and the highest point on the island at 93 metres (305 ft), is to the north. Just below it within the same park is the **Koxinga Memorial Hall** (郑成功纪念馆; Zhengchenggong Jinianguan; open daily 8am–5pm; admission included with Sunlight Rock), with a mixture of 17th-century artefacts and a large dose of Taiwan-related propaganda. *For details on Koxinga see pages 28–9.*

Some of the finest buildings on Gulangyu are situated in the area immediately uphill from the main ferry pier – on Fujian Lu, Lujiao Lu and Longtou Lu (the latter is also a good bet for restaurants). A little further west is the long-closed **Xiamen Museum** at 43 Guxin Lu, whose beautiful cupolas are visible

*The Koxinga statue on the eastern tip of Gulangyu gazes out across the sea to nearby Taiwan.*

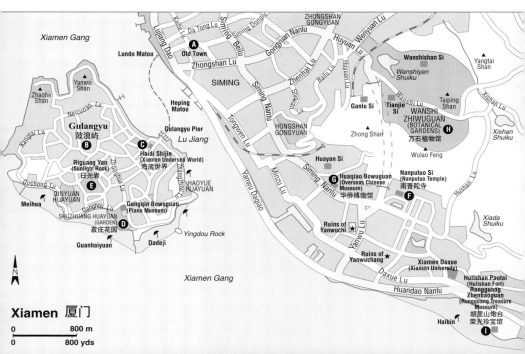

**Xiamen** 厦门

0     800 m
0     800 yds

*Skyscraper on the seafront at Xiamen, one of China's wealthiest cities.*

**BELOW:** the western waterfront district of Xiamen, near the Gulangyu ferry pier, is the most interesting part of the city.

from a distance. This is one of the island's most fascinating structures, dating from 1907, with its domes sprouting from perfectly proportioned octagonal bases. The architect has incorporated elements from Armenian churches, a famous mosque in Jerusalem and the Parthenon, along with many traditional Chinese features, that all seem to blend into a homogenous end result.

## City sights

Back on Xiamen Island, the tourist sights are to be found to the southeast of the city centre. The **Nanputuo Temple ⓕ** (南普陀寺; Nanputuo Si; open daily 8am–5pm; entrance fee) is always busy, and on a still day it is wrapped in a blue veil of incense smoke. Structures nearest to the main road have suffered the most unsympathetic renovation, but the further you move up the hill, the more atmospheric (and quieter) the place becomes.

Few visitors seem inclined to venture into the **Overseas Chinese Museum ⓖ** (华侨博物馆; Huaqiao Bowuguan; open daily 9am–4.30pm; entrance fee), so you are likely to have the outstanding collection of bronzes pretty much to yourself.

The museum seems to have inherited many private collections over the years, including some fabulous 3,000-year-old pieces. It also provides a rare opportunity to see some fine works from the generally ignored late 19th and early 20th centuries. The rest of the museum is also of interest, with the three galleries on the ground floor charting the story of the Fujianese diaspora and their subsequent role as benefactors to their ancestral villages (*for more on the Overseas Chinese, see pages 60–1*).

On the hill behind, the **Wanshi Botanical Gardens ⓗ** (万石植物馆; Wanshi Zhiwuguan; open daily 6.30am–6.30pm; entrance fee) is one of China's oldest and best, famous for its collection of tropical and subtropical trees and shrubs.

A trip around the ring road encircling the island makes a popular excursion. Local tour groups line up to gaze through strategically located coin-operated telescopes at Taiwan's outlying islands. The best views, however, are from the other major attraction on the coast road, **Hulishan Fort ⓘ** (胡里山炮台; Hulishan Paotai), which dates from Qing times, and reopened in 2006 as part of the **Rongguang Treasure Museum** (荣光珍宝馆; Rongguang Zhenbaoguan; entrance fee) The impressive cannons, originally imported from Germany in 1891 to defend Xiamen against pirate attacks, were used a few decades later to sink a Japanese battleship and are still in place on the firing platform. The five-gallery museum includes ancient swords and other weapons including artillery pieces, ancient fossils and mineral specimens from around the world.

## Northwest to Yongding

The rugged, mountainous countryside inland from Xiamen is attractive and surprisingly unspoilt, and the city makes a logical starting point for a trip northwest into **Yongding County** (永定), home to some little-known wonders of the world – the thousands of *tulou*, or fortified earth clan dwellings, built by the Hakka people. Yongding itself is approximately five hours from Xiamen by bus.

## TRANSPORT TO/FROM FUJIAN

**Flights**: Xiamen and Fuzhou airports handle a few international flights – *see page 351.* Both have flights to cities all over China.

**By Train and Bus**: Overlanding from Hong Kong or Guangdong is easier by bus (9 hrs from Shenzhen): rail links are slow (14 hrs Guangzhou–Xiamen). Rail is a better bet if travelling between Fujian, Jiangxi or Hunan. The Xiamen–Hong Kong ferry no longer operates.

## GETTING AROUND FUJIAN

Note there are no trains between Xiamen, Quanzhou and Fuzhou.

**Xiamen**: Trains to Yongding (2 fast trains daily, 3 hrs), Wuyishan (3 daily, 13½ hrs) and Nanchang (4 daily, 17 hrs). There are frequent buses to Fuzhou (3 hrs), Quanzhou (2 hrs), Yongding (5 hrs) and several daily to Shantou and Chaozhou in Guangdong (3½–4 hrs).

**Fuzhou**: Trains to Wuyishan (6 daily, 5½ hrs) and Nanchang (11 daily, 12–13 hrs). Buses to Shenzhen and Guangzhou (several daily, 9 hrs). Frequent buses to Xiamen (3 hrs), Quanzhou (2 hrs) and Wuyishan (6–8 hrs).

**Quanzhou**: Frequent buses go to Xiamen and Fuzhou (both 2 hrs), Yongding and Wuyishan.

### TIP

Unless you are in Xiamen on business, avoid visiting Xiamen in the second week of September: at this time, almost every hotel bed in the city is likely to be booked up for the annual CIFIT International Fair for Investment and Trade, one of China's three largest such events.

---

Designed to house an entire clan, a *tulou* is a communal complex constructed of earth and set in a circle around a central courtyard. Thousands of these unique dwellings are scattered across rural Yongding, although only a few are readily accessible to visitors. The best-known *tulou* is **Zhencheng Lou** ❷ (振城楼; open daylight hours; entrance fee), on the edge of Hekeng, a short bus ride east of Yongding. Built in 1912, the *tulou* contains more than 200 rooms set in concentric circles around an inner courtyard, which houses the ancestral shrine where guests are traditionally received. With their tall outer walls, *tulou* like Zhencheng Lou were designed to protect clan members from marauding bandits, with a courtyard well, a food store and animal pens allowing for a period of self-sufficiency in case of lengthy conflict. As with neighbouring

**BELOW:** the inner courtyard at Zhencheng Lou.

**BELOW:** a performance at the opening of the Maritime Silk Route festival in Quanzhou.

*tulou*, Zhencheng Lou has four storeys of galleried rooms divided into eight sections to form an octagonal *bagua*, a potent symbol of protection in Daoism.

## QUANZHOU

You could spend weeks exploring old **Quanzhou** ➌ (泉州), on the mid-Fujian coast between Xiamen and Fuzhou, where it seems that every stone is steeped in undiluted history. The earliest finds date back some 5,000 years, and every dynasty has contributed to Quanzhou's fascinating cultural tapestry. Even new buildings follow height and design standards to keep them in harmony with the past.

The starting point for exploration of the city's historic area must be the **Ashab Mosque** (清净寺; Qingzhen Si / Qinjing Si; open daily 8am–6pm; entrance fee) at 113 Tumen Jie. Completed in the year 1009, it collapsed in an earthquake in 1607, but its stone foundations provide testimony to Quanzhou's heyday as a cosmopolitan city with many thousands of foreign residents, the majority of them Muslim traders. This was one of seven mosques in the city, and it is said to be

the only one in China built along traditional Islamic, rather than Chinese, lines. Excellent English-language signs help to bring alive the past for the (rather rare) foreign visitor.

Quanzhou has long enjoyed a rich cultural life, with its own creative twist on everything from kung fu to music. The city is famous for its locally crafted puppets, and the **Puppet Museum** (木偶博物馆; Mu'ou Bowugun; open daily 9am–6pm; entrance fee) on Tumen Jie behind the mosque has a wide range of marionettes and glove puppets: the best are works of art with hand-carved heads and exquisite garments. Enquire here about performance schedules.

The **Guan Di Temple** (关帝庙; Guan Di Miao), only a few minutes' walk southeast of the mosque along Tumen Jie, is small and plain, but worshippers jostle for space to make offerings almost round the clock. Most evenings see a local opera troupe in front of the temple.

Keep your eyes open for the Xun Pu Nu women, who dress their hair in an elaborate style reminiscent of southern India and Sri Lanka. They come from a village called **Xun Pu**, about half an

hour away, and are said to be descendants of Arab merchants who married local women 1,000 or more years ago. They make the trip to Quanzhou to stock up on items that they can resell to make a profit in their home town.

Islam was not the only foreign religion to reach Quanzhou, as you soon realise on the ground floor of the **Maritime Museum** (海外交通史博物馆; Haiwai Jiaotongshi Bowuguan; open daily 8am–6pm; entrance fee) on the northeast side of town at Dongmenwai, opposite the Xiao Xiang Gymnasium. Nestorian crosses, carved fragments from Hindu temples, stones bearing the star of David, Arabic inscriptions and even remnants of a 7th-century Manichean shrine compete for attention in this fascinating display. On the upper floor you will find a masterly survey of China's seafaring history and a sizeable display devoted to the remarkable expeditions of Admiral Zheng He. Imaginative layout and lively exhibits make this one of China's best museums, fully worthy of its UNESCO sponsorship. All labels are translated into English.

Quanzhou has many fine temples, but the 7th-century **Kaiyuan Temple** (开元寺; Kaiyuan Si; Dongduan, Xi Jie; open daily 6am–6pm; entrance fee), in the northwest of town, is the undoubted highlight. Built in 686, at one time this Buddhist temple had 3,000 resident monks. Restoration has been carried out with a light and sympathetic hand, and the stonework and venerable banyans have the unmistakable patina acquired over centuries. The carvings are outstanding even in a province that has an international reputation for inspired craftsmanship. Take time to admire the quirky pillar carvings and such notable features as the 86 winged figures that bear up the roof of one of the prayer halls like angels in a medieval European cathedral. Two pagodas to the east and west of the main building were originally of wood, but in the 13th century they were rebuilt in stone, skilfully worked by the finest craftsmen of the day to resemble wood. The resulting artistic and technical triumph is classified as one of great national importance.

## Around Quanzhou

If time permits, venture 2 km (1½ miles) outside of this small city to the woodlands of **Qingyuan Shan National Park**

*The traditional Islamic design of the Ashab Mosque in Quanzhou is unusual: most Chinese mosques are almost indistinguishable from Chinese temples.*

**BELOW:** Guandi Temple, Quanzhou.

*Quanzhou's Maritime Museum is one of the best museums in China, with an unusually large number of labels and captions in English.*

(清源山国家公园; Qingyuanshan Guojia Gongyuan). Grottoes, calligraphic inscriptions and statues are scattered around the park's 62 sq km (24 sq miles). The most famous feature is a powerful Song Dynasty carving of the philosopher Laozi on a 5.5-metre (18-ft) boulder.

Quanzhou's bridge-builders deserve a special study. Around 30 km (20 miles) south of the city stands a medieval engineering masterpiece, the 2.25-km (1½-mile) **Anping Pedestrian Bridge** (安平桥; Anping Qiao). The height of engineering and aesthetics is represented by **Luoyang Bridge**, 10 km (6 miles) west of the city. Built in 1059, this is lavishly decorated with pagodas and statues that make it a real work of art. Just as significant, it is one of the first examples of successful biological engineering: live oysters were placed between the stones to bind them together like natural super-glue, to quote Fujian commentator Dr Bill Brown.

## FUZHOU

**Fuzhou ❹** (福州) is one of China's more visitor-friendly provincial capitals, sometimes called the banyan city for the trees that line the streets, their aerial roots hanging down in elegant curtains almost to the ground. It's a clean and well-maintained sort of place, but there is little in the way of sights.

**Wuyi Square ❹** (五一广场; Wuyi Guangchang) is the focal point of new Fuzhou. One of China's last Mao statues presides over the tree-shaded square where decorous couples of all ages waltz their way gracefully through an hour or more of Strauss favourites before work in the morning, or after dinner in the evening. The future direction of the city is easily seen in the new high-rises along Wuyi Zhonglu (to Mao's right), dominated by the Shangri-La Hotel complex. Facing the chairman is the city's cultural centre and opera house.

Directly behind the Mao statue is the modest **Jade Hill** (Yu Shan), and on its western flank stands the 10th-century **Bai Ta ❸** (White Pagoda) commanding views over the city. Further west, beyond the major shopping thoroughfare of Bayiqi Zhonglu, is **Wu Shan** (Black Hill), crowned with the corresponding **Wu Ta ❸** (Black Pagoda), an ancient granite structure dating back to the 8th century.

Fuzhou has five major temples.

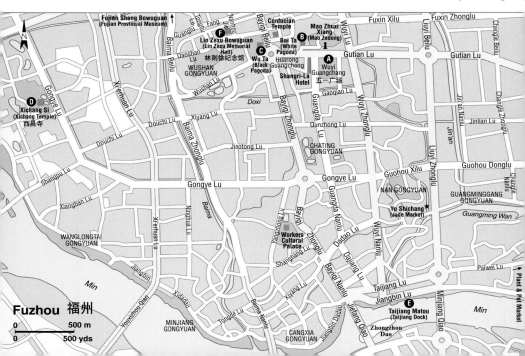

**Fuzhou 福州**

0   500 m
0   500 yds

although not all were open to the public at the time of writing. **Xichang Temple** D (西昌寺; Xichang Si) is the largest and oldest, dating back to pre-Tang times, although it has been much restored in recent times thanks to donations from prosperous overseas residents. Situated off Gongye Lu some 1.5 km (1 mile) west of the centre near the Min River, the buildings epitomise Fujian style at its most flamboyant. Upturned eaves have elaborate curlicues, and Fuzhou's finest craftsmen have incorporated auspicious symbols in the myriad decorative features. Older buildings are of mellow, lichen-covered stone, while more recent ones are encrusted with gaudy mosaics. Venerable magnolia trees bear blossoms like lamps.

Like most Chinese cities, Fuzhou is very much a place in transition. But despite the new buildings and the abundance of reinforced concrete, local colour still abounds in the older areas, where pavements are annexed for multiple purposes – drying laundry, preparing food, cooking, eating, minding children in sturdy rattan playpens and snoozing in S-shaped bamboo recliners. Fuzhou women are famous for their loud voices, and this is where you hear them in full cry.

At least 2,000 years ago Fuzhou was the cradle of China's shipbuilding industry, a tradition that still flourishes in the **Ma Wei Shipyard** (马尾造船厂; Mawei Zaochuanchang). Sections of the river-bank area have been attractively renovated, and boat tours operate from **Taijiang Dock** E (Taijiang Matou) on the river at the southern end of Wuyi Nanlu.

Walking up to the lookout point to watch the shipping on the fast-flowing Min River here, you pass the cement tableau that immortalises one of Fuzhou's most famous sons, Lin Zexu (1785–1850), best-known for precipitating the Opium War of 1840. But a visit to the **Lin Zexu Memorial Hall** F (林则徐纪念馆; Lin Zexu Bowuguan; open daily 8am–noon, 1.30pm–5.30pm; entrance fee), back in the centre of town – just north of Wu Shan at 16 Aomen Lu – reveals Lin as a multi-talented scholar, poet and inventor. The historic detail is somewhat selective, but the museum and its surrounding garden have been tastefully renovated, creating a quiet and

*Xichang is the largest and oldest of Fuzhou's temples.*

**BELOW:** the Tai Jiang Building on the banks of the Min River, Fuzhou.

**BELOW:** fabulous scenery at Wuyi Shan.

enjoyable oasis in the heart of the city. From the upper floor it is easy to understand the principle of one of Lin's many innovations, the firewall that protects neighbouring buildings in crowded areas.

To the east of the city the land rises to the wooded slopes of **Gu Shan**. Horrendously crowded at weekends, it makes for a pleasant escape at other times.

## WUYISHAN

The highland area encompassed by the **Wuyishan Scenic District** ❺ (武夷山风景区; Wuyishan Fengjingqu) covers almost 1,000 sq km (390 sq miles) around Mount Wuyi in the north of Fujian province. The government has designated a sizeable portion of this region for hotels, restaurants and other facilities for holidaymakers, while access to the 29,000-hectare (72,000-acre) nature reserve at its core remains restricted. Serious walkers, scientists and nature-lovers spend weeks exploring this unspoilt region, although most package tours do a quick round of the major attractions within a couple of days. The most popular sights are within a few kilometres of each other, and there is talk of linking them by electric trains in an effort to reduce pollution from tour buses.

The outside world first heard of the unique natural riches of this region in 1798, when a French botanist returned home bearing scientific specimens. Other international plant collectors followed, and, as interest grew, the xenophobic authorities became increasingly concerned, and banned foreigners altogether.

Restrictions have since eased, and in 1999 UNESCO officially declared Wuyishan's nature reserve a World Heritage Site on account of its rich and unique biodiversity. With elements of both temperate and subtropical biological zones, it is indeed home to an impressive variety of flora and fauna: over 3,000 plant species, 475 vertebrate species and more than 4,500 species of insects.

**Wuyishan City** ❻ (武夷山市) has about 60,000 inhabitants, many of whom were relocated here from the Yangzi Basin, while others have accepted substantial inducements to move out of the nature reserve into the "new town" area.

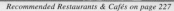

*Recommended Restaurants & Cafés on page 227*

The entrance to the reserve is just 10 km (6 miles) southwest of the city.

Most visitors to Wuyishan climb up to some of the most famous vantage points and strange rock formations. The **Heavenly Tour Peak**, **Tiger Roaring Rock**, **Thread of Sky**, **Water Curtain Cave** and **King Peak** will occupy a couple of half-days. But Wuyishan has considerable man-made claims on your time, as humans have inhabited this region for at least 4,000 years and left substantial remains of all kinds. The extraordinary "hanging coffins", mostly made from whole trees, are wedged in caves high up on cliff faces. Carbon dating has revealed that they are more than 3,000 years old, but no one has yet explained how or why they were installed in such seemingly inaccessible locations.

## Nine Bend Stream

Rain or shine, the raft trip down **Nine Bend Stream** (the Jiuqu River; 九曲溪; Jiuqu Xi) is an essential part of the Wuyi experience. It is customary to tip the boatmen about 100 percent of the ticket price as you board, otherwise you might find yourself getting rather wet. Sit at

ease on one of the six bamboo armchairs secured to the raft – actually a pair of rafts, each made from eight bamboo trunks and lashed together. You are in good hands: boatmen have undergone a three-year government training course before receiving their operator's licence. They are thoroughly versed in hands-on rivercraft, the ways of sandbanks, rapids, deep pools – 35 metres (115 ft) or more – and shallows, plus local myths and legends. It's tempting to assume that the front poler controls your destiny as you progress downstream, but in fact the man at the rear does most of the hard work and the steering, while the man at the front is responsible for the commentary. Throughout the 80-minute trip you are likely to be regaled by almost non-stop tales of the curious rock formations and anecdotes about celebrities who have taken the raft trip.

## Lost City

It is well worth the 35-km (22-mile) journey south from Wuyishan City to the **Minyue Kingdom Museum** ❼ (敏岳 王国馆; Minyue Wangguoguan; open

*Chinese tea is traditionally sold in small drums, with labels indicating the quality and price. The tea industry has remained important in China – it is worth around Rmb 30 billion each year.*

**BELOW:** harvesting the tea crop in the Fujian hills.

## Fujian Tea

Tea is central to every aspect of life in China, and for at least 1,800 years the Wuyishan area has produced some of China's finest. The word "tea" itself derives from the Fujianese (Minnan) *te* – an indication that this region was the original source for the tea purchased by Europeans in the 17th century (the Cantonese word *cha* was also used and reflects the fact that most of the tea trade went via Guangzhou).

Some Fujian tea, most notably Da Hong Bao (Big Red Robe), is so rare that it is virtually unobtainable. Back in 1999 a Hong Kong connoisseur reportedly paid Rmb 150,000 for 20 grams, since when there has been no word of any being sold. However, the government has allegedly promised a small quantity to China's first gold medallist in the 2008 Olympics.

*River rafting at Nine Bend Stream (the Jiuqu River) in the heart of the Wuyi Shan region.*

**BELOW:** Wuyi Shan is popular with Chinese tour groups.

daily 7am–6pm; entrance fee), site of Chengcun, the ancient lost capital of the Minyue Kingdom.

In Western Han times, the Minyue Kingdom became increasingly powerful until, in 202 BC, the Emperor Qinshihuang was so concerned about this potential rival state that he destroyed it, leaving very little behind. Archaeologists began excavating the site in 1980, but work has been sporadic, and only a small portion of the lost city's 50 hectares (124 acres) have so far been uncovered.

The entrance fee covers admission to the museum and the site across the road, where you can get a sense of the sheer scale of the moat and fortifications, the royal audience halls and the enormous heated bathing pools. Visitors were obliged to bathe before an audience with the ruler: this ritual of purification was a sign of respect, but it also ensured that no one entered the audience chamber bearing a hidden weapon. Rulers took simple but effective precautions against surprise attacks. Stairs were constructed from hollow bricks that reverberated when trodden upon, thus raising the alarm when intruders were around the palace.

Before you leave, taste the sweet spring water that still comes from the 2,000-year-old well. The three topmost ceramic rings lining the well have been replaced, but nothing else has changed since it was sunk.

Only a minute's walk from the museum, the Ming Dynasty village of **Cheng Cun**（陈村）is a worthwhile stop, if time allows, especially if you can catch one of the daily variety shows that include some numbers that are said to be in "ancient Min style".

The region abounds with interesting villages that have barely changed in centuries. In 2002, the administrator of **Xia Mei** village, about 45 minutes by bus from Wuyishan City, saw the tourism potential in this once-flourishing centre of the regional tea trade. Rich merchants and tea growers spent their money on magnificently decorated courtyard homes, some 40 of which survived the Cultural Revolution more or less intact. As you walk through the market that lines both banks of the canal, it's easy to imagine the non-stop procession of laden barges leaving the slipways on the first stage of their journey to the West. ❑

# RESTAURANTS & CAFÉS

## Restaurants

Average price for a meal for one, with one drink:
$ under US$12 (under Rmb 100)
$$ US$12–20 (Rmb 100–60)
$$$ over US$20 (over Rmb 160)

Fujianese cuisine features strong, salty flavours and lots of seafood. Xiamen, and to a lesser extent Fuzhou, have plenty of Western food options in international hotels as well as the ubiquitous fast-food chains.

### Fuzhou

#### An Tai Restaurant
39 Jipi Lu, Gulou District, beside An Tai Bridge. Tel: 0591 8755 0890. $
No English menu, but on the first floor everything is laid out around the cooking stations, so point to whatever you fancy. Try deep-fried sand worms and a small "basket" of purple rice.

#### Bang Mian and Bian Rou
68 Hot Spring Branch Road. $
The stools and tables are plastic, and pink toilet roll takes the place of napkins, but it's spotlessly clean and unbeatable value. Make your selection – peanut and sesame sauce or hot chilli sauce with noodles or dumplings.

#### EZ Cafe
Shangri-La Hotel, 9 Xin Quan Nanlu. Tel: 0591 8798 8888. $$
The international buffet has all the customary Shangri-La flair, complete with chocolate fountain. Don't miss out on the fresh Nori rolls – they disappear as fast as the chef can make them.

#### Podian
46 Zhu Zi Fang. $
Tucked away alongside the Fuzhou Public Security Bureau, this is a noisy favourite with off-duty officers, not to mention off-duty chefs drawn by the creative cooking. Try the pork simmered very slowly in soy and vinegar. No English menu, but a smile wins plenty of help.

#### Yong He
31 Pagoda Street (Ta Xiang). $
Founded in 1934, this tiny hole in the wall is a Fuzhou icon. Chewy yet silken smooth, the fishballs (Yu Wan) and finely minced pork balls (Rou Wan) are served in paper bowls with plastic spoons. Help yourself to the warm vinegar, on the table in a small teapot.

### Quanzhou

#### Ho An Por
Liu Guan Lu. $
Anywhere in Quanzhou's food street is a sure bet; Ho An Por is famous for its leaf-wrapped, steamed rice dumplings.

#### Quanzhou Hotel
22 Zhuang Fu Xiang.
Tel: 0595 2228 9958.
www.quanzhouhotel.com $$
Local seafood is superb. Just let the staff tailor a menu to your budget.

### Xiamen

#### Samrat
69 Jiang Tou Beilu.
Tel: 0592 555 7699. $$
Local expatriates call the place Indiana John's. A favourite spot to hang out from 5.30pm until late, with the resident DJ kicking off his Latin-style set at 9.30pm. Feast on Indian chicken tikka, palak paneer and naan.

#### Sofitel Plaza
19 Hubin Beilu.
Tel: 0592 507 8888. $$
Make believe you're on the Left Bank in Paris as you sip Betjeman and Barton tea and nibble on a pastry on the oh-so-French tea terrace.

#### Tutto Bene
1–16 Jianye Lu (opposite Marco Polo Hotel).
Tel: 0592 504 6026. $$$
Grills and pizzas, pastas and salads are all beautifully prepared by the Italian owner-chef. Admirable selection of wines. Leave room for the delectable tiramisu.

#### Lujiang Restaurant
Lujiang Hotel, 54 Lujiang Dao
Tel: 0592 202 2922. $$
Rooftop dining – either indoors or al fresco – in the heart of the city, with great views over the harbour and Gulangyu. Good dim sum available all day plus Cantonese buffet and Fujian specialities.

#### Xiang Lu Grand Hotel
18 Changhao Lu, Huli.
Tel: 0592 569 9555. $$
Xiamen's largest hotel, the Xiang Lu Grand promises an inexpensive, non-stop buffet, plus very competitively priced and varied food in the many outlets dotting its 2,000-seat atrium.

### Wuyishan

#### Lao Zi Hao
Wuyishan Nong Jia Yin Can Yin. Tel: 0599 525 2257. $$$
In this rustic restaurant, one of many started by farmers to cater to nature reserve visitors, dine on local produce in a straw-roofed bamboo hut. Wild game is available in season, but local mushrooms are the delicacy in these parts.

#### Wuyi Tea Hotel
Wuyi Mountain National Tourist Resort. Tel: 0599 525 6777. www.teahotel.net $$$
There's a long history of cooking with tea leaves in this area. Opt for the Tea Banquet and you can expect to sample fried tender tea leaves, fish with Rougui Tea, and wulong tea pancake. Pay in advance.

# The Taiwan Dispute

K nown in China as the "renegade province", the island of Taiwan – officially called the Republic of China – is the last missing piece in the PRC puzzle and a fascinating amalgam of southern Fujian, aboriginal and various other mainland Chinese cultures. Though sizeable communities of Fujianese fishermen began settling the island in the 16th century, and it was officially admitted into the Chinese Empire (as a prefecture of Fujian province) in 1684 following the exploits of Koxinga and Shi Lang (see page 29), it was not until 1949 that it became of paramount importance to the rival armies vying for control of China.

It was at this time, after the communists had finally defeated Chiang Kaishek's nationalist forces, that the remnants of the Guomindang army retreated across the Taiwan Strait, inundating the island with almost 2 million "mainlanders" and seizing complete military and political control. As the last bastion of the Republic of China ruled by the Nationalists, Chiang intended to use it as a base for the military to regroup before reclaiming mainland China and, in the process, changed the face of Taiwan for ever. From the time Chiang named himself president in 1950 until his death in 1975, the mainlanders monopolised positions of authority and insti-

tuted hegemonic policies that still have resonance today. Opposition parties and Taiwanese language (the southern Fujian dialect) were banned, and Chiang diverted resources to defend the island from communist attacks and ultimately, he hoped, to regain control of the whole of China again.

The early days of nationalist rule were grim on most fronts: all forms of domestic dissent were brutally suppressed, and the island's inhabitants lived in constant fear of a communist invasion. The tiny islands of Kinmen and the Matzu archipelago, huddled just off the Fujian coastline, quickly became Cold War flashpoints, suffering heavy PRC bombardments through most of the 1950s. In August 1954, the nationalist government sent 15,000 troops to Matzu, instigating a massive artillery assault by the communists. The shelling continued steadily until 1956, when the United States supplied the nationalists with weaponry that successfully countered the communist offensive, and the bombing continued only sporadically until August 1958, when PRC forces staged a wider offensive against Matzu and Kinmen and threatened to invade the main island of Taiwan. The US responded by deploying its Seventh Fleet to the Taiwan Strait, providing naval aircraft that enabled the nationalists to regain control of the region's airspace. Eventually a curious agreement was made whereby the communists would only bomb the islands on odd-numbered days if US warships stayed away from the mainland coast – the alternate-day shelling continued until 1978.

Though Chiang's staunchly anti-communist Taiwan remained a vital buffer in the American-led fight against red expansion throughout the 1960s, by the early 1970s its political influence began to wane. When Mao Zedong's PRC was admitted into the United Nations in 1971, Chiang withdrew his Republic of China rather than share a seat. The following year, US President Richard Nixon made his historic visit to the PRC, initiating a rapprochement that ultimately led President Jimmy Carter to shift US recognition to the mainland in 1978, effectively severing formal relations with Taiwan. Since then, most of the world has done the same, and as of 2007 only 25 small states still officially recognise the island (in exchange for large sums of financial aid).

But as Taiwan's political clout was declining, it was quickly gaining economic power, undergoing one of the most rapid and complete transformations from developing-nation status to a fully developed economy

**LEFT:** sending a strong message to China.
**RIGHT:** Lee Teng-hui, president of Taiwan 1988–2000.

the world has ever seen. Following the launch of an export-orientated economic strategy in the 1960s, the island became the world's fastest-growing economy between 1960 and 1970, averaging a staggering 9.7 percent growth in annual GNP. In the 1980s, Taiwan started to produce high-end electronics, and is now one of the world's biggest exporters of computer components – a major factor contributing to its current status as the world's 17th-largest economy.

In recent decades, Taiwan has also undergone substantial political changes, evolving from the totalitarian Chiang Kaishek regime into the world's only Chinese democracy. Following Chiang's death in 1975, opposition to one-party rule and nationalist corruption grew, with academics and students starting to contest local elections. However, the government continued to resist change, and in December 1979 (now led by Chiang's son, Chiang Ching-kuo) it forcibly suppressed a mass protest in the southern city of Kaohsiung, later trying eight members of the opposition and sentencing most of them to lengthy jail terms. Though the government continued to crack down on dissidents over the next five years, the so-called Kaohsiung Incident and the subsequent trials helped to garner widespread public sympathy for the fledgling democracy movement. In response to mounting domestic and US pressure for reforms, President Chiang finally ended martial law in July 1987 and lifted press restrictions in January 1988.

Later that year, Taiwan got its first native-born president, nationalist Chairman Lee Teng-hui, who continued the programme of reforms and formally ended hostilities with China in 1991. Five years later, the country held its first free presidential election, won by incumbent Lee despite an overwhelming campaign of intimidation from China, which provocatively tested missiles close to the island to express its outrage over Lee's mounting independence tendencies.

In 2000, the nationalists lost their grip on power when Chen Shui-bian of the Democratic Progressive Party took over. The peaceful transfer of power to a lawyer who had largely built his reputation by defending the dissidents who were tried after the Kaohsiung Incident was widely seen as a sign that Taiwanese democracy had finally come of age.

Since then, the question of Taiwan's political identity has been the prevailing issue. About 75 percent of Taiwanese claim to support what has become known as the "status quo" – whereby Taiwan remains effectively independent and runs its own affairs without formally declaring independence and upsetting its much larger neighbour. Although 15 percent of the population supports an outright declaration of independence and 10 percent advocates reunification with mainland China, neither of these options appears to be viable for the foreseeable future, and with both Taiwan and the PRC enjoying prolonged prosperity, the status quo looks set to continue. ❑

# THE SOUTHERN INTERIOR

**The interior provinces of Jiangxi and Hunan lie off the main tourist trail, but both are rich in scenic beauty. They also share a starring role in modern Chinese history**

Journey north from Guangzhou or Xiamen and you are likely to notice a number of changes: grimier towns, poorer-looking people, fewer cars, bumpier roads – all illustrating the divide between the rich south and less-rich interior. By the time you reach the landlocked provinces of Jiangxi and Hunan, the difference is quite pronounced, although the main urban centres of Nanchang and, especially, Changsha are almost on a par with their southern counterparts (the contrast is even more obvious if you travel west into Guizhou). And there is one other change you may notice as you travel northwards – the food becomes a lot spicier.

Out-of-the-way Jiangxi is one of China's more obscure corners, well removed from the tourist trail. It is under-rated: take the time to explore its quiet backwaters, with numerous ancient villages set amid the green hills. In the north is the fabulous mountain scenery of Lushan. Close by, where the land slopes down to the Yangzi River, is Poyang Lake – one of the most peaceful places in China; its adjoining wetlands are an important sanctuary for birdlife. Jingdezhen, to the east, is famous for its porcelain, while there is more beguiling scenery in the southwestern reaches of the province around Jinggangshan, forever associated with the early Chinese communists.

Neighbouring Hunan is also steeped in communist history, with Mao's home town, Shaoshan, still attracting hordes of devotees as well as the plain curious. Changsha is a lively city, but the most interesting areas are in the west and northwest of the province: the area around Zhangjiajie is fantastically scenic – with dramatic mountains and caves at Tianmen, and the awe-inspiring limestone pinnacles of Wulingyuan. Further south is the picturesque old river town of Fenghuang, gradually waking up to its considerable tourist potential. ❏

**LEFT:** red peppers drying on a tiled roof, Hunan. **TOP:** limestone scenery at Zhangjiajie, Hunan. **ABOVE LEFT:** Jingganshan, Jiangxi.
**ABOVE RIGHT:** Mao tat for sale at Shaoshan, Hunan.

*Recommended Restaurants & Bars on page 243*

# JIANGXI

Hemmed in by mountains to the south
and the Yangzi to the north, Jiangxi is a
backwater with a revolutionary past, home
to China's "porcelain capital" and the
beautiful Lu Shan highlands

**S**panning the lengthy Ganjiang Valley from the banks of the Yangzi in the north to the lightly populated mountainous area along the border with Guangdong in the south, seldom-visited Jiangxi province's historic and natural riches belie its reputation as one of China's long-forgotten backwaters.

Bounded by mountains on three sides, the rugged topography has kept it largely isolated from the wealthier neighbouring coastal provinces. However, over the centuries, the territory of modern-day Jiangxi has been the epicentre of some of China's most defining cultural, intellectual and political revolutions, from the 12th-century ascendancy of Neo-Confucian thought to the 20th-century rise of Chinese communism and the formation of the Red Army. Classical Chinese poets and communist revolutionaries have sought succour or refuge in its mountains: Tang Dynasty poet-officials Bai Juyi and Li Bo wrote gushing odes to the beauty of the mist-shrouded mountains of **Lushan** in the north, while Mao Zedong and Zhu De made the densely foliated southern passes around **Jinggangshan** their base during the pivotal 1928 battles against the nationalists.

Located along the Yangzi in the north of the province is the atmospheric port city of **Jiujiang**, which offers calming views of the mighty river as well as a chance of catching street performances of Jiangxi opera. The ancient kiln town of **Jingdezhen** in Jiangxi's northeast, has for more than 1,000 years been China's leading producer of fine porcelain and today draws droves of collectors.

## Nanchang

Jiangxi's capital, **Nanchang ❶**（南昌）, until recent years known primarily for it role in Chinese communism's history, is now at the forefront of another revolution: the rapid economic upsurge of China's so-called "second-tier" cities, many of them capitals of interior provinces that are now benefiting from the spread of investment inland from the more developed coastal areas such as

**LEFT:** trees in the mist, Lushan.
**BELOW:** the Dongjin bridge at Ganzhou in southern Jiangxi.

*Chinese New Year kumquat tree.*

Guangdong and Fujian. Nanchang has steadily reinvented itself as a hub of commerce, industry and transport, at the same time shedding many of its grey, Soviet-inspired stylings for a greener image as a city of sprawling gardens, sidewalk cafés and historic structures. It is a curious blend of classical Chinese landmarks, sombre revolutionary monuments and gleaming new commercial buildings.

The city's premier historic site is the nine-storey **Tengwang Pavilion ⒶA** (滕王阁; Tengwang Ge; 36 Fang Gu Jie; open summer 7.30am–7pm, winter 8am–4.30pm; entrance fee), which towers majestically over the Gan River. At night, a multicoloured array of lights brings its graceful flying eaves to life. Originally built on the same site in AD 653 to commemorate the appointment of a Tang Dynasty prince (known as "Tengwang") as governor of Nanchang, it was immortalised later in a poem by noted Tang-era poet Wang Bo, who vividly described a banquet held in celebration of the pavilion's first reconstruction. The present incarnation, said to be the 29th, was completed in 1989 and is surrounded by a garden of elegant pavilions and gently weeping willows.

On a small islet to the south of the pavilion is the **Jiangxi Provincial Museum ⒷB** (江西省博物馆; Jiangxi-

sheng Bowuguan; 2 Xinzhou Lu; open Mon–Fri 9am–4.30pm, Sat–Sun 9am–5pm; entrance fee), with Chinese-language exhibits covering the neolithic period to the communist revolution; porcelain buffs will appreciate the comprehensive timeline of Jingdezhen porcelain on the third floor, with excavated examples outlining the art form's evolution from the Song to the Qing dynasties.

Towards the eastern end of bustling **Minde Lu**, the street with the bulk of Nanchang's hippest bars, clubs and restaurants, is **Youmin Temple C** (佑民寺; Youmin Si; 181 Minde Lu; open daily 7am–5pm; entrance fee), a Buddhist temple first built in AD 503 but repeatedly destroyed over the centuries – most recently in the 1960s by a remarkably combative local contingent of Red Guards. The temple's three main halls have been restored and it is again an active place of worship, with resident monks performing daily votive rituals.

## Revolutionary sights

Across Minde Lu from the temple is **August 1 Park D** (八一公园; Bayi Gongyuan; open summer 6am–9pm, winter 6am–6pm), a breezy patch of greenery surrounding a tranquil lake where paddleboats can be rented. Further east, tucked away on a side street off Minde Lu, is **Zhu De's Former Residence E** (朱德旧居; Zhu De Jiuju; 2 Huayuanjiao Jie; open daily 8am–5.30pm; entrance fee), the grey brick house where the revered communist revolutionary and guerrilla tactician lived in March of 1927 – just months before he and comrades Zhou Enlai and He Long led 30,000 communist troops in the abortive 1 August rebellion against nationalist forces. Despite its failure, the uprising is considered the first major conflict of the Chinese Civil War, and, as such, 1 August (*bayi* in Mandarin Chinese) has come to be celebrated as the anniversary of the People's Liberation Army's formation. Though Zhu De's old quarters contain little more than a few black-and-white photos and some personal items such as weapons, the **1 August Uprising Museum F** (八一纪念馆; Bayi Jinianguan; 380 Zhongshan Lu; open daily 8am–5.30pm; entrance fee), a short distance to the south on Zhongshan Lu, houses a more

**TIP**

At the Tengwang Paviliion, take the lift to the top storey, where there are regular performances of classical Chinese music and opera; from there you can work your way back down, pausing to enjoy the river views from the upper balconies.

**BELOW:** Nanchang's Tengwang Pavilion.

**TIP**

Climb to the top of the seven-storey Shengjin Ta (Golden Rope Pagoda) for commanding views of Nanchang.

## GETTING TO JIANGXI

**Flights**: Nanchang is the main airport, with flights to most cities in China.

**By Train and Bus**: Rail connections with Fujian and Hunan, and north to Wuhan, Nanjing and Shanghai are reasonable. Buses run to Changsha, Wuhan, Shanghai, Xiamen, Guangzhou and other cities.

## GETTING AROUND JIANGXI

**Nanchang**: The fastest trains to Jiujiang (12 daily) take 2½ hours, while buses take 2 hours. Trains and buses to Jingdezhen (several daily) both take 4 hours. There are frequent buses to

Lushan (1½ hours), and 3 daily to Jingganshan (5–8 hours).

**Jiujiang**: Trains to Nanchang (12 daily) take 2½ hours. There are frequent buses to Lushan (1 hour), and hourly departures to Jingdezhen (2 hours).

**Lushan**: There are buses every 40 minutes or so from Nanchang (1½ hours). Similarly frequent buses run from Jiujiang (1 hour).

**Jingdezhen**: Trains to Nanchang (5 daily) take 7 hours. There are numerous buses to Jiujiang (2 hours), and 3 daily to Nanchang (3½ hours).

complete collection of photos, illustrated maps and paintings chronicling the communists' early revolutionary activities in Jiangxi. Exhibits have limited English captions, but it is fairly easy to follow the revolutionaries' trajectory from Nanchang to Jinggangshan: on the top floor the pivotal events are depicted in massive oil paintings, the most evocative of which portrays the historic handshake between Mao Zedong and Zhu De as

they united their respective units to form the Fourth Red Army in Jinggangshan.

But Nanchang's grandest tribute to the uprising is without doubt **1 August Square** **G** (八一广场; Bayi Guangchang), China's largest public square after Beijing's Tiananmen Guangchang. The vast expanse of concrete on the eastern side of Bayi Dadao (1 August Avenue), the city's main traffic artery, is one of the country's most overwhelming examples

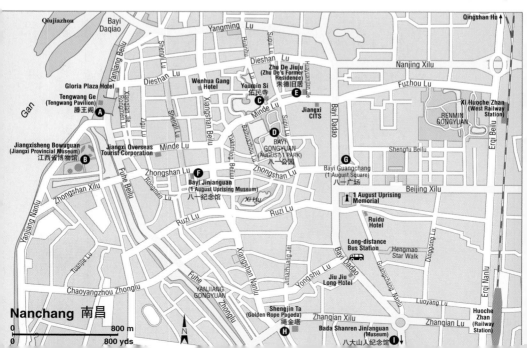

**Nanchang 南昌**

of Soviet-inspired megalomania. The square's southern half is dominated by the **1 August Uprising Memorial**, an imposing obelisk which tapers into a sculpture of a bayoneted rifle adjoining a red-tiled flag emblazoned with the Chinese characters for 1 August. The monument, adorned with bold reliefs of the armed proletarian struggle at its base, is Chinese-style socialist realism at its most melodramatic.

In the city's southern section, down a busy market street just off Zhanqian Xilu, is the magnificent **Golden Rope Pagoda**  (绳金塔; Shengjin Ta; 1 Shengjin Ta Jie; open daily 8am–6pm; entrance fee), which at a height of almost 59 metres (194 ft) is Nanchang's tallest ancient structure. According to legend, when the original Tang Dynasty pagoda was being built workers unearthed an iron chest filled with precious objects, including four bundles of golden rope – hence the tower's name. The tower has repeatedly been destroyed and was last rebuilt in 1713.

A 5-km (3-mile) taxi ride south of here, next to a grassy lakeside park, is the **Bada Shanren Museum**

(八大山人纪念馆; Bada Shanren Jinianguan; 259 Shinpu Lu; open daily 8.30am–4.30pm; entrance fee), dedicated to the emotionally charged art of the widely imitated 17th-century calligrapher and painter Zhu Da, a roaming Buddhist monk commonly known by the Daoism-inspired name Bada Shanren.

## Jiujiang and Poyang Hu

In Jiangxi's northwest corner, tucked between the Yangzi's southern bank and the northern fringe of Poyang Hu – China's largest freshwater lake – is the port city of **Jiujiang** ❷ (Nine Rivers) (九江). Its location at the confluence of a formidable network of rivers combined with the centuries-old trade in porcelain from nearby Jingdezhen meant Jiujiang prospered, reaching its zenith in the 19th century as an official treaty port. The city continues to profit from its location, though today it benefits as much from its proximity to the mountain resort of Lushan as it does from river trade: just two hours by bus from Nanchang, the town is the main staging point for trips to Lushan National Park and the surrounding scenic areas.

*Commemorating the early Chinese communists at the 1 August Uprising Memorial.*

**BELOW LEFT:** park musician.
**BELOW:** Mao befriends the peasants in this socialist realist painting.

*Siberian white cranes at Poyang Lake, one of the best birdwatching sites in China – especially in autumn and winter when migrating species are present in huge numbers.*

**BELOW:** the Daoist shrine at the Immortals Cave, Lushan.

Jiujiang itself is a pleasant town, with a scenic walkway beside riverfront Binjiang Lu offering the chance to stroll along the Yangzi – and to visit some historic landmarks on its southern bank. Heading east from the centre, the first such structure you will encounter is the **Xunyang Tower** (寻阳楼; Xunyang Lou; open daily 8am–6pm; entrance fee), a four-storey wooden reconstruction of a wine house originally built on the same site during the Tang Dynasty.

A few hundred metres further east from here is the **River Lock Pagoda** (锁江塔; Suojiang Ta; open daily 8am–6pm; entrance fee), a seven-storey pagoda first built in 1586 and for centuries the first structure boatmen would spot as they passed the city from the east – as such, it has become one of the best-known symbols of Jiujiang.

Occupying much of the city's western area is the **Gantang Lake** (甘棠湖; Gantang Hu), a natural body of water that is flanked in the north by a long promenade, the site of spontaneous folk-art performances during the warmer months: take a summer afternoon stroll here and you are likely to see some lively street offerings of traditional Jiangx opera. Straddling a tiny islet in the north of the lake, and connected to the promenade by a crooked bridge, is the graceful **Misty Water Pavilion** (烟水亭; Yanshui Ting; open summer 8am–9.30pm; winter 8am–5.30pm; entrance fee), originally built on the same spot in AD 815 under the direction of prolific Tang Dynasty poet-official Bai Juyi.

In addition to being a crucial overflow reservoir when the Yangzi bursts its banks each summer, the expansive **Poyang Lake ❸** (鄱阳湖; Poyang Hu) is widely regarded as one of the world's most important wetlands, providing a sanctuary for large concentrations of several endangered species of waterfowl. The **Poyang Lake National Nature Reserve** (鄱阳湖 国家级自然 保护区; Poyanghu Guojieji Ziranbaohuqu), situated around the minuscule village of **Wucheng** (吴城), is considered by many birdwatchers to be one of Asia's supreme avian spectacles, attracting six species of cranes each winter. The main attraction is the critically endangered Siberian white crane, the most aquatic of all cranes – 95 percent of its 4,000-strong population spends the winter here each year.

## Lushan (Guling)

Rising abruptly from the Yangzi and Poyang Hu basins, **Lushan ❹** (Cottage Mountains) (庐山) is among China's time-honoured natural treasures, for centuries lauded by the literary elite. This beautiful area is filled with ancient Buddhist and Daoist temples, with elegant pavilions where eminent masters once meditated. As one of the places where the traditional Chinese aesthetic approach towards harmony with nature was refined, Lushan's misty landscapes have been the subject of thousands of poems, calligraphic works and paintings. Its role as one of the most important spiritual and intellectual centres of Chinese civilisation was recognized by UNESCO in 1996 when it was named as a World Heritage Site. In the mid-19th century the village of **Guling** (牯岭) was developed into a hill retreat for Western expatriates, and on

*Recommended Restaurants & Bars on page 243*

he surrounding hillsides there are hundreds of European-style stone holiday houses that were built during this time.

The bus journey up the winding road from Jiujiang takes just over an hour and offers dramatic views of the hills and the giant lake to the east. If you are not with a tour you can hire a taxi or jump on one of the minibuses that run a circuit of the most famous attractions. From Guling, one of the most rewarding walks starts along the road leading downhill to the southwest of the village. After passing the placid **Harp-like Lake** (如琴湖; Ruqin Hu), where the **Nine Harps Pavilion** (Jiuqin Ting) casts a serene reflection over the calm waters from an islet in the lake's centre, carry on along the fir-tree lined **Floral Path** until you reach a right-hand turn-off leading to the **Immortals' Cave** (仙人洞; Xianren Dong) – a grotto which, according to legend, was once inhabited by Tang Dynasty Daoist master Lu Dongbing, revered as one of China's "eight immortals". Inside the cave is a venerated Daoist shrine where resident monks regularly recite incantations and perform finger-gesture rituals.

For another accessible walk, head south from the bus station along busy Hexi Lu, past several European-style stone buildings, until you come to the left-hand fork for Hedong Lu – continue south along this road for a few minutes to reach the **Meilu Villa** (美庐别墅; Meilu Bieshu; open summer 7.30am–6pm; winter 8am–5.30pm; entrance fee), from 1934–48 the summer residence of nationalist leader Chiang Kaishek, who named the villa after his wife, Song Meiling. Back on Hexi Lu, continue south for another 15 minutes to reach the **People's Hall** (人民剧院; Renmin Juyuan; open daily 8am–5.30pm; entrance fee), often called the **Lushan Conference Site**, where in 1959 the Communist Party's Central Committee held its explosive eighth plenary session, which came to be known as the Lushan Conference.

In the far southeast of the Lushan area, at the foot of **Five Old Men Peak** (Wulou Feng), is the **White Deer Grotto Academy** (白鹿洞书院; Bailudong Shuyuan; open daily 8am–5.30pm; entrance fee), one of ancient China's four greatest centres of higher learning. Originally the haunt of Tang Dynasty poet Li

**TIP**

The easiest way to see Lushan's many natural attractions in one day is to join a tour starting in Jiujiang: every hotel in the city offers them, and those listed in this book *(see page 362)* can provide you with an English-speaking guide.

**BELOW:** red tassels and "lucky" padlocks on a Lushan peak.

# The Long March

The Long March, widely celebrated as one of the 20th century's most extraordinary human and military triumphs, retains a legendary quality that resonates far beyond China's borders. The monumental retreat of the country's ragtag Red Armies from better-equipped and numerically superior nationalist forces spanned several thousand kilometres of arduous terrain, leaving over four-fifths of an estimated 100,000 communist revolutionaries dead. Despite devastating military defeats, malnourishment and sickness, this supreme effort galvanised support for the communist cause in the countryside, and historians herald it as the defining event in their long struggle towards victory in 1949.

In a broad sense, the achievement includes the retreat of three separate Red Armies from southern and central China and their ultimate unification in the northerly province of Shaanxi in October 1936. But the term "Long March" most commonly refers to the calamitous one-year journey of the First Front Red Army from its final stronghold in Jiangxi province's southeast to Shaanxi province, led by Communist Party officials such as Mao Zedong, Zhu De, Zhou Enlai and Deng Xiaoping. Between October 1934 and October 1935, the ill-equipped forces sliced a broad swathe across southern and western China, cutting

through 11 provinces and negotiating some of the country's most unforgiving topography. Distance estimates vary wildly, but Mao's official figure of 25,000 li (12,500 km, or about 8,000 miles) is increasingly considered by independent historians to be hyperbolic, with more rigorous recent calculations of about 6,000 km (3,700 miles).

After being driven from their base in the southern Jiangxi village of Ciping in January 1929, Red Army forces under Mao's command in 1930 established the Chinese Soviet Republic around the southeastern Jiangxi city of Ruijin, close to the border with Fujian. Despite thwarting four nationalist attempts to unseat his troops between 1930 and 1933, Mao was temporarily relieved of command in July 1934 for political reasons, and his guerrilla tactics were replaced with frontal attacks on Chiang Kaishek's nationalist forces that resulted in heavy communist casualties. In August 1934, upon receiving information that Chiang's troops were planning a major offensive against Ruijin, the communist leadership decided to retreat and give its embattled troops time to regroup. Following several diversionary assaults, in October 1934 a 130,000-strong Red Army force led by Bo Gu and German adviser Otto Braun (known in Chinese as Li De) attacked a nationalist perimeter near Yudu, with some 86,000 soldiers and 11,000 administrative personnel breaking through the lines – marking the beginning of the Long March.

One month later, after marching west through Hunan and Guangdong provinces and into Guangxi, the Red Army encountered heavy nationalist reinforcements at the Xiang River, losing well over 40,000 troops in only two days – a defeat that allowed Mao to regain military control at a January 1935 party conference in Zunyi, Guizhou.

Henceforth, Mao and supporter Zhu resumed their guerrilla methods, breaking the army into smaller units and taking circuitous routes as they zigzagged their way through the treacherous mountains and rivers of Yunnan and Sichuan. In addition to the geographical barriers, these remote areas also presented obstacles such as regional warlords and ethnic minority tribes who were hostile to the mostly Han Chinese communist troops. After repelling numerous ambushes from Tibetans and bands of Muslim Hui Chinese, Mao's remaining force of 8,000 crossed into Shaanxi in October 1935, setting up a new base in the city of Yan'an, where they eventually united with the Second Front Red Army and the remnants of the Fourth Front Red Army. ❏

**LEFT:** depiction of the Long March at Jinggangshan.

o, who kept a white deer as a pet, the cademy's importance grew over the enturies, reaching its apex during the outhern Song Dynasty (1127–1279), vhen it was rebuilt and expanded by pre-minent neo-Confucianist Zhu Xi, who odified what is now widely considered o be the Confucian canon.

## ingdezhen

o the east of Poyang Hu, about 90 min-tes by bus from Jiujiang, is **Jingdezhen** ❺ (景德镇), a grimy but venerable town hat has been producing porcelain for some ,700 years. During the Yuan, Ming and Qing dynasties it was China's "porcelain apital", the world's leading innovator and xporter of fine porcelain and ceramics. orcelain is still the city's main industry – s evidenced by the scores of kilns that ominate the skyline, sending plumes of lack smoke into the air each day.

Porcelain also brings tourism, and vis-tors flock to the **International Trade Market** (国贸市场; Guomao Shichang) ext to Jiefang Lu, about 200 metres 660 ft) south of the city's central square, o marvel at the staggering array of reations for sale – and to pick up some argains. For a view of the city – and the moky kiln towers that dominate the usty streets – climb to the top of **Dragon Pearl Pavilion** (龙珠阁; Longzhu Ge; Zhonghua Beilu; open daily 8.30am–5.30pm; entrance fee), vhich also houses the **Imperial Por-celain Museum**, three floors of mostly Ming-era wares. The **Museum of Ceramics History** (陶瓷历史博物馆; Taoci Lishi Bowuguan; open summer 8am–5.30pm, winter 8am–5pm; entrance ee) is at the northern end of Guyao Lu, quiet, forested lane on Jingdezhen's western outskirts. The museum's exhib-tion of unearthed porcelain is somewhat overshadowed by the grand Ming-style ompound of wooden buildings and gar-lens in which it is displayed, and by the rtisans engaged in various stages of he production process. Look out for the eculiar **Temple of the Kiln God** and an mazingly well-preserved Southern Song Dynasty kiln.

## Jinggangshan (Ciping)

Celebrated as the cradle of the Chinese revolution, the rugged mountains of **Jinggangshan** ❻ (井岗山), along Jiangxi's southwestern border with Hunan, provided essential shelter for the embryonic Chinese Red Army divisions during fierce fighting with the national-ists in the late 1920s and early 1930s. It was to these mountains that the main communist armies fled after failed urban uprisings, consolidating their forces and developing their distinctive brand of rural-based revolution and guerrilla warfare. The village of **Ciping** (茨坪) served as a base for Mao Zedong and Zhu De after they united their divisions to form the Fourth Red Army in 1927.

The **Former Revolutionary Head-quarters** (革命旧居群; Geming Jiuju-qun; Nanshan Lu; open summer 7.30am–6pm, winter 8am–5.30pm; entrance fee) houses a collection of restored mud houses where some of the communist leaders lived and planned their battles in 1928. Inside the compound are the for-mer living quarters of Mao, Zhu, Chen Yi and a few others.

*An example of Jingdezhen porcelain. The town has been producing ceramics for over 1,700 years.*

**BELOW:** porcelain delivery, Jingdezhen.

*One of the waterfalls at the Five Dragon Pools, in the green mountains outside Ciping.*

**BELOW:** the Monument to the Revolutionary Martyrs, Ciping.

About 1 km (⅔ mile) north of here, atop Beishan (North Hill), just off Wuling Lu, is a massive Soviet-style complex centred on the **Monument to the Revolutionary Martyrs** (烈士纪念堂; Lieshi Jiniantang; open daily 8am–5pm; entrance fee). Spanning the entire hillside, the circuit of monuments commemorating the revolution draws legions of red-flag-waving Chinese tourists and makes for a fascinating hour's walk. The circuit culminates at the hilltop, where the martyrs' monument faces south over Ciping towards **Five Fingers Peak** (五指峰; Wuzhi Feng), Jinggangshan's most famous mountain. At the base of the monument are series of relief sculptures depicting defining events, such as the unification of Red Army units. The path leading to the exit runs through a somewhat surreal sculpture park filled with larger-than-life busts and statues of a host of influential revolutionaries – look for the likeness of a young Mao dressed in traditional Chinese clothing.

Continue along the main road to the south to reach the **Revolutionary Museum** (井岗山博物馆; Jinggang-shan Bowuguan; open summer 7.30am–5.30pm, winter 8am–5pm; entrance fee); two floors filled with black-and-white photographs, maps and battle plans, none labelled in English.

There are several scenic attractions in the mountains around Ciping, but none as spectacular as the **Five Dragon Pools** (五龙潭; Wulong Tan; open daily 8am–6pm), a sequence of eight waterfalls plunging down a steep gorge, each section spilling into a crystal-clear pool of water. The falls are about 7 km (4½ miles) north of Ciping; from the entrance a series of steps follows the cascade down the canyon, while a cable-car carries tourists back to the top.

## Ganzhou

A few hours south of Jinggangshan by bus and a short haul from the Guangdong border is **Ganzhou ⑦** (赣州) once a strategic port and now one of the world's major producers of tungsten. Straddling a peninsula where two minor rivers, the Gongjiang and the Zhangjiang, meet to form the beginning of the Gan River, the riverfront area has for centuries been heavily fortified, and many of the historic battlements still remain. A crenellated wall stretches for several kilometres along the peninsula's northern, river-facing side, with a string of guard towers concentrated near the confluence of the two waterways. The two best-preserved of these are the **Jianchun Men** and the **Dongjin Men**, both city gates facing the Gongjiang just east of the peninsula's tip.

Between the gates, and stretching 400 metres (1,300 ft) across the Gong River, is the **Dongjin Bridge** (东津桥; Dongjun Qiao), Ganzhou's most enduring historic landmark. The rare pontoon bridge, one of several originally built here during the Southern Song Dynasty, is made of wooden planks piled atop dozens of paddle boats tethered together with iron chains. The bridge, which gives excellent views back towards the city's battlements, still supports a steady stream of locals, who use it to reach the village on the river's far side.

# RESTAURANTS & BARS

## Restaurants

Average price for a meal for one, with one drink:
**$** under US$12 (under Rmb 100)
**$$** US$12–20 (Rmb 100–160)
**$$$** over US$20 (over Rmb 160)

Jiangxi is part of China's spice belt, and chillis feature heavily in local cuisine. In the Yangzi region of the north, fish are more prevalent.

### Jingdezhen

**Tang Ren Jie**
Corner of Xincun Xilu.
Tel: 0798 822 5777. **$**
Upmarket dining venue specialising in spicy Jiangxi fare with an eye towards presentation. Wide range of cold starters and fiery meat and vegetable mains – ask for low-spice if you don't have a tolerance for chilli peppers. Reservations recommended.

### Jinggangshan (Ciping)

**Lao Kejia**
23–25 Tian Jie.
Tel: 0796 656 6999. **$**
Owned by the nearby Eden Plaza Hotel, this welcoming place is known for its Hakka (Kejia) cuisine, especially its fish and mountain vegetable dishes.

**Xi Jiang Yue**
22 Tian Jie.
Tel: 0796 655 9199. **$**
Unpretentious joint next to Lao Kejia which prides itself on staple dishes once favoured by communist revolutionaries. Try Hongjun Cai (Red Army Vegetable), a delectable local item.

### Jiujiang

**Xunyang Lou Restaurant**
910 Binjiang Lu.
Tel: 0792 856 2968. **$**
This excellent restaurant prepares tasty fish, tofu and vegetable dishes for surprisingly reasonable prices. Book ahead in summer for a second-storey table with Yangzi River views.

### Lushan (Guling)

**Farmer Vegetables Restaurant**
25 Hexi Lu. **$**
Alongside Hexi Lu, this unassuming family-run restaurant serves up basic Chinese food. The freshwater fish with a side order of steamed mountain fungus is recommended.

**Soil Restaurant**
11 Guling Jie.
Tel: 0792 828 5588. **$$**
Another restaurant with a reputation for fresh local vegetable dishes and fiery stir-fries. Located in the heart of town and easy to spot with its English sign.

### Nanchang

**Atrium Café**
88 Yanjiang Beilu.
Tel: 0791 673 8855. **$$**
On the ground floor of the Gloria Plaza Hotel, with good-value breakfast, lunch and dinner buffets of Chinese and authentic Western food. Puts on a fabulous spread of cakes, cookies and chocolates for lunch and dinner.

**Hao Yuan Lai**
175 Minde Lu.
Tel: 0791 639 5678. **$**
The speciality here is steak, served up sizzling on fajita-style plates in a mild black-pepper sauce – a hit with Nanchang residents. A variety of steamed buns and dim sum snacks is also wheeled around on trolleys.

**Hongni Shaguo**
Tengwang Pavilion, South Gate. Tel: 0791 670 4888. **$**
This friendly establishment next to the Tengwang Pavilion is one of the best places to try the Jiangxi take on delicacies such as savoury *hongshao ruyu* (soy-braised mullet).

**Hunan Wang Caiguan**
99 Supu Lu.
Tel: 0791 623 8433. **$**
Facing Bayi Park, this immensely popular restaurant has some of Jiangxi's most authentic Hunanese cuisine.

**Ming Chao**
146 Bayi Dadao.
Tel: 0791 639 0283. **$**
Across Bayi Dadao from the long-distance bus station, this long-running local favourite is known primarily for the zesty Jiangxi-style soups that simmer in the big bronze cauldron out front.

**Spinach**
431 Minde Lu.
Tel: 0791 678 7116. **$$–$$$**
Trendy hang-out with Chinese and Western-style food, including a range of blended fruit juices. Occasional evening acoustic sets from young musicians.

## Bars

### Nanchang

**Base**
131 Rongmen Lu.
Tel: 0791 883 4165.
Small, homey pub with a selection of bottled European beers. Favoured by local expats for televised sporting events.

**Escape Bar**
122 Dinggong Lu.
Tel: 1370 709 2592.
This welcoming pub has a pool table and an outdoor patio. Located in a new up-and-coming bar district.

**Mayflower**
88 Minde Lu.
Tel: 1317 783 8168.
Nanchang has a vibrant dance scene, and this is the city's longest-running and best-known venue.

# HUNAN

Hunan is best-known as the birthplace of Mao Zedong, and monuments to the man litter the landscape around his home village of Shaoshan. Further afield lies the second-largest lake in China and the vertiginous scenery of Wulingyuan

here are two main reasons to visit Hunan: the bizarre and the beautiful, in the form of the village where Mao was born and China's first national park – gazetted early on by Hunanese leaders in Beijing for its soaring, jagged beauty. Hunan is a large province with a total area of 211,800 sq km (81,775 sq miles) and a population of 65 million, which includes Tujia, Miao, Yso, Dong, Bai, Hui and Zhuang ethnic groups. Mountains form natural barriers to three sides of this inland province, with China's second-largest lake, Dongting, and the mighty Yangzi River providing a watery northern frontier. The province is traditionally an agrarian place, famous for its rice, vegetables and fiery food.

The 20th century saw Hunan produce a number of famous communist sons, from Mao himself to ex-premier Zhu Rongji and Hua Guofeng, Mao's lookalike and briefly empowered successor. While China roars ahead, Mao's legacy is more visible in Hunan than anywhere else in China, thanks to countless statues and an elaborate tourist trail that steers visitors around every facet of his youth and his return as leader.

Mao used to say that the red-hot food made for great "red" patriots, and Hunan's fiery cuisine is often compared to the more famous cuisine of neighbouring Sichuan province. Both make extensive use of chillies, to cleanse the palate and to cope with the humid climate – somewhat counter-intuitively, hot foods such as red chilli peppers dry out and cool down the body, making it easier to handle the heat and dampness. However, while Sichuanese recipes frequently call for chilli bean paste, Hunan dishes are normally made with fresh chilli peppers, including the seeds and membranes, which contain most of the heat. Poultry and meat dishes are popular.

Although it is industrialising fast, Hunan still produces China's highest yields of rice, and is the nation's second-largest supplier of beef, pork and mutton. Meanwhile, its lakes provide an abundance of fish and shellfish.

**Main attractions**
YUEYANG TOWER
HUNAN PROVINCIAL MUSEUM, CHANGSHA
SHAOSHAN
HENG SHAN
WULINGYUAN SCENIC RESERVE
TIANMEN MOUNTAIN
FENGHUANG

**LEFT:** the dramatic route up to Tianmen Cave. **BELOW:** a collection of Mao badges.

*Hunan's cuisine is
the hottest in China.*

# YUEYANG, DONGTING HU
# AND NORTHEASTERN HUNAN

Northeastern Hunan is dominated by China's second-largest lake, Dongting Hu, home to the ancient sport of dragon-boat racing.

Situated at the point where the Yangzi meets Dongting Hu is **Yueyang ❶** (岳阳), a historic waterside town on the transit route between Hunan and Jiangxi. Yueyang makes for a good northern entrance/exit point into Hunan, either via the Yangzi or by rail – it's a major stopping point for river vessels and trains. Though much of the town is now nondescript and modern, the parts that retain the old rambling lakeside feel make it a

worthwhile stopover. Getting around is straightforward: Bailing Lu run east–west, past the bus station and then through the main part of city and down to the lake, where it intersects with Dongting Lu extending north–south along the lake shore.

**Yueyang Tower** (岳阳楼; Yueyang Lou; open daily May–Sept 7am–7pm; Oct–Apr 7.30am–6.30pm; entrance fee on Dongting Bei Lu stands out as the premier tourist attraction in town, a classically designed temple tower on three floors with long, swooping lines. The tower was built without a single nail around AD 217 on the shores of the lake. It initially served as a military reviewing

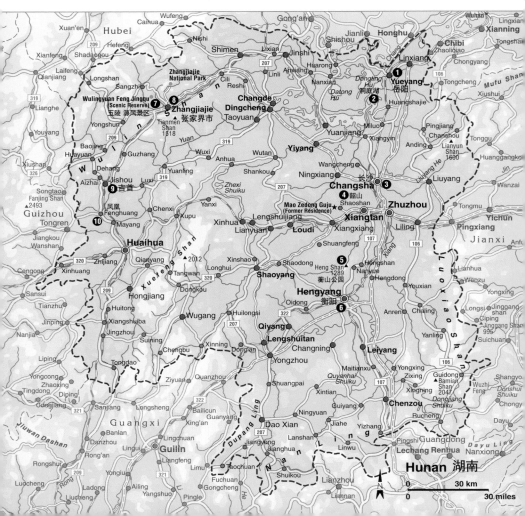

Hunan 湖南

tand and became known as Yueyang Tower in the Tang Dynasty, before being ebuilt in 1045, moved backwards 20 metres (65 ft) in 1880 and partially renovated in 1983. As well as a tomb, and the tandard Hunanese Mao memorabilia, ook out for an elderly chap who will cut he outline of your face on a black card or a small fee with amazing, if often unflattering, accuracy.

Old buildings are something of an endangered species in Yueyang, so head down Dongting Nanlu from the Yueyang Tower to get a greater understanding of what this lakeside community used to be ike. A 10-minute walk will bring the Cishi Pagoda (词史塔; Cishi Ta) into view. Built in 1242 and accessed via a side alley called Baota Xiang, this ancient brick building is in a dilapidated state with trees sprouting out of t, and there is no access into the interior. It is a picturesque sight nonetheless, and the side streets around here are full of character.

## Dongting Hu

The tiny island of **Junshan Dao** (居山岛), accessible by ferry from the pier beyond Yueyang Tower on Dongting Beilu, is the other reason Yueyang is on the Chinese tourist map. It sits in the **Dongting Hu** ❷ (洞庭湖), a vast expanse of chocolate-brown water 3,700 sq km (1,430 sq miles) in size.

Once a Daoist retreat reminiscent of Putuoshan, the sacred island off the coast of Zhejiang south of Shanghai, Junshan is best-known these days for its exclusive *yinzhen cha*, or silver needle tea, a bitter green tea that costs around Rmb 40 a cup or Rmb 270 for a tin's worth. Tea bushes dominate most of the hilly hinterland of this 2.6-sq km (1-sq mile) isle. The island is highly manicured and operates as a park, with temples, wells, pavilions and an area where, for a fee, you can watch caged, emaciated monkeys play the guitar and read newspapers; in short, the island is a familiar effort to create "historical tourism" out of nothing.

Dongting Hu and the surrounding waterways also gave the world the sport of dragon boating – the narrow, wooden vessels that careen speedily through the water, stroked to the beat of a drum *(see following page).*

*Yueyang's Cishi Pagoda is in urgent need of renovation. There is no public access, and the tower is surrounded by houses with residents' washing hanging out to dry.*

**BELOW:** classical design at Yueyang Tower.

**Flights**: Changsha is the only large airport, with flights to most cities in China.

**By Train and Bus**: Hunan lies on the main Guangzhou–Beijing line and rail connections with Guangdong, and north to Wuhan, Nanjing and Shanghai are frequent. Buses run to Guangzhou, Wuhan and other cities.

**GETTING AROUND HUNAN**
**Changsha**: There are frequent buses to Shaoshan (2 hours). There are regular trains to Zhangjiajie (6 hours, 7 daily; note that some go the long way round and take much longer than 6 hours). There are also trains to Shaoshan (3 hours, 1 daily).

**Yueyang**: There are frequent trains and buses to Changsha (1½–2 hours), and 1 daily bus to Zhangjiajie (7 hours).

**Shaoshan**: There are frequent buses to Changsha (2–3 hours). One train per day departs for Changsha (3 hours).

**Zhangjiajie**: Buses depart for Fenghuang (4 hours, 2 daily). There are trains to Changsha (6 hours, 7 daily).

**Fenghuang**: There are regular buses to Jishou, which take 1 hour from the bus station in the new town. There are frequent buses to Haihua (2 hours). Jishou and Haihua are both well connected by train with Changsha (8–9 hours).

*With taxis so cheap, most tourists will find Chinese city buses more trouble than they are worth. Long-distance buses, on the other hand, are often the best way to travel from city to city.*

**BELOW & BELOW RIGHT:** the dragon boat festival near Yueyang.

## MAO'S HOMELAND

Mao Zedong is Hunan's biggest draw by far, for domestic tourists at any rate. The Great Helmsman spent his formative years here – at Shaoshan, the village of his birth, then at Changsha, where he studied. When you tire of the endless memorabilia in this east-central part of the province, the nearby attractions of Nanyue and Heng Shen, one of China's most sacred mountains, are within easy reach.

## Changsha

The provincial capital **Changsha** ❸ (长沙) is by far the largest city in Hunan, with a population of over 6 million. Along with Hengyang, it is the province's principal transport hub. Orien-

## Dragon Boat Racing

**D**ragon boating, which can trace its ancestry back to the landlocked province of Hunan, has become a major international sport, with races held from Hawaii to Hokkaido. The origins hark back to 278 BC, when the former state of Chu was being attacked by the soon to be all-powerful Qin armies. Living around the shores of the lake of Dongting Hu was a famous poet and proud Chu nationalist, Qu Yuan. As the Qin forces approached, he drowned himself so as to avoid the spectacle of imminent defeat. Hundreds of locals leapt into their boats to try and save his life – but to no avail. These same fishermen would return later to throw pork and *zongzi* (sticky rice wrapped in leaves) into the river to placate Qu's spirit.

To this day all over China, the fifth day of the fifth lunar month commemorates this event with dragon-boat festivals on as many waterways as possible, including the Miluo River south of Yueyang, with boisterous spectators, competitive teams and large quantities of *zongzi*.

*Recommended Restaurants & Cafés on page 257*

tation is relatively easy, as the majority of the city sits to the east of the Xiang River, with the main throughfare, Wuyi Dadao, conveniently splitting the city between north and south. To the west of the river, in more rural surroundings, lies the university. The city was named Changsha – "long sand isle" – after a shoal in the river.

While at first sight it is not the most enticing of places, further investigation reveals a city with a fair amount to offer, even if there is very little that is ancient in modern-day Changsha. Evidence of 3,000 years of settlement was virtually destroyed by the Guomindang, who torched the old city during the 1940s in the face of the conquering Japanese.

Mao moved from Shaoshan to Changsha at the age of 18, and his legacy runs throughout the city and is the main focus for tourism. Nonetheless, it is the **Hunan Provincial Museum** Ⓐ (湖南省博物馆; Hunansheng Bowuguan; 50 Dongfeng Lu; open daily Apr–Nov 8am–6pm, Dec–Mar 8.30am–5.30pm; entrance fee) that stands out as the best sight in town. The first settlements in the Changsha area date back 5,000 years, and the gigantic concrete museum housing more than 110,000 artefacts is rightly famous for its 2,100-year-old Western Han tombs, corpses and coffins, as well as Shang- and Zhou-era bronzes discovered in the region. To the left of the museum entrance is **Martyrs' Park** (烈士公园; Lieshi Gongyuan; open daily 6am–10.30pm), a giant expanse of greenery in the city centre.

Turning to Mao-related tourism, **Clearwater Pool** Ⓑ (清水潭; Qingshui Tang; open daily 8.30am–5pm; entrance fee) on Bayi Lu is the must-see area on the Mao trail in the city. The site contains the first Chinese Communist Party provincial headquarters, established by Mao in 1921, as well as a house where the future leader lived for two years. There is also a rather tatty museum dedicated to glorifying the young Mao and crucifying the Cuomindang. All are set in pleasant lakeside parklands. You'll know when you've found the place – a 7-metre (24-ft) high aluminium alloy statue rears up just inside the entrance.

In the south of the city near the river, the arched, dark-grey **First Teacher's Training School** Ⓒ (open 8am–5.30pm;

*Tang-dynasty lacquerware box at the Hunan Provincial Museum.*

*Furong Square in the heart of downtown Changsha.*

entrance fee), on Shuyuan Lu, was where the future leader spent a few years studying between 1913 and 1918. The site is not overly inspiring and is a replica, as the original building was destroyed in the 1940s.

To the west beyond the Xiang River and above the university, sits **Yuelu Shan park D** (岳麓山公园; Yuelu Shan Gongyuan), best reached by taxi from the city centre. A walk to the top of the hill takes just over an hour and affords great panoramas across Changsha. The university where Mao used to study is at the bottom of the mountain, and to this day the area is teeming with students enjoying the green surroundings. North of the university is the **Yuelu Academy** (岳麓书院; Yuelu Shuyuan; open daily 8am–5.30pm; entrance fee), full of courtyards and rooms where many of China's great literati once studied – the establishment was founded in the Song Dynasty.

Thirty-five minutes northwest of Changsha by bus is a shrine to another great communist hero, Lei Feng. An orphan thanks to Japanese soldiers, Lei died aged 22, having been run over by a truck. A year later, his legend was made

by the authorities with the "discovery" of his diaries, which revealed him to have been the perfect communist hero – a man who shared everything he had, and fought all forms of oppression whether they were from the Japanese or Chinese nationalists. Even in today's market-driven China, 5 March remains "Learn from Lei Feng Day". The **Lei Feng Memorial Museum** (雷锋纪念馆; Leifeng Jinianguan) serves to glorify his life, and the brick house next door was where this selfless martyr grew up. Take bus No. 12 from Changsha to the terminus, then catch minibus No. 15 to the Leifeng Township. The museum is a couple of minutes' walk from the bus terminal.

## Shaoshan

The village of **Shaoshan 4** (韶山), which translates as "little mountain", lies 130 km (80 miles) southwest of Changsha. Come rain or shine, expect to see an armada of mainland tourist buses at this quasi-religious site – the village where Mao was born. Nothing can prepare you for the old-world propaganda and tack that lies in store in this otherwise peaceful area of Hunanese countryside – a

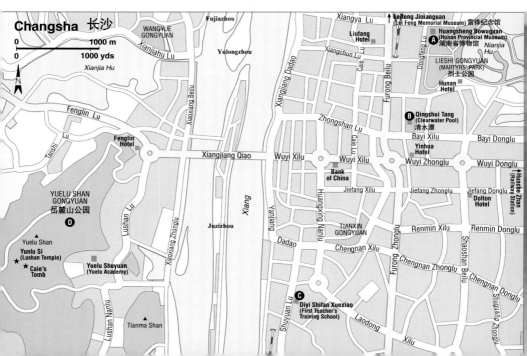

throwback and a must-see in China's fast-changing society. A fantastically persistent trade of minibuses act as shuttles between the handful of Mao tribute sites scattered around the old section of town (note that the bus and train stations are in the new part of town, some 5km/3 miles distant). The streets are lined with every Mao-connected trinket imaginable (and many more unimaginable ones besides). To this day, even though the Party might have its misgivings about Mao, he nevertheless serves as *the* brand of the Chinese Communist Party, and so his birthplace can be considered the Chinese communist equivalent of Bethlehem.

The Shaoshan experience can be done as a day trip, with both trains and buses arriving in the morning and departing in the late afternoon. As many as 3 million people a year make the pilgrimage to the principal sights – the Former Residence and nearby childhood School of Mao – situated beneath a monumental bronze statue of the man which presides over the village.

The mud-walled **Former Residence** (毛泽东故居; Mao Zedong Guju; open daily 8am–5.30pm), where Mao was born on 26 December 1893 and brought up

with his two brothers, is surprisingly large, facing south with pines behind and paddy terraces in front. Inside are detailed descriptions in both Chinese and English of every section of the house, including the rooms of his brothers Mao Zemin and Mao Zetan, who both died fighting for their beliefs. This experience is designed to be absolutely humbling, removing any doubt that Mao was a flesh-and-blood human being and heavily toning down the glorified, quasi-celestial being that has transcended reality. This seems to fit with the current administration's line that declares that Mao was "human like the rest of us", and humans make mistakes – in Mao's case, a legacy of being "30 percent wrong and 70 percent right". However, on leaving the residence, the human Mao gives way to the god-like Mao in the form of stall after stall selling an astounding assortment of trinkets and paraphernalia. Next door to the Former Residence is the rather dull **Na'Nan School** (open daily 8am–5.30pm; entrance fee) where Mao began his studies.

Slap bang in the middle of the village is the **Bronze Square**, where, in something

*Locals claim Changsha's ferris wheel, built in 2004 and situated next to the Helong Stadium on Furong Nanlu, is the world's largest. However, at an albeit impressive height of 120 metres (393 ft), it is lower than London's Millennium Eye, and both are set to be eclipsed by a new super-wheel under construction in Beijing.*

**BELOW LEFT:**
*Quotations from Chairman Mao Tse-tung*, the famous "Little Red Book".

## The Cult of Mao

The cult of Mao was a pervasive, propaganda-fuelled phenomenon that etched the leader as a deity in the minds of most Chinese. Although Mao had been the prevailing figure in revolutionary posters since the early 1950s, the trend towards a full-blown personality cult began to take on epic proportions after his 1962 launch of the Socialist Education Movement, which employed the mass dissemination of politicised socialist art to stem what he perceived as anti-revolutionary tendencies in the countryside.

By the mid-1960s, Mao's image was ubiquitous, dominating didactic posters emblazoned in red. Workers and students alike wore badges with his portrait, and after the 1966 publication of *Quotations from Chairman Mao* – commonly known as the "Little Red Book" – even his words were on the lips of every student and soldier. Mao's increasing paranoia encouraged him to harness the power at his disposal to launch the disastrous Cultural Revolution in 1966.

Following his death, the power of the personality cult rapidly waned, but even today the Chairman's image is undoubtedly China's most prevalent, adorning all the country's banknotes and overlooking the main squares of major cities. And anyone who visits his hometown of Shaoshan will be see for themselves how old habits die hard.

*A 1960s picture of Mao visiting his homeland.*

**BELOW:** bowing to the Chairman in Shaosan's Bronze Square.

reminiscent of Turkmenistan or North Korea, tour groups line up to bow. Across from the Mao statue is the **Museum of Comrade Mao** (毛泽东纪 念馆; Mao Zedong Jinianguan; open daily summer 7.30am–5.30pm, winter 8am–5pm), which gives visitors a quick rundown in timeline fashion of the life of the Great Helmsman. Next to this is **Mao's Ancestral Temple** (毛氏宗祠; Maoshi Zongci; open daily 8am–5.30pm; entrance fee), which traces Mao's ancestry back to a Ming patriot who fought the Mongols.

In nearby Shao Park, a maze of little rooms act as little Mao museums, each of them accessed via a beautiful path ascending an intricately landscaped hill. Former offices, another residence, the literally breathtaking Yan'an Pagoda, and countless photographs of his life history – Mao meeting an assortment of foreign leaders and going about his various duties – make for an in-depth meander through his career. As with all the sights in Shaoshan, photography is restricted; however, for a modest fee, and provided you don't attempt to touch him, you can have your photo taken with a realistic wax Mao, who sits happily enjoying a cigarette at the top of the park.

To the east of the village is **Dripping Water Cave** (滴水洞; Dishui Dong; open daily 8am–5.30pm; entrance fee), where Mao and his entourage decamped for a fortnight in 1966, amid the Cultural Revolution. Set at the back of a forested, watery park where patriotic music blares from speakers secreted in fake rocks, the cave is more of a dacha. At the end of the tour there is another photo opportunity, this time alongside a lifelike Mao mannequin.

Finally, on a rutted road 2 km (1¼ miles) south of town is a chairlift (open daily 8am–5.30pm; entrance fee) which ascends the impressive mountain of **Shao Shan**. Make sure you start your descent from the summit before 4.30pm, as the path is rugged and difficult to negotiate in the dark.

## Heng Shan

Approximately 120 km (75 miles) south of Mao's home territory is **Heng Shan ❺** (衡山), one of China's most sacred Daoist mountains and probably the third-most worthwhile sight in all of Hunan after Shaoshan and Zhangjiajie. There is plenty of hiking and temple viewing to keep any-

one occupied for a couple of days. The mountain, the highest part of a range that stretches from Hengyang northwards all the way to Changsha, is accessed from the town of **Nanyue** (南岳), rather than the village of Heng Shan.

First impressions of Nanyue are deceptive – another semi-modern, dull town with few distinguishing features. Peek further and an old town emerges, and as this is the main access point for Daoist pilgrims to the holy mountain, there is a pervasive sense of old China – not to mention a remarkable number of incense shops. Right in the centre of town is **Nanyue Temple** (南岳大庙; Nanyue Damiao; open daily 7am–7pm; entrance fee), an avowed classic of the Tang and Qing dynasties (though parts of it have been rebuilt). The temple has three courtyards, perfectly maintained roofing, ornate carvings and a good claim to being one of the very best-preserved temples in all of southern China.

Heng Shan rises just to the north of Nanyue and can be reached from the town on foot: allow around five hours to reach Wishing Harmony Peak (Zhurong Feng), the highest point, and another three hours

to descend back to Nanyue: in all it's a full day's hike. Alternatively there are frequent minibuses which travel all the way to the summit, or a cable-car to the top of an adjacent peak from approximately halfway up. The area is encompassed by **Heng Shan Park** (衡山公园; Heng Shan Gongyuan), entrance to which involves a modest fee. There are countless small Daoist temples and pagodas, which climb all the way to the 1,290-metre (4,232-ft) summit. The main trails are well endowed with vendors and food stalls, so bringing your own supplies is not necessary – although it's always advisable to carry water. In winter Heng Shan should only be attempted with proper planning and, preferably, with prior experience on mountains. This is one of the few places in southern China where you can rely on seeing snow.

Four km (2½ miles) east of Nanyue is a beautiful waterfall and cave complex, with a worthwhile 20-minute hike to the top of the fall.

## Hengyang

There is absolutely no need to make a point of stopping over in the dreary city

**TIP**

If you decide to climb to the summit of Heng Shan, be careful not to set your goal too high in winter. The loftiest accommodation is halfway up the mountain and the temples are locked after dark. Between November and April temperatures drop sharply after 5pm.

**BELOW:** Zhurong Daoist Temple on the icy summit of Heng Shan.

of **Hengyang ❻** (衡阳) south of Heng Shan, but given its status as a transport nexus – it is on the main road and rail routes to both Guilin and Guangzhou – you might have to hole up here for a night awaiting an onward bus or train. One way to pass the time is to hang out in the main square outside the train station, where, in the evenings, a cacophony of music blares out from competing sets of speakers, dancers waltz and twirl in competing unison, rollerbladers whizz by, and shuttlecocks launch into the air in a frenzy of action. It certainly beats kicking your heels in the grimy waiting halls of the train station.

## NORTHWESTERN HUNAN

This corner of Hunan, close to the border with Hubei, is home to a clump of beautiful forested mountains shaped by the region's karst geology, the limestone spires and pinnacles climbing vertically from the lush subtropical greenery of verdant valleys. Zhangjiajie, as this region as a whole is often known, is a popular spot with domestic visitors, although there are plenty of opportunities to get off the beaten track. In the far

west lies the Xiangxi Tujia and Miao Nationalities Autonomous Prefecture, where many of Hunan's ethnic minorities are concentrated.

### Zhangjiajie (Wulingyuan)

The UNESCO World Heritage Site of **Wulingyuan Scenic Reserve ❼** (五陵源风景区; Wulingyuan Feng Jingqu; entrance fee) is home to some of the most stunning scenery in China. This is exceptionally beautiful landscape, with mature forests, crystal-clear lakes, limpid streams and, rising above all, the karst topography: the quartzite sandstone crags and canyons here are simply breathtaking. The area shelters a remarkable variety of plants (over 3,000 species, including more than 500 species of tree) and some rare animals – including a few clouded leopards, various monkeys, and 1-metre (3-ft) long giant salamanders.

Prosperous **Zhangjiajie City ❽** (张家界市; Zhangjiajie Shi) is the regional hub and lies some 33 km (21 miles) south of Wulingyuan (the main point of access to the reserve itself is Zhangjiajie Village). A short taxi ride south of Zhangjiajie City brings you to what is purported to be the world's longest **cable-car** run (open daily 8am–5.30pm), which climbs the spectacular face of **Tianmen Shan** (天门山) – a vertiginous panorama of rock shards festooned in forest and often shrouded in mist. The cable-car runs for a distance of 7.5 km (4½ miles), rising 1,300 metres (4,260 ft) in elevation. It is an impressive piece of engineering, a feat reflected in the high ticket price – although this also includes transport access to the base of **Tianmen Cave** (天门洞; Tianmendong), where 1,000 steps lead up to the gargantuan 400-metre (1,300-ft) high, 200-metre (660-ft) wide natural archway. In 1999, three fighter jets flew through this hole in the mountain on live television.

A one-hour bus ride from Zhangjiajie City (last bus at 6.30pm) lies **Zhangjiajie Village** (张家界村; Zhangjiajie Cun), the most popular springboard for exploring the Scenic Reserve. The entrance to the protected area is close to the market (a good place to look for local souvenirs

*Hunan is one of the major rice-producing provinces of China.*

**BELOW:** the cable-car to Tianmen Shan.

*Recommended Restaurants & Cafés on page 257*

such as weaving and wooden carvings). From here there are two easy four-hour trails along the valley floor, as well as far more extensive options. Peace and tranquillity cannot be guaranteed as the area is popular with tour groups, although if you hike deep into the reserve and avoid some of the main paths, you'll have the spectacular soaring scenery to yourself. One of the most popular routes up onto the peaks is the **Bailong Lift**, an elevator attached to a cliff face below Yuanjiajie which shoots up 326 metres (1,070 ft) in just two minutes.

## Xiangxi Tujia and Miao nationalities autonomous prefecture

Most of Hunan's ethnic minorities are concentrated in the autonomous prefecture of **Xiangxi Tujia**, close to the borders with Guizhou and Chongqing Shi. Each ethnic group has its own distinct culture, and the entire area is wonderfully green and wild. Better still, very few visitors head to this neck of the woods, and a hike off one of the main roads will guarantee astonished looks from the local people you encounter.

Unlike many other parts of China, it seems unlikely that the road network will be improved any time soon in this corner of Hunan – which is good thing if you're looking for a taste of the untouched China of old (though the long bumpy bus journeys are hard work).

The capital of the Prefecture is **Jishou** ❾ (吉首), at the southern end of the Wuling Shan range. Visitors only tend to pass through here en route to the more interesting Miao settlements such as **Aizhai** (矮寨) 15 km (9 miles) to the west, which is picturesquely framed by precipitous mountains. The principal Hunan–Sichuan highway climbs here to a height of 440 metres (1,440 ft), with gradients as steep as 60 degrees. **Dehang** (德夯), another appealing Miao village, is a short distance further west, and makes a fine base for treks into the countryside – the highlight of which is twelve imposing waterfalls, with drops of around 190 metres (625 ft).

**Wangcun Village** (王村村), about 90 km (56 miles) to the west of Zhangjiajie, is a 2,000-year-old community at the juncture of the Mengdong and Yuanshui rivers. The village consists of a 2.5-km (1½-mile)

*The Bailong lift at Wulingyuan Scenic Reserve.*

**BELOW:** two of the limestone pillars at Wulingyuan.

*Miao handicrafts are sold in the tourist markets of Fenghuang. Western Hunan has significant populations of various minority groups.*

**BELOW:** stepping across the Tuo River in Fenghuang.

street paved with stone slabs, flanked by an ancient stone wall and the exotic buildings of the Tujia people.

## Fenghuang

Around 53 km (33 miles) south of Jishou is the ancient and beguiling riverside town of **Fenghuang** ⑩ (Phoenix Town) (凤凰), home to Miao and Tujia minorities. Fenghuang is one of Hunan's most beautiful towns and is certainly worth a visit if you are en route between Hunan and Guangxi. The Tuo River runs through the old district (the town dates back to 248 BC), surrounded by the red sandstone city walls and grand old gateways, while Ming- and Qing-style architecture lines up along the elegant intersecting stone-paved streets. The architectural styles of the Miao and Tujia ethnic groups are much in evidence. Fenghuang has woken up to its tourist potential in recent years and become very popular with tour groups, so things can get rather crowded, particularly in the summer months. Despite the tourist hordes and the money they bring, many of the buildings are in a poor state of repair, however – although for some this

only adds to the town's mesmerising lost-in-the-clouds aura.

The focus for tourism is pedestrianised **Dongzheng Jie**, which follows the river northwestwards from the 18th-century **East Gate Tower** (Dongmenlou) and is flanked by the old city wall. Just the other side of the gate is the impressive **Hongqiao Bridge**, a covered bridge of similar vintage. The Tuo River is straddled by several bridges, and its depth is sufficiently shallow to allow two sets of **stepping stones**, accessed from halfway along Dongzheng Jie, to provide an alternative means of crossing. Exploring the warren of narrow alleyways on both sides of the river is rewarding, with many small temples waiting to be discovered, and traditional shops selling all manner of goods.

Cottage industries abound; walk out of the north city gate and you'll come across silverware workshops, *mao tai* distilleries, native handicraft shops and the dyehouses instrumental in creating the deep-blue tones of the local clothing. On the boundaries of town is the **Huashan National Forest Park** (花山国家森林 公园; Huashan Guojie Senlin Gongyuan). ❏

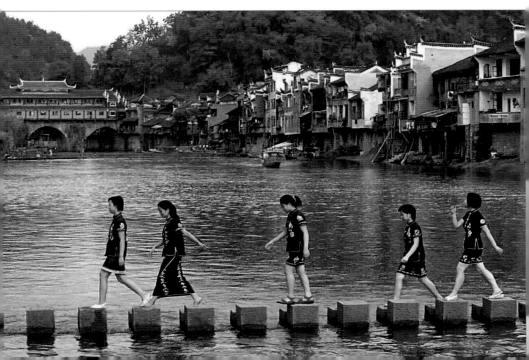

# RESTAURANTS & CAFES

## Restaurants

Average price for a meal for one, with one drink:
$ under US$12 (under Rmb 100)
$$ US$12–20 (Rmb 100–160)
$$$ over US$20 (over Rmb 160)

Hunan is famous for its spicy food, and local restaurants indulge in a liberal use of chillis with everything. Similar to Sichuanese cuisine, it has become popular across China.

### Changsha
For an eclectic range of restaurants (including some reasonable attempts at western-style food), the area around the eastern end of Wuyi Dadao is the best bet. There are also plenty of cafés around here. Another cluster of eateries can be found near the giant ferris wheel on Furong Nanlu. For fast-food chains, the shopping area around Huangxing Lu is the place.

A chain of bakeries from Macau – Padaria New Mario – comes complete with the famous Macanese egg tarts, though sadly minus the coffee. One of the bakeries is just to the left of the entrance to the Hunan

Provincial Museum.

### Huogongdian
105 Wuyi Dadao (city centre). Tel: 0731 412 0580. Another branch is at 78 Pozi Jie (near the Xiang River). $–$$
With traditional red frontage, either branch of Huogongdian (the name translates as Fire Palace, appropriately enough given the eye-watering heat of much of the food) is a great place to sample a wide range of local specialities. Inside a whirlwind of ladies with trolleys bring round all sorts of appetising Hunanese morsels. Make sure you try the cured chilli beef. Mao himself praised the smelly tofu when he dropped by in 1959.

### Illy Café
Zhongshan Lu. $
The Illy pumps out top espressos, has free internet, a surprisingly wide range of foreign beer, and rather tasty spaghetti bolognese.

### Shaoshan
Shaoshan is touristy and there is no shortage of restaurants cashing in, mostly concentrated around the main square. Prices are relatively high. All serve traditional dishes such as Mao Family Braised Pork.

### Yueyang
#### Xinjiang
Dongting Beilu. $
If you have had enough of Hunanese food, a good option is the Xinjiang restaurant next to Agricultural Bank of China. It's a friendly place to sit outside with barbecues brought to your table to roast spicy kebabs. Try the fresh Xinjiang noodles.

Around the Yueyang Tower on Dongting Beilu there are scores of good fish restaurants, for which the town is famous.

### Nanyue (Heng Shan)
There are numerous restaurants around the

tourist centre on Dong-shan Lu. The best restaurant in town is the two-storey Three Star which has local dishes such as Heng Shan tofu and delicious local noodles, with the water for the tea taken from the mountain behind. The restaurant can count former president Jiang Zemin as one of its past customers.

### Fenghuang
The riverside streets on both sides of the Tuo River are full of small restaurants, bars and cafés, and there's a cluster of street food stalls around Hong Qiao bridge.

**RIGHT:** condiments accompany the main dishes.

# THE SOUTHWEST

From Guilin to Guizhou, tropical Xishuangbanna to snowy Himalayan peaks, there is a huge amount to see in China's fascinating southwestern corner

The southwest is many travellers' favourite part of China, and it isn't hard to understand why. In terms of scenery and cultural diversity, this region is hard to beat, and exploring its riches gives a greater sense of adventure, a more complete "travel experience". Much of the southwest lies outside the mainstream Han Chinese world, and therefore looks and feels quite different from the rest of China.

Guangxi is southern China's only Autonomous Region, in recognition of the fact that the Zhuang minority comprise around a third of the population. However, compared with the minority groups elswhere in the southwest, the Zhuang are more assimilated into modern Chinese life and, therefore, Guangxi is less known for its cultural aspects than for its incredible scenery. The Li River around the city of Guilin winds its way lazily through an astonishing landscape, familiar to anyone who has set eyes on a classical Chinese scroll painting. To the north, a scenic route leads via the stunning Long-

sheng rice terraces to Guizhou, while the overland route through southern Guangxi to Vietnam is another fascinating journey.

Guizhou, one of the poorest parts of China, is home to a fabulous array of minority groups with their exotic architecture and festivals. The landscape across much of the province is wild and mountainous and travel is often rough, with poor accommodation and terrible roads, but can be extremely rewarding for the hardy.

Finally, much of southern Yunnan feels more like Laos or Thailand than China, with elaborate Buddhist temples, jungles and minority peoples. Beyond the pleasant provincial capital, Kunming, the land rises to the easternmost ridges of the Himalayas. Here you will find the magical cities of Dali and Lijiang, both set against dramatic mountains and within easy reach of some of the best trekking in China. The far northwest around Zhongdian is culturally part of Tibet, and marketed as "Shangrila" to tourists seeking adventure. ❏

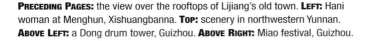

**PRECEDING PAGES:** the view over the rooftops of Lijiang's old town. **LEFT:** Hani woman at Menghun, Xishuangbanna. **TOP:** scenery in northwestern Yunnan. **ABOVE LEFT:** a Dong drum tower, Guizhou. **ABOVE RIGHT:** Miao festival, Guizhou.

*Recommended Restaurants & Bars on pages 284–5*

# GUANGXI

**Guangxi is historically one of China's poorest and most isolated provinces, but also one of its most beautiful. The famous scenery around the city of Guilin is the biggest attraction, though visitors will be rewarded by veering off the beaten track**

**D**ominated by weathered limestone peaks and plunging valleys, Guangxi is historically one of China's most isolated provinces. As such, it has become a repository for many of the nation's smaller ethnic groups – the Yao, Zuang and Dong, among others. Guilin, in the northeast of the province, is one of China's most famous sights – a place where the city and its surrounding landscape meld into one, while to the south along the Li River towards Yangshuo, the fantastical karst scenery grows ever more spectacular. In the far north are the awesome rice terraces of Longsheng, while the deep south offers more wonderful scenery en route to Vietnam.

## GUILIN

The area around **Guilin ❶** (桂林) has been attracting tourists for over 1,000 years. Drawn by the ethereal beauty of the karst landscape, poets, artists and admirers have showered praise upon the natural wonders of its remarkable mountains, caves, lakes and rivers. The city was named after the local osmanthus (or cassia) trees, whose scent wafts through the streets each autumn.

Historical records put Guilin's founding at 214 BC, when Qin Shi Huangdi, the first emperor of a united China, ordered the construction of the Ling canal to connect the Yangzi plains with Southeast Asia, via the Li and Zhu rivers. The canal, one of the world's oldest, still exists, and a 34-km (21-

mile) stretch can be seen at Xing'an, 65 km (40 miles) northwest of Guilin.

Guilin has been a significant political and cultural centre since the Tang Dynasty (618–906), but its golden years arrived during the Ming Dynasty (1368–1644), after Zhu Shouqian, the son of the founding Ming emperor who was appointed ruler of this part of China, set up his court in Guilin. Three hundred years later, in 1647, Guilin fleetingly became a base for the fleeing Ming court when the Manchus swept them out of power. Another three centuries later, as

**Main attractions**

GUILIN
LI RIVER CRUISE
YANGSHUO
LONGSHENG RICE TERRACES
ZUO RIVER AND LONGRUI
   NATURE RESERVE
DETIAN FALLS
SILVER BEACH, BEIHAI

**LEFT:** Guilin's amazing limestone landscape draws the tourists.
**BELOW:** dock at Beihai in the steamy south.

*The Sun and Moon pagodas on Fir Lake in central Guilin.*

the Japanese invaded, hundreds of thousands of north Chinese sought safety in Guilin. In 1949 it was one of the last Guomindang (nationalist) strongholds to fall to the communists.

At first glance there is little to see of Guilin's rich history – almost the entire city was razed by the Japanese army in 1944. When it was rebuilt, there was little to distinguish it from any other mid-sized Chinese city – apart from the unusual sight of limestone peaks in the city centre. Over 4 million people live in the municipality of Guilin, which extends over 30,000 sq km (12,000 sq miles) but the city proper is home to 700,000 people in 58 sq km (22 sq

miles). Along with Beijing, Shanghai and Xi'an, Guilin is on the must-see list for domestic tourists, so the city's visitor numbers have grown with every boom in the economy since the 1980s. Since 1999 the municipal government has invested in a beautification programme, which includes the restoration and reconstruction of historical landmarks. Silted-over rivers and moats have been dredged, new road bridges built to ease congestion, view-blocking buildings demolished and hundreds of trees planted.

The modern city parameters are defined by Zhongshan Lu to the west and the **Li River** (漓江; Li Jiang) to the east. The long-distance bus station, the rail-

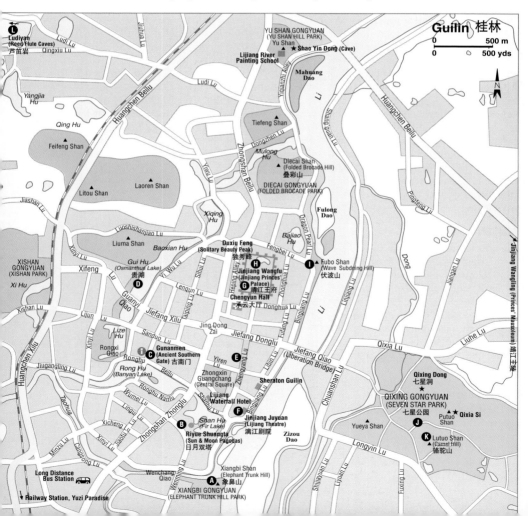

way station and a number of tourist hotels are located on Zhongshan Nanlu, while the central part of town is located in the grid of streets between Zhongshan Zhonglu and Binjiang Lu, which runs alongside the Li River. This was the location of the ancient city of Guilin, which at one time was surrounded by a moat and marked out by strategically chosen peaks.

You can trace the outline of the old city by following the banks of the river and the restored waterways of Fir Lake (Shan Hu), Banyan Lake (Rong Hu) and Osmanthus Lake (Gui Hu). Strolling under the osmanthus and willow trees in the early morning provides a peaceful glimpse of the city, and the lakes are attractively dotted with islets and hump-back bridges.

## City sights

Guilin's landmark **Elephant Trunk Hill** Ⓐ (象鼻山; Xiangbi Shan) is a good place to start a walk around the city. Located slightly south of the centre, on the river bank where the Li meets the smaller Taohua Jiang, the hill distinctly resembles a limestone elephant sipping

from the river. It is situated within a small **park** (open daily 7am–7pm; entrance fee), the entrance to which is on Minzhu Lu. If you have the energy, climb the 200-metre (650-ft) hill and catch your breath inside the Puxian Pagoda, which was built more than 500 years ago. The pagoda provides a good vantage point across the city.

From Elephant Trunk Hill, head north over Wenchang Bridge and pass Fir Lake (Shan Hu) and the twin **Sun and Moon pagodas** Ⓑ (日月双塔; Riyue Shuangta; open daily; entrance fee). At night the colourful lights of the 40-metre (131-ft) pagodas add glittering gold and silver reflections to Fir Lake.

Follow the lake to reach Shanhu Lu, and then continue along neighbouring Banyan Lake (Rong Hu) until you reach Rongxi Bridge. Across the road, to the right of the Guilin Tourism Bureau, is an authentic remnant of the old city, the **Ancient Southern Gate** Ⓒ (古南门; Gunanmen), built during the Tang Dynasty and expanded in Ming times, when Guilin became the provincial capital. It was once part of the city walls, so the oldest part of the gate is a modest

*A trip on a bamboo raft is the best way to appreciate Elephant Trunk Hill.*

**BELOW:** Solitary Beauty Peak.

**TIP**

If you time an evening stroll well, you can take in the odd sight of the world's largest outdoor man-made waterfall at the Lijiang Waterfall Hotel. At 8pm every evening the hotel's 76-metre (250-ft) wide and 42-metre (138-ft) high exterior glass wall briefly, and somewhat bizarrely, turns into huge cascading falls, accompanied by gaudy bright lights and loud music.

**BELOW:** acrobatics displays are very popular in China.

stone tunnel. A Ming-style single-storey building now sits on top of the wall. From here the lakeside promenade turns right and heads north along Yiwu Lu following the banks of **Osmanthus Lake D** (贵湖; Gui Hu), the former moat that forms the western border of the old city and runs parallel with the Li River.

To explore the city centre, turn right at Guanyi Bridge and head east along Jiefeng Lu. As you enter the middle section of the city's grid layout, the lakeside fairy lights give way to neon lights and Guilin is suddenly indistinguishable from any medium-sized Chinese city. The main hub of activity is the area around Central Square (Zhongxin Guangchang), built in 1999 south of the intersection of Jiefang Lu and the city's other main thoroughfare, Zhongshan Lu. In this downtown area department stores, stalls and restaurants are open until late. Between Central Square and the Li River, pedestrianised **Zhenyang Lu E** runs south from Jiefeng Lu to Nanhuan Lu. Popularly referred to as "walking street", this area is geared towards tourists, with a selection of restaurants, bars, galleries and fairly kitsch souvenir stalls. Its loca-

tion one block in from the Sheraton Guilin and the Lijiang Waterfall Hotel makes it a convenient place to dine if you have limited time in Guilin.

On the waterfront Binjiang Lu, the **Lijiang Theatre F** (漓江剧院; Jinjiang Juyuan) has a changing programme of evening shows that often feature Guangxi's minorities. Evening boat trips along the city's restored waterways, and other tours, can be booked at the numerous agents along Binjiang Lu, or through hotel tour desks.

## Princes' City

The most historic area of Guilin is the **Jinjiang Princes' Palace G** (靖江王府; Jinjiang Wangfu; open daily 8.30am–5pm; entrance fee), a short stroll north of the city centre. Its walls, gates and halls follow the classic lines of a Ming Dynasty city. Tour guides will always stress that it was built 34 years before the larger Forbidden City, but unlike Beijing's palace, most of what you see today has been reconstructed in the last 20 years or so.

First built in 1372 as the palace of Zhu Shouqian *(see page 263)*, the palace was

*Recommended Restaurants & Bars on pages 284–5*

## GETTING TO GUANGXI

**Flights**: Guilin and Nanning are connected with most cities in China.

**By Train and Bus**: Guangxi lies on the Beijing–Hanoi railway, with other long-distance routes between Guangzhou and Yunnan crossing the province. Sleeper buses run from Guilin (and Yangshuo) to Guangzhou, Changsha and other cities.

## GETTING AROUND GUANGXI

**Guilin**: There are regular bus services to Yangshuo (1–1½hrs, every 20 minutes,), Longsheng (1½ hrs, hourly) and Nanning (4–4½hrs, every 15 minutes). There are trains to Nanning (4–6 hours, 10 daily).

**Yangshuo**: There are frequent minibuses to Guilin (1–1½ hours). The nearest railway station is Guilin, from where there are many onward connections.

**Longsheng**: Buses depart every 15 minutes to Guilin and take 1½ hours. Guilin is the nearest railway station.

**Nanning**: There are frequent bus services to Beihai (2½ hours) and Guilin (4½ hours). There are trains to Pingxiang (3½ hours, 6 daily) and Guilin (5 hours, 10 daily). There is one bus per day to Pingxiang (4 hours).

**Pingxiang (Vietnam border)**: There are bus services to local towns, and trains to Nanning (3½ hours, 6 daily).

**Beihai**: There is a daily train to Nanning (3½ hours). Buses run to Guilin (7 hours), and Nanning (2½ hours).

*Flower bouquets outside Chengyun Hall in Jinjiang Princes' Palace.*

home to the next 12 generations of Jinjiang princes until the end of the dynasty in 1644. When the Ming court fled south, they tried to establish a Southern Ming Dynasty from here, but in 1650 the Manchus drove them out of Guilin and the city was destroyed.

Parts of the original city walls are still in place, and some original stone carvings and balustrades have been recovered and restored. The main palace in the centre of the complex, **Chengyun Hall** (承云大厅; Chengyun Daiting), houses a small exhibition about the 14 princes who lived here down the centuries.

Guilin's ancient city within a city has its very own karst mountain inside its walls (included in entrance fee). **Solitary Beauty Peak** (独秀峰; Duxiu Feng) rises up above the Ming buildings, and climbing the 300 or so steps to the pagoda at the top rewards you with the delightful view enjoyed by princes and poets over the centuries. At the western foot of the peak is the entrance to the **Peace Grotto** (平石窟; Pingshiku; included in entrance fee), a network of caves and passages where the princes once worshipped their ancestors. Today the portraits of the 14 princes line the underground walkway, which leads to a gallery and souvenir shop.

During the Qing Dynasty, the former palace became an examination centre, and exam booths and a Confucian temple were built near the north wall. After

**BELOW:**
statue at the Jinjiang Princes' Mausoleum.

*The distinctly camel-like profile of Camel Hill.*

**BELOW:** inside the Seven Star Park caves.

travelling to Guilin, scholars prayed for academic success at the temple before being confined to small three-sided booths for two days while they took exams.

Solitary Beauty Peak played a role in modern Chinese history during the Northern Expedition in the 1920s, when the Guomindang set out to break the control of warlords over the impoverished southwest. In 1921 Sun Yatsen, who was leading the North Expeditionary Army, established his headquarters at the foot of the peak, and a monument beside nearby Crescent Pond commemorates his time of residence here.

Since the 1930s the site of the Jinjiang Princes' City has been home to the Guangxi Normal University Teacher's Training College, and the reconstruction has taken place around the campus.

## Fubo Shan and other peaks

Around 200 metres (660 ft) east, within a small riverside park along Fengbei Lu, lies **Wave Subduing Hill** ❶ (伏波山; Fubo Shan; open daily 7am–7pm; entrance fee), also known as Whirpool Hill. The compact park at the foot of the peak includes a number Qing relics,

including a huge 2-ton bronze bell and a giant bronze wok encased in stone. On the south side of the park is the **Cave of the Returned Pearl** (Huangzhu Dong), with its Sword Testing Stone, a 3-metre (10-ft) stalactite. Buddhist sculptures and prayers, carved during the Tang and Song dynasties, can be seen on **Thousand Buddha Rock** (千佛岩; Qianfo Yan) at the foot of the peak.

A short, steep climb up the steps takes you to a small viewing platform on the summit, from where you can see the hills of **Folded Brocade Hill** (叠彩山; Diecai Shan; open daily 8am–6.30pm; entrance fee), so called because when this group of hills catch the changing daylight they are said to resemble piles of folded fabric. There are plenty of pavilions from which to stop and take in the views. Halfway up, the Wind Cave cuts through the limestone from north to south and is home to Buddhist carvings from the Tang and Song dynasties.

Located a few kilometres north, **Yu Shan** distinguishes itself from other city peaks with an art school and gallery. Ignore the unattractive concrete amphitheatre in front of the entrance to **Yu Shan Park** (open daily; entrance fee) and enjoy the 8,000-sq metre (2-acre) classical garden that is home to the **Lijiang River Painting School**. Students attend the school's Guilin Landscape Painting Research Institute to paint the classic scenes first-hand. Established by noted 20th-century artists Xi Beihong and Guan Shanyue, the school has a permanent collection and a retail gallery. **Shao Yin Cave** runs through the foot of Yu Shan, and the Buddhist carvings within include a figure of Guanyin dating from the Northern Wei Dynasty.

## Seven Star Park

Across the Li River from the city centre and reached via Liberation Bridge (built in 1999) lie the scenic peaks of **Seven Star Park** ❷ (七星公园; Qixing Gongyuan; open daily 7am–7pm; entrance fee). The park within which they are set allows you to sample all the city's natural

attractions in one manageable 40-hectare (100-acre) site. It is a pleasant mix of landscaping, caves and temples set amid the seven peaks, which lie in the shape of the Big Dipper constellation.

Walk through **Qixia Temple** towards **Putuo Shan** and follow the steps up the hill to the entrance of **Qixing Dong** (七星洞; entrance fee included), which is a network of caves within the peak. The subterranean journey begins in a large cavern, with walls covered with centuries-old inscriptions and poems, as well as some more recent items including a sample of Mao's calligraphy. A paved path through the caves takes you through the stalactites and stalagmites. Ceilings are high, and guides will turn on the lights and explain what the different shapes are supposed to represent. It is easy to spend an hour or two in the caves before heading back into the daylight and the well-maintained gardens.

Visitors are clearly drawn to the oddly shaped **Camel Hill** Ⓚ (骆驼山; Lutuo Shan); in a province crammed full of strangely shaped rocks that sometimes barely fit the name that's supposed to describe their shape, it does in fact look uncannily camel-like. In front of the hill, people queue up to stand in the footsteps of former US president Bill Clinton and be photographed at a plinth commemorating a speech he made about the environment during his 1998 visit to Guilin. Near the foot of the hill you will find the park's zoo; it is a miserable place and best avoided.

## The Reed Flute Caves

The **Reed Flute Caves** complex Ⓛ (芦笛岩; Ludiyan; open daily 8.30am–4.30pm; entrance fee) is located about 7 km (4 miles) northwest of the city centre and is the most dramatic of Guilin's cave systems. The caves were named after the reeds growing nearby which were traditionally used to make musical instruments. At the entrance, cave staff wait for a group of 40 or so visitors to form, and then, megaphones in hand, lead the way inside. Pagodas, chandeliers, mushrooms, giant pillars, fish and even Santa Claus have all been spotted in the speleothems in these labyrinthine passageways, gaudily illuminated with multicoloured lights. The paths are wet,

**TIP**

River cruises down the Li River *(see p273 for a description)* from Zhujiang port (or city-centre Binjiang Lu when the water is higher in summer) take around 6 hours and include lunch on board and a bus back to Guilin. There are also cheaper cruises from Xingping and Caoping further south. If you are in a hurry, frequent Yang-shuo-bound minibuses depart from points along Zhongshan Lu and from outside the railway station.

**BELOW:** roadside souvenir stall between Guilin and Yangshuo.

*The sculpture garden at Yuzi Paradise, spread over 60 hectares (150 acres) of attractively landscaped parkland.*

**BELOW:** the picnic sculptures at Yuzi Paradise.

narrow and winding but open out to impressive caverns with underground pools and lakes, the most impressive of which is the vast Crystal Palace of the Dragon King.

Guilin's Ming rulers are buried some 10 km (6 miles) east of the ancient city at the **Jinjiang Princes' Mausoleum** (靖江王陵; Jinjiang Wangling; open daily; entrance fee). This final resting place of princes, generals, lieutenants and families that inhabited the Jinjiang Princes' Palace is a peaceful spot, surrounded by pine and birch trees. More than 300 tombs are thought to spread over 100 sq km (39 sq miles), but so far only the 15th-century altar palace of Prince Zhuangjiang and his wife has been restored. Statues of animals and court officials line the path to the altar palace, and inside there is an exhibition (labelled in Chinese only) featuring a small collection of artefacts including gold, silver, jade, pottery and porcelain.

At nearby **Yao Shan** (903 metres/ 2,960 ft) there is an amusement park and a chairlift ride (or taxi) to the mountain top for some grand views of the surrounding area.

## Yuzi Paradise

Further out of the city, on the road to Yangshuo, the mountains of Guilin are an inspired setting for the sculpture park at **Yuzi Paradise ❷** (愚自乐园; Yuzi Leyuan; open daily 8.30am–6pm; www.yuzi-paradise.com; entrance fee). Situated 30 km (18 miles) south of Guilin city, this bold project was instigated in 1996 by a Taiwanese tycoon with a passion for sculpture and a desire to leave a lasting legacy. The juxtaposition of modern art against a backdrop of misty mountains makes for a wonderful visual experience. Huge contemporary sculptures are spread over 60 hectares (150 acres) in a landscape of winding paths, lakes, modern architecture and the odd karst outcrop. Over the last decade during eight international sculpture symposia hosted at Yuzi, more than 200 artists from 47 countries have made their contributions, including Taiwan's Ju Ming, China's Zhu Yu, British sculptor Allen Jones and Eberhard Eckerle from Germany.

Yuzi is a fascinating place to explore for at least half a day – and if you have more than a passing interest in art you

will want to stay longer. At the 3,000-sq metre (32,000-sq ft) workshop, sculptors, potters and artists busy themselves casting, carving and creating. An exhibition gallery shows smaller pieces in a variety of media by contemporary artists; art courses are available if you book ahead. A music park dedicated to the late Chinese singer Teresa Tang adds an aural angle to the sculpture park.

Golf buggies will ferry you around, or you can walk or hire bikes. There is also a children's area to explore with logs to clamber on, oversized see-saws and giant arty-looking climbing frames.

Between all this art and beauty you can dine on reasonably priced fusion cuisine at the Hotel of Modern Art's restaurant. Shuttle buses for Yuzi Paradise leave the main Guilin bus station every 20 minutes.

## AROUND GUILIN

The extraordinary beauty of the countryside south of Guilin is no secret, and a steady stream of riverboats make the scenic journey along the Li River between Guilin and Yangshuo. The landscape in this region is dominated by the outlandish limestone pinnacles rising sheer from the otherwise flat terrain of paddy fields. Farmhands in conical hats work the rice terraces, while on the river, villagers fish from bamboo rafts using trained cormorants. This is the classic Chinese landscape familiar from so many scroll paintings, and for many visitors, this region represents a quintessential taste of China. It's a year-round destination, but the summer months are perhaps the best time to visit: the landscape is a vivid green and there is a greater chance of clear (ie non-hazy) weather, despite the fact that it is the wettest season. It is very hot, however.

## North of Yangshuo

The stretch of river between **Yangdi** ❸ (杨堤) and **Xingping** ❹ (兴坪) has the best views of the Li landscape. If you opt to travel between Guilin and Yangshuo by road, it is also possible to join a boat at Xingping for a short river trip. From Yangshuo, there are local buses every 20 minutes for the one-hour journey to Xingping, which was the main town in the area 400 years ago. Surrounded by seven peaks on the east side of the river, it is worth allow-

*Xiongsen, just outside Guilin, is the world's biggest farm for rare animals, with an astonishing total of 1,300 tigers (as well as hundreds of bears and other species) bred for their body parts used in Chinese medicine. The international ban on tiger products has meant that nothing can be sold – yet: Xiongsen is banking on this being about to change. Somewhat shamefully, the complex has become a tourist attraction: at feeding time, crowds gather to watch a tiger kill a cow or other prey.*

**BELOW:** the majestic Li River.

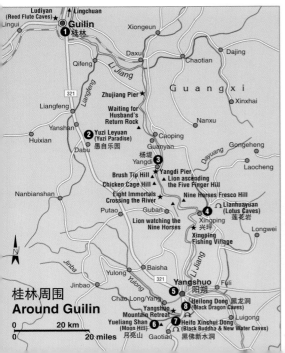

*Yangshuo is one of China's leading rock-climbing centres.*

**BELOW:** strolling along Xi Jie, Yangshuo's main drag.

ing some time to stroll through the oldest part of Xingping, where traditional houses line narrow, unpaved footpaths. From Xingping there are pleasant boat trips to the adjoining, well-preserved fishing village. Commercialisation is creeping into Xingping, but at present it is still only a brief stop for coach trips; if the lack of English menus and the quiet, dusty streets appeal, you will find a few basic hotels along the main street.

Three km (2 miles) outside Xingping are the **Lotus Caves** (莲花岩; Lianhuayan; open daily; entrance fee). Tickets are available from a booth by the bus station. The entrance includes a guide, who will turn on the multi-coloured lights within the 600-metre (2,000-ft) underground passageway and point out a multitude of hard-to-discern animal shapes.

## Yangshuo

Situated 60 km (37 miles) downstream from Guilin, **Yangshuo ❺** (阳朔) has long enjoyed a prime position on the backpacker trail. These days, though, there are thousands upon thousands of foreign and domestic tourists of all bud-

gets occupying its hostels, guest houses and hotels throughout the year. Despite all this, it somehow manages to retain a riverside country town feel, and for most tourists remains one of the most enjoyable destinations in all of China. The great appeal is the opportunity it provides to slow down, bike or hike and explore the Chinese countryside that is otherwise only glimpsed from trains and buses.

**Xi Jie ❹** (West Street) is the centre of the independent tourist scene. Most visitors arrive either at **Yangshuo Quay ❸** at the bottom of the street, or at the bus station on the corner of Diecui Lu and Pantao Lu. Chengzhong Lu has a few pavement cafés and small hotels. Gui Hua Lu and Xianqian Lu are the centre of the rock-climbing community.

Every afternoon the tour boats from Guilin pull up at the Ming-style steps on the quayside and hundreds of day-trippers disembark for a quick tour of the town, before most board their tour buses back to Guilin. One of the sights on the tour is Xi Jie itself. As the original backpacker area of Yangshuo, for domestic Chinese tour groups Xi Jie's cafés, bars and shops with their foreign customers

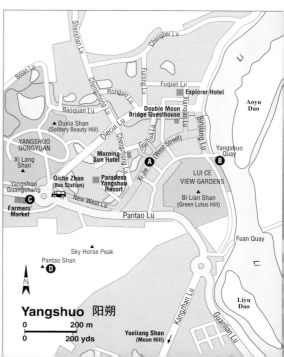

Yangshuo 阳朔

GUANGXI
Maps on pages 271, 272
273
Recommended Restaurants & Bars on pages 284–5

re of as much interest as the peaks, Ming Dynasty rooftops and cobblestones.

For Westerners, Yangshuo is one of the easiest places in China to spend time. There's a good selection of reasonably priced accommodation in the town, a wide choice of clean, inexpensive restaurants with foreigner-friendly food, cheap beer and excellent Yunnan coffee.

Shopping can easily consume many hours here, with shops selling a vast range of souvenirs, minority handicrafts, embroidery, textiles, art and jewellery. Surprisingly, urban offerings include Asian-inspired interior design, CDs and DVDs. Yangshuo's clothes shops offer everything from Beijing 2008 T-shirts, tie-dye and minority batiks, to branded sports shoes and designer clothing.

To inspect the region's produce, visit the local **farmers' market** ⓒ, which is held daily in Yangshuo, just off Pantao Lu near the junction with Diecui Lu. Nearby **Pantao Shan** ⓓ, which is covered in transmitters and known by locals as TV Tower Hill, is an easy 30–40-minute climb, where you are rewarded with a full panorama of the town and the surrounding landscape.

## Exploring the countryside

Cycling is one of the easiest ways to escape into the peace of the countryside around Yangshuo. There are some straightforward routes along the **Yulong River** (玉龙河; Yulong He), but unless you are sure of your route then hiring a local guide will keep you on track (see Travel Tips). Ideal for cyclists, the terrain between the peaks is mostly banana-pancake-flat. Most routes will take you on roads and dirt tracks alongside the fields where buffaloes are the beast of burden and farmers struggle to eke a living from their land.

**Moon Hill** ⑥ (月亮山; Yueliang Shan; open daily; entrance fee to summit) is one of the most popular destinations from Yangshuo. If you are cycling, it is reached either by a straightforward 10-km (6-mile) trip south along the road, or via a more circuitous route east out of Yangshuo past yellow-mud brick farms and village houses. As the only hill with a moon-shaped hole at the top, it's also an easy landmark to aim for. The 50-metre (164-ft) hole was once a cave, and looks particularly magical when the moon itself shines through. Moon Hill

**TIP**

Yangshuo's small army of mainly female bicycle guides can usually be found around the bike hire shops and cafés on Xi Jie, dressed smartly in polo shirts and trousers. Most speak good English and will charge around Rmb 20–30 per hour or Rmb 100–50 per day to act as your guide. If you want to go further than Yulong River, hiring a guide will ensure you don't get lost and will definitely enhance your day out.

**BELOW LEFT:** a cruise along the Li River is the best way to appreciate the incredible landscape.

## Li Riverboat Trips

A boat trip on the Li River is a highlight of a trip to China. The most popular journey is to sail the 80 km (50 miles) from Guilin down to Yangshuo, through the heart of the incredible karst scenery which has made the region famous. For most of the year, boats leave from the tourist port at Zhuijiang Pier, south of the city.

The cruise passes through the karst landscape's endlessly fascinating spires, along near-vertical cliffs that shoot up from the flat plains. It's a relaxing way to take in the peaks and catch a glimpse of life along the river bank. This is the timeless scenery that Tang Dynasty poet Han Yu famously described as a blue ribbon pinned down by mountains serving as jade hairpins.

En route guides will intermittently point out the names that the poets have bestowed on the peaks, some of which have equally imaginative translations: Waiting for Husband's Return; Lion Ascending the Five Finger Hill; Chicken Cage Hill; Eight Immortals Crossing the River; Lion Watching the Nine Horses. As you approach the town of Xingping, fellow passengers will pull out Rmb 20 notes to compare the real thing with the peaks that appear on the back of the note. The journey takes three to five hours, depending on the water level, with transport back to Guilin by bus.

**BELOW:** cormorant
fishing on the Li
River at Yangshuo.

has also become a magnet for climbers
who can often be seen silhouetted against
the opening – the Chinese describe their
feats as "ballet in the air".

The hill itself towers 230 metres (755
ft) over the surrounding paddy fields,
with dozens of souvenir stalls and cafés
clustered around its base. Those who
climb the 800-odd steps to the top are
rewarded with unforgettable views.

Nearby are two popular cave complexes that rely less on coloured lights
for effect and more upon the visitor's
sense of adventure. **Black Buddha Cave**
and **New Water Cave** ❼ (黑佛新水洞;
Heifo Xinshui Dong) were discovered in
1991, and the 1½-hour or 3-hour tours
will involve some scrambling along lad-
ders and wading through mud. About 3
km (4 miles) down the road, the **Black
Dragon Caves** ❽ (黑龙洞; Heilong
Dong) can be explored by boat or by
kayak if you arrange your tour with a
guide or agent in Yangshuo in advance.

The easiest place to hike or bike without a guide is alongside the **Yulong
River**. Head south out of town along the
main Pantao Lu, on the road to Moon
Hill, and turn right at **Workers' Bridge**
(Gongnong Qiao). From here the road is
mainly unpaved. The route takes you
past the Yangshuo Mountain Retreat and
numerous hamlets including Chao Long
and Chao Yang. The trail runs parallel to
the river for about 12 km (7½ miles)
upstream to **Yulong Qiao** – a particularly
photogenic humpbacked stone bridge
that is said to be over 400 years old. If
you take a right here you will reach the
town of **Baisha**, which has a market
every third day. From Baisha, it is a 9-km
(5½-mile) cycle ride back to Yangshuo
along the main highway.

Alternatively, you can combine hiking
or biking with a bit of messing about on
the river. Entrepreneurial villagers operate bamboo rafts from a series of stations
along the Yulong (although at around
Rmb 150 for two hours, this is more
costly than most activities). The rafts follow the design of the simple fishing boat
of the region, comprising bamboo poles
lashed together – though these are wide
enough to accommodate two deckchairs,
an umbrella and your bicycles. Passengers are provided with life jackets and
can lean back while they are punted along
for an hour or two. Most rafts are

## Cormorant Fishing

Traditionally, Li River fisherman used
cormorants to catch fish. With tied
necks, the birds were unable to swallow
any fish they caught and the catch was
squeezed back up their necks by the
fisherman. These days, however, rather
than actually fishing for a living, there is
far more money to be earned in
demonstrating the technique to tourists.
Tours are available from hotels and Xi Jie
travel agents. Alternatively, head down
the quayside in the evening and you can
join a one-hour boat trip which follows
the trail of fishermen accompanied by
their cormorants on bamboo rafts for a
fishing demonstration by lamplight. It is a
curious but fascinating sight, though
it can feel like a bit of a forced performance when shared with so many
other tourists.

quipped with water pistols, and you may ven have the option of being serenaded y a girl dressed in minority costume vho sings through a blowhorn. If you refer to paddle your own boat, most ravel agents or guides can arrange kayak rips on the rivers around Yangshuo.

Climbing for beginners or experts can e arranged through one of the cafés or pecialist guide shops around Guihua Lu nd Xianqian Lu in Yangshuo. These nformal information exchanges are also he best places for adventure-sports nthusiasts to find out about more chal- enging routes for caving, kayaking and 10untain biking.

## mpressions of Liu Sanjie

angshuo's scenery provides the back- rop to a world-class musical perfor- nance at 8pm every night, just down the ver from the main town. **Impressions f Liu Sanjie** was devised and directed y China's renowned film director hang Yimou – best known for films uch as *Raise the Red Lantern*, *Hero* and *Iouse of the Flying Daggers* – and re- ells a Guangxi folk tale that was made opular throughout China by a film made

in 1960 called *Third Sister Liu*. The Li River and the riverside provides the stage, and 12 tastefully lit karst moun- tains are the perfect arena for this love story. Audiences enjoy a sweeping 2-km (1¼-mile) panorama of the show from a riverbank theatre stand, and spectacular scenes include hundreds of bamboo rafts gliding across the river to create a river ballet. Most of the 500-plus cast are local farmers and fishermen. Up to 2,000 people see the show every night, many travelling down from Guilin.

## NORTHERN GUANGXI

The road north from Guilin leads to minority areas, dramatic scenery and, eventually, the back door into Guizhou province.

## Longsheng rice terraces

The spectacular rice terraces at **Longji Tit- ian**（龙脊梯田）and **Jingkeng**（金坑） are 700 years old, reach a height of 800 metres (2,620 ft) from the valley base and are popularly referred to as the Dragon's Back. Different seasons pro- duce varying effects. Spring provides the most striking time, when the fields are

*The great arch that gives Moon Hill its name. A climb to the top is well worth the effort for one of the most awe-inspiring views in China.*

**BELOW:** a performance of Zhang Yimou's *Impressions of Liu Sanjie*.

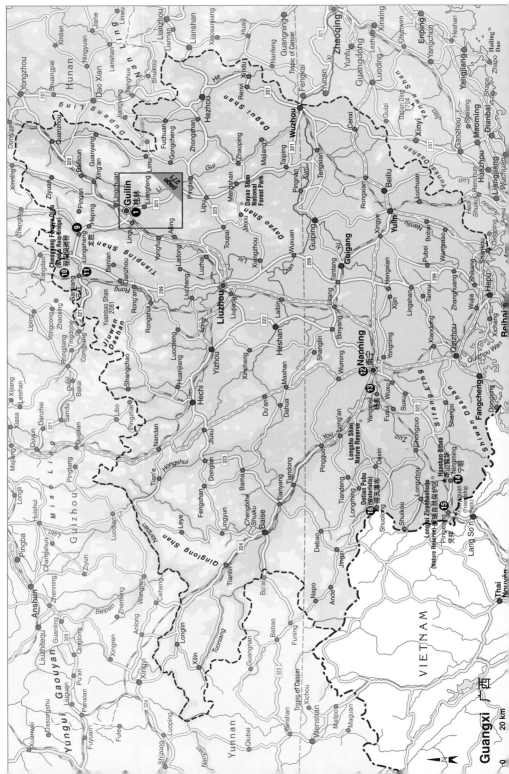

full of water, but a winter snowfall, or beds of emerald green rice shoots in summer, can be just as memorable. Bamboo pipes ferry water to the myriad paddy fields.

The town of **Longsheng** ❾ (龙胜), 90 km (56 miles) north of Guilin (1½ hours by bus), is the gateway to the terraces, but since rustic accommodation and good food is easily found at the sights themselves, there is little reason to stay here. Most tour groups visit the terraces at **Pingan** (平安) (*see below*), 29 km (18 miles) east of Longsheng, although the terraces at **Jingkeng**, 35 km (22 miles) from Longsheng, cover a larger area and are less visited, making them a more tranquil place to spend the night. Basic three-storey pinewood guest houses dot the trails.

The Yao village of **Da Zai** (大寨), at the base of the terraces, has a ticket office (entrance fee) and is the starting point for walks to the three viewpoints above. Although a local guide is not essential, it is time-saving, and they will porter your bags (expect to pay in the region of Rmb 40–50 for a half day). Yao women are famed for their long hair, and, tradition-ally, the number of times it is knotted reveals the number of children they have.

A steep 1½–2-hour trek leads to viewpoint No. 3. Viewpoint No. 1 is a further 1-hour walk across the terraces and conveniently sports the Panorama Guest House at the same location. A few minutes further on there are several other places to stay. However, although this area is quite isolated, it can get busy with hiking groups at the weekends. All of the accommodation provides great views of viewpoint No. 2. Sunrise lights up the staircase of water-filled paddies to surreal and dramatic effect.

The 3–4-hour walk from viewpoint No. 1 to the popular Zuang village of **Pingan** is also highly recommended. This undulating trail passes through the interesting Zhongliu village and offers beautiful vistas along the way. Before descending into Pingan, visits can be made to the two viewpoints that overlook the village. From Pingan, a 1-hour circuit incorporating these two vantage points runs through the terraces. On a moonlit night, if there is water in the terraces below viewpoint No. 2, it is said that the shape of the paddies resembles seven

*The northern areas of Guangxi bordering Guizhou province are home to several minority groups, including the Yao. As in most of these ethnic groups, Yao women weave and embroider their own festival costumes.*

**BELOW:** the beautiful Jingkeng rice terraces.

*The Dragon's Back (or Dragon Spine) Terraces at Longsheng are a spectacular sight, and one which changes dramatically with the seasons.*

stars and the moon. Pingan has a good supply of guest houses and restaurants.

From Pingan a road leads down to a parking area where infrequent buses ply the route to Longsheng. There is a ticket office here if you are entering the terraces at Pingan. However, by descending a stone path and then crossing a bridge, the Yao village of Huanglo, on the main road, can be reached. From here buses to Longsheng or Da Zai are frequent. Another option is to walk from Pingan to the traditional **Old Zuang Village** and then on to **Golden Zuang Village**, which is again on the main road. There are also some waterfalls in the area.

## North to Sanjiang

The next place of interest heading north is the **Chengyang Wind and Rain Bridge** ❿ (程阳风雨桥; Chengyang Fengyu Qiao; entrance fee), located 20 km (12 miles) from the town of Sanjiang (*see below*). This is an area populated by the Dong, a minority famous for their unique wind-and-rain bridges and drum towers (*see page 94*). Chengyang's famed bridge was built in the early 1900s, and, as with all traditional Dong structures, wooden pegs were used in its construction in preference to nails. There is also a large drum tower beside the river. The entrance fee allows access to the bridge and the village of Chengyang, where there are several cheap places to stay. The valley is very picturesque, and large wooden wheels slowly rotate gathering water to irrigate the surrounding fields. Panoramic views of bridge and village can be achieved by walking up to the pagoda set on an adjacent hill. The Firecracker Festival here takes place in the village on the seventh day of the first lunar month, although there are plenty of similarly pyrotechnic festivals in other villages throughout the year.

**Sanjiang** ⓫ (三江) itself isn't of great interest, but is the place to catch a bus into the southeastern corner of Guizhou Province, picturesque home to various colourful minority groups (*see pages 287–299 and 300–301*).

## SOUTHERN GUANGXI

The steamy southern reaches of Guangxi are well removed from the tourist trail, although in places the scenery on offer is not vastly inferior to the famous Guilin karst. The main interest is in the route to Vietnam, but the seaside town of Beihai is not without charm.

### Nanning

Guangxi's provincial capital, **Nanning** ⓬ (南宁), is a major transport interchange between the south and southwest of China and Vietnam, and is full of many of the ethnic minorities that people the province. It has a certain deep-south border flavour – many hotel signboards are in Vietnamese, and shops are stocked with consumables imported from Hanoi.

The city is laid out on a large scale around the Yong River, and its bus stations are scattered around the edges of the urban area. **Chaoyang Lu**, the main commercial artery, leads south from the railway station to Yongjiang Bridge, and is lined with hotels and department stores on both sides. The oldest part of town lies west of Chaoyang Lu, in the maze of narrow streets around Xinhua Jie. It's

here on Jiefang Lu that you'll find the **Xinhui Academy** (新会书院; Xinhui Shuyuan; open daily 9am–noon, 1pm–4.30pm), a guildhall built by Guangdong businessmen in the early Qing Dynasty. Constructed in the typical southern Chinese Lingnan style, it's possibly the best-kept old building in Nanning, with fine roof sculptures.

The **Provincial Museum** (省博物馆; Sheng Bowuguan; open daily 8am–11.30am, 2.30–5pm; entrance fee) has no English signage, and can be hard to find. It's the squat communist-era building on the southeast corner of Minzu Square. The main exhibit is a collection of bronze drums and other items cast by people of the **Dongson culture**, a mysterious civilisation which existed in the Guangxi, Yunnan and northern Vietnam region around 2,000 years ago. They were a trading people: Dongson artefacts have been found as far away as Indonesia and Myanmar. The bronze drums were used as emblems of leadership, and many examples feature detailed figurines of people, cattle and frogs.

The upper floor of the building has displays on the clothing and customs of Guangxi's present-day ethnic groups. Don't miss the museum's landscaped garden: traditional houses, granaries and towers of the Zhuang, Yao, Miao and other nationalities are set amidst bamboo and fishponds.

**Renmin Park** (人民公园; Renmin Gongyuan; open daily dawn–dusk; entrance fee) is laid out around **Zhenning Fort** (镇宁炮台; Zhenning Baotai; open daily dawn–dusk; entrance fee). Inside, you can climb steps to reach a German-built cannon dating from 1890. It would have had a clear field of fire over Nanning's old town. The need for defence was very real: Nanning has been on the invasion route of French, Vietnamese and Japanese armies, as well as home-grown rebels. The magazines around the gun emplacement hold a double exhibition of Chinese heroes and trick mirrors, although any connection between the two is not made apparent. The pleasant park also includes a lake and aviary.

The **Qingxiushan Scenic Area** (青秀山风景区; Qingxiushan Fengjingqu; open daily dawn–dusk; entrance fee) is located on the southeastern edge of

*Palm-lined walkway between the lakes at Nanning's Renmin Park.*

**BELOW LEFT:** Zhuang minority dancers at the Guangxi Provincial Museum, Nanning.
**BELOW:** Nanning railway station.

*Dongson artefact at Nanning's Provincial Museum.*

**BELOW:** the Chinese gateway, with the French Customs House beyond, at the Friendship Pass on the Vietnamese border.

town, at the terminus of the No. 10 bus. The zone near the main gate features a traditional wind-and-rain bridge over 500 metres (1,640 ft) long, built by a team of Dong craftsmen. At the far end of the beauty spot is a Guanyin temple, a nunnery, a Thai garden and two pagodas set amid hillside orchards and flower nurseries. The nine-storey Longxiang Pagoda is built in Ming style and is beautifully illuminated after dark.

Thirty kilometres (20 miles) west of Nanning along the Yong River, the rural backwater of **Yangmei** ⑬ （杨美） makes a pleasant excursion. The town made its living from river trade, and most houses date back to Qing times, its period of greatest prosperity. It's worth a wander, although limited transport options mean that the expedition becomes a day trip: there are trains and ferries from Nanning, but in each case there is only one departure per day, at 8.30am.

## Towards the Vietnam border

Some 200 km (125 miles) southwest of Nanning en route to the Vietnamese border, the country town of **Ningming** ⑭ （宁明） is the jumping-off point for a boat trip along the scenic **Zuo River** （左江; Zuo Jiang). Take a 15-minute motorcycle taxi ride from the train station to Panlong village, entry point to the **Longrui Nature Reserve** （陇瑞自然保护区; Longrui Ziranbaohuqu）, which protects the habitat of the rare white-headed leaf monkey. The muddy landing stage is a five-minute walk from the ticket office. Entry to the river area involves a fixed fee, while the boatman's fee is negotiable.

The slow-paced sailing gives you time to appreciate activity on the river bank – water buffalo tethered beneath bamboo groves, girls washing clothes in the river, villagers boarding rafts – as well as towering limestone cliffs. An hour or so downriver you reach **Huashan Bihua** （华山碧华）, a vertical rock face daubed with hundreds of crimson stick figures. Depicting scenes of hunting and farming, the paintings were made by the Luoyue people and are thought to date from the early Han period.

From Ningming, buses follow mint-scented village roads for 40 km (25 miles) to **Pingxiang** ⑮ （凭祥） a small river

town focused on cross-border trade. Shops close surprisingly early for a Chinese town, but food is available at a small night market opposite the railway station.

It's worth visiting the **Friendship Pass** (友谊关; Youyiguan) on the Vietnamese border 30 minutes south of Pingxiang by taxi or pedicab, even if you're not crossing into Vietnam. Graced by two imposing landmarks – a colonial French Customs house and a ceremonial Chinese gateway – the crossing straddles a narrow pass between tall, misty mountains. Cracked stone steps lead up to vantage points on either side. Formerly known as Zhennan Pass, its name was changed to Youyi (Friendship) Pass in 1965, just in time for China to supply the Vietnamese with armaments during the Vietnam War. Inside the French-era building, faded photographs show Mao Zedong trading jokes with Ho Chi Minh, but friendship hasn't always been in great supply: within 15 years the two neighbours were at war with each other.

A picturesque route to follow is that from **Chongzuo** (崇左) north to **Daxin** (大新). Limestone crags gather ever closer together as the bus traverses lush fields between villages. Daxin is the nearest large town to the **Detian Falls** **⑯** (得天瀑布; Detian Pubu), and there are cheap hotels near the bus station.

Reaching the waterfalls requires several changes of transport. First, take a motorcycle taxi from Daxin's bus station to a point further west where shared minivans wait for passengers. For a few yuan the van will take you on a hairpin journey across mountains to Suolong, a tiny town with a marketplace nestled under a cliff, where you'll have to pick up another motorcycle taxi for the remaining distance. This final section runs alongside the broad, shallow Guichun River which marks the boundary between China and Vietnam. The taxi driver will stop for you to take photos at scenic points.

Surrounded by green karst peaks, the **waterfalls** (open dawn–dusk; entrance fee) are impressive: a wide meeting of overlapping cascades which plunge 60 metres (200 ft) into the river, throwing up great clouds of mist. A bamboo raft will take you into the spray for a small fee. Above the falls, a path beside rapids leads to an antique boundary stone inscribed in Chinese and French. A scruffy bazaar on

*The rock face at Huashan Bihua is covered with red figures dating back over 2,000 years.*

**BELOW:** karst peaks hem in the Detian Falls.

*The old French marker stone at the Vietnamese border, close to the Detian Falls.*

the Vietnamese side sells perfume and confectionery. There is no official presence here, and it's easy to walk past the bazaar into Vietnam, although you can go no further than the river.

## The southern coast

Guangdong and Guangxi played pass-the-parcel with **Beihai ❼** (北海) until 1965, when it was permanently incorporated into the latter. The city experienced an aborted economic boom in the mid-1990s which left it with more than the usual amount of half-finished buildings and highways to nowhere, but the lure of its beaches is drawing a growing number of holidaymakers, and plans are in train for a golf course and other tourist infrastructure.

Formerly known by its Cantonese name, Pakhoi, the city became a treaty port in 1876, and Western powers quickly established themselves with schools, trading houses and consulates. **Zhongshan Lu and Zhuhai Lu**, two parallel streets of 1920s-era shophouses, form the nucleus of the old town. Occasional plaques relate historical details such as the story of the Japanese-run

Maruichi pharmacy, an attack on which was used as a pretext for Japanese military action in the 1930s. Although some shophouses have been refaced in white bathroom tiles, the favoured material of modern Chinese construction, the overall effect is not spoiled.

Other relics of the treaty port era, including a Customs house and post office, are found on connecting streets. Built in tropical-colonial style, the former British Consulate sits in the grounds of No. 1 Middle School on Beijing Lu. A European church – shockingly restored with bathroom tiles – can be found on the other side of the same compound. The influence of missionaries was strong, and Beihai still has a sizeable community of Roman Catholics.

**Beibuwan Lu** marks the centre of town, with hotels, shopping malls and the main bus station. Local Anglophiles hold an "English corner" in the McDonald's here from 8–10pm on Mondays.

From the junction of Beibuwan Lu and Sichuan Lu, bus No. 3 runs south for 10 km (6 miles) to **Silver Beach** (北海银滩; Beihai Yintan), where a row of new resort hotels face the seafront.

Recommended Restaurants & Bars on pages 284–5

The greyish-white sandy beach extends along the shore for a total of 24 km (15 miles), and it is very popular: tens of thousands of people set out their deck-chairs on summer weekends. Opposite the bus stop, there is a shaded boardwalk backed by cafés and palm trees.

The road between the beach and the city centre is bordered by upscale apartment complexes which could almost be termed Miami-style if not for the washing hanging to dry from their balconies. Just west of the beach, the **Beihai International Ferry Port** (北海港客运站; Beihaigang Keyunzhan) has ferry services to Hainan and to **Weizhou Island**, an offshore isle which is China's largest volcanic island. Besides a pair of Gothic-style churches built by the French, the island is visited for its coastal scenery of caves and coral reefs. Boats leave Beihai at 8.30am, returning from Weizhou at 3pm. There is also a ticket office in town on Sichuan Lu.

**Beihai Underwater World** (北海海底世界; Beihai Haidi Shijie; open 8am–5.30pm; entrance fee) is one of China's largest aquariums, with viewing tunnels which allow you to walk through the world of sharks and stingrays. Star attraction is a turtle that is more than 100 years old, and there are also crocodiles, dugongs and seals. The educational indoor complex is located in Beihai Seaside Park, behind a well-used city beach close to the Qing Dynasty Puduzhen Temple.

The **Exhibition Centre of Pearls, Shellfish and Coral** (水产馆; Shuichan Guan; Sichuan Nanlu; open 8.30am–9pm; entrance fee) has smaller-scale exhibits and focuses more on the pearls, which long provided Beihai its livelihood. It has some beautiful live coral displays. At the time of writing, a four-dimensional "Oceanorama" was being constructed next door.

Waishadao, on the city's north shore, has been branded Waisha Seafood Island and has a dozen waterfront restaurants built in Thai and European styles. Further west, the No. 2 bus line terminates at the main harbour and fish market, busy with ocean-going fishing boats. The neighbourhood is home to ethnic Chinese boat people who fled Vietnam in the 1970s, and though many still live in shanty accommodation, they have one of the city's best viewing points for sunsets. ❑

*Silver Beach is one of the most pleasant urban beaches in the region, even if you don't require a swing chair to appreciate it.*

**BELOW:** a street of 1920s shophouses, Beihai.

# RESTAURANTS & BARS

## Restaurants

Average price for a meal for one, with one drink:
$ under US$12 (under Rmb 100)
$$ US$12–20 (Rmb 100–60)
$$$ over US$20 (over Rmb 160)

Guangxi cuisine lacks a clear identity – there is a strong Cantonese influence in the east and south, while things get increasingly spicy further inland. Guilin has a reputation for outlandish zoological delicacies, and Nanning's most famous dish is its dog hot-pot.

### Guilin

Restaurants are clustered around Central Square (Zhongxin Guangchang) and along Zhongshan Zhonglu heading south from the square.

### Aunt
5/F Niko Niko Do Plaza, Zhongshan Lu. $
From the shopping centre's top floor overlooking People's Square, Aunt restaurant has one of the largest selections of Chinese food. In fact, it operates more like a food court, which makes it easy to try lots of inexpensive new dishes.

### The Coffee Store
Zhengyan Lu/Yiren Lu. $
Coffee shop on pedestrianised street with open-air seating. Choose from their range of snack food and large choice of coffees.

### Forest Gump
17 Yiren Lu.
Tel: 0773 286 3038. $
Modest Chinese restaurant with branches across the city – and no apparent connection to the film of the same name. Good choice of dishes and friendly staff.

### Left Bank Café
18 Binjiang Lu.
Tel: 0773 288 2259. $
With a firm emphasis on food hygiene, this café is located along Li River with views of Seven Star Park. An ambitious range of offerings includes steaks, burgers, pizzas and fried rice served in a dimly lit dining room.

### Natural Café
24–25 Yiren Lu.
Tel: 0773 283 8866. $$
Large restaurant offering Western staples such as spaghetti, sandwiches, steaks and chops, not to mention Chinese dishes and curries.

### Two Pigs Asian Fusion
Hotel of Modern Art (HOMA), Yuzi Paradise, Dabu Township, Yanshan District.
Tel: 0773 386 9100. $$
Immaculately presented fresh food in arty modern restaurant, with noodles, Thai, sushi and burgers all available. Some cuisine fusions are less than successful; but the food is high-quality and remarkably good value. Drop by for a meal if you're visiting the sculpture park.

### Yi Yuan Restaurant
106 Nanhuan Lu. $
Tasty Sichuan food is a good choice for dinner after a stroll alongside Guilin's lakes. A useful menu clearly ranks the chilli-factor of the dishes. Groups may need to book ahead to get a table.

### Zhengyang Tang Cheng
Zhengyang Lu.
Tel: 0773 285 8553. $
Popular local restaurant whose range of dishes includes a few local specialities. Try their Guilin noodles, hotpots and as many dishes as you can.

### Yangshuo

There are numerous restaurants, cafés and bars (often all under one roof) along Xi Jie (West Street).

### 7th Heaven Café
93 Xi Jie.
Tel: 0773 882 6101. $
All the Yangshuo café favourites plus the added bonus of a selection of medicinal Chinese soups. Friendly service from pleasant staff.

### Café del Moon
Xi Jie. $
Two-storey café offering balcony tables, a good vantage point for watching the world go by. Pizzas, pasta and burgers are on the menu, along with some exceptional ice cream.

### Café Too
7 Cheng Zhong Lu.
Tel: 0773 882 8342. $
This café incorporating a second-hand bookstore/book exchange is a quiet spot to gather information. Serves a satisfying choice of local dishes, including hotpots, and there's an extensive menu of Western food. Breakfast, pages-long in all its permutations, is good value.

### Chuan Jia Ren Restaurant
Xi Jie. $$
Specialising in local dishes, this is a fine place to sample local favourites like Beer fish, Li River snails and spicy ribs.

### Drifters
58 Xi Jie.
Tel: 0773 882 1715. $
Australian-owned bar/café with a long menu of filling meals.

Weekly specials and good range of desserts.

### Everest Camp
9 Gui Ha Lu.
Tel: 0773 890 1166. **$**
Small, friendly café with some tasty Chinese dishes and a selection of burgers and Western snacks. Slightly cheaper than most of the cafés on Xi Jie. Internet also available.

### Le Vôtre
79 Xi Jie.
Tel: 0773 882 8040. **$$**
A restored Ming Dynasty building with a large outside terrace houses something unusual in provincial China – an upmarket French restaurant. Imported ingredients and distinctly French dishes, including *salade niçoise*, croissants and chocolate mousse.

### Nanning

### Kangaroo Bar
Beibuwan Xilu.
Tel: 0779 303 2786. **$**
The expat-run Kangaroo Bar has become popular with young locals, who use it as a place to meet up before heading off to the nightclubs, and its forecourt is buzzing in the evenings. Besides food, the bar has a pool table.

### Tibetan Cafe
Junction of Nanning's Dongge Lu and Gecun Lu. **$**

The cosy Tibetan Café has momo dumplings, Indian curries and ethnic wall hangings above the dark-wood tables, though alas, no yak cheese makes it this far south.

### V-Touch Restaurant
43-12 Xinmin Lu.
Tel: 0771 263 6388. **$**
V-Touch Restaurant has a helpful picture menu and English-speaking staff. The house special is hotpot, and there are vegetarian options. Spend over Rmb 50 and you can elect to play darts with the waitresses to win a glass of plum wine!

### White Dragon Restaurant
Renmin Park. **$$$**
Located inside peaceful Renmin Park, the White Dragon Restaurant specialises in seafood which is on display in outdoor tanks. Tables overlook the willow-fringed lake.

### Beihai

### Tommy's Place
Waishadao.
Tel: 0779 208 7020. **$**
Tommy's Place, a two-storey venue behind the seafood restaurants on the north shore, has its own micro-brewery and an East/West menu which includes steaks and pan-Asian dishes. Outdoor seating completes the picture.

### Xin Yu Guang Su
4 Jinxing Huayuen, Beibuwan Donglu.
Tel: 0779 205 2769. **$**
Stylish Xin Yu Guang Su serves up spicy Taiwanese dishes and exotic shaved-ice creations. For an extra few yuan, the Taipei-born owner will divine your future with the aid of a basket full of fortune sticks.

### Guilin
There's a selection of bars on "walking street" between Central Square and the river.

### Club 100% Baidu
Binjiang Lu.
Full-on nightclub close to the Li River and Jiefang Bridge.

### Yangshuo
Cafés and bars stay open late in Yangshuo, and it's easy to hang out for hours over after-dinner coffee or drinks. There's also a growing number of bars on and around Xi Jie with live music at night; with such a dense concentration of venues, it's simply a case of wandering down the street and seeing which place or sound appeals.

### Bar 98
42 Gui Ha Jie.
As the night wears on, Bar 98 attracts a late-night crowd with its live music acts and a quality sound system.

### Buffalo Bar
50 Xianqian Lu.
Friendly bar that runs regular quiz nights and plays movies late into the night.

**RIGHT:** an array of healthy local dishes.

*Recommended Restaurants & Bars on page 299*

# GUIZHOU

This often overlooked corner of southern China is fabulously rich in minority traditions, while its mountainous landscape is punctuated by limestone pinnacles, waterfalls and dense forest

Guizhou, with its fascinating minority cultures and dramatic landscapes, is one of the most rewarding parts of southern China to explore. Within the 171,000 sq. km (66,000 sq. miles) of this remote and mountainous backwater, only around five percent of the land is flat. Much of the terrain lies at an altitude of around 1,000 metres (3,300 ft) or higher, enough to make it cool and rainy much of the time – and positively frigid in winter – while the highest peaks reach to almost 3,000 metres (9,900 ft). The rugged terrain and thin limestone soils go a long way to explaining why the population of 39 million have the lowest GDP of any province in the country. Agriculture is the mainstay, although Guizhou also has an abundance of mineral resources.

## A land apart

The Han established marginal control over the region during the Tang Dynasty (618–907), when tribal chiefs sent tribute to the Emperor, but it was only during the Ming dynasty (1368–1644), with the establishment of military garrisons and migrations of poor peasants looking for new land, that greater central authority was achieved. The local population frequently revolted against the corrupt administration of both the Ming and the Qing dynasties: instances of unrest took place every few years, although the Miao Rebellion that occurred from 1854 to 1873 was certainly the longest and most widespread.

During the 1930s, the Red Army spent many months trudging through the demanding terrain in attempts to evade the pursuing Guomindang forces. Most of the minority peoples the marchers encountered were so poor they had to share clothes, and it was not uncommon to see peasants working naked in the fields. With the founding of the People's Republic of China, land redistribution followed, and, despite numerous setbacks and hardships, the autonomous minority prefectures are increasingly gaining control over their own affairs.

Mountainous terrain, miserable weather and a rural population largely bypassed

**Main attractions**

ZHAOXING AND SURROUNDINGS
DONG VILLAGES
MIAO VILLAGES AROUND KAILI
ZHENYUAN AND THE
   WUYANG RIVER
HUANGGUOSHU WATERFALL
ZHIJIN CAVES
CAO HAI LAKE

**LEFT:** The Miao festival costumes feature lavish amounts of silver. **BELOW:** scenery near Fanjing Shan in the northeast.

*Guizhou's numerous minority festivals often take place in remote areas, with rough roads and poor transport.*

**BELOW:** village children on a Dong wind-and-rain bridge.

by the booming economy are the prime characteristics associated with this corner of China – and that means that you can travel for days without seeing a foreign face. But it is these realities that, sometimes indirectly, make it such a rewarding place to visit. The terraced landscape offers some of the most spectacular karst scenery in the world, while the impoverished minority groups retain many of their fascinating traditions. But

be warned – to explore this province and its peoples requires a certain degree of perseverance and a sense of adventure. Very few people speak English, transportation can be rough, and food and accommodation basic.

## Guiyang: precious sun

Any visit to Guizhou is likely to involve passing through the provincial capital of **Guiyang ❶** (贵阳). In Putonghua, this

industrial city's name means, rather aptly, "precious sun".

Located in a basin surrounded by mountains, Guiyang was developed as an administrative centre during the Ming Dynasty, although real growth only began during the war with Japan. Nationalist forces were pushed west into the region and developed the communications and other infrastructure which helped haul it into the modern world. Today, the city has a population of over 3 million, and countless new skyscrapers are trying to break through the cloud and find that elusive sunshine. For all its efforts at modernisation, Guiyang is only just beginning to provide the services and facilities that foreign travellers might expect, and realistically there are few reasons to linger when the countryside offers so much more.

The main sights in the city can be explored in a day or two. **Qianling Park** Ⓐ (黔灵公园; Qianling Gongyuan; open daily 6.30am–10pm; entrance fee), in the northwest, is worth a visit. Beyond the tacky amusement park near the entrance are trails and a cable-car leading up the hill to **Hongfu Monastery** Ⓑ (弘福寺; Hongfu Si), a refuge was originally con-

structed in 1673 by the Zen Buddhist monk Chishong. A statue of Guanyin is set in a floral courtyard, and the buildings have been lovingly restored since their desecration during the Cultural Revolution, while cheap vegetarian food is available on-site. Further north there is a lake with attendant monkeys and a cave.

There are a few attractions in the city centre. The three-storey, 20-metre (66-ft) **Wenchang Pavilion** Ⓒ (文昌阁; Wenchang Ge; open daily; entrance fee) was built in 1596 and is a key historical relic, as is the **Jiaxiu Pavilion** Ⓓ (甲秀楼; Jiaxiu Lou), which sits on a rock in the middle of Nanming River. Constructed to inspire scholars in their studies, this late 16th-century pagoda now has a bridge that leads to the **Cuiwei Gardens** (粹惟园; Cuiweiyuan; open daily; nominal fee) on the south bank. **Renmin Square** Ⓔ (人民广场; Renmin Guangchang), with its massive statue of Chairman Mao, is only a short walk west along the same side of the river. During the day and early evening locals indulge in various forms of dance in front of the Great Helmsman, and the occasional folk performance can also be seen here. Cross

**TIP**

The CITS office in Guiyang is buried down a side-road at the junction of Hequn Road and Central Yanan Road.

**BELOW:** the Jiaxiu Pavilion, Guiyang.

*Bullfights traditionally accompany the Miao lusheng festivals.*

the river again along Zunyi Lu, and the Ming Dynasty **Qianming Temple ⓕ** (黔明寺; Qianming Si) can be visited, although at the time of writing it was closed for renovation.

Further afield are two scenic spots that allow for urban escape. **Huaxi Park** (花溪公园; Huaxi Gongyuan; open daily dawn–dusk; entrance fee) is 17 km (11 miles) south of the city and contains a series of hills and streams, along with pavilions, bridges, pagodas and gardens. **Baihua Lake** (百花湖; Baihuahu; open daily; entrance fee), 22 km (14 miles) northwest of Guiyang, is punctuated by more than 100 small limestone islands which create a mystical environment.

Both places are 30 minutes by bus from the city centre.

A nearby minority village of note is **Zhenshan** (珍山), situated close to Huaxi Park. Home to the Bouyei minority, it is surrounded by water on three sides and dates from 1600, when General Li Renyu was sent here on a mission by the Emperor and ended up marrying a Bouyei girl: the entire population are reputedly 17th-generation descendants of this couple. The village has a museum documenting its history.

## The Dong heartlands

The Dong minority, famous for their exotic-looking drum towers and wind-

Guizhou 贵州

and-rain bridges, are concentrated in an area that straddles the area between the far southeast of Guizhou and northeast Guangxi, and their cultural capital, **Zhaoxing ❷** (肇兴), is one of the most entrancing places in southern China. In addition to the five impressive drum towers and an equal number of wind-and-rain bridges, virtually all other buildings are traditional fir-wood three-storey structures that house farm animals on the ground floor. Early in the morning and late in the afternoon, a steady stream of man and beast ebbs and flows through the streets. Many of the inhabitants routinely dress in their colourful tribal clothing, although this is at its best during a festival *(see panel, page 292)*, when the small theatres opposite each of the drum towers stage performances. Whenever you visit, Zhaoxing is always fascinating.

For a good view of the town, head for Zhaoxing Middle School, situated in the northwest corner of town. The surrounding countryside also offers visual treats as the rice terracing ascends to great heights. The friendly village of **Pingshan** (平山), perched on the top of a mountain (at the end of a track that peels off to the left of the main road heading east), affords wonderful views of the next valley. Shortly before reaching this turn-off, a track to the right leads to **Tangan** (唐安), a village overlooking the Zhoaxing Valley with a picturesque wind-and-rain bridge and a large drum tower. A trail leads from here to the village of **Sha Ge** (厦格), which has three drum towers, with a cemetery above the village and a shrine below. The trail continues through the rice terraces and back round to Zhaoxing – a 4-km (2½-mile) stroll that takes a leisurely three hours. The large village of **Ji Tang** (济堂), 3 km (1¾ miles) southwest of Zhaoxing, is also worth a visit, and has two drum towers. It is possible to hire transport for the entire day, taking in all of the villages mentioned, for around Rmb 150.

A popular route to Zhaoxing is by the twice-daily bus from **Sanjiang** *(see page 278)*, 98 km (61 miles) to the south in Guangxi. This beautiful four-hour journey follows the valley of the Duliu River as it passes through a number of Dong villages before rising into mountains contoured with terracing from top to bottom. In the past, a stop in the town of **Diping** (地坪) would have been recommended,

*Strikingly exotic drum towers are a feature of many Dong villages.*

**BELOW:** magnificent wind-and-rain bridges can still be seen in the Dong areas of southeast Guizhou. The name simply relates to the protection these covered structures give from the elements.

*Guardian spirits on a drum tower at Pingshan. Dong culture, like that of other minority groups in Guizhou, retains a strong element of ancient animist religion.*

**BELOW:** traditional indigo garments worn by the Dong at festivals.

but its principal attraction – a particularly large wind-and-rain bridge – was swept away by flash floods in 2004.

The nearest large town from Zhaoxing is **Congjiang** ❸ (丛江), a regional transport hub 60 km (37 miles) to the southwest. The town itself is of little interest, and while many of the villages en route may be worth a visit, most are beginning to lose their traditional feel to the concrete mixer. The best time to tour this region is certainly during the Lusheng festival season, which runs from the middle of the seventh to the middle of the eighth lunar month. A short drive north of Congjiang is the village of **Yintang** (印堂), still very much wrapped in the past.

One of the best Sunday markets in Guizhou can be found at the town of **Rongjiang** ❹ (榕江), a 2½-hour journey up the Guiyang road from Congjiang. The variety of products on sale is mindboggling – a pile of dead rats proves the efficacy of a poison, while at the stall opposite, satellite dishes are for sale. The Dong from the surrounding villages are often seen selling charcoal, and many more are there to shop. A wide array of unusual street food is also available

(including rats). Even if you can't make the Sunday market, Rongjiang is still a pleasant enough place to break your journey. There are a couple of hotels near the bus station, and the night market has good cheap food.

For a manageable day excursion, head west to **Bakai** ❺ village (八开). The hour-long bus trip also passes through the villages of **Dujiang** (杜江) and **Layou**, which are both on the river. For a more adventurous expedition, catch a bus to **Tingdong**, 23 km (14 miles) along the road to Congjiang, and then arrange your own transport to visit the villages of **Xindi** (新地) and **Zengchong** (曾崇). The former is famous for having the region's largest drum tower and the latter for having the oldest. Regardless of these superlatives, these picturesque villages are surrounded by spectacular scenery. Although the furthest is only 23 km (14 miles) off the main road, a combination of dirt track and motor tricycle make for a hard slog. You'll need to make a very early start to complete this trip in a day, so be prepared to stay overnight with your driver in one of the villages if necessary.

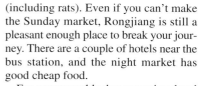

## Dong Festivals

Two of the largest Dong festivities, observed in villages right across the Dong areas, are Cai Ge Tang, held on the second day of the first lunar month, and Tai Guan Ren, held on the following two days. Cai Ge Tang commemorates the death of a female freedom fighter known euphemistically as Sasui, or "grandmother". Events take place in front of the shrines dedicated to her honour.

The Tai Guan Ren festival is shared by two neighbouring villages. A man from one village impersonates "Guan Ren", a government official who hands out money and is accompanied by girls dressed in their finest clothes. A parade of locals from the other village dressed as goblins, soldiers, fishermen and various animals ensues, after which traditional songs are sung under the drum tower.

## Kaili and the Miao areas

Out of a total population of around 8 million, approximately half of the Miao minority live in Guizhou. Various subdivisions are scattered throughout the province, but the greatest concentration is in and around the city of **Kaili** ❻ (凯里), 195 km (120 miles) east of Guiyang. This is a fairly typical Chinese city, with wide boulevards bisecting the centre and new developments springing up all over. Although Kaili has little in the way of sights, its range of accommodation and restaurants makes it a good base for visiting the local Miao settlements.

**Langde Shang** (朗德上) is probably the most appealing of traditional Miao villages within easy reach of Kaili. Approximately 30 km (19 miles) to the south of Kaili, along the road to Leishan, is a small turning on the right. A short walk past the ubiquitous waterwheels leads to Langde village, a well-preserved heritage site. It is famed as the place where Lu Dadao sparked the Miao uprising *(see page 32)* against the corrupt Qing rulers in 1853. The cobblestoned village square is frequently used for cultural performances laid on for the daily

bus tours of Chinese tourists intent on seeing a snapshot of local customs. Although somewhat contrived, these displays give a taste of different aspects of Miao culture in a postcard-perfect setting. It is interesting to see the otherwise sleepy village explode into life in expectation of such a visit. There is a basic guest house for those who wish to investigate further.

Heading south along the main road, **Leishan** (雷山) is a nondescript town, from where **Xijiang** ❼ (西江) can be accessed, purportedly the largest Miao village in existence, with over 1,200 households. Both places are famous for their Miao New Year festivals.

To the northeast of Kaili, the villages of **Shidong** ❽ (施洞) and **Taijiang** (台江) are well known as centres for the Sister's Meal Festival, and the former is also the best place to see the Miao Dragon Boat festival. *For more on these and other Miao festivals, see the panel on page 295.*

Along the road that runs alongside the Kaili–Guiyang expressway are several villages that come to life during the Chinese New Year holidays. Lusheng

**TIP**

The CITS office in Kaili (open daily 9am–5.30pm) is located in a courtyard shared by the Yingpanpo National Hotel. It's a useful place to pick up maps and find out about festivals in the area – schedules and locations often change from year to year.

**BELOW:** wooden Dong house at Pingshan, complete with satellite dish.

**TIP**

To arrange rafting trips on the Wuyang River, try the Wu Yang Feng Qing travel agency (tel: 0855-386 9108), located close to the bus station in the town of Shibing.

festivals move between the villages of **Yatang** (雅堂), **Zhouxi** (州西) and **Lian Dao Wan**, the last of which takes place on the banks of a small river that meanders through the surrounding mountains. The small town of **Xiasa**  (下沙) is also an interesting place to visit during this period. Also known as the "sports town", traditional New Year dragon dances are performed along with bull-fights held in an impressive earthen arena. Beside the river, dog fights can be seen, although they are fairly innocuous affairs.

## Zhenyuan and north of Kaili

A Han garrison settlement for the last 2,000 years, the town of **Zhenyuan** ⑩ (镇远) is ranged photogenically along the deep, green valley of the Wuyang River a short train journey (1 hour 40 minutes) northeast of Kaili. Its **Black Dragon Cave** (黑龙洞; Heilong Dong; open daily 6.30am–7.30pm; entrance fee) is in fact a collection of Buddhist and Daoist temples and pavilions that cling to the rock face on the opposite side of the river from the historic old town. The complex, dating from 1530, gives good views of **Zhusheng Bridge** (竹生桥; Zhusheng Qiao) on which sits **Kuixing Pavilion** (魁星楼; Kuixing Lou). Beside the bridge, on the edge of the old town, a steep climb up a paved path provides even better views. At the top, the old city walls seem to offer less protection than the karst mountains on which they were built. Following a path to the left and then down the hill leads to the small **Sigong Temple** (Sigong Si), from where a descent back into the town is possible. The Han Dragon Boat racing festival (on the fifth day of the fifth lunar month) is the town's major festival.

For more water-based activities a cruise along the **Wuyang River** (舞阳河; Wuyang He) is recommended. They can be arranged at the large town of **Shibing** ⑪ (施秉), 40 km (19 miles) west of Zhenyuan: a typical two-hour excursion downstream costs about Rmb 200 for the boat, and another Rmb 20 for transport to the dock. Upriver tours costing the same price are only one-way, but a connecting bus takes travellers on to Zhenyuan. Limestone pinnacles along the route, with such fanciful names as Sitting Frog, Hungry Tiger and Elephant's Face, form several gorges, and their image is reflected onto the placid waterway. River rafting is

**BELOW:** a Miao village in the hills north of Kaili appears to have changed little in the past 100 years.

also an option. For a fast connection to Kaili, Shibing train station is a 20-minute drive out of town.

A further 75 km (47 miles) along the road west to Guiyang is **Chong'an** ⑫ (重安), famous for its market, which is held every five days. Covering the entire village, it is a colourful affair, with Miao women stirring vats of indigo dye whilst Chinese techno music pounds away in the background. This is also where the Gejia minority can be seen. Until 1993 the Gejia were classified as a sub-group of the Miao. Now an independent minority, this people are recognised at festival time by their orange-and-blue costumes that historically are copies of the Qing uniforms of the Han soldiers they married. There are many Gejia villages within walking distance of Chong'an.

There are a couple of guest houses west of the settlement beside the river. This is also a good place to swim. Further west is a chain suspension bridge dating from 1873, and 5 km (3 miles) further is a scenic spot named **Shengu Pool** (神瞽湖; Shenguhu). Another Gejia village on the way to Kaili is **Matang** (麻塘), which is renowned for its batik.

## Northern Guizhou

Northern Guizhou has more land under cultivation than other parts of the province and is an important tobacco- and fruit-growing area. It is also known for the production of Maotai and other Chinese wines. Industrial development is ever increasing, and mineral reserves are abundant. Ethnically, it is less diverse than other areas, and in the far north the geography is more akin to the fertile Sichuanese basin than the limestone uplands of Guizhou. The region around Chishui is heavily forested and famed for its waterfalls and varied plant life.

The city of **Zunyi** ⑬ (遵义), 160 km (100 miles) north of Guiyang, is the second-largest in the province and holds a pivitol place in the annals of the Chinese Communist Party (CCP): a conference held here in 1935, during the Long March, propelled Mao to the leadership. The main reason to visit is to wallow in Long March and other CCP nostalgia. The **Zunyi Conference Site** (遵义会议址; Zunyi Huiyizhi; open daily 8.30am–6pm; entrance fee) contains a series of period buildings where politburo leaders were housed, a Catholic church, a Soviet bank and a large

*Fitting an ornate silver headdress at a lusheng festival.*

**BELOW LEFT:** a gathering of Small Flowery Miao at the Nankai lusheng festival in southwestern Guizhou *(see page 298).*

## Miao Festivals

The Miao are famous for their festivals, with hundreds taking place around Guizhou during the course of a year. The most famous are the **lusheng festivals**, at which young girls don their traditional costumes and dance to the music of the lusheng pipes (long reed pipes made from bamboo). These festivities are mainly occur from October to April, particularly in January and February when agricultural work is at a minimum. Often accompanied by bullfights, they are held at a designated site called a "flower ground", which could be anything from the local basketball court to a picturesque natural setting, and are real community events: the gatherings are traditionally an opportunity for young people to find suitable marriage partners – the Miao call this "fishing".

A more ritualised courtship takes place from the 15th to 17th days of the third lunar month at the **Sister's Meal festival**, with the symbolic exchange of sticky rice and other gifts between prospective partners. It is centred around the Miao villages of Shidong and Taijiang to the northeast of Kaili. Shidong is also the best place to catch the **Miao Dragon Boat festival**, commemorating the slaying of a dragon that once terrorised the local population, while **Miao New Year** takes place over a five-day period around the end of the tenth lunar month.

*The Zunyi conference, which saw Mao regain overall control of the communist armies, was one of the key events of the Long March. The event is commemorated at the Conference Site, with various artefacts, memorabilia and art.*

**BELOW:** dancing to the lusheng pipes.

exhibition hall. To make sense of the various photographs, maps and memorabilia it is important to have done some research before arriving, since all information is in Chinese. The area surrounding the site is pleasant enough, with parks and old buildings, and nearby **Phoenix Hill Park** (凤凰山公园; Fenghuangshan Gongyuan) has a huge **Monument to the Martyrs of the Red Army** (红军烈士纪念坤; Hongjun Lieshi Jinianbei).

In the far northeast of Guizhou is **Fanjing Shan** (梵净山), a remote nature reserve centred on the eponymous peak (2,572 metres/8,438 ft), and known for its population of golden monkeys. It is normally accessed from the town of Tongren, and it is possible to stay at Jinding Si monastery near the top of the mountain.

## West to Anshun

The western side of Guizhou has large coal and iron ore deposits, and so industrial development is more prevalent in this area. Apart from the draw of Huangguoshu waterfall this region is less travelled than the east and south of the province. Still, there are many other attractions that warrant attention.

The city of **Anshun** ⑭ (安顺), which developed as a trading centre in the 13th century, is linked to Guiyang, 105 km (65 miles) away by expressway, making day trips from the capital a possibility. However to explore properly the area's notable attractions – a striking array of waterfalls and caves – it's better to stay in Anshun. The Sunday market here occupies several streets in the northwest of the city and sees plenty of Bouyei people in attendance. On a mound in the city centre is the Ming Dynasty **White Pagoda** (白塔; Bai Ta), and beside the plaza north of this landmark is an active Catholic church built in 1867. Near to the dock on Hongshan Reservoir, in the north of the city, lies another Ming monument, the **Wen Temple** (文化庙; Wenhua Miao), which has some well-preserved stone carvings and a small teashop.

The **Longgong Caves** ⑮ (龙宫洞; Longgong Dong; open daily 7am–8pm; entrance fee) are 23 km (14 miles) from Anshun, making for an easy excursion. Visitors can choose between a series of boat tours and guided walks through the colourfully lit caves. The main trail passes a medicinal garden before leading

*Recommended Restaurants & Bars on page 299*

eventually to Guanyin Cave, where there are three statues of the goddess Guanyin, and Buddha Cave, where a couple of large Buddha statues are flanked by many smaller ones. It is possible to continue on foot and by boat to an exit further up the valley. However, the guides, whose services are included in the entrance fee, work at an Olympian pace and may well dictate the exit strategy. Minibuses leave regularly from Anshun, taking around 45 minutes.

## Huangguoshu waterfall

At 78 metres (256 ft) high and 101 metres (331 ft) wide, **Huangguoshu waterfall** ⓰ (黄果树瀑布; Huangguoshu Pubu) is the largest in China (open daily 8am–6pm; entrance fee). Best seen after heavy rains (which can be at almost any time in this part of China), it is certainly an impressive sight. From the park entrance a circuit can be taken that involves walking through a cave behind the cascading water. Known as **Water Curtain Cave**, there are several "windows", which allow views through the falls. Excellent views can also be had from the string of restaurants in the village that is perched on the cliff facing the falls.

Huangguoshu is part of a waterfall and cave network, and there are several beauty spots worth seeing in the vicinity. Located 8 km (5 miles) to the south (take a motorised tricycle from Huangguoshu), the **Star Bridge Scenic Area** (天星桥风景区; Tianxingqiao Fengjingqu; open daily 8am–6pm; entrance fee) is a collection of pools, lakes, rivers and caves set in a stone forest. The perfect place for a picnic, the karst scenery demands a leisurely morning or afternoon's attention. Particularly imposing is **Tainxing Cave**, with large stalactites and stalagmites illuminated in a huge chamber. The **Silver Chain Falls** are also not to be missed. A path links all of these features, although the cable-car can save the effort of the final ascent, which leads to the exit on the main road.

Other notable cataracts are **Lousitan**, 1 km (⅔ mile) downstream from Huanggshou, and **Dishuitan**, 5 km (3 miles) west of the main falls, where a series of cascades cover a vertical distance of 410 metres (1,345 ft). Just north of the village is **Steep Slope Falls** (open daily 8am–6pm; entrance fee), 105 metres (344 ft)

**TIP**

If you fancy biding your time at the Huangguoshu Waterfall, there are places to stay on the road that leads up to the entrance of the falls. Minibuses shuttle between city of Anshun and the falls at 20-minute intervals for the hour-long ride.

**BELOW:** dramatic Huangguoshu waterfall in full flow.

*Black-necked cranes at Caohai Lake. Together with Poyang Lake in Jiangxi (see page 238), this is one of China's best birdwatching sites. Attempts to drain the lake in the 1950s and 1960s fortunately proved unsuccessful.*

**BELOW:** golden statue at the Longgong Caves.

wide and 23 metres (75 ft) high. The surrounding park is home to peacocks and a variety of native bird species.

## Zhijin Caves

The most magnificent cave system in Guizhou is without doubt found near the town of **Zhijin** (织金), 125 km (80 miles) north of Anshun. The numerous caverns of the **Zhijin Caves** ⑰ (织金洞; Zhijin Dong; open daily 8am–5pm; entrance fee) are impressive in their scale, extending into the hillside for several kilometres; at its broadest, the complex extends some 175 metres (574 ft), and reaches a vertical height of 150 metres (492 ft). Leviathan stalactites and stalagmites have names in honour of their immensity. The largest chamber has a volume of 50,000 sq metres (538,000 sq ft).

Tracksuited guides should dispel any notion that the 2-hour tour might be conducted at a less than rigorous pace. The caves are 22 km (14 miles) from Zhijin and can be reached by minibus or taxi.

## The far west

Described as the "Sea of Coal", this part of the province becomes ever more mountainous as you approach the border with Yunnan, with extensive rice terraces etched into the steep valley sides.

Around the town of **Luizhi** ⑱ (六枝) are gathered several villages belonging to the Long Horned Miao. Their name comes from the wooden combs around which an ancestor's hair is wrapped to create incredible hairstyles. **Suoga** village (梭嘎) is the starting point for the "dancing on the slope" festivities that take place from the fourth to the 14th day of the first month of the lunar calendar. The festival circulates around the other villages over the 10-day period. **Longga**, 2.5 km (1½ miles) further up the mountain is another Long Horned Miao village worth a visit around this time.

**Liupanshui** ⑲ (六盘水), 174 km (108 miles) from Guiyang, is an undeniably ugly city famous for coal mining, and best avoided but for the three-day Small Flowery Miao festival held on the 13th to the 15th of the second lunar month. The event takes place near the village of **Nankai** (南开), 37 km (23 miles) northeast of town. Hairdos are again the defining physical feature of this sub-group, red wool being piled on the head to form a huge bouffant. Another one-day flower dance takes place on the fifth of the fifth lunar month. Rail is the best mode of transport for connections to Guiyang and west into Yunnan.

In the far northwest of the province, within walking distance of the town of Weining, is **Caohai Lake** ⑳ (草海), a 20-sq km (8-sq mile) wetland teeming with migratory bird life during the November to March wintering season. It is considered one of the best birdwatching destinations in Asia. Among the 179 species recorded are protected birds such as the black-necked crane, white stork, golden eagle, imperial eagle, white-tailed sea eagle, Eurasian crane and white spoonbill. Buses leave from Liupanshui for the 2½-hour journey to the backwoods town of **Weining**, from where its a 5-minute taxi ride to the lake. Pole boats can be hired – you will be plagued by touts at the lakeside – and are the easiest way to navigate the waterways. ❑

# RESTAURANTS & BARS

## Restaurants

Average price for a meal for one, with one drink:
**$** under US$12 (under Rmb 100)
**$$** US$12–20 (Rmb 100–160)
**$$$** over US$20 (over Rmb 160)

Food in Guizhou is hot and spicy, with chillies commonly being the ingredient used to fuel the fire. In the towns and cities and at festivals, kebab, noodle and hotpot stalls provide cheap and interesting dining opportunities. However, dog-lovers may want to check any suspicious-looking meat, as this animal is viewed as a tasty morsel by the minority peoples.

Lacking foreign visitors, most restaurants in Guizhou have neither English signs nor menus. Therefore, hotel restaurants are easier to locate. KFCs (Kentucky Fried Chicken outlets) and various other foreign-based imposters can be found in the main cities.

All this makes eating in local establishments a real, and at times challenging, experience. When selecting food, a visit to the kitchen might help make things clearer.

### Guiyang

For local fare try walking from the railway station along Zunyi Lu: there are plenty of stalls along the side streets.

#### Howard Johnson Plaza Hotel

29 Zaoshan Lu. Tel: 0851 651 8888/ 810 8888. **$$**
If you are pining for those back-home foods, the "all you can eat international buffet" in the ground floor restaurant should satisfy, providing great value in a 5-star setting. The à la carte menu is comprehensive and reasonably priced. A Cantonese restaurant is also to be found on the third floor.

#### Merrylin Restaurant

First floor, Motel 168, 2, Guiyang Shi Shenghu Lu Tel: 0851 821 7692. **$$–$$$**
An upmarket and sophisticated establishment, with attentive staff to boot, offering good-quality Chinese and Japanese fare and a comprehensive selection of Chinese wine. The menu is in Chinese, but pictures come to the rescue.

### Kaili

#### Bobo Simple Restaurant

Beijing Donglu.
Tel: 0851 826 0299. **$**
Pleasant setting, where the young movers and shakers come to eat, drink and be merry. The choice of Chinese cuisine is extensive – although no English menus unfortunately – as is the line-up of fresh juices and other beverages. You'll find Bobo's entrance down a side street off the main road.

### Zhaoxing

#### The Haixing Pub

Zhaoxing main street. **$**
This trendy hang-out in a two-storey Dong house is a great place to watch rustic life go by. Stop off here for good local food as well as the only pizza you are likely to find outside Guiyang.

## Bars

Although **Guiyang** has a lively nightlife scene with lots of discos, karaoke bars and nightclubs, such establishments are spread out across the city. The Shangri-La Bar on Hequn Lu is one that's popular with the young crowd. Generally speaking, Fushui Lu has many bars and restaurants.

In **Kaili**, there are many bars along Qingping Nanhu west of the city centre, although they are dark and fairly uninviting.

**RIGHT:** noodle soup is part of the staple diet of millions of Chinese.

# THE MINORITIES OF SOUTHWEST CHINA

**The minority groups of southwestern China, with their magnificent costumes and colourful festivals, have retained their identity and traditions into the present day**

The swathe of southern China from western Hunan province through Guizhou, parts of Guangxi and much of Yunnan is home to a large concentration of minority peoples, remnants of a larger population that has been displaced by the Han Chinese over the course of many centuries. Minority groups have thus tended to retreat to relatively remote and infertile highland regions (a trend accelerated by persecution following the rebellions of the 19th century), and this in turn has reinforced their isolation from modern China: a strong sense of identity and tradition has survived to the present day, and it is this that makes a visit to a minority village – particularly at festival time – a rewarding, authentic experience.

The largest minority group is the Zhuang of Guangxi and eastern Yunnan, although they are relatively integrated into mainstream Chinese life compared with the other main groups – the Miao (numbering over 8 million, most of whom are concentrated in Guizhou), the Yi (Yunnan), Dong (southern Guizhou), Dai (southern Yunnan), Bai (Dali region) and Naxi (Lijiang region). There are dozens of smaller groups scattered around the region.

Having suffered varying degrees of persecution in the past, all China's minority populations are now guaranteed freedom to retain their language and customs by the Chinese constitution. That isn't to say that they are on an equal footing to the Han, although this is perhaps less to do with any direct discrimination than the fact that it is difficult for these communities, with their strong sense of tradition, to break out from the cycle of rural poverty.

**ABOVE:** the Lisu are one of the numerous small groups in western Yunnan.
**RIGHT:** a Gejia tribal from eastern Yunnan in full festival finery.

**ABOVE:** The Miao's fabulously exotic silver headdresses contribute to the sense of occasion at festivals, and are complemented by silver jewellery and ornaments patterned with symbolic designs. These days only a small proportion of the silver is pure, and silver plate is often used. Many villages still possess a silversmith.

**ABOVE:** the Naxi people of northwestern Yunnan are a matriarchal society; inheritance is passed on to daughters rather than sons. Music is important; the well-known Naxi Orchestra in Lijiang performs music dating back to the Song Dynasty.

**RIGHT:** like most of Yunnan's minority groups, the Bai are predominantly Buddhist, but with influences from a wide range of other religions – including Daoism and even Christianity. The Miao, Yi, Dong and others have retained their animist traditions; most villages still have a shaman to communicate with the spirits and protect against malevolent forces. Ancestor worship is also important.

## MINORITY COSTUME

The Miao and other minority groups (such as the Yi, *pictured above*) are known for their colourful festivals – a time when the community comes together, with the people (mainly the women) resplendent in traditional costume.

Most striking of all are the remarkable silver headdresses worn by Miao girls at the lusheng festivals. There are several Miao subgroups, each of which has its own distinctive costume. Some, such as the wonderfully named Small Flowery Miao, specialise in gigantically bouffant hairdos, while the Long-Horned Miao tie their hair around wooden horns projecting from the sides of the head.

*For more on festivals see pages 292, 295 and 368–70.*

**RIGHT:** Many of the minority groups in Guizhou have maintained their traditional textiles, with dyeing, weaving and embroidery continuing to be a cottage industry. Natural indigo dye is used by the Dong, Miao and Bouyei of eastern Guizhou, who extract it from various indigenous plants. Miao women still weave their festival attire on their own looms, while the embroidered designs are also done by hand. The lack of a written script has resulted in a rich textile culture, where embroidered symbols and motifs represent stories.

**LEFT:** Naxi pictographic script. Most of the minority groups of southern China do not possess a written script, a significant factor in their isolation. In terms of spoken language, the various Miao subgroups share a common ancestral tongue affiliated to the Miao-Yao branch of the Sino-Tibetan languages, although differing dialects mean it is not mutually intelligible. The minorities of southern Yunnan, as well as the Zhuang, speak languages of the Tai-Kadai language family related to Thai. The large Yi minority speak a Tibeto-Burman language.

# CENTRAL AND SOUTHEAST YUNNAN

Yunnan's genial capital, Kunming, is a favourable introduction to this varied corner of Yunnan, home to the China's largest freshwater lake, immaculate terrace-top villages and yet more dramatic limestone scenery

**Main attractions**
KUNMING
BAMBOO TEMPLE
WESTERN HILLS
STONE FOREST
JIANSHUI
YUANYANG AND LUCHUN
RICE TERRACES

**BELOW:** like so many Chinese cities, Kunming is modernising rapidly.

With its laid-back atmosphere, lack of pollution and pleasant climate, Kunming is a common favourite among Chinese cities. As provincial capital of Yunnan, it also has a good range of accommodation and restaurants. There are some fascinating temples in the nearby hills, while further afield – heading southeast in the direction of the Vietnamese border – is the famous Stone Forest, a couple of ancient cities, and what many people consider to be China's most spectacular example of rice terracing.

## KUNMING

It has become almost a travel-writing cliché that **Kunming ❶** (昆明), little more than a decade ago, was home to charming alleys lined with quaint wooden buildings and bustling market areas – and that those days are long gone. The city is today home to an estimated 8 million people, its skyline punctuated by office blocks, its boulevards lined with shopping complexes and billboards. But all is not lost, with pockets of the old Kunming surviving here and there, and other factors combining to create an environment refreshingly removed from the average Chinese city.

One front on which Kunming continues to distinguish itself from other urban sprawls is the relative absence of pollution. At an altitude of 1,890 metres (6,200 ft), its climate is also unusually temperate, which has earned it the nickname Spring City. When most Chinese cities toil in palls of haze, sweating through oven-like summers and rugging up for frigid, rainy winters, Kunming generally wakes up to temperate, sunny mornings. The winters are mild, but the altitude ensures that the summers are pleasantly cool. Plants thrive in the springlike weather, and the city is famed for its year-round floral displays. Coupled with a local economy that has so far failed to succumb to the inflationary pressures of China's coastal metropolises, it is small surprise that the city is emerging as one of the most popular places for foreign students to master Mandarin.

## GETTING TO YUNNAN

**Flights**: Kunming is an important regional centre and is connected with most cities in China, as well as to Thailand. Dali, Lijiang and Jinghong also benefit from good air connections.

**By Train and Bus**: Yunnan is fairly well connected by rail to the rest of China, a vital link over the years. There are trains between Kunming and most cities in China. Long-distance buses are a less popular option.

## GETTING AROUND CENTRAL YUNNAN

**Kunming**: Buses to the Stone Forest at Shilin run every 30 minutes between 8am and noon and take 2 hours. Buses to Hekou run twice daily (12 hours) and to Yuanyang three times daily (6–7 hours). There are trains to Shilin (8 daily 1½–2 hours). The train service from Kunming to Hekou on the Vietnamese border has been suspended. *For trains to Dali and other destinations in Yunnan see pages 316, 324 and 338.*

**Stone Forest**: Minibuses on the return journey to Kunming leave in the afternoon when full.

**Tonghai/Jianshui**: Frequent buses run from between Tonghai to Kunming and Jianshui (both 2 hours).

**Hekou**: To Kunming take 12–15 hours (2 daily).

**Yuanyang**: Buses leave for Kunming 3 times daily (6–7 hours); there are also buses to Hekou (4 hours) and Gejiu (1 hour).

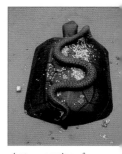

*A stone carving of a snake winding around a tortoise at the Daoist Three Purity (Sanqing) Pavilion west of Lake Dianchi. Snakes and tortoises are symbols of longevity and, traditionally, anyone who touches the carving will live to a ripe old age.*

**BELOW:** Yuantong Si, Kunming's main Buddhist temple.

Little is known of Kunming's early history. It acquired its name after the Mongols swept through China, establishing the Yuan Dynasty (1271–1368), and made it the provincial capital rather than Dali, the former regional seat of power under the Nanzhao Kingdom. What is now Cuihu Lake and the Yunnan University campus emerged as the heart of the city in the following centuries, even though there are no reminders of this today. In fact, most of Kunming's still extant historical sites lie some way from what must have been the traditional city centre. This can largely be explained by the Panthay Rebellion of the mid-19th

*Traditional dwelling in the old part of the city, east of the Provincial Museum.*

century, in which Hui Chinese Muslims rose up in an attempt to establish their own kingdom. In the process they laid siege to Kunming four times, and on occasion forces loyal to Du Wenxiu, the self-proclaimed Sultan of Dali, took control of the city. When the revolt was put down by Qing forces, tens of thousands of Chinese Muslims were driven into exile in Burma, Laos and Thailand.

## City sights

Today, the city's most ancient landmarks are the **East Pagoda Ⓐ** (东寺塔; Dongsi Ta) and **West Pagoda Ⓑ** (西寺塔; Xisi Ta; both open 9am–8.30pm; entrance fee). The latter dates back to the Tang Dynasty, though the East Pagoda is a 19th-century reconstruction. Both are situated south of Jinbi Lu, not far from the busy commercial district that fans out from the corner of Shulin Jie.

Head directly north from the West Pagoda and you'll pass through the city's traditional Muslim quarter. Unfortunately, Kunming has laid siege to this part of town much in the way the Chinese Muslims laid siege themselves during the Panthay Rebellion. The city's old

mosque was torn down in the 1990s, and its newer replacement has removed some of the character from the area. Nonetheless, the community has not disappeared altogether, and a number of Hui restaurants still remain.

Continue north and you end up in the heart of what was once the old quarter. Veer left onto Wuyi Lu to reach the **Yunnan Provincial Museum Ⓒ** (云南省博物馆; Yunnansheng Bowuguan; open daily 9am–5pm; entrance fee), with its extensive collection of Yunnan bronzeware, Buddhist artefacts and exhibitions on the province's minority cultures. The city's other museum, the **Kunming City Museum Ⓓ** (昆明市博物馆 Kunmingshi Bowuguan; open Tues–Sun 10am–5pm; entrance fee), is located on the east side of town, across the river on Tuodong Lu. It houses an eclectic collection ranging from bronzes to dinosaur bones and fossils, but also has interesting sections on the history of Kunming and Dianchi Lake.

**Yuantong Temple Ⓔ** (圆通寺; Yuantong Si; open daily 8am–5pm; entrance fee), on the north side of the city, has been Kunming's most important Bud-

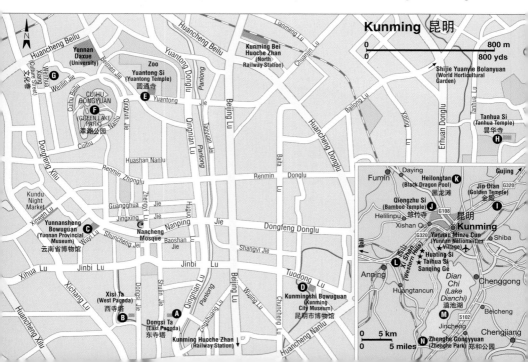

*Recommended Restaurants & Bars on page 311*

dhist temple for more than 1,000 years, although the current structure has seen more than its fair share of renovations, including a major refurbishment in 2006. It features a courtyard garden with resident turtles (symbols of longevity) swimming in a pool, and a rear altar with a golden Buddha statue that is said to have been donated by Thailand.

A few hundred metres west of the temple is **Green Lake Park ⑥** (翠湖公园; Cuihu Gongyuan; open dawn–dusk; entrance fee), an attractive leafy space that is popular with the locals. Very much like parks elsewhere in China, it is a place for group exercises and t'ai chi, among other traditional pursuits. On weekends the park fills up with families, who spill out onto the lake in paddle boats. The Cuihu area is close to Yunnan University, and the youthful crowds now have a university district shopping and dining precinct in **Wenhua Xiang**, or Culture Street **⑥** (文化巷). Weekends are particularly lively, and when the weather is fine many of the restaurants set up tables and chairs alfresco.

Kunming's most spectacular historical attraction is **Tanhua Si ⑪** (昙华寺; open daily 8am–5pm; entrance fee), a lofty pagoda located approximately 3 km (2 miles) east of the city centre down Renmin Lu. An active Buddhist place of worship dating back to 1634, it is named after a species of magnolia tree that grows in its front courtyard – another popular spot for t'ai chi and communal exercises. The courtyards surrounding the pagoda contain Buddha images and bas-reliefs of Chinese classical texts. A climb to the seventh floor of the pagoda provides splendid views of the city on a clear day.

## DAY TRIPS FROM KUNMING

If Kunming is not quite as charming as it was just a decade or so ago, the surrounding areas more than compensate. Within easiest reach are the city's surrounding temples, and these can be visited individually by hiring a taxi. The **Golden Temple ①** (金殿; Jin Dian; open daily 8am–5pm; entrance fee) is a Daoist temple complex 7 km (4 miles) east of town on Mingfengshan. A Ming Dynasty structure, it dates back to the turn of the 16th century, though the "gold" plating is actually bronze.

*Hui porcelain with Islamic inscription. Kunming has a large Hui population.*

**BELOW:** Kunming is well known for its flowers, which flourish in the city's mild climate.

*The clay sculptures at the Bamboo Temple depict* luohan *holy men in a variety of astonishing action poses. The larger-than-life figures variously surf amid sea monsters or grimace in surreal fashion.*

**BELOW:** city youth.
**RIGHT:** Lake Dianchi.

Downhill from the Golden Temple, to which it is linked by cable-car, is the **World Horticultural Garden** (世博园; Shiboguan; open daily 8am–5pm; entrance fee). Created for Kunming's horticultural exposition in 1999, the large park is modestly scenic; within its landscaped acres are masses of colourful local blooms, rare species of tree, a tea plantation, some peculiar topiary and a themed area relating to ethnic minorities.

The **Bamboo Temple ⊙** (筇竹寺; Qiongzhu Si; open daily 8am–6pm; entrance fee), around 12 km (7½ miles) northwest of town, is the most popular of Kunming's nearby temple sights, and famed for its array of extraordinary sculptures. Dating back to the Tang Dynasty, this Chan (Zen) Buddhist monastery was reconstructed during the 1880s, with the help of inspired Sichuanese artists (notably Li Guangxiu) who created the 500 clay sculptures of *luohan – arhats*, or "holy men" – each recognisably distinct from the other, and said to embody a Buddhist virtue.

The **Black Dragon Pool ⊙** (黑龙滩; Heilongtan; open daily 8am–6pm; entrance fee), around 11 km (7 miles) north of Kunming, is disappointing by comparison, despite its reputation. Flanked by a Daoist temple and a botanical garden with camellias, rhododendrons and azaleas, it makes for a pleasant stroll, but can be skipped on a tight itinerary.

## The Western Hills and Lake Dianchi

**The Western Hills ⊙** (西山; Xishan), which rise to a height of 2,350 metres (7,700 ft) to the west of Kunming and Dianchi Lake, have three more temples of note, though the crowds can be overwhelming, particularly during Chinese holidays. While the temples are interesting enough, it is the views of **Lake Dianchi ⊙** (滇池湖) – particularly on a sunny day – that tend to steal the show. At 340-sq km (130-sq miles), this is one of the largest freshwater lakes in China, extending for 40 km (25 miles) end to end. Unfortunately, green algae, caused by agricultural run-off, threatens the future of the lake, a problem that has refused to go away despite reported government spending in the vicinity of around US$2 billion in recent years.

*Recommended Restaurants & Bars on page 311*

Environmentalists have campaigned for the relocation of some of the 250 factories that continue to operate around the lakeside.

All the same, Dianchi continues to look impressive from a distance, and the hike to three temples in the Western Hills provides some good viewing opportunities. To do this – rather than book a tour in Kunming – take a taxi to **Huating Temple** (华亭寺; Huating Si; open daily 8am–6pm; entrance fee) at the base of the hills, Kunming's largest Buddhist temple. The original structure is thought to date back to the 1300s, but it has been through several reconstructions since. Some of the statuary here is notable, with impressively large gilded Buddhas in the main hall.

From Huating Temple, a forest path makes upwards, some 2 km (1¼ miles), to the Chan Buddhist **Taihua Temple** (泰华寺; Taihua Si; open daily 8am–6pm; entrance fee), although the way is easier to find by the road. The Taihua complex features a pond and a pavilion for viewing Lake Dianchi, making it a perfect place to rest for a while, before continuing up the more than 1,000 steps

to **Sanqing Ge** (三清阁), a Daoist temple with tremendous views.

It is also possible to walk up the road to the **Tomb of Nie Er** (聂耳墓; Nieermu), a famed early 20th-century singer. Nearby you can take a chairlift, or a tram, to the highest lookout point at **Dragon Gate** (龙门; Longmen). The walk up here involves negotiating your way through a series of vertiginous corridors and grottoes that were chipped from the cliff face by Qing Dynasty monks – if you are claustrophobic, scared of heights or don't like crowds, it is best avoided.

The chairlift also rattles downhill to the lakeside **Yunnan Nationalities Village** (云南民族村; Yunnan Minzu Cun; open daily 8am–7pm; entrance fee), a village that features all 25 of Yunnan's minorities in traditional dress, dancing and singing. Most foreign visitors find the attraction tacky, though it is a staple on the Chinese tour-bus circuit.

At the southern end of the lake is **Zhenghe Park**  (郑和公园; Zhenghe Gongyuan), where a massive pavilion commemorates the Chinese eunuch explorer traditionally known in the West

**TIP**

A good way to beat the crowds in the Western Hills is to travel by foot, the way pilgrims of yore did, rather than by tourist bus as most people tend to do. Begin at Huating Si and follow the temple trail through the forest. The uppermost reaches around the Dragon Gate do get crowded, however.

**BELOW:** the Stone Forest.

**TIP**

To explore the Stone Forest and its limestone grottoes relatively undisturbed, it is advisable to stay overnight and make the most of the early morning and late afternoon hours – before the tour buses have arrived and after they have left. Sunset can be especially magical.

**BELOW RIGHT:**
Kublai Khan.

as Cheng Ho (1371–1433). Zheng He, a Chinese Muslim, is thought to have been born close by, within sight of the lake. When the Ming came to power in 1368, Yunnan was one of the last Muslim strongholds of the Mongol Yuan Dynasty. The Ming, however, soon established effective control over the region, and in the process a young Zheng He was captured, castrated and sent to the imperial court as a eunuch. As a favourite of the Emperor Yongle, he later became China's greatest navigator, visiting more than 30 Asian and African countries (see also page 27). A mausoleum in the park has displays relating to Zheng's life.

### The Stone Forest

Some 126 km (78 miles) southeast of Kunming and reached by frequent minibuses is the region's most famous tourist attraction, the **Stone Forest ❷** (石林; Shilin; open daily 8.30am–7pm; entrance fee). So famous, in fact, that many visitors complain that the "forest" of bizarre limestone rock formations has become a circus, with cheek-by-jowl crowds, designated walking trails and Sani minority tour guides and souvenir-

sellers hiding behind every rock. To a certain extent, this is true. The crowds can be maddening, but the otherworldly rocks – some of which tower more than 30 metres (100 ft) high – are still a sight to behold, particularly early in the morning and late in the afternoon. Around 10 km (6 miles) to the north is the **Black Stone Forest** (Naigu Shilin), slightly less spectacular but with far fewer tourists.

## SOUTHEAST TO LUCHUN AND THE VIETNAM BORDER

It is an epic trip from Kunming south to the Vietnamese border, and one only for those with plenty of time and patience. While new highways are under construction in other parts of the province, this area of south central Yunnan is still a long way from having good roads, so be prepared for some slow and uncomfortable journeys.

### Tonghai and Jianshui

The old city of **Tonghai ❸** (通海) lies at the southern end of the central Yunnan lakes region, approximately 200 km (125 miles) to the south of Kunming. Orientation is simple: in the centre there is a

## The Mongol Legacy

Into the 21st century the 7,000 inhabitants of the village of Xinmen, 15 km (9 miles) west of Tonghai, remain firmly Mongolian. Visiting the village gives a fascinating glimpse of another culture, displaced by thousands of kilometres from its homeland (in fact Yunnan is as geographically distant from Mongolia as it is possible to be within China). Just as it was eight centuries ago, the Mongolian relationship with the Hui (Chinese Muslims), is fractious to say the least – though there has been no serious fighting between rival villages in recent years. The ideal time to visit Xinmen would be during the Nadam Mongolian sporting tournament – unfortunately it only takes place every third October (2008 and 2011 are the next scheduled events)

This poor community is gradually enriching itself through the successful cultivation of honey melons in addition to the agricultural staples of rice, tobacco and vegetables. The ethnic mix has been diluted in the past 60 years as it has become commonplace for Han Chinese to marry Mongols. There is talk, too, of the local government establishing a Mongolian theme park here, so try to visit before Xinmen becomes Disneyfied. At the back of the village is a temple glorifying the three great Mongol leaders from yesteryear, Genghis, Kublai and Mangil Khan, with stone tablets on the walls recording their history.

*Recommended Restaurants & Bars on page 311*

drum tower from where roads head in the four compass-point directions. The best thing to do is head to the south of the centre to the green hills where the 2,000-year-old **Xiu Shan Park** (秀山公园; Xiu Shan Gongyuan) is located. A steep-stepped climb through the trees leads past several secluded temples to reach the 1,466-metre (4,810-ft) summit, with views of the whole area including Qilu Lake. Near the top, the **Gushing Lotus Temple** (涌金寺; Yongjin Si) is a wonderful place to bring a book and while away a few hours. Back in town, head to Gudong Lu, where Muslim hawkers sell bric-a-brac antiques.

**Xinmen** village (薪门) can be seen in a half-day from Tonghai, a short half-hour bus ride away. More than 750 years ago one rampaging Kublai Khan passed through this settlement and founded a garrison whose descendants are still much in evidence *(see panel opposite)*.

The ancient city of **Jianshui** ❹ (建水), a further 80 km (50 miles) south of Tonghai, is one of the best-preserved old cities in southeastern Yunnan, famous for its old walls. Horse-drawn carts can take visitors from the old town's east to west gates. At the former stands the forbidding red Ming Dynasty tower, **Chaoyang Lou**. Jianshui is unquestionably a beautiful, well-preserved city, though things are changing as the place gets spruced up. **Han Lin Jie** is a pleasant old-style shopping street, while the **Confucian Academy** makes for a nice stroll along a lovely lake. The **Zhu' Clan Gardens**, formerly owned by the city's richest family, is another major tourist draw, comprising 42 courtyards and 214 rooms in an area measuring 20,000 sq m (5 acres), set in the centre of the old town.

## Yuanyang and Luchun

The scenic road south from Jianshui to Yuanyang winds along vertiginous ridges and mountains of rice terraces, with villages perched on the lofty slopes. From **Yuanyang Nansha** ❺ (元阳南沙; Yuanyang new town), a road winds up above the Red River to **Yuanyang Xinjie** (元阳新街; the old town), which offers stunning panoramic views from its central square. The old town is a good base for exploring some of the surrounding villages.

*Deep-fried yoghurt wafers (rubing), a Yunnanese speciality.*

**BELOW:** the Confucian Academy, Jianshui.

*Swallows Cave is colourfully lit in typical Chinese style. Atypically, it also features an underground restaurant.*

**BELOW:** the Yuanyang rice terraces.

The journey west from Yuanyang to Luchun has some of the very best scenery in all of southern Yunnan, but very few tourists make it here. Stunningly steep and vibrant-green terraced paddy fields, which contrast amazingly with the deep red of the soil, clasp onto every available spot on the mountainside. They are tended to by the Hani tribe, who live in mushroom-shaped mud-and-thatch houses. While many other rice terraces in China have fallen into disrepair, these are in fantastic condition and attain an electric-green colour as the rice flowers between November and April. If you walk among the terraces, keep to the walls or you'll end up with mud up to your knees and an irate farmer on your tail.

Five hours southwest of Yuanyang, among the steep mountains of south central Yunnan, is the busy town of **Luchun** ❻ (绿春), which straddles a dramatic section of rice terraces. Way off the main tourist trail, this interesting town has a more overt ethnic mix than most settlements in the region, and many locals sport traditional costume on a day-to-day basis. Ancient mini-vans and electric eight-seater contraptions ply the main street and provide the easiest means of getting around town. There are some attractive gardens right in the centre, just beyond the market. Wrap up warm at night; the temperature drops as the sun slides behind the terraced hills.

## To the Vietnam border

From Jianshui, the long and winding road to Vietnam heads east, then southeast. To reach the border takes the best part of a day by bus. Alternatively there is a flood-prone narrow-gauge railway linking Jianshui with Kaiyuan for onward train connections to the border town of Hekou. It's a picturesque, though very slow, journey.

**Swallows Cave** (燕子洞; Yanzi Dong; open daily 8am–5pm; entrance fee) is located 30 km (18 miles) east of Jianshui on the road to the to the tin capital of Yunnan, **Gejiu** ❼ (个旧). While there are countless signs of neolithic man's existence here, the caves (which feature an underground restaurant) are most famous for their swifts, which nest here in their thousands and make a deafening din. The Bird Nest Festival on 8 August is the only day of the year that people are allowed to collect the disused nests, highly-prized for bird's-nest soup; watched by huge crowds, sinewy local Yi men clamber unaided up 60-metre (197-ft) cliffs to snaffle up the nests.

The final, long stretch of road follows the Red River (Yuan Jiang) to **Hekou** ❽ (河口), the border town – the frontier is literally a couple of minutes from the train and bus station across a bridge. Vietnamese visas cannot be obtained at the border; the nearest place to get them is at the Camellia Hotel Travel Agency in Kunming. Across the border, the town of **Lao Cai** (老街) has a gargantuan animal market, some shabby hotels and a train station 3 km (2 miles) away with two services a day to Hanoi. A popular pastime around Hekou is kayaking on the Naxi River. A 3½-hour trip with the current takes kayakers 32 km (20 miles) down river amid subtropical rainforest, ending at the border where the clear Nanxi joins up with the muddy Red River. ❑

# RESTAURANTS & BARS IN KUNMING

## Restaurants

Average price for a meal for one, with one drink:
**$** under US$12 (under Rmb 100)
**$$** US$12–20 (Rmb 100–160)
**$$$** over US$20 (over Rmb 160)

Yunnan cuisine features a diverse range of flavours reflecting influences from Indo-China and Burma as well as Sichuan and the Hui (Chinese Muslim) community. Many dishes are sour/spicy combinations.

The most famous dish is "crossing the bridge noodles", a hot noodle soup. Kunming is also well known for its coffee, and its street food (especially the Muslim varieties) can be very good – try the streets south of the Nancheng Mosque.

In Kunming there is a large number of restaurants and cafés around the Camellia Hotel on Dongeng Donglu. Wenlin Jie, close to Yunnan University, has emerged as the most popular eating and drinking district for the growing expatriate population, with Chapter One probably its most in demand watering-hole.

### 1910 La Gare du Sud
8 Houxin Jie.
Tel: 0871 316 9486. **$$**
Colonial-style restaurant with a garden area for

diners serving a mix of Yunnan specialities and Chinese cuisine staples. An English menu is available, and prices are far more reasonable than you might assume from the appearance of the venue. It's best to go to 1910 by taxi (ask for *huoche nanzhan canting*), as it is situated on a small alley south of Jinbi Lu and difficult to find even with a map.

### Ban Thai Restaurant
18/F, Sakura Hotel, 29 Dongfeng Donglu.
Tel: 0871 316 5888. **$$**
Kunming's best Thai restaurant, with Thai chefs and great Siam-themed décor. Opposite the Thai Consulate.

### Belvedere International Restaurant
Greenlake Hotel, 6 Cuihu Nanlu. Tel: 0871 515 8888.
**$$–$$$**
With lakeside views, the 24-hour Belvedere is the perfect place for a blow-out Western meal. But it also features an "open kitchen" rice/noodle centre serving the famous Yunnan "over-the-bridge noodles".

### The Brothers Jiang
1 Jinbi Qianjie (corner of Jinbi Lu and Shulin Jie). Tel: 0871 537 8206. **$–$$**
The Brothers Jiang is so popular that there are now branches scattered around town, such as at

Dongfeng Donglu and Renmin Zhonglu. The speciality of the house is "over-the-bridge noodles", which you order by buying a ticket at the front door. Note that the army of plates that turn up at your table are not nibbles but, along with the noodles, are meant to be mixed into the broth when it arrives.

### Guangyi Restaurant
68–70 Beimen Jie.
Tel: 0871 513 9548. **$$**
This Yunnan Minorities restaurant is quite a treat, though it can get very crowded. In a traditional setting, with a lovely courtyard area, one of the favourites is the Naxi hot-pot, containing Yunnan's famous cured ham.

### Mamafu
60 Dongfeng Donglu.
Tel: 0871 312 0036. **$$**
Mamafu, very close to the Kunming and Camellia hotels, is a popular spot with foreign travellers and local office workers alike. Dishes are a mixture of Sichuan-style classics and Thai-inspired stir-fries, while a few alfresco tables provide the perfect spot for a late afternoon beer.

### Salvador's
76 Wenlin Jie, Wenhua Xiang.
Tel: 0871 536 3525. **$$**
Salvador's is a foreign-run café and restaurant

with excellent Tex-Mex cuisine, homemade ice cream and free wireless Internet. Situated on lively "Culture Alley" in the university district, it is a firm fixture with both foreign and local students.

## Bars

### Chapter One
146 Wenlin Jie.
Tel: 0871 536 5635.
A short walk from Salvador's, this is Kunming's first English pub, and features a splendid upstairs seating area. The walls are stacked with reading material and the pub grub is good.

### The Hump Bar
3rd Floor, Jinbi Plaza (corner of Jinbi Lu and Shulin Jie).
Tel: 0871 364 0359.
While it won't win any awards for its décor, this is a convivial spot which attracts backpackers and locals alike, and its huge balcony area, with views of neon-lit downtown Kunming, is a great spot for an evening beer.

### Speakeasy
445 Dongfeng Xilu.
Tel: 0871 532 7047.
Late-night bar/club with pool tables and occasional live performances by indie bands from all over China. The clientele is a mix of local Chinese hipsters and expatriates.

# XISHUANGBANNA

Xishuangbanna is where China begins to blend with Southeast Asia, complete with jungle reserves, wild elephants and a population dominated by ethnic minorities who have little in common with the Han Chinese

**Main attractions**
JINGHONG
SANCHAHE NATURE RESERVE
GANLANBA
TROPICAL BOTANICAL GARDENS
BUPAN AERIAL WALKWAY
BAMBOO SHOOT PAGODA

**LEFT:** the golden pagoda at the Dai Minority Park, Ganlanba.
**BELOW:** forest views from the Bupan Aerial Walkway.

own in Yunnan's deep south is China's little slice of Southeast Asia, a tropical nugget cushioned between Laos and Myanmar (Burma). Fittingly exotic-sounding Xishuang-banna (the name is derived from the Thai *Sip Sawng Panna*, meaning 12 rice-growing districts) is populated by 14 minorities, the most populous of whom are the Dai, who speak a language closely related to Thai and account for around 34 percent of the autonomous prefec-ture's 830,000-strong population. Most of the Dai are Theravada Buddhists, and their exotically shaped pagodas add to the overall sense of being in Southeast Asia rather than China. Other minorities include the Jinuo, the Hani or Akha, the Bulang and the Yi.

For tourists – and the majority of these are Chinese these days – the prefecture's colourful minorities are the leading draw, and many villages have inevitably been transformed into parodies of themselves, with daily water-splashing festivals (cel-ebrated in Thailand in April as Songkhran) and staged song-and-dance routines. In un-touristed areas, many old villages have been rebuilt Han-style with proceeds from the lucrative local rubber industry. All the same, this is a large area, and, with a little effort, it is not difficult to find relatively unspoilt minority villages.

Local roads have been falling into dilapidation in anticipation of the com-pletion of a new set of highways, includ-ing the long-anticipated Kunming to Bangkok route, which will supersede the current road to Mengla when it opens in 2009. The region will undoubtedly see a considerable increase in tourist traffic when this highway opens, with Chinese tourists using it as a springboard to Chi-ang Mai, and foreign backpackers and Thai tourists taking advantage of the increased accessibility from northern Thailand into Laos and Xishuangbanna.

## JINGHONG AND ITS SURROUNDINGS

Once a sleepy town lining the Mekong River (known locally as the Lancang

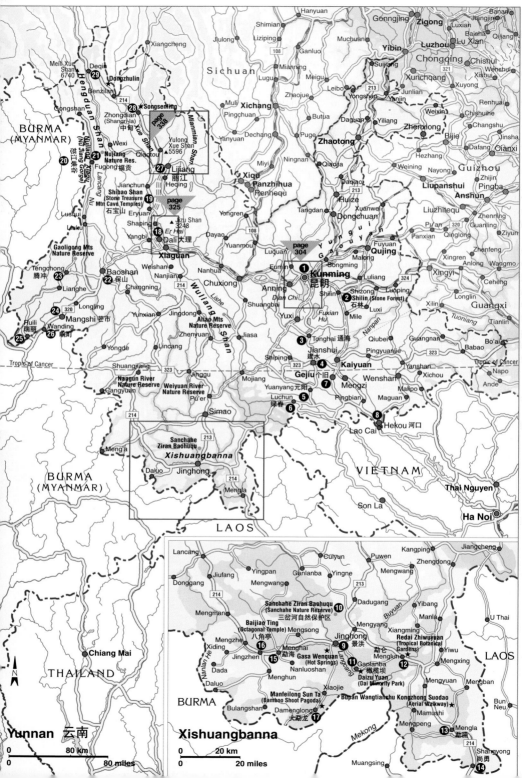

Jiang), the prefectural capital **Jinghong** (景洪) ❾ is today a rapidly expanding city of close to half a million inhabitants that echoes to the boom of construction and the honk of traffic. All the same, it has a decidedly different atmosphere to Han cities to the north, with palm-lined boulevards and a lively street-side dining culture. All signs are bilingual, using Chinese characters and the cursive Burmese-looking Dai script, and it is a pleasant city to stroll around, with a large number of leafy parks and a colourful mix of cultures – including traders from Myanmar and Thailand.

The city sits on the southwest bank of the Lancang River, which heads downstream into Laos to become the Mekong. Streets radiate out from central Peacock Lake – the peacock being the symbol of the Dai people. Jinghong is not rich in tourist attractions – the chief sights are the parks and backstreet markets selling goods from Burma and Thailand – but it is worth spending a day exploring nonetheless.

In the city centre, **Peacock Lake Park** (孔雀湖公园; Kongquehu Gongyuan) features an artificial lake and in the late afternoons and evenings is crowded with local strollers. Off Jinghong Xilu, the **Tropical Flower and Plants Garden** (热带花卉园; Redai Huahuiyuan; also known as the Botanical Gardens; open daily 7.30am–6pm; entrance fee) does not compare with the sprawling equivalent in Menglun (*see page 318*), but still has more than 1,000 examples of Xishuangbanna's native flora in an area of around 80 hectares (200 acres). Adjoining the park is a traditional medicine centre with its own botanical garden.

About 1 km (⅔ mile) southwest of the centre is the **National Minorities Park** (勐巴拉纳西公园; Mengbalanaxi Gongyuan; open daily 8.30am–6pm, Wed and Sat evenings until 11pm; entrance fee), which is avoided by most foreign tourists due to its somewhat tacky song and dance performances. Nonetheless, the lush park makes a very pleasant setting, and if you're prepared to join in with the spirit of the occasion it can be an enjoyable evening.

The **Jinsha Night Market** (金沙夜市场; Jinsha Yeshichang) can be found underneath the left (ie north) side of the new Xishuangbanna Bridge. It is a lively place in the evenings, with diners flocking to the area to enjoy barbecue dishes that are very similar to those found in Laos or in northeast Thailand. There are several places selling beer and other drinks, and even a special outdoor massage section.

**Manting Park** (曼听公园; Manting Gongyuan; also known as Chunhuan Park; 1 Manting Lu; open daily 8am–11.30pm; entrance fee), 2 km (1¼ miles) southeast of the city centre, has multiple pagodas, peacocks and evening cultural shows daily from 7pm. It used to be a separate village where royal slaves were kept but has now been absorbed into Jinghong.

Just north of the park is **Wat Manting** (曼听佛寺; Manting Fosi; entrance fee), Xishuangbanna's largest Buddhist monastery. Red and gold predominate colourwise in this giant temple, with traditional Thai-style sloping roofs and large dragon statues protecting the entrance. Photography is not allowed, and visitors are

*The modern Xishuangbanna Bridge over the Lancang (Mekong) River, Jinghong.*

**BELOW:** palm-lined street in Jinghong.

TIP

Xishuangbanna is a moderate-risk area for malaria, together with the other border areas of Yunnan, and also the rural areas of southern Guangxi and Hainan Island. The risk is far lower in the cooler, drier winter months. If travelling in these areas, particularly in summer, take the usual precautions – use plenty of insect repellant and cover skin as much as possible.

**BELOW:** a young Buddhist monk playing mah-jong.
**BELOW RIGHT:** a Dai woman prepares sticky rice.

**GETTING TO / FROM XISHUANGBANNA**
**Kunming to Jinghong**:

**Flights**: There are 4–6 flights per day between Kunming and Jinghong (1 hour), and from Jinghong to Bangkok, Chiang Mai and Lijiang.

**By Bus**: Sleeper buses between Kunming and Jinghong depart every 30 minutes (4–8pm), journey time 10 hours. Other long-distance routes are Jinghong to Dali (17 hours) and Ruili (24 hours). There are no railways.

**Onward travel to Laos and Thailand**: Taking the bus from Jinghong to Luang Phrabang and Vientiane in Laos, Chiang Mai and Bangkok in Thailand is now a possibility. Departures run at least once daily and currently take around 20 hours to Luang Phrabang, but times will shorten as the new road opens. There are also river boats on the Lancang (Mekong) – *see page 320.*

**GETTING AROUND XISHUANGBANNA**
**Buses from Jinghong** run every 20 minutes or so to Ganlanba (40 minutes), Sanchahe (1½ hours), Menglun (2 hours), Mengla (4–5 hours), Menghai (45 minutes), Damenglong (3½ hours).

asked to be quiet, respectful and take their shoes off when entering the prayer hall. Most people here are Buddhists of the Southeast Asian Theravada school. Similarly impressive and just a shade smaller is **Wat Chienglarn**, past the Dai Garden Hotel on Manting Lu.

## Villages around Jinghong

Travelling out of town, you will encounter minority villages everywhere, some within walking distance of Jinghong. Continue along Manting Lu all the way and there is a dirt path leading to the Liusha River. Take the bamboo bridge, cross a vegetable plot and turn right into a Dai village with houses set on stilts and hugely welcoming people. Head onto paddy fields and you'll pass a temple and a golden stupa, before returning via a choice of two bridges downstream. Alternatively, after heading through the vegetable plot, turn left and follow the road to Monkey Hill Park, after which there is a cable-car across the Lancang River and then a walk across the new bridge back

into town. Exploring on your own can be fun, but hiring a guide to visit a Dai village will provide a more intimate glimpse of village life, as most of the guides (check first) speak Dai. Guides can be hired in Jinghong at the Mei Mei Café or the Forest Café.

Several kilometres west of Jinghong, the **Gasa Hot Springs** (嘎洒温泉; Gasa Wenquan) are popular with locals, particularly in the evenings.

## Sanchahe Nature Reserve

Better known locally as Wild Elephant Valley, the **Sanchahe Nature Reserve ⓿** (三岔河自然保护区); Sanchahe Ziran Baohuqu), some 50 km (30 miles) north of Jinghong, is one of Xishuangbanna's most popular attractions – 359 hectares (887 acres) of tropical rainforest, with a cable-car ride, herds of wild elephants, a small zoo and some touristy performing elephant shows. The number of elephants in the reserve is disputed, with local estimates ranging from 70 to 300. Sightings of herds larger than 12 animals are rare. The most reliable way of seeing the elephants is to stay overnight at the basic and overpriced "treehouse" bungalows,

which overlook a small stream that the elephants frequent for a wash and a frolic in the evenings and early mornings. You will need a guide if you want to leave the well-marked trails near the bungalows, as a ground-level encounter with a herd of wild elephants is not recommended.

One of the the highlights of the reserve is a cable-car trip over the jungle, which lasts for some 40 minutes over a distance of more than 2 km (1¼ miles). From the cable-car terminus a half-hour walk leads to the rear entrance of the park, from where a minibus can take you back to the main entrance. At the departure point for the cable-car is a small zoo area, with a troop of black gibbons, a couple of snake cages, and a small enclosure with some giant lizards, which the locals claim are indigenous to the region. The butterfly enclosure is aflutter with colourful wings from spring right through the summer wet season, but almost deserted from late autumn and through the winter dry season. Immediately before the cable-car is an aviary.

About half an hour beyond Elephant Valley is the **Dadugan Tea Plantation** (大渡岗万亩茶园; Dadugan Wanmu

*A black racket-tailed treepie, one of the many tropical species that thrive in southern Yunnan.*

**BELOW:** a Xishuangbanna village in the wet season.

Chayuan), which sprawls across the rolling hills and which locals claim is the largest of its kind in all China, attracting traders of green tea from Hong Kong, Taiwan, South Korea and Japan every harvest season. Very few travellers or Chinese tourists visit the plantation. In mid- to late spring the fields come alive with locals picking the fresh tips of green tea, but at other times of the year it is simply a quiet, picturesque place for a walk. The plantation is accessed via the winding old road to Simao, which is now virtually unused and makes a good cycling route.

## EAST OF JINGHONG

**Ganlanba ⓫** (橄榄坝; also known as Menghan) is a nondescript town on the Lancang River around an hour southeast of Jinghong. It is situated in the heart of a fertile plain that has long been an important agricultural zone for the Dai people. Visitors will find the flat terrain ideal for cycling. Some travellers visit the **morning market** here, but it is essentially a sprawling wet market, and definitely not for the squeamish. The main items on sale are agricultural products,

*The Hani are one of the region's main minority groups, with a population of around 1.2 million scattered around southern and western Yunnan. Together with the Yi and Lisu, they form part of the Tibeto-Burman linguistic family.*

**BELOW:** water-splashing festivities.

such as pork and vegetables, but don't be surprised to see the occasional dog or goat. It's only worth a short visit, and there is really nothing to buy.

Ganlanba's chief attraction is the the **Dai Minority Park** (傣族园; Daizu Yuan; open 24 hours; entrance fee), best visited in the morning, when the bus-loads of Chinese tourists are at the Botanical Gardens in Menglun. The park here is actually comprised of five traditional village communities that in 1999 the government decided to preserve by combining them into an enclosed tourist attraction – most of the original family homes here have been, or are in the process of being, rebuilt. The mornings are peaceful, and it is possible to walk around the five villages undisturbed, though they also seem to be deserted of locals. In the afternoon the place is flooded with crowds of tourists on golf carts, and the daily shows of singing and dancing and water-splashing are in full swing. The largest of the temples in the cultural village – **Chunman Dasi Temple** – is well worth a visit, as it has been renovated in fine style, with a gold-leaf stupa. In each of the five villages are guest houses, offering an inexpensive opportunity to overnight and dine with a local Dai family.

Some people opt to avoid the cultural village altogether, and instead take a ferry across the river, where there is a collection of small villages and banana plantations. It's best to do this by bicycle, which can be hired in Jinghong, where there are at least two good shops for mountain-bike hire close to Mei Mei Café. Either ride the bikes to Ganlanba (it's a pleasant two-hour ride) or put them on the roof of a local bus.

### Menglun

There's not much to **Menglun ⓬** (勐仑), which lies some 90 km (55 miles) east of Jinghong, other than its function as a pit stop on the road to Laos and the splendid **Tropical Botanical Gardens** (热带植物园; Redai Zhi-wuyuan) down by the Luosuo River (open daily 8am–midnight; entrance fee).

The largest garden of its kind in all China, it features more than 3,000 examples of the local flora labelled in both Chinese and Latin over an area of more than 900 hectares (2,250 acres). It is best to visit in the afternoon, when the tour buses have all returned to Ganlanba for Dai minority performances, but do not expect to have the gardens to yourself. It is possible to stay overnight inside the park at a guest house with a swimming pool.

## To the Laos border

The route south from Menglun to Mengla traverses one of the wilder parts of Xishuangbanna, an area which has retained plenty of its forest cover. Some 100 km (62 miles) distant, **Mengla** ⑬ (勐腊) is an ugly town set in some of the most lush, pristine, wild areas of Xishuangbanna – and the last major dwelling en route to Laos; the border is a bumpy 90-minute ride away. The four-hour journey from Menglun to Mengla is a fairly gruelling ordeal along potholed roads through the hills, although the scenery eventually becomes stunning rainforest. Use bikes with trolleys as taxis

to get around Mengla. There are hot springs just outside town.

The **Bronze Spire Pagoda** (青铜尖顶塔; Qingtongjian Dingta) is the town's stand-out tourist attraction, founded over 1,000 years ago and rebuilt in 1759. Its shiny jutting roof marks the only inspiring addition to this otherwise moribund skyline. A quiet road runs north from Mengla through picturesque forested scenery to Yaoqu; some 25 km (16 miles) along the way is the **Bupan Aerial Walkway** (补蛙望天 树空中索道; Bupan Wangtianshu Kongzhong Suodao), which is strung between the trees approximately 40 metres (130 ft) above the ground, allowing for close-up views of the forest canopy.

Heading south to Laos, **Shangyong** ⑭ (尚勇) is the final village before the border. The village is full of the Miao minority, with their dark-blue traditional clothing and markings on their forearms. These Miao (known as Hmong across the border) backed the wrong side in the Vietnam War – after the conflagration ended they were savagely repressed, with thousands heading from Vietnam and Laos into this part of China.

*Many place names in Xishuangbanna are rendered confusingly similar by the common use of the prefix "Meng", which has come to mean, simply, "small town". Meng was traditionally the name for the Dai noble class and it also referred to the areas under their dominion.*

**BELOW:** a remote Dai village in Mengla county.

**TIP**

Access from Xishuang-
banna to northern
Thailand is possible via
a daily flight from
Jinghong to Chiang Mai,
and passenger boats
(two or three per week)
along the Mekong from
Jinghong to Chiang
Saen (visas for Laos
and Myanmar are not
necessary on this
route). Laos can be
reached from Mengla
(visa available on arrival
at the border), but the
200-km (125-mile) road
trip to the border can
take all day due to the
poor road conditions.

**BELOW:** elephants
can still be seen
in Xishuangbanna
jungles.

Just beyond Shangyong and 6 km (4 miles) from the border is **Mo Han** (边贸站), also called Bian Mao Zhan, which translates as "Frontier Trade Station". There is basic accommodation here, and transport is available to the border, which closes mid-afternoon. Visas can be obtained from the Lao Consulate in Kunming *(see page 381)*. Just across the border is the small village of Ban Boten, but for accommodation and other facilities you will have to head further, to the small town of Luang Namtha.

## WEST OF JINGHONG

Around 50 km (30 miles) west of Jinghong, the dusty, modern town of **Menghai ⑮** (勐海) cannot be recommended to travellers as anything more than a possible lunch stop en route to the market towns of Menghun and Xiding further west. The **Xiding morning market** on Thursdays and the **Menghun morning market** on Sundays have superseded the once-popular but now modernised Damenglong morning market. The Xiding market is mostly Akha, while the Menghun market is largely Dai. The swirl of minorities at the mar-

kets is a colourful sight, but it's a good idea not to go with too high expectations. These are agricultural markets for outlying villages and they trade mostly in vegetables, spices, meats and other foodstuffs, along with a host of everyday items that range from shoes and bedding to cheap electronics. Locals are accustomed to foreigners turning up with cameras, though it is no easy feat to get good shots in the scrum. Noodle soups and barbecued meats are available for the adventurous, but it's best to eat before and after the market.

Around 10 km (6 miles) from Xiding on the road back to Menghai, a sign points the way to a little-visited **Bulang** village (布朗), home to about 70 families who live in traditional stilted houses. The hills in the distance mark the border with Myanmar. The village has a small, neglected Buddhist temple, and a museum (Culture Exchange and Exposition Centre of Bulang People), which as yet only sports a couple of photographs and a monograph about the Bulang, one of China's most recently recognised minorities, with a population of some 85,000. Like most of the villages in the region, it

*Recommended Restaurants & Cafés below*

is possible to negotiate with the locals to stay overnight for a nominal fee – usually in the form of a tip before you leave. A new village area is being built next to the museum – the main village is below it.

On the road back to Jinghong, about 19 km (12 miles) before Menghai, is the **Jingzhen Octagonal Temple ⑯** (八角亭; Baijiao Ting; open daily 8am–6pm; entrance fee), which is worth a visit. It gets its name from a stupa in the forecourt, which was founded in 1701, but most of the temple complex is a relatively recent reconstruction, as it suffered badly in the turbulent years of the Cultural Revolution. Today the temple serves as a monastic school for teaching boys in the nearby village of Jingzhen how to read Dai – very few Dai girls are taught.

## Damenglong

A bumpy, dilapidated road heads from Jinghong to the small town of **Damenglong ⑰** (大勐龙) in Xishuangbanna's deep south close to the Burmese border – the 70 km (43 miles) taking anywhere from 3 to 5 hours by bus or car. The **Sunday market** used to be a major draw but has rather less in the way of local

colour these days. The chief attraction in the vicinity is the **Bamboo Shoot Pagoda** (曼飞龙笋塔; Manfeilong Sun Ta), nestled beside Manfeilong village about 30 minutes' walk from downtown Damenglong. Founded in 1204, and the most famous stupa in Xishuangbanna, it is said to commemorate a visit to the region by the Sakyamuni Buddha, and an oversize footprint in a niche on the stupa is said to be his.

The **Damenglong to Bulangshan trek** is popular with backpackers. From Damenglong, you need to get transport to Manguanghan – taxis will do it for around Rmb 30. Most people stay overnight in a Hani village called **Weidong** (卫东), though the villagers here have seen a little too much trekker traffic and are not as welcoming as they were in times past. The walk is around seven hours long, although the road is now paved and usually vehicles will stop and offer walkers lifts. The walk to Bulangshan is around four hours, but transport from there to Menghai is erratic (one bus a day) and on a very bumpy road. The road from Menghai to Jinghong is good, and buses do it in less than an hour. ❑

*The Bamboo Shoot Pagoda near Damenglong dates back to 1204.*

# RESTAURANTS & CAFÉS

## Restaurants

In southern parts of Yunnan you are likely to encounter fresh fish roasted with lemongrass, chicken boiled with sour bamboo shoots, and pork cooked in bamboo tube.

### Jinghong
### Forest Café
Ganlanba Nanlu (diagonal to Mei Mei's), Jinghong. Tel: 0691 213 6957. **$** Home-made bread, Western and Chinese fare, and tasty combinations

for fruit shakes make this a popular choice.

### Mei Mei's
Top of Jinde Xilu (near roundabout). Tel: 0691 212 7324. **$** The original backpackers' hang-out, with all the reference material you could wish for on getting around Xishuangbanna, plus standard banana-pancake fare: that's what sums up Mei Mei's, a comfortable, laid-back yet intimate café in the centre of town. Has Internet access as well as books in English, and

guides for trekking can also be arranged.

### Night Market
Mekong Bridge. **$**
Just to the north side of the new bridge is the finest dining experience in Jinghong. Open-air stalls abound where you select the freshest of produce which is then typically cooked to Dai traditions: in other words heavy on the lemongrass and a veritable taste explosion. Do not miss the rice cupped in a hollowed out pineapple. Get here before 9pm to sample the best of the produce, the river fish especially.

### Menghai
### Sichuan Flavour Restaurant
Xiangshan Xinjie (5 minutes from the train station).
Tel: 0691 665 4409. **$$**
If you're after something spicy in Menghai, try the Sichuan Flavour – though try not to overdo the chillies... Alternatively, plenty of tasty Muslim snack food is available in the streets around the nearby mosque.

• • • • • • • • • • • • • • • •
*Average price for a meal for one, with one drink:*
***$** = under US$12 (Rmb 100),*
***$$** = US$12–20 (Rmb 100–60),*
***$$$** = over US$20 (Rmb 160).*

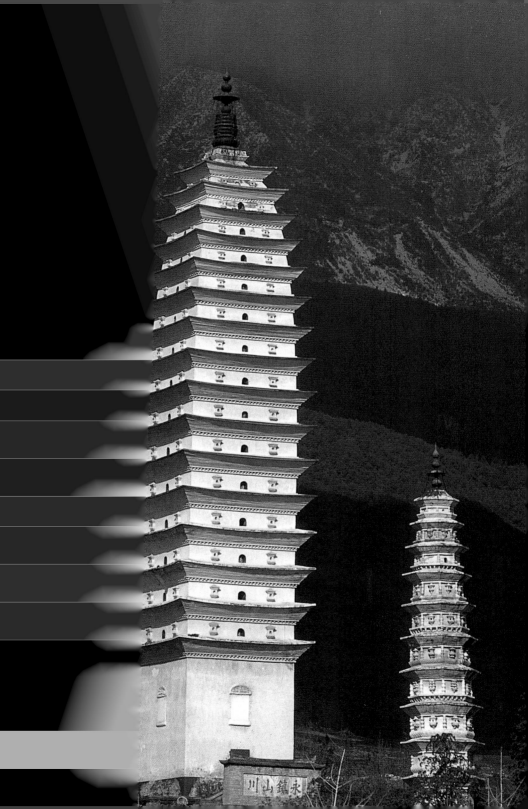

Recommended Restaurants, Cafés & Bars on page 335

# DALI AND THE BURMA ROAD

Dali is a city to woo all comers, perched between
the blue waters of Er Hai Lake and the temple-
studded Cangshan range. West of Dali snakes
the historic Burma Road, one-time lifeline
to the outside world

The ancient mule tracks winding
their way through the hills from
Kunming to the Burmese border
were once an important staging post on
the trade route between China, Burma
and India, and much later, during World
War II, the route became a vital supply
line – the famous Burma Road. On the
way, before the land descends to the
Mekong and Salween valleys, is the
wonderfully relaxing city of Dali, popular among Chinese and Western visitors
alike for its dramatic setting and cultural
heritage. The Three Parallel Rivers Area
west of Dali is one of the wildest and
most spectacular parts of China. In the
far west, the tropical areas close to the
Burmese border are essentially an extension of the Xishuangbanna region
described in the previous chapter. Over
the centuries, this corner of China has
absorbed a range of cultural influences
and the region has become a homeland
for the Dai, Jingpo and Bai people,
among other smaller minorities.

## DALI

**Dali ⑱** (大理), an ancient walled town
some 400 km (250 miles) west of Kunming, is one of the most picturesque destinations in all of China. Flanked on one
side by the 4,000-metre (13,000-ft) Cangshan Mountains and on the other by Er
Hai, Yunnan's second-largest lake, Dali
has a location that is rivalled by few other
historical sites in the region. And, at an
altitude of 1,900 metres (6,200 ft), it has
a year-round temperate climate. Small

surprise, then, like Yangshuo in Guangxi,
it was one of the earliest places to be discovered by pioneering backpackers when
China first opened up to individual travel
back in the early 1980s. Much has
changed in the old town since then: the
handful of laid-back cafés on Huguo Lu
that once welcomed Asia overlanders
have blossomed into a host of popular
establishments offering pizzas, cheese-
cake and sometimes dubious Chinese cuisine, while the street itself has been
renamed Yangren Jie, or "Foreigners'
Street" – a draw for the bus-loads of Chi-

**Main attractions**

DALI (OLD CITY)
THREE PAGODAS
ER HAI LAKE
CANGSHAN MOUNTAINS
NU JIANG GORGE
HESHUN XIANG
RUILI

**LEFT:** the
spectacular
pagodas outside
Dali. **BELOW:** Bai
dancers at a tea
ceremony.

The restaurants, cafés and bars of Dali cater primarily to Western backpackers.

**BELOW:** souvenir shops in Dali.

nese tourists who make mass incursions through the city walls on a daily basis. Nevertheless, Dali retains much of its charm – despite burgeoning real-estate developments – and makes a perfect base for exploration of the nearby lake- and mountainside attractions.

Independent travellers need to be aware that in popular local parlance there are actually two Dalis. The old walled town, where almost all foreign visitors stay, is known as **Dali Gucheng** (大理古城; Dali old city), while the newer, larger Dali, around 20 minutes south of the old city by road, is usually marked on maps as **Xiaguan** (下关), but sometimes as just "Dali" and sometimes as Dali Shi (Dali City). Whatever it is called, it's a less than charming urban sprawl. Most buses from Kunming and Lijiang terminate at Xiaguan rather than Dali Gucheng, but taxis are available for the final leg at around Rmb 30.

## Ancient capital

The walled town of Old Dali that exists today is a legacy of the Nanzhao Kingdom, which began to coalesce during the period of China's Southern and Northern dynasties in the 5th and 6th centuries AD. Yunnan's centre of power shifted west from Kunming during this period to a collection of six *zhao*, or kingdoms, that were home to the Bai minority. By the time the Tang Dynasty was in its ascendancy, a local chieftain named Piluoge (697–748) had unified all six kingdoms and established the Nanzhao (literally, "southern kingdom", 738–902), with Dali as its capital.

Repulsing a Tang attempt to bring the city under its subjugation, at the height of its power, Nanzhao's territories stretched north into Sichuan, south into Burma and southeast into northern Vietnam. But by the latter decades of the 9th century, as the Tang Dynasty began to wane, the Bai people's domain also began to crumble. Internecine conflict broke out, and when a Bai official led a coup in 939 the Nanzhao contracted to the Dali Kingdom, which effectively held sway over the region corresponding to today's autonomous Bai prefecture.

## Sights in Old Dali

It is possible to get a glimpse of some Nanzhao historical treasures at the small **Dali Museum** Ⓐ (大理博物馆; Dali Bowuguan; open daily 8am–5.30pm; entrance fee) on Cangping Lu. The museum was also the headquarters of Du Wenxiu, an ethnic Hui Muslim who led the Panthay Rebellion (1856–73) against the Qing Dynasty and was executed for his efforts. A better selection of historical artefacts can be found in Xiaguan at the Dali Bai Autonomous Prefecture Museum (*see page 329*).

The Dali Museum is just a short stroll from the **South Gate** Ⓑ (南门; Tonghaimen), also called Nanmen, Dali's best-preserved section of old city walls. The gate is largely a reconstruction, as the original walls were badly damaged in the Panthay Rebellion, and restoration efforts did not begin until the 1990s.

All four city gates and the walls that link them are worth a look; the walls themselves feature a total of 45 battlements, while the **North Gate** Ⓒ (北门; Anyuanmen, also called Beimen) has some surviving woodcarvings. Not far from the South Gate, straddling **Fuxing Lu** – now a very busy tourist street, chock-a-block with souvenir shops – is the Qing **Wuhualou**, or Tower of Five Glories.

Continuing north along Fuxing Lu, on Yu'er Lu, is **Yu'er Park** Ⓓ (玉耳公园; Yu'er Gongyuan; open daily 8am–5.30pm; entrance fee), a tranquil garden where old people gather to gossip away the time amid rockeries and minuscule ponds. Two blocks on and to the left, on Pingdeng Lu (Equality Street) is a small **Catholic church**, a legacy of early – and largely unproductive – proselytising efforts by missionaries bent on converting Dali's Buddhist Bai inhabitants.

Dali's most spectacular and famous nearby attraction is the San Ta Si, more popularly known as the **Three Pagodas** Ⓔ (三塔寺; Santa Si; open daily 8am–7pm; entrance fee), which are around

*Inside the bell tower immediately to the west of Dali's Three Pagodas.*

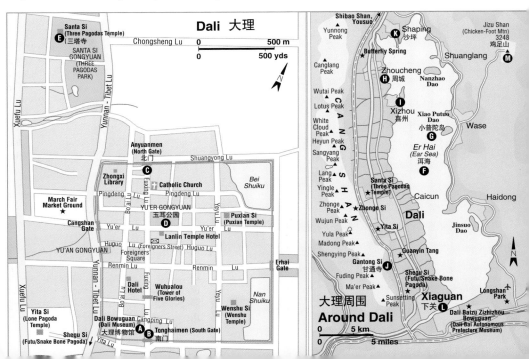

*Performing dance troupe outside Dali's South Gate.*

**BELOW:** a Bai Temple set against Er Hai Lake.
**BELOW RIGHT:** cormorants are still used by fishermen on the lake to secure their quarry.

1 km (⅔ mile) north of town. Well over 1,000 years old, the exact date of construction of the fluted towers is uncertain, but they are known to be of Nanzhao/Tang Dynasty provenance. The central tower (Qianxunta) is 69 metres (230 ft) tall and has 16 tiers, while its two flanking structures have 10 tiers and stand at 43 metres (141 ft). The pagodas were restored in 1979, after miraculously surviving earthquakes and the vicissitudes of nature for centuries, but the Chongsheng Monastery they once stood guard over is long gone. Excavations of the monastery, also in 1979, unearthed a treasure trove of gold Buddhas, bronzes and silverware, some of which can be viewed in a small **museum** (included in the entry fee).

Although the Three Pagodas are the picture-postcard scene most associated with Dali, there are a couple of other Nanzhao-era pagodas still standing. Not far west of Dali's South Gate is Hongsheng Temple's **Lone Pagoda** (一塔寺; Yita Si), another 16-tiered tower but slightly smaller than the largest of the Three Pagodas, at 46 metres (150 ft). Closer to Xiaguan is **Futu Pagoda** (蛇骨塔; Shegu Si), which also goes by the name of the Snake Bone Pagoda. The popular name for this Nanzhao-era temple is entwined with a legend of a local hero who died in battle with a huge python that once preyed on the inhabitants of Dali.

## AROUND DALI

Dali's most obviously compelling natural attraction is **Er Hai ⑥** (洱海), or "Ear Sea", a 250-sq km (100-sq mile) lake that was named for its size and shape. On the kind of sunny day that is commonplace during Dali's pleasant spring and autumn months, the lake is a profound shade of aquamarine, and when the weather turns colder it is crowned from the far side by the snow-frosted peaks of the Cangshan Mountains. Numerous streams tumble down off the steep mountain slopes into the lake, and the locals say that no matter how extreme the weather, the area neither floods nor runs short of water.

Not so long ago, the only boats that traversed the Er Hai were fishing vessels and small ferries plying the waters in coordination with local market days in the various nearby villages. The relatively recent large-scale influx of tourists has changed that, and most of the lake traffic today can

be accounted for by gaudy, often noisy, sightseeing boats. Countless outlets (including many of the popular guest houses) in town can organise tickets for the tour boats, which leave from Taoyuan Pier, but the more interesting option is to head to the wharf just east of Dali at **Caicun** village (彩村)– anyone who wants to do some exploring on the other side of the lake is advised to take a hired bicycle to the wharf.

Theoretically, there is a daily ferry from here to the village of **Wase** (挖色), a picturesque Bai settlement on the eastern side of the lake, but in reality the ferry runs rarely now (cars, motorbikes and a lakeside road having put it out of business), and most visitors charter a boat. Wase has a small *zhaodaisuo*, or guest house, for travellers who want to overnight, but it is a rough-and-ready affair. Just offshore from Wase is **Little Putuo Island G** (小普陀岛; Xiao Putuo Dao), which derives its name from the mythical mountain home of Guanyin, the Chinese goddess of compassion. There is a small statue of the goddess – who is said to guard the lake's waters – in a temple on the crown of the small island.

Several kilometres north of Wase is the fishing village of **Shuanglang** (爽朗), which has perhaps the best views of the lake and the mountains on the far side. Unfortunately, **Nanzhao Island** (南诏岛; Nanzhao Dao) is a tacky adjunct to the Er Hai boat cruises, and best avoided.

Rounding the northern tip of the lake, the road – which has been jarringly renamed Er Hai Beach Boulevard, with cavalier disregard for the fact there is no beach – passes the relatively nondescript Jiangwei village to the south, before making a sharp right turn and passing **Butterfly Spring**. The latter – once a charming pond shaded by an acacia tree and locally famed for its butterflies – has become an obligatory stop on the tour-bus lake circuit, and is awash with souvenir stalls.

Nearby **Zhoucheng H** (周城), a Bai village that looks much as Dali did three decades ago, is a far more enticing prospect. The men of the village dress in rural Chinese style, but the women still sport traditional red vests and bonnet-like headwear. The houses here are also traditional – mostly in *sanfang*, or court

*Policemen stand to attention in Dali.*

**BELOW:** Bai vendors at Putuo Island, Er Hai Lake.

yard style, with upturned eaves, and fronted by cobbled streets.

Continuing on in the direction of Old Dali, the road passes **Xizhou ❶** (喜州), another traditional Bai village. A renowned southern Silk Route trading town during the Ming Dynasty, Xizhou was for many centuries the richest settlement in the area, and many of the sprawling houses with multiple courtyards are still standing and inhabited.

## The Cangshan Mountains

The beautiful **Cangshan mountain range** flanks the western side of Er Hai Lake, providing a splendid backdrop to the Dali area. The Cangshan can be considered one of the outlier ranges of the eastern Himalayas, and rises to an impressive 4,122 metres (13,523 ft) at its highest point. Around 400 metres (1,300 ft) above the lakeshore on these verdant slopes is **Zhonghe Temple** (中和寺; Zhonghe Si), largely notable for its views of Dali and the lake. It is a very steep, sweaty climb, but most people today opt for the cable-car that whisks passengers to the temple in minute. From Zhonghe, the 11-km (7-mile) hike south along a scenic trail to

**Gantong Temple ❿** (甘通 寺; Gantong Si) is the chief attraction of the mountains. The trail is shaded most of the way, and there are some superb views. Gantong is a Nanzhao-era temple, but only one hall now remains of what was once a huge 36-hall Buddhist place of worship. From Gantong, it is a relatively easy hike downhill to the **Guanyin Tang** (观音堂), which has a shrine to the goddess of compassion perched on a boulder in its courtyard. The temple is by the roadside, making it easy to jump on a bus, or – if you are lucky – a taxi back to Dali.

## Markets

The colourful market days in the Bai villages around Dali – which sell everything from fabrics and vegetables to chickens and ponies – shift from village to village according to days of the week. But, no matter how short your stay, there is almost guaranteed to be one somewhere within striking distance. Xizhou, a short 17-km (11-mile) taxi ride (or 1–1½ hours by bicycle) north of Dali, has an early morning market.

It is less lively, however, than the weekly Monday market at **Shaping ❿** (沙坪), around 13 km (8 miles) further north. Minibuses to the weekly market are a regular cottage industry in Dali, as are boat trips to the **Wase** market, which takes place every five days (the 5th, 10th, 15th, and so on). On Fridays the village of **Yousuo** (右所), which is around 1½ hours north of Dali by local bus, holds a sprawling market that is the least touristed – in fact there are often no tourists at all; subsequently, very few people in Dali know of it, and finding the right bus to go there is something of a challenge.

## Xiaguan

Causing no end of confusion for foreigners, **Xiaguan ❿** (下关) is often referred to locally as Dali Shi, or Dali City. Although the city has a large number of hotels and restaurants, it is little more than a transit point for Old Dali and the other attractions around Er Hai and on the mountainside, as well as destinations further west (*see page 331*). The only

*Having a haircut at Shaping market.*

**BELOW:** All the markets held in the Bai villages surrounding Dali tend to get under way in the midmorning (9am–10.30am) and winds down between 4pm and 5.30pm.

Recommended Restaurants, Cafés & Bars on page 335

ttraction worth mentioning is the **Dali Bai Autonomous Prefecture Museum** 大理白族自治州博物馆; Dali Baizu Zizhizhou Bowuguan; open 8am–5.30pm; entrance fee), near the Er Hai Dock, located at the east end of Erhai Nanlu in the Xiaguan Town region of Dali City. It was built in 1986, and has a total area of 3 hectares (8 acres). A "garden-style" museum, it is of interest mostly for its examples of the local architecture, but it also houses some interesting bronzes and other Nanzhao-era artefacts.

## Sacred Mountains

ntrepid travellers might be tempted by any of three sacred mountains in the vicinity of Dali, and each is accessible from Xiaguan by bus. The most famous of them of is **Jizushan** Ⓜ (鸡足山; Chicken-Foot Mountain), which rises to a lofty 3,248 metres (10,656 ft) to the north of the town of Binchuan, around 90 km (56 miles) northeast of Xiaguan. In its heyday, this Buddhist mountain retreat was home to a disputed number of monasteries – the locals will tell you 108 or perhaps 360, both auspicious Buddhist numbers. Construction reached its peak

at the height of the Nanzhao era, but fell into decline with the kingdom, and then hit rock bottom many centuries later when the Red Guards went on the rampage during the Cultural Revolution. Nevertheless, some monasteries remain and are today active again, providing heated – though very basic – lodging for travellers who wish to lodge close to the summit and rise at the crack of dawn to the see the sunrise.

Some 115 km (70 miles) north of Dali near the village of Shaxi is **Shibaoshan** ⑲ (石宝山; Stone Treasure Mountain), home to a series of cave temples. The grottoes themselves are poised above a small temple, and contain exquisite Buddhist statuary.

**Weibaoshan** (巍宝山) is a Daoist mountain retreat around 85 km (53 miles) south of Dali (old city), and some of the original temples here are still standing. Access is via the nearby village of **Weishan** (巍山), another former Nanzhao stronghold noted for its massive main city gate and traditional town centre – for anyone looking to see Yunnan as it was before the tourists arrived, it is a perfect getaway.

*The tranquil Daoist temple at Weibaoshan.*

**BELOW:** pool with a view.

**TIP**

Access to the Nu Valley is not quite as difficult as it might sound, though don't expect many comforts along the way – accommodation is extremely limited, food is basic, and many of the villages are only accessible by foot, even though a sealed road now serves much of the valley.

**BELOW:** dramatic scenery on the Nu Jiang (Salween) River.

## The Nu Jiang Gorge

Well off the beaten track, close to the Myanmar border northwest of Dali, the **Nu Jiang Gorge** ⑳ (怒江峡谷; Nujiang Xiagu) is a 320-km (200-mile) gorge and UNESCO World Heritage Site, described by the United Nations body as the "epicentre of Chinese biodiversity". The Nu Jiang River itself (known in Myanmar as the Salween) is the westernmost watercourse of the so-called "Three Parallel Rivers Area", where it runs close to two other major rivers, the Lancang (the Mekong) and the Jinsha (the main headwater of the Yangzi). All three run north to south in parallel, each of the deep valleys separated by huge mountain ridges. All three rivers have their origins in Tibet. Plans to construct dams for hydroelectric power have brought controversy to this little-known corner of the planet, causing the Beijing government to put all dam projects officially on hold. Still, rumours of planned dam projects continue to percolate from the region, which is inhabited mostly by two minorities that are converts to Christianity – the Nu and the Lisu (a tribe also native to the Golden Triangle, a remote mountainous region bordering Myanmar, Thailand and Laos) while the inhabitants deep in the valley are mostly Tibetan.

This dramatically remote and scenic area can be accessed from **Fugong** ㉑ (福贡), which is served by 12-hour overnight buses from Xiaguan; the trip can be broken up with an overnight stopover in Baoshan *(see below)*. From Fugong, it is a couple of hours by bus to **Liuku** (六库), a nondescript county seat with onward access into the valley.

## THE BURMA ROAD

Through history there must have been many Burma Roads. After all, the 832-km (520-mile) highway that snakes west from Kunming to Ruili on the border with Myanmar is no more than a sealed, modern-day equivalent of the fabled southwest Silk Route. According to Chinese records as early as 400 BC the route saw the shipment of goods from Sichuan to as far afield as India and Afghanistan. The modern road that supplanted the mule track of old has its origins as a supply route during the second Sino-Japanese War (1931–1945), when the nationalists put some 200,000 labourers to work on a road from

Kunming to the border, connecting with the British-built road to Lashio in what was then British Burma. It is believed that hundreds perished building it, though the road proved to be a lifeline in the fight against the Japanese. Today, sleeper buses ply the bitumen between Kunming and Ruili in around 14 or 15 hours (on a good run). Unless you are in a hurry to get to Myanmar, however, a few overnight stopovers en route are recommended: this little-travelled corner of Yunnan rewards even the briefest of forays.

## Baoshan

Some 120 km (75 miles) and around 5 hours west of Xiaguan, the city of Baoshan ㉒ (保山) was for two millennia the last major Chinese outpost on one of the strands of the southern Silk Route, though for the vast majority of that time it was known as Yongchang. The mighty Lancang Jiang (澜沧江), the Chinese section of the Mekong River, is crossed some 60 km (37 miles) before the town.

Most travellers sensibly use Baoshan merely as an overnight stop, and save a longer stay for Tengchong, which is a little over 3 hours (160 km/100 miles) dis-

tant by bus via a new road that takes a far less circuitous, and less scenic, route than that which it replaced. Today, the city of 750,000 inhabitants looks very much like any other third- or second-tier Chinese city, and its few historical attractions are of fairly recent provenance.

Baoshan itself is a small hill in the city suburbs with a pagoda and a shrine to the memory of Zhuge Liang, the legendary military strategist of the Three Kingdoms era, who led the Southern Expedition from the Kingdom of Shu (present-day Chengdu), and entered Chinese folklore for his games of wile with the leader of the Nanmen ("southern barbarian") tribal leader Meng Huo.

Around 3 km (2 miles) to the south of town is a more contemporary military site, the large **Graveyard of National Heroes** (国殇墓园; Guoshang Muyuan) which commemorates the thousands of Guomindang soldiers killed in their attempt to wrest nearby Tengchong from the Japanese. The events of the time are also explored in the museum at Heshun (see page 333).

Baoshan's other main attraction is the very low-key **Taibo Shan Park** (太保

*A Lisu woman uses a rope bridge to cross the Nu Jiang (Salween) River in the far west of Yunnan.*

**BELOW LEFT:**
Chinese troops on the Burma Road during World War II.

## The Burma Road

Now a modern highway with tunnels and bridges making quick work of the rough terrain, the route between Kunming and the Burmese border at Ruili has a long and eventful history. Mention of the Burma Road brings to mind its most famous incarnation as China's lifeline to the outside world during World War II. With the Japanese in control of all of its seaports, this 1,145-km (715-mile) cobbled road from Kunming to the British railhead at Lashio in northern Burma was used to transport supplies to the struggling Nationalist (KMT) forces. Built in the late 1930s by 200,000 Chinese labourers using only rudimentary tools, the road symbolised the desperate fight against the Japanese invaders. The eastward continuation of the route into Assam (India) was built under the command of General "Vinegar Joe" Stillwell *(see margin, page 332)*.

Although mountainous, the route lies just south of the impassable peaks that mark the beginning of the Tibetan lands, and has been a conduit for both trade and invasion for centuries. In AD 97, the Burmese king sent tribute via this route to the Emperor of the Eastern Han Dynasty. In 1254, Burmese forces on elephant-back fought the army of Kublai Khan in Baoshan. During the 18th century, the Chinese Emperor Qianlong, obsessed with high-quality Burmese jade, used it, unsuccessfully, to attempt a full-scale invasion.

*The Stillwell Road, built during World War II, extended the Burma Road westwards to Assam in India – a 765-km (478-mile) route through extremely rugged terrain. There has been talk of reopening the road to facilitate trade between India and China.*

**BELOW:** Lisu minority people at the Kuoshijie Festival, Tengchong.

山公园; Taiboshan Gongyuan), a small, lightly forested park around a few minutes from town by taxi, with a small pavilion and some pleasant walks.

A worthwhile detour is the **Reclining Buddha Temple** (卧佛寺; Wofo Si), set deep in the countryside 16 km (10 miles) to the north of town. The restored marble figure measures over 6 metres (20 ft) in length, and the temple dates back some 12 centuries.

## Tengchong

**Tengchong ㉓** (腾冲) lies on a plain at an altitude of around 1,600 metres (5,250 ft), around 6 hours from Baoshan by bus. As little as a decade ago, much of the city was built of wood, but the old architecture is rapidly being pushed aside by the real-estate developers.

**Dieshuihe** (叠水河瀑布) is a 30-metre (100-ft) waterfall on the Daying River, and just a short taxi ride from the city centre – in fact, the locals like to say that Tengchong is China's only city with a waterfall inside the city limits. However, this is not what draws increasing numbers of Chinese tourists to the city. For them, the chief attraction is the geothermal

delights – 97 volcanic cones, some still active, more than 80 natural hot springs and even some geysers.

Increasingly today travellers skip the city hotels altogether in favour of that geothermal activity, and go straight to **Rehai** (热海; open daily 7.30am–11pm; entrance fee), around 10 km (6 miles) northeast of town – an inexpensive taxi ride. Other than a small collection of hotels and a couple of the star attractions, Rehai is surprisingly undeveloped. There are well-marked trails, designated bathing pools with entry tickets, and a vast steaming pool known as the **Big Boiling Pot** (Dadunguo), where locals boil eggs in temperatures of more than 96°C (200°F). There are also quieter trails passing many more natural pools and hissing vents.

A few kilometres further north is the **Volcano Park** (火山公园; Huoshan Gongyuan; open daily 8am–7pm; entrance fee), where the main attraction is **Dakong-shan** (大空山), or Big Empty Mountain. Steps have been carved into the mountainside, and a stiff walk takes visitors to the lip of the now dormant volcano's cone. The summit also has splendid views of the surrounding volcanic peaks – most of which

re dormant. It is also possible to climb to the peaks of nearby **Xiaokongshan** – small Empty Mountain – and **Heikong-han** – Black Empty Mountain.

The village of **Heshun Xiang** (和顺乡), recently named one of the 10 most picturesque villages in China and now scheduled for development as a tourist site, lies 6 km (4 miles) west of Tengchong. Its winding cobblestone streets are lined with handsome traditional houses of some opulence, constructed by Heshun's native sons upon their return from perilous journeys into Burma as jade merchants. During World War II, Chinese troops were billeted here, and their HQ had been turned into a fascinating **museum** chronicling the struggle by the Chinese, with assistance from American military units, to oust the Japanese invaders. The museum holds weapons, uniforms and other equipment from both sides of the fierce battle which took place in Tengchong when the Japanese were ousted from southern Yunnan in 1944.

Heshun Xiang is also the home town of the Chinese philosopher **Ai Sipi**, who tutored Mao Zedong, and his home has been converted into another museum.

## Mangshi Region

**Mangshi ㉔** (芒市), around 500 km (310 miles) west of Kunming, and 3 hours by bus from Tengchong, is the capital of the Dehong Dai and Jingpo Autonomous Prefecture. Less than half of the local inhabitants are Han; the rest are largely either Dai or Jingpo, who are known as the Kachin in Myanmar. The city itself is often confusingly referred to as Luxi, even though the airport – the border region's only air connection with the outside world – is known as Mangshi.

Like Dali, there are two Mangshi cities – the old town and the new town – though in this case they are adjacent to each other, and a real effort has been made with many of the recently constructed buildings to reproduce the Dai minority charm of the old quarters in the northern and eastern districts. But, despite the city's soporific, tropical charm, with its hints of neighbouring Myanmar, Laos and Thailand, Mangshi offers little reason to linger. The **Puti Temple** on Zhengnan Lu is a somewhat ramshackle affair, while **Wuyun Si**, or Five Clouds Temple, on Wuyun Lu, is a little more rewarding. Also of minor interest, on Youyi Lu, is

*Rapeseed cultivation adds a splash of colour to the landscape west of Dali.*

**BELOW & BELOW LEFT:** southwestern Yunnan is a largely Buddhist region.

*Ruili, on the riverine border with Myanmar, has a remote, edge-of-the-world feel.*

**BELOW:** Ruili is a major jade centre.

the **Shubao Ta**, or Tree-Wrapped Pagoda, where there is a small pagoda that has succumbed to the embrace of the local vegetation – rather like a miniature version of Ta Phrom at Angkor, Cambodia.

## Ruili

It is around six hours by bus from Tengchong (or two from Mangshi) to **Ruili ㉕** （瑞丽）, a busy city of around 110,000 on the Myanmar border. The city is a somewhat odd exercise in stark contrasts between the bold and modern style of Chinese architecture – blue-tinted glass facades, rocket-like spires and post-Soviet bas-reliefs – and downmarket bamboo and tin structures that seem inspired by another world somewhere over the border. Still, the downtown area is not without charm, with its leafy boulevards and haphazard Burmese culinary influence in the cafés. Not far from the Dai-influenced government guest house, which features a lovely garden area, there is a busy night market, and in fact the entire downtown area has a late-night party atmosphere – with some inevitable hints of sleaze. The main attraction for Chinese tourists is the city's sprawling **Jade Market** （珠宝街；

Zhubao Jie) – said to be among the busie in the world, and no place to spend mone unless you really know your jade.

Bicycles are available for hire inex pensively in the city centre, and it is pos sible to cycle out to several Dai Buddhi temples. On the road east of Ruili i **Wanding ㉖** （畹町）, a sleepy borde post that achieved fame in the late 1930 as the main supply route for the Britis from Burma to southwestern China, i **Jiele Jinta** （姐勒金塔）, the Golde Pagoda. Some 200 years old, its spir reaches 40 metres (130 ft) into the air. A cycling trip to the southwest of town i the direction of Nongdao is more reward ing, however. Around 5 km (3 miles) ou of town – and impossible to miss thank to the signs – is the **Hansha Zhuang** （喊萨奘寺）, a miniature wooden mor astery with a Buddha inside. Around km (4 miles) further is a perfectly whi pagoda on a hillside that provides view of the area – **Leizhuangxiang**. Betwee downtown Ruili and the border is **Non gan Jinya Ta** （弄安金鸭塔）, or mor popularly in English, the Golden Duc Temple, a Thai-influenced stupa with golden Buddha image.

# RESTAURANTS, CAFÉS & BARS

## Restaurants

Average price for a meal for one, with one drink:
$ under US$12 (under Rmb 100)
$$ US$12–20 (Rmb 100–60)
$$$ over US$20 (over Rmb 160)

### Dali (Dali Gucheng/ Old Dali)

Dali has no shortage of restaurants catering to backpackers, but very few regional Chinese restaurants. On upper Renmin Lu, though, there is a profusion of kitchen-style eateries – many of these don't even have menus (or English names), but a little creative pointing and gesturing can result in a superb meal at a bargain price. In the evenings, on the corner of Fuxing Lu and Huguo Lu, a collection of stalls offer barbecued lamb, chicken and beef.

### An Caife Beag

215 Renmin Lu. Tel: 0872 267 0783. $
This cozy, unostentatious café (the name is Gaelic, and translates as "a small cafe") on lower Renmin Lu serves Dali's best breakfasts, and also has a selection of Chinese dishes.

### King's Park Kitchen

5 Huguo Lu. Tel: 0872 266 4082. $$
King's serves up the best Cantonese cuisine in town, though it is a good idea to call in in advance if you want fish dishes – in Dali, fish on short order tend be small and bony. The restaurant is in a courtyard at the far end of Huguo Lu, just before the Number Four Guest House.

### La Stella's Pizzeria

21 Huguo Lu. Tel: 0872 267 9521. $
Located on upper Huguo Lu, or Foreigner's Street, Stella's is the only restaurant in Dali that serves wood-fired pizzas. On sunny afternoons, people make a beeline for the alfresco seating area.

### Li Jia Baizu Fengwei

75 Renmin Lu. $
The name translates as the Li Family Bai Minority Cuisine Restaurant, and this is the most popular pick-and-choose restaurant on Renmin Lu. Fresh wild vegetables and mushrooms adorn the entrance, while cured meats hang indoors. There are also credible Sichuan dishes, though – as in most local restaurants aimed at Chinese tourists – no English menu.

### Shuangqiao Yuan

98 Renmin Lu. Tel: 0872 266 4938. $
Shuangqiao Yuan, or Double-Bridge Garden, is perhaps Dali's most in-demand restaurant specialising in Bai Minority cuisine, which is strong on fish from the lake, *doufen* – yellow-bean noodles – and wild vegetables from the mountainside. It has no English sign, but is easily recognisable as the Tang Dynasty themed place on the corner of Renmin Lu and Fuxing Lu.

### Ruili

As in most of remote southwestern Yunnan, recommendable sit-down restaurants are hard to come by in Ruili, though the adventurous will find plenty to experiment with. Jiegang Lu has a number of Burmese restaurants, but many travellers complain of stomach upsets after eating there. The **New Kaitong Hotel** has two Chinese restaurants that are reliable, including a very good Sichuan restaurant. On the southern section of Jiegang Lu, **Huafeng Market** has some excellent food stalls proffering a good range of regional Chinese cuisines as well as Burmese fare – the Chinese offerings are the safest.

## Bars

### Dali

### Bad Monkey

74 Renin Lu.
The most popular bar in Dali for both visitors and foreign residents, the Bad Monkey has a reputation for raucous late-night parties. However, show up earlier in the evening and you'll find a good place to knock back a few drinks and meet people.

### Bird Bar

22 Renmin Lu. Tel: 0872 266 1843.
Dali's longest-running bar is something like a sprawling living room, and a popular refuge for bohemian writers and artists from Beijing and Shanghai. Service standards are best described as aloof, but on the plus side, the Bird Bar supplies a fascinating insight into Dali's alternative scene.

### The Lazy Lizard

223 Renmin Lu.
The Lazy Lizard is a German-run bar with Dali's largest selection of imported beers. If the psychedelic décor is too disturbing for you, wander out to the courtyard area out at the back that in the colder winter months is often the setting for impromptu fireside parties.

# NORTHWESTERN YUNNAN

In northwestern Yunnan, where China runs into Tibet, the scenery takes on a grandiose scale, from the deepest canyon on Earth to the mountain valley of Shangri-la

The diversity and scenery for which Yunnan is famous reaches its high point in the northwest, both in terms of culture and – literally – in terms of geography. The Naxi and Tibetan "minorities" form the majority in these parts, and have recorded their significant cultural and historical achievements in their own written languages. The landscapes are magnificent: the southeasternmost corner of the Tibetan plateau extends into the area, and the surrounding Himalayan peaks reach altitudes of over 6,000 metres (22,000 ft).

## LIJIANG

With its backdrop of snow-capped mountains and its rich local culture, twisting cobblestone lanes and vaulted stone footbridges crossing rushing canals of clear water, **Lijiang ㉗** (丽江) has always fascinated visitors. Some 160 km (100 miles) north of Dali at a cooling altitude of 2,400 metres (7,800 ft), the town lies at the foot of the Jade Dragon Snow Mountain, whose towering peaks offer a hint of what awaits further north.

Lijiang is composed of two distinct districts, separated by the pine-forested Lion Hill. New Lijiang (pop. 200,000), founded in the 1950s, is a modern Chinese city, with the ubiquitous tinted glass and dull tile-clad buildings that characterise its ilk all over China. East of Lion Hill, the ancient city of Lijiang (pop. 50,000), although hardly untouched by the outside world, provides a striking architectural and cultural contrast to the new town.

The settlement here has flourished for centuries as a caravan stop for those travelling to and from Tibet. It was Kublai Khan who gave the town its name ("beautiful river") when his troops passed through here in 1253, and the Khan also introduced Chinese music to the Naxi, initiating a unique musical tradition which still flourishes. During the Ming Dynasty, Lijiang experienced a cultural golden age when the ruling Mu family established a series of monasteries following Tibetan Buddhist teachings in the surrounding hills. It is, however, the

**Main attractions**
LIJIANG OLD TOWN
JADE DRAGON SNOW MOUNTAIN
TIGER LEAPING GORGE
LUGU LAKE
ZHONGDIAN (SHANGRI-LA)
THE FAR NORTHWEST (DEQIN)

**LEFT:** Jade Dragon Snow Mountain from Lijiang's Black Dragon Pool Park. **BELOW:** taking the canoe across Lugu Lake.

*Naxi flute player. This matriarchal society has a strong tradition of musicianship, and Lijiang's Naxi Orchestra (see pages 300 and 340) is a well-established tourist attraction.*

## GETTING TO NORTHWESTERN YUNNAN

There are several daily **flights** between Lijiang and Kunming, and also at least one daily to Guangzhou, Shenzhen, Shanghai and Chengdu. Zhongdian (Shangri-la) is linked to Kunming by 4 daily flights, and there are also flights to Guangzhou and Lhasa.

Frequent **buses** run between Lijiang and Dali (3 hours) and Kunming (8–12 hours) – sleeper buses are an option on the latter route.

## GETTING AROUND NORTHWESTERN YUNNAN

**Lijiang**: Buses run to Zhongdian (Shangri-la) roughly every hour and take 5 hours, stopping at Qiaotou for Tiger Leaping Gorge. There are also buses to Ninglang (6–8 daily, 4 hours); Jinjiang (for the rail line north to Sichuan; 3–4 daily, 8 hours); Lugu Lake (at least 1 daily; 7–8 hours).

**Zhongdian (Shangri-la)**: There are buses to Lijiang (hourly, 5 hours), Deqin (4 daily, 6 hours) and Dali (hourly 8 hours).

old town, known as Dayan (the name means "big ink stone" – a reference to the town's slate-coloured roofs, as seen from one of the many surrounding hilltops), that attracts modern visitors.

The local inhabitants of Lijiang, the Naxi, are a branch of the Qiang people of Tibet, who left the northwest of China 2,000 years ago and settled in this fertile, temperate plain. Numbering around 300,000, theirs is a matriarchal society, that is, the women have a dominant role in all major aspects of life, in commercial dealings, landownership and rearing of children. The men are traditionally gardeners, horsemen and musicians. With a religious tradition based on Tibetan shamanism, a unique written language which uses pictographs, and a flourishing literary and musical tradition, they are one of the most sophisticated of Yunnan's minorities.

During the 1930s many foreign explorers and botanists came to the region to catalogue its varied and unique plant and animal species. The most eccentric and prolific was Joseph Rock, an Austro-American botanist who lived here for more than 30 years, collecting and photographing plant and animal specimens,

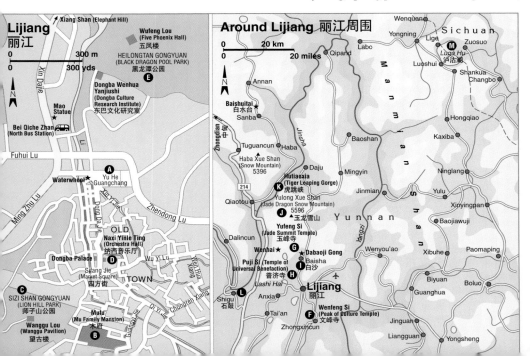

Recommended Restaurants on page 347

translating the written language, writing articles for *National Geographic* and esoteric scholarly works for Harvard University. Rock was reluctantly evacuated when Mao's communist forces arrived in 1949. A collection of his photographs is on display at the Dongba Palace in Lijiang.

In 1996, the Lijiang Valley was shaken by a devastating earthquake, which measured 7.2 on the Richter scale and claimed the lives of more than 300 people. The brick-and-wood architecture in the old town fared better than the concrete buildings of the new. Two years later, the old town and some surrounding sites were added to the UNESCO World Heritage list, resulting in greater local attention to both preservation and tourism.

While all construction in the old town must now be in the traditional style, a growing number of former homes are given over to shops and restaurants to cater to the needs of the ever-expanding tourism industry: Lijiang is now extremely popular with Chinese tourists, and the nearby airport has put the area within the reach of large tours groups. It may be well and truly on the map, but the old town – free of any motor vehicles – remains a magical place for a stroll. There are helpful signs with directions and background information in English on almost every street corner.

## City sights

A walk through Lijiang might logically start at **Yu He Square Ⓐ** (Yu He Guangchang), noted for its huge waterwheels, and located at the northern edge of the old town. It is possible to see much of the old town without passing through **Sifang Market Square** (四方街; Sifang Jie), the most commercialised part of the city. To do so, head south from Yu He Square and take Xin Yijie, which runs to the east of Dong Dajie (the main drag). This smaller street crosses Wuyi Jie, which climbs into the more tranquil eastern section of the old city. Tiny food shops and small groceries are built into the fronts of the old Naxi homes with carved wooden doors leading into central courtyards of intricate tile work. Massive wooden posts frame the scene, and stairways wind to the latticework balconies. To complete the 3-km (2-mile) circuit, turn right onto Wen Hua Xiang and walk through this quiet residential neighbour-

*Lijiang's appeal is considerably enhanced by its magnificent mountain backdrop.*

**BELOW:**
the view across Dayan, Lijiang's old town.

hood before turning right onto Chongren Xiang, then right again onto Qi Yijie. The second street on the left, Guangyi Jie, leads to the entrance of the Mu Palace.

The **Mu Family Mansion** ❷ (木府; Mufu; open 8.30am–6pm; entrance fee) is a recreation of a Ming-style palace commemorating the rule of the Mu family, who governed Lijiang in the name of the Yuan, Ming and Qing emperors from 1254 until 1723. This series of six large pavilions in a walled compound was financed by the World Bank and constructed soon after the earthquake in 1996. It's not unpleasant but doesn't really fit into the ambience of the rest of old Lijiang. Leaving the back of the Mu Palace, it's a short but steep walk up to the **Lion Hill Park** ❸ (师子山公园; Sizi Shan Gongyuan; open 6.30am–6pm; entrance fee) and the **Wanggu Lou Pavilion** (望古楼; Wanggu Lou). The pavilion was constructed recently in traditional Chinese style, a five-storey wooden tower which affords a superb view over the old town. Leaving Lion Hill Park from the northeast entrance, bear left to return to Yu He Square, or

bear right to descend into **Si Fang market square**. In addition to many tour groups, souvenir shops and sidewalk cafés, you're likely to find some traditional folk-dancing performances, or possibly a Tibetan warrior in full regalia, astride his horse, employed as a photo opportunity. Turning left up Dong Da Jie leads quickly back to Yu He Square.

While the recent changes to overcome Lijiang are undeniable, they have strengthened a Naxi cultural revival which flourishes in the arts, particularly music. The 23 Tang Dynasty songs which Kublai Khan bequeathed to the Naxi were lost elsewhere in China and have survived only here. Performances of this music, augmented with original Naxi folk music, take place at the **Naxi Orchestra Hall** ❹ (纳西音乐厅; Naxi Yinle Ting), opposite the Dongba Palace on Dong Da Jie.

A short walk north of the square, following the stream, is the **Black Dragon Pool Park** ❺ (黑龙潭公园; Heilongtan Gongyuan; open 6.30am–8.30pm; entrance fee). This park, where willow and chestnut trees line pathways which meander around a small lake, is home to some architectural treasures, notably the **Five Phoenix Hall** (五凤楼; Wufeng Lou), built in the 17th century and moved here 30 years ago from the Fuguousi Temple outside Lijiang. This magnificent structure gets its name from the elongated eaves terminating in eight flaring roof points on each of three storeys. Viewed from any angle, five of these wooden "phoenixes" are visible. Inside the hall, a statue of Sanduo, the Naxi god of war, glowers ominously.

Between this hall and **Elephant Hill** (象山; Xiang Shan), which offers a rigorous but rewarding climb, the **Dragon God Temple** (龙神寺; Longshen Si) is an elegantly ambling single-storey complex with small interior courtyards which now serve as gallery spaces. A gently arching bridge reaches over a pool, in which stands the white-marble **Moon Embracing Pavilion**, from which one can enjoy a picture-perfect view of the traditional architecture, superb land-

**BELOW:** in the heart of the old city.

scaping and the majestic Jade Dragon Snow Mountain *(see page 342).*

Outside the back gate of the park you'll find the **Dongba Culture Research Institute** （东巴文化研究室; Dongba Wenhua Yanjiushi; open 8.30am–6pm; entrance fee). Dongba is the name of the Naxi shamanistic cult which governed spiritual life here before the assimilation of Buddhism and Daoism. The museum has excellent collections of the ritual clothing and accoutrements used by the shamans, as well as a collection of painted scrolls and manuscripts written in their pictographic language.

## AROUND LIJIANG

Monasteries, forests, soaring mountain peaks and reputedly the deepest canyon in the world – the environs of Lijiang provide some of the highlights of any visit to China.

### The temples

The hills surrounding Lijiang are home to several monasteries established by the Mu rulers in the 17th century. At their peak, the monasteries were occupied by hundreds of monks following the Gelugpa (Yellow Hat) sect of Tibetan Buddhism. Unfortunately, the Tibetan connection attracted the wrath of the authorities in the early 1950s, and during the Cultural Revolution any religious observance was attacked, leading to the depopulation and desecration of these temples. Some of the defaced religious objects have been restored, and a scattering of resident monks remain, but today these holy places are attractive for their artistic merit and beautiful forested surroundings.

**Peak of Culture Temple ❺** （文峰寺; Wenfeng Si) is located 8 km (5 miles) southwest of Lijiang. Situated amidst fruit orchards and forests, it is built in the shade of huge trees and draws water from a nearby spring. The murals are well restored, the architecture harmonious and the atmosphere peaceful.

**Jade Summit Temple ❻** （玉峰寺; Yufeng Si) is located 11 km (7 miles) northwest of town in a pine forest above the village of Baisha. The temple is built in several terraced levels. The temple's architecture is striking, featuring carved wooden doors, restored frescoes and geometrically perfect courtyards connected

*The Naxi Orchestra perform Tang- and Song-dynasty music as well as their own folk songs.*

**BELOW:** the Mu Family Mansion.

*Dr Ho sells herbal remedies to curious tourists from his home in Baisha village, 9 km (6 miles) north of Lijiang. As he is only too happy to point out, a surprising array of celebrities have made it to this remote spot.*

**BELOW:** scenery on the road north to Zhongdian.

by stone pathways. The highest terrace has been constructed around the famous Camellia Tree of 20,000 Blossoms, which illuminates the place in early spring.

**The Temple of Universal Benefaction** (普济寺; Puji Si) is only 5 km (3 miles) northwest of town, but the climb is up steep, winding goat paths. A courtyard within the temple contains two immense crab apple trees and some interesting Tibetan Buddhist iconography, and there are splendid views across the valley below.

Further out, 11 km (7 miles) north of Lijiang, the village of **Baisha** (白沙) was the capital of the Naxi people until the arrival of Kublai Khan in 1253, when Lijiang was established. It is now a typical Naxi village, and an easy bicycle ride from Lijiang. Of interest in the village is the **Dabaoji Gong**, a temple complex featuring a syncretic blend of Tibetan Buddhist, Daoist and even Naxi Dongba iconography. The murals are sombre, even bizarre, to the first time observer, featuring a menagerie of demons, giants, demigods, and scenes of the underworld.

As an alternative to visiting the temples, a good way to explore the countryside is to cycle to **Lashi Lake** (拉市海; Lashi Hai). The lake is only 5 km (3 miles) west of town and can be cycled around in a full day, stopping along the way at the villages which surround it.

## Jade Dragon Snow Mountain

The poetically named **Jade Dragon Snow Mountain** (玉龙雪山; Yulong Xueshan; entrance fee) in fact refers to a range of 13 peaks which are almost emblematic of Lijiang. The Alpine meadows in the area are famed for their wide variety of plants, both ornamental and medicinal. The highest peak reaches 5,600 metres (18,300 ft), and was first climbed in 1963. While the south side of the mountains step gracefully down to the Lijiang plain, the northern edge plunges almost vertically to the Yangzi River, forming the famous Tiger Leaping Gorge (*see page 343*). To reach the higher elevations, you can choose between three chairlift routes. These are hugely popular with visiting Chinese, and long queues and tour buses are almost always a factor.

Another way to enjoy this beautiful area is to visit **Wenhai** (文海), an Alpine lake and wetland, where a community-based ecotourism zone has been estab-

Recommended Restaurants on page 347

lished in conjunction with foreign NGOs. It's a four-hour trek or pony ride to reach Wenhai Lake, which lies southwest of the peaks at an altitude of 3,100 metres (9,300 ft). Visitors are accommodated either in the Wenhai Ecolodge (tel: 0139-0888 1817) or at other home-stay operations in this Naxi village. Depending on the season, Wenhai is good for birdwatching or admiring the wild flowers which thrive here. Local guides can take you further up the mountain for spectacular views.

## Tiger Leaping Gorge

Perhaps even more renowned than the Jade Dragon Snow Mountain is the remarkable **Tiger Leaping Gorge** Ⓚ (虎跳峡; Hutiaoxia), where the surging Jinsha River (a headwater of the Yangzi) cuts a 4,000-metre (12,000-ft) gorge between the Jade Dragon and Haba Snow mountains. The gorge takes its name from the local tale of a tiger that eluded pursuing hunters by leaping across the narrow gorge. The easiest access point to the gorge is from Qiaotou, 100 km (60 miles) from Lijiang, where the Xiao Zhongdian River joins the Jinsha. The route to Qiaotou is excep-

tionally scenic – terraced fields bordered by brick farmhouses and walnut trees covering the hills. From Qiaotou it is possible to follow the road downstream about 30 km (20 miles), cross the Jinsha by ferry and return by road to Lijiang from the town of Daju. The halfway piont along the gorge is Walnut Grove, which sits 2,000 metres (6,600 ft) above the waterline and looks across at a sheer 4,000-metre (13,200-ft) cliff.

For those so able, the best way to enjoy Tiger Leaping Gorge is to trek the high trail, which is usually done from Qiaotou to Walnut Grove. The trek can take two or three days, and the small family-run guest houses along the route assure that food and a bed are never more than two hours' walk away. Ponies are available for hire, either to carry you or your bags. Maps listing the guest houses en route can easily be found in Lijiang, but be careful to check on current conditions as well. While the high trail has been improved and is generally well marked, it requires your serious attention, and should not be attempted when rainfall or high winds are likely. For the serious trekker, trails lead up from the

*Ferry across the turbulent Jinsha Jiang at the entrance to Tiger Leaping Gorge.*

**BELOW:** a Yi minority "Tiger Procession".

gorge to the Alpine meadows of **Haba Snow Mountain** (哈巴雪山; Haba Xueshan), almost as impressive as the Jade Dragon range, with not a chairlift or tour bus in sight.

North of the gorge is an incredible geological phenomenon known as **Baishuitai** (白水台), an area of calcified limestone that gleams bright-white against the green forests and terraced fields – itself resembling the rice terraces. According to Naxi tradition, the gods deposited Baishiutai as a lesson in how to terrace their fields. The area abounds with traditional Naxi and Li towns and villages.

## Shigu

Leave Lijiang to the west and you encounter a rather different geology. After crossing a dry stony plain, you arrive at the town of **Shigu**  (石鼓), 40 km (25 miles) from Lijiang. Shigu is named after the most famous local sight, the Stone Drum, which is in fact a cylindrical marble tablet inscribed with a history of the defeat of a Tibetan army by Naxi and Han forces in 1548. Another noteworthy event in Chinese history took place here in 1936. Eighteen thousand Red Army soldiers, fleeing nationalist forces in what was to become the Long March, found themselves stranded on the banks of the river at Shigu. Aided by locals, they crossed in small boats over a period of four days.

History aside, Shigu is an attractive spot to spend a day. The Stone Drum rests in an ornate pavilion surrounded by willow trees. Nearby, a chain-link suspension bridge – built during the Qing Dynasty when tea caravans from southern Yunnan passed through en route to Tibet – still functions. A short walk up Cloud Mountain (Yu Shan) provides wonderful views over the first bend in the Yangzi, the point where the mighty river (correctly termed the Jinsha Jiang at this point) executes an abrupt left turn to swing round to the northeast. Around 120 km (75 miles) downstream it turns back around to the south, forming a gigantic loop around Lijiang, before gradually easing east and north again on its long journey to central China and the East China Sea.

## Ninglang and Lugu Lake

East and somewhat north of Lijiang, one enters the **Ninglang Yi Autonomous County** (宁蒗彝族自治县; Ninglang Yizu Zizhixian). The Yi people, who number nearly 400,000, typically dwell at higher elevations than their Naxi neighbours, in small villages consisting of log cabins. Prior to 1949, they were feared by people outside their group for their frequent raids and a tradition of enslaving their prisoners. Those days are gone, and the Yi are now known for their conservative adherence to traditional lifestyles and colourful dress. Yi women are recognisable for their impressive headgear, an enormous piece of stiff, black, rectangular felt.

Beyond the county seat at Ninglang, where there is a good **museum** devoted to Yi culture, one enters Yongning district, the home of yet another minority, the Mosuo, who inhabit the area around **Lugu Lake**  (泸沽湖; Lugu Hu; entrance fee). The lake is nestled against

*Reading the unique Yi script. The Yi language is Tibeto-Burman, but the written form bears no resemblance to other languages in that group, or to Chinese. Most Yi live in Ninglang County, northeast of the Lijiang area.*

**BELOW:** Tiger Leaping Gorge.

the border between Yunnan and Sichuan, 240 km (145 miles) by road from Lijiang. Surrounded by mountains and dotted with islets, this 50-sq km (20-sq mile) lake, which reaches depths of 80 metres (240 ft), is considered by many to be Yunnan's most magnificent natural beauty spot. The scenery, coupled with the interest generated by the false reputation for sexual frivolity on the part of Mosuo women, has caused the beauty of the place to become somewhat tainted. The small town nearest the lake, **Luoshui** (落水), is now little more than an overpriced tourist trap, with the attendant buses and sleazy karaoke bars. It's best to move rapidly through Luoshui to **Lige** (里格), on the north side of the lake. Simple accommodation is available, and boat rides on the lake are easily arranged. The market town of **Yongning** (永宁), which lies on a fertile plain about 20 km (12 miles) west of the lake, is frequented by Yi, Mosuo, Naxi and Lisu people. It's a good place to enjoy the views of nearby Lion Mountain and take in the traditional atmosphere.

## THE FAR NORTHWEST

Following the road north from **Qiaotou** (桥头), the rolling hills of walnut and spruce suddenly give way to a plateau of grasslands, with towering snow-covered mountains on the horizon. This area is both geographically and culturally Tibetan. Called the Deqin Tibetan Autonomous Prefecture, it lies at a base altitude of 3,000 metres (9,000 ft). With white *chorten* (the Tibetan word for pagoda or stupa) festooned with colourful prayer flags, and long-haired yak grazing amidst Alpine wild flowers, the area offers a stark contrast to the lower parts of Yunnan.

### Zhongdian (Shangri-la)

The town of **Zhongdian** ㉘ (中甸) lies some 200 km (120 miles) north of Lijiang. A long-time Tibetan settlement, known to the locals as Gyeltang, it has been re-branded by the Chinese tourism authorities as **Shangri-la**, based on a somewhat dubious claim that the best-selling 1933 novel, *The Lost Horizon*, set in a paradisiacal Himalayan mountain valley, was based on the area *(see panel on page 346)*. As in Lijiang, this official promotion has certainly spurred domestic tourism. On the positive side, it has given the indigenous people, a branch of Tibetans known as Khampa, a renewed pride in all aspects of their culture. Confusingly, Zhongdian's airport is often listed as "Deqin" or "Deqing" (even though it is nowhere near the town of Deqin).

The **old town**, located on the southern edge of Zhongdian, is full of new restaurants and cafés, souvenir emporia, and rustic guest houses. Muddy alleys have become cobbled lanes, and Tibetan folk dancing takes place around a central square in the evenings, with visitors enthusiastically joining the circle. On a hill behind the old town, a 23-metre (70-ft) **golden prayer wheel** is pushed by locals, launching their prayers heavenwards. Beside the spiritual benefits, the spot offers a fine view over the old town.

About 5 km (3 miles) north of town, in the village of **Songzhanling**, lies **Songsenling**, (松赞林寺; Sumtseling

*The far northwest of Yunnan lies within the Tibetan cultural sphere, and the lamaist temples of the region are filled with fierce-looking protector deities.*

**BELOW:** a Yi woman wearing the distinctive traditional hat.

*Remote and tranquil, Lugu Lake is one of the highlights of northern Yunnan.*

**BELOW RIGHT:**
snowy Himalayan peak above the upper Nu Jiang valley, northwestern Yunnan.

Gompa in Tibetan; open daily 7am–4pm; entrance fee), a sprawling monastery of the Gelugpa (yellow hat) sect. The monastery was established in the 17th century, totally destroyed during the 1950s, and rebuilt in the 1980s. The central building of the complex bears a striking resemblance to the Potala Palace in Lhasa, and is tended by hundreds of monks, especially at festival times, making it the largest Tibetan lamasery in Yunnan. The main temple has four storeys, with the ground-floor walls covered with imposing frescoes depicting Tibetan legends and views of the cosmos. The village has several Tibetan houses converted into hotels, and given the ease of transport into town, staying in the village of Songzhanling is a good way to appreciate Zhongdian.

Just a few kilometres north of Songzhanling, the **Napa Hai Nature Reserve** （纳帕海自然保护区; Napa Hai Ziran Baohuqu; open daily 9am–6pm; entrance fee) is a seasonal lake which fills during the summer monsoon season. The area is a bird-watchers' paradise, and serves as a migration point for the rare Black-necked crane. Ponies are available for hire here, and are quite useful for exploring this wide area of wild flowers and grazing yak.

## North to Deqin

The road from Zhongdian to Deqin consists of 190 km (115 miles) of fantastic mountain scenery tempered by moments of serious vertigo. Reaching altitudes of 4,000 metres (13,200 ft), with sharp curves and precipitous drops, it is an incredible engineering feat and an unforgettable journey. The road is now fully surfaced, although cobblestones are wisely used on the steepest sections. The road is often closed due to snow in the winter. Midway on this trip, a chance to catch your breath is offered at the town of **Benzilan** （奔子兰）, in a wooded valley at the relatively low altitude of 1,900 metres (6,200 ft). About 20 km (12 miles) beyond Benzilan lies a reconstructed monastery, **Dongzhulin** （东竹林寺） which is both aesthetically pleasing and lively with monastic devotees, including a *tulku*, or incarnate lama. At the former site of Dongzhulin monastery, which was dynamited by the PLA in the 1950s, a Tibetan **Buddhist**

## Selling Shangri-La

In 2001 the State Council, a lofty arm of the Chinese bureaucracy, announced that new research had proven that James Hilton's 1933 novel *Lost Horizon*, set in a remote and idyllic Himalayan valley, was in fact based on the area surrounding the town of Zhongdian. They declared that the area was now known officially as Shangri-la, and a campaign of tourist promotion followed. In fact, Hilton never saw the Himalayas, and the name of his hidden valley is probably based on the Tibetan word *shambala*, meaning paradise.

Nonetheless, this bold rebranding exercise, aided by a new airport with direct flights to Beijing and Shanghai, and the creation of a new "old town", has proved to be a dramatic success. Tourist arrivals have increased tenfold, and the cobblestone streets of the "old town" are filled with shops and guest houses which are more attractive than the typically sterile concrete avenues of Chinese Zhongdian. After years of repression, the local Tibetans are encouraged to revel in their culture and religion, and despite some misgivings the locals generally consider tourism less of a threat than the alternatives of mining and logging. In any case, the name change means little to them – they still refer to their town as Gyeltang, its original Tibetan name.

nunnery is home to more than 100 female devotees.

The town of **Deqin** ㉙ (德钦), called Atunze by the Tibetans, is so far pleasantly undeveloped. There is a thriving local market and an old Tibetan section at the north end of the town, which looks much like the old town of Zhongdian did before it became Shangri-la. The town really consists of one street four blocks long, and its atmosphere, while authentic, will not detain you more than a few hours. Although accommodation is available here, an alternative is to continue about 8 km (5 miles) towards Meili Snow Mountain, where several acceptable guest houses have been built above a row of *chortens* (Tibetan Buddhist reliquaries) with a stunning view of the Kawa Karpa range. Within walking distance is the **Feilaisi Temple** (飞来寺), known as Nak Trashi to the Tibetans, which houses a statue of the mountain's guardian deity. Indeed it is this mountain range, called **Meili Xue Shan** (梅里雪山) by the Chinese and Kawa Karpo by the Tibetans, which attracts both visitors and Tibetan pilgrims to the area. The highest peak in Yunnan, at an altitude of 6,740 metres (22,100 ft), it has never been climbed, in spite of several attempts by serious climbers. In 1991, a team of Japanese and Chinese mountaineers perished in their attempt to scale the mountain.

To reach the mountain from Deqin, one first descends the winding road to the Mekong River, which the Chinese call Lancang Jiang, meaning winding river. Shortly before the bridge crosses the river, near a pavilion containing rows of prayer wheels, an entrance fee is collected. A base camp, which has several decent guest houses, lies at the foot of the mountain. From here, it's a pleasant 8-km (5-mile) climb, or pony ride, to the foot of the **Mingyong glacier** (明永冰川; Mingyong Pingchuan), where a small temple sells snacks and drinking water. The mountain is heavily forested, and you'll meet many Tibetan pilgrims making the climb. Another route, from the village of Yubeng, slightly to the south, leads to the **Fairy Waterfall** (雨崩神瀑; Yubeng Shenpu), which is also venerated by the Tibetans – its spray is not only cooling but washes away bad fortune. ❑

*The Tibetan Monastery of Dongzhulin in the hills above Zhongdian.*

# RESTAURANTS

## Restaurants

### Lijiang old town

#### Lamu's House of Tibet

56 Xinyi Jie. Tel: 0126 000 8380. $

A convivial place to sample both Tibetan and Naxi dishes, not to mention the Western and Chinese standards.

#### Le Petit Lijiang Book Café

50 Chongren Xiang, Qiyi Jie. Tel: 0888 511 1255. $$

Feast on the Western and Chinese dishes either seated in the courtyard or inside this old Lijiang home. A knowledgeable Belgian-Chinese couple also offer travel services and some interesting books for sale.

#### Sakura Café

123 Cuiwen Xiang (near Sifang Square). $$

Located on one of Lijiang's canals, the speciality here is Korean food, and both the hotpots and Korean barbecue are good. Japanese, Chinese and Western dishes also served.

### Lijiang new town

#### Mao's Kitchen (Mao Jia Fandian)

Hua Ma Jie. Tel: 0888 518 7668. $$

Near the Black Dragon Pool, and a 10-minute walk from the waterwheel at the entrance to the old town, Mao's Kitchen dishes up a slice of Mao Zedong nostalgia in Lijiang. Be warned, the cuisine of the Chairman's home province of Hunan is very, very spicy! English menus are available.

### Outside Lijiang

#### Qing Song Lijiang

Situated between Lijiang and Lashi Lake. $

The Qing Song consists of a huge traditional courtyard and nicely decorated dining rooms over two floors, some with great views of the Jade Dragon Snow Mountain. Naxi cuisine is served exclusively. Every evening, a group of elderly Naxi ladies from the nearby village come to dance in the courtyard, and diners are welcome to join them. No English menus available.

● ● ● ● ● ● ● ● ● ● ● ● ● ● ●

*Average price for a meal for one, with one drink:*

**$** = under US$12 (Rmb 100),
**$$** = US$12–20 (Rmb 100–60),
**$$$** = over US$20 (Rmb 160).

# TRAVEL TIPS

# T RANSPORT

# GETTING THERE AND GETTING AROUND

## GETTING THERE

### By Air

Hong Kong is the main international airport for the region, but various other airports across southern China are now handling international flights: Macau, Shenzhen, Guangzhou, Sanya, Xiamen, Fuzhou and Kunming are all linked with cities around East and Southeast Asia. Note that international flights into Shenzhen, Macau or Guangzhou can often be cheaper than equivalent flights into Hong Kong.

### From the UK and Europe

There is a wide choice of airlines with direct and indirect flights between London and Hong Kong, as well as flights from Amsterdam, Paris, Frankfurt, Rome and other European airports. A recent arrival on the scene is Hong Kong's own Oasis Airlines, which offers a low-cost, no-frills deal (but a direct flight). Flight time between London and Hong Kong is 10–12 hours. There are also flights from Paris to Guangzhou.

### From the US and Canada

Several airlines fly direct between North America and Hong Kong, and a few fly direct to Guangzhou. A flight from New York to Hong Kong takes around 16 hours, 12 hours from Vancouver.

### From Australia and New Zealand

Hong Kong is a major destination from Australia, and direct services operate from Melbourne, Sydney, Canberra, Perth, Adelaide and Brisbane. China Southern flies direct from Sydney to Guangzhou. Many other regional carriers also fly via their airline's hub city.

Flights are more limited to and from New Zealand, but there are direct services to Hong Kong from Auckland.

### From Bangkok

Several airlines operate flights between Bangkok and the southern Chinese cities of Kunming, Jinghong, Guangzhou, Shenzhen, Xiamen and Fuzhou. There are also flights to Macau and, of course, Hong Kong.

### From Singapore

Other than the frequent flights to Hong Kong operated by several airlines, there are services to Macau, Shenzhen, Guangzhou, Kunming, Xiamen and Fuzhou. Tiger Airways (www.tigerairways.com) also flies daily to Haikou (Hainan Island) in the summer and autumn months (check website for winter schedule), from as little as US$25 one-way (plus taxes).

### Regional Airports

#### Hong Kong

Hong Kong International (www.hongkongairport.com) is by far the largest in southern China. Transport links are excellent. The Airport Express (AEL) is a comfortable train service that runs every 10 minutes and takes only 20 minutes to reach the city (the journey by road via taxi or bus around twice as long). There is a free shuttle service between the AEL stations and the major hotels. Flying out, you can check in at the AEL Central and Kowloon stations 90 minutes before departure.

The airport is also linked by rapid direct coach service to destinations in Guangdong. While there are several operators, CTS (ctsbus.hkcts.com) has the best coverage. A one-way ticket to Shenzhen costs HK$60.

#### Macau

There are scheduled flights between Macau International Airport (www.macauairport.com; tel: (853) 861 111) and Bangkok, Jakarta, Kaohsiung, Kota Kinabalu, Kuala Lumpur, Male, Manila, Seoul, Singapore and Taipei.

The airport is situated on the east side of Taipa Island, and is linked by bridges to the downtown area. It generally takes less than 30 minutes to get from the airport to anywhere in Macau. For transport to and from the airport there are authorised taxis and the regular AP1 bus, which serves major hotels, the ferry terminal and the border gate.

Two ferry companies run very frequent high-speed vessels to Hong Kong (55–75 minutes) almost 24 hours a day. The ferries are very busy at weekends, so book in advance if possible (see also page 353).

If you prefer helicopters, East Asia Airlines (tel: 2108 9898 in Hong Kong; tel: 727 288 in Macau) operates daily every 30 minutes, 9.30am–10.30pm, using helipads on the Macau Ferry Terminal at the Shun Tak Centre in Hong Kong and at the Ferry Terminal in Macau. The choppers seat 10 and the flight takes 16 minutes.

#### Shenzhen

Shenzhen International Airport (www.szairport.com) is now one of China's busiest and handles flights to/from Bangkok, Ho Chi Minh City, Kuala Lumpur, Nagoya (Japan), New York, Seoul, Singapore and Tokyo.

The airport is 35 km (20 miles) west of downtown Shenzhen. Hotel (and other) shuttle buses take around 30 minutes, and also go to Hong Kong Airport. Line One of the city's metro is presently being

## Useful Words

These basic words are useful for finding your way around China; compass points, in particular, feature heavily on street names.

| north | bei | 北 |
|---|---|---|
| south | nan | 南 |
| east | dong | 东 |
| west | xi | 西 |
| central | zhong | 中 |
| road/street | lu/jie | 路/街 |
| rail station | huoche zhan | 火车站 |
| bus station | qiche zhan | 汽车站 |
| ferry | dulun | 渡轮 |
| mountain | shan | 山 |
| river | he | 河 |
| lake | hu | 湖 |
| sea | hai | 海 |
| village | cun | 村 |
| town | zhen | 镇 |
| city | cheng shi | 城市 |

extended in phases from Shijie Zhi Chuang to the airport, with the final section to the airport scheduled to be completed at the end of 2010.

### Guangzhou

Guangzhou is well connected to the rest of China, Asia and further afield through its new airport (Baiyun), which opened in 2004, 30 km (18 miles) north of the city centre.

Within the region there are direct flights to/from Bangkok, Fukuoka, Hanoi, Ho Chi Minh City, Jakarta, Kuala Lumpur, Kota Kinabalu, Kuching, Manila, Osaka, Penang, Phnom Penh, Phuket, Seoul, Singapore, Tokyo, Vientiane and Yangon.

Further afield there are flights between Guangzhou and Amsterdam, Atlanta, Cairo, Cincinnati, Dallas, Dubai, Frankfurt, Los Angeles, Melbourne, Nairobi, Paris and Sydney. The list is constantly growing as the airport expands.

CAAC shuttle buses connect the city with the airport (one hour), leaving from the China Southern Airlines office at 181 Huanshi Donglu (tel: 020 8668 2000), near the main train station. A taxi to the airport will cost around Rmb 100.

### Xiamen and Fuzhou

Fujian's two large cities both have international airports, although **Xiamen** is better-served by both international and domestic flights. There are international flights between Xiamen and Bangkok, Jakarta, Kuala Lumpur, Manila, Nigata, Osaka, Penang, Seoul, Singapore, Taipei and Tokyo. Xiamen's airport is a 10-minute taxi hop from the city.

**Fuzhou** has a smaller airport. There are flights to Bangkok, Kuala Lumpur, Osaka and Singapore.

### Hainan Island

Direct flights operate between the resort of **Sanya** and Seoul, Moscow and Singapore. There are also flights between the provincial capital **Haikou** and Singapore.

### Kunming and Jinghong

Kunming's airport, just 3 km (2 miles) from the city centre, is connected with Bangkok, Chiang Mai, Hanoi, Singapore, Vientiane and Yangon (Rangoon). Jinghong, in southern Yunnan, has flights to Bangkok and Chiang Mai.

## Overland Routes

The opening of southwestern China's three international borders has facilitated some interesting routes into tropical southeast Asia. A new road between Kunming and Bangkok, due for completion at some point before 2010, will open up these areas still further.

### Burma (Myanmar)

A border crossing with Burma (Myanmar) opened in 1996, but the Burmese discourage foreigners from using it. Visas are available at the Myanmar Consulate in Kunming, but you can only enter Myanmar by land if you join a tour group – either in Kunming or in Ruili – and will not be allowed to enter the country as an independent traveller. For up-to-date information check at the Myanmar Consulate in Kunming (see page 381).

### Laos

Independent travellers can enter Laos from the border post at Mohan in Mengla County, eastern Xishuangbanna (buses run from Mengla). On the Lao side of the border is the vilage of Boten (Luang Nam Tha Province). Visas are available at the Lao consulate in Kunming (see page 381), or on the border itself. Heading into China from Laos is less straightforward – you'll need to arrange your visa in advance as none are available at the border. There are also passenger boats along the Mekong between Jinghong and Chiang Saen in Thailand.

### Vietnam

A twice-weekly train service connects Beijing and Hanoi (38 hours) via the Friendship Pass on Guangxi's border with Vietnam. The train can be boarded at a number of cities in southern China, including Nanning,

Changsha and Guilin. There is also a twice-weekly rail service (15 hours) between Kunming and the Hekou/Lao Cai border post in southern Yunnan.

It is also possible to cross the border on foot at the Friendship Gate (Dong Dang, Vietnam/Pingxiang, China – note that the railway at Dong Dang is several kilometres from the border). You can also walk across at Hekou/Lao Cai.

Neither Vietnamese nor Chinese visas are available at these border posts – you will need to obtain a Vietnam visa in Beijing, Hong Kong or Kunming (see page 381). Heading in the other direction, you can buy your Chinese visa in Hanoi.

## GETTING AROUND

*For details on getting around see also the blue Transport panels within individual chapters in the Places chapters. What follows is an overview of regional transport, both long-distance and within cities.*

### Domestic Flights

A plethora of local airlines – China Southern Airlines, China Eastern Airlines, Dragonair and a whole host of others – means that there are plenty of flights connecting China's cities. *See individual chapters chapters for details, and the panel on page 352 for sample fares.* Fares are more expensive from Hong Kong. Tickets are usually very easy to obtain and generally sold one-way, with return fares simply being twice the one-way fare.

### Chinese Railways

The Chinese rail network extends an impressive 53,400 km (32,500 miles). Average train speed is not high, although increasing due to modernisation and investment; modern air-conditioned trains are increasingly in evidence on the major routes such as Guangzhou to Beijing and Shanghai, and the Guangzhou–Shenzhen route features extremely rapid trains imported from Spain.

### Seating/sleeping options

There is no first or second class on Chinese trains, but instead four categories: *ruanwo* or soft-sleeper; *ruanzuo* or soft-seat; *yingwo* or hard-sleeper, and *yingzuo* or hard-seat. The soft-seat class is usually only available for short journeys. If available, ask for the air-conditioned class *(yu kong-tiao)* when buying a ticket. Long-distance

## Car Hire

Self-drive car hire is now possible in China, but given the chaos on the roads and serious congestion in cities, hiring a car with a driver is a far better bet. Avis China has both options in Guangzhou, Shenzhen, Xiamen and Changsha.

trains normally only have soft-sleeper or hard-sleeper facilities. The soft-sleeper class has 4-bed compartments with soft beds, and is recommended, particularly for long journeys. The hard-sleeper class has open, 6-bed compartments. The beds are not really hard, but are not very comfortable either, and it's all rather cramped. Seat tickets for long-distance trains generally include a seat reservation at no extra charge, although this is not always essential for the hard-seat category. If you do not have a reservation you may occupy any vacant seat of the appropriate class, but be prepared to give it up to a passenger with a reservation for that seat. At busy times, "standing only" hard-seat tickets may be sold beyond the seating allocation.

### On-board facilities

There is always boiled water available from boilers on the trains – bring/buy your own mug and tea, coffee, packet noodles, etc. There are washrooms in the soft-sleeper and hard-sleeper classes. The toilets, regardless of which class, are not usually very hygienic (but better on the new air-conditioned trains). Bring your own toilet paper. Most trains have dining cars, and almost all have a trolley catering service – often available on station platforms, too.

### Tickets and reservations

Trains are often fully booked, so it is advisable to get a ticket in advance

(the usual maximum advance period is 5 days). This is particularly true during the main travel season – Chinese New Year, and the 1 May and 1 October holiday periods.

The price depends on the type of seat or berth, and also on the speed (and modernity) of the train. Reservations can be made at the station (some have special foreigners' ticket offices), through travel agencies or at your hotel. When boarding a train, allow plenty of time, as finding the platform can be tricky.

In Hong Kong, tickets can be purchased through travel agents, hotels, CTS offices or at the Intercity Passenger Services Centre at Hung Hom railway station (open daily 6.30am–7.30pm; tel: 2947 7888). In provincial cities, large hotels and the CTS office can help get train tickets.

A comprehensive English translation of the complete Chinese Railways timetable is available from the website at www.chinatt.org, either in PDF format for £9 ($20), or as a printed version for £15–18 ($33–44). A useful booking form in both English and Chinese is provided for purchasing train tickets: fill out your request, hand it to the booking clerk, and it could help avoid many a misunderstanding. A handy website for easy-to-use train timetable information is www.cnvol.com.

### Long-Distance Buses

Long-distance buses are the most important means of transport in many parts of China. Note that in most towns, there is more than one bus station, and large cities have several. Journeys can be slow and uncomfortable – although with the large-scale road improvement across southern China, times are decreasing.

There are regular breaks, often at roadside foodstalls. Most overnight journeys involve sleeper-buses, which

come equipped either with bunk beds or reclining seats which fold flat.

You will usually find simple restaurants and accommodation near the bus stations. Some buses have numbered seats, but it is not usually necessary to book a ticket or seat in advance. Modern buses with air-conditioning are frequently available in the tourist centres.

### Ferries

There is a wide choice of services on ferries and fast hydrofoils between Hong Kong and many Guangdong cities – including Guangzhou (2 hours by hydrofoil), Shekou (for Shenzhen) and Zhuhai. There are also longer routes – to Shantou (14 hours; daily), Xiamen (20 hours; 5 weekly), and Shanghai (60 hours; 1 weekly). Most departures are from the China Ferry Terminal at the China Hong Kong City Building (the lurid gold building), Canton Road, Tsim Sha Tsui.

Travellers heading to Macau from Hong Kong will find a variety of rapid vessels speeding throughout the day and night from both the China Ferry Terminal in Tsim Sha Tsui (Kowloon) and the Hong Kong Macau Ferry Terminal in the Shun Tak Centre, Sheung Wan, on Hong Kong Island. Jetfoils and catamarans make the journey in under an hour. There are also ferries running between Macau and Shenzhen (Shekou) and other cities in Guangdong.

For information on schedules from Hong Kong, call 2859 3333 or 2736 1387/2516 9581.

**Getting to Hainan Island by ferry**
There are no ferries to Hainan from Hong Kong. Ferries operate between Haikou and Haian, Xuwen, Zhanjiang, Shenzhen and Guangzhou, and to Beihai in Guangxi. The ticket office is at 7 Haifu Lu. Tel: 0898 6535 1557 or 0898 6621 0596.

## Typical Economy-Class Domestic Airfares in Chinese Rmb (one-way)

| From Hong Kong to: | Changsha: 875 | Kunming: 1,410 | Nanchang: 1,640 |
|---|---|---|---|
| Haikou: 1,750 | Guiyang: 1,105 | | Changsha: 1,600 |
| Sanya: 1,900 | Guilin: 800 | **From Fuzhou to:** | Guiyang: 1,750 |
| Xiamen: 1,675 | Nanning: 1,065 | Haikou: 1,750 | Kunming: 1,000 |
| Nanchang: 2,210 | Kunming: 1,410 | Sanya: 1,865 | |
| Changsha: 1,980 | | Nanchang: 1,675 | **From Kunming to:** |
| Guiyang: 2,170 | **From Guangzhou to:** | Changsha: 875 | Haikou: 1,220 |
| Guilin: 1,865 | Haikou: 840 | Guiyang: 1,295 | Sanya: 2,325 |
| Nanning: 2,055 | Sanya: 915 | Guilin: 1,715 | Nanchang: 2,285 |
| Kunming: 2,130 | Xiamen: 800 | Nanning: 2,135 | Changsha: 1,105 |
| | Nanchang: 875 | Kunming: 2,360 | Guiyang: 570 |
| **From Shenzhen to:** | Changsha: 840 | | Jinghong: 800 |
| Haikou: 840 | Guiyang: 990 | **From Guilin to:** | Dali: 570 |
| Sanya: 1,065 | Guilin: 800 | Haikou: 1,600 | Lijiang: 645 |
| Nanchang: 950 | Nanning: 840 | Sanya: 1,675 | Zhongdian: 1,015 |

### Cruises

An alternative to independent travel is to take a cruise along the south China coast; vessels leave from Hong Kong and Shanghai and call in at destinations such as Beihai, Guangzhou, Sanya and Xiamen. Shore excursions are usually organised as optional extras, allowing you to pick and choose your itinerary. Routes change with the seasons, so check with travel agents or with the cruise line direct. Operators include:

**Costa Cruises**, tel: (HK) 3528 5328
http://www.costacruisesasia.com
**Seabourn Cruises**,
http://www.seabourn.com
**Star Cruises**, tel: (HK) 2317 7711
http://www.starcruises.com.hk

### Cycling

With the increase in car ownership, there are rather fewer bicycles on Chinese roads these days, but cycling is still a good way to get around, with most cities being relatively flat and many equipped with bike lanes (although heavy traffic and bad driving can be a problem). Rental outlets catering to foreigners are concentrated in cafés and guesthouses in the main traveller centres; in other places, hotels are your best bet.

Rates should be around Rmb 5 per hour and up to Rmb 40 per day. Shop around, as these can be highly variable. You will usually be required to leave a deposit of up to Rmb 500 and some form of ID. Ask for a receipt, try to avoid leaving your passport, and make sure you have checked your bicycle's brakes, gears and tyre pressure before renting. You must use the designated parking areas, where your bike will be kept safe for a small

**ABOVE:** Hong Kong's efficient MTR (metro) has been used as a blueprint for similar systems in Guangzhou and Shenzhen.

fee. Cycle helmets can be hard to find, and night-time cycling can be hazardous due to a lack of cycle lights.

Another option is to choose a specialised bike tour *(see pages 377–8)*. Riding a bike comes into its own when exploring an area of natural beauty. The area around Yangshuo in Guangxi is fantastic for cycling– the extraordinary karst landscape is just minutes by bike from the town centre, along quiet roads and trails.

### City Transport

#### Hong Kong

**Hong Kong** has an efficient, cheap and user-friendly metro system (the MTR). Buses and minibuses are also good. A ride on one of Hong Kong Island's clanking old trams is a recommended way of seeing the city. Kowloon is linked to the New Territories via suburban rail lines (East Rail, also known as the KCR, and

West Rail). In addition to the famous cross-harbour Star Ferry, numerous ferries operate between Central and the outlying islands. It is worth buying an **Octopus stored-value card**, valid on all forms of public transport and available from MTR stations.

Taxis are cheap and usually easy to find, although things can sometimes get complicated if you wish to take a taxi from Hong Kong Island to Kowloon or vice versa – some drivers won't oblige. Many drivers can speak some English and know the main hotels and tourist spots, but this isn't always the case: to avoid problems, take your destination written down in Chinese. If you encounter difficulties, all cabs are equipped with a radio telephone, and somebody at the control centre should be able to translate.

#### Macau

There is no metro system in Macau, but buses and minibuses are adequate, and traffic jams not generally too bad. Taxis are even cheaper than in Hong Kong.

#### Mainland cities

Shenzhen and Guangzhou have efficient metro systems *(see pages 157 and 171 for details)*. Chinese buses can be rather daunting for the uninitiated, and most tourists are far more likely to get around by **taxi**: an average in-town journey should cost no more than about Rmb 20. If possible, have your destination written in Chinese characters (ask at your hotel), as cabbies are unlikely to speak English. Many cabs have a metal grill or thick plastic screen dividing the back seats and the driver, which is a bit disconcerting when you first hop in. Traffic jams can be a nightmare in many Chinese cities.

### Sample Rail Fares in Chinese Rmb (one-way)

Unless otherwise indicated, the fares listed below are for express trains with air-conditioning – slower trains without air-conditioning are, of course, cheaper. Return fares are double the single fare.

*Fares from left to right: hard-seat, soft-seat, hard-sleeper, soft-sleeper (n/a = not available).*

| Guangzhou–Hong Kong | | | |
|---|---|---|---|
| n/a | HK$190 | n/a | n/a |

| Guangzhou–Shenzhen | | | |
|---|---|---|---|
| 76 | 101 | n/a | n/a |

| Guangzhou–Changsha | | | |
|---|---|---|---|
| 99 | n/a | 183 | 276 |

| Guangzhou–Guilin | | | |
|---|---|---|---|
| 116 | n/a | 215 | 326 |

| Guangzhou–Nanning | | | |
|---|---|---|---|
| 94 | n/a | 185 | 286 |

| Guangzhou–Kunming | | | |
|---|---|---|---|
| 194 | n/a | 353 | 539 |

Other sample fares:

| Nanning–Guilin | | | |
|---|---|---|---|
| 65 | n/a | 101 | 153 |

| Nanning–Kunming | | | |
|---|---|---|---|
| 97 | n/a | 181 | 274 |

| Kunming–Dali (non-express) | | | |
|---|---|---|---|
| 45 | n/a | 93 | 136 |

# A CCOMMODATION

# HOTELS IN SOUTHERN CHINA

### Choosing a Hotel

Southern China has a range of accommodation that encompasses everything from some of the world's best five-star hotels in Hong Kong to backpacker-friendly lodgings in Yunnan. Almost everywhere, the impact of the growing tourism and business-travel industries can be seen in the rapidly improving standard of accommodation. The likes of Starwood, InterContinental, Shangri-La and Accor have established impressive flagship five-star hotels across China, while good-quality Chinese-owned and managed hotels are increasingly easy to find.

**Luxury hotels** abound in the largest cities. Hong Kong is in a class of its own, but there are some spectacular properties elsewhere in the region, including the Venetian in Macau (part of the casino complex). Even remote Lijiang, in northwestern Yunnan, has a luxurious five-star at the Banyan Tree Lijiang.

---

**BELOW:** international-standard accommodation at Dadonghai, Hainan.

In the **middle price range**, various chain hotels are appearing, catering to the 21st-century Chinese business traveller. The larger cities have a good choice of well-priced modern hotels. There is considerable variety in the quality of rooms, amenities and value for money in this class of hotel, so if in doubt ask to see a room before you commit.

The best **budget hotels** and guest houses are in popular tourist areas in places like Yangshuo, Dali and Lijiang, where they primarily cater to backpackers. Elsewhere, very cheap accommodation can be harder to find – traditionally, budget hotels are discouraged from taking foreigners, although this is starting to change with the advent of new budget chains such as Accor's Ibis and China brand Motel 168; these offer a modern clean room for under Rmb 200. In Hong Kong, budget accommodation is practically non-existent outside the guest houses of Chungking Mansions and other similar blocks along Nathan Road in Tsim Sha Tsui.

If you are planning to stay in the countryside in remote rural areas such as Guizhou and Yunnan, you may be able to find lodgings in small guest houses or with families.

Outside Hong Kong, tour groups usually stay in comfortable hotels, either international brands or locally owned properties more used to dealing with groups from Tianjin or Shanghai than Toronto or Sussex. You can, nonetheless, expect a decent standard.

Rates at all but the cheapest hotels are subject to a 10–15 percent service surcharge. Outside high season it is usually possible to get better rates through travel agents, websites or by contacting the hotel directly. It is often possible to bargain the price down at the reception desk.

In 2006 YHA China joined the International Youth Hostels Federation, with online booking at www.iyhf.org.

### What to expect

Most hotel rooms have two single beds. Checkout is normally at noon. Many establishments have pretensions of luxury in their ostentatious marble-clad lobbies, but this often contrasts sharply with the shabby state elsewhere in the hotel. As a rule, you will get more for your money away from the large cities.

Lone female travellers are very much in the minority and may be treated with puzzlement outside five-star hotels. Prostitution is obvious in many hotels in China, and some "health clubs" and "spas" are for men only. If you are staying in a hotel catering to business travellers and located outside of the main tourist areas, don't be surprised to see a price list with a basket of delightfully named "uncomplimentaries" in your room.

## ACCOMMODATION LISTINGS

*Hotels are listed in alphabetical order within price categories.*
*Towns and cities are listed in the order in which they appear in the book.*

# HONG KONG

### Hong Kong Island

**Four Seasons Hong Kong**
8 Finance St, Central
Tel: 3196 8888. Fax: 3196 8899
www.fourseasons.com
Raising the bar for luxury, this glamorous new hotel uses light and harbour views to maximum effect. Its French and Cantonese restaurants have already won international acclaim. **$$$$$**

**Grand Hyatt**
1 Harbour Rd, Wan Chai
Tel: 2261 0222. Fax: 2802 0677
www.hongkong.grand.hyatt.com
The high-rollers' hotel of choice on Hong Kong Island. This glitzy five-star hotel is adjacent to the convention centre and hence is popular with businesspeople and delegates. The luxury factor is even higher since it opened The Plateau, an amazing 7,000-sq. metre (80,000-sq. ft) spa. **$$$$$**

**Mandarin Oriental**
5 Connaught Rd, Central
Tel: 2522 0111. Fax: 2810 6190
www.mandarinoriental.com
A Hong Kong institution for the last four decades, the Mandarin holds its own in the face of competition from newer properties. Wonderful combination of impeccable service, grand atmosphere and beautiful décor. Major renovations were completed in 2006. **$$$$$**

**Conrad Hong Kong**
Pacific Place,
88 Queensway, Admiralty
Tel: 2521 3838. Fax: 2521 3888
www.conrad.com.hk
Towering above the Pacific Place complex in Admiralty, this elegant, modern business hotel is located on floors 40 to 61. Its luxurious rooms are some of the most spacious in this class. **$$$$**

**Island Shangri-La**
Pacific Place,
Supreme Court Rd, Central
Tel: 2877 3838. Fax: 2521 8742
www.shangri-la.com/island

Regularly acclaimed as one of the best hotels in Hong Kong, this is a glamorous retreat from the bustle of the city. Exceptional restaurants add to the hotel's deserved reputation. **$$$$**

**J.W. Marriott Hotel**
1 Pacific Place
88 Queensway, Admiralty
Tel: 2810 8366. Fax: 2845 0737
www.marriotthotels.com/hkgdt
Classic modern luxury hotel with Marriott's signature clear in high standards of service and smart décor. **$$$$**

**Excelsior**
281 Gloucester Rd,
Causeway Bay
Tel: 2894 8888. Fax: 2895 6459
www.mandarinoriental.com/excelsior
A very popular hotel managed by Mandarin Oriental. Great location in Causeway Bay overlooking the yacht club and harbour. Still the best four-star hotel in Hong Kong. **$$$**

**Park Lane Hong Kong**
310 Gloucester Rd,
Causeway Bay
Tel: 2293 8888. Fax: 2576 7853
www.parklane.com.hk
A tourist favourite near Victoria Park and right in the thick of the shopping district. **$$$**

**Bishop Lei International House**
4 Robinson Rd, Mid-Levels
Tel: 2868 0828. Fax: 2868 1551
www.bishopleihtl.com.hk
Small, hospitable hotel whose Mid-Levels location is extremely convenient. The best rooms have views of skyscrapers and the harbour. Budget rate is offered for the most basic rooms. **$$–$$$**

**Charterhouse**
209–219 Wan Chai Rd
Tel: 2833 5566, Fax: 2833 5888
www.charterhouse.com
Middle-of-the-road three-star hotel located on the border of Wan Chai and Causeway Bay. Compact but pleasant rooms

furnished in a neoclassical style. **$$–$$$**

**Cosmopolitan Hotel**
387–397 Queen's Rd East,
Wan Chai
Tel: 3552 1111. Fax: 3552 1122
www.cosmopolitanhotel.com.hk
A four-star hotel with a contemporary feel. Guests booking with the hotel are guaranteed a full 24 hours for their money, regardless of check-in time. **$$**

**Emperor (Happy Valley)**
1 Wang Tak St, Happy Valley
Tel: 2893 3693. Fax: 2834 6700
www.emperorhotel.com.hk
Tucked away in a residential part of Happy Valley, close to the racecourse. Good value – if you can bear to be more than five minutes from the city centre. **$$**

**Novotel Century Harbourview**
508 Queen's Rd West, Western
Tel: 2974 1234. Fax: 2974 0333
www.accorhotels-asia.com
In the heart of Western District, the Novotel is comfortable, bright and modern. Rooftop pool with interesting views. **$$**

**Novotel Century Hong Kong**
238 Jaffe Rd, Wan Chai
Tel: 2598 8888. Fax: 2598 8866
www.accorhotels-asia.com
A good-value choice in this price bracket. Undistinguished, but a convenient good-quality hotel midway between Wan Chai and Causeway Bay. **$$**

**The Wesley**
22 Hennessy Rd, Wan Chai
Tel: 2866 6688. Fax: 2866 6633
www.hanglung.com
A location between the shopping centres of Admiralty and the Wan Chai nightlife is a big plus for this hotel. Bright welcoming lobby, limited dining facilities. **$$**

**Wharney Guangdong Hotel**
57–73 Lockhart Rd, Wan Chai
Tel: 2861 1000. Fax: 2865 1010
www.gdhhotels.com
Good-value business hotel located in the heart of the

Wan Chai entertainment district. **$$**

**Ibis North Point**
138 Java Rd, North Point
Tel: 2588 1111. Fax: 2204 6677
www.accorhotels-asia.com/
This neat, clean, no-frills modern hotel has proved popular with tourists and business travellers.**$**

**Mount Davis Youth Hostel**
Mount Davis, Western District
Tel: 2788 3105. Fax: 2788 1638
www.yha.org.hk
Basic accommodation with a beautiful hilltop location and wonderful harbour views. Free shuttle bus to/from Central (Shun Tak Centre; runs approximately every two hours). **$**

### Kowloon

**InterContinental**
18 Salisbury Rd, Tsim Sha Tsui
Tel: 2721 1211. Fax: 2739 4546
www.interconti.com
Formerly the Regent, this is the most glamorous modern hotel on the Tsim Sha Tsui waterfront. Delightful rooms, wonderful harbour views, exceptional restaurants and superb spa. **$$$$$**

**The Peninsula**
Salisbury Rd, Tsim Sha Tsui
Tel: 2920 2888. Fax: 2722 4170
www.peninsula.com
Established in the 1920s,

### PRICE CATEGORIES

$: under HK$500
$$: HK$500–1,000
$$$: HK$1,000–1,500
$$$$: HK$1,500–2,000
$$$$$: over HK$2,000
Prices are for a standard double room at peak season (no breakfast)

PRICE CATEGORIES

PRICE CATEGORIES

$: under HK$500
$$: HK$500–1,000
$$$: HK$1,000–1,500
$$$$: HK$1,500–2,000
$$$$$: over HK$2,000
Prices are for a standard
double room at peak
season (no breakfast)

The Pen is Hong Kong's only
historic hotel and arguably
the best. Potted palms and
string quartets in the lobby;
world-class restaurants and
bars, plus a Clarins spa –
this place oozes class and
elegance. The ultimate
choice. $$$$$

**Kowloon Hotel**
19–21 Nathan Rd,
Tsim Sha Tsui
Tel: 2929 2888. Fax: 2739 9811
www.thekowloonhotel.com
Across the road from The
Peninsula, this is a good
hotel in an excellent
location. $$$$

**Kowloon Shangri-La**
64 Mody Rd, Tsim Sha Tsui East
Tel: 2721 2111. Fax: 2723 8686
www.shangri-la.com/kowloon
Superb luxury hotel on Tsim
Sha Tsui waterfront.
Excellent restaurants and
views. Short walk to KCR
and MTR stations and Star
Ferry. $$$$

**Langham Hotel**
8 Peking Rd, Tsim Sha Tsui
Tel: 2375 1133. Fax: 2375 6611
www.langhamhotels.com
Solid five-star hotel with
handy location close to Star
Ferry, China Ferry and
cruise terminal. Five
minutes from railway
stations. $$$$

**Langham Place Hotel**
555 Shanghai St, Mong Kok
Tel: 3552 3388. Fax: 2384 3670
www.langhamhotels.com/
langhamplace/
This glamorous new hotel
is leading the revival of
Mong Kok with five-star
class. Plush rooms feature
the latest technology, which
contrasts with striking art,
sculpture and architecture
reflecting Chinese tradition.
$$$$

**Marco Polo Gateway**
Harbour City, 13 Canton Rd,
Tsim Sha Tsui
Tel: 2113 0888. Fax: 2113 0022
www.marcopolohotels.com
A good-quality tourist hotel,
part of the Harbour City
shopping centre and cruise
terminal. $$$$

**Sheraton Hong Kong Hotel
& Towers**
20 Nathan Rd, Tsim Sha Tsui
Tel: 2369 1111. Fax: 2739 8707
www.sheraton.com/hongkong

Lively five-star hotel close
to Star Ferry, KCR, MTR
and Nathan Road shopping
areas. Great restaurants
and bars, popular with
locals, tourists and
business travellers alike.
$$$$

**Holiday Inn Golden Mile**
50 Nathan Rd, Tsim Sha Tsui
Tel: 2369 3111. Fax: 2369 8016
www.goldenmile.com
Ever-popular tourist hotel in
the middle of Nathan Road
– the tourist golden mile of
Tsim Sha Tsui. $$$

**The Minden**
7 Minden Ave, Tsim Sha Tsui
Tel: 2739 7777. Fax: 2739 3777
www.theminden.com
Small, friendly boutique
hotel in the heart of Tsim
Sha Tsui's newest nightlife
district. The European feel
is enhanced by a terrace
bar-restaurant. Functional
and comfortable
accommodation. Quality
fabrics and original art add
a luxurious touch. $$$

**Miramar**
118–130 Nathan Rd,
Tsim Sha Tsui
Tel: 2368 1111. Fax: 2369 1788
www.miramarhk.com
An unpretentious and
friendly hotel with an indoor
pool, in the heart of things

a stone's throw away from
Tsim Sha Tsui's best bars
and restaurants. $$$

**Kimberley Hotel**
28 Kimberley Rd, Tsim Sha Tsui
Tel: 2723 3888. Fax: 2723 1318
www.kimberleyhotel.com.hk
Reliable three-star hotel,
two minutes from bustling
Nathan Road. There's a
good choice of restaurants
and bars in nearby
Knutsford Terrace. $$

**The Salisbury YMCA**
41 Salisbury Rd, Tsim Sha Tsui
Tel: 2268 7000. Fax: 2739 9315
www.ymcahk.org.hk
Book ahead at this
upmarket YMCA. Rooms are
hotel-style and many enjoy
panoramic views of the
harbour. Large indoor pool,
good restaurant and a range
of sports and child-friendly
facilities. Great location,
too. $$

**Chungking House**
4&5/F Block A, Chungking
Mansions, 40 Nathan Rd,
Tsim Sha Tsui
Tel: 2366 5362. Fax: 2721 3570
There are cheaper deals in
the area, but in the dark
corridors and grim
stairwells of Chungking
Mansions this is the only
establishment approved by
the HKTB. $–$$

# MACAU

## City

**Mandarin Oriental Macau**
956–1110 Avda Amizade
Tel: 2856 7888. Fax: 2859 4589
www.mohg.com
The Mandarin remains
Macau's classiest hotel.
Full five-star facilities and
superb spa in garden
setting. $$$$$

**Grand Emperor Hotel**
288 Avda Comercial de Macau
Tel: 2888 9988. Fax: 2888 9933
www.grandemperor.com

PRICE CATEGORIES

$: under MOP$500
$$: MOP$500–1,000
$$$: MOP$1,000–1,500
$$$$: MOP$1,500–2,000
$$$$$: over MOP$2,000
Prices are for a standard
double room at peak
season (no breakfast)

Luxurious new hotel (and
casino) overlooking Nam
Van Lake with its
mesmerising fountain. Part
of the new breed of themed
Vegas-style hotels, the
Grand Emperor attempts to
recreate the style and
elegance of historic
European palaces. $$$$

**Pousada de São Tiago**
Avda da Republica
Tel: 2837 8111. Fax: 2855 2170
www.saotiago.com.mo
This piece of Macanese
history includes part of a
17th-century Portuguese
fortress built for its
commanding views. Dark
wood, marble, chandeliers
and white linen add to the
historic ambience. Good
restaurants, an outdoor
swimming pool and a
delightful terrace. $$$$

**Lisboa**
2–4 Avda de Lisboa
Tel: 2837 7666. Fax: 2856 7193
www.hotelisboa.com
Despite being
overshadowed by the
opening of its near-
namesake, the enormous
Grand Lisboa) in late 2007,
this gaudy hotel remains
something of an icon of
Macau, and famous for its
casino. Rooms are grand
and the décor highly ornate.
$$$

**Ritz Hotel**
Rua do Comendador,
Kou Ho Neng
Tel: 2833 9955. Fax: 2831 7826
www.ritzhotel.com.mo
Small luxury hotel with five-
star facilities located on
Penha Hill. The bland exterior
belies ornate, spacious
interiors. Many rooms have

good views. Facilities include
mini-golf, squash and tennis.
$$$

**Hotel Royal**
2–4 Estr da Vitoria
Tel: 2855 2222. Fax: 2856 3008
www.hotelroyal.com.mo
Convenient mid-range hotel
at the foot of the Colina da
Guia, in a quiet area close
to the centre. Spacious,
rooms and indoor pool. $$$

**Pousada de Mong Ha**
Colina de Mong-Ha
Tel: 2851 5222. Fax: 2855 6925

www.ift.edu.mo/pousada/
Tucked away on a hillside below 19th-century ruins, this romantic boutique hotel has beautifully decorated rooms with Portuguese and Oriental style. Great value. **$$**

**Hotel Sintra**
Avda D. João IV
Tel: 2871 0111. Fax: 2851 0527
www.hotelsintra.com
Sister hotel to the Lisboa, the Sintra is a pleasant, low-key three-star alternative. Rooms were renovated in 2004 and are large and comfortably

furnished. An excellent location for central Macau. A shuttle runs to the Lisboa. **$$**

## Taipa/Coloane

**Venetian Resort Hotel Macau**
Cotai strip. Tel: 2882 8888.
www.venetian-macao.com
Lavish new hotel in this spectacular themed resort complex on the Cotai strip. The gigantic space includes some 3,000 suites featuring Italian marble fittings, over 30 restaurants and 350

shops. And a casino, of course. **$$$–$$$$**

**Westin Resort**
1918 Estrada de Hac Sa, Coloane
Tel: 2887 1111. Fax: 2887 1122
www.westin-macau.com
Luxury hotel overlooking the sea. Guest rooms terrace down towards the beach, and the extensive recreation facilities include an 18-hole golf course on the resort's roof, and a spa. **$$$–$$$$**

**Grand View Hotel**
142 Estr Governador Albano de Oliveira, Taipa
Tel: 2883 7788. Fax: 2883 7777

www.grandview-hotel.com
De luxe hotel in the heart of Taipa Island. Great value, and fascinating views of Macau Jockey Club's racetrack. Handy for the airport. **$$$**

**Pousada de Coloane**
Praia de Cheoc Van, Coloane. Tel: 2888 2144. Fax: 2888 2251
www.hotelpcoloane.com.mo/
A long-time favourite with Hong Kong residents, recent renovations have greatly brightened up this family-run hotel that provides a peaceful retreat. **$$**

# SHENZHEN & THE PEARL RIVER DELTA

## Shenzhen

**Crowne Plaza**
9026 Shennan Xilu
Shenzhen 518053
Tel: 0755 2693 6888
Fax: 0755 2693 6999
www.crowneplaza.com
With a faux European shopping arcade and a style to resemble that of a Venetian building, the 400-room Crowne Plaza is Shenzhen's first five-star themed hotel – and reminiscent of the Las Vegas-style behemoths springing up in Macau. Located to the west of town, close to the theme parks. **$$$$**

**Four Points by Sheraton Shenzhen**
Futian Free Trade Zone
5 Guihua Lu
Shenzhen 518038
Tel: 0755 8359 9999
Fax: 0755 8359 2988
www.fourpoints.com
A 10- minute walk from Huanggang port – China's busiest land port – the well-appointed Sheraton comes equipped with supremely comfortable beds. **$$$$**

**Holiday Inn Donghua Shenzhen**
Donghua Park, Nanyu Lu
Shenzhen 518053
Tel: 0755 8619 3999
Fax: 0755 2664 5282
www.ichotelsgroup.com
The 352-room Holiday Inn was the first international hotel to venture into the

Nanshan district, Shenzhen's theme-park centre. **$$$$**

**Marco Polo**
Temeisi Plaza
Fuhua Yilu, Futian CBD
Shenzhen 518048
Tel: 0755 8291 0114
Fax: 0755 8291 0129
www.marcopolohotels.com
The 391-room Marco Polo first opened its doors in August 2006. Well located in Futian district, one of Shenzhen's major shopping areas. **$$$$**

**Novotel Bauhinia Shenzhen Hotel**
Qiaocheng Donglu
Shenzhen 518040
Tel: 0755 8282 9966
Fax: 0755 8282 9111
www.novotel.com
Well-appointed hotel close to Shenzhen HighTech Industrial Park and the China International Garden and Flower Exhibition. **$$$$**

**Best Western Shenzhen Felicity Hotel**
1085 Heping Lu
Shenzhen 518010
Tel: 0755 2558 6333
Fax: 0755 2556 1700
www.bwsz.net
Hong Kong's Lo Wu border is just minutes away from this standard upper mid-range hotel. Overlooks Hong Kong and the Shenzhen River. **$$$**

**Nanhai Hotel**
1 Gongye Yilu
Nanhai Boulevard, Shekou

Shenzhen 518069
Tel: 0755 2669 2888
Fax: 0755 2669 2440
Conveniently located for Shenzhen Airport and the jetfoil to Hong Kong, this hotel has a good range of facilities, including a swimming pool. **$$$**

**Hailian Hotel**
12 Yingchun Lu
Shenzhen 518005
Tel: 0755 2518 0888
Fax: 0755 2518 0218
In the Lo Wu district near the border, the Hailian is probably the best three-star choice in Shenzhen. **$$**

## Dongguan

**Sheraton Dongguan Hotel**
5256 Provincial Highway
Houjie Town
Dongguan 523962
Tel: 0769 8598 8888
Fax: 0769 8590 8888
www.sheraton.com
For those who love to shop, the choice in Dongguan is obviously the 500-room Sheraton, adjacent to Ming Cheng shopping centre in the heart of the busy Houjie district. **$$$**

## Zhongshan

**Shangri-La**
16 Qiwan Beilu
Eastern Area, Zhongshan
Tel: 0760 838 6888
Fax: 0760 838 6666
www.Shangri-la.com
Located in the middle of

Zhongshan and 15 minutes from the port, this 463-room hotel is the best place to stay in town. **$$$$**

## Zhuhai

**Harbour View Hotel and Resort**
47 Middle Lover's Lane
Zhuhai 519015
Tel: 0756 332 2288
Fax: 0756 337 1385
www.harbourviewhotel.com/eng/jdjs
Just five minutes from Jiuzhou Ferry Terminal, the 381-room Harbour View is a self-contained hotel with excellent recreational facilities. **$$**

## PRICE CATEGORIES

Price categories are for a standard double room in high season (no breakfast):
**$** = under US$30 (Rmb 240)
**$$** = US$30–50 (Rmb 240–400)
**$$$** = US$50–100 (Rmb 400–800)
**$$$$** = US$100–150 (Rmb 800–1200)
**$$$$$** = over US$150 (Rmb 1200)

TRANSPORT

ACCOMMODATION

ACTIVITIES

A – Z

LANGUAGE

# GUANGZHOU

**China Marriott Hotel**
Liuhua Lu
Guangzhou 510015
Tel: 020 8666 6888
Fax: 020 8667 7288
www.Marriott.com
The lobby is always busy, which is not surprising considering this hotel is directly opposite the China Trade Exhibition Centre and is one of the rare few in Guangzhou with direct metro access. **$$$$**

**Dong Fang Hotel**
120 Liuhua Lu
Guangzhou 510016
Tel: 020 8666 9900
Fax: 020 8666 2775
www.dongfanghotel-gz.com
For a hotel with character and an old-style feel, there's none better in Guangzhou than the Dong Fang, with gardens inviting enough to attract even non-walkers. **$$$$**

**Shangri-La Pazhou**
Suite 2001, North Tower, The Hub
1068 Xingang Donglu
Hai Zhu District
Guangzhou 510335
Tel: 020 8923 1188
Fax: 020 8923 1185
www.shangri-la.com
If you are in town for business, you can't beat the 730-room Shangri-La Pazhou, which opened late 2006, right on the doorstep of the mass transit railway. **$$$$**

**White Swan Hotel**
1 South Shamian Island
Guangzhou 510133
Tel: 020 8188 6968
Fax: 020 8186 1188
www.whiteswanhotel.com
With its atrium lobby encapsulating Southern China's most famed landscapes, the White Swan Hotel captures the spirit of historic Shamian Island. **$$$$**

**Asia International Hotel**
326 Section 1, Huanshi Donglu
Guangzhou 510060
Tel: 020 6128 8888
Fax: 020 6120 6666
www.aihotel.com
Resembling a brightly lit spaceship, Asia International's Sky Café Revolving Restaurant is the city's highest, and offers the most panoramic views of the city. **$$$**

**Chime Long Hotel**
Yingbin Lu, Panyu
Guangzhou 511430
Tel: 020 8478 6838
www.chimelonghotel.com
Home to two (caged) white tigers and a flock of flamingos, the lobby of the Chime Long Hotel resembles the Safari and Crocodile Park just outside the hotel's gate. **$$$**

**Donlord International Hotel**
63 Guangzhou Bei Dadao, Tianhe
Guangzhou 510040
Tel: 020 8333 8989
Fax: 020 8335 0467
www.donlord-international-hotel-guangzhou.hotelgate24.com
This 239-room hotel is well-equipped for families and business travellers, and conveniently located for the Tianhe shops, the scenic Baiyun hills and Guangzhou's East Railway Station. **$$$**

**The Garden Hotel**
368 Huanshi Donglu
Guangzhou 510064
Tel: 020 8333 8989
Fax: 020 8335 0467
www.gardenhotel-guangzhou.com
The Garden Hotel's rooms soothe the senses with their restful colour schemes, as does the garden, where guests are invited to listen to the sounds of the waterfall. **$$$**

**Hotel Landmark Canton**
8 Qiaoguang Lu
Haizhu Square
Guangzhou 510115
Tel: 020 8335 5988
Fax: 020 8333 6197
www.hotel-landmark.com.cn
Located right on the Pearl River and in the middle of Haizhu Square, the 672-room Hotel Landmark also includes apartments and offices. **$$$**

**Rosedale Hotel & Suites**
348 Jiang Nanda Zhonglu
Guangzhou 510245
Tel: 020 8441 8888
Fax: 020 8442 9645
www.rosedalegz.com.cn
The only four-star hotel in the Haizhu district, this 399-room Sino-foreign joint venture prides itself on its philosophy of "considerate service". **$$$**

**China Merchants Hotel**
111-8 Liuhua Lu
Guangzhou 510010
Tel: 020 3622 2988
Fax: 020 3622 2680
www.cbw.com
Facing Liu Hua Lake, the 240-room China Merchants Hotel is handy for business as it is located right next to the Chinese Export Commodities Fair. **$$**

**Globelink Hotel**
208 Yuexiu Nanlu
Guangzhou 510100
Tel: 020 8389 8888
Fax: 020 8389 8866
www.globelinkhotel.com.cn
The 247-room Globelink is right next to a complex containing 800 restaurants, bars and other entertainment venues. **$$**

**Guangzhou Haitao Hotel**
208–210 Huangpu Lu
West Tianhe District
Guangzhou 510623
Tel: 020 8759 8888
Fax: 020 8759 5030
www.miramar-group.com
The Haitao's main attraction is its centrality: this 156-room hotel, part of the Miramar group, is just a few minutes' walk from the heart of the city. **$$**

**Liuhua Hotel**
194 Huanshi Xilu
Guangzhou 510017
Tel: 020 8666 8888
Fax: 020 8666 7828
www.lh.com.cn
The 414-room Liuhua is close to the biggest apparel wholesale market in southern China and the Chinese Export Commodities Fair Complex, thus placing it in the city's logistic centre. **$$**

**Ocean Hotel**
Longkou Xilu
Guangzhou 510061
Tel: 020 8759 6988
Fax: 020 8759 7988
www.oceanhotel.com.cn
Close to the airport, the Ocean Hotel has geared itself towards business travellers with its extensive conference facilities, but those with a hankering for snooker can also indulge themselves here. **$$**

# ELSEWHERE IN GUANGDONG

## Qingyuan

**Royal Crown Hotel**
8 Fengming Lu
Tel: 0763 387 8888
The new Royal Crown Hotel is located in the southern half of town, beside the main bus station. It's one of the new breed of clean and comfortable middle-price bracket Chinese hotels, and very convenient if you are taking the morning bus to Feilaixia. **$$**

## Shaoguan

**Royal Regent Hotel**
2 Beijiang Lu
Tel: 0751 821 0218
The Royal Regent Hotel is a cut above the average three-star hotel in terms of

interior design, with small rooms furnished in pleasing contemporary style. Its location is also good, just south of the railway station forecourt and overlooking the river. **$$**

## Chaozhou

**Chaozhou Hotel**
Crossroads of Chaofeng Lu and Yonghu Lu
Tel: 0768 233 3333
Chaozhou's high rollers hang out at the large and opulent Chaozhou Hotel, their expensive cars blocking the pavement outside. The lobby is suitably grand, and the hotel incorporates restaurants, a gym and conference rooms. Easy to find, directly opposite the bus station. **$$**

## Shantou

**Grand Harbour View Hotel**
18 Haibin Lu
Tel: 0754 854 3838
The recently renovated Grand Harbour View Hotel

stands beside the Stone Fort at the eastern end of the waterfront promenade. The guest rooms and restaurants enjoy sea views. **$$**
**Shantou Guest House**
10 Haibin Lu
Tel: 0754 891 8593
The Shantou Guest House is made up of a group of low-rise buildings in a garden set back from the promenade. Although lacking direct sea views, it is friendly, peaceful and within walking distance of the ferry pier. **$**.

## Huizhou

**West Lake Hotel**
10 Haibin Lu
Tel: 0754 891 8593
The West Lake Hotel occupies a prime spot overlooking Huizhou's famous water feature. Although its lobby is somewhat redolent of the 1980s, the building is well maintained. The restaurants on the higher floors have some of the

city's best views across the lake. **$$**
**South Hotel**
12 Erling Beilu
Tel: 0752 227 7888
The South Hotel is opposite the bus station but still within walking distance of West Lake. Rooms are large, clean and good value. **$**

## Kaiping

**New World Hotel**
62 Shuguang Xilu
Tel: 0750 850 7777
Of the several hotels clustered around Kaiping's long-distance bus station, the New World is the newest and smartest (which isn't saying much). One end of the hotel is above a very noisy karaoke bar, so ask for a quiet room to ensure a good night's sleep. **$**

## Yangchun

**Yue Hua Hotel**
40 Donghu Xilu
Tel: 0662 776 8888
The largest-scale hostelry in Yangchun, the Yue Hua

Hotel is located in the centre of the town's shopping area. As well as Chinese and Western restaurants it has an in-house foot-massage centre. **$$**
**Golden Roc Hotel**
2 Chengdong Dao
Tel: 0662 773 8889
The Golden Roc Hotel is used by Western couples visiting to adopt local children, and as such it is accustomed to English-speaking guests. Convenient for buses to Chunwan. **$$**

## Zhanjiang

**Hai Bin Hotel**
32 Haibinsan Lu
Xiashan
Tel: 0759 228 6888.
Set in gardens at the northern end of the waterfront, the Hai Bin Hotel claims to be the largest in western Guangdong, and plays host to visiting state leaders. Rooms are large and come with sea views. **$$$**

# HAINAN ISLAND

## Haikou

**HNA Hotel**
Haikou International Commercial Centre, 38 Datong Lu
Tel: 0898 6679 6999
hkhicc@public.hk.hi.cn
Spacious rooms and public areas and a landscaped garden all add up to proper four-star qualities. In the heart of Haikou's financial

and municipal centre, the location is also great for shops and restaurants. **$$$**
**Sheraton Haikou Resort**
199 Binhai Lu, Haikou
Tel: 0898 6870 8888
www.sheraton.com/haikou
For a laid-back location fronting a sandy coast, a few minutes from Holiday Beach and a just a few more into the city centre,

this resort is a first for Haikou, offering genuine fine dining and a cigar bar. A snooker table, spa and sprawling sea-view pool add to its allure. **$$$**
**International Financial (Jasper) Hotel**
29 Datong Lu
Tel: 0898 6653 6999
www.jasperhotels.com.cn
This downtown Haikou 234-room hotel, at the junction of the city's main thoroughfares, claims to be four-star but is closer to three. Clean and comfortable with friendly staff, though; get past the cherub-studded fountain at its entrance and you are onto a winner. **$$**

## Qixianling

**Paradise Rainforest Spa & Resort**
Qixianling National Forest Reserve, Baoting County

Tel: 0898 8388 8888
www.hainanparadise.com
Probably the island's best non-coastal spa nestles under the seven jagged

## PRICE CATEGORIES

Price categories are for a standard double room in high season (no breakfast):
**$** = under US$30 (Rmb 240)
**$$** = US$30–50 (Rmb 240–400)
**$$$** = US$50–100 (Rmb 400–800)
**$$$$** = US$100–150 (Rmb 800–1,200)
**$$$$$** = over US$150 (Rmb 1,200)

**BELOW:** resort accommodation at Yalong Bay.

TRANSPORT
ACCOMMODATION
ACTIVITIES
A – Z
LANGUAGE

peaks of Mount Qixianling. Private balcony hot-spring-fed tubs are standard, and landcaped public pools are plentiful. An exceptional Chinese restaurant offers some lesser-known Hainanese specialities. **$$$**

### Dongjiao

**Hainan Prima Resort**
Yelin Bay, Wenchang
Tel: 0898 6353 8222
www.hainanprimaresort.com
The best of Dongjiao's beachfront accommodation offers small low-rise blocks or wooden bungalows, up to three-star standard. A good restaurant, friendly staff, and fishing and aquatic activities all add up to a winner. **$$**

### Sanya Area

**Eadry Resort**
Yuya Lu, Sanya City
Tel: 0898 8860 9999
www.eadryresort.com
Billed as a five-star hotel, this is not far off. With views over the fishing harbour and of Liuhuitou Hill, Eadry is in the heart of Sanya City, with main shopping streets five minutes away on foot. A very good restaurant and polite, helpful staff make staying here a pleasure. **$$$**

### Dadonghai

**Rendezvous Baohong Hotel**
18 Haiyun Lu
Tel: 0898 8898 9221
Contemporary comfort rules in this new resort. Interior décor and outdoor pool make a pleasant setting. **$$$**

**Royal Garden Resort Hotel**
Luling Lu
Tel: 0898 8822 8888
A few steps away from Dadonghai beach, which can be seen from many balconies. This popular hotel is spotlessly clean, if a little lacking in character. **$$**

### Yalong Bay

**Hilton Sanya Resort & Spa**
Yalong Bay National Resort District
Tel: 0898 8858 8588

www.sanya.hilton.com
The most stylish of the big three consecutive international resorts, right on Yalong Bay, although the downside of its chic rooms – chocolate-brown and ivory, with orange highlights – is the slightly smaller size. A sprawling spa, with lots of open areas, is secluded from the rest of the resort. **$$$$$**

**Marriott Sanya Resort & Spa**
Yalong Bay National Resort District
Tel: 0898 8856 8888
marriott.com/SYXMC
Very open and tropical in design, from the moment you step into the breezy lobby with its whirling ceiling fans. Like at the Hilton and the Sheraton, there is a kids' club and swimming pool, making it a good family choice. Bright rooms offer free broadband for laptop users. The new Quan spa is well rated. **$$$$$**

**Sheraton Sanya Resort**
Yalong Bay National Resort District
Tel: 0898 8855 8855
www.sheraton.com/sanya

Currently the only hotel in the vicinity with a shopping arcade, the Sheraton is where the Miss World candidates stayed when Sanya hosted three competitions a few years ago. Mature grounds and clever landscaping makes corners of the garden and resort pool feel secluded. Rooms are much plainer than the grand lobby. **$$$$$**

### Nanshan

**Tree House**
Nanshan Park
Tel: 0898 8883 7936
www.treehousesofhawaii.com
Bring out your inner child, or bring the children to possibly Hainan's most unusual accommodation, built into tamarind trees along a sand dune behind virgin beach, in Nan Shan Park itself. Rooms are spartan but, like the shared bathrooms, well kept. Ventilation is natural, and all windows have insect screens. Restaurant and on-site security. **$$$$**

# FUJIAN

### Xiamen

**Marco Polo Xiamen**
8 Jianye Lu, Hubin Bei
Tel: 0592 509 1888
www.marcopolohotels.com
Good location in the north of the city alongside Xiamen's City Hall and Cultural Centre. Dragonair and Cathay Pacific offices, Bally and Max Mara shops set the tone for this gracefully ageing hotel facing Yuandang Lake. **$$$$$**

**Sheraton**
386-1 Jiahe Lu
Tel: 0592 552 5888
www.sheraton.com/xiamen
Opened in mid-2006, this is Xiamen's first hotel with spectacular glass staircase, 48 suites, a two-storey presidential suite, internationally managed spa, Wine and Cigar Bar and one of Asia's longest international Open Kitchen buffet spreads. **$$$$$**

**Xianglu Grand**
18 Changhao Lu, Huli District
Tel: 0592 569 9555
www.xianglugrand.com
Everything looks inward in this 1,500-room hotel built around a huge enclosed landscaped atrium. Opened in 2006, it is geared to large-scale conventions and weddings, with promised live entertainment, massive spa, fitness centre and 25-metre (82-ft) swimming pool. **$$$$$**

**Crowne Plaza Harbourview**
12-8 Zhenhai Lu
Tel: 0592 202 3333
www.crowneplaza.com
This was Xiamen's first internationally managed hotel, but pioneer days are past and it is beginning to show its age. Nonetheless, it remains a comfortable place to stay. **$$$$**

**International Seaside**
199 Island Ring Road
Tel: 0592 595 9999
www.seaside.cn

Set on green lawns, low-rise buildings with big balconies overlook the Taiwan Straits. The hotel's connection by enclosed corridor to the International Conference and Exhibition Centre ensures full-house signs at trade-fair times. **$$$$**

**Mandarin**
101 Yuehua Lu, Huli District
Tel: 0592 602 3333
www.xmmandarin.com
Famous for its chateau-style main building and its night-time bright lights, bar and karaoke. The garden setting is unrivalled: 7,000 sq. metres (8,400 sq. yds) of private grounds scattered with quiet villas. **$$$$**

**Lujiang Harbourview**
54 Lujiang Lu
Tel: 0592 202 2922
Fax: 0592 202 4644
www.lujiang-hotel.com
This 1920s old-colonial-style hotel faces the Gulangyu Ferry and backs onto Xiamen's pedestrian

shopping street. Exquisitely renovated in 2004, it incorporates WiFi and other 21st-century amenities while maintaining the original ambience. Even the cheapest rooms are great value, but splash out on a sea-view suite for at least one night in a vast room with open balcony. **$$$**

**Huaqiao**
70–74 Xinhua Lu
Tel: 0592 266 0888
www.xmhqhotel.com.cn
This cavernous, state-owned time-warp of a hotel offers what is probably the city's cheapest presidential suite (US$100 in 2006) and a nightclub managed by Hong

**ABOVE:** Xiamen's Lujiang Hotel.

Kong entrepreneurs who describe it as Xiamen's "most luxurious, offering you comfort and joy". **$**

### Yongding

**Ke Lai Deng Hotel**
Yongding Earth Building, National Culture Village
Tel: 0597 553 1295
kelaideng@163.com
www.ydtu.com/jiudian22.asp
Very basic, but the best option hereabouts. Bring your own toiletries, toilet paper and towel. The family who run it are very friendly, even proffering a bilingual menu for your evening meal – which is killed and cooked while you wait. Ideal location only one minute's walk from the largest Tulou village. **$**

### Quanzhou

**Quanzhou Hotel**
22 Zhuang Fu Xiang
Tel: 0595 2228 9958
www.quanzhouhotel.com
Soviet-style rambling buildings offer few creature comforts apart from outstanding local food. If the old building is too spartan for your taste, ask to see a room in the new one. **$$$**

### Fuzhou

**Shangri-La**
9 Xinquan Nanlu
Tel: 0591 8798 8888
Fax: 0591 8711 9148
www.shangri-la.com
Opened in 2006, this hotel sets a high standard for all the newcomers queuing to open in Fuzhou. Expect to find all the de luxe touches associated with Asia's favourite brand and a few local extras, like miniature jasmine shrubs blooming in your room. **$$$$**

**Golden Resources International**
59 Wenquan Gongyuan Lu
Tel: 0591 708 8888
Good choice for the discerning in the city's financial and commercial centre, next to Fuzhou International Exhibition Centre and surrounded by the Hot Spring Park. **$$$**

**International Seaman's Club**
8 Luoxingta Lu, Mawei District
Tel: 0591 8368 2276
Rooms and food are very local, and it's at least a half-hour bus ride to the city centre, but the place is clean and inexpensive.

Extras include darts, gym, garden and history on all sides: this is where the opium was burnt during the Opium Wars and it is also on the doorstep of Mao Wei Shipyard, the cradle of China's modern shipbuilding industry. **$**

### Wuyishan

**Mountain Villa**
Wuyi Palace, Wuyigong
Tel: 0599 525 1888
Visiting VIPs stay in the best of these interlocking low-rise buildings that blend beautifully into the landscape, with birdsong and chattering waterfalls providing the background music. A strong contender for inclusion among China's best hotels for its ambience, facilities and service. **$$$$**

**Scenery Golf Club**
Wuyishan Tourism Resort
Tel: 0599 523 6587
www.wysgolf.com
Golfers will appreciate this 123-room clubhouse, where balconies overlook the 27-hole international golf course. **$$$$**

**Shanghai Yun'An**
Wuyishan County Tourism District
Tel: 0599 525 3789
Its riverside setting makes this small and friendly hotel uniquely attractive. However, it also boasts the best electronic equipment in the city thanks to the electronics factory that has invested heavily in it. If possible, take

an executive room overlooking the river. **$$$**

**Yi Li**
12 Huandao Lu,
County Tourism Holiday Resort
Tel: 0599 525 2358
This hotel is geared to Chinese tour groups, but mid-week off-season, it's virtually deserted. Sit in solitary splendour in the echoing dining room as you sample a traditional Chinese breakfast (tip: bring your own supply if you need a morning caffeine jolt or muesli). Rooms are basic, but all have en suite bathrooms and free broadband. **$$$**

**Tea Hotel**
National Tourist Resort
Tel: 0599 525 6777
www.fujian-tea.com
This traditional courtyard style hotel encloses meandering streams and tea-houses in Japanese, Korean and Taipei style. Leisure options include disco and billiards. Good value for the abundant atmosphere. **$$**

# JIANGXI

### Nanchang

**Gloria Plaza Hotel**
88 Yanjiang Beilu
Tel: 0791 673 8855
Fax: 0791 673 8533
www.gphnanchang.com
Well-maintained, five-star chain hotel that attracts foreign businesspeople and Western couples planning to adopt Chinese babies. Rooms are spacious with king-sized beds, and many command excellent views of the Ganjiang and

Tengwang Pavilion. The café has good-value buffet breakfasts, lunches and dinners. **$$$**

**Ruidu Hotel**
399 Guangchang Nanlu
Tel: 0791 620 1888
Fax: 0791 620 1999
Situated on Bayi Square's southeastern corner, next to the Bank of China, this four-star hotel has reasonably priced doubles, many with sweeping views of the square. Expansive suites are great value, with

airy living areas and an extra children's bedroom. **$$$**

**Jiu Jiu Long Hotel**
122 Bayi Dadao
Tel: 0791 886 6555
Fax: 0791 629 5299
Just across the road from the long-distance bus station and a short walk from the train station, this delightful three-star hotel is Nanchang's best bargain, with slick doubles, conscientious staff and breakfast included in the

room rate. Ideal for independent travellers. **$**

**Wenhua Gong Hotel**
222 Xiangshan Beilu
Tel: 0791 678 6966
Fax: 0791 678 6976
Features a curious

assortment of cavernous rooms, many fitted with amazing period furniture. While ageing slightly, the de luxe rooms and suites are good value. $

### Jiujiang

**S&N International Hotel**
116 Nanhu Lu
Tel: 0792 877 8999
Fax: 0792 877 8000
www.yuanzhou.com.cn
Owned by the Smile & Natural Group, this five-star hotel is great value, with giant, airy rooms and heavenly king-sized beds. Most doubles have views of Nan Lake in the city centre, and breakfast and internet access is included in the room rate. $$$

**Chevalier Hotel**
68 Binjiang Lu
Tel: 0792 823 3388
Fax: 0792 812 1288
In the heart of Jiujiang near the Yangzi's fortified banks, this four-star hotel is reasonably priced, with large rooms offering the town's best views of the legendary river. All rooms have computers that can access the internet for a Rmb 50 surcharge. $$

### Lushan (Guling)

**Lushan Hotel**
70 Hexi Lu
Tel: 0792 829 5201
Fax: 0792 828 1330
www.lushanhotel.cn
A 15-minute walk south down scenic Hexi Lu from the bus station and the centre of Guling village, this is the best conventional hotel in the Lushan area, with breezy, well-furnished standard rooms in a large stone mansion. The affordable suites yield great views of the surrounding greenery. $$

**Lushan Villa Hotel**
182 Zhihong Lu
Tel: 0792 828 2927
Fax: 0792 828 2387
In a quiet garden behind the sprawling Meilu Villa complex, and accessible via a side street just off Hedong Lu – a 10-minute walk south of the bus station – is this collection of quaint rooms in renovated stone and wood cottages first built in 1896 by the American Protestant Episcopal Church. $$

**Guling Hotel**
7 Hexi Lu
Tel: 0792 829 5388
Fax: 0792 828 2209

About 150metres/yds down Hexi Lu from the bus station, and opposite the pedestrian mall that leads to Guling Jie, this comfortable hotel is the easiest to find without the help of a taxi driver and is a short walk from Guling village. $

### Jingdezhen

**Jinsheng Hotel**
71 Zhushan Zhonglu
Tel: 0798 827 1818
Fax: 0798 827 1158
Though only a two-star establishment, the Jinsheng's best rooms feel a notch higher and can often be had at steep discounts. The restaurant serves up tasty Chinese standards, and the hotel is only a 10-minute walk from the main porcelain market. $

### Jinggangshan (Ciping)

**Eden Plaza Hotel**
Building C, Tian Jie
Tel: 0796 656 6666
Fax: 0796 656 6662
One of Jiangxi's newest and best, this four-star hotel has five-star comfort and is the province's biggest

accommodation bargain. Standard doubles are big and bright, with super-comfy beds, large-screen TVs and computers with internet access for no extra charge. Bathrooms are modern, with marble fittings. $$$

**Jin Ye Hotel**
18 Hongjun Beilu
Tel: 0796 655 8118
Fax: 0796 655 4011
Near most of Ciping's main sights, this modern three-star hotel has spotlessly clean rooms with spacious bathrooms – the best are in the new wing to the rear. From the bus station it's a walk of less than 10 minutes. $$

### Ganzhou

**Gan Dian Hotel**
29 Hongqi Dadao
Tel: 0797 820 2388
Fax: 0797 820 2399
Heads above the rest of Ganzhou's hotels in terms of comfort and location, with plush rooms that cost far less than their equivalent in bigger Chinese cities. Conveniently located near the town's centre point, Nanmen (South Gate) Square. $$

# HUNAN

### Yueyang

**Highsun Hotel**
39 Baling Xilu
Tel: 0730 831 8888
The Highsun Hotel is a bit past its best but is still the most luxurious option in Yueyang. American invested with a white colonial façade and a white stretch limo outside plus two restaurants, KTV, business centre and large rooms make this a top choice with rooms starting at 360Rmb, even if it falls far short of its claims to be the 21st-best foreign invested hotel in the whole country. $$$

**Snow Lily Hotel**
Dongting Beilu, opposite the Yueyang Ferry Wharf
Tel: 0730 832 1633
Though not getting any

younger, this place is remarkable value with very accommodating staff. $

### Changsha

**Zhong Ou Grand Hotel**
30 Dongfeng Lu
Tel: 0731 453 5566
In between Martyr's Park and the Hunan Provincial Museum is the popular Zhong Ou Grand Hotel – the building has a giant plastic lobster on one side. Clean rooms with IKEA-type wood furnishings are slightly small. Good seafood and a decent bar downstairs. $$$

**Civil Aviation Hotel**
47 Wuyi Donglu
Tel: 0731 417 0288
With the CAAC office in the same building, large rooms, and many great Hunanese restaurants nearby, this

hotel is a decent choice. $$

**Hunan University Foreign Students Guest House**
Base of Yuelu Mountain
Tel: 0731 882 3942
For those seeking greener surroundings this place to the far west of town is a good, cheap bet with clean, spartan rooms. $

**Xinxing Hotel**
1 Wuyi Donglu
Tel: 0731 417 7288 ext. 201
Only for those with an awkwardly timed train connection there are hotel rooms right by the Changsha station. The air-conditioned rooms tend to go fast. $

### Shaoshan

**Shaoshan Binguan**
16 Guyuan Lu
Tel: 0732 568 2309

Hotel options are limited in Shaoshan are limited, and the best bet is the state-owned Shaoshan Binguan where all top dignitaries stay when coming to pay their respects. There are a few restaurants dotted around the village, but the easiest option is to eat at the hotel and, having bought all the Mao trinkets you could ever need, why not tuck into the hotel's speciality: Mao's braised pork in brown sauce.
$$$

## Nanyue

**Shouyue Hotel**
Next to bus station
Remarkable value in
Nanyue is the Shouyue
Hotel very near the bus
station, with clean rooms,
and even spartan suites
going for a song. **$**

## Hengyang

**Huatian Hotel**
20 Renmin Lu
Tel: 0734 828 8688
The biggest, flashiest hotel

in Hengyang – a 10-minute
taxi ride from the train
station – the Huatian
contains all mod cons. **$$$**

## Zhangjiajie

**Bao Feng Hu Hotel**
Bao Feng Hu, Wulingyuan District
Tel: 0744 561 9999
A four-star hotel set in a
leafy location with a bar,
restaurant and internet. Set
outside the busy city centre
on a hillside rooms have
good sweeping views of the
surroundings. **$$$$**

**Xiangdian International
Hotel**
Zhangjiajie Forest Park
Zhangjiajie Village
Tel: 0744 571 2999
In Zhangjiajie Village,
Xiangdian International Hotel
is a huge complex with pools
and pavilions. It is expensive
though, with some rooms
being not all that big. **$$$$**

**Dragon International Hotel**
46 Jiefang Lu
Tel: 0744 561 7888
An explosion of new hotels
in Zhangjiajie City has led to
a price war with many

pleasant, modern rooms
going for low-budget sums.
Higher up the price scale,
the Dragon International
Hotel is the flashest place in
town with a big swimming
pool (for an additional fee),
business centre, bars, KTV
and restaurants. **$$$–$$$$**

**Noble Hotel**
23 Huilong Lu
The Noble Hotel, centrally
located on bustling Huilong
Lu, to the right of the bus
station has dark-wood-
furnished rooms and
friendly, polite service. **$$**

# GUANGXI

## Guilin

**Lijiang Waterfall Hotel**
1 Shanhu Beilu
Tel: 0773 282 2881
Fax: 0773 282 2891
www.waterfallguilin.com
One of the newest hotels in
the city centre, the
luxurious Lijiang Waterfall
Hotel is located close to
Elephant Trunk Hill and
Shan Hu, and has some
rooms over looking the Li
River. The 646-room hotel
has Chinese, Japanese,
Korean and Western
restaurants and an indoor
swimming pool. **$$$$$**

**Sheraton Guilin Hotel**
15 Binjiang Lu
Tel: 0773 282 5588
Fax: 0773 282 5598
Sheraton.Guilin@sheraton.com
www.sheraton.com/guilin
Located beside the Li River
and convenient for all major
sights, the Sheraton is the
only internationally managed
five-star hotel in Guilin, with
high service standards and
English skills in evidence.
High-speed internet access
is available in all of its 430
spacious and comfortable
rooms. **$$$$$**

**Hotel of Modern Art
(HOMA)**
Yuzi Paradise
Dabu Township
Yanshan District
Tel: 0773 386 9100
Fax: 0773 386 9200
yuzi@yuzi-paradise.com
www.hotelofmodernart.com
A stay at this unique
boutique hotel built within

the Yuzi Paradise sculpture
park allows you to
experience art and nature
away from urban trappings.
A spa and fusion
restaurant were added in
2006. **$$$$**

**Golden Elephant Hotel**
36 Binjiang Lu
Tel: 0773 280 8888
Fax: 0773 280 9999
Korean managed hotel
beside Elephant Hill Park
caters mainly to East Asian
market. 73 rooms. Useful
three-star option. **$$$**

**Guilin Fubo Hotel**
27 Binjiang Lu
Tel: 0773 256 9898
Fax: 0773 282 2328
fubo@public.glptt.gx.cn
www.fubohotel.com
Tired but friendly three-star
hotel located on Li River
close to Fubo Hill. Not
worth the high season rate
but an acceptable basic
hotel if discounted. **$$$**

**Universal Hotel**
1 Jiefang Donglu
Tel: 0773 282 8228
Fax: 0773 282 3868
htlunivs@public.glptt.gx.cn
Solid mid-range hotel
located at convenient
crossroads for major
sights. Friendly staff plus
bar and restaurant with
views of river compensate
for faded interiors. **$$$**

**Guilin Backstreet Youth
Hostel**
3 Renmin Lu
Tel: 0773 281 9936
guilinhostel@hotmail.com
This newly converted four-
storey building has clean,

functional rooms, with
concrete floors and rattan
blinds brightened up by
touches of Chinese décor.
Doubles with en suite
bathrooms, air-con and TV
available, as well as
dorms. There is a laid-back
café with comfortable
sofas and cheap internet.
Good location in central
Guilin. **$**

**Guilin Flowers Youth
Hostel**
6 Shanzhi Xiang, Block 2,
Zhongshan Nanlu
Tel: 0773 3839625
Fax: 0773 3845275
yhaguilin@yahoo.com.cn
www.yhaguilin.com
Across the road from the
railway station and 500
metres/yds from the long-
distance bus station, this
hostel is popular with
independent budget
travellers. Bar with pool
table is social centre of
hostel. Dorms and twin
rooms available. **$**

## Yangshuo

**Paradesa Yangshuo Resort**
116 Xi Jie
Tel: 0773 882 2109
Fax: 0773 882 2106
Email: glpysr@gl.gx.cninfo.net
www.paradiseyangshuo.com
Now known as the
Paradesa (rather than
Paradise), this
internationally managed
resort has the best
facilities in Yangshuo. Set in
its own grounds, which
include a small lake and

picturesque bridges and
willows, Paradesa has an
outdoor swimming pool.
Reasonable guest rooms
include choice of family
rooms and easy access
rooms on the ground floor.
**$$$$**

**Yangshuo Regency
Holiday Hotel**
117 Xi Jie
Tel: 0773 881 7198
Fax: 0773 881 7199
regency163@163.net
www.ys-holidayhotel.com
A 10-minute stroll from the
quayside, this four-star
hotel caters to a mix of
foreign and domestic tour
groups with its 70 clean
guestrooms. Dark public
spaces, but large picture
windows in the rooms

TRANSPORT

ACCOMMODATION

ACTIVITIES

A – Z

LANGUAGE

provide light and good views. **$$$**

**Explorer Hotel**
40 Xianqian Jie
Tel: 0773 882 8116
Fax: 0773 882 7816
jimmyqin@hotmail.com
Dark Chinese woodcarving is featured in the design of this quiet 26-room hotel. Its modest clean rooms offer more space than nearby guest houses. **$$**

**Morning Sun Hotel**
4 Cheng Zhonglu
Tel: 0773 881 3899
Fax: 0773 881 3898
info@morningsunhotel.com
www.morningsunhotel.com
Tucked away on a quiet street two minutes from Xi Jie (West Street), this clean, modern hotel, new in 2002, incorporates traditional Chinese design elements. Its 23 comfortable rooms are grouped around an open courtyard with gallery, café and tour desk on the ground floor. **$$**

**Yangshuo Mountain Retreat**
Wang Gongshan Jiao
Fenglou Cunwei
Gao Tian
Tel: 0773 877 7091
Fax: 0773 877 7092
angel_zhao@altec.com.cn

www.yangshuomountainretreat.com
If you want to wake up looking at the mountains and start experiencing nature the moment you step out of the door, this is the place. Located outside the main town, this comfortable 22-room lodge with a garden on the Yulong river bank is well placed for hiking and biking. River-view rooms with balconies are a treat. **$$**

**Double Moon Bridge Guest House**
38 Xianqian Jie
Tel: 0773 882 8116
Fax: 0773 882 7816
webmaster@dmbhotel.com
www.dmbhotel.com
Small family-run guest house has mix of basic rooms, doubles and triples with aircon. Simple bathroom attached to rooms. **$**

**Yangshuo Outside Inn**
Chao Long Village
Tel: 0773 881 7109
www.yangshuo-outside.com
Traditional yellow-brick farmhouses have been restored and basic mod cons (such as electricity, showers and toilets) added to offer an authentic experience of rural China, 5 km (3 miles) outside

Yangshuo. Twelve of the 18 rooms have en suites. Relax in the wooden teahouse/beer garden or explore the countryside. Family rooms also available. **$**

## Nanning

**Nanning Hotel**
38 Minsheng Lu
Tel: 0771 210 3888
This top-end hotel, opposite the Parkson department store and surrounded by new shopping malls, has a no-smoking lobby which will give non-smokers a rare sense of respite. Facilities include a sauna and swimming pool. **$$$**

**Phoenix Hotel**
63 Chaoyang Lu
Tel: 0771 211 9666
A grand, imposing edifice which has all the usual hotel amenities plus a surrounding gaggle of restaurants and massage centres. With large, expensively furnished rooms, it represents great value for money. Free internet in some rooms. **$$**

**Minhang Hotel**
82 Chaoyang Lu
Tel: 0771 209 9000

The Minhang Hotel is small, as are its rooms, but these are clean and as yet unspoilt by wear and tear. The hotel is well located for both the railway station and the bus ticket office. **$**

## Beihai

**Shangri-La Hotel Beihai**
33 Chating Lu
Tel: 0779 206 2288
www.shangri-la.com/beihai
Beihai's large Shangri-La Hotel, an island of Western-style service in China, enjoys a sea view setting on the city's quiet north shore. Although the rooms are showing their age a little, the communal facilities and gardens are well kept. **$$$**

**Liang Gang Hotel**
10 Beibuwan Donglu
Tel: 0779 208 6666
The Liang Gang Hotel is sought after not so much for its amenities as for its convenient position on Beihai's main street. Rooms at the back are very quiet despite the hotel's central location. There is a popular teahouse on the ground floor. **$$**

# GUIZHOU

## Guiyang

**Howard Johnson Plaza Hotel**
29 Zaoshan Lu
Tel: 0851 651 8888/810 8888
Fax: 0851 651 7777/810 7777
hjphgz.guiyang@hojoplaza.com
www.hojochina.com
The city's only five-star hotel to date, the HJ is very affordable, offers all that one might expect from a quality chain, and is a real rest-stop for the weary traveller. There is a Cantonese restaurant on the third floor and a Western restaurant on the ground floor. Located in the northwest of Guiyang, it is a stone's throw from Qianling Park. **$$$**

**Guizhou Park Hotel**
66 Beijing Lu
Tel: 0851 682 3888

Fax: 0851 682 4397
slaes@gzhotel.com
www.gz-hotel.com.cn
This 400-room, four-star hotel beside Quinling Park has a bowling alley, disco and billiard room. Restaurants offer both Chinese and Western cuisine. **$$**

**Tongda Hotel**
Zunyi Lu
Tel: 0851 582 0567
sales@public.gzzt.net.cn
Well located opposite the railway station and close to the bus station. A revolving restaurant on the 28th floor offers Guizhou hotpot and city views. **$-$$**

**Motel 168**
2 Guiyang Shi Sheng Hu Lu
Tel: 0851 821 7692
Fax: 0851 821 7696
www.motel168.com
Very swish, modern and

centrally located, this new hotel is part of the Merrylin chain. With free internet, an English news channel on TV, and a good restaurant on the first floor, this is excellent value. **$**

## Kaili

**Blue Sky Hotel**
Beijing Donglu (facing the central roundabout)
Tel: 0855 807 5980
The Blue Sky is centrally situated and has double and triple rooms. **$**

**Gui Tai Hotel**
Beijing Donglu (by the central roundabout)
Tel: 0855 8269888/382 1688
Fax: 0855 826 9818
This 11-floor, three-star hotel is a good choice located right in the heart of the city. The satellite TV

has one English news channel, and the complimentary breakfast has elements more familiar to the Western eye than most, with coffee, toast and jam. **$**

## Zhenyuan

**Ming Cheng Hotel**
Xingshang Jie
Tel: 0855 572 6018
Even though this hotel has no English sign, it is not difficult to find as it is on

the main road through the old town. Expect the arrival of a foreigner to be met with surprise. Rooms are standard with good showers. **$**

### Zhaoxing

**Lulu's Homestay**
Tel: 0855 613 0112
Fax: 0855 613 0588
luxinfeng@china.com.cn
This traditional Dong house has cheap double rooms and shared hot showers,

and staying here is a real experience (in a good way!). Public balconies on each floor have good views, and the ground-floor restaurant has vegetarian and vegan options as well as Dong specialities (although one may wish to avoid the "cow pie", which is the animal's first stomach). Mr Lu, the owner, can provide information about the area and can also organise transport for day trips. The more upmarket Zhaoxing

Hotel is twice the price but lacks atmosphere. **$**

### Anshun

**Minzu Hotel**
Tashan Donglu
Tel: 0853 335 3555/334 8666
Fax: 0853 335 1758
Otherwise known as the "People's Hotel". Standard doubles with baths invite a long soak. A bowling alley, pool-like sauna bath and cavernous Chinese restaurant are on-site. **$**

### Huangguoshu

**Huangguoshu Hotel**
Midway between Huangguoshu village and the bus stop. Located just before the main entrance to the waterfall, this is the best option in the area. The standard doubles are a bit tatty, but the hotel is set in expansive grounds, and its huge outdoor pool is inviting in hot weather. Rates include breakfast. **$$**

# YUNNAN

### Kunming

**Harbour Plaza Kunming**
20 Hong Huaqiao
Tel: 0871 538 6688
Fax: 0871 538 1189
www.harbour-plaza.com
With a great location not far from Green Lake Park (Cuihu Gongyuan), the Hong Kong-managed Harbour Plaza is the pick of Kunming's accommodation (the city is still awaiting the invasion of brand-name five-star outlets that is taking place elsewhere in China). Rooms come in standard, superior and de luxe varieties, and with either city- or park-view aspects. For executive travellers, the Harbour Club floors sport a lounge and personalised business services. **$$$**
**Kai Wah Plaza International Hotel**
157 Beijing Lu
Tel: 0871 356 2828
Fax: 0871 356 2828
www.kaiwahplaza.com
Formerly the Westin, the Kai Wah is the Harbour Plaza's leading competitor, with similar rates and services, and for golfers the added attraction of an out-of-town 71-par golf course (free shuttle-bus services are provided). A gleaming 525-room tower in the heart of the downtown area (not far from the railway station and around 15 minutes by taxi from the airport), the hotel

has five executive floors and a good selection of de luxe and superior rooms, along with "panorama suites" that have good views of a rather less than overwhelming cityscape. **$$$**
**Kunming Green Lake Hotel**
6 Cuihu Nanlu
Tel: 0871 515 8888
Fax: 0871 515 3286
www.greenlakehotel.com.cn
One of Kunming's original state guest houses, the Green Lake has an enviable waterside location next to Green Lake Park and has been tastefully refurbished, yet some guests complain that it does not quite live up to its promise. But travellers who enjoy varied four to almost five-star standards and service Chinese-style will find it easily the most charming of Kunming's more well-heeled accommodation options. **$$$**
**The Kunming Hotel**
145 Dongfeng Donglu
Tel: 0871 316 2063
Fax: 0871 313 8220
The Kunming – in its day, the first four-star hotel in Yunnan province – is another long-running hotel that has been given a face-lift. It has a good location, very close to the popular Camellia Hotel and to the railway station, well-appointed rooms and staff who are accustomed to dealing with foreign guests. **$$$**

**New Era Hotel**
99 Dongfeng Lu
Tel: 0871 362 4999
Fax: 0871 363 6556
The New Era is fairly typical of the upmarket Chinese hotels that have sprung up around the nation over the last decade – grand, ostentatious and somewhat lacking in intimacy. However, it's situated in what remains of the old Muslim quarter, and the environs are interesting to explore on foot. Discounts are usually available on request if you have not booked in advance. Locals rate the hotel for its regional cuisines – notably the Chaozhou, Huaiyang (Zhejiang and Suzhou) and Sichuan restaurants. **$$$**
**Dianchi Garden Hotel & Spa**
37 Dianchi Lu
Tel: 0871 433 2888
Fax: 0871 433 2999
www.spagardenhotel.com/hotel/english/index.asp
The sprawling Dianchi Garden – complete with gardens – is an exercise in opulence, though more of the kind beloved by Chinese tour groups. In its favour is its peaceful location next to Dianchi Lake and a spa swimming pool. The hotel is just 8 km (5 miles; around Rmb 15 by taxi) from downtown, making it the best of both worlds. **$$**
**Horizon Hotel**
432 Qingnian Lu
Tel: 0871 318 6666
Fax: 0871 318 8888

The 440-room Horizon is a centrally located luxury hotel that is popular with tour groups and business travellers. The atmosphere is somewhat impersonal, but it does have some highly rated restaurants, such as the 28th floor Ziyun Tian – a revolving Cantonese restaurant that claims to be the biggest and highest in southwest China. **$$**
**Kunming Sakura Hotel**
25 Dongfeng Donglu
Tel: 0871 316 5888
Fax: 0871 316 5888
www.sakurahotel.cn/en
The Sakura Hotel used to be a branch of the Holiday Inn group, but is now locally managed. It's a reliable

### PRICE CATEGORIES

Price categories are for a standard double room in high season (no breakfast):
**$** = under US$30 (Rmb 240)
**$$** = US$30–50 (Rmb 240–400)
**$$$** = US$50–100 (Rmb 400–800)
**$$$$** = US$100–150 (Rmb 800–1,200)
**$$$$$** = over US$150 (Rmb 1,200)

four-star option with a central location not far from the railway station. The rooms have the appearance of a well-appointed business hotel, but it's a popular choice with tour groups all the same. The Sakura has some of Kunming's best dining, including the city's top Thai restaurant, Ban Thai. **$$**

### Camellia Hotel
154 Dongfeng Donglu
Tel: 0871 316 3000
Fax: 0871 314 7033
www.kmcamelliahotel.com
Kunming's long-standing and most famous hotel among backpackers – it has very inexpensive dormitory accommodation – also has a good selection of three-star rooms that are perhaps the best choice for anyone who

**ABOVE:** Tiger Leaping Gorge.

doesn't want to splash out on five-star accommodation. Rooms may not be luxurious, but they're comfortable and clean, and the common areas of the hotel are good places to meet other travellers and exchange information. English-speaking staff can provide information on almost anything you need to know about Kunming and further afield – a large range of foreigner-oriented tours (avoid lengthy delays in souvenir shops) are also available.
**$–$$**

## Stone Forest

### Stone Forest Hotel
2 Longquan Lu,
Stone Forest Town, Lunan County
Tel: 0871 779 5401
Fax: 0871 779 5414
Very few foreigners (except for the occasional tour group) stay at this "villa-style resort" out at the Stone Forest, but it's a restful retreat from the hubbub of Kunming – at least after the tourist buses all start to pull out late in the afternoon. Rooms are basic, as is the English of the staff, but it's a taste of off-the-beaten-track China within easy striking distance (80 km/50 miles) of Kunming.
**$–$$**

## Jinghong

### Xishuangbanna New Tai Garden Hotel
61 Minhang Lu
Tel: 0691 216 6999
New Tai Garden Hotel is a very clean, pricey, swish option, all styled in super-sized Dai architecture. Its location is a 10-minute taxi ride from the centre of town and sprawls across large parkland. The complex includes a swimming pool, two tennis courts and a restaurant. **$$$**

### Golden Banna Hotel
Mengle Dadao, Jinghong Tourism and Vacation Area (by Manting Park and the Ethnic Cultural Garden)
Tel: 0691 212 4901
It's a big clump of concrete, but inside, the Golden Banna Hotel represents good value for money with well-equipped rooms. The three different restaurants offer a decent variety of Chinese cuisine and the swimming pool is never crowded. **$–$$**

### Crown Hotel
Jinghong Nanlu
Tel: 0691 212 8888/9888
With lovely wooden floors, a large swimming pool ringed by palm trees and sizeable rooms with balconies, the Crown Hotel is a garden oasis with Dai-influenced architecture and the best-value three-star hotel in Xishuangbanna.

**$–$$**.

### Banna Hotel
Ganlaba Lu (to the right of the Forest Café)
Tel: 0691 213 2052
Slap bang in the centre of town, this place is the best-value offering in town and is swollen by backpackers most of the time. Most rooms have TV and air-con plus private bathrooms. **$**

## Dali Gucheng (Dali old town)

### Asia Star Hotel Dali
Fifteen minutes' walk from the South Gate (Tonghaimen/Nanmen)
Tel: 0872 267 9999
Fax: 0872 267 1699
Out of town (a 15-minute walk from the South Gate), the Asia Star is a relatively luxurious accommodation option in a destination still dominated by budget guest houses. Rooms are well appointed and come in "mountain view" and "lake view" varieties – in the colder months, when the Cangshan Mountains are frosted with snow, the former is the better choice. That said, the hotel's pretensions to four-star luxury stretch credulity somewhat. The shuttle-bus service into Dali is not reliable, so it's best to hire bicycles if you're heading into town for dinner or drinks. **$$**

### Landscape Hotel
96 Yu'er Lu
Tel: 0872 266 6188
Fax: 0872 266 6189
www.landscapehotel.com/index.html
This boutique hotel in a refurbished Bai Minority house is Dali's most ambient place to stay. In the heart of the old city, the Landscape has superb Bai-themed rooms with views of the town's jostling, crazy-tiled rooftops, and an atmospheric courtyard area that is lit up at night with lanterns. **$$**

### Dali San Ta Yuan Hotel
San Ta Yuan
Tel: 0872 267 6521
Fax: 0872 266 6280
www.santayuan.com
Located north of town in Dali's picturesque Three

Pagodas area, the San Ta Yuan (three pagodas) Hotel gets mixed reviews from travellers, but is not without charm. The Bai-themed décor and fittings are not as well maintained as they might be, and the English ability of the staff is minimal, but there is no denying that it is a relaxing retreat from the tourist crowds. A 10-minute taxi ride is required to get into town, however. **$**

### Jim's Tibetan Hotel
13 Yuxiu Lu (just outside the South Gate)
Tel: 0872 267 7824
Fax: 0872 267 7823
Jim's is not a luxury hotel, but it is probably the best accommodation choice in Dali. It has a great location just outside the South Gate of the Old Town, easy walking or cycling distance to the cafés and bars, and is extremely foreigner-friendly, with budget tours to Dali's attractions. The Tibetan-themed rooms are tasteful and clean, and most come with delightful balconies. **$**

### MCA Guest House
58 Renmin Lu (100 metres/yds south of the South Gate)
Tel: 0872 267 3666
Fax: 0872 267 1999
www.mcahotel.com
The MCA is a standby with backpackers, but that's no reason to turn your nose up at the place. It is tastefully appointed throughout, very foreigner-friendly and extremely reasonably priced. **$**

## Xiaguan (Dali New Town)

### Manwan Hotel
Cangshan Lu
Tel: 0872 218 8188
Fax: 0872 281 1742
An impersonal four-star hotel popular with tour groups and strictly speaking the best of Dali's hotels, the great disadvantage of the Manwan is that it is located in Xiaguan, Dali's drab, modern sister city. Rooms are relatively luxurious in the conservative style of

second-tier Chinese city hotels. Taxis to Dali Old Town take around 20 minutes and cost Rmb 30. **$$**

## Baoshan

**Landu Hotel**
146 Baoshan Xilu
Tel: 0875 212 1888
Fax: 0875 212 1990
www.landuhotel.com
The Landu, an opulent monster of a hotel, is Baoshan's best. Chandeliers and marble aside, it is very much a standard Chinese three-star hotel. Very little English is spoken here, and foreign guests mostly consist of the occasional adventurous tour group. **$$**

## Mangshi

**Mangshi Hotel**
58 Youyi Lu
Tel: 0692 212 2169
Fax: 0692 212 2301
Formerly the state guest house, the Mangshi Hotel is a sprawling – and very charming – place to stay, in a slightly run-down tropical style. Prices vary considerably depending on the wing of the hotel and when it was renovated. **$–$$**

## Tengchong

**Rehai Grand Hotel**
Rehai
Tel: 0875 515 0366
Fax: 0875 515 0356
The Rehai, just 12 km (8 miles) southwest of Tengchong (a 15-minute taxi ride), is a good accommodation alternative to the Tengchong Hotel, even if the staff are less used to having foreign guests. It has hot-spring water piped into the hotel, as do even the cheaper hotels in this area. The three-star rooms here are acceptable. The hotel tends to get booked out during busy Chinese holiday periods. **$$**
**Tengchong Hotel**
12 Guanting Xiang
Tel: 0875 512 5634
Fax: 0875 512 3566

The Tengchong is a relatively high-standard Chinese *bingguan*, or guest house, that offers substantial discounts on its already reasonable room rates on request. Rooms are on a par with three-star hotels elsewhere in southern China, and the friendly staff do their best to accommodate foreign visitors – who have become more frequent in recent years. **$$**

## Ruili

**New Kaitong International Hotel**
2 Biancheng Lu
Tel: 0692 414 9528
Fax: 0692 414 9526
The New Kaitong is an impersonal three- to four-star hotel favoured by Chinese and Burmese businesspeople. Discounts are available on request. The hotel's Chinese restaurants are the best in town. **$$**

## Lijiang

**Banyan Tree Lijiang**
Yuerong Lu, Shuhe,
Gucheng District
Tel: 0888 533 1111
Fax: 0888 533 2222
www.banyantree.com
Five-star luxury comes to northwestern Yunnan. Situated north of Lijiang on the way to Shuhe village, this resort property has 55 individual pavilions, a spa, swimming pool and a view of the Jade Dagon Snow Mountain. Tasteful, immaculate, exclusive. **$$$$$**
**Grand Lijiang Hotel**
Xinyi Jie
Tel: 0888 512 0888
Fax: 0888 512 7878
Well located next to the waterwheel square on the way to the Black Dagon Pool, the four-star Grand Lijiang is a modern, well-equipped hotel with fine views across to the mountains and the old town. Good service and a pleasant restaurant beside the stream. **$$$**
**Jian Nan Chun Hotel**
8 Guang Yi Jie

Tel: 0888 510 2222
Fax: 0888 510 2988
hotel@jnchotel.com
www.jnchotel.com
A four-star hotel located in the centre of the Old Town. Favoured by visiting dignitaries, it is built in traditional Chinese style, however the rooms are decidedly modern. **$$$**
**Homy Hotel**
Guang Yi Jie
27 Xin Yuan Xiang
Tel: 0888 518 9698
A tastefully restored courtyard home; 20 rooms with all amenities and an excellent restaurant. **$$**
**Swiss Snow Inn**
34 Sifang Jie
Tel: 0888 518 4862
Fax: 0888 518 4851
swisssnowinn@yahoo.com.cn
www.swisssnowinn.com
A beautifully renovated old Naxi courtyard house in the centre of the old town. Sixteen rooms, all with attached baths. **$$**
**Mu Shi Guest House**
22 Ji Shan Xiang
Xinyi Jie
Tel: 0888 512 6492
liguo_628@sina.com
www.lijiangmuzi.com
A typical courtyard house converted into a guest house in a quiet neighbourhood of the Old Town. Friendly staff. Clean and simply furnished. **$**
**Ping An Inn**
Xinyi Jie
Tel: 0888 512 5834
Another nice old Naxi courtyard house. Simple but authentic and pleasant. **$**

## Zhongdian

**Banyan Tree Ringha**
Hong Po Village
Jiantang Town
Tel: 0887 533 1111
Fax: 0887 533 2222
ringha@banyantree.com
www.banyantree.com/ringha
Thirty-two Tibetan farmhouses transformed into uber-de luxe lodges and suites, with fireplaces and private spas. Located 20 km (12 miles) from Zhongdian near the Tibetan monastery of Da Bao Si.

Masseuses from Thailand, chefs from Bali and Tibetan trekking guides. Crème de la crème, including the prices. **$$$$$**
**Songtsam Hotel**
Songzhanling Village
Tel: 0887 828 8889
Fax: 0887 828 8887
songtsam@yahoo.com.cn
www.songtsam.com
A large Tibetan home which has been converted into an attractive 20-room hotel in the village adjacent to the Songzhanling Monastery, 3 km (2 miles) out of town. Great for exploring this famous monastery and the the village as well as trekking in the nearby hills. **$$$**
**Tibet Café and Inn**
Changzhen Lu
Tel: 0887 823 0019
Fax: 0887 823 0342
shangbala2005@yahooo.com.cn
A variety of rooms, internet café and good hearty Western, Tibetan and Chinese food. Tibetan travel permits and jeep trips are arranged here. *The* travellers' hang-out. **$**

## Deqin

**Rainbow Grand Hotel**
Nanping Lu
Tel: 0887 841 4248
A modern four-storey hotel near the bus station in Deqin. Clean and warm, with a decent attached restaurant. **$$**
**Deqin Tibetan Hotel**
86 Nanping Lu
Tel: 0887 841 2031
qmdj@hotmail.com
Moderately priced and quiet, with nice views. Trekking information is provided. **$**

### PRICE CATEGORIES

Price categories are for a standard double room in high season (no breakfast):
**$** = under US$30 (Rmb 240)
**$$** = US$30–50 (Rmb 240–400)
**$$$** = US$50–100 (Rmb 400–800)
**$$$$** = US$100–150 (Rmb 800–1,200)
**$$$$$** = over US$150 (Rmb 1,200)

# **A**CTIVITIES

# CULTURAL ACTIVITIES, NIGHTLIFE, CHILDREN'S ACTIVITIES, SHOPPING, SPORTS AND TOURS

## CULTURAL ACTIVITIES

### Chinese Opera

Chinese opera performaces can be seen in virtually every town across southern China, most frequently during festivals. In the countryside, look out for more spirited shows, sometimes put on for temple festivals and weddings.

In general, traditional opera is increasingly being shunned by the younger generation, but the over-50s still love it. We have listed some of the main venues in larger cities; for other venues try asking at your hotel or from travel agencies.

### Shenzhen (Guangdong)

**Shenzhen Opera House**
Xinyuan Lu (junction of Dongmen Lu and "Walking Street")
A large modern arts complex also containing a small cinema and other performance spaces.
**Shenzhen Grand Theatre**
5018, Shennan Donglu, Luohu District. Tel: 0755 8326 2745.
Hosts performances by the Beijing Opera Company.

### Guangzhou (Guangdong)

**Sun Yatsen Memorial Hall**
**Yuexiu Hill**
Occasional performances of opera from around the whole of China, in this grand traditional octagonal building.

### Chaozhou (Guangdong)

This culturally rich city has its own form of opera considered to be less strident in style than the Beijing tradition. The best place to hear opera here is an occasional performance in Xihu Park, during festivals.

### Xiamen (Fujian)

The Xiamen Municipal Gezai Opera Troupe performs a Taiwanese form of folk opera, known as Gezai, or Xiangju.
No. 1, Xianfengying, Xiamen. Tel: 0592 202 2073.

### Nanchang (Jiangxi)

Tengwang Pavilion, about 1 km (⅔ mile) west of Youmin Si, overlooking the Gan River, sometimes gives performances of local opera. Tel: 0791 677 3005.

### Kunming (Yunnan)

There is no dedicated opera house in Kunming, but the city does have several operatic troupes, who give impromptu performances in front of the Workers' Cultural Hall and in Cuihu Park at weekends. Also worth checking out the Yunnan Arts Theatre on Dongfeng Xilu for similar events.

## Festivals – National

Holidays such as **National Day** and **International Labour Day** are fixed on the modern Chinese calendar, but most traditional festivals and events are determined by the lunar calendar, which means the date varies slightly from year to year. The following list of events highlights the major national festivals, but each region has its own special days and events.

At Chinese New Year and during the week-long May and October holidays travel in China can be difficult; many attractions become impossibly overcrowded and rail and air tickets difficult to obtain.

### January/February

The most important festival time is the **Lunar New Year**, or **Spring Festival**, which usually falls in late January or early February. Public buildings are festooned with coloured lights, people from all over China travel to reunite with family and friends, debts are settled, and food is consumed – lots of it. In recent years, a more relaxed atmosphere has brought the revival of old Spring Festival traditions, such as giving *hongbao* – small, red envelopes containing money – to children and young adults. Temple fairs feature martial arts demonstrations, stand-up comedy, home-made toys and, of course, food.

### April

On the 12th day of the third lunar month, at the beginning of April, the Chinese honour their deceased ancestors by observing **Qingming**, sometimes referred to as the "grave-sweeping" day. It is much less impressive nowadays, as people are cremated instead of being buried. Qingming is a time for remembering ancestors, but also for revelling on a warm spring day.

### May/June

**International Labour Day** on 1 May is a week-long public holiday. Following hot on its heels is **Youth Day**, a commemoration of the May 4 Movement of 1919, reflected by large editorials and government hoopla in the official press.

**International Children's Day** is celebrated in earnest on 1 June by letting classes out early and treating children to outings at public parks.

### July/August

1 July is the **Anniversary of the Communist Party**, which was

TRANSPORT

founded in Shanghai in 1921. This means very little to the average citizen but plenty of fun for high-level Party members.

The fifth day of the fifth lunar month (in June or July) brings the **Dragon Boat Festival**, with dragon-boat races in many cities. It commemorates the memory of Qu Yuan (340–278 BC), a poet in the days of the Kingdom of Chu, who, rather than submit to political pressure, drowned himself in the Miluo River, in Hunan (where there is a particularly large festival, *see below*). To prevent the fish from eating his body, the people threw glutinous rice cakes *(zongzi)* into the river. Nowadays, these *zongzi* are simply eaten to mark the occasion.

1 August is the **Anniversary of the People's Liberation Army**. Inaugurated in 1927 and formerly marked by enormous parades, it is now celebrated mainly in the media.

### September/October

The timing of the **Mid-Autumn Festival** again depends on when the moon reaches its fullest, usually around mid-September. The shops do great business in "moon cakes" – pastries filled with gooey sesame paste, red-bean and walnut filling. *Tang yuan*, glutinous rice-flour balls with sweet fillings in sugar syrup, and *yuè bing*, a cake baked specifically for this occasion, are also eaten. In the tradition of poets, this is the time to drink a bit of wine and toast the moon.

Late September is normally the time when Chinese communities celebrate the memory of **Confucius**.

1 October is the PRC's birthday, **National Day**, celebrated with a one week public holiday.

The **Double-Ninth Festival** takes place on the ninth day of the ninth lunar month. The number nine signifies *yang* (male energy), and various displays of virility – contests of strength, mountain climbing, etc – mark the occasion.

### December

**Christmas** is gaining momentum as a consumer celebration. Christian churches hold special services that draw thousands of spectators. In Beijing, for example, it is fashionable to exchange greeting cards and presents, while Santa Claus makes the odd shop appearance.

### Local Festivals in the South

The south is the most ethnically diverse region of the country, home to nearly half of China's 56 ethnic

groups. Reflecting this wide cultural range, the area has a lively and colourful array of festivals and customs celebrated throughout the year. Some of the events are exclusive to just one area or town, and dates vary – check with local branch of the China Travel Service (CTS). The Dong, Miao and other minorities in **Guizhou province** have a notably rich festival tradition *(for more details see pages 292, 295 and 300–1)*.

The number of local festivities in southern China makes it impossible to list them all. What follows is an outline of the major events of interest to tourists.

### Hong Kong and Macau

Hong Kong's **International Film Festival** is held every spring. Book ahead, as tickets sell out fast (you can buy online on www.hkiff.org.hk). In April or May, fishermen celebrate the **birthday of Tin Hau**, the goddess of the sea, by decorating their boats in bright colours and visiting Tin Hau temples. The **Cheung Chau Bun Festival** (usually in May) is one of the most exciting local festivals; costumed figures parade on stilts or ride in floats across the island. The **Mid-Autumn Festival** (also known as the Moon Festival) takes places between mid-September and early October, and is one of the most attractive events; the parade of lanterns is at its best in Causeway Bay's Victoria Park.

In Macau the biggest annual event is the **Macau Grand Prix**, which starts in front of the Lisboa Hotel and runs for 6 km (4 miles) around the city streets over the third weekend in November (www.macau.grandprix.gov.mo). Macau also has its own public holiday, the **Special Administrative Region Establishment Day**, on 20 December (Hong Kong marks its SAR day on the 1 July).

### Guangdong

In Guangzhou, Chinese New Year festivities include a spectacular **flower festival**. The **Double-Ninth Festival** (ninth day of the ninth lunar month) is marked with a mass climbing of the Baiyun Hills to the north of the city. The **China Tourist Art Festival** and the **Guangdong Happy Festival** take place in Guangzhou every September and October, with colourful displays and events throughout a four-week period.

Regional festivals include the June/July **Lychee Festival** in Conghua, with singing and dancing. The **birth of Tin Hau** is marked in coastal towns on the 23rd day of the third lunar month. Around the time of

the Mid-Autumn festival, the city of Meizhou hosts a colourful **Hakka Folk Festival**.

### Hainan Island

The **International Coconut Festival** is held in Haikou and several other towns on the island during the first ten days of April. It's primarily a trade fair, but also has some side-attractions for visitors, including dragon-boat races, martial arts contests, as well as Miao and Liu ancestral ceremonies.

### Fujian

Fujian celebrates all the major Chinese festivals, especially the Spring (Lunar New Year) and Mid-Autumn festivals. In addition, these seafaring people have a number of local deities, most importantly Mazu (the goddess of the sea, known as Tin Hau to the Cantonese); the main **Mazu Festival** takes place on the 23rd day of the third lunar month (there is a smaller Mazu festival on the ninth day of the ninth lunar month). It is primarily a religious event that attracts pilgrims from far afield, but also involves displays of local arts and crafts, as well as folk song and dance performances.

The province has many local festivals, like the picturesque **Quanzhou Lantern Festival** on the 15th day of the Lunar New Year. The Tulou and other ancestral villages have their own annual celebrations, but there seems to be no central source of information about these. One of the most unusual local events is the **Xiamen Bobing (Cake Gambling) Festival** in the eighth lunar month, shortly before the Mid-Autumn Festival. Every spring in even years brings the **Xiamen International Piano Festival**.

### Jiangxi

The **Jingdezhen International Pottery and Porcelain Festival** takes place through the month of October, with exhibitions and various events.

### Hunan

The **Yueyang International Dragon Boat Festival** is held on the Miluo River on the fifth day of the fifth lunar month. This is one of the planet's largest dragon-boat events, with more than 100 teams from all over the world competing in the races.

### Guangxi

The **Nanning International Folk Song Festival** takes place on the third day of the third month of the lunar calendar. Comprising performances by local musicians and others from across China and abroad, the festival is based on a song festival traditionally held in the countryside by the Zhuang and other regional ethnic groups; it also involves displays of costumes and folk handicrafts.

The **Guilin Scenery Tourism Festival** in the first week in November was introduced in the early 1990s to boost the attractions for visitors in one of China's most popular tourist areas. The festival focuses on the cultural and natural highlights of the region, with folk art, singing and dancing.

### Guizhou

Guizhou has a fantastic array of colourful festivals. Practically every Miao and Dong minority village indulges in a so-called *lusheng* festivity through the year – *for more details see pages 292, 295 and 300–1*. It is worth checking websites *(see below)* for up-to-date details of upcoming events so that you can time your visit to take one in. However, it's always best to check things out the day before, and get more specific local information. Actual locations often involve a long hike along dirt tracks from the nearest village, so be prepared.

The **Guizhou Azalea Festival** takes place in the village of Jinpo, Guanxi county, during 8–25 April, based on the abundance of azalea varieties in the region, with a natural azalea forest in the northeast of Guizhou (between Qianxi and Dafang counties). In homage to the glories of the flower, the festival offers ethnic dancing and musical shows, as well as bullfighting and local foodstalls.

The following websites have updated timetables of festivals in Guizhou. It is advisable to compare specific festivals dates to get the most definitive results.

www.travelchinaguide.com
www.gzcyts.com
www.chinahighlights.com
www.chinaplanner.com

### Yunnan

The **Water Splashing Festival** is celebrated in Xishuangbanna for a week in mid-April. Based on a Buddhist New Year celebration, the festival predictably involves lots of getting wet, with people throwing little bags of water over each other in a spirit of goodwill. There are also dragon-boat races, fireworks and candlelit lamps filling the streets.

The biggest festival in the Dali area is the **Torch Festival**. A Yi minority festival that falls on the 24th

**ABOVE:** New Year festivities in Haikou.

day of the sixth lunar month, the festival is now celebrated – with gusto – by the Bai minority in Dali Old Town. Elaborately decorated torches are carried through the town in the evening, amidst much singing and general merriment. This festival is also celebrated by the Naxi minority further north in Lijiang.

On the third lunar month, the **Third Month Fair** turns Dali Old Town into a vast market for all kinds of produce – notably herbal medicines – from all over Yunnan. The fair is also marked by dragon dances and horse races.

The Naxi's most important festival is called **Sanduojie**, which honours Sanduo, the Naxi's guardian spirit and god of war. Respects are paid to his statue at the Jade Summit Temple outside Lijiang. At this time, the eighth day of the second lunar month, the huge camellia tree is in full blossom. Later in the day, traditional orchestras play throughout the old city.

The Han Chinese festival honouring ancestors, called the **Hungry Ghosts** or All Souls festival, is celebrated with verve in Lijiang – and a few days earlier than elsewhere in China, on the 12th through the 14th days of the seventh lunar month. All of Dayan is decorated with elaborate paper lanterns, and small candlelit floats are placed in the town's streams.

In Zhongdian, the **Horse Racing Festival**, held on the fifth and sixth days of the fifth lunar month, is one of the best of Yunnan's many festivals. Aside from the races, there are demonstrations of acrobatic riding skill and dancing performances from the several ethnic groups in the area. Horse-trading also takes place, with Tibetan merchants arriving from afar in their traditional finery.

### Concerts

There are regular performances of Western classical and traditional Chinese music in various cities. Hong Kong has world-class classical orchestras, including the Hong Kong

Philharmonic and the Hong Kong Chinese Orchestra, and concerts are held at the **Hong Kong Cultural Centre** (10 Salisbury Road, Tsim Sha Tsui; tel: 2734 2009); recitals (sometimes free) are held at the **Hong Kong Academy for Performing Arts** (1 Gloucester Road, Wan Chai; tel: 2584 8500).

The most common traditional music of southern China is *sizhu* ("silk and bamboo"), comprising groups of musicians playing bamboo flutes and plucked and bowed-drawn stringed instruments, creating a smooth sound that is often easier on Western ears than other Chinese music. Around the coast of southern Fujian, particularly in Quanzhou and Xiamen, you can hear ensembles playing *nanguan* ballads. Female vocalists sing sad love songs to the accompaniment of flutes and lutes, creating a refined and peaceful sound.

In many areas – notably in places like Guizhou province with its large numbers of minority people – you can see stage shows of local dances and songs.

## NIGHTLIFE

### Bars, Discos and Karaoke

Nightlife is increasingly a feature of modern China, and the southern cities are particularly lively, especially in wealthier centres such as Guangzhou, Shenzhen and Xiamen. Numerous bars and pubs have opened in recent years, and are now meeting places for affluent youths. The cosmopolitan buzz of Hong Kong and Macau nightlife is as enjoyable as ever, and the latter's burgeoning casino scene *(see page 371)* is a world of its own. Restaurants, bars and cafés generally remain open until midnight or even later. Check the monthly expat magazines in Guangzhou and other large cities for the latest listings.

Karaoke is a ubiquitous form of entertainment in China, although somewhat on the wane in recent years. The Japanese-style singalong bars caught on in the 1990s, considerably increasing the planet's off-key harmonies. Most are easily recognised by the letters "OK" amongst the characters for their names. Some of these are pricey, with the clientele being rich businessmen, and can be fronts for prostitution; such hostess-style bars are illegal and can fleece customers, so beware.

Discos are popular throughout China. Many hotels have their own, which are frequented by well-off local youths, and most stay open until the early hours of the morning.

### Guangdong

Listings: Shenzhen page 165, Guangzhou page 179.

Shenzhen's main nightlife area is the Futian District in the west of the city, although there are also plenty of bars and clubs in the central Dongmen area and around Luo Hu (Lo Wu) on the border with Hong Kong. Most of the venues are large and loud, incorporating a nightclub, karaoke lounge and disco; there are also a few smaller places for a quiet drink. Clubs and upmarket bars open at around 8pm and are busiest around midnight. Shenzhen's port town of Shekou, about 45 minutes away by cab, has more girlie bars and the like, but regular nightlife is also in evidence.

Guangzhou is a booming city, with burgeoning nightlife to match. The liveliest areas are north of the Culture Park (Wenhua Gongyuan), between Xiajiu Lu and Changshou Lu, and in the east of the city, with many bars in and around Times Square. Typical venues are large, mixed entertainment clubs, though also range to the other extreme, with some very poky drinking dens (many bars come and go at short notice; see http://guangzhou.asiaxpat.com).

### Hainan

There are no individual bars worth singling out for recommendation – hotel and resort bars are the best bet. The wharfside area of Sanya City is seedy. For better nightlife options, get out of Sanya altogether and head for the nearby resort areas of Dadonghai and upmarket Yalong Bay.

### Fujian

If you're looking for bright lights and scintillating nightlife, Fujian is likely to disappoint. Xiamen is the most lively place, with a few new night spots opening around the new bar area of Bai Lu Zhou. First to open was You and I, then came The Glass House, with others opening all the time; people are attracted by the pretty lakeside outdoor seating area. Havana is an old favourite: this Spanish-style house with garden has a band on Friday and Saturday nights attracting a good party crowd from 8pm until about 4am.

Park Latin used to be centre of Xiamen's nightlife and it is still regarded as the hottest place. La Bamba disco has so far held its own, and it remains packed every night of the week. True Love, Xiamen's first dating pub, still has its adherents and it remains very successful.

The new generation of hotels have beautiful bar concepts, especially the Sofitel, where lobby parties with Parisian DJs have really put the place on the map. The Sheraton also put a great deal of thought into its novel lobby-bar-lounge-bar concept.

Fuzhou has surprisingly few places to go at night for such a sizeable city, though bars and clubs are beginning to appear around Dong Jie.

### Jiangxi

Listings (Nanchang): page 243.

Nanchang, the capital of Jiangxi province, has a sprinkling of bars and cafés in the Donghu district; the trendiest nightclubs though are in the bustling social hub of Minde Lu.

### Hunan

Changsha boasts that it has the finest cuisine in China (though it's not the only city to say that), but its

nightlife is not so renowned. There are a few bars dotted along Jiefang Xilu, as well as Western-style nightclubs such as the Hot Rock Pub (Gushi Deba) on the corner of Jiefang Donglu and Shaoshan Beilu.

### Guangxi

Listings (Guilin, Yangshuo, Nanning): page 285.

Guilin's entertainment tends to be of the tour-group spectacle variety, with ethnic groups performing rather tacky song and dance shows. One city nightclub, Dada Hui, has quite a trendy following among expats; it's on the corner of Yiren Lu and Zhongshan Lu (Rmb 15 cover charge). Otherwise, your best bet for a fun night out is Yangshuo, which is packed with lively bars and clubs. Most are clustered along the main street, Xie Jie, notably the MC Blues Bar.

Nanning is not so well known for its nightlife, but it does put on a range of weird and wonderful so-called minority displays, such as pole climbing, stilt soccer and Chinese rugby. One city bar currently in with the expat community is the Kangaroo Bar.

### Guizhou

Guiyang has a lively nightlife scene with lots of discos, karaoke bars and nightclubs spread around the city. The Shangri-La Bar on Hequn Lu is popular, while Fushui Lu has many bars and restaurants.

There are many bars along Qingping Nanhu west of the city centre in Kaili.

### Yunnan

Listings: Kunming page 311, Dali page 335.

Kunming has a good reputation as one of the most relaxed cities in China, with plenty of laid-back bars

## Macau's Casinos

The rapidly expanding number of casinos in Macau are clustered into two main zones – the reclaimed land NAPE on the southern end of the Macau Peninsula, and the Cotai strip linking the islands of Taipa and Coloane. Customers will need to be reasonably smartly dressed to enter a casino. All are open 24 hours. The minimum age is 18.

Some of the major casinos are:

**Emperor Palace Casino**
Grand Emperor Hotel,
288 Avenida Commerical De Macau
Tel: 2888 9988

**Grand Waldo Casino**
Avenida Marginal Flor
de Lotus, Taipa
Tel: 2888 6888
**Greek Mythology Casino**
New Century Hotel, 889 Avenida
Padre Tomas Pereira, Taipa
Tel: 2883 5223
**Casino Lisboa**
2–4 Avenida de Lisboa
Tel: 2837 5111
**Casino Macau Palace**
Avenida da Amizade, Outer Harbour
Tel: 2834 6701
**Casino Marina**
Pousada Marina Infante, Aterro

COTAI, Marina da Taipa Sul, Taipa
Tel: 2883 8333
**Casino Oriental**
Mandarin Oriental, 956–1110
Avenida da Amizade. Tel: 2856 4297
**Pharoah's Palace Casino**
The Landmark Macau,
555 Avenida da Amizade
Tel: 2878 8111
**The Sands Casino**
Avenida da Amizade. Tel: 2888 3388
**Venetian Casino**
Cotai Strip. Tel: 2882 8888
**Wynn Casino**
Rua Cidade de Sintra, NAPE.
Tel: 2888 9966

and clubs, particularly around Wenlin Jie, near Yunnan University, a popular area with local expats. Dali and Lijiang are full of bars catering to Western tourists.

## Cinema

Chinese cinema has certainly arrived on the scene in recent years with the international success of films like *Crouching Tiger, Hidden Dragon* and *Hero*, but unless you speak Chinese your options will be limited to Hong Kong and Macau as far as going to the cinema is concerned. A few cinemas in other large cities and provincial centres occasionally show English-language films with Chinese subtitles, or other films with English subtitles, but most screenings of foreign films are dubbed.

## CHILDREN'S ACTIVITIES

One of the main challenges of taking children on holiday in China is the sheer scale of the place, and the long journeys involved. The quickest way to get around is by air, and although it's the most expensive form of transport, there are some discounts available for children (usually up to age 12) and student fares, plus you might save on hotel costs. The railway system is extensive and an excellent way to travel with kids, with a variety of long-distance and high-speed services available, dining cars and sleepers, and generally more space for youngsters, plus the sideshow of other passengers and the moving scenery from out the window. Take plenty of games, books, etc, to keep younger kids amused though, as the novelty of the journey may wear off after a few hours. The key advice is to plan well ahead, especially if travelling during peak holiday times or public holidays, when everything is fully booked.

Although there may not be as many child-friendly facilities here as in the West, the Chinese love kids. Foreign families, particularly those with blond-haired, blue-eyed children, are likely to get plenty of friendly attention – possibly more, in fact, than you might want. Be prepared for locals making a fuss of small children.

Eating out with the family is the norm for the Chinese. Traditional Chinese restaurants, in fact, will be a fascinating experience for kids of all ages; with their array of exotic dishes, colourful décor and lively atmosphere. Some of the fast-food chain restaurants in the cities –

particularly KFC outlets – have small children's playgrounds inside.

In southern China, the biggest attractions for kids are likely to be the theme parks, of which there are a growing number, particularly in and around the major cities.

### Hong Kong and Macau

Hong Kong has plenty on offer for children. For a start, it has its own Disneyland (tel: 1 830 830; www.hongkongdisneyland.com), featuring all the famous faces as well as rides; there's also Ocean Park, on the south side of Hong Kong Island, offering exotic animals as well as various stomach-churning rides. A trip on the Star Ferry and the incredible views across to Hong Kong Island will appeal, and at 8pm every night the sound-and-light show from the Tsim Sha Tsui waterfront is utterly spectacular. Another sure-fire winner is a trip on the Peak Tram up to The Peak, and the views from the top (where there is also a Madame Tussaud's waxworks). A cable-car ascends Lantau's lofty mountains to Po Lin Monastery and the big Buddha statue. Various museums in Kowloon are also popular with kids.

Macau has a new harbourside area, Fisherman's Wharf, which is a multi-billion dollar, Las Vegas-style complex of entertainment centres, shops and restaurants, as well as Aladdin's Fort, offering an "Arabian-style market" with rides for younger kids (and more attractions being built, including a watersports park).

Various Hong Kong festivals, such as the Cheung Chau Bun Festival (usually in May) and the Dragon Boat Festival (usually in June) are a riot of colour and excitement.

### Guangdong

Seven-year-olds of all ages are likely to enjoy Guangdong's theme parks, where the more Caucasian-looking will probably be deemed attractions in themselves by Chinese visitors.

To the west of Shenzhen are a cluster of theme parks – Window of the World, Splendid China and China Folk Culture Village *(see page XXX)* – and there are others around Guangzhou. Note that the Shenzhen Safari Park, hardly a bastion of animal rights, is not recommended to anyone, and the same applies to Chinese zoos in general.

River cruises in Guangzhou are a good option in a city not over-endowed with juvenile entertainment.

### Hainan

All the main beaches in southern Hainan have large inflatable toys for

hire, alongside dinghies and canoes for older kids. Most resort hotels have a kids' pool and slides – the better ones have children's activity centres, with scheduled programmes during peak seasons.

Away from the beaches, some excursions to explore the landscape and discover the wildlife will appeal to older children: Monkey Island – inhabited by some 1,500 macaques – is worth a day trip *(see page 204)*; also the Hainan Tropical Wildlife Park and Botanical Garden, near Haikou *(see page 201)*.

### Fujian

Fujian is no easier or more challenging than anywhere else in China or elsewhere when it comes to travelling with children. Chinese generally love children and parents find doors opening and officials smiling on all sides when they have youngsters with them. Baby-sitters are usually readily available among hotel staff. Food is, however, likely to be a problem with picky eaters outside Fuzhou and Xiamen. Outdoorsy teenagers will certainly enjoy the wide range of open-air activities widely available. Hard-core mallers, however, might find time hanging heavily on their hands.

### Jiangxi

Nanchang is the only place in Jiangxi that is well suited for travelling with kids – a reflection of its function as a centre for baby adoption. The Gloria Plaza Hotel is accustomed to guests with small children and will allow two kids under age 12 to stay in the same room with their parents for no additional charge. Complimentary cribs are also available.

### Hunan

Changsha is home the world's second-largest ferris wheel and a couple of theme parks: Windows of the World and Martyrs Park, both with roller coasters and the like. The remarkably long cable-car ride up Tianmen Shan in the northwest of the province is exciting, as is the Bai Long lift, an elevator that travels up a cliff face *(see pages 254–5)*, and the scenery in this area is dramatic.

### Guangxi

The ethereal landscapes around Guilin appeal to everyone – and a relaxing Li River cruise is an ideal way to see the amazing peaks for those with children.

Yangshuo is one of the best places in China to visit with children. In the mornings it's common to see families grouped around a table enjoying an inexpensive breakfast, from a menu with enough choice for even the fussiest of eaters. The novelty of visiting farms and seeing buffaloes in rice fields is often more interesting than the landscape for many city kids, and there's a chance to incorporate a host of activities, notably cycling – ideal, as the terrain between the limestone peaks is very flat (see page 377).

### Yunnan

Very few visitors travel in Yunnan with children, but in destinations such as Kunming and Dali the obstacles are not formidable, even if there is a relative lack of child-oriented activities to keep the kids amused. Remoter destinations, such as the Burma Road, could be hard work with younger children. In Dali, activities that children might enjoy include the Cangshan Cable-Car, boat trips on the lake and cycling excursions – particularly on the far side of the lake (accessible by ferry), where traffic is relatively light.

## SHOPPING

### What to Buy

#### Hong Kong

Typically "Chinese" goods such as silk, jade and porcelain are still cheaper and of a better quality in Hong Kong than elsewhere. Though it may not be the bargain basement it once was, for many visitors to the territory this shoppers' paradise offers one of the most compelling activities of their trip. The choice varies – if you are lucky, the shelves are well stocked and you can find excellent and well-cut silk articles being sold very inexpensively; if the supply has dried up, you will only find meagre remnants.

#### Elsewhere in southern China

Jiangxi's famous porcelain is available all over the province, but for the best deals Jingdezhen, China's porcelain capital, is the place to buy. The city centre is full of shops, but the best selection and prices can be found at the Guomao Shichang (International Trade Market) next to Jiefang Lu.

If you are visiting Fujian, the number-one souvenir that people take home is the local tea, with numerous outlets to choose from. Ten Fu Tea's flagship store in Fuzhou is a good place to buy, with lots of nice packages. Tea is also a popular choice in Hainan, along with local pepper and coconut products.

In Guangxi caligraphy and classic landscape paintings are the big item, unless you're in the market for some snake wine.

In Yunnan you could pick up some of the fermented pu'er tea, renowned all over China as an aid to digestion. Alternatively, head to Dali for marble, which has patterns that strongly resemble the traditional Chinese brush landscapes. Boai Lu is a good place to shop for marble, while stores on Huguo Lu (Foreigners' Street) have a good selection of batiks, as fabric or ready-made items. In the northwest of the province there are some interesting art galleries showing Dongba-inspired paintings in modern style. Copies of these are available inexpensively and make a great gift or souvenir.

#### Genuine or fake?

Apart from genuine craft and souvenir items, shoppers are often tempted by low prices for everyday items and clothing. Be warned that low prices are often matched by low quality, and that pirated DVDs and "designer" labels are still being peddled in places. Better-quality goods that are produced for export are mostly sold in the "Friendship Stores" (Youyi Shangdian), as well as in many hotel shops.

It is worth looking for local products in the smaller towns or in the places where ethnic minorities live. These will be difficult to find anywhere else in China. The most usual articles on offer are craft objects for everyday use or specially worked or embroidered garments.

### Import and Export

Antiques that date from before 1795 may not be legally exported (regulations cover six different categories of antiques: books, curios, furniture, calligraphy and paintings, porcelain and jewellery). Those that can be taken out of China must carry a small red seal or have one affixed by the Cultural Relics Bureau. All other antiques are the property of the People's Republic of China and, without the seal, will be confiscated without compensation. Beware of fakes; producing new "antiques" (and the seal) is a thriving industry.

You should not export, or even buy in the first place, objects made from wild animals, especially from ivory. The majority of Western countries ban the import of ivory objects, and will confiscate them without compensation.

See also A–Z section, page 380.

### Bargaining

In many shops, bargaining can be an essential strategy for buying goods at a reasonable price. It is not advisable in the state-owned shops and warehouses, but at souvenir stands it is a good idea to haggle, as many goods are overpriced.

Check prices first at state-operated stores, such as the Friendship Store, before buying a similar item in a hotel shop or on the free market. And in the free market, bargain, and be stubborn – but friendly – if interested in an item.

Bargaining usually begins with the shopkeeper suggesting a price and the buyer responding with a lower one. The starting price is often 30 to 50 percent higher than the price that shopkeepers will eventually accept, so be persistent. Look for missing buttons, stains and other flaws, keep smiling, but walk away if you find the price unacceptable.

In Hong Kong the once-common practice of bargaining for goods is a dying art. Price differences are usually so marginal that it is hardly worthwhile trying to bargain, and it is a complete waste of time in department stores and modern shops. Elsewhere, shopkeepers who are not used to bargaining may react impatiently to your efforts. However, you might get a better deal by paying in cash rather than with a credit card. Small, family-run shops might be more amenable to bargaining, and in markets it is perfectly acceptable, but even here it is highly unlikely that you'll reduce the asking price by more than about 10 to 20 percent.

### Where to Shop

**Department stores**: Almost every town has a department store selling everyday products, from toothpaste to bicycles. However, the quality, style and sizes of items are often lacklustre.

Some large department stores are state-owned, but there are many privately owned small shops selling products from Hong Kong, including relatively high-quality clothing. There is an increasing number of luxury shopping malls in China, where you can find designer labels and a wealth of choice, particularly in large cities such as Guangzhou.

**Markets**: Food items such as fruit, vegetables, fish and meat are sold at markets. You may also find wicker baskets, metalwork and clothes. Look out for antiques/curio markets where you can sift through diverse memorabilia and knick-knacks.

### Hong Kong

Hong Kongers are insatiable shoppers, and the territory is a paradise for retail therapy, with a huge range of goods for sale from a huge range of outlets – from colourful night markets to glitzy malls, multi-storey department stores to bustling narrow streets of antiques and bric-a-brac. It's no longer the bargain basement it once was, however; prices of electronic goods, in particular, are now far closer to those of the West than they were 20 years ago.

The prime shopping centres are the malls of Central, Admiralty and Causeway Bay on Hong Kong Island and Tsim Sha Tsui in Kowloon. Shopping goes on until late seven days a week.

Hong Kong has some of the world's most glitzy and glamorous shopping malls; the best-known are The Landmark and the shiny IFC Mall in Central, Pacific Place in Admiralty and City Plaza in Taikoo Shing further east on the island. In Kowloon the enormous Ocean Terminal and Harbour Centre complexes can keep you busy for hours if not days.

Department stores range from luxury emporiums such as Lane Crawford (IFC Mall) and the upmarket Japanese store Seibu (Pacific Place), to long-established local department stores like Sincere and Wing On, where most residents tend to shop. However, it's the mainland Chinese department stores that are most worthy of exploration, even if you don't intend to buy; these include Arts & Crafts (the most upmarket of all), Yue Hwa (301–309 Nathan Road, Central) and Chung Kiu Chinese Products emporiums.

Hong Kong has a number of lively and interesting shopping markets, well worth a visit even if only to soak up the sights and atmosphere; the pick of the bunch include: Cat Street, off Hollywood Road in Central/Western; Stanley Market, on the south side of the island; Temple Street, Hong Kong's most popular night market, runs from Jordan to Yau Ma Tei in Kowloon; Tung Choi Street is a busy street market in Mong Kok and is less tourist-oriented than Temple Street; the Jade Market, located under the flyover near Kansau Street in Yau Ma Tei, specialises in jewellery.

### Macau

Macau is a good place to buy Chinese antiques and artefacts, and an excellent place to buy well-crafted Asian furniture in wood or wicker. Hong Kong expats often buy their furniture here and have it delivered to Hong Kong. Shipping prices are reasonable. Many antique stores are clustered in **Rua de São Paulo**, the busy lane which leads up to the facade of São Paulo. You are free to bargain hard here. Otherwise, Macau has well-priced wines, brandies and ports.

### Shenzhen

Shenzhen is now a major shopping destination for Hong Kongers. There is a wide variety of merchandise at prices much lower than you will ever find in Hong Kong. Designer clothing and accessories can be bought for less than a fifth of the price in Europe or North America.

**Lo Wu Commercial City**, immediately on the right as you emerge from customs, is the place everyone heads to, a vast shopping mall packed with electronics, jewellery, clothes and all kinds of chinoiserie. Shops are generally open seven days a week from about 10am until 8 or 9pm. Most people venture no further, but there are also some great bargains to be had in the main shopping area of **Dongmen** in the centre of Shenzhen (take the new subway, or find a taxi). You'll also find the best tailors here, clustered together in **Bu Cheng**.

Whatever you are buying, remember to bargain hard!

### Guangzhou

Don't expect the glitz and variety of goods available in Hong Kong, but Guangzhou does offer interesting shopping and good bargains. It is considered to have the widest range of goods of all Chinese cities, from silk products to arts and crafts and musical instruments, many of which are imported from other parts of the country. The main shopping areas in Guangzhou are Zhongshan Wulu, Beijing Lu, Renmin Nanlu, Zhongshan Silu and Xiajiu Lu-Shangjiu Lu. The main open-air market is at Qingping Lu, near Shamian Island.

There are several large department stores in Guangzhou with a wide array of foreign merchandise, at prices lower than in Hong Kong, and often lower than Shenzhen. Recommended stores include: Nanfang Dasha (49 Yanjiang Xilu); Xihu Lu Baihuo Dasha, on Xihu Lu; Xin Da Xin, at the corner of Beijing Lu and Zhongshan Wulu; the government-owned Friendship Store, on the ground floor of the Marriott China Hotel; and the Kwangchow Friendship Store, at 369 Huanshi Donglu, opposite the Garden Hotel.

Here are a few suggestions for the best things to buy in Guangzhou: antiques (Daihe Lu Market); bird cages (new ones at the Bird Market at the Dongfeng Lu entrance of Liuhua Park); clothing and textiles (biggest variety is to be found at the government-owned Friendship Stores); jade (most reliable at established shops like the Jade Shop, Baoli Yuqi Hang, Guangzhou Antique Shop and the jewellery shops of the China, Garden and White Swan hotels); Mao memorabilia (Daihe Lu antique market, Friendship Stores, and the stamp market in People's Park); paper cuts (from the Renshou Temple in Foshan); pearls (Guangzhou Gold and Silver Jewellery Centre (109 Dade Lu) and Sun Moon Hall (Equatorial Hotel, Renmin Beilu)); and seals (have your name engraved in Chinese characters on a seal, called a chop in colonial English, at the basement floor of the White Swan Hotel).

### Hainan

Coconut products – mostly the edible variety – are popular souvenirs and available everywhere. Local coffee, green tea and spices – particularly pepper – are sold in larger souvenir shops and department stores, notably in Xinlong, where most are grown. Coconut and shell souvenirs are ubiquitous but mostly tacky.

### Fujian

Tea is the number-one souvenir to take home from Fujian. It seems that every few metres someone is selling local tea. Stop and sample as the mood takes you, but don't feel pressure to buy. If you are not sure, go to one of the big chain shops: Ten Fu Tea's flagship store in Fuzhou, opposite the Shangri-La Hotel, sells exquisitely packaged and novelty teas to suit every budget, and the shop itself is beautifully designed to make a delightful experience out of a simple shopping excursion. Shoushan stone (a rare type of alabaster in every shade of red through to brown and orange) is found only in a small area of Fujian. Local carvers do incredibly intricate work, and their finished miniature landscapes command colossal prices.

Decorative combs made from buffalo horn are much-prized traditional Fujian souvenirs, but good workmanship is increasingly hard to find. "Bodiless lacquer" is another Fujian speciality: the featherlight vases range from palm size to 2 metres (6½ ft) high or more.

### Jiangxi

Jiangxi's prized porcelain is available all over the province, but for the best deals Jingdezhen – China's porcelain capital – is the place to buy. While the city centre is saturated with shops, the widest selection and the cheapest prices can be found at the Guomao Shichang (International Trade Market) next to Jiefang Lu, about 200 metres (220 yards) south of the central square.

### Hunan

In the land of Mao, Hunan offers more Great Helmsman tack and "memorabilia" than you can shake a stick at, with Shaoshan being the centre of this red commerce. Whether it's watches, paperweights, statues, paintings, or little red books, your every Mao whim is catered for in Shaoshan.

Another big-ticket item readily available almost everywhere in Hunan for the adventurous drinker is snake wine. While all of China imbibes this stuff, Hunan is especially famous for it – papaya, wolfberry and angelica are all added to the dead snake mix before the concoction is left to mature for anywhere between three months to a year. A bottle with snake inside will cost around Rmb 300, and the burning sensation from the 45 percent alcohol content will stay with you for quite some time. More pricey are options with up to three snakes inside for that super slithery taste.

### Guangxi (Guilin)

Shops around the major hotels are geared up for the stream of tourists that pass though here for a brief stay. Classical-style paintings of the Guilin landscape and calligraphy are popular choices. Stalls and booths on Walking Street offer miscellaneous souvenirs, and clothes

**ABOVE:** with tourism developing rapidly in China, souvenirs are easy to find.

and shoes are available on Yiren Lu and Zhongshan Lu around Central Square.

Guilin's culinary speciality is locally made chilli sauce, which livens up its otherwise fairly dull cuisine. Shopkeepers will delight in offering you Guilin's famous snake wine.

Yangshuo's shops are touristy but can keep anyone interested in minority artwork, textiles or jewellery happily occupied.

### Guizhou

Green tea is a good buy. The fiery alcoholic beverage Maotai is also readily available. In Guiyang, Qiancuihang, located on Beijing Lu in front of the Guishou Park Hotel, has good-quality batik, paintings, masks and minority handicrafts. It's a large shop catering to tourists but is well worth a visit. Miao women occasionally sell embroidered textiles in a courtyard near the CITS office in Kaili. There are also a couple of shops selling minority wares near to the entrance. Miao traders also operate throughout the region, although you may need to go to their home to view their merchandise. Machine-produced items will obviously be cheaper than those that have been meticulously sewn. Check the stitching to reveal the production method used. Beware of buying silver jewellery on the street, since much of it is fake.

### Yunnan

Dali's most famous product is its marble. On Boai Lu, rows of stalls offer the marble cut into thin slabs and framed. The patterns in the marble produce effects that bear a remarkable resemblance to traditional Chinese brush landscapes. Prices range from around Rmb 400 per piece. Stores on Huguo Lu (Foreigners' Street) have good selections of minority batiks, which can be purchased

either as strips of cloth or made into shirts, skirts and bags. Bai and Yi minority jewellery are also popular purchases. Yunnan is also famous in China for its fermented pu'er tea, which comes in musty blocks and is allegedly good for the digestion. It is widely available in Kunming and in Dali. The local coffee is good but suprisingly difficult to buy outside the department stores in Kunming.

In Xishuangbanna, apart from tea, coffee, medicinal herbs, jade, wood carvings and handicrafts, you may also buy various ethnic souvenirs, such as bags, dolls, woven items and paintings, and you may even have Dai-style garments tailored. Jinghong's night market on Mengla Lu is open from 7pm until midnight.

Near the entrance to the Mu Palace in Lijiang, some interesting art galleries show Dongba-inspired paintings in modern style. Elsewhere, copies of these ancient religious artefacts make a unique and inexpensive gift.

In Zhongdian there are some good shopping opportunities along Chongzheng Lu for Tibetan art, such as thangka religious paintings, engraved silver swords, and Tibetan jewellery made from amber, turquoise and coral. Initial offering prices are not to be taken seriously.

## SPORTS

### Golf

Hitting the little white ball into the hole is the new craze for China's growing population of well-heeled business executives and their expat chums, and southern China has some of the country's most spectacular golf courses, the region around Shenzhen in particular (see Golf feature on page 158).

### Guangdong (Shenzhen)

**Mission Hills**, 1 Mission Hills Road; tel: 0755 2802 0888 www.missionhillsgroup.com
**Noble Merchant**, Shahe Donglu, Nanshan District; tel: 0755 2690 9999
**Sand River**, 1 Bai Shi Road, Nanshan District; tel: 0755 2690 0111
**Xili**, Tang Lang Village, Xili District; tel: 0755 655 2888; www.xiligolf.com

### Hainan

Golf courses in Hainan have a good reputation. Haikou's best are **West Coast Golf** (128 Binhai Lu; tel: 0898 6870 3180; www.westgolf.com.cn) and **Meishi Mayflower International Golf Club** (88 Binhai Lu; tel: 0898 6871 8888; www.meishi-mayflower.com).
In the Sanya area, **Sun Valley Sanya Golf Club** (Bohou Village, Yalong Bay; tel: 0898 8856 4488; www.sunvalleysanya.com) is rated as one of the best. Nearby is **Yalong Bay Golf Club** (Bohou Village, Yalong Bay; tel: 0898 8856 5039; www.yalongbaygolfclub.com).

### Fujian

Wuyishan has a 27-hole course, Fuzhou and Xiamen each have several nearby courses.

### Jiangxi

Jiangxi's top golf course is in Liantang, a Nanchang suburb about 40 minutes by taxi from the city centre.
**Nanchang Greenwood Golf Resort**
828 Golf Resort, Liantang; tel: 0791 583 8828; www.828hotel.com

**BELOW:** Southern China has some world-class golf courses.

### Guangxi

The largest golf course in Guangxi is Guilin Merryland Golf Club, Zhi Ling Road, Xing'an, Guilin, www.merry-land.com.cn, located north of the city.

### Yunnan

Golf courses are sprouting up in Kunming, Dali and Lijiang. Kunming's **Spring City Golf and Lake Resort** (Tel: 0871 767 1888) features a mountain course designed by Jack Nicklaus and a lake course designed by Robert Trent-Jones Jr. The **Dali Stone Mountain Golf Club** (Tel: 0871 808 1899) is the latest arrival to the Yunnan golf circuit, and has scenic location poised over the Erhai Lake, close to the Three Pagodas.
**Jade Dragon Snow Mountain Golf Course**, tel: 0888 516 3666; www.jadedragongolfclub.com.
Located at the foot of the mountain, this claims to be the longest golf course in the world. Green fees are about US$145 on weekdays, $160 at weekends.

### Hiking

Hong Kong has some excellent hiking routes. The ridge walk along the spine of Hong Kong Island is highly recommended, and
One of the best hikes in southern China is the holy mountain of Heng Shan in Hunan province. It is very popular with Chinese tour groups, so avoid weekends and holidays in these places, as the crowds and congestion can ruin the appeal. The Wuyi Shan area of Fujian and the Wulingyuan area of Hunan are also wonderfully scenic. Apart from

individual climbs (such as the ascent of Moon Hill), the famous karst scenery around Guilin is more usually explored by bicycle – or as a rock-climbing exercise – than as a hike.
Guizhou and Yunnan offer endless possibilities for hikers. In the former, the most rewarding hikes are between the minority villages in the east and south of the province. In Yunnan, tropical Xishuangbanna also offers treks between minority villages, as well as more demanding jungle treks, best organised through tour operators in Jinghong. Further north, the Cangshan Mountains west of Dali and, most famously, Tiger Leaping Gorge near Lijiang have tremendous hiking. Tours are possible and can be arranged through hotels and guest houses, but most people trek independently. Longer treks in the spectacular mountains of the remote northwest, or in the similarly remote Nu Jiang Gorge area, require proper preparation.

### Other Activities

### Guangdong

Watersports are available at the Xiaomeisha resort area to the east of Shenzhen. Also close to Shenzhen, various outdoor activities, including horse-riding, are on offer at the Xili Lake Holiday Village close to the well-known golf course. The nearby Window of the World theme park has an indoor ski centre.
**Xili Lake Holiday Village**; tel: 0755 2651 1743.
**Window of the World Indoor Ski Area**, Nanshan District, Shenzhen; tel: 0755 2660 8000.

### Hainan

All seaside resorts either have their own watersports service or work with a reputable operator. One of the best is available at **Yalong Bay Underwater World**, tel: 0898 8856 5588; www.underwatersightseeing.com

### Fujian

Wuyishan has many opportunities for water- and mountain sports – including white-water rafting, trekking, horse-riding and kayaking. Xiamen's annual International Marathon first took place in 2003 and in 2006 attracted some 21,000 participants.

### Guangxi (Yangshuo)

Yangshuo is one of the best places in China for outdoor pursuits – from a gentle bike ride to rock climbing on the region's limestone peaks.

**Cycling:** bicycles, tandems and mountain bikes are available to hire. Charges start from Rmb 10 per day plus a Rmb 300 deposit. A guide can combine a bus trip to a start off point with a hike or a bike ride followed by a spot of rafting.

**Bamboo rafting:** various enterprises have set up along the Yulong River offering the chance to mess about on the river for a few hours. The cost is around Rmb 180 for two hours.

**Rock climbing:** the region's limestone crags offer some great climbs that have been developed over the last decade. There are over 200 bolted climbs in the surrounding mountains. Experienced guides, courses and equipment hire are offered by a number of companies based around Xian Qian Lu Gui Ha Lu. The best guidebook to use is *Yangshuo Rock Climbs* by Paul Collis – available at all climbing shops. **China Climb**, the longest-established climbing company in Yangshuo, is based at The Lizard Lounge on Xian Qian Lu; www.chinaclimb.com The Karst Café at 42 Xian Qian Jie is a friendly place to find climbing information; www.karstclimber.com

**Caving:** trips to the caves around Yangshuo can be arranged a travel agent or on an ad hoc basis with a freelance guide. If you are a serious caver, ask at the rock-climbing cafés and shops.

**Kayaking:** most of the Yangshuo tour operators will offer kayaking with half-day trips for Rmb 150.

**Mountain biking:** for more technical mountain-bike information try the

climbing shops above and X-climber (29 Guiha Lu, tel/fax: 0773 881 4499), which rents out better quality mountain bikes for experienced riders.

**Hot-air ballooning:** A trip in a hot-air balloon above the karst scenery costs around Rmb 750 per hour. Operated by the Guilin Yangshuo Flying Balloon Club, most tour operators in the area sell these tours to anyone who is "not in a bad physical or spiritual condition".

### Yunnan

*see Hiking section, opposite.*

## TOURS AND AGENCIES

There are countless travel agencies within and outside China that handle domestic travel arrangements. Prominent among the agencies is **China International Travel Services** (**CITS**), with branches throughout China. **China Travel Services** (**CTS**) is a similar organisation, which also caters to foreigners. The efficiency of both organisations still leaves a lot to be desired. Neither functions as a tourist information service – they only exist to sell tours – although some branches are far more helpful than others.

If you go directly to an agency in the area you are visiting, savings may be possible. Sometimes agencies such as CITS may hold transport and entertainment tickets, even when such tickets are "sold out". Prices will be higher than at source, however.

There are also small-scale, unlicensed tour operators, whose prices may be cheaper. Reportedly, some of these use unroadworthy vehicles, take their customers to shops and restaurants that give the guides "backhanders" (though this probably also happens with licensed operators), and demand mark-ups of 100 percent or more for tickets to tourist sites.

### China National Tourism Offices

www.cnto.org
**Australia**, 19/F, 44 Market St, Sydney, NSW 2000; tel: 9299 4057; fax: 9290 1958.
**Singapore**, 1 Shenton Way, #7-05 Robina House, Singapore 068803; tel: 221 8681; fax: 221 9267.
**United Kingdom**, 4 Glenworth St, London NW1 5PG; tel: 020 7935 9787; fax: 020 7487 5842.
**United States**, 350 Fifth Avenue, Suite 6413, Empire State Building,

New York, NY 10118; tel: 888 760 8218; fax: 212 760 8809. Also at 550 North Brand Boulevard, Suite 910, Glendale, California, CA 91203; tel: 818 545 7507; fax: 818 545-7506.

### UK tour operators

**Abercrombie & Kent**: St George's House, Ambrose Street, Cheltenham, Gloucestershire, GL50 3LG; tel: 01242 547700; www.abercrombiekent.co.uk
**Cox & Kings**: Gordon House, 10 Greencoat Place, London SW1P 1PH; tel: 020 7873 5000; www.coxandkings.co.uk
**CTS Horizons**: CTS House, above 7 St Martin's Lane, London WC2H 9DL; tel: 020 7836 9911; www.ctshorizons.com
**Kuoni**: Kuoni House, Dorking, Surrey, RH5 4AZ; tel: 01306 47002; www.kuoni.co.uk
Kuoni operates in China as SKY Travel, www.skytravel.com.hk, and is one of the most experienced tour operators in the region.
**Regent Holidays**: 15 John St, Bristol, BS1 2HR; tel: 0870 499 0911; www.regent-holidays.co.uk
Long-standing China specialist.
**Voyages Jules Verne**: 21 Dorset Square, London NW1 6QG; tel: 0845 166 7003; www.vjv.co.uk

### US tour operators

**Abercrombie & Kent**: 1520 Kensington Road, Suite 212, Oak Brook, Illinois, IL 60523-2156; tel: 800 554 7016; www.abercrombiekent.com
**Asian Pacific Adventures**: 6065 Calvin Avenue, Tarzana, CA 91356; tel: 800 825 1680/818 881 2745; www.asianpacificadventures.com
**Backroads**: 801 Cedar St, Berkeley, CA 94710-1800; tel: 510 527 1555; www.backroads.com
**Bike China Adventures**, tel: 1388 2266 575, or toll-free in the US on 1 800 818 1778; http://bikechina.com. Specialist company offering bike tours all over China, including in the provinces of Yunnan, Guangdong, Guizhou and Hunan. The tours are custom-made or private, in small groups of between one and eight people.

### Hong Kong tour operators

There are hundreds of tour agencies in Hong Kong offering guided tours to China. China Travel (www.chinatravel.com) is reliable, while CTS has a couple of branches, where they arrange tours, tickets and visas for travel to the mainland, although they don't provide a tourist information service:

**Central**: G/F, CTS House, 78–83 Connaught Road, Central; tel: 2853 3533.
**Kowloon**: 1/F, Alpha House, 27 Nathan Road, Tsim Sha Tsui; tel: 2315 7106.

*For tourist information in Hong Kong and Macau see page 384.*

### Macau

**CITS**: Avenida da Praia Grande 429, Centro Comercial da Praia Grande, Sala 201; tel: 2897 5183. Local branch of China International Travel Services, can book tours, transportation and visas for China.

### Guangdong

The most comprehensive sightseeing tours are run by **China Travel** (www.chinatravel.com). Call their offices in Shenzhen (tel: 0755 5180 646) or Hong Kong (tel: 2155 2088) for information.

In Hong Kong, **International Cyclists to Asia** (tel: 2454 9191; www.mountainbikingasia.com) runs two-wheeled trips around the backwaters of Guangdong, and elsewhere around China and neighbouring countries.

### Hainan

Sanya Holiday operates tours all over the island; tel: 0898 8825 5203; www.sunnysanya.com

### Fujian

Branches of CITS outside China are the most likely starting points for an English-speaking tour of Fujian. Hotel tour desks can usually provide a guide and an itinerary of sorts at short notice.
The **China Youth Travel Service** (CYTS) has established a good reputation for itself in recent years. Its Xiamen branch works in association with Xiamen Youth Southeast Travel Agency and claims to be able to handle international and domestic air reservations and ticketing, coach and train tickets, tours to Quanzhou and other nearby attractions as well as city tours. Supplement for English-language guides – Rmb 200 over and above the basic charges. They have a tour desk at the Sofitel Plaza Xiamen. www.xmtravel.com.cn

### Jiangxi

There are several travel agents and tour operators in Nanchang, but most are geared towards domestic tourists and cannot arrange itineraries with English-language guide services. As such, the options are limited to the

Jiangxi CITS and the Jiangxi Overseas Tourist Corp, both of which can arrange English-language tours of the entire province.
**Jiangxi CITS** (Mon–Fri 8am–noon and 2.30–6pm), 368 Bayi Dadao (behind the Jiangxi Hotel); tel: 0791 620 2259.
**Jiangxi Overseas Tourist Corporation**, 502 Minde Lu; tel: 0791 218 9289.

### Hunan

As in Jiangxi province, opportunities for English-language tours are limited.
**CITS**, 11/F, Xiaogyuan Building, Wuyidong Lu, Changsha; tel: 0731 228 0442.
**CTS**, 6/F, Xintian Office Building, Chezhanbei Lu, Changsha; tel: 0731 228 699.
Hunan Tourism Office website: www.hnt.gov.cn/english/

### Guangxi

#### Guilin
In Guilin, signing-up tours may offer the simplest solution to sightseeing when you have limited time. They can also be cost-effective – bear in mind that some entrance fees cost Rmb 60 or more. All major hotels have their own tour desks.
**CITS**, 19 Binjiang Lu, Guilin; tel: 0773 288 2727.

#### Yangshuo
There is certainly no shortage of tour operators along Xie Jie (West Street), and a lot of the hotels and guest houses have their own tour desk offering essentially the same tours, day trips and activities. Yangshuo's Tourist Information Service Centre has branches throughout the town.

**Uncle Sam's Travel**, 42 Xie Jie; tel/fax: 0773 882 8061; email: samszhang@hotmail.com
**Lisa's Café**, 71 Xie Jie. Helpful tour desk at back of popular café.

Australian-owned company **Bike Asia** (http://www.bikeasia.com) can be found on the 2nd floor, 42 Guihua Lu; tel: 0773 882 652. It offers Western-standard mountain-bike hire from its town premises, in addition to a range of guided tours.

### Guizhou

**Minorities-Guizhou Travel** at 2-20-4, Meijia Building, 53 Zhanghua Beilu, Guiyang (tel: 0851 685 1623) operates group tours to minority areas for foreign visitors. Knowledgeable and attentive guides speak English, French and German. Transportation is good, and

itineraries vary in length of time and places visited. Their website at www.minogz.com also gives information about local festivals.

Although there are many sightseeing tours to the waterfall at Huangguoshu, they are grossly overpriced and may not even have a competent English-speaking guide. The entrance fee for some attractions includes a Chinese-speaking guide. Invariably they are there as a minder and to hasten you through the location rather than to provide much in the way of information.

River rafting is popular along the Wuyang River north of Kaili in eastern Guizhou. Contact the **Wu Yang Feng Qing Travel Agency** on the corner of Huancheng Donglu and Buxing Jie and ask for Mr Jiang Qian Ling, who speaks English; tel: 0855 386 9108.

### Yunnan

Although practically every hotel in Kunming offers sightseeing tours and travel bookings, by the far the best place to do this is the travel agency at the **Camellia Hotel** at 154 Dongfeng Donglu (tel: 0871 316 6388; www.kmcamelliahotel.com/English/Travel-1.asp), which has many years' experience of catering to foreign tourists, and has a vast range of tours and other services (the Stone Forest tour with no stops at souvenir shops is very popular). Other popular tours offered include glacier walks at Mount Meili Shan, minority tours in western Yunnan, and overland trips to Tibet via Zhongdian (Shangri-la).

The **Xishuangbanna China International Travel Service** in Jinghong caters for for foreign tourists. Tel: 0691 672 3638; www.lmrbt.com

Almost all hotels in Dali and Lijiang offer guides and ticket booking services. In Lijiang, the **Tourist Reception Center** on Dong Dajie, near the waterwheel square, can arrange online bookings and issue air tickets.

**Lijiang Qi Dian Adventures**, 44 Xing Ren Xiang, Wuyi Jie, Lijiang. Tel: 130 1347 2550; www.ljqd.com

**Khampa Caravan**, Beimen Jie, Zhongdian. Tel: 0887 828 8648 or 828 8907; www.khampacaravan.com Specialises in adventure tours to remote areas of the far northwestern corner of Yunnan.

# A – Z

# A HANDY SUMMARY OF PRACTICAL INFORMATION, ARRANGED ALPHABETICALLY

## **A** dmission Charges

Nearly all museums, galleries, temples and similar attractions in China charge a small entry fee. Entrance to privately owned sites, theme parks, etc, is more expensive. Admission to all beaches is free; parks usually charge a nominal fee. Discounts for foreign students are rare, although a few museums and cultural events, mostly in Hong Kong and Macau, offer a small reduction (with an ISIC – International Student Identity Card).

### *Hong Kong and Macau*

Government-owned museums and galleries are good value; average charges in Hong Kong are around HK$10 for adults and HK$5 for seniors and students, with similar prices in Macau. Children under three are free, and many museums are free to all on Wednesdays. The HK$30 Museum Pass gives one week's unlimited access to six of Hong Kong's most popular museums.

## **B** udgeting for Your Trip

Daily expenses are broadly the same as elsewhere in China, though Hong Kong and Macau are slightly more

expensive. An average US$150 per day to include travel, meals, accommodation and typical activities should be ample, though this does vary from one region to another. Accommodation will be your largest daily expense, accounting for just over half your budget on average. If you show up at a hotel without a booking and offer to pay in cash, you might be able to haggle for a lower rate. Bargaining for a wide range of products and services is something of a Chinese institution in fact, though you should prepare your tactics in advance *(see Shopping, page 373)*.

Food is extremely good value; if you're on a tight budget, food stalls and market snack bars are usually very cheap; they might look a bit grubby, but the food is often pretty good. Upmarket hotels, particularly Western chains, often serve huge buffet breakfasts which, although expensive, should see you through most of the day. Also, look out for special menus and budget set menus at cafés and restaurants. "Business lunch" set menus are great value.

Transport is very reasonably priced *(see Transport, page 351)*. In many cities you can hire bicycles from some of the larger hotels.

## Business Hours

Most offices, shops and businesses are open 9am–6pm, though some may close for an hour at lunch and some shops stay open later (until 10pm), particularly in larger cities. Tea shops seem to operate almost round the clock. Government offices are usually open Mon–Fri, from 8.30am to 5.30pm, with a lunch break from noon to 1.30pm. However, many banks – especially the foreigner-friendly Bank of China – are now open seven days a week, from 8am to 6pm, with no lunch break. Bank of China ATMs accept most international credit cards. Expect to wait if you change money at a bank.

Bars and restaurants are free to choose their own opening times and stay open until late, particularly in and around Hong Kong and Macau, where you can join the all-night drinking and partying if you've got the stamina (and money). In Macau, after midnight most of the action is centred around the 24-hour casinos.

Major tourist attractions are usually open every day, though museums tend to close one day during the week, generally Monday or Tuesday, and are sometimes shut for lunch.

## CLIMATE CHART

### Guangzhou

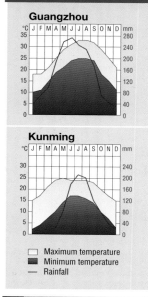

### Kunming

☐ Maximum temperature
■ Minimum temperature
— Rainfall

## Climate

Much of southern China has a humid subtropical climate, with mild to warm winters, long hot summers and plenty of rain.

Given their low latitude, **coastal areas** have surprisingly cool temperatures during the short winter season, and although climate charts show this as the dry season, the weather can be grey and drizzly at times, especially in the east of the region. Only on the southern coast of Hainan Island is the weather reliably warm (24°C/75°F and above) in the January–March period. Late March to early June is a time of rising heat and humidity, and a lot of rain interspersed with drier spells. From June to mid-September, temperatures are uniformly high (above 30°C/86°F), rain can be torrential and the humidity is uncomfortable. There is also the risk of typhoons in late summer. October through to December sees the best weather – drier, less humid and pleasantly warm. Hong Kong is often blessed with perfect weather in November, although a few days without rain sees the pollution levels creep up – this is particularly unpleasant in the Pearl River Delta.

**Inland** there tends to be even more rain, and flooding can disrupt travel plans in the summer months. Guizhou province is notorious for its rain. Higher elevations are obviously going to be cooler and generally wetter. Winter temperatures are significantly lower away from the coast, and most areas can expect frost on a few occasions in winter, more frequently the further north you are. The higher reaches of Wuyi Shan, Heng Shan, Wulingyyuan and Lu Shan receive occasional snowfalls in winter.

**Yunnan province** experiences rather different weather from the rest of the region, and Kunming (at an altitude of 1,900 metres/6,200 ft) has probably the most pleasant climate of any city in China, with springlike temperatures for most of the year, and plenty of sunshine. Xishuangbanna, together with southern Hainan Island, is the only truly tropical region of China, with high temperatures throughout the year and a dry sunny winter season.

The best months for touring the region as a whole are April, May, September and October. Hong Kong and much of the coast is pleasant from October to December. Xishuangbanna is perfect at any time between November and March. Kunming, Dali and Lijiang can be cool in winter, but the clear weather makes for tremendous mountain views at this time of year.

## Crime and Safety

Your chances of being a victim of crime are extremely low; China is one of the safest countries for visitors in all of Asia. Nevertheless, as one of the most rapidly booming regions of the world, southern China is also starting to suffer from the associated rise in crime, particularly in cities such as Guangzhou and Shenzhen.

You can minimise potential risk by following the same precautions as you would when on holiday anywhere else in the world. Be particularly vigilant when you're out on the street, especially in crowded places, such as bus and train stations and markets, where pickpockets and bag-slashers can be a problem. Avoid dimly lit city streets at night.

Chinese police (Public Security Bureau, or PSB) wear green uniforms and caps. Make it clear from the outset that you want a loss report to claim on your insurance policy, otherwise you might find yourself bogged down in a lengthy bureaucratic procedure to investigate the crime. Most PSB stations should have an English-speaker to hand, but if you can take someone with you who speaks Chinese, it will probably help. The PSB are generally friendly towards foreigners.

Load your hotel concierge's phone number into your mobile phone, and note it separately on a piece of paper to carry with you, as few police officers speak English.

## Customs Regulations

### Visas & Passports

All foreigners must acquire an entry visa before arrival in China, although those visiting Hong Kong or Macau only do not usually require a visa. If you are part of an organised group, the tour operator will usually obtain your visa for you. Individual travellers can apply at any Chinese embassy or at the CTS office in Hong Kong (see page 378). The procedure is straightforward, taking about a week (quicker in Hong Kong), depending on the latest regulations. A 30-day single-entry visa is usually issued. Your passport must be valid for six months after the expiry date of the entry visa.

If your visa expires while you are in China, it can be extended by the local Public Security Bureau (Gongan Ju), the ubiquitous police. However, make sure you visit them before it expires, because fines for overstaying your welcome can be steep, negotiations long and frustrating and, depending where you are, it may take some time to get the stamp you seek.

Nowadays, most of the country is open to foreigners, except some border areas and military zones.

### Customs

On arrival, each traveller must complete a health declaration form.

Tourists can freely import two bottles of wine or spirits and 400 cigarettes, as well as foreign currency and valuables for personal use without restrictions. The import of weapons, ammunition, drugs and pornographic literature is prohibited.

On departure, antiques such as porcelain, paintings, calligraphy, carvings and old books must carry the red lacquer seal of an official antique shop. Otherwise, they can be confiscated by the customs officials

## Emergencies

For ambulance, police or fire you can call one number throughout the country: **112**. As long as you speak clearly you should be understood. Most operators speak some English and French.

For police, fire and ambulance services in Hong Kong, dial **999**. In Macau call **999** for emergencies, or **919** for police.

without compensation *(see also Shopping, page 373)*.

Hong Kong is a free port, so you can bring as many gifts as you like in and out of the territory. Duty-free allowances for visitors are 200 cigarettes and 50 cigars or 250 g tobacco and 1 litre of wine or spirits.

## **D** isabled Travellers

Facilities for physically disabled visitors are generally rare or non-existent throughout the region. Steps and rough paths are commonplace at all tourist sites, and there are few ramps or special entrances for wheelchairs. Travel is only feasible at all if you're with an organised group, and even then, it's not a comfortable experience. Nevertheless, the needs of disabled visitors are beginning to be considered, with special legislation being introduced in recent years. Newly built luxury hotels in bigger cities now comply with new regulations regarding facilities for the disabled. Ask at the China National Tourist Offices and CITS *(see page 377)* for information about special trips for people with disabilities.

## **E** lectricity

Electricity in China is 220 volts, 50 cycles AC. Don't forget to take an international adaptor which can accommodate different-style plugs; the most common are two flat-pin, also three flat-pin plugs (in Hong Kong and Macau). Hotels of three-star standard and above should have adaptors to borrow, also cheaply available at larger department stores. If travelling away from tourist centres, it is worth taking battery-operated equipment.

## Embassies and Consulates

### Hong Kong

**Australia**, 21–24/F, Harbour Center, 25 Harbour Road, Wan Chai; tel: 2827 8881.
**Canada**, 11/F, Tower One, Exchange Square, 8 Connaught Place, Central; tel: 2810 4321.
**Japan**, 46/F, Tower One, Exchange Square, Central; tel: 2522 1184.
**New Zealand**, Rm 6505, Central Plaza, 18 Harbour Road, Wan Chai; tel: 2877 4488.
**Singapore**, Unit 901, 9/F, Tower One, Admiralty Centre, 18 Harcourt Road, Admiralty; tel: 2527 2212.
**United Kingdom**, 1 Supreme Court Road, Admiralty; tel: 2901 3000.
**United States**, 26 Garden Road; tel: 2523 9011.

### Guangzhou

**Australia**, 12/F Development Centre, No. 3 Linjiang Lu, Zhujiang New City; tel: 020 3814 0111; email: guangzhou.consular@dfat.gov.au
**Cambodia**, Room 811, Garden Hotel (Tower), 368 Huangshi Donglu; tel: 020 8333 8999/804/808; email: cambodia@public.guanzhou.gd.cn
**Canada**, Room 801, China Hotel Office Tower, Liuhua Lu; tel: 020 8666 0569; email: ganzu.consular-consulaire@international.gc.ca
**United Kingdom**, 7/F, Guangdong International Hotel, 339 Huanshi Donglu; tel: 020 8314 3000; email: Guangzhou.Consular@fco.gov.uk
**United States**, 1 Shamian Nanjie, tel: 020 8121 8000.
**Vietnam**, 2/F, B Building North, Hotel Landmark Canton Qiaoguang Lu; tel: 020 8330 5910/5911 6801; fax: 020 8330 5915.

### Kunming

**Laos**, Room 3226, Camellia Hotel, 145 Dongfeng Donglu; tel: 0871 317 6623.
**Myanmar**, Room B 503, 5/F, Longyuan Haozhai, 166 Weiyuan Jie; tel: 0871 364 1268; email: info@mcg-kunming.com
**Thailand**, 1/F, Kunming Hotel (South Building), 145 Dongfeng Donglu; tel: 0871 316 8916.
**Vietnam**, 2/F, Bestway Hotel, 157 Beijing Lu; tel: 0871 351 5889.

## Etiquette

Although Chinese politeness has always been a formal behaviour that follows strict rules, in some situations Chinese people can seem quite impolite by Western norms. Nevertheless, as a visitor you are advised to remain polite.

For the Chinese, it is bad to lose face, especially in front of a foreigner. Take care not to do this to anyone; any criticism or complaint should be made tactfully.

It is usually not the custom in China to greet someone with a handshake, though it is commonly used with foreigners. Moreover, embracing or kissing when greeting or saying goodbye is highly unusual. Chinese people do not, on the whole, show their emotions in public.

If you are visiting China on business, be aware that it is as important for the Chinese to make and keep good connections *(guanxi)* as it is for foreigners. Expect lots of gifts and invitations. The wining and dining of guests *(qinke)* is an old Chinese tradition and is still used today to thank friends for a favour or to make new business contacts. If invited, you are obliged to return the invitation. For this reason, you are not expected to share the restaurant bill and to insist may cause embarrassment.

It is considered normal in China to eat noisily and belch during a meal. This does not mean, however, that a foreign guest needs to do likewise. An increasing number of Chinese, particularly in the larger cities, do not find this behaviour very pleasant either. In many simple restaurants, bones and other remnants are thrown on the table or the floor, instead of being left on the side of the plate. It is also quite common for people to spit.

## **G** ay and Lesbian Travellers

Officially, homosexuality is outlawed in China, but in practice it is becoming more widely accepted and tolerated by both the authorities and society as a whole. Most of the major cities in the south, particularly Hong Kong and Macau, have one or two gay bars and clubs. Hong Kong held

**BELOW:** Yalong Bay on the southern coast of Hainan.

its first Pink Parade in October 2004, and the city's Gay and Lesbian film festival has become part of the alternative arts calendar (November, see www.hklgff.hk/index.html).

# H ealth and Medical Care

The most frequently reported health problem is diarrhoea, as it is throughout Eastern Asia. The best prevention is to ensure maximum hygiene while travelling, especially in restaurants and roadside snack bars. Never eat raw, uncooked, or partially cooked food other than in the top hotels. Animal or human excrement is still frequently used as fertiliser, so bacteria on uncooked vegetables can easily be ingested. If travelling independently on a tour group, acquire chopsticks and a tin bowl with lid for train journeys and meals in small roadside restaurants. Drink only boiled or bottled water, even though the tap water is drinkable in some places, including Hong Kong. Reduce exposure to insects; wear long sleeves and trousers outdoors during twilight hours. There is a small malaria risk in rural areas.

For up-to-date advice on health hazards, including bird flu (avian influenza) see www.fco.gov.uk.

A selection of hospitals and clinics are listed below. The Hong Kong expat website http://hongkong.asiaxpat.com, which also covers Guangzhou, Macau and other Asian cities, has more.

### Medical Treatment

**Hong Kong**
**Adventist Hospital**, 40 Stubbs Rd, Happy Valley; tel: 2574 6211.
**Central Medical Practice**, 1501 Prince's Building, Central; tel: 2521 2567.
**Hong Kong Central Hospital**, 1B Lower Albert Rd, Central; tel: 2522 3141.

**Queen Elizabeth Hospital**, 30 Gascoigne Rd, Kowloon; tel: 2958 8888.
**Queen Mary Hospital**, Pokfulam Rd, Hong Kong; tel: 2816 6366.

**Macau**
**Kiang Wu Hospital**, Estrada Coelho do Amaral; tel: 2837 1333.
**S. Januário Hospital**, Estrada do Visconde de S. Januário; tel: 2831 3731.

**Shenzhen**
**Shenzhen People's Hospital**, Dongmen Beilu; tel: 2553 3018.

**Guangdong**
**The Can Am International Medical Centre**'s hotline in Guangzhou (tel: 020 8386 6988) is staffed 24 hours a day.
**Guangzhou No. 1 People's Hospital**, 602 Renmin Beilu; tel: 020 8108 2090.

**Fujian**
**Fujian Provincial Hospital**, No. 134 Dong Dajie, Fuzhou; tel: 0591 8755 7768.
**Lifeline Medical System**, 123 Xidi Villa Hubin Beilu, Xiamen City; tel: 0592 532 3168 (24 hours); email: lifelinexiamen@yahoo.com
**Union Hospital Affiliated to Fujian University of Medical Science**, No. 11 Xinquan Lu, Fuzhou; tel: 0591 8335 7896, ext. 8291, 8292.

**Jiangxi**
The best medical care can be found in Nanchang, where you should be able to consult a physician who speaks some English. Located in the heart of the city, and recommended by expats, is the **First Hospital of Nanchang** at 128 Xiangshan Beilu.

**Guangxi**
Guilin's Renmin Hospital is situated just off Wenming Lu.

## Pharmacies

Chemists are plentiful; those in larger towns and cities also offer basic medical advice, though you'll probably need to take a good phrase book or a Chinese-speaker with you, as few staff will speak English. The more upmarket hotels may also have a clinic for their guests. A wide range of health products, including antibiotics and contraceptives, is available over the counter.

**Yunnan**
The local emergency hotline is 316 5603, but very little English is spoken. The US Embassy in Beijing recommends the Hospital of the Kunming Medical College at 153 Xichang Lu, Kunming; tel: 0871 532 4888, emergency hotline: 0871 532 4590; and the Yunnan First People's Hospital, Jinbi Lu, Kunming; tel: 0871 363 4031/172.

### Dental Treatment

**Hong Kong**
Dr James Woo & Associates, 908 Crawford House, 70 Queens Road Central, Hong Kong; tel: 852 2869 6986. A US-trained practice.

**Macau**
Dr Diana Yuk Tan Ho, Avda Praia Grande, Talent Commercial Centre 7/A; tel: 335 213. US-qualified.

**Guangdong**
Kai Yi (Sunshine) International Dental Clinic, 5/F Ice Flower Hotel, 2 Tianhe Beilu, Guangzhou; tel: 020 3886 4821/3387 4278.

## I nternet

Once ubiquitous, numbers of internet cafés (wangba) in large cities in China have tumbled dramatically in recent years as the authorities have cracked down on licences. Those there are may be hard to find, as they often do not have signs in English. Once logged on, be prepared to find your access to the airwaves obstructed by the government's firewall (nicknamed "The Great Wall"), which habitually blocks the BBC, CNN and other Western networks.

Many hotels will provide in-room internet access. Even budget hostels will often have free wireless service. Many cafés and bars in larger cities provide free wireless internet for those with wireless-enabled laptops.

Look in the vicinity of colleges and universities for cheaper places; youth hostels have cheap internet access.

**BELOW:** reality TV has spawned increasingly bizarre game shows in China.

## Left Luggage

The bigger hotels will usually have somewhere safe for guests to leave their luggage. Otherwise, most airports, bus and train stations have reasonably secure left-luggage facilities available for a small fee, though they may only be open during daylight hours.

## Maps

Maps with place names in both English and Chinese are useful. If you can point at a place name written in Chinese characters, many a misunderstanding can be avoided.

Insight Guides produce several *Fleximaps* to Chinese cities, including Hong Kong, Macau, Shenzhen and Guangzhou. For more details, see www.insightguides.com.

You can buy street maps of most cities in kiosks, bookstalls, hotel shops, etc, as well as in bus and train stations and airports. These are usually in Chinese; others with explanations in English can be found in bigger cities, in bookshops and in larger hotels.

In Hong Kong, the Tourist Board has free Welcome Packs, which include maps that show airport, seaport and border crossings from the Chinese mainland.

## Media

### Newspapers

The English-language *China Daily* is published every day except Sunday. It is moderately informative, but toes the party line. Same-day editions are available only in large cities; elsewhere, it'll probably be several days late.

Overseas editions of the *China Daily* are published in Hong Kong and the United States. Hong Kong also produces the highly influential English-language daily *South China Morning Post*, as well as the *Hong Kong Standard*. International newspapers and magazines can usually be found in the larger hotels. Guangzhou now publishes magazines aimed at expats, which are a good source of local information, news and events. They are free in most hotels, bars and restaurants.

Most large hotels sell foreign-language newspapers and journals, including the *International Herald Tribune*, *The Times*, *Asian Wall Street Journal*, *Time*, *Newsweek*, *Far Eastern Economic Review* and many more. Foreign online newspapers are not generally jammed, except for the BBC online News in Chinese.

### Television and Radio

There are few options available to English-speaking audiences, all broadcasting from Hong Kong. The one dedicated English-language radio channel is RTHK. If you bring a short-wave radio, the BBC World Service (www.bbc.co.uk/worldservice) is available 24 hours a day; you can also listen to Asian-focused programmes on the Voice of America (www.voanews.com/english/asia.cfm), Radio Canada (www.rcinet.ca/rci/en) and Radio Australia (www.abc.net.au/ra).

For local news, Hong Kong's two TV stations, TVB and ATV, each broadcast one English-language channel and one Chinese-language channel. If you are staying in a hotel you should have access to a good selection of regional and international broadcasters in English.

As for the mainstream Chinese TV output, it's all pretty poor, ranging from pro-government news and propaganda programmes to tacky entertainment shows and dated Hollywood and Chinese movies.

### Money

The Chinese currency is the *renminbi* (people's currency), often abbreviated to **Rmb**. The basic unit is the *yuan* (colloquially, *kuai*). Ten *jiao* (colloquially, *mao*) make one yuan; 10 *fen* make one *jiao*. Thus, 100 fen make one yuan. Notes are currently issued for 1, 2, 5, 10, 20, 50 and 100 yuan. Coins come in 1 yuan, 5 jiao, 1 jiao and 5 fen.

Hong Kong and Macau have retained their separate currencies, the Hong Kong dollar and pataca. Hong Kong dollars are also widely accepted in Guangzhou and Shenzhen, but if you are staying more than a day in mainland China it is worth changing your money to Chinese currency.

Major currencies are accepted in banks and hotels. Global network-connected ATM machines (Cirrus, Plus) can be found in major cities and tourist towns – try branches of the Bank of China, major hotels and department stores. **Citibank** also has a presence in Hong Kong and Guangzhou, and its ATMs usually accept lots of different cards. Money can also be withdrawn on credit from Bank of China ATMs that accept Visa and MasterCard, which are quite widespread in larger towns and cities.

Don't expect to use credit cards much outside the major cities. Train and bus tickets must be purchased in cash, but plane tickets can be bought with credit cards.

### Exchange rates

In July 2007, Rmb 7.5 = US$1, Rmb 15.5 = £1 sterling. The Hong Kong dollar is pegged to the US dollar at HK$7.8 to US$1. HK$15.9 = £1 sterling. The Chinese yuan is similar in value to the Hong Kong dollar: Rmb 1 = HK$1.03. Macanese Patacas are pegged to the Hong Kong dollar: MOP$1 = HK$0.97 or Rmb 0.94.

## Photography

Taking photographs or videos of military installations is prohibited. As in other countries, some museums, palaces or temples will not allow photographs to be taken, or will charge a fee. At other times, photography is allowed, but without using a flash.

### Postal Services

Domestic mail delivery is exceedingly fast and cheap in China, and it puts most Western postal services to shame. Within some cities, there is often same-day delivery; between large cities, delivery is usually overnight. International mail, too, is efficient.

Express mail (EMS) is available to the majority of international destinations, as are private international courier services. Note

### Public Holidays

Official Chinese state holidays:
**1 January** New Year's Day
**1 May** Labour Day
**1 October** National Day
Most shops and offices close down for a week or so during Chinese New Year, and for a few days around Labour Day and National Day.

In addition, **Hong Kong** has the following public holidays:
**March/April** Good Friday and Easter Monday; Ching Ming Festival (5 April)
**May/June** Dragon Boat Festival; Buddha's Birthday (lunar); Labour Day (1 May)
**1 July** SAR Establishment Day
**September/October** The day following Mid-Autumn Festival
**1 October** National Day (two days)
**October** Chung Yeung Festival
**25 December** Christmas (two days)

In **Macau**, the SAR Establishment Day is on **20 December** instead of the 1 July holiday.

that large parcels must be packed and sealed at the post office.

For general delivery or poste restante services, you should visit the central post office. Card members can also use American Express offices for receiving mail.

## Public Toilets

Few public conveniences exist, and in general they are of the squat-over-a-hole variety and are not for the squeamish. Carry your own toilet paper and hand cleanser, as public toilets seldom provide either. The smarter hotels' loos could well be signed "Oasis"; foreigners popping in to "spend a fen" are unlikely to have their progress barred. The rare public pay toilets are generally cleaner than free ones; some – very heavily used – are in bus and train stations.

## R eligious Services

Officially, the People's Republic encourages atheism. However, there are Buddhist and Daoist temples and places of worship throughout the country, as well as mosques in the Muslim areas and in all large cities, which have regular prayers at the prescribed times. Catholic and Protestant churches can also be found in most big cities.

## S tudent Travellers

Students do not benefit from many travel discounts in Hong Kong, Macau and the mainland. Some cultural events offer slightly reduced ticket prices for students with identification (see Budgeting for Your Trip, page 379).

## T elecommunications

### Telephone/fax

Domestic long-distance calls are cheap; international calls are expensive. Local calls in China from hotels are usually free. International calls made from hotels typically have high surcharges added to China's already high call rates. IP (Internet Phone) cards are the cheapest way to phone abroad; these can be bought at news-stands and hotels in large cities. You call a local number, enter a PIN code and then the number you wish to dial abroad. Most IP calls are much cheaper than standard phonecards and can be used for long-distance calls within China.

Like many nations expanding their domestic telephone networks, China's telephone numbers can change at short notice. If you hear a

peculiar ringing sound on the line and can't get through, the number may have changed.

Hong Kong is known for having one of the most advanced telecommunications systems in the world. It also has one of the highest rates of mobile-phone penetration. Mobile phones can be rented at Hong Kong International Airport. To avoid roaming charges on your own mobile, pick up a pre-paid SIM card, widely available in telephone company shops and convenience stores. Also see Internet, page 382.

## Tipping

Officially, it is still illegal to accept tips in China (but not in Hong Kong and Macau, see below). Moreover, for a long time, it was considered patronising. Tourists and visitors in recent years, however, have changed attitudes in areas such as Guangzhou and Shanghai. It's also become the custom for travel groups to give a tip to Chinese tour guides and bus drivers. If you are travelling with a group, ask the guide, who is responsible for the "official" contacts of the group, whether a tip is appropriate, and how much.

Tipping is still uncommon in most restaurants and hotels, although it is accepted in the top-class ones. As part of the ritual any gift or tip will, at first, be firmly rejected.

### Hong Kong and Macau

Tipping is customary in Hong Kong bars, restaurants and hotels. Though a 10 percent service charge is often added to restaurant bills, a further 5 percent is usually added, to go direct to the staff. Taxi drivers do not expect to be tipped, but rounding up the fare to the nearest dollar or two is appreciated. In Macau, Shenzhen and Guangzhou, tipping is increasingly common practice.

## Tour and Travel Agents

See Activities, page 377–8.

## Time Zone

All of southern China is in the same time zone as Beijing: eight hours ahead of GMT and 13 hours ahead of EST. There is no daylight-savings time, so from early April to late October, when Europe and the US put their clocks forward by one hour, Hong Kong is seven hours ahead of London and 12 hours ahead of New York.

## Tourist Information

The idea of providing free tourist information has not yet taken off in China, with the exception of larger hotels in the big cities, who often have information desks with brochures, etc. Hong Kong and Macau also have government-run tourist boards, where you can pick up useful material and up-to-date advice. On the mainland, the China Travel Service (CTS) is the state travel agency; it has branches everywhere, for arranging tours and tickets for events, though it does not offer a tourist information service.

### HKTB visitor centres

● **International Airport** (only accessible to arriving visitors): 7am–11pm daily.
● **Lo Wu Terminal Building**: Arrival Hall, 2/F, 8am–6pm daily.
● **Hong Kong Island**: Causeway Bay MTR station (Near Exit F), 8am–8pm daily.
● **Kowloon**: Star Ferry Pier, Tsim Sha Tsui, 8am–8pm daily.
**Visitor Hotline** (multilingual); tel: 2508 1234 8am–6pm daily. Tourist information is available at www.DiscoverHongKong.com.

### Macau

**The Macau Government Tourist Office** runs offices at the Macau Ferry Terminal in Hong Kong and upon arrival in Macau. There is also a useful **tourist information centre** on the Largo do Senado square, open 9am–6pm daily. Visitors can contact the tourist hotline, tel: 853 2833 3000, or view the website: www.macautourism.gov.mo.

## W hat to Bring

Personal toiletries such as anti-perspirant are hard to find on the mainland, as are sanitary towels and tampons, toilet paper and soap (which are rarely provided in public loos), though all are easily bought in Hong Kong and Macau. Sunblock and sunglasses are important if you're going to the tropical regions or high altitudes. If travelling long distances overland, bring a few weighty books to help pass the hours. It's also worth bringing some cheap mementoes from home: postcards, stamps and small coins, etc – to satisfy the curiosity of locals whom you're likely to meet. Other practical items if you're travelling for a long time off the beaten track include: penknife, sewing kit, first-aid kit, ear-plugs and sleeping mask, universal plug adaptor and universal sink adaptor.

# LANGUAGE

# UNDERSTANDING THE LANGUAGE

### Forms of Chinese

The use of English is steadily increasing in China, but on the whole you will still find it difficult to meet people away from the big hotels and business and tourist centres who speak any English, never mind German or French. Group travellers generally have translators with them in case of communication problems. But if you are travelling on your own, it is worth taking a dictionary and learning some standard Chinese (known in the West as Mandarin Chinese and in China as *putonghua*, meaning common language).

Over a billion people in China, and many other Chinese in Southeast Asia and North America, speak Mandarin Chinese. Yet within China the situation is complicated by the fact that in many parts of the country – particularly in the south – a dialect form of the language is spoken which bears little relation to Mandarin. The Cantonese spoken in Hong Kong and Guangzhou is one such dialect, and is almost completely incomprehensible to Mandarin speakers. A native of Guangzhou who has not learned Putonghua, or Mandarin, cannot understand a Beijing speaker, and Cantonese is as unintelligible to a speaker of Mandarin as Dutch is to an English-speaker. Despite minor grammar and vocabulary differences, the dialects of China are united by Chinese characters, which make it possible for anyone to read a newspaper countrywide, even if the pronunciation they give the characters they are reading in their native dialect differs widely from region to region.

In southern China, particularly Guangxi and further west, people speak what is called Southern Mandarin. It is, however, by no means easy to understand, even for native speakers of "standard" Mandarin. Coastal southern China is dominated by the tonally complex dialects of Fujian (Hokkien), Chaozhou (Teochew) and Guangdong (Cantonese), which are the dialects spoken mostly in overseas Chinese communities. Other dialects include Hakka, which is spoken in pockets throughout southern China, wherever the migratory Hakka (Kejia, or "guest people") have settled, and the dialect of Hainan Island, which is related to Hokkien. The minority dialects of southern China are largely little related to the Chinese dialects, and tend to be closer to Thai, Burmese or Tibetan, usually depending on the border region they are closest to. This is no reason, however, to leave a Mandarin phrasebook at home: Standard Mandarin is the lingua franca of the Chinese Empire, and prevails throughout the entirety of southern China.

### Language and Writing

Written Chinese is a language of symbols or images. Each symbol represents a one-syllable word, but there is no phonetic link: Chinese characters were originally derived from pictures or symbols representing objects or concepts, so there is no correlation between their apperance and the sound that they represent. This means that, although Cantonese and other dialects such as that used in Fujian sound very different from Mandarin, the words are all represented by exactly the same characters.

There are in total more than 47,000 symbols, though modern Chinese uses only a fraction of these. For a daily newspaper, between 3,000 and 4,000 symbols are sufficient. Scholars know between 5,000 and 6,000. Many symbols used to be quite complicated, but reforms were introduced in the People's Republic in 1949 to simplify the written language and boost literacy. Today, these simplified symbols are used throughout mainland China, although in Hong Kong and Taiwan, independence from the PRC has meant that the complex forms are still used.

Many Chinese words are composed of two or more symbols or single-syllable words. For instance, the Chinese word for film is *dian-ying*, and is made up of the two words: *dian* for electricity and *ying* for shadow. To make reading easier, the pinyin system joins syllables which together form words.

### Pinyin

Standard Chinese is based on the pronunciation of the northern dialects, particularly the Beijing dialect. There is an officially approved roman writing of standard Chinese, called Hanyu Pinyin (the phonetic transcription of the language of the Han people). Pinyin is used throughout the People's Republic; many shops and public facilities show names both in symbols and in pinyin.

Most modern dictionaries use the pinyin system. (Taiwan, however, usually uses the older Wade-Giles transliteration system.) This transcription may at first appear confusing: the city of Xiamen, for example, is pronounced *shee-amen*. It would definitely be useful to familiarise yourself a little with the

## Styles of Calligraphy

In the history of Chinese calligraphy, there are four basic styles of writing. The first is the archaic *xiao zhuan* (small-seal script), established in the Qin Dynasty (221–206 BC) and which is meticulous and laborious.

The square *li shu*, with its clear brushstrokes, was established in the Han Dynasty and used in official writing. Many of the inscriptions on steles of ancient Chinese classics are done in this style.

*Cao shu* ("grass" or cursive style), in which brushstrokes are often joined together in one continuous flow, was developed as a quicker and simpler alternative to the more formal scripts. More so than any other style, the flamboyance of *cao shu* is a form of individual expression.

Finally, *kai shu* is a combination of the more formal *li shu* and the more expressive *cao shu*, and is the basis of today's standard calligraphic script.

Calligraphy is still highly esteemed, practised by housewives and politicians alike. Even the old masters will claim they are but students of this fine art.

pronunciation of pinyin *(see below)*. Even when asking for a place or street name, you need to know how it is pronounced, otherwise you won't be understood. This guide uses the pinyin system throughout for Chinese names and expressions.

## Names and Forms of Address

Chinese names usually consist of three, or sometimes two, syllables, each with its own meaning. Traditionally, the first syllable is the family name, the second or two others are personal names. For instance, in Deng Xiaoping, Deng is the family name, Xiaoping the personal name. The same is true for Fu Hao, where Fu is the family name, Hao the personal name.

Until the 1980s, the address *tongzhi* (comrade) was common, but today *xiansheng* and *furen*, the Chinese equivalent of Mr and Mrs, are more usual. A young woman, as well as female staff in hotels and restaurants, can be addressed as *xiaojie* (Miss). Address older men, especially those in important positions, as *xiansheng* or *shifu* (Master).

## Pronunciation

The pronunciation of the consonants is similar to English *(see below)*. The i after the consonants ch, c, r, sh, s, z, zh is not pronounced; it indicates that the preceding sound is lengthened.

**Pinyin/Phonetic/Sound**
a/a/f**a**r
an/un/r**un**
ang/ung/l**ung**
ao/ou/l**ou**d

c/ts/ra**ts**
ch/ch/**ch**ange
e/er/d**ir**t
e (after i, u, y)/a/tr**a**m
ei/ay/m**ay**
en/en/w**hen**
eng/eong/**ng** has a nasal sound
er/or/hon**our**
h/ch/lo**ch**
i/ee/k**ee**n
o/o/b**o**nd
q/ch/**ch**eer
r/r/**r**ight (but with the tip of the tongue turned up and back onto the palette)
sh/sh/**sh**ade
u/oo/sh**oo**t
u (after j, q, x, y)/as German ü/**ü**ber
x/sh/as in **sh**eep
z/ds/re**ds**
zh/dj/**j**ungle

The consonants **b, d, f, g, j, k, l, m, n, p, s, t, w** and **y** are pronounced as in English.

**In Cantonese:**
similar to Mandarin except:
**e** as in l**e**t
**o** as in g**o**
**ou** as in n**o** (thus Guangzhou is pronounced "Gwang-joe" in Cantonese, but "Gwang-jow" – ie rhyming with c**ow** – in Mandarin)
**au** as in c**ow**
**ai** as in b**uy**
**c** similar to **ch**ip
**ng** as in lying, but further back in the mouth

## Tones

It is sometimes said that Chinese is a monosyllabic language. At first sight, this seems to be true, since each character represents a single syllable that generally indicates a specific concept. However, most words are made up of two or three syllables, sometimes more. In the Western sense, spoken Chinese has only 420 single-syllable root words, but tones are used to differentiate these basic sounds, which often makes it very difficult for foreigners to learn the language. Tone is never used within a sentence to indicate stress as in many European languages; instead, each word has a distinct pitch that goes higher, lower or stays flat within each word. For instance, if one pronounces the syllable *mai* with a falling fourth sound (mài) it means to sell; if it is pronounced with a falling-rising third sound, it means to buy. The meaning of a word is given by the symbol, but the tone is not.

Mandarin has four tones and a fifth, "neutral" sound: The first tone, indicated by the symbol ¯ is spoken high pitched and even, the second (´) rising, the third (ˇ) falling and then rising, and the fourth sound (`) falling.

first sound (high, even) *tā*: **he**
second sound (rising) *má*: **hemp**
third sound (falling and then rising) *mǎ*: **horse**
fourth sound (falling) *mà*: **to complain**

There is no standard agreement as to how many tones there are in **Cantonese** – some say as many as nine – but most people use six in daily life. The Yale transliteration system is one of the less complicated, and classifies these six main tones as follows:
1: high – indicated by the grave accent symbol: à
2: middle/level (no symbol)
3: low – indicated by the underline symbol: a̱
4: high-rising – indicated by an acute accent symbol: á
5: low-falling – indicated by a grave accent symbol and an underline: à̱
6: low-rising – indicated by an acute accent symbol and an underline: á̱

For the new learner, just hitting three tones to boost their intelligibility is a triumph – but be warned, it isn't easy!

## Grammar

The Chinese sentence structure is simple: subject, predicate, object. The simplest way of forming a question is to add the question particle "ma" to the end of a statement. It is not usually possible to know from a Chinese word whether it is a noun, adjective or another form, singular or plural: it depends on the context.

There are some differences between Mandarin and Cantonese grammar, however.

| English | Pinyin (Mandarin) | Cantonese translit. (phonetic) | Characters |
|---|---|---|---|
| **BASIC EXPRESSIONS** | | | |
| Hello | Nǐ hǎo | náy hó | 你好 |
| How are you? | Nǐ hǎo ma? | láy gáy hó à mah? | 你好吗？ |
| Thank you | Xièxie | dàw je | 谢谢 |
| Goodbye | Zài jiàn | joy ginn | 再见 |
| My name is… | Wǒ jiào… | ngáw giu | 我叫… |
| My last name is… | Wǒ xìng… | síu sing | 我姓… |
| What is your name? | Nín jiào shénme míngzi? | láy giu màt yé méng ah? | 你叫什么名字？ |
| What is your last name? | Nín guìxìng? | chéng man gwai sing? | 你贵姓？ |
| I am very happy… | Wǒ hěn gāoxìng… | ngáw hó fai lawk… | 我很高兴… |
| All right/fine/good | Hǎo | gáy hó | 好 |
| Not all right | Bù hǎo | ng hai gáy hó | 不好 |
| Can you speak English? | Nín huì shuō Yīngyǔ ma? | láy sìk ng sìk gáwng yìng mán aa? | 你会说英语吗？ |
| Can you speak Chinese? | Nín huì shuō Hànyǔ ma? | láy sìk ng sìk gáwng dùng wáa? | 你会说汉语吗？ |
| I cannot speak Chinese | Wǒ bù huì Hànyǔ | ngáw ng sìk gáwng dùng wáa | 我不会汉语 |
| I do not understand | Wǒ bù dǒng | ngáw ng mìng | 我不懂 |
| Do you understand? | Nín dǒng ma? | náy mìng ng mìng ah? | 你懂吗？ |
| What is this called? | Zhège jiào shénme? | lày gaw giu màt yé ah? | 这个叫什么？ |
| How do you say…? | … zěnme shuō? | dím yéung duk lày gaw? | …怎么说？ |
| Please/Excuse me | Qǐng | ng gòy | 请 |
| Never mind/no problem | Méi guānxì | mó man tài | 没关系 |
| Sorry | Duìbùqǐ | deui ng jew | 对不起 |
| **PRONOUNS** | | | |
| Who/who is it? | Shéi? | bìn gaw? | 谁？ |
| My/mine | Wǒ/wǒde | ngáw ge | 我/我的 |
| You/yours (singular) | Nǐ/nǐde | láy/láy ge | 你/你的 |
| He/his | Tā/tāde | kéui/kéui ge | 他/他的 |
| She/hers | Tā/tāde | kéui/kéui ge | 她/她的 |
| We/ours | Wǒmen/wǒmende | ngáw day/ngáw day ge | 我们/我们的 |
| You/yours (plural) | Nǐmen/nǐmende | láy day/láy day ge | 你们/你们的 |
| They/theirs | Tāmen/tāmende | kéui day/kéui day ge | 他们/他们的 |
| You/yours (respectful) | Nín/nínde | láy/láy ge | 您/您的 |
| **TRANSPORT AND TRAVEL** | | | |
| Where is it? | zài nǎr? | hái bìn do? | 在哪？ |
| Do you have it here? | Zhèr… yǒu ma? | láy do…yáu mó? | 这…有吗？ |
| No/it's not here/ there aren't any | Méi yǒu | may oh | 没有 |
| Hotel | Fàndiàn/bīnguǎn | jáu dim | 饭店/宾馆 |
| Restaurant | Fànguǎnr | jáu làu | 饭馆 |
| Bank | Yínháng | ngàn hàwng | 银行 |
| Post office | Yóujú | yàu gúk | 邮局 |
| Toilet | Cèsuǒ | chi sáw | 厕所 |
| Airport | Fēijīchǎng | fày gày chèung | 飞机场 |
| Bus | Gōnggòng qìchē | bàa sí/chèung tò hay | 公共汽车 |
| Taxi | Chūzū qìchē | dìk sí | 出租汽车 |
| Bicycle | Zìxíngchē | dàan chè | 自行车 |
| Railway station | Huǒchē zhàn | fó chè jaam | 火车站 |
| Bus station | Qìchē zhàn | chèung tò hay chè jaam | 汽车站 |
| Ticket | Piào | piu | 票 |
| Embassy | Dàshǐguǎn | daai si gún | 大使馆 |
| Consulate | Lǐngshìguǎn | lìng si gún | 领事馆 |
| Passport | Hùzhào | wu jiu | 护照 |
| Visa | Qiānzhèng | chìm jing | 签证 |
| Pharmacy | Yàodiàn | yeuk fàwng | 药店 |
| Hospital | Yīyuàn | yi yéwn | 医院 |
| Doctor | Dàifu/yīshēng | yi sàng | 大夫/医生 |
| Translate | Fānyì | fàan yik | 翻译 |
| **SHOPPING** | | | |
| How much? | Duōshǎo? | gáy dàw? | 多少？ |
| How much does it cost? | Zhège duōshǎo qián? | gáy dàw chín? | 这个多少钱？ |
| Too expensive, thank you | Tài guì le, xièxie | taai gwai laa, dàw je | 太贵了，谢谢 |
| Very expensive | Hěn guì | hó gwai | 很贵 |
| Do you have…? | Nín yǒu… ma? | yáu mó? | 你有…吗？ |
| I want/I would like | Wǒ yào/wǒ xiǎng yào | ng gòy ngáw you | 我要/我想要 |

TRANSPORT

ACCOMMODATION

ACTIVITIES

A – Z

LANGUAGE

| English | Pinyin (Mandarin) | Cantonese translit. (phonetic) | Characters |
|---|---|---|---|
| I want to buy... | Wǒ xiǎng mǎi... | ngáw séung máai... | 我想买... |
| Where can I buy it? | Nǎr néng mǎi... ma? | bìn do háw yí máai dó? | 哪能买...吗? |
| This/that | Zhège/nèige | lày gaw/gáw gaw | 这个/那个 |
| A little (bit) | Yìdiǎnr | yàt dī | 一点 |
| Too much/too many | Tài duō le | taai | 太多了 |
| A lot | Duō | hó dàw | 多 |
| Few | Shǎo | yàt dī | 少 |

**MONEY MATTERS, HOTELS, COMMUNICATIONS**

| | | | |
|---|---|---|---|
| Money | Qián | chín | 钱 |
| Chinese currency | Rénmínbì | Renminbi | 人民币 |
| One yuan/one kuai | Yī yuán/yī kuài | yat yuàn | 一元/一块 |
| One jiao/one mao | Yì jiāo/yì mǎo | yat gawk | 一角/一毛 |
| One fen | Yī fēn | yat fán | 一分 |
| Traveller's cheque | Lǚxíng zhīpiào | léui hàng jì piu | 路行支票 |
| Credit card | Xìnyòngkǎ | seun yung kàat | 信用卡 |
| Foreign currency | Wàihuìquàn | ge day fàwng | 外汇券 |
| Where can I change money? | Zài nǎr kěyǐ huàn qián? | hái bìn do wun chín? | 在哪可以换钱? |
| I want to change money | Wǒ xiǎng huàn qián | ngáw yiu wun chín | 我想换钱 |
| What is the exchange rate? | Bǐjià shì duōshǎo? | hai gáy dàw deui wun léut? | 比价是多少? |
| We want to stay for one (two) nights | Wǒmen xiǎng zhù yì (liǎng) tiān | ngáw day séung zhu yat (yi) táu | 我们想住一(两)天 |
| How much is the room per day? | Fángjiān duōshǎo qián yì tiān? | gáy dàw chín yi táu? | 房价多少钱一天? |
| Room number | Fángjiān hàomǎ | fáwng ho máa | 房间号码 |
| Single room | Dānrén fángjiān | dàan yàn | 单人房间 |
| Double room | Shuāngrén fángjiān | sèung yàn | 双人房间 |
| Reception | Qiántái/fúwùtai | jip doy chew | 签台/服务台 |
| Key | Yàoshì | sáw sì | 钥匙 |
| Clothes | Yīfu | yè fuk | 衣服 |
| Luggage | Xínglǐ | hàng láy | 行李 |
| Telephone | Diànhuà | dìn wáa | 电话 |
| Long-distance call | Chángtú diànhuà | chèung to dìn wáa | 长途电话 |
| International call | Guójì diànhuà | gawk jai dìn wáa | 国际电话 |
| Telephone number | Diànhuà hàomǎ | dìn wáa ho máa | 电话号码 |
| Telegram | Diànbào | dìn bo | 电报 |
| Computer | Diàn nǎo | dín ló | 电脑 |
| Check email | Chá diànxìn | tái háa ngáw ge dìn jí yàu sèung | 查电信 |
| Use the Internet | Shàng wǎng | séung máwng | 上网 |
| Letter | Yì fēng xìn | seun | 一封信 |
| Air mail | Hángkōng xìn | hùng yàu | 航空信 |
| Postage stamp | Yóupiào | yàu piu | 邮票 |

**TIME**

| | | | |
|---|---|---|---|
| When? | Shénme shíhou? | gáy sì? | 什么时候 |
| What time is it? | Xiànzài jídiǎn zhōng? | yi gàa gáy dím jùng? | 现在几点钟? |
| How long? | Duōcháng shíjiān? | gày noy? | 多长时间? |
| One/two/three o'clock | Yī diǎn/liǎng diǎn/sān diǎn zhōng | yàt (yi, sàam) dím jùng | 一点/两点/三点钟 |
| Early morning/morning | Zǎoshang/shàngwǔ | jiù tao jó/jiù jó | 早上/上午 |
| Midday/afternoon/ evening | Zhōngwǔ/xiàwǔ/wǎnshang | jùng ng/haa jau/ye máan | 中午/下午/晚上 |
| Monday | Xīngqīyī | sìng kày yàt | 星期一 |
| Tuesday | Xīngqīèr | sìng kày yi | 星期二 |
| Wednesday | Xīngqīsān | sìng kày sàam | 星期三 |
| Thursday | Xīngqīsì | sìng kày say | 星期四 |
| Friday | Xīngqīwǔ | sìng kày ńg | 星期五 |
| Saturday | Xīngqīliù | sìng kày luk | 星期六 |
| Sunday | Xīngqītiān/xīngqīrì | sìng kày yat | 星期天/星期日 |
| Weekend | Zhōumò | jàu mut | 周末 |
| Yesterday/today/ tomorrow | Zuótiān/jīntiān/míngtiān | kàm yat/gàm yat/tìng yat | 昨天/今天/明天 |
| This week/last week/ next week | Zhègexīngqī/shàngxīngqī/ xiàxīngqī | ne gaw sìng kày/ seung gaw sìng kày/ haa gaw sìng kày | 这个星期/ 上个星期/ 下星期 |
| Hour/day/week/month | Xiǎoshí/tiān/xīngqī/yuè | jùng tàu/yat táu/sìng kày/yewt | 小时/天/ 星期/月 |
| January/February/March | Yīyuè/èryuè/sānyuè | yàt yewt/yi yewt/sàam yewt | 一月/二月/三月 |

| English | Pinyin (Mandarin) | Cantonese translit.(phonetic) | Characters |
|---|---|---|---|
| April/May/June | Sìyuè/wǔyuè/liùyuè | say yewt/ng yewt/luk yewt | 四月/五月/六月 |
| July/August/September | Qīyuè/bāyuè/jiǔyuè | chàt yewt/baat yewt/gáu yewt | 七月/八月/九月 |
| October/November/ December | Shíyuè/shíyīyuè/shíèryuè | sap yewt/sap yàt yewt/ sap yi yewt | 十月/十一月/十二月 |

**EATING OUT**

| | | | |
|---|---|---|---|
| Restaurant | Cāntīng/fànguǎn'r | jáu làu | 餐厅/饭馆 |
| Attendant/waiter | Fúwùyuán | fuk mo yèwn | 服务员 |
| Waitress | Xiǎojiē | seeu jé | 小姐 |
| Eat | Chī fàn | sik | 吃饭 |
| Breakfast | Zāofàn | jó chàan | 早饭 |
| Lunch | Wǔfàn | ng chàan | 午饭 |
| Dinner | Wǎnfàn | màan faan | 晚饭 |
| Menu | Càidān | choy dàan | 菜单 |
| Chopsticks | Kuàizi | faai jí | 筷子 |
| Knife | Dāozi | dò | 刀子 |
| Fork | Chāzi | chàa | 叉子 |
| Spoon | Sháozi | gàng | 勺子 |
| Cup/glass | Bēizi/bōlíbēi | buì | 杯子/玻璃杯 |
| Bowl | Wǎn | wún | 碗 |
| Plate | Pán | díp | 盘 |
| I want... | Wǒ yào... | ngáw séung yiu... | 我要... |
| I did not order this | Zhège wǒ méi diǎn | lày gaw mm hai ngáw geeu gé | 这个我没点 |
| I am a vegetarian | Wǒ shì chī sù de rén | ngáw sik jàai ge | 我是吃素的人 |
| I do not eat any meat/fish | Wǒ suǒyǒude ròu hé yú, dōu bù ch | Ngáw ng sik yuk/yéw | 我所有的肉和鱼, 都不吃 |
| Beer | Píjiǔ | bè-jáu | 啤酒 |
| Red/white wine | Hóng/bái pútaojiǔ | hung/baak pò tò jáu | 红/白葡萄酒 |
| Liquor | Bái jiǔ | jáu jìng | 白酒 |
| Mineral water | Kuàngquánshuǐ | kawng chèwn séui | 矿泉水 |
| Soft drink | Yǐnliào | hay séui | 饮料 |
| Cola | Kělè | hor háu hor lòck | 可乐 |
| Tea | Cháshuǐ | chàa | 茶水 |
| Fruit | Shuǐguǒ | séui gwáw | 水果 |
| Bread | Miànbāo | min bàau | 面包 |
| Yoghurt | Suān nǎi | sèwn láai | 酸奶 |
| Fried/boiled egg | Chǎo/zhǔ jīdàn | cháau/saap dáan | 炒/煮鸡蛋 |
| Rice (steamed) | Mǐfàn | baak faan | 米饭 |
| Soup | Tāng | tàwng | 汤 |
| Stir-fried dishes | Chǎo cài | cháau coi | 炒菜 |
| Beef/pork/lamb/chicken | Niú/zhū/yáng/jī ròu | ngàu yuk/jèw yuk/yèung yuk/gài | 牛/猪/羊/鸡肉 |
| Fish | Yú | yéw | 鱼 |
| Vegetables | Shūcài | sàw choy | 蔬菜 |
| Spicy/sweet/sour/salty | Là/tián/suān/xián | laat/tìm/sèwn/yìm | 辣/甜/酸/咸 |
| Hot/cold | Rè/liáng | yit/dung | 热/凉 |
| Green tea/red tea | Lùchá/hóngchá | luk chàa/hùng chàa | 绿茶/红茶 |
| Coffee | Kāfēi | gaa fè | 咖啡 |
| Can we have the bill, please | Qǐng jié zhàng/mǎidān | ng gòy ngáw yiu màai dàan | 请结帐/买单 |
| Bar | Jiǔbā | ju bàa | 酒吧 |
| Cigarette | Xiāngyān | hèung yìn | 香烟 |

**Specialities**

| | | | |
|---|---|---|---|
| Peking Duck | Běijīng kǎoyā | bàk gìng hàau aap | 北京烤鸭 |
| Hotpot | Huǒ guō | fo wò | 火锅 |
| Phoenix in the Nest | Fèng zài wōlǐ | fúng zòi wò lèi | 凤在窝里 |
| Mandarin fish | Tángcù guìyú | tòng cou gwai yu-ee | 糖醋贵鱼 |
| Thousand layer cake | Qiān céng bǐng | cin cáng beng | 千层饼 |
| Lotus prawns | Ǒu piàn'r xiārén | áau pin háa ján | 藕片虾仁 |
| Homestyle cooking | Jiā cháng cài | zè sóeng coi | 家常菜 |

**Appetizers**

| | | | |
|---|---|---|---|
| Deep-fried peanuts | Zhá huāshēngmǐ | yàu jàa fàa sàng | 炸花生米 |
| Boiled peanuts | Zhǔ huāshēngmǐ | jéw fàa sàng | 煮花生米 |
| Soft beancurd | Bàn dòufu | Bàn dáu fu | 拌豆腐 |
| "Hairy" green beans | Máo dòu | máau dáu | 毛豆 |
| Mashed cucumber | Pái huángguā | paak wóng gwàa | 拍黄瓜 |
| Pressed beancurd strips | Dòufu sī | dáu fu si | 豆腐丝 |

TRANSPORT

ACCOMMODATION

ACTIVITIES

A – Z

LANGUAGE

| English | Pinyin (Mandarin) | Cantonese translit. (phonetic) | Characters |
|---------|-------------------|-------------------------------|------------|
| **Meat dishes** | | | |
| Spicy chicken with chillies/peanuts | Làzi jīdīng/gōngbào jīdīng | gùng baau gài dìng | 辣子鸡丁/宫保鸡丁 |
| Pork with egg and "tree ear" fungus | Mùxū ròu | muk sèui juk | 木须肉 |
| Shredded pork with bamboo shoots | Dōngsǔn ròusī | dùng seong juk si | 冬笋肉丝 |
| Beef in brown sauce | Hóngshāo niúròu | gùng siù au juk | 红烧牛肉 |
| Sizzling "iron plate" beef | Tiěbǎn niúròu | tit baan au juk | 铁板牛肉 |
| **Seafood** | | | |
| Prawns with cashew nuts | Yāoguǒ xiārén | jiù gu háa ján | 腰果虾仁 |
| Carp in brown sauce | Hóngshāo lǐyú | gùng siù lèi yu-ee | 红烧鲤鱼 |
| Boiled prawns | Shuǐzhǔ xiārén | jéw hàa | 水煮虾仁 |
| Stir-fried prawns | Qīngchǎo xiārén | cháau hàa | 清炒虾仁 |
| Hot and sour squid | Suānlà yóuyú juàn | sèwn laat yàu yéw | 酸辣鱿鱼卷 |
| **Vegetable dishes** | | | |
| Spicy "dry" green beans | Gānbiān biǎndòu | gon bìn pìn dáu | 干煸扁豆 |
| Spicy beancurd with chilli | Málà dòufu | màa lát dáu fu | 麻辣豆腐 |
| Stir-fried egg and tomato | Xīhóngshì chǎo jīdàn | fàan ké chàau dáan | 西红柿炒鸡蛋 |
| Clay pot with beancurd soup | Shāguō dòufu | sàa gwàw dáu fu | 砂锅豆腐 |
| Sour cabbage with "glass" noodles | Suāncài fěnsī | syùn coi fan si | 酸菜粉丝 |
| Potato, aubergine and green pepper | Dì sān xiān | dei sàam sin | 地三鲜 |
| **Staple food** | | | |
| Plain rice | Bái fàn | baak faan | 白饭 |
| Fried rice | Dàn chǎo fàn | cháw faan | 蛋炒饭 |
| Noodles | Miàntiáo | min | 面条 |
| Pancakes | Bǐng | béng | 饼 |
| Stuffed pasta parcels | Jiǎozi | gàau jí | 饺子 |
| meat/vegetable filling | ròu xiàn/sù xiàn | juk haàm/sou haàm | 肉馅/素馅 |
| Steamed meat buns | Bāozi | bàau | 包子 |
| "Pot stickers" (fried *jiaozi*) | Guōtiē | wò tìp | 锅贴 |
| Egg pancake | Jiān bǐng | jìn béng | 煎饼 |
| Wonton soup | Húndùn | wàn tàn | 馄饨 |
| Soy milk | Dòu jiāng | dau jèung | 豆浆 |
| Deep-fried dough sticks | Yóutiáo | yàu jàa gwái | 油条 |
| **NUMBERS** | | | |
| Zero | Ling | lìn | 零 |
| One | Yī | yàt | 一 |
| Two | Èr | yi | 二 |
| Three | Sān | sàam | 三 |
| Four | Sì | say | 四 |
| Five | Wǔ | ng | 五 |
| Six | Liù | luk | 六 |
| Seven | Qī | chàt | 七 |
| Eight | Bā | baat | 八 |
| Nine | Jiǔ | gáu | 九 |
| Ten | Shí | sap | 十 |
| Eleven | Shíyī | sap yàt | 十一 |
| Twelve | Shíèr | sap yi | 十二 |
| Twenty | Èrshí | yi sap | 二十 |
| Thirty | Sānshí | sàam sap | 三十 |
| Forty | Sìshí | say sap | 四十 |
| Fifty | Wǔshí | ng sap | 五十 |
| One hundred | Yībǎi | yàt baak | 一百 |
| One hundred and one | Yībǎi língyī | yàt baak ling yàt | 一百零一 |
| Two hundred | Liǎng bǎi | léung baak | 两百 |
| Three hundred | Sān bǎi | sàam baak | 三百 |
| Four hundred | Sì bǎi | say baak | 四百 |
| Five hundred | Wǔ bǎi | ng baak | 五百 |
| One thousand | Yīqiān | yàt chìn | 一千 |
| One thousand and one | Yīqiān língyī | yàt chìn ling yàt | 一千零一 |
| One million | Yīwàn | yàt màan | 一万 |

# FURTHER READING

## History and Politics

**Hong Kong: A Cultural and Literary History**. Michael Ingham. Beneath the surface of Hong Kong's image.

**A History of Hong Kong**. Frank Welsh. A comprehensive but readable account of the history of Hong Kong to 1997.

**Macau: The Imaginary City**. Jonathan Porter. A recent and readable study of Macau's history and its commercial, cultural and social links with China.

**Mao: The Unknown Story**. Jung Chang, Jon Halliday. Thought-provoking and searingly critical appraisal of the Mao era. Essential reading for anyone interested in the evolution of modern China.

**Sons of the Yellow Emperor**. Lynn Pan. Tells the fascinating story of China's overseas diaspora.

**The Southern Expansion of the Chinese People**. Charles P. Fitzgerald. Authoritative and comprehensive examination of China's expansion to the south.

**The Nanhai Trade: Early Chinese Trade in the South China Sea**. Wang Gungwu. Seminal account of China's early links with Southeast Asia.

**God's Chinese Son**. Jonathan Spence. An account of the Taiping Rebellion in central and southern China during the mid 19th century.

**The Chinese**. Jasper Becker. Fine analysis of contemporary China and of what makes the country tick.

**The China Dream: The Elusive Quest for the Greatest Untapped Market on Earth**. Joe Studwell. Salutary observations and cautionary tales for those contemplating doing business in China.

**The End of Empire in the Far East**. John Keay. Explores the legacy of the British Empire in Asia with some fascinating detail, and a new afterword on the remarkable development of the Chinese economy.

## Travel Literature

**Across Yunnan: A Journey of Surprises**. Archibald John Little. Recent reprint of a classic travel account dating from 1910.

**Hong Kong**. Jan Morris. Wonderfully insightful text from the doyenne of modern travel writers.

## Literature

**Noble House**. James Clavell. Historical fiction at its best, based on the early British banking tycoons in Hong Kong.

**A House by the River**. Sid Smith. Whitbread prize winning novel set among the Yi minority in South China in the early 20th century

## Feedback

We do our best to ensure the information in our books is as accurate and up-to-date as possible. The books are updated on a regular basis, using local contacts, who painstakingly add, amend and correct as required. However, some mistakes and omissions are inevitable and we are ultimately reliant on our readers to put us in the picture. We would welcome your feedback on any details related to your experiences using the book "on the road". Maybe we recommended a hotel that you liked (or another that you didn't), as well as interesting new attractions, or facts and figures you have found out about the country itself. The more details you can give us (particularly with regard to addresses, e-mails and telephone numbers), the better. We will acknowledge all contributions, and we'll offer an Insight Guide to the best letters received.

Please write to us at:
Insight Guides
PO Box 7910
London SE1 1WE
United Kingdom
Or send e-mail to:
insight@apaguide.co.uk

## Other Insight Guides

*Insight Guides* cover nearly 200 destinations, providing information on culture and all the top sights, as well as superb photography. Titles which highlight China include:

**Insight Guide: China**, a companion to the present volume, captures the essence of China with incisive text and memorable photography.

**Insight City Guide: Hong Kong** surveys the SAR with insightful text and superb photography. **Insight City Guide: Shanghai** does the same for the booming city to the east.

**Insight Smart Guide: Hong Kong** is part of a new series of guides packed with listings and recommendations.

**Insight Fleximaps** (titles include Hong Kong, Macau, Shenzhen, Guangzhou, Shanghai) are the perfect on-the-spot companions. Text, photographs and maps are all carefully cross-referenced for maximum practicality in this superbly portable format.

# ART & PHOTO CREDITS

4 Corners/SIME/Luca Da Ros 70
4 Corners/Massimo Borchi 123
Peter Adams/Jon Arnold 336
AFP/Getty Images 155
AGE Fotostock/SuperStock 166, 167
Alamy 285
Art Archive 20, 22, 37
Asian Art & Archaeology Inc./Corbis 4C, 23
Bohemian Picture Makers/Corbis 169
Massimo Borachi/4 Corners 140
Adrian Bradshaw/Corbis 59, 239
Derek Brown/Alamy 143T
Bridgeman Art Library 24
Mark Cawardine/Nature Picture Library 53R
Sam Chambers 231TR, 244, 247T, 247, 252, 254, 255T, 263
China Tourism Press/Getty Images 9TR, 100/101, 232, 253
CPA Media 25, 26 L&R, 28, 30, 33, 34, 35L&R, 252T, 308
Croquet-Zouridakis 17CR, 111, 115, 119, 129T, 170T, 239
Dbimages/Alamy 299
Danita Delimont/Alamy 324BL&R
Andrew Dembina 199R, 200, 201, 202T, 204, 209, 210, 211
Gertrud & Helmut Denzau 186T
Digital Vision/SuperStock 343
EPA/Corbis 53L, 205T, 225
Alain Evrard/Robert Harding/Alamy 76
Eyepress/Corbis 38
Firefly Productions/Corbis 10BL
Lee Foster/Alamy 180
Bert Freeman/Alamy 77
Yves Gellie/Corbis 10TR
Getty Images 7CL, 12/13, 19, 56, 93, 131T, 131, 230, 238T, 248L, 255, 278, 291, 376
Jim Goodman/CPA 1, 73, 81, 256T, 305, 309, 310T, 310, 315T, 315, 316L, 319, 321T, 331T, 332, 338T, 343, 345, 346T, 376
Leo Haks Collection 27
Tim Hall/Axiom 106
Dallas & John Heaton 262
David Henley/CPA 6TL, 42/43, 79, 86, 302, 305T, 309T, 342T, 370
David Henley/CPA/Apa 3, 4, 5T, 7TR, 8C, 9CR&BR, 10BR, 11TR&BR, 17CR, 75, 80, 85, 92, 94, 95, 103CL&BR, 149TR,BR&BL, 153, 154, 155T, 157, 159T, 159, 160T, 160, 161T, 161, 162T, 162, 163, 169T, 171T, 172, 173T, 173, 174T, 175T, 176T, 177, 179, 183T, 183, 186, 187L&R, 189, 191T, 191, 192T, 193T, 194T, 196, 198T, 199L, 201T, 202, 203L, 205, 206, 207T, 208T, 208, 210T, 212, 213, 214T, 215T, 216T, 218T, 218, 219, 221T, 221, 222T, 223T, 223, 225T, 226T, 235T, 246, 248T, 254T, 264T, 265T, 267T, 272T, 272, 273, 275T, 278T, 279T, 279, 280, 281T,

281, 282T, 282, 283T, 283, 292, 354, 359, 361, 375, 381
Mark Henley/Panos 64R
Peter Holmshaw 39T, 303, 339t
Nigel Hicks 117, 121, 124, 127T
Tim Hill/Cephas 203R
John Holmes/FLPA 45
Hong Kong Tourist Board 112T
David Hosking/FLPA 317T
Hulton-Deutsch Collection/Corbis 331
ImagineChina 2/3, 7TL, 16, 55, 67, 74, 138T, 156, 181, 187T, 194, 195T, 215, 220, 226, 249T, 256, 289, 306R, 312, 313, 317, 318, 320, 324T, 334T
Richard Jones/Rex Features 64L
Richard Jones/Sinopix/Apa 7CR, 39, 103TR, 107CL&BR, 116T, 116, 118T, 119T, 135, 137T, 141T, 141, 143, 145
Cao Jingjian/CPA 14/15, 286, 294
JTB Photo Communications/Alamy 74, 88
Catherine Karnow 7BL, 142, 165
Taras Kovaliv/Apa 89, 107TR, 113T, 117T, 122T, 125L&R, 130
Krause & Johansen/SuperStock 7BR, 216, 217T
Yann Layma/Getty Images 6BR
Ming Li/Photolibrary 324
Liu Liqun/Corbis 224
Ken Lucas/Ardea 49
James Marshall/Corbis 57
Mary Evans Picture Library 31, 190
Iain Masterton/Alamy 184
Kees Metselaar/Alamy 353
Minden Pictures/FLPA 52
Brice Minnigh 9TL, 36, 235, 237T, 237L, 238, 240, 241T, 241, 242T, 242
Manfred Morgenstern 29, 32, 40TL&BR, 41TR&BL
Ben Nakayama 271
Kazuyoshi Nomachi/Corbis 233
National Palace Museum 87
David Noton/Getty Images 110
Richard Nowitz/Apa 231BR, 251
Panorama Media/Alamy192
PanoramaStock/Robert Harding Picture Library 69, 98/99, 146/147, 148, 170, 171, 250T
Photobank, Singapore 6BL
Michael Pitts/Nature Picture Library 48
Private Archive 60TR
Redlink 62, 63, 152, 176, 344
Reuters/Corbis 54, 65, 197, 248/249, 275, 382
G.P. Reichelt 129
Hans Georg Roth/Corbis 126
Bob Sacha/Corbis 239, 257
Joel Sartore/Getty Images 46R
Scala 21
Anup Shah/Nature Picture Library 51
Sinopix 5B, 288T, 288, 290T, 293,

295T, 295, 296, 304T, 316R, 318T, 324T
Peter Spurrier 163T, 188T, 188, 263, 280T
Ed Stokes 127, 128,
Rick Strange 128T
Chris Stowers/Panos 228, 229
Keren Su/Corbis 8BL, 47, 68
SuperStock 96/97, 184T, 193, 266, 269, 274
Bjorn Svensson/SuperStock 174
Tim Thompson/Apa 60CL
Zhang Tianlin/CPA 286
TopFoto 175
Robert van der Hilst/Corbis 58
Graham Uden 8T, 112, 120
Graham Uden/Corbis 265
Julia Wardlow/Eye Ubiquitous 71
Bill Wassman/Apa 11TL, 114T, 126T, 137, 334
Dr. Myrna Watanabe/Still Pictures 50
Werner Forman Archive 92
David Wilkinson 7BC, 10TL,17BL, 102, 134, 139, 268, 277T, 277, 291T, 292T, 296T, 297, 298, 307, 322, 323, 325T, 326T, 326BL&R, 327T, 328T, 328, 329, 337, 339, 340, 341T, 341, 343T, 344T, 345T, 347T
Rod Williams/Nature Picture Library 44
Ruth Williams 158TR&BL, 267, 268T, 270T, 270
Corrie Wingate 329T
Xinhua Photo/Corbis 245, 306L
Michael S. Yamashita/Corbis 66
Zhang Yaobing/CPA 46L, 258/259, 330, 346
How Hwee Young/Corbis 72

## PICTURE SPREADS

**Pages 82–83 Chinese Medicine**
Peter Hessel 82/83T, Corbis 82BL, National Palace Museum 82CR, David Wilkinson 82TL, Alamy 83BL, Richard Jones/Sinopix/Apa 83BR, Mike Theiler 83TR.
**Pages 90–91 Chinese Opera**
Bodo Bondzio 90/91T, 91 BR, Wendy Chan/Getty Images90CR, David Henley/CPA/Apa 90B, Pat Aithie/Ffotograf 91BL, A. Carroll/Eye Ubiquitous 91CR, Reuters/Corbis 91TR.
**Pages 300–301 The Minorities of Southwest China**
Tang Zhongfa/CPA300–301T, Jim Goodman/CPA 300 TL&BC, 301TR&B, David Henley/CPA/Apa 300BR, Yann Layma/Getty Images 301CR.

**Map Production:** Phoenix Mapping and Stephen Ramsay

©2007 Apa Publications GmbH & Co. Verlag KG (Singapore branch)

**Production:** Linton Donaldson